THIRD EDITION

THE PRACTICE OF COMPUTING USING PYTHON

GLOBAL EDITION

William Punch

Richard Enbody

Pearson

Boston Columbus Indianapolis New York San Francisco Hoboken
Amsterdam Cape Town Dubai London Madrid Milan Munich Paris Montréal Toronto
Delhi Mexico City São Paulo Sydney Hong Kong Seoul Singapore Taipei Tokyo

Vice President, Editorial Director, ECS: Marcia Horton
Acquisitions Editor: Matt Goldstein
Editorial Assistant: Kristy Alaura
Acquistions Editor, Global Editions: Murchana Borthakur
Vice President of Marketing: Christy Lesko
Director of Field Marketing: Tim Galligan
Product Marketing Manager: Bram Van Kempen
Field Marketing Manager: Demetrius Hall
Marketing Assistant: Jon Bryant
Director of Product Management: Erin Gregg
Team Lead, Program and Project Management: Scott Disanno
Program Manager: Carole Snyder
Project Editor, Global Editions: K.K. Neelakantan
Senior Manufacturing Controller, Global Editions: Jerry Kataria
Senior Specialist, Program Planning and Support: Maura Zaldivar-Garcia
Cover Designer: Lumina Datamatics
Manager, Rights and Permissions: Rachel Youdelman
Project Manager, Rights and Permissions: William Opaluch
Inventory Manager: Meredith Maresca
Media Project Manager: Dario Wong
Media Production Manager, Global Editions: M Vikram Kumar
Full-Service Project Management: Jogender Taneja, iEnerziger Aptara®, Ltd.
Cover Photo Credit: Marietjie/Shutterstock

Credits and acknowledgments borrowed from other sources and reproduced, with permission, in this textbook appear on appropriate page within text. Reprinted with permission.

Pearson Education Limited
Edinburgh Gate
Harlow
Essex CM20 2JE
England

and Associated Companies throughout the world

Visit us on the World Wide Web at:
www.pearsonglobaleditions.com

Authorized adaptation from the United States edition, entitled The Practice of Computing Using Python, 3rd Edition, ISBN 978-0-13-437976-0, by William F. Punch and Richard J. Enbody published by Pearson Education © 2017.

British Library Cataloguing-in-Publication Data

A catalogue record for this book is available from the British Library

10 9 8 7 6 5 4 3 2 1

ISBN 10: 1-292-16662-2
ISBN 13: 978-1-292-16662-9
Typeset by iEnerziger Aptara®, Ltd.
Printed in Malaysia (CTP-VVP)

To our beautiful wives Laurie and Wendy and our kids Zach, Alex,
Abby, Carina, and Erik,
and our parents.
We love you and couldn't have done this
without your love and support.

BRIEF CONTENTS

CONTENTS

VIDEONOTES

PREFACE

A FIRST COURSE IN COMPUTER SCIENCE IS ABOUT A NEW WAY OF SOLVING PROBLEMS computationally. Our goal is that after the course, students when presented with a problem will think, "Hey, I can write a program to do that!"

The teaching of problem solving is inexorably intertwined with the computer language used. Thus, the choice of language for this first course is very important. We have chosen Python as the introductory language for beginning programming students—majors and non-majors alike—based on our combined 55 years of experience teaching undergraduate introductory computer science at Michigan State University. Having taught the course in Pascal, C/C++, and now Python, we know that an introductory programming language should have two characteristics. First, it should be relatively simple to learn. Python's simplicity, powerful built-in data structures, and advanced control constructs allow students to focus more on problem solving and less on language issues. Second, it should be practical. Python supports learning not only fundamental programming issues such as typical programming constructs, a fundamental object-oriented approach, common data structures, and so on, but also more complex computing issues such as threads and regular expressions. Finally, Python is "industrial strength" forming the backbone of companies such as YouTube, DropBox, Industrial Light and Magic, and many others.

We emphasize both the fundamental issues of programming and practicality by focusing on data manipulation and analysis as a theme—allowing students to work on real problems using either publicly available data sets from various Internet sources or self-generated data sets from their own work and interests. We also emphasize the development of programs, providing multiple, worked out, examples, and three entire chapters for detailed design and implementation of programs. As part of this one-semester course, our students have analyzed breast cancer data, catalogued movie actor relationships, predicted disruptions of satellites from solar storms, and completed many other data analysis problems. We have also found that concepts learned in a Python CS1 course transitioned to a CS2 C++ course with little or no impact on either the class material or the students.

Our goals for the book are as follows:

- Teach problem solving within the context of CS1 to both majors and nonmajors using Python as a vehicle.
- Provide examples of *developing* programs focusing on the kinds of data analysis problems students might ultimately face.
- Give students who take no programming course other than this CS1 course a practical foundation in programming, enabling them to produce useful, meaningful results in their respective fields of study.

WHAT'S NEW, THIRD EDITION

We have taught with this material for over eight years and continue to make improvements to the book as well as adapting to the ever changing Python landscape, keeping up to date with improvements. We list the major changes we have made below.

Anaconda: One of the issues our students ran into was the complexity associated with getting Python packages, along with the necessary pre-requisites. Though tools like `pip` address this problem to some extent, the process was still a bit overwhelming for introductory students.

Thus we switched to the **Anaconda** distribution made freely available from Continuum Analytics. They make available a full distribution with more than 100 modules pre-installed, removing the need for package installation.

Appendix A, newly written for Anaconda, covers the installation process.

SPYDER: Another benefit of the Anaconda distribution is the SPYDER Integrated Development Environment. We have fully adopted SPYDER as our default method for editing and debugging code, changing from the default IDLE editor. SPYDER provides a full development environment and thus has a number of advantages (as listed at the Spyder git page, `https://github.com/spyder-ide/spyder/blob/master/README.md`).

- Integrated editor
- Associated interactive console
- Integrated debugging
- Integrated variable explorer
- Integrated documentation viewer

SPYDER is a truly modern Python IDE and the correct way for students to learn Python programming.

Chapter 1 has been rewritten, incorporating the SPYDER IDE and using SPYDER is sprinkled throughout the book. Appendix A provides a tutorial on SPYDER.

IPython: Anaconda also provides the iPython console as its interactive console. IPython is a much more capable console than the default Python console, providing many features including:

- An interactive history list, where each history line can be edited and re-invoked.
- Help on variables and functions using the "?" syntax.
- Command line completion

Every session of the book was redone for the iPython console and iPython's features are sprinkled throughout the book. Further, a tutorial on the use of iPython is provided in Appendix A.

Debugging help: Debugging is another topic that is often a challenge for introductory students. To address this need, we have introduced a "What's Wrong with My Code" element to the end of chapters 1, 2, 4, 5, 6, 7, 8, 9, and 11. These provide increasingly detailed tips to deal with new Python features as they are introduced. An overall tutorial is also provided in the **new Appendix C**.

As SPYDER provides a debugger, use of that debugger is used for all examples.

Pylab updated: We have incorporated graphing through `matplotlib/pylab` into the book since the first edition, but this module has changed somewhat over the years so the "Visual Vignettes" at the end of chapters 1, 2, 5, 7, 9, and 13 have been updated and somewhat simplified. In particular the discussions of NumPy have been removed except for where they are useful for graphing. Appendix D has also been updated with these changes.

Web-based GUIs: Building Graphic User Interfaces (GUIs) is a topic many students are interested in. However, in earlier editions we hesitated to focus on GUI development as part of an introductory text for a number of reasons:

- The extant `tkinter` is cross platform, but old and more complex to work with than we would like for an introductory class.
- Getting a modern GUI toolset can be daunting, especially cross platform.
- Just **which** GUI toolset should we be working with?

A discussion with Greg Wilson (thanks Greg!) was helpful in resolving this problem. He suggested doing Web-based GUIs as a modern GUI approach that is cross-platform, relatively stable and provided in modern distributions like Anaconda.

What that left was the "complexity" issue. We choose to use the package `flask` because it was relatively less complex, but more importantly was easily modularized and could be used in a template fashion to design a GUI.

Thus, we wrote some simple GUI development in `flask` at the end of chapters 4, 6, 7, 9, 10, and 15. We also wrote a **new Appendix E** as a tutorial for development of web-based GUIs.

Functions Earlier: One of the common feedback points we received was a request to introduce functions earlier. Though we had purposefully done strings first, as a way to start working with data, we had sympathy for those instructors who wanted to change the order and introduce functions before strings. Rather than pick a right way to do this, we **rewrote Chapter 5** so that it had no dependencies on Chapter 4, the string chapter. Instructors are now free to introduce functions anytime after Chapter 2 on control. Likewise Chapter 4 on strings has no dependencies on Chapter 5, the functions chapters. Thus the instructor can choose the order they prefer.

Online Project Archive: We have established an online archive for Python CS1 projects, `http://www.cse.msu.edu/~cse231/PracticeOfComputingUsingPython/`. These describe various projects we have used over the years in our classes. This site and its contents has been recognized by the National Center for Women & Information Technology (NCWIT) and was awarded the 2015 NCWIT EngageCSEdu Engagement Excellence Award.

New Exercises: We added 80 new end-of-chapter exercises.

Other changes: We have made a number of other changes as well:

- We updated Chapter 16 with a discussion about Python Numbers and the various representations that are available
- We moved the content of some of the chapters in the "Getting Started" part to the "Data Structures and Functions" part. This is really just a minor change to the table of contents.
- We fixed various typos and errors that were either pointed out to us or we found ourselves as we re-read the book.

ACKNOWLEDGMENTS FOR THE GLOBAL EDITION

Pearson would like to thank and acknowledge the following people for their contributions to the Global Editions.

Contributor
Abhinava Vatsa

Reviewers
Debajyoti Bera, Indraprastha Institute of Information Technology, Delhi
Shivani Pandit
Somitra Sanadhya, Indraprastha Institute of Information Technology, Delhi

PREFACE TO THE SECOND EDITION

The main driver for a second edition came from requests for Python 3. We began our course with Python 2 because Python 3 hadn't been released in 2007 (it was first released in December 2008), and because we worried that it would take some time for important open-source packages such as NumPy and MatPlotLib to transition to Python 3. When NumPy and MatPlotLib converted to Python 3 in 2011 we felt comfortable making the transition. Of course, many other useful modules have also been converted to Python 3—the default installation now includes thousands of modules. With momentum building behind Python 3 it was time for us to rewrite our course and this text.

Why Python 3? The Python community decided to break backward compatibility with Python 3 to fix nagging inconsistencies in the language. One important change was moving the default character encoding to Unicode which recognizes the world-wide adoption of the language. In many ways beyond the introductory level, Python 3 is a better language and the community is making the transition to Python 3.

At the introductory level the transition to Python 3 appears to be relatively small, but the change resulted in touching nearly every page of the book.

One notable addition was:

- We added a set of nine **RULES** to guide novice programmers.

We reworked every section of this text—some more than others. We hope that you will enjoy the changes. Thanks.

BOOK ORGANIZATION

At the highest level our text follows a fairly traditional CS1 order, though there are some differences. For example, we cover strings rather early (before functions) so that we can do more data manipulation early on. We also include elementary file I/O early for the same reason, leaving detailed coverage for a later chapter. Given our theme of data manipulation, we feel this is appropriate. We also "sprinkle" topics like plotting and drawing throughout the text in service of the data manipulation theme.

We use an "object-use-first" approach where we use built-in Python objects and their methods early in the book, leaving the design and implementation of user-designed objects for later. We have found that students are more receptive to building their own classes once they have experienced the usefulness of Python's existing objects. In other words, we motivate the need for writing classes. Functions are split into two parts because of how Python handles mutable objects such as lists as parameters; discussion of those issues can only come after there is an understanding of lists as mutable objects.

Three of the chapters (3, 10, and 13) are primarily program design chapters, providing an opportunity to "tie things together," as well as showing how to design a solution. A few chapters are intended as supplemental reading material for the students, though lecturers may choose to cover these topics as well. For background, we provide a Chapter 0 that introduces some general concepts of a computer as a device and some computer terminology. We feel such an introduction is important—everyone should understand a little about a computer, but this material can be left for reading. The last chapters in the text may not be reached in some courses.

BOOK FEATURES

1.0.1 Data Manipulation

Data manipulation is a theme. The examples range from text analysis to breast cancer classification. The data.gov site is a wonderful source of interesting and relevant data. Along the way, we provide some analysis examples using simple graphing. To incorporate drawing and graphing, we use established packages instead of developing our own: one is built-in (Turtle graphics); the other is widely used (MatPlotLib with NumPy).

We have tried to focus on non-numeric examples in the book, but some numeric examples are classics for a good reason. For example, we use a rational numbers example for creating classes that overload operators. Our goal is always to use the best examples.

1.0.2 Problem Solving and Case Studies

Throughout the text, we emphasize problem solving, especially a divide-and-conquer approach to developing a solution. Three chapters (3, 10, and 13) are devoted almost exclusively to program development. Here we walk students through the solution of larger examples. In addition to design, we show mistakes and how to recover from them. That is, we don't simply show a solution, but show a *process of developing* a solution.

1.0.3 Code Examples

There are over 180 code examples in the text—many are brief, but others illustrate piecemeal development of larger problems.

1.0.4 Interactive Sessions

The Python interpreter provides a wonderful mechanism for briefly illustrating programming and problem-solving concepts. We provide almost 250 interactive sessions for illustration.

1.0.5 Exercises and Programming Projects

Practice, practice, and more practice. We provide over 275 short exercises for students and nearly 30 longer programming projects (many with multiple parts).

1.0.6 Self-Test Exercises

Embedded within the chapters are 24 self-check exercises, each with five or more associated questions.

1.0.7 Programming Tips

We provide over 40 special notes to students on useful tips and things to watch out for. These tips are boxed for emphasis.

SUPPLEMENTARY MATERIAL ONLINE

- For students
  - All example source code
  - Data sets used in examples

The above material is freely available at www.pearsonglobaleditions.com/punch

- For instructors
  - PowerPoint slides
  - Laboratory exercises
  - Figures (PDF) for use in your own slides
  - Exercise solutions

Qualified instructors may obtain supplementary material by visiting www.pearsonglobaleditions.com/punch. Register at the site for access. You may also contact your local Pearson Education sales representative

W. F. Punch
R. J. Enbody

BREAKTHROUGH

To improving results

MyProgrammingLab™

Through the power of practice and immediate personalized feedback, MyProgrammingLab helps improve your students' performance.

PROGRAMMING PRACTICE

With MyProgrammingLab, your students will gain first-hand programming experience in an interactive online environment.

IMMEDIATE, PERSONALIZED FEEDBACK

MyProgrammingLab automatically detects errors in the logic and syntax of their code submission and offers targeted hints that enables students to figure out what went wrong and why.

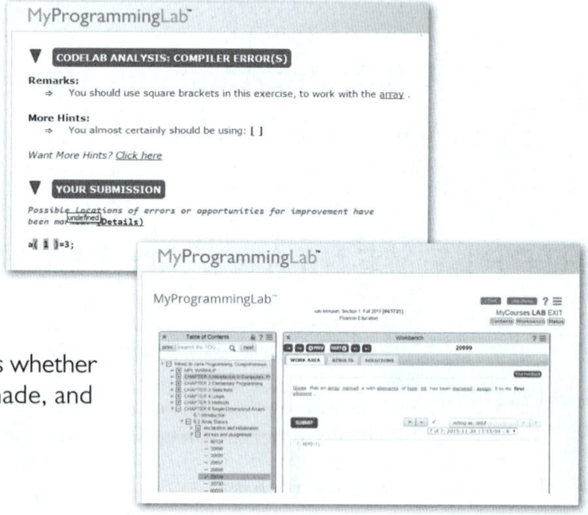

GRADUATED COMPLEXITY

MyProgrammingLab breaks down programming concepts into short, understandable sequences of exercises. Within each sequence the level and sophistication of the exercises increase gradually but steadily.

DYNAMIC ROSTER

Students' submissions are stored in a roster that indicates whether the submission is correct, how many attempts were made, and the actual code submissions from each attempt.

PEARSON eTEXT

The Pearson eText gives students access to their textbook anytime, anywhere.

STEP-BY-STEP VIDEONOTE TUTORIALS

These step-by-step video tutorials enhance the programming concepts presented in select Pearson textbooks.

For more information and titles available with **MyProgrammingLab**, please visit **www.myprogramminglab.com**.

ALWAYS LEARNING

PEARSON

PART 1

Thinking About Computing

CHAPTER 0

The Study of Computer Science

> Composing computer programs to solve scientific problems is like writing poetry. You must choose every word with care and link it with the other words in perfect syntax.
>
> James Lovelock

0.1 WHY COMPUTER SCIENCE?

It is a fair question to ask. Why should anyone bother to study computer science? Furthermore, what is "computer science"? Isn't this all just about programming? All good questions. We think it is worth discussing them before you forge ahead with the rest of the book.

0.1.1 Importance of Computer Science

Let's be honest. We wouldn't be writing the book and asking you to spend your valuable time if we didn't think that studying computer science is important. There are a couple of ways to look at why this is true.

First, we all know that computers are everywhere, millions upon millions of them. What were once rare, expensive items are as common place as, well, any commodity you can imagine (we were going to say the proverbial toaster, but there are many times more computers than toasters. In fact, there is likely a small computer *in* your toaster!). However, that isn't enough of a reason. There are millions and millions of cars, and universities don't require auto mechanics as an area of study.

Second, Computers are not only common, but they are also more universally applicable than any other commodity in history. A car is good for transportation, but a computer can be used in so many situations. In fact, there is almost no area one can imagine where a computer would *not* be useful. That is a key attribute. No matter what your area of interest, a computer could be useful there as a *tool.* The computer's universal utility is unique, and learning how to use such a tool is important.

0.1.2 Computer Science Around You

Computing surrounds you, and it is computer science that put it there. There are a multitude of examples, but here are a few worth noting.

Social Networking The tools that facilitate social networking such as Facebook or Twitter are, of course, computer programs. However, the tools that help study the interactions within social networks involve important computer science fields such as *graph theory.* For example, the Iraqi dictator Saddam Hussein was located using the graph theoretic analysis of his social network.

Smartphones Smartphones are small, very portable computers. Apps for smartphones are simple computer programs written specifically for smartphones.

Your Car Your car probably hosts dozens of computers. They control the engine, the brakes, the audio system, the navigation, and the climate control system. They determine if a crash is occurring and trigger the air bags. Some cars park automatically or apply the brakes if a crash is imminent. Fully autonomous cars are being tested, as are cars that talk to each other.

The Internet The backbone of the Internet is a collection of connected computers called *routers* that decide the best way to send information to its destination.

0.1.3 Computer "Science"

> Any field that has the word science in its name is guaranteed thereby not to be a science.
>
> Frank Harary

A popular view of the term "computer science" is that it is a glorified way to say "computer programming." It is true that computer programming is often the way that people are introduced to computing in general, and that computer programming is the primary reason many take computing courses. However, there is indeed more to computing than programming, hence the term "computer science." Here are a few examples.

Theory of Computation

Before there were the vast numbers of computers that are available today, scientists were thinking about what it means to do computing and what the limits might be. They would ask questions, such as whether there exist problems that we can conceive of but cannot compute. It turns out there are. One of these problems, called the "Halting Problem,"[1] cannot be solved by a program running on any computer. Knowing what you can and cannot solve on a computer is an important issue and a subject of study among computer scientists that focus on the theory of computation.

Computational Efficiency

The fact that a problem is computable does not mean it is easily computed. Knowing roughly how difficult a problem is to solve is also very important. Determining a meaningful measure of difficulty is, in itself, an interesting issue, but imagine we are concerned only with time. Consider designing a solution to a problem that, as part of the solution, required you to sort 100,000 items (say cancer patient records, or asteroid names, or movie episodes, etc.). A slow algorithm, such as the sorting algorithm called the Bubble Sort, might take approximately 800 seconds (about 13 minutes); another sorting algorithm called Quick Sort might take approximately 0.3 seconds. That is a difference of around 2400 times! That large a difference might determine whether it is worth doing. If you are creating a solution, it would be good to know what makes your solution slow or what makes it fast.

Algorithms and Data Structures

Algorithms and data structures are the currency of the computer scientist. Discussed more in Chapter 3, algorithms are the methods used to solve problems, whereas data structures are the organizations of data that the algorithms use. These two concepts are distinct: a general approach to solving a problem (such as searching for a particular value, sorting a list of objects and encrypting a message) differs from the organization of the data that is being processed (as a list of objects, as a dictionary of key-value pairs, as a "tree" of records). However, they are also tightly coupled. Furthermore, both algorithms and data structures can be examined independently of how they might be programmed. That is, one designs algorithms and data structures and then actually implements them in a particular computer program. Understanding abstractly how to design both algorithms and data structures independent of the programming language is critical for writing correct and efficient code.

Parallel Processing

It may seem odd to include what many consider an advanced topic, but parallel processing, using multiple computers to solve a problem, is an issue for everyone these days. Why? As it turns out, most computers come with at least two processors or CPUs (see Section 0.6), and many come with four or more. The Playstation4(TM) game console uses a special AMD chip with a total of eight processors, and Intel has released its new Phi card with more than 60 processors! What does this mean to us, as both consumers and new computer scientists?

[1] http://www.wired.com/2014/02/halting-problem/

The answer is that new algorithms, data structures, and programming paradigms will be needed to take advantage of this new processing environment. Orchestrating many processors to solve a problem is an exciting and challenging task.

Software Engineering

Even the process of writing programs itself has developed its own subdiscipline within computer science. Dubbed "software engineering," it concerns the process of creating programs: from designing the algorithms they use, to supporting testing and maintenance of the program once created. There is even a discipline interested in representing a developed program as a mathematical entity so that one can *prove* what a program will do once written.

Many Others

We have provided but a taste of the many fields that make computer science such a wonderfully rich area to explore. Every area that uses computation brings its own problems to be explored.

0.1.4 Computer Science Through Computer Programming

We have tried to make the point that computer science is not just programming. However, it is also true that for much of the book we will focus on just that aspect of computer science: programming. Beginning with "problem solving through programming" allows one to explore pieces of the computer science landscape as they naturally arise.

0.2 THE DIFFICULTY AND PROMISE OF PROGRAMMING

If computer science, particularly computer programming, is so interesting, why doesn't everybody do it? The truth is that it can be hard. We are often asked by beginning students, "Why is programming so hard?" Even grizzled programming veterans, when honestly looking back at their first experience, remember how difficult that first programming course was. Why? Understanding why it might be hard gives you an edge on what you can do to control the difficulty.

0.2.1 Difficulty 1: Two Things at Once

Let's consider an example. Let us say that, when you walk into that first day of Programming 101, you discover the course is not about programming but French poetry. French poetry?

Yes, French poetry. Imagine that you come in and the professor posts the following excerpt from a poem on the board.

A une Damoyselle malade

Ma mignonne,
Je vous donne
Le bon jour;
Le séjour
C'est prison.

Clément Marot

Your assigned task is to translate this poetry into English (or German, or Russian, whatever language is your native tongue). Let us also assume, for the moment, that:

(a) You do not know French.
(b) You have never studied poetry.

You have two problems on your hands. First, you have to gain a better understanding of the syntax and semantics (the form and substance) of the French language. Second, you need to learn more about the "rules" of poetry and what constitutes a good poem.

Lest you think that this is a trivial matter, an entire book has been written by Douglas Hofstadter on the very subject of the difficulty of translating this one poem ("Le Ton beau de Marot").

So what's your first move? Most people would break out a dictionary and, line by line, try to translate the poem. Hofstadter, in his book, does exactly that, producing the crude translation in Figure 0.1.

My Sweet/Cute [One] (Feminine)

My sweet/cute [one] (feminine)
I [to] you (respectful) give/bid/convey
The good day (i.e., a hello, i.e., greetings).
The stay/sojourn/ visit (i.e., quarantine)
{It} is prison.

A une Damoyselle malade

Ma mignonne,
Je vous donne
Le bon jour;
Le séjour
C'est prison.

FIGURE 0.1 Crude translation of excerpt.

The result is hardly a testament to beautiful poetry. This translation does capture the syntax and semantics, but not the poetry, of the original. If we take a closer look at the poem, we can discern some features that a good translation should incorporate. For example:

- Each line consists of three syllables.
- Each line's main stress falls on its final syllable.
- The poem is a string of rhyming couplets: *AA, BB, CC, ...*
- The semantic couplets are out of phase with the rhyming couplets: *A, AB, BC, ...*

Taking some of these ideas (and many more) into account, Hofstadter comes up with the translation in Figure 0.2.

My Sweet Dear	**A une Damoyselle malade**
My sweet dear,	Ma mignonne,
I send cheer –	Je vous donne
All the best!	Le bon jour;
Your forced rest	Le séjour
Is like jail.	C'est prison.

FIGURE 0.2 Improved translation of excerpt.

Not only does this version sound far more like poetry, but it also matches the original poem, following the rules and conveying the intent. It is a pretty good translation!

Poetry to Programming?

How does this poetry example help? Actually, the analogy is pretty strong. In coming to programming for the first time, you face exactly the same issues:

- You are not yet familiar with the syntax and semantics of the language you are working with—in this case, of the programming language Python and perhaps not of *any* programming language.
- You do not know how to solve problems using a computer—similar to not knowing how to write poetry.

Just like the French poetry neophyte, you are trying to solve two problems simultaneously. On one level, you are just trying to get familiar with the syntax and semantics of the language. At the same time, you are tackling a second, very difficult task: creating poetry in the previous example and solving problems using a computer in this course.

Working at two levels, the meaning of the programming words and then the intent of the program (what the program is trying to solve) are the two problems the beginning programmer has to face. Just like the French poetry neophyte, your first programs will be a bit clumsy as you learn both the programming language and how to use that language to solve problems. For example, to a practiced eye, many first programs look similar in nature to the literal translation of Hofstadter's in Figure 0.1. Trying to do two things simultaneously is difficult for anyone, so be gentle on yourself as you go forward with the process.

You might ask whether there is a better way. Perhaps, but we have not found it yet. The way to learn programming is to program, just like swinging a baseball bat, playing the piano, and winning at bridge; you can hear the rules and talk about the strategies, but learning is best done by doing.

0.2.2 Difficulty 2: What Is a Good Program?

Having mastered some of the syntax and semantics of a programming language, how do we write a good program? That is, how do we create a program that is more like poetry than like the mess arrived at through literal translation?

It is difficult to discuss a good program when, at this point, you know so little, but there are a couple of points that are worth noting even before we get started.

It's All About Problem Solving

If the rules of poetry are what guides writing good poetry, what are the guidelines for writing good programs? That is, what is it we have to learn in order to transition from a literal translation to a good poem?

For programming, it is *problem solving*. When you write a program, you are creating, in some detail, how it is that *you* think a particular problem or some class of problems, should be solved. Thus, the program represents, in a very accessible way, your thoughts on problem solving. Your thoughts! That means, before you write the program you must *have* some thoughts.

It is a common practice, even among veteran programmers, to get a problem and immediately sit down and start writing a program. Typically that approach results in a mess, and, for the beginning programmer, it results in an unsolved problem. Figuring out how to solve a problem requires some initial thought. If you think before you program, you better understand what the problem requires as well as the best strategies you might use to solve that problem.

Remember the two-level problem? Writing a program as you figure out how to solve a problem means that you are working at two levels at once: the problem-solving level and the programming level. That is more difficult than doing things sequentially. You should sit down and think about the problem and how you want to solve it *before* you start writing the program. We will talk more about this later, but rule 1 is:

Rule 1: Think before you program!

A Program as an Essay

When students are asked "What is the most important feature a program should have?" many answer, "It should run." By "run," they mean that the program executes and actually does something.

Wrong. As with any new endeavor, it is important to get the fundamentals correct right at the beginning. So **RULE 2** is

> **Rule 2:** A program is a human-readable essay on problem solving that also happens to execute on a computer.

A program is an object to be read by another person, just as any other essay. Although it is true that a program is written in such a way that a computer can execute it, it is still a human-readable essay. If your program is written so that it runs, and even runs correctly (notice we have not discussed "correctly" yet!), but is unreadable, then it is really fairly worthless.

The question is why? Why should it be that people must read it? Why isn't running good enough? Who's going to read it anyway? Let's answer the last question first. The person who is going to read it the most is you! That's correct, *you* have to read the programs you are writing all the time. Every time you put your program away for some period of time and come back to it, you have to re-read what you wrote and understand what you were thinking. Your program is a record of your thoughts on solving the problem and you have to be able to read your program in order to work with it, update it, add to it, and so on.

Furthermore, once you get out of the academic environment where you write programs solely for yourself, you will be writing programs with other people as a group. Your mates have to be able to read what you wrote! Think of the process as developing a newspaper edition. Everyone has to be able to read each others' content so that the edition, as a whole, makes sense. Just writing words on paper isn't enough—they have to fit together.

Our goal is to write programs that other people can read, as well as be run.

0.2.3 The Promise of a Computer Program

A program is an essay on problem solving and that will be our major focus. However, it is still interesting that programs do indeed run on a computer. That is, in fact, one of the unique, and most impressive parts about a program. Consider that idea for a moment. You can think of a way to solve a problem, write that thought down in detail as a program, and (assuming you did it correctly) that problem gets solved. More importantly, the problem can be solved again and again because the program can be used *independent of you*. That is, your thoughts not only live on as words (because of the essay-like nature of the program), but also as an entity that actually implements those thoughts. How amazing is that! Do you have some thoughts about how to make a robot dance? Write the program, and the robot dances. Do you have some ideas on how to create music? Write the program, and music is written automatically. Do you have an idea of how to solve a Sudoku puzzle? Write the program, and every puzzle is solved.

So a computer program (and the computer it runs on) offers a huge leap forward, perhaps the biggest since Gutenberg in the mid-1400s. Gutenberg invented moveable type, so that the written word of an individual—that is, their thoughts—could be reproduced independently of the writer. Now, not only can those thoughts be copied, but also implemented to be *used* over and over again.

Programming is as open, as universally applicable, as the thoughts of the people who do the programming, because a program is the manifest thought of the programmer.

0.3 CHOOSING A COMPUTER LANGUAGE

We have selected a particular programming language, the language called Python, for this introductory text. You should know that there are lots of programming languages out there. Wikipedia lists more than 500 programming languages (here is a list of the top 100[2]). Why so many languages, and why Python for this text?

0.3.1 Different Computer Languages

If a program is a concrete, runnable realization of a person's thoughts, then it makes sense that different people would create languages that allow them to better reflect those thoughts. In fact, computer scientists are crazy about languages, which is why there are so many. Whatever the reason that some language was created—and there can be many reasons—they all reflect some part of the creator's view of how to best express solving problems on a computer. In fact, computer scientists are specifically trained to write their own language to suit their needs—a talent few other disciplines support so fully!

So given all these languages, why did we pick Python?

0.3.2 Why Python?

> I set out to come up with a language that made programmers more productive.
>
> Guido van Rossum, author of Python

There are three features that we think are important for an introductory programming language:

- The language should provide a low "cognitive load" on the student. That is, it should be as easy as possible to express your problem-solving thoughts in the mechanisms provided by the programming language.
- Having spent all your time learning this language, it should be easy to apply it to problems you will encounter. In other words, having learned a language, you should be able to write short programs to solve problems that pop up in your life (sort your music, find a file on your computer, find the average temperature for the month, etc.).

[2] http://www.tiobe.com/index.php/content/paperinfo/tpci/index.html

- The programming language you use should have broad support across many disciplines. That is, the language should be embraced by practitioners from many fields (arts to sciences, as they say) and useful packages, collections of support programs, should be available to many different types of users.

So how does Python match up against these criteria?

Python Philosophy

Python offers a philosophy: *There should be one—and preferably only one—obvious way to do it.* The language should offer, as much as possible, a one-to-one mapping between the problem-solving need and the language support for that need. This is not necessarily the case with all programming languages. Given the two-level problem the introductory programmer already faces, reducing the programming language load as much as possible is important. Though Python does have its short cuts, they are far fewer than many other languages, and there is less "language" one has to remember to accomplish your task.

A "Best Practices" Language

One of our favorite descriptions of Python is that it is a "best practices" language. This means that Python provides many of the best parts of other languages directly to the user. Important data structures are provided as part of the standard language; iteration (described later) is introduced early and is available on standard data structures; packages for files, file paths, the Web, and so on are part of the standard language. Python is often described as a "batteries included" language in which many commonly needed aspects are provided by default. This characteristic means that you can use Python to solve problems you will encounter.

Python Is Open Source

One of Python's most powerful features is its support from the various communities and the breadth of that support. One reason is that Python is developed under the *Open Source* model. Open Source is both a way to think about software and a culture or viewpoint used by those who develop software. Open Source for software is a way to make software freely available and to guarantee that free availability to those who develop new software based on Open Source software. Linux, a type of operating system, is such a project, as are a number of other projects, such as Firefox (web browser), Thunderbird (mail client), Apache (web server), and, of course, Python. As a culture, Open Source adherents want to make software as available and useful as possible. They want to share the fruits of their labor and, as a group, move software forward, including the application areas where software is used. This perspective can be summarized as follows:

> A rising tide lifts all boats.

Each person is working explicitly (or implicitly) as part of a larger group towards a larger goal, making software available and useful. As a result of Python's Open Source development, there are free, specialized packages for almost any area of endeavor including: music, games, genetics, physics, chemistry, natural language, geography, and others. If you know Python and can do rudimentary programming, there are packages available that will support almost any area you care to choose.

0.3.3 Is Python the Best Language?

VideoNote 0.1
Getting Python

The answer to that question is that there is no "best" language. All computer programming languages are a compromise to some degree. After all, wouldn't it be easiest to describe the program in your own words and just have it run? Unfortunately, that isn't possible. Our present natural language (English, German, Hindi, whatever) is too difficult to turn into the precise directions a computer needs to execute a program. Each programming language has its own strengths and weaknesses. New programmers, having mastered their first programming language, are better equipped to examine other languages and what they offer. For now, we think Python is a good compromise for the beginning programmer.

0.4 WHAT IS COMPUTATION?

It can be difficult to find a good definition for a broadly used word such as "computation." If you look, you will find definitions that include terms such as "information processing," "sequence of operations," "numbers," "symbols," and "mathematical methods." Computer scientists interested in the theory of computation formally define what a computation is, and what its limits are. It is a fascinating topic, but it is a bit beyond our scope.

We will use an English language definition that suits our needs. In this book we will define a computation as:

> *Computation* is the manipulation of data by either humans or machines.

The data that is manipulated may be numbers, characters, or other symbols.

0.5 WHAT IS A COMPUTER?

The definition of a computer then is

> A *computer* is something that does computation.

That definition is purposefully vague on *how* a computer accomplishes computation, only that it does so. This imprecision exists because what counts as a computer is surprisingly diverse. However, there are some features that almost any system that does computation should have.

- A computer should be able to *accept input*. What counts as input might vary among computers, but data must be able to enter the computer for processing.
- If a computer is defined by its ability to *do computation*, then any object that is a computer must be able to manipulate data.
- A computer must be able to *output data*.

Another characteristic of many computers is their ability to perform computation using an assembly of only simple parts. Such computers are composed of huge numbers of simple parts assembled in complex ways. As a result, the complexity of many computers comes from the organization of their parts, not the parts themselves.

0.5.1 Computation in Nature

There are a number of natural systems that perform computation. These are areas of current, intense investigation in computer science as researchers try to learn more from existing natural systems.

The Human Brain

When electronic computers were first brought to the public's attention in the 1950s and even into the 1960s, they were often referred to as "electronic brains." The reason for this was obvious. The only computing object we had known up to that time was the human brain.

The human brain is in fact a powerful computing engine, though it is not often thought of in quite that way. It constantly takes in a torrent of input data—sensory data from the five senses—manipulates that data in a variety of ways, and provides output in the form of both physical action (both voluntary and involuntary) as well as mental action.

The amazing thing about the human brain is that the functional element of the brain is a very simple cell called the *neuron* (Figure 0.3).

Though a fully functional cell, a neuron also acts as a kind of small switch. When a sufficient signal reaches the *dendrites* of a neuron, the neuron "fires" and a signal is transmitted down the *axon* of the neuron to the *axon terminals*. Neurons are not directly connected to one another; rather, the dendrites of one neuron are located very close to the axon terminals of another neuron, separated by a space known as the *synapse*. When the signal reaches the axon terminal, chemicals called *neurotransmitters* are secreted across the synapse. It is the transmission of a signal, from neurotransmitters secreted by the axon terminals of one neuron to the dendrites of a connecting neuron that constitutes a basic computation in the brain.

Here are a few interesting facts about neuronal activity:

- The signal within a neuron is not transmitted by electricity (as in a wire), but by rapid chemical changes that propagate down the axon. The result is that the signal is very much slower than an electrical transmission down a wire—about a million times slower.

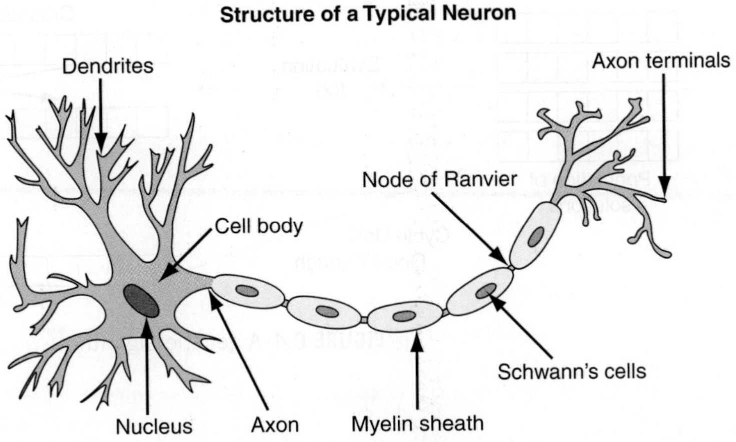

FIGURE 0.3 An annotated neuron. [SEER Training Modules, U.S. National Institutes of Health, National Cancer Institute.]

- Because the signal is chemical, a neuron must typically recover for a millisecond (one-thousandth of a second) before it can fire again. Therefore, there is a built-in time delay to neuronal firing.
- A neuron is "fired" in response to some combination of the number of signals that are received at its dendrite (how many other neurons are firing in proximity) and the strength of the signal received (how much neurotransmitter is being dumped into the synapse).

One thing to note is how *slow* the neuron is as a switch. As you will see in Section 0.6.2, electronic switches can act many millions of times faster. However, what the brain lacks in terms of speedy switches, it makes up for in sheer size and complexity of organization. By some estimates, the human brain consists of of 100 billion (10^{11}) neurons and 100 trillion (10^{14}) synapses. Furthermore, the organization of the brain is incredibly complicated. Scientists have spent hundreds of years identifying specific areas of the brain that are responsible for various functions, and how those areas are interconnected. Yet for all this complexity, the main operational unit is a tiny, slow switch.

Scientists have been fascinated by the brain, so much so that there is a branch of computer science that works with simulations of *neural networks*, networks consisting of simple switches such as those found in the brain. Neural networks have been used to solve many difficult problems.

Evolutionary Computation

The evolution of biological species can be viewed as a computation process. In this view, the inputs of the computational process are the environmental variables the biological entity is

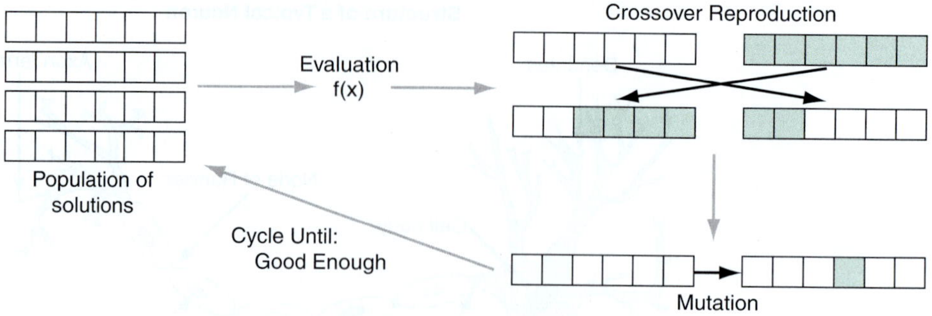

FIGURE 0.4 A genetic algorithm.

subjected to; the computational process is the adaptation of the genetic code and the output is the adaptation that results from the genetic code modification.

This point of view has been incorporated into approaches known as *genetic algorithms*. These techniques take the concepts of simple genetics, as proposed by Gregor Mendel, and the processes of evolution as described by Charles Darwin, and use them to compute.

The basic parts of a genetic algorithm, shown in Figure 0.4, are:

- A way to *encode* a solution in a linear sequence, much like the sequence of information contained in a chromosome. This encoding depends on the problem, but it typically consists of parameters (struts for a bridge, components for a circuit, jobs for a schedule, etc.) that are required to constitute a solution.
- A method to *evaluate* the "goodness" of a particular solution, called the *evaluation function* and represented as f(x) in the diagram.
- A *population* of solutions often initially created by random selection of the solution components, from which new solutions can be created.
- Some genetic *modification* methods to create new solutions from old solutions. In particular, there is *mutation*, which is a modification of one aspect of an existing solution and *crossover*, which combines aspects of two parent solutions into a new solution.

The process proceeds as follows. Each solution in the population is evaluated to determine how fit it is. Based on the fitness of the existing solutions, new solutions are created using the genetic modification methods. Those solutions that are more fit are given more opportunity to create new solutions; less fit solutions are given less opportunity. This process incorporates a "survival of the fittest" notion. Over time, better and better solutions are evolved that solve the existing problem.

Genetic algorithms and other similar approaches have been used to solve many complex problems such as scheduling, circuit design, and others.

FIGURE 0.5 NACA (National Advisory Committee for Aeronautics) High-Speed-Flight Station Computer Room. [NASA/Courtesy of nasaimages.org]

0.5.2 The Human Computer

The common use of the word "computer" from around the seventeenth century to about World War II referred to *people*. To compute difficult, laborious values for mathematical constants (such as π or e), fission reactions (for the Manhattan Project), and gun trajectory tables, people were used (Figure 0.5). However, using people had problems.

A classic example of such a problem was created by William Shanks, an English amateur mathematician, who in 1873 published π calculated to 707 decimal places. The calculation by hand took 28 years. Unfortunately, he made a calculation error at the 528th digit that made the last two years of calculation a waste of time. His error wasn't found until 70 years later using a mechanical calculator.

The U.S. Army's Ballistics Research Laboratory was responsible for the creation of gun trajectory tables. Each new artillery piece required a table for the gunner to use to calculate where the round would land. However, it took significant human effort to make these tables. Kay Mauchly Antonelli, a mathematician from the University of Pennsylvania and one of the six original programmers of the ENIAC, the first general-purpose electronic digital computer, said, "To do just one trajectory, at one particular angle, usually took between 30 to 40 hours of calculation on this [mechanical] desk calculator." These tables exceeded 1800 entries and required up to four years to produce by hand.[3]

It was obvious that something had to be done. People were neither accurate enough nor fast enough, to do this kind of calculation. A more modern, faster, and accurate approach was needed.

0.6 THE MODERN, ELECTRONIC COMPUTER

Although there may be many notions of a computer, we all know what a modern computer is. We read e-mail on it, text message each other, listen to music, play videos, and play games on them. The design of these computers was first conceived around World War II to solve those tedious calculation problems that humans did so slowly, especially the Army's ballistics tables. How do electronic computers work? What makes them so special?

0.6.1 It's the Switch!

Modern digital computers use, as their base component, nothing more complicated than a simple switch. Very early computers used mechanical switches or relays; later versions used vacuum tubes, and finally, modern computers use transistors (see Figure 0.6).

FIGURE 0.6 Vacuum tube, single transistor, and chip transistor (the dot). [Reprint Courtesy of International Business Machines Corporation, copyright © International Business Machines Corporation].

A switch's function is pretty obvious. It is either on or off. When turned on, electricity flows through the switch and when turned off, no electrical flow occurs. Using a switch and its on/off property, you can construct simple logic circuits. In logic, we have only two states: True and False. In our logic circuit, we translate True and False to the physical process of a switch. The True condition is represented by a current flowing through the circuit and

[3] http://www.comphist.org/pdfs/Video-Giant%20Brains-MachineChangedWorld-Summary.pdf

False is represented by lack of current flow. Though we will cover Boolean logic in more detail in Chapter 2, there are two simple combinations of switches we can show: the ***and*** and ***or*** circuits.

For the Boolean ***and***, a True value results *only* if both of the two input values are True. All other combinations of input have a False output. In the ***and*** circuit, we connect two switches together in series as shown in Figure 0.7. Electricity can flow, that is, the circuit represents a True value, only if *both* switches are turned on. If either switch is turned off, no electricity flows and the circuit represents a False value.

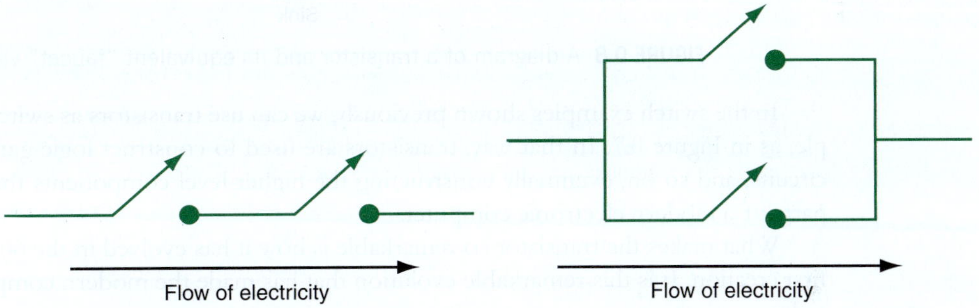

FIGURE 0.7 Switches implementing an ***and*** gate (left) and an ***or*** gate (right).

We can do the same for the Boolean ***or***. An ***or*** is True if *either one or both* of its inputs are True; otherwise, it is False. In the ***or*** circuit of Figure 0.7, we connect two switches together in parallel. Electricity can flow if *either* switch is turned on, representing a True value. Only when both switches are turned off does the circuit represent a False value.

Similar Boolean logic elements, usually called logic *gates*, can be constructed from simple circuits. The amazing thing is that using only simple logic circuits, we can assemble an entire computer. For example, an ***and*** and ***or*** gate can be combined to make a simple circuit to add two values, called an *adder*. Once we can add, we can use the adder circuit to build a subtraction circuit. Further, once we have an adder circuit we can do multiplication (by repeated addition), and then division, and so on. Just providing some simple elements like logic gates allows us to build more complicated circuits until we have a complete computer.

0.6.2 The Transistor

Although any switch will do, the "switch" that made the electronic computer what it is today is called a *transistor*. The transistor is an electronic device invented in 1947 by William Shockley, John Bardeen, and Walter Brattain at Bell Labs (for which they eventually won the Nobel Prize in Physics in 1956). It utilized a new technology, a material called a semiconductor, that allowed transistors to supersede the use of other components such as vacuum tubes. Though a transistor has a number of uses, the one we care most about for computer use is as a switch. A transistor has three wires with the names Source, Sink, and Gate. Electricity flows from the Source to the Sink. If there is a signal, a voltage, or current, on the Gate, then electricity flows—the switch is "on." If there is no signal on the Gate, no electricity flows—the switch is "off." See Figure 0.8.

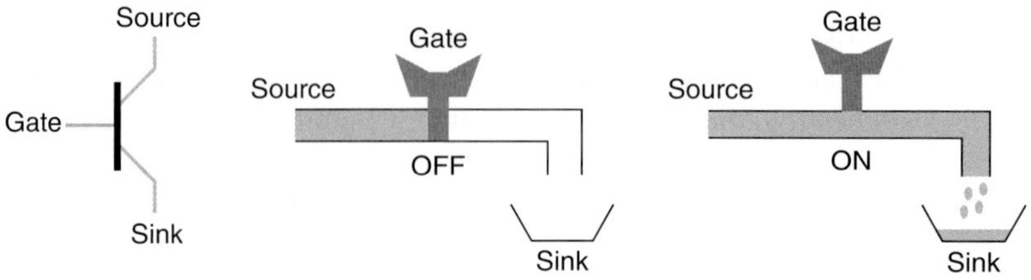

FIGURE 0.8 A diagram of a transistor and its equivalent "faucet" view.

In the switch examples shown previously, we can use transistors as switches, for example, as in Figure 0.7. In that way, transistors are used to construct logic gates, then larger circuits, and so on, eventually constructing the higher-level components that become the parts of a modern electronic computer.

What makes the transistor so remarkable is how it has evolved in the 60 years since its first creation. It is this remarkable evolution that has made the modern computer what it is today.

Smaller Size

The size of a transistor has changed dramatically since its inception. The first Shockley transistor was very large, on the order of inches (see Figure 0.9). By 1954, Texas Instruments was selling the first commercial transistor and had shrunk the transistor size to that of a postage stamp.

However, even the small size of individual transistor components was proving to be a limitation. More transistors were needed in a smaller area if better components were to be designed. The solution was the *integrated circuit*, invented by Jack Kilby of Texas Instruments

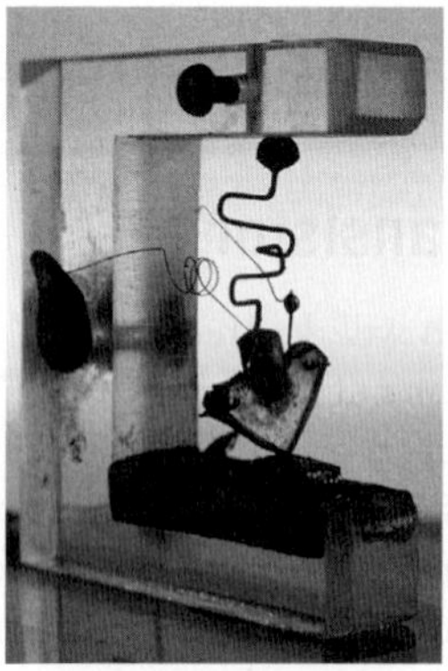

FIGURE 0.9 The Shockley transistor—the first transistor. [Image courtesy of Science & Society Picture Library/Getty Images.]

FIGURE 0.10 Kilby's first integrated circuit (left) and the Intel 4004 microprocessor (right). [Image courtesy of Texas Instruments (left). Image courtesy of Intel Corporation (right).]

in 1958–1959 (for which he won the 2000 Nobel Prize in Physics); see Figure 0.10. The integrated circuit was a contiguous piece of semiconductor material upon which multiple transistors could be manufactured. The integrated circuit allowed many transistors to be embedded in a single piece of material, allowing a more complex functional circuit on a very small area. By 1971, Intel managed to manufacture the first complete computer processing unit (or CPU) on a single chip, a microprocessor named the Intel 4004 (see Figure 0.10). It was approximately the size of a human fingernail (3 × 4 mm) with 2300 transistors. By this time, the size of the transistor on this microprocessor had shrunk to 10 microns, the width of the a single fiber of cotton or silk.

The shrinkage of the transistor has continued. Today, the size of a transistor has reached amazingly small levels. Figure 0.11 shows an electron microscope picture of an IBM

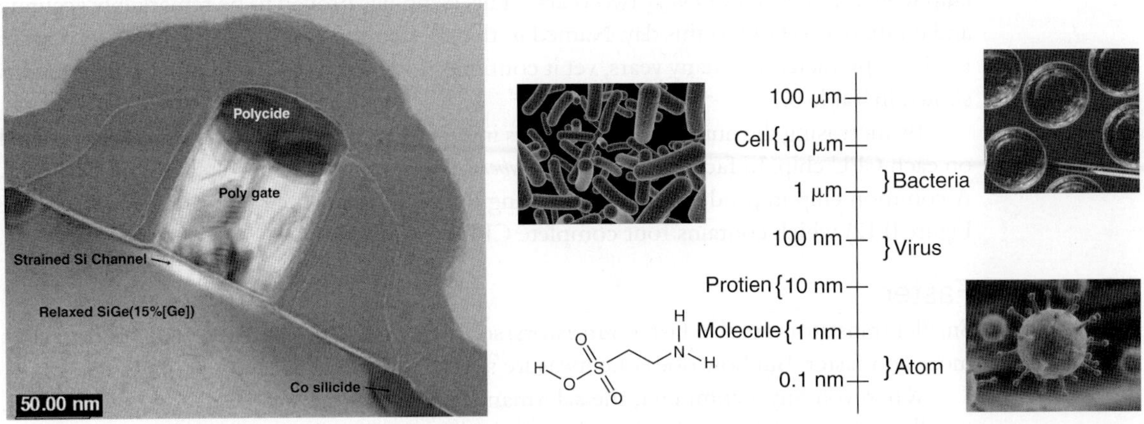

FIGURE 0.11 A photomicrograph of a single 50 nm IBM transistor (left) and a scale small items (right). [Reprint Courtesy of International Business Machines Corporation, copyright © International Business Machines Corporation (left) Sebastian Kaulitzki/Shutterstock (right)].

Year	Transistor Count	Model
1971	2,300	4004
1978	29,000	8086
1982	134,000	80286
1986	275,000	80386
1989	1,200,000	80486
1993	3,100,000	Pentium
1999	9,500,000	Pentium III
2001	42,000,000	Pentium 4
2007	582,000,000	Core 2 Quad
2011	2,600,000,000	10-core Westmere
2014	3,000,000,000	Apple A8X (iPad2)
2015	5,560,000,000	18-core Xeon Haswell

TABLE 0.1 Transistor counts in Intel microprocessors, by year.

transistor gate that is 50 nanometers wide, 50×10^{-9} meters, a thousand times smaller than transistors in the Intel 4004. That is more than 10 times smaller than a single wavelength of visible light. It is approximately the thickness of a cell membrane and only 10 times larger than a single turn of a DNA helix. Current transistors are nearly a third that size at 14 nm with smaller devices being tested in labs.

Quantity and Function

As the size of a transistor shrank, the number of transistors that could be put on a single chip increased. This increase has been quite dramatic. In fact, there is a famous statement made by the founder of Intel, Gordon Moore, that predicts this amazing trend. In 1965, Moore predicted that the number of transistors that can be placed inexpensively on a single chip would double about every two years.[4] This trend has proven to be remarkably accurate and continues to hold to this day. Named in the popular press as "Moore's Law," its demise has been predicted for many years, yet it continues to hold true. A summary of this trend is shown in Table 0.1.

By increasing the number of transistors in a CPU, more functionality can be introduced on each CPU chip. In fact, recently the *number* of CPUs on a single chip has also increased. A common chip in production at the writing of this book is the quad-core processor (see Figure 0.12) which contains four complete CPUs.

Faster

Smaller transistors are also faster transistors, so smaller transistors provide a doubling factor: more and faster. But how does one measure speed?

When you buy a computer, the salesman is more than happy to tell you how fast it is, usually in terms of how many "gigahertz" the computer will run. The value the salesman mentions is really a measure of a special feature of every computer called its *clock*. The clock

[4] The original estimate was one year, but was later revised upward.

FIGURE 0.12 Intel Nehalem Quad Core Processor. [Courtesy of Intel Corporation.]

of a computer is not much like a wall clock, however. Rather, it is more like a drummer in a band. The drummer's job in the band is to keep the beat, coordinating the rhythm of all the other members of the band. The faster the drummer beats, the faster the band plays. The components on a CPU chip are like the band—they need something to help them coordinate their efforts. That is the role of the clock. The clock regularly emits a signal indicating that the next operation is to occur. Upon every "beat" of the clock, another "cycle" occurs on the chip, meaning another set of operations can occur.

Therefore, the faster the clock runs, the faster the chip runs and, potentially, the more instructions that can be executed. But how fast is a gigahertz (GHz)? Literally, 1 gigahertz means that the clock emits a signal every nanosecond, that is, every billionth of a second (10^{-9}). Thus, your 1 GHz computer executes instructions once every nanosecond. That is a very fast clock indeed!

Consider that the "universal speed limit" is the speed of light, roughly 186,282 miles/second (299,792,458 meters/second) in a vacuum. Given that an electrical signal (data) is carried at this speed, how far can an electric signal travel in a nanosecond? If we do the math, it turns out that an electric signal can only travel about 11.8 inches. Only 11.8 inches! At 2 GHz, it can only travel 5.9 inches; at 4GHz, only 2.95 inches. Consider that 5.9 inches is not even the width of a typical computer board! In fact, at the writing of this book a further doubling of speed of present computers is limited by the distance electricity can travel.

Given a measure of the speed of a computer, how does that translate to actual work done by the computer? The process of measuring computing operations, known as "benchmarking," can be a difficult task. Different computing systems are better or worse, depending on how you measure the benchmark. However, manufacturers do list a measure called *instructions per second* or *IPS*. That is, it's a measure of how many instructions, such as an addition, can be done every second. In Table 0.2, we can see how the measure of increased clock rate affects the IPS (MIPS is millions of IPS). One interesting note is that, since about 2000, the

Year	CPU	Instructions/second	Clock Speed
1971	Intel 4004	1 MIPS	740 kHz
1972	IBM System/370	1 MIPS	?
1977	Motorola 68000	1 MIPS	8 MHz
1982	Intel 286	3 MIPS	12 MHz
1984	Motorola 68020	4 MIPS	20 MHz
1992	Intel 486DX	54 MIPS	66 MHz
1994	PowerPC 600s (G2)	35 MIPS	33 MHz
1996	Intel Pentium Pro	541 MIPS	200 MHz
1997	PowerPC G3	525 MIPS	233 MHz
2002	AMD Athlon XP 2400+	5,935 MIPS	2.0 GHz
2003	Pentium 4	9,726 MIPS	3.2 GHz
2005	Xbox360	19,200 MIPS	3.2 GHz
2006	PS3 Cell BE	10,240 MIPS	3.2 GHz
2006	AMD Athlon FX-60	18,938 MIPS	2.6 GHz
2007	Intel Core 2 QX9770	59,455 MIPS	3.2 GHz
2011	Intel Core i7 990x	159,000 MIPS	3.46 GHz
2015	Inel Core i7 5960X	238,310 MIPS	3.0 GHz

TABLE 0.2 Speed (in millions of IPS or MIPS) and clock rates of microprocessors, by year.

clock speed has not increased dramatically for the reasons mentioned previously. However, the existence of multiple CPUs on a chip still allows for increases in IPS of a CPU.

0.7 A HIGH-LEVEL LOOK AT A MODERN COMPUTER

Now that you know something about the low-level functional elements of a computer, it is useful to step up to a higher-level view of the elements of a computer, often termed the computer's *architecture*. The architecture is used to describe the various parts of the computer and how they interact. The standard architecture, named after the stored program model of John von Neumann, looks something like the following (see Figure 0.13):

- **Processor:** As we have mentioned, the processor is the computational heart of a computer. Often called the CPU (Central Processing Unit), it can itself consist of a number of parts including the ALU (Arithmetic and Logic Unit), where logical calculations are done; local fast storage, called the cache; connections among components, called the bus, as well as other elements.
- **Main Memory:** A processor needs data to process, and main memory is where data is stored. Main memory is traditionally volatile; that is, when power is turned off, data is lost. It is also called RAM = Random Access Memory, that is, retrievable in any order. Use of non-volatile memory is increasing, especially in portable devices.

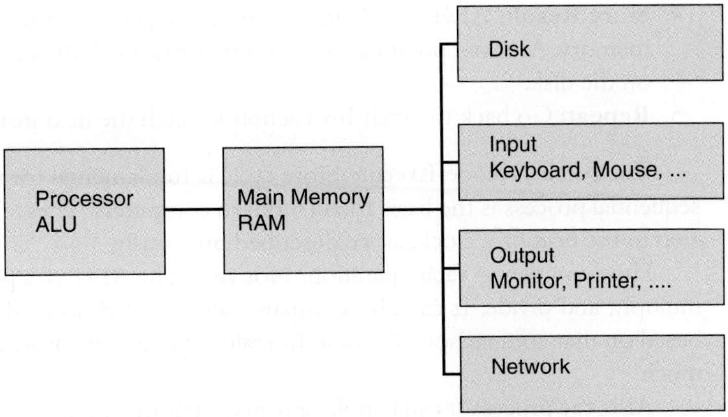

FIGURE 0.13 A typical computer architecture.

- **Disk:** The disk is for permanent (non-volatile) storage of data. The disk is also known as the "hard drive." Data must be moved from the disk to main memory before it can be used by the processor. Disks are relatively slow, mechanical devices that are being replaced by non-mechanical memory cards in some portable devices.
- **Input/Output:** These devices convert external data into digital data and vice versa for use and storage in the computer.
- **Network:** A network is needed to communicate with other computers. From the viewpoint of the processor the network is simply another input/output device.

Consider a simple operation `theSum = num1 + num2`. The `theSum`, `num1`, and `num2` terms are called *variables*, readable names that contain values to be used in a program. The statement adds the two numbers stored in `num1` and `num2` to produce a result which is stored in `theSum`. Assume that `num1` and `num2` represent numbers that are stored on the disk and that the result `theSum` will also be stored on the disk. Assume that the instruction itself, `theSum = num1 + num2`, also resides on the disk. Here is how it works:

1. **Fetch Instruction:** When the processor is ready to process an instruction, it fetches the instruction from memory. If the instruction is not in memory but on the disk, the memory must first fetch it from the disk. In this way, the instruction `theSum = num1 + num2` will move from the disk through memory to the processor.
2. **Decode Instruction:** The processor examines the instruction ("decodes" it) and sees that operands `num1` and `num2` are needed, so it fetches them from memory. If `num1` and `num2` are not in memory, but on the disk, the memory must first fetch them from the disk.
3. **Execute Operation:** Once the processor has both the instruction and the operands, it can perform the operation, addition in this case.

4. **Store Result:** After calculating the sum, the processor will store the resulting sum in memory. At some point before power is turned off, the data in memory will be stored on the disk.
5. **Repeat:** Go back to Fetch Instruction to fetch the next instruction in a program.

The Fetch-Decode-Execute-Store cycle is fundamental for all computers. This simple, sequential process is the basis for all modern computers. These four steps are done in lock-step to the beat of a clock, as we described previously.

How complex is each operation? Not very. The ALU of a processor can add, subtract, multiply, and divide. It can also compare values and choose which instruction to do next based on that comparison. That's it. In reality, it is slightly more complex than that, but not much.

Also, the processor can handle only two types of operands: integers and floating points. For our purposes, you can think of floating-point values as fractional values represented in decimal notation, for example, 37.842. There will be a separate ALU for integers and a separate one for floating-point numbers, called the FPU = Floating-Point Unit.

The important concept is that everything a computer does boils down to a few simple operations, but at billions of operations per second, the result is significant computational power.

0.8 REPRESENTING DATA

The underlying element of a computer is typically a switch, usually a transistor. Given that, what is the most obvious way to represent data values? The obvious choice is binary. Binary values can only be either 1 or 0, which corresponds to the physical nature of a switch, which is on or off. What is interesting is that we can represent not only numbers in binary, but music, video, images, characters, and many other kinds of data also in binary.

0.8.1 Binary Data

By definition, a digital computer is binary, which is base 2. Our normal number system is decimal, base 10, probably because we have 10 fingers for counting. People haven't always worked in base 10. For example, the ancient Babylonians (2000 BC) used base 60 (sexagesimal) for the most advanced mathematics of that time. As a result, they are the source of modern time-keeping and angle measurement: 60 seconds in a minute, 60 minutes in an hour, and 360 degrees in a circle. For decimals we use ten digits: 0, 1, 2, 3, 4, 5, 6, 7, 8, 9. For sexagesimal the Babylonians used sixty digits: 0, 1, 2, 3, ..., 58, 59. For binary there are only two digits: 0, 1.

Why binary? Two reasons, really. As we have said, the first reason is the hardware being used. Electronic transistors lend themselves very naturally to base two. A transistor is either on or off, which can be directly translated to 1 or 0. However, the second reason is that two digits are easy to store and easy to operate on. Storage devices in binary need a medium that has two states: a state called "one" and another state "zero." Anything with two states can become digital storage. Examples include high/low voltage, right/left magnetism, charge/no-charge, on/off, and so on. For example, main memory has small capacitors that hold a charge (1) or not (0). Disks are magnetized one way (1) or the other (0). CDs and DVDs reflect light one way (1) or the other (0).

Manipulations of the underlying data can also be done simply using electronic gates that we discussed previously, that is, the Boolean logic: and, or, not. Because such logical circuits can be extremely small and fast, they can be implemented to do calculations quickly and efficiently. For example, the adder circuit we discussed previously that adds two binary digits or *bits* (bit = BInary digiT) can be done with logical circuits: sum = (A and (not B)) or ((not A) and B)). From such simple logic all arithmetic operations can be built. For example, subtraction is the addition of a negative value, multiplication is repeated addition, and division can be done using the other three operations. A choice can be made based on the value of a bit: choose one thing or another. That choice bit can be calculated using any arbitrary logical expression using the logical operators: and, or, not. Therefore, the entire ALU (and the rest of the computer) can be built from the logical operators: and, or, not.

0.8.2 Working with Binary

A brief look at the binary representation of numbers and characters provides useful background for understanding binary computation. Because our world is a world of decimal numbers, let's look at representing decimals in binary. We begin with a review of place holding in decimals, by taking you back to elementary school. For example, consider the number 735 in base 10 (written as 735_{10}). Notice in the last line how the exponents start at 2 and work down to 0 as you move from left to right.[5]

$$\begin{aligned}735_{10} &= 7\ \textit{hundreds} + 3\ \textit{tens} + 5\ \textit{ones}\\ 735_{10} &= 7 * 100 + 3 * 10 + 5 * 1\\ 735_{10} &= 7 * 10^2 + 3 * 10^1 + 5 * 10^0\end{aligned}$$

In binary we only have two digits: 0, 1. Also, our base is 2 rather than 10. Therefore, our rightmost three places are fours, twos, ones. As with base 10, the exponents will decrease as we move from left to right—in this case: 2, 1, then 0. Using the previous notation, but working backwards from the last line to the first line, let us determine what 101 in binary (101_2) is in base 10 (decimal).

$$\begin{aligned}101_2 &= 1 * 2^2 + 0 * 2^1 + 1 * 2^0\\ 101_2 &= 1 * 4 + 0 * 2 + 1 * 1\\ 101_2 &= 4 + 0 + 1\\ 101_2 &= 5_{10}\end{aligned}$$

[5] We use an asterix(*) to represent multiplication.

In a similar way, any decimal integer can be represented in binary. For example,

$$1052_{10} = 10000011100_2$$

Fractions can be represented using integers in the scientific notation that you learned in science classes:

$$1/8 = 0.125 = 125 * 10^{-3}$$

The mantissa (125) and exponent (-3) are integers that can be expressed and stored in binary. The actual implementation of binary fractions is different because the starting point is binary, but the principle is the same: binary fractions are stored using binary mantissas and binary exponents. How many bits are allocated to mantissa and how many to exponents varies from computer to computer, but the two numbers are stored together.

There are four important concepts that you need to know about representation:

- All numbers in a computer are represented in binary.
- Because of fixed, hardware limits on number storage, there is a limit to how big an integer can be stored in one unit of computer memory (usually 32 or 64 bits of storage).
- Fractions are represented in scientific notation and are approximations.
- Everything is converted to binary for manipulation and storage: letters, music, pictures, and so on.

0.8.3 Limits

We have covered the representation of numbers in binary. Let's look at limits. Most computers organize their data into *words* that are usually 32 bits in size (though 64-bit words are growing in use). There are an infinite number of integers, but with only 32 bits available in a word, there is a limited number of integers that can fit. If one considers only positive integers, one can represent 2^{32} integers with a 32-bit word, or a little over 4 billion integers. To represent positive and negative integers evenly, the represented integers range from negative 2 billion to positive 2 billion. That is a lot of numbers, but there is a limit and it is not hard to exceed it. For example, most U.S. state budgets will not fit in that size number (4 billion). On the other hand, a 64-bit computer could represent 2^{64} integers using a 64-bit word, which in base 10 is 1.8×10^{19}: a huge number—over 4 billion times more than can be stored in a 32-bit word.

Fractional values present a different problem. We know from mathematics that between every pair of Real numbers there are an infinite number of Real numbers. To see that, choose any two Real numbers A and B, and $(A + B)/2$ is a Real number in between. That operation can be repeated an infinite number of times to find more Real numbers between A and B. No matter how we choose to represent Real numbers in binary, the representation will always be an approximation. For example, if you enter 19/5.0 into Python, it will be calculated as 3.7999999999999998 instead of the expected 3.8 (try it!). The approximation is a feature of storage in binary rather than a feature of Python.

Bits, Bytes, and Words

Computer words (as opposed to English words) are built from *bytes*, which contain 8 bits so one 32-bit word is made of 4 bytes. Storage is usually counted in bytes, for example, 2 GB of RAM is approximately 2 billion bytes of memory (actually, it is 2^{31} bytes, which is 2,147,483,648 bytes). Bytes are the unit of measurement for size mainly for historical reasons.

0.8.4 Representing Letters

So far we've dealt with numbers. What about letters (characters): how are characters stored in a computer? Not surprisingly, everything is still stored in binary, which means that it is still a number. Early developers created ways to map characters to numbers.

First, what is a character? Characters are what we see on a printed page and are mostly made from letters (a, b, c, ...), digits (0, 1, 2, ...), and punctuation (period, comma, semicolon, ...). However, there are also characters that are not printable such as "carriage return" or "tab" as well as characters that existed at the dawn of computing to control printers such as "form feed." The first standardized set of computer characters was the ASCII (American Standard Code for Information Interchange) set developed in 1963. ASCII served the English-speaking world, but could not handle other alphabets. As computing became more universal the restrictions of the 128 ASCII characters became a problem. How could we handle the tens of thousands of Chinese characters? To address this problem a universal encoding named Unicode was first defined in 1991 and can handle over 1 million different characters. One implementation of Unicode is UTF-8 which is popular because it is backward compatible to the ASCII encoding that dominated the first 30 years of computing. Currently over 85% the pages on the World Wide Web use UTF-8. It is the default character representation for Python 3. For those reasons this text will use UTF-8.

Table 0.3 has part of the UTF-8 encoding showing some English characters, some symbols, and some control characters. The table shows a mapping between numbers and

Char	Dec	Char	Dec	Char	Dec	Char	Dec
NUL	0	SP	32	@	64	`	96
SOH	1	!	33	A	65	a	97
STX	2	"	34	B	66	b	98
ETX	3	#	35	C	67	c	99
EOT	4	$	36	D	68	d	100
ENQ	5	%	37	E	69	e	101
ACK	6	&	38	F	70	f	102
BEL	7	'	39	G	71	g	103
BS	8	(	40	H	72	h	104

TABLE 0.3 Table of UTF-8 characters (first few rows).

characters. Each character has an associated number, that is "A" is 65 while "a" is 97. Knowing this relationship, we can interpret a set of numbers as characters and then manipulate those characters just as we would numbers. We'll talk more about this topic in Chapter 4.

0.8.5 Representing Other Data

You must get the idea by now: what computers can represent is numbers. If you want to represent other data, you must find a way to encode that data as numbers.

Images

How to store an image? If the image is discrete—that is, built of many individual parts—we can represent those individual parts as numbers. Take a close look at your monitor or TV screen (with a magnifying glass, if you can). The image is made up of thousands of very small dots. These dots, called *pixels* (short for picture elements), are used to create an image. Each pixel has an associated color. If you put a lot of these pixels together in a small area, they start to look like an image (see Figure 0.14).

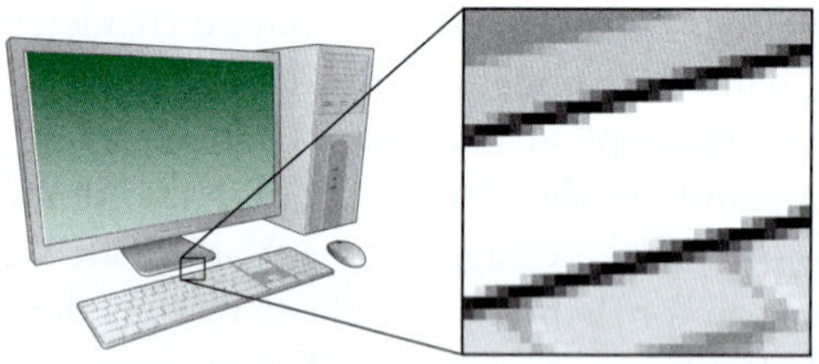

FIGURE 0.14 A computer display picture with a close-up of the individual pixels. [Juliengrondin/Shutterstock]

Each pixel can be represented as a location (in a two-dimensional grid) and as a color. The location is two numbers (which row and which column the pixel occupies), and the color is also represented as a number. Although there are a variety of ways to represent color, a common way is to break each color into its contribution from the three basic colors: red, green, and blue. The color number represents how much of each basic color is contributed to the final color. An 8-bit color scheme means that each color can contribute 8 bits, or $2^8 = 256$ possible shades of that color. Thus, a 24-bit color system can represent 2^{24} different colors, or 16,777,216.

The quantity of pixels is important. Standard analog television (extinct as of the writing of this book) used 525 lines of pixels, with each line containing 480 pixels, a total of

252,000 pixels. High-definition television has 1920 × 1080 pixels for a total of 2,073,600, a much higher resolution and a much better image.

Music

How to represent music as numbers? There are two types of musical sound that we might want to capture: recorded sound and generated sound. First, let's look at recording sound. A sound "wave" is a complex wave of air pressure that we detect with our ears. If we look at the shape of this sound wave (say with an oscilloscope), we can see how complex the wave can be. However, if we record the height of that wave at a very high rate—say, at a rate of 44,100 times/second (or 44kHz, the sampling rate on most MP3s)—then we can record that height as a number for that time in the sound wave. Therefore, we record two numbers: the height of the recorded sound and the time when that height was recorded. When we play sound back, we can reproduce the shape of the sound wave by creating a new sound wave that has the same height at the selected times as the recorded sound at each point in time. The more often we "sample" the sound wave, the better our ability to reproduce it accurately. See Figure 0.15 for an example.

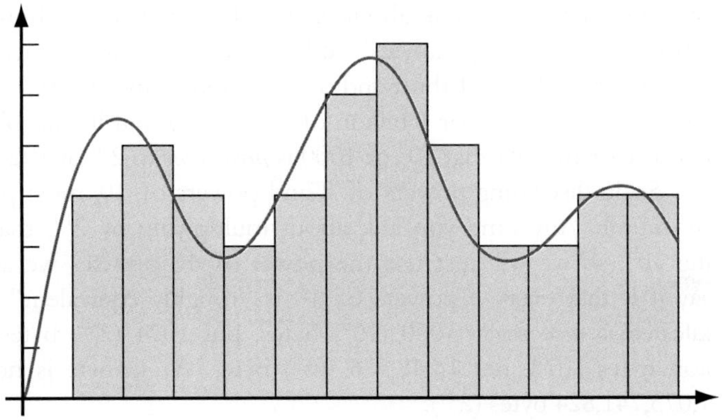

FIGURE 0.15 A sound wave and the samples of that sound wave (green bar height) over time.

To generate our own new sound, we can write computer programs that generate the same data, a wave height at some point in time, and then that data can be played just like recorded sound.

0.8.6 What Does a Number Represent?

We've shown that all the data we record for use by a computer is represented as a number, whether the data is numeric, text, image, audio, or any other kind of data. So how can you tell what a particular recorded data value represents? You cannot by simply looking at the bits. Any particular data value can be interpreted as an integer, a character, a sound sample, and so on. It depends on the use for which that data value was recorded. That is, it depends on the *type* of the data. We will talk more of types in Chapter 1, but the type of the data indicates for what use the data values are to be used. If the type is characters, then the numbers represent UTF-8 values. If the type is floating-point, then the numbers represent the mantissa and exponent of a value. If the type is an image, then the number would represent the color of a particular pixel. Knowing the type of the data lets you know what the data values represent.

0.8.7 How to Talk About Quantities of Data

How much data can a computer hold, and what constitutes "a lot" of data? The answer to that question varies, mostly depending on when you ask it. Very much like Moore's law and processing speed, the amount of data that a commercial disk can hold has grown dramatically over the years.

Again, there are some terms in common usage in the commercial world. In the context of data amounts, we talk about values like "kilobytes" (abbreviated KB) or "megabytes" (abbreviate MB) or "gigabytes" (abbreviated GB), but the meaning is a bit odd. "Kilo" typically refers to 10^3 or 1 thousand of something, "mega" 10^6 or 1 million of something, and "giga" usually to 10^9 or 1 billion of something, but its meaning here is a little off. This is because of the fact that 10^3 or 1000 is *pretty close* to 2^{10} or 1024.

So in discussing powers of 2 and powers of 10, most people use the following rule of thumb. Any time you talk about multiplying by 2^{10}, that's pretty close to multiplying 10^3, so we will just use the power of 10 prefixes we are used to. Another way to say it is that every 3 powers of 10 is "roughly equivalent" to 10 powers of 2. Thus a kilobyte is not really 1000 (10^3) bytes, but 1024 (2^{10}) bytes. A megabyte is not 1 million bytes (10^6), but 1,048,576 (2^{20}) bytes. A gigabyte is not 1 billion bytes (10^9), but 1,073,741,824 bytes (2^{30}).

0.8.8 How Much Data Is That?

At the writing of this book, the largest standard size commercial disk is 1 terabyte, 1 trillion bytes (10^{12}). On the horizon is the possibility of a 1 petabyte, 1 quadrillion (10^{15}) bytes. Again, the growth in disk sizes is dramatic. The first disk was introduced by IBM in 1956 and held only 4 megabytes. It took 35 years before a 1 gigabyte disk was made, but only 14 more years until we had 500 gigabyte disks, and only two more years until a 1 terabyte (1,000 gigabyte) disk was available. A petabyte disk (1,000,000 gigabytes) may happen soon.

So, how big is a petabyte? Let's try to put it into terms you can relate to:

- A book is roughly a megabyte of data. If you read one book a day every day of your life, say 80 years, that will be less than 30 gigabytes of data. Because a petabyte is 1 million gigabytes, you will still have 999,970 gigabytes left over.
- How many pictures can a person look at in a lifetime? If we assume 4 megabytes per picture and 100 images a day, after 80 years that collection of pictures would add up to 30 terabytes. So your petabyte disk will have 970,000 gigabytes left after a lifetime of photos and books.
- What about music? MP3 audio files run about a megabyte a minute. At that rate, a lifetime of listening—all day and all night for 80 years—would consume 42 terabytes of space. So with a lifetime of music, pictures, and books, you will have 928,000 gigabytes free on your disk. That is, almost 93% of your disk is still empty.
- The one kind of content that might overflow a petabyte disk is video. For DVDs the data rate is about two gigabytes per hour. Therefore, the petabyte disk will hold about 500,000 hours worth of video. If you want to record 24 hours a day, 7 days a week, the video will fill up your petabyte drive after about 57 years.

Of course, why stop there? More prefixes have been defined:

- exa is $2^{60} = 1{,}152{,}921{,}504{,}606{,}846{,}976$
- zetta is $2^{70} = 1{,}180{,}591{,}620{,}717{,}411{,}303{,}424$
- yotta is $2^{80} = 1{,}208{,}925{,}819{,}614{,}629{,}174{,}706{,}176$

Does anything get measured in exabytes or even zetabytes? Yes, it does though such a large measure is not (yet) applied to the the capacity of a single device. It is, however, applied to global measures such as Internet traffic.

Cisco Systems Inc., one of the leading providers of network equipment, has provided a white paper on the growth of Internet traffic. Their 2014–2019 forecast[6] made the following report:

- In **2014**, global internet traffic was 59.9 exabytes **per month**. By **2019** they estimate that rate will climb to 168 exabytes per month.
- By **2019**, global internet traffic will reach 2 zetabytes/year.

The storage company EMC has sponsored the IDC Digital Universe study to estimate the amount of data in use. Figure 0.16 shows a decade of estimates that reach 8 zettabytes by 2015 and their study estimates that to grow to 35 zettabytes by 2020. As fanciful as those numbers seem, they illustrate a practical use of the term zettabyte.

---

[6] http://www.cisco.com/c/en/us/solutions/collateral/service-provider/ip-ngn-ip-next-generation-network/white_paper_c11-481360.html

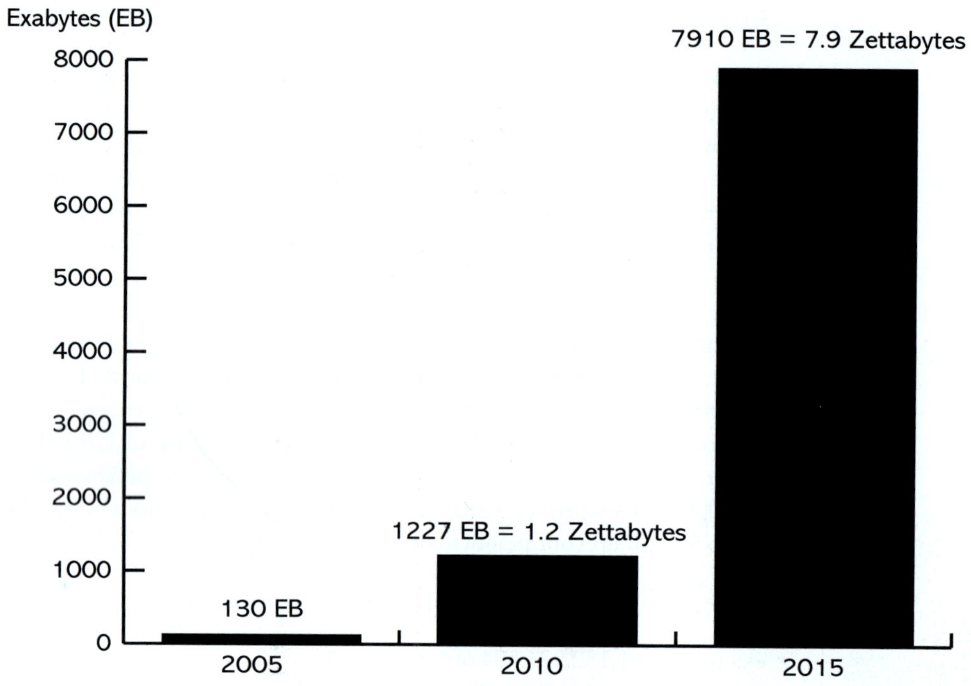

FIGURE 0.16 Estimates of data created and stored. [Data from The 2011 IDC Digital Universe Study]

0.9 OVERVIEW OF COMING CHAPTERS

This text is divided into five parts. The first gets you started on Python, computing, and problem solving. With that in hand, we get down into details in the next part where we develop both the Python language and problem-solving skills sufficient to solve interesting problems. The third part provides more tools in the form of Python built-in data structures, algorithm and problem-solving development, and functions. Part 4 shows you how to build classes—your own data structures. The final part includes more on Python.

Summary

In this chapter, we considered ways that data can be represented and manipulated—at the hardware level. In subsequent chapters, we will introduce ways in which you, as a programmer, can control the representation and manipulation of data.

PART 2

Starting to Program

CHAPTER 1

Beginnings

> A good workman is known by his tools.
>
> Proverb

OUR FIRST STEPS IN PROGRAMMING ARE TO LEARN THE DETAILS, SYNTAX, and semantics of the Python programming language. This necessarily involves getting into some of the language details, focusing on level 1 (language) issues as opposed to level 2 (problem solving) issues. Don't worry: we haven't forgotten that the goal is to do effective problem solving, but we have to worry about both aspects, moving between levels as required. A little proficiency with Python will allow us to write effective, problem-solving programs.

Here are our first two **RULES** of programming:

> **Rule 1:** Think before you program!
> **Rule 2:** A program is a human-readable essay on problem solving that also happens to execute on a computer.

1.1 PRACTICE, PRACTICE, PRACTICE

Let's start experimenting with Python. Before we get too far along, we want to emphasize something important. One of the best reasons to start learning programming using Python is that you can easily experiment with Python. That is, Python makes it easy to try something out and see the result. Anytime you have a question, simply try it out.

Learning to experiment with a programming language is a very important skill and one that seems hard for introductory students to pick up. So let's add a new **RULE**.

> **Rule 3:** The best way to improve your programming and problem skills is to practice!

Problem solving—and problem solving using programming to record your solution—requires practice. The title of this section is the answer to the age-old joke:

> **Student:** How do you get to Carnegie Hall?
> **Teacher:** Practice, practice, practice!

Learning to program for the first time is not all that different from learning to kick a soccer ball or play a musical instrument. It is important to learn about fundamentals by reading and talking about them, but the best way to *really* learn them is to practice. We will encourage you throughout the book to type something in and see what happens. If what you type in the first time doesn't work, who cares? Try again; see if you can fix it. If you don't get it right the first time, you will eventually. *Experimenting* is an important skill in problem solving, and this is one place where you can develop it!

We begin with our first QuickStart. A QuickStart shows the development of a working program followed by a more detailed explanation of the details of that program. A QuickStart gets us started, using the principal of "doing" before "explaining." Note that we ask you to try some things in the Python shell as we go along. Do it! Remember **Rule 3**. (To get Python see Appendix A.)

1.2 QUICKSTART, THE CIRCUMFERENCE PROGRAM

Let's start with a simple task. We want to calculate the circumference and area of a circle given its radius. The relevant mathematical formulas are:

- circumference $= 2 * \pi * radius$
- area $= \pi * radius^2$

To create the program, we need to do a couple of things:

1. We need to prompt the user for a radius.
2. We need to apply the mathematical formulas listed previously using the acquired radius to find the circumference and area.
3. We need to print out our results.

Here is Code Listing 1.1. Let's name it `circumference.py`. The ".py" is a file *suffix*.

PROGRAMMING TIP

Most computer systems add a suffix to the end of a file to indicate what "kind" of file it is—what kind of information it might store: music (".mp3"), pictures (".jpg"), text (".txt"), etc. Python does the same and expects that a Python file have a ".py" suffix. The Spyder editor (see Appendix A) is pretty helpful in that it, by default, saves the files you edit with a ".py" suffix. However, if you choose to save it as a ".txt" file or something else, then the Spyder's color scheme for your code disappears. Those colors are useful in that each color indicates a type of thing (green for strings, purple for keywords) in the program, making it more readable.

Code Listing 1.1

```
# calculate the area and circumference of a circle from its radius
# Step 1: prompt for a radius
# Step 2: apply the area formula
# Step 3: Print out the results

import math

radius_str = input("Enter the radius of your circle: ")
radius_int = int(radius_str)

circumference = 2 * math.pi * radius_int
area = math.pi * (radius_int ** 2)

print ("The cirumference is:",circumference, \
      ", and the area is:",area)
```

Important: The line numbers shown in the program are *not* part of the program. We list them here only for the reader's convenience.

Before we examine the code, let's illustrate how the program runs with two different input radii to confirm that it works properly.

The easiest way to run a program is to open that program in the SPYDER editor, then select Run → Run (F5). If you haven't saved the file yet, you will be prompted where to save it. Then, you will see a `runfile` message in the iPython console. The `runfile` *imports* the file into the shell and runs it. Note that every time you run the program, the iPython console shell prints the `runfile` line, indicating that the shell is restarting and running your program.

You can choose some "obvious" values to see if you get expected results. For example, a radius value of 1 results in the area having the recognizable value of $\pi = 3.14159\ldots$. Although not a complete test of the code, it does allow us to identify any gross errors quickly. The other case has a radius of 2 that can be easily checked with a calculator:

```
In  [1]: runfile('/Users/user/python/file.py', wdir='/Users/user/python')

Enter the radius of your circle: 1
The cirumference is: 6.283185307179586 , and the area is: 3.141592653589793


In  [2]: runfile('/Users/user/python/file.py', wdir='/Users/user/python')

Enter the radius of your circle: 2
The cirumference is: 12.566370614359172 , and the area is: 12.566370614359172
```

1.2.1 Examining the Code

Let's examine the circumference.py code line-by-line. In this first example, there are many topics that we will touch on briefly, but will be explained in more detail in subsequent chapters. Note that we number only every fifth line in the code listing. Here is a walk through of this code.

Lines 1–4: Anything that follows a pound sign (#) is a comment for the human reader. The Python interpreter ignores it. However, it does provide us as readers some more information on the intent of the program (more on this later). Remember **RULE 2**. Comments help make your document easier to understand for humans.

Line 6: This line imports special Python code from the math *module*. A module is a Python file containing programs to solve particular problems; in this case, the `math` module provides support for solving common math problems. Modules are described in more detail in Section 1.4.1. Python has many such modules to make common tasks easier. In this case we are interested in the value π provided by the math module, which we indicate in the program using the code `math.pi`. This is a naming convention we will explore in more detail in Section 1.8, but essentially the code `math.pi` means—that within the module named `math` there is a value named `pi`, with a "." separating the module and value name.

Line 8: This line really has two parts: the Python code to the right of the = sign and the Python code on the left:

- On the right, `input` is a small Python program called a *function*. Functions (see Chapter 8) are often-used, small program utilities that do a particular task. The `input` function prints the characters in quotes, "Enter the radius of your circle:", to the Python shell and waits for the user to type a response. Whatever the user types in the shell before pressing the Enter key at the end is *returned*, that is, provided as input to a program.
- On the left side of the = is a *variable*. For now, consider a variable to be a name that is associated with a value. In this case, the value returned from `input` will be associated with the name `radius_str`. (Programmers traditionally shorten "string" to "str".)

  Think of the = as a kind of glue, linking the values on the right side with the variable on the left. The = is called an *assignment statement*; we will have more to say about assignment in Section 1.5.1.

Line 9: The user's response returned by `input` is stored as a sequence of characters, referred to in computer science as a *string* (see Chapter 4). Python differentiates a sequence of characters, such as those that constitute this sentence, from numbers on which we can perform operations such as addition, subtraction and so on. Strings are differentiated from numbers by using quotes, single or double quotes are acceptable ("hi mom" or `'monty'`). For this program we want to work with numbers, not characters, so we must convert the user's response from a string of characters to numbers. The *`int`* function takes the value associated with the variable `radius_str` and returns the integer value of `radius_str`. In other words, it converts the string to an integer. As in the previous line, the value returned by ***int*** is associated with a variable using the assignment statement. For example, if `radius_str` holds the string of characters `"27"`, the ***int*** function will convert those characters to the integer 27 and then associate that value the new variable name `radius_int`.

The difference between the characters `"27"` and the number 27 will likely seem strange at first. It is our first example of value *types*. Types will be described in more detail in Section 1.6, but for now, let's say that a type indicates the kinds of things we can do to a value and the results we obtain.

Line 11: Here we calculate the circumference using the following formula:

`circumference = 2 *` *pi* `* radius`

While +, -, and / mean what you expect for math operations (addition, subtraction, and division), we use the * symbol to represent multiplication as opposed to · or ×. This is to avoid any confusion between "x" and × or "." and "·". The integer 2, the value associated with the variable `math.pi`, and the value associated with the `radius_int` are multiplied together, and then the result is associated with the variable named `circumference`. As you will later see, the ordering is important: the mathematical expression on the right-hand side of the equal sign is evaluated, and then the result is associated with the variable on the left-hand side of the equal sign.

Line 12: Similarly, we calculate the area using the formula listed previously. There isn't a way to type in an exponent (superscript) on a keyboard, but Python has an exponentiation operator `**` by which the value on the left is raised to the power on the right. Thus `radius_int ** 2` is the same as `radius_int` squared or $\texttt{radius\_int}^2$. Note that we use parentheses to group the operation. As in normal math, expressions in parentheses are evaluated first, so the expression `math.pi * (radius_int ** 2)` means square the value of `radius_int`, then take that result and multiply it by *pi*.

Lines 14 and 15: We print the results using the Python ***print*** statement. Like the `input` statement, ***print*** is a function that performs a much used operation, printing values to the user console. The print statement can print strings bracketed by quotes (either single or double quotes) and a value associated with a variable. Printable elements are placed in the parentheses after the ***print*** statement. If the element being printed is quoted, it is printed exactly as it appears in the quotes; if the element is a variable, then *the value associated with the variable* is printed. Each object (string, variable, value, etc.) that is to be printed is separated from other objects by commas. In this case, the ***print*** statement outputs a string, a variable value, another string, and finally a variable value. The backslash character (\) indicates that the statement continues onto the next line—in this case, the two-line ***print*** statement behaves as if it were one long line. Stretching a statement across two lines can enhance readability—particularly on a narrow screen or page. See Section 1.4.3.

1.3 AN INTERACTIVE SESSION

An important feature of Python, particularly when learning the language, is that it is an *interpreted* language. By interpreted we mean that there is a program within Python called the interpreter that takes each line of Python code, one line at a time, and executes that code. This feature allows us to try out lines of code one at a time by typing into the Python shell. The ability to experiment with pieces of code in the Python shell is something that really helps while you're learning the language; you can easily try something out and see what happens. That is what is so great about Python—you can easily explore and learn as you go.

Consider our circumference program. The following code shows a session in a Python shell in which a user types each line of the program we listed previously to see what happens. We also show a few other features, just to experiment. *Open up a Python shell and follow along by trying it yourself.* The comments (text after #, the pound sign), are there to help walk you through the process. There is no need to type them into the Python shell.

```
In  [1]: import math
In  [2]: radius_str = input("Enter the radius of your circle: ")
Enter the radius of your circle: 20
In  [3]: radius_str # what is the value associated with radius_str
Out [3]: '20'

In  [4]: radius_int = int(radius_str) # convert the string to an integer
In  [5]: radius_int # check the value of the integer
Out [5]: 20                      # look, no quotes because it is a number

In  [6]: int(radius_str) # what does int() return without assignment (=)
Out [6]: 20

In  [7]: radius_str # int() does not modify radius_str!!
Out [7]: '20'

In  [8]: math.pi # let's see what value is associated with math.pi
Out [8]: 3.141592653589793

In  [9]: circumference = 2 * math.pi * radius_int # try our formula
In  [10]: circumference
Out [10]: 125.66370614359172

In  [11]: area = math.pi * radius_int ** 2 # area using exponentiation
In  [12]: area
Out [12]: 1256.6370614359173

In  [13]: math.pi * radius_int ** 2 # area calculation without assignment
Out [13]: 1256.6370614359173

In  [14]: print("Circumference: ", circumference, ", area: ", area)
Circumference:  125.66370614359172 , area:  1256.6370614359173
```

Within the Python shell, you can find out the value associated with any variable name by typing its name followed by the Enter key. For example, when we type `radius_str` in the shell as shown in the example, `'20'` is output. The quotes indicate that it is a string of characters, `'20'`, rather than the integer 20.

Interestingly, Python treats single quotes (`'20'`) the same as double quotes (`"20"`). You can choose to designate strings with single or double quotes. It's your choice!

We can see that after the conversion of the string to an integer using the `int` function, simply typing `radius_int` results in the integer 20 being printed (no quotes).

We can also try the expression `int(radius_str)` without assigning the result to `radius_int`. Note that `radius_str` is unchanged; it is provided as a value for the `int` function to use in its calculations. We then check the value of *pi* in the `math` module named `math.pi`. Next we try out the circumference and area formulas. The area calculation is then performed using the exponentiation operator (`**`), raising `radius_int` to the second power. Finally, we try the **`print`** statement. Remember **RULE 3.**

An advantage of Python over other languages such as C, C++, and Java is the Python shell. Take advantage of this feature because it can greatly enhance your learning of what the Python language can do. If you wonder about how something might or might not work, try it in the Python shell!

1.4 PARTS OF A PROGRAM

RULE 2 describes a program as an essay on problem solving that is also executable. A program consists of a set of *instructions* that are executed sequentially, one after the other in the order in which they were typed. We save the instructions together in a *module* for storage on our file system. Later, the module can be *imported* into the Python interpreter, which runs programs by executing the instructions contained in the module.

1.4.1 Modules

- A *module* contains a set of Python commands.
- A module can be stored as a file and *imported* into the Python shell.
- Usage:

```
import module # load the module
```

Hundreds of modules come with the standard Python distribution; the math module and many more can be found and imported. You can even write your own modules and use them as tools in your own programming work!

1.4.2 Statements and Expressions

Python differentiates code into one of two categories: *expressions* or *statements*. The concept of an expression is consistent with the mathematical definition, so it may be familiar to you.

Expression: A combination of values and operations that creates a new value that we call a *return value*, that is, the value returned by the operation(s). If you enter an expression into the Python shell, a value will be returned and displayed; that is, the expression `x + 5` will display 7 if the value of `x` is 2. Note that the value associated with `x` is not changed as a result of this operation!

Statement: Does not *return a value*, but does perform some task. Some statements may control the flow of the program, and others might ask for resources; statements perform a wide variety of tasks. As a result of their operation, a statement may have a *side effect*. A side effect is some change that results from executing the statement. Take the example of the *assignment statement* `my_int = 5` (shown in the following example). This statement does not have a *return value*, but it does set the value associated with the variable `my_int` to 5, a *side effect*. When we type such an assignment into the Python shell, no value is returned, as you can see here:

```
In  [1]: my_int = 5 # statement, no return value but my_int now has value 5
In  [2]: my_int
Out [2]: 5

In  [3]: my_int + 5 # expression, value associated with my_int added to 5
Out [3]: 10

In  [4]: my_int # no side effect of expression, my_int is unchanged
Out [4]: 5
```

However, after we type the assignment statement, if we type the variable `my_int`, we see that it does indeed now have the value of 5 (see the example session). A statement never returns a value, but some statements may have a side effect. You will see more of this behavior as we explore the many Python statements.

PROGRAMMING TIP

Knowing that an expression has a value but a statement does not is useful. For example, you can print the value generated by an expression, for example, `print(x + 5)` (as long as `x` has a value). However, if you try to print a statement, Python generates an error. If no value is returned from a statement, then what will be the print output? Python avoids this by not allowing a statement to be printed. That is, it is not allowable syntax.

```
In  [1]: print(x + 5) # printing an expression
7
In  [2]: print(y = x + 5) # trying to print a statement
TypeError: 'y' is an invalid keyword argument for this function
```

There are a number of instances of entering expressions and statements into the Python shell in the previous examples. Whenever an expression was entered, its return value was printed on the following line of the console. Whenever a statement was entered, nothing was printed: if we wanted to see what a statement changed (side effect), we, the programmers, have to inquire about the change.

1.4.3 Whitespace

When we type, we usually separate words with what is typically called *whitespace*. Python counts as whitespace the following characters: space, tab, return, linefeed, formfeed and vertical tab. Python has the following rules about how whitespace is used in a program:

- Whitespace is *ignored* within both expressions and statements.
  For example, `Y=X+5` has exactly the same meaning as `Y   =   X  +   5`.
- *Leading* whitespace, whitespace at the beginning of a line—defines *indentation*. Indentation plays a special role in Python (see the following section).
- Blank lines are also considered to be whitespace, and the rule for blank lines is trivial: blank lines are allowed anywhere and are ignored.

Indentation

Indentation is used by all programmers to make code more readable. Programmers often indent code to indicate that the indented code is *grouped together*, meaning those statements have some common purpose. However, indentation is treated uniquely in Python. Python *requires* it for grouping. When a set of statements or expressions needs to be grouped together, Python does so by a consistent indentation. Grouping of statements will be important when we discuss control statements in Chapter 2.

Python requires consistency in whitespace indentation. If previous statements use an indentation of four spaces to group elements, then that must be done consistently throughout the program.

The benefit of indentation is *readability*. While other programming languages encourage indentation, Python's whitespace indentation *forces* readability. The disadvantage is that maintaining consistency with the number of spaces versus tabs can be frustrating, especially when cutting and pasting. Fortunately, Python-aware editors such as SPYDER automatically indent and can repair indentation.

PROGRAMMING TIP

SPYDER provides a command under the Source → Fix Indentation menu to help fix indentation. If you are having problems with indentation, or if Python is complaining about irregular indentation, try this command to repair the problem.

Continuation

Long lines of code—those wider than the width of a reasonably sized editing window—can make reading code difficult. Because readability is very important (remember **RULE 2**), Python provides ways to make long lines more readable by splitting them. Such splitting is called a *continuation*. If a single statement runs long, that statement can be continued onto another line (or lines) to help with readability. That is, a continued line is still a single line, it just shows up over multiple lines in the editor. Indicate a continuation by placing a backslash character (\) at the end of a line. Multiple-line expressions can be continued similarly. In this way, a long line that may be difficult to read can be split in some meaningful and readable way across multiple lines. The first program in this chapter, `circumference.py`, used such a backslash character in the print statement.

1.4.4 Comments

> Let us change our traditional attitude to the construction of programs: Instead of imagining that our main task is to instruct a computer what to do, let us concentrate rather on explaining to human beings what we want a computer to do.
>
> Donald Knuth[1]

We will say many times, in different ways, that a program is more than "just some code that does something." A program is a document that describes the thought process of its writer. Messy code implies messy thinking and is both difficult to work with and to understand. Code also happens to be something that can run, but just because it can run does not make it a good program. Good programs can be read, just like any other essay. Comments are one important way to improve *readability*. Comments contribute nothing to the running of the program because Python ignores them. In Python, anything following a pound character (#) is ignored on that line. However, comments are critical to the readability of the program.

There are no universally agreed-upon rules for the right style and number of comments, but there is near-universal agreement that they can enhance readability. Here are some useful guidelines:

- The *why* philosophy: "Good comments don't repeat the code or explain it. They clarify its intent. Comments should explain, at a higher level of abstraction than the code, what you're trying to do."[2] (*Code Complete* by McConnell)
- The *how* philosophy: If your code contains a novel or noteworthy solution, add comments to explain the methodology.

1.4.5 Special Python Elements: Tokens

As when learning any language, there are some details that are good to know before you can fully understand how they are used. Here we show you the special keywords, symbols, and characters that can be used in a Python program. These language elements are known generically as *tokens*. We don't explain in detail what each one does, but it is important to note that Python has special uses for all of them. You will become more familiar with them as

[1] Excerpt from "Literate Programming" by Donald E. Knuth in *The Computer Journal*, 27(2), pp. 97–111. Published by Oxford University Press, © 1984.

[2] Excerpt from "Code Complete: A Practical Handbook of Software Construction, 2e" by Steve McConnell. Published by Microsoft Press, © 2004.

we proceed through the book. More importantly than what they do is the fact that Python reserves them for its own use. You can't redefine them to do something else. Be aware they exist so that you don't accidentally try to use one (as a variable, function, or the like).

Keywords

Keywords are special words in Python that cannot be used by you to name things. They indicate commands to the Python interpreter. The complete list is in Table 1.1. We will introduce commands throughout the text, but for now know that you cannot use these words as names (of variables, of functions, of classes, etc.) in your programs. Python has already taken them for other uses.

and	del	from	not	while
as	elif	global	or	with
assert	else	if	pass	yield
break	except	import	print	class
exec	in	raise	continue	finally
is	return	def	for	lambda
try	True	False	None	

TABLE 1.1 Python keywords.

Operators

Operators are special tokens (sequences of characters) that have meaning to the Python interpreter. Using them implies some operation, such as addition, subtraction, or something similar. We will introduce operators throughout the text. The complete list is in Table 1.2. You can probably guess many of them, but some of them will not be familiar.

+	-	*	**	/	//	%
<<	>>	&	|	^	~	
<	>	<=	>=	==	!=	<>
+=	-=	*=	/=	//=	%=	
&=	|=	^=	>>=	<<=	**=	

TABLE 1.2 Python operators.

Punctuators and Delimiters

Punctuators, also known as delimiters, separate different elements in Python statements and expressions. Some you will recognize from mathematics; others you will recognize from English. We will introduce them throughout the text. The complete list is in Table 1.3.

(	)	[	]	{	}
,	:	.	`	=	;
'	"	#	\	@	

TABLE 1.3 Python punctuators.

Literals

In computer science, a *literal* is a notation for representing a fixed value, which is a value that cannot be changed in the program. Almost all programming languages have notations for atomic values such as integers, floating-point numbers, strings, and Booleans. For example, 123 is a literal; it has a fixed value and cannot be modified. In contrast to literals, variables are symbols that can be assigned a value that can be modified during the execution of the code.

1.4.6 Naming Objects

> The practitioner of ... programming can be regarded as an essayist, whose main concern is with exposition and excellence of style. Such an author, with thesaurus in hand, chooses the names of variables carefully and explains what each variable means. He or she strives for a program that is comprehensible because its concepts have been introduced in an order that is best for human understanding, using a mixture of formal and informal methods that reinforce each other.
>
> Donald Knuth[3]

If writing a program is like writing an essay, then you might guess that the names you use in the program, such as the names of your variables, would help greatly in making the program more readable. Therefore, it is important to choose names well. Later we will provide you with some procedures to choose readable names, but here we can talk about the rules that Python imposes on name selection.

1. Every name must begin with a letter or the underscore character (_):
   - A numeral is not allowed as the first character.[4]
   - Multiple-word names can be linked together using the underscore character (_), for example, `monty_python`, `holy_grail`. A name *starting* with an underscore is often used by Python and Python programmers to denote a variable with special characteristics. You will see these as we go along, but for now it is best to *not* start variable names with an underscore until you understand what that implies.
2. After the first letter, the name may contain any combination of letters, numbers, and underscores:
   - The name cannot be a *keyword* as listed in Table 1.1.
   - You cannot have any delimiters, punctuation, or operators (as listed in Tables 1.2 and 1.3) in a name.

[3] Excerpt from "Literate Programming" by Donald E. Knuth in *The Computer Journal*, 27(2), pp. 97–111. Published by Oxford University Press, © 1984.

[4] This is so that Python can easily distinguish variable names from numbers.

3. A name can be of any length.
4. UPPERCASE is different from lowercase. For example,
   - `my_name` is different than `my_Name` or `My_Name` or `My_name`.

1.4.7 Recommendations on Naming

Because naming is such an important part of programming, conventions are often developed that describe how to create names. Such conventions provide programmers with a common methodology to make clear what the program is doing to anyone who reads it. These conventions describe how to name various elements of a program based on their function, in particular when to use various techniques to name elements (capitalize, uppercase, leading underscore, etc.). It is a bit beyond us at this point to fully discuss these standards as we are not yet familiar with the different kinds of elements in a Python program, but we will describe the rules as we go along. However, for those that are interested, we will be using the standard that Google uses for its Python programmers, the *Google Style Guide for Python* which is similar to Python's PEP 8, the *Style Guide for Python Code*.[5] While we follow those guidelines, it is wise to not follow them to the point where readability is impinged. In that spirit we pull our next rule straight from PEP 8:

> **Rule 4:** A foolish consistency is the hobgoblin of little minds.

That rule is actually a quote from Ralph Waldo Emerson: "A foolish consistency is the hobgoblin of little minds, adored by little statesmen and philosophers and divines. With consistency a great soul has simply nothing to do." Emerson implies that rules are useful to follow, but sometimes not.

1.5 VARIABLES

A *variable* is a name you create in your program to represent "something" in your program. That "something" can be one of many types of entities: a value, another program to run, a set of data, a file. For starters, we will talk about a variable as something that represents a value: an integer, a string, a floating-point number, an so on. We create variables with meaningful names because the purpose of a good variable name is to make your code more readable. The variable name *pi* is a name most would recognize, and it is easier to both read and write than 3.1415926536. Once a variable is created, you can store, retrieve, or modify the data associated with that variable. Every time you use your variable in a program, its value is retrieved by Python and used in that variable's place. Thus, a variable is really a way to make it easier to read the program you are writing.

[5] http://google-styleguide.googlecode.com/svn/trunk/pyguide.html

PROGRAMMING TIP

It is often useful to describe your variable using a multiword phrase. The recommended way to do this, according to the *Google Style Guide*, is called "lower_with_under". That is, use lowercase letters to write your variable names, and connect the words together using an underline. Again, it is useful to avoid using a leading underline to your variable names for reasons that will become clear later. It is also useful to avoid capital letters, as the style guide will have something to say about when to use those later. Thus "radius_int" or "circumference_str" would be good variable names.

How does Python associate the value of the variable with its name? In essence, Python makes a list of names (variables, but other names as well) that are being used right now in the Python interpreter. The interpreter maintains a special structure called a *namespace* to keep this list of names and their associated values (see Figure 1.1). Each name in that list is associated with a value, and the Python interpreter updates both names and values during the course of its operation. The name associated with a value is an *alias* for the value, that is, another name for it. Whenever a new variable is created, its name is placed in the list along with an association to a value. If a variable name already exists in the table, its association is updated.

1.5.1 Variable Creation and Assignment

How is a name created? In Python, when a name is first used (assigned a value, defined as a function name, etc.) is when the name is created. Python updates the namespace list with the new name and its associated value.

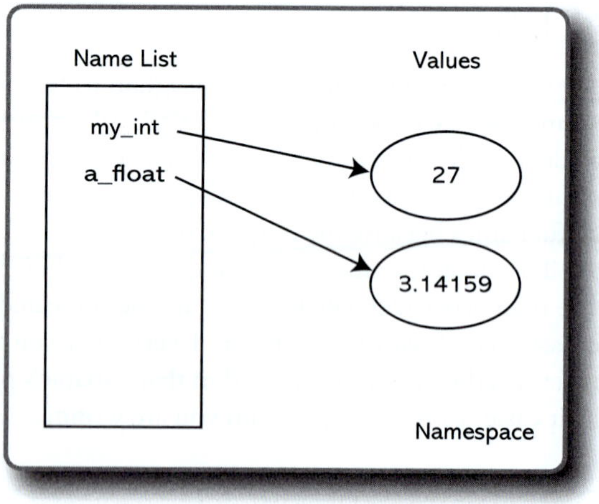

FIGURE 1.1 Namespace containing variable names and associated values.

Assignment is one way to create a name such as a variable. The purpose of assignment is to associate a name with a value. The symbol of assignment for Python is the equal (=) sign. A simple example follows:

```
my_int = math.pi + 5
```

In this case, 5 is added to the value of the variable associated with `math.pi`, and the result of that expression is associated with the variable `my_int` in the Python namespace. It is important to note that the value `math.pi` is **not** modified by this operation. In fact, assignment does not change any values on the right-hand side. Only a new association is created by assignment: the association with the name on the left-hand side.

The general form of the assignment statement is the same as in mathematics:

left-hand side = right-hand side

Although we use the familiar equal sign (=) from mathematics, its meaning in programming languages is different! In math, the equal (=) indicates equality: what is on the left hand side of the equal sign (=) has the same value as what is on the right-hand side. In Python, the equal sign (=) represents *assignment.* Assignment is the operation to associate a value with a variable. The left-hand side represents the variable name, and the right hand side represents the value. If the variable does not yet exist, then the variable is created and placed in the namespace table; otherwise, the variable's value is updated to the value on the right-hand side. This notation can lead to some odd expressions that would not make much sense mathematically, but make good sense from Python's point of view, such as:

```
my_var = my_var + 1
```

We interpret the previous statement as follows: get the value referred to by `my_var`, add 1 to it, and then associate the resulting sum with the variable `my_var`. That is, if `my_var`'s value was 4, then after assignment its value will be updated to be 5. More generally, the process is to evaluate everything in the expression on the right-hand side first, get the value of that expression, and associate that value with the name on the left-hand side.

Evaluation of an assignment statement is a two-step process:

1. Evaluate the expression on the right-hand side.
2. Take the resulting value from the right-hand expression and associate it with the variable on the left-hand side. (Create the variable if it doesn't exist; otherwise update it.)

For example:

```
my_var = 2 + 3 * 5
```

First evaluate the expression on the right-hand side, resulting in the value 17 (remember, multiplication before addition), then associate 17 with `my_var`; that is, update the namespace so that `my_var` is an alias for 17 in the namespace. Notice how Python uses the standard mathematical rules for the order of operations: multiplication and division before addition or subtraction.

In the earlier assignment statement

```
my_var = my_var + 1
```

notice that `my_var` has two roles. On the right-hand side, it represents a value: "get this value." On the left-hand side, it represents a name that we will associate with value: "a name we will associate with the value."

With that in mind, we can examine some assignment statements that do not make sense and are thus not allowed in Python:

- `7 = my_var + 1` is illegal because 7, like any other integer, is a literal, not a legal variable name, and cannot be changed. (You wouldn't want the value 7 to somehow become 125.)
- `my_var + 7 = 14` is illegal because `my_var + 7` is an expression, not a legal variable name in the namespace.
- Assignment cannot be used in a statement or expression where a value is expected. This is because assignment is a statement; it does not return a value. The statement `print(my_var = 7)` is illegal because print requires a value to print, but the assignment statement does not return a value.

Check Yourself: Variables and Assignment

1. Which of the following are acceptable variable names for Python?
   (a) xyzzy
   (b) 2ndVar
   (c) rich&bill
   (d) long_name
   (e) good2go

2. Which of the following statement(s) best describe a Python namespace?
   (a) A list of acceptable names to use with Python
   (b) A place where objects are stored in Python
   (c) A list of Python names and the values with which they are associated
   (d) All of the above
   (e) None of the above

3. Give the values printed by the following program for each of the labeled lines.

```
int_a = 27
int_b = 5
int_a = 6

print(int_a)       # Line 1
print(int_b + 5)   # Line 2
print(int_b)       # Line 3
```

   (a) What is printed by `Line 1`?
   (b) What is printed by `Line 2`?
   (c) What is printed by `Line 3`?

1.6 OBJECTS AND TYPES

In assignment, we associate a value with a variable. What exactly is that value? What information is important and useful to know about that value?

In Python, every "thing" in the system is considered to be an *object*. In Python, though, the word "object" has a very particular meaning. An object in Python has

- an *identity*
- some *attributes*
- zero or more names

Whenever an object is created by Python, it receives an identification number. If you are ever interested in the number of any object, you can use the `id` function to discover its ID number. In general, the ID number isn't very interesting to us, but that number is used by Python to distinguish one object from another. We will take a brief look at the ID here because it helps explain how Python manages objects.

Notice that in addition to the ID number, an object can also have a name or even multiple names. This name is not part of the object's ID but is used by us, the programmers, to make the code more readable. Python uses the namespace to associate a name (such as a variable name) with an object. Interestingly, multiple namespaces may associate different names with the same object!

Finally, every object has a set of attributes associated with it. Attributes are essentially information about the object. We will offer more insight into object attributes later, but the one that we are most interested in right now is an object's type.

In Python, and in many other languages, each object is considered an example of a *type*. For example, 1, 27, and 365 are objects, each of the same type, called *`int`* (integer). Also, 3.1415926, 6.022141×10^{23}, 6.67428×10^{-11} are all objects that are examples of the type called floating-point numbers (real numbers), which is the type called *`float`* in Python. Finally, "spam", 'ham', "'fred"' are objects of the type called strings, called *`str`* in Python (more in Chapter 4).

Knowing the type of an object informs Python (and us, the programmers) of two things:

- *Attributes* of the object tell us something about its "content". For example, there are no decimal points in an integer object, and there are no letters in either an integer object or a float object.
- *Operations* tell us something about actions that can be done with the object. For example, we can divide two integer objects or two float objects, but the division operation makes no sense on a string object.

If you are unsure of the type of an object in Python, you can ask Python to tell you its type. The function `type` returns the type of any object. The following session shows some interaction with Python and its objects:

```
In  [1]: a_int = 7
In  [2]: id(a_int)
Out [2]: 16790848
```

```
In  [3]: type(a_int) # because 7 is an integer, a_nt is of type int
Out [3]: int

In  [4]: b_float = 2.5
In  [5]: id(b_float) # note that b_float's ID is different than a_int's ID
Out [5]: 17397652

In  [6]: type(b_float) # because 2.5 is Real, b_float is of type float
Out [6]: float

In  [7]: a_int = b_float # associate a_int with value of b_float
In  [8]: type(a_int)
Out [8]: float       # a_int is now of type float

In  [9]: id(a_int) # a_int's now has the same ID as b_float
Out [9]: 17397652
```

Notice a few interesting things in the example session:

- When we ask for the ID (using `id`), we get a system dependent ID number. That number will be different from session to session or machine to machine. To us, the ID number is hard to remember (though not for Python). That's the point! We create variable names so that we can remember an object we have created so we don't *have* to remember weird ID numbers. We show the ID here to help explain Figure 1.2.
- The information returned by a call to the `type` function indicates the type of the value. An integer returns *`int`*, a floating-point object returns *`float`*, and so on.
- Most important, the type of an object has *nothing* to do with the variable name; instead it specifies only the *object* with which it is associated. In the previous Python session, an int object (`a_int = 7`) and a floating-point object (`b_float = 2.5`) associated (respectively) with `a_int` and `b_float`. We then assign the floating-point object to the variable named `a_int` using `a_int = b_float`. The type of object associated with `a_int` is now float. The name of the variable has nothing to do with the type of object with which it is associated. However, it can be useful if the name *does* say something about the associated object for those who must read the code. In any case, Python does not enforce this naming convention. We, as good programmers, must enforce it. Note that the ID of the object associated with `a_int` is now the same as the ID of the variable `b_float`. Both names are now associated with the same object.

Figure 1.2 shows the namespace with two assignments on the left side and a third assignment on the right.

Python (and therefore we) must pay particular attention to an object's type because that type determines what is "reasonable" or "permissible" to do to that object, and if the operation can be done, what the result will be. As you progress in Python, you will learn

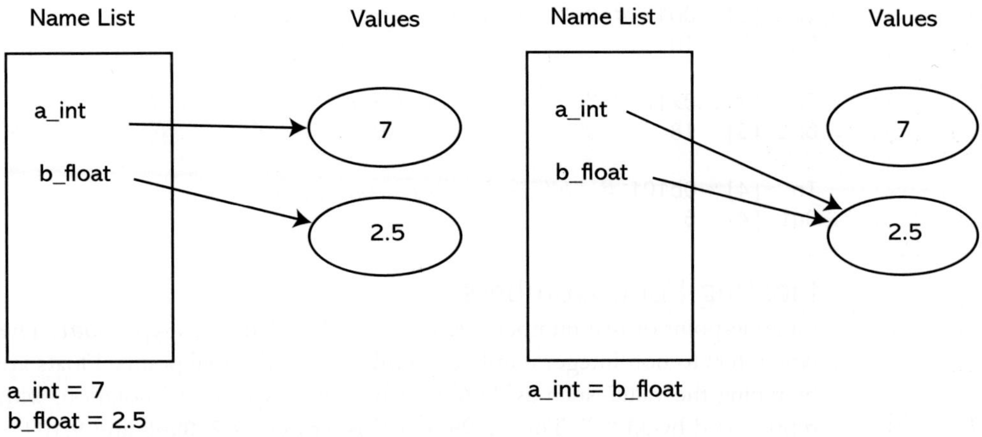

FIGURE 1.2 Namespace before and after the final assignment.

more about predefined types in Python, as well as how we can define our own types (or, said in a different way, our own *class*. See Chapter 11).

The following sections describe a few of the basic types in Python.

1.6.1 Numbers

Python provides several numeric types. We will work a lot with these types during these early chapters because they relate to numeric concepts that we are familiar with. You will add more types as we move through the book.

Integers

The integer type is designated in Python as type `int`. The integer type corresponds to our mathematical notion of integer. The operations we can perform are those that we would expect: + (addition), − (subtraction), * (multiplication), and / (division, though there are some complications about division /—[see Section 1.7]) as well as a few others. In Python, integers can grow to be as large as needed to store a value, and that value will be exact, but really big integers can be slower to operate on.

How big an integer can you make? Give it a try.

Integers can be written in normal base 10 form or in other base formats—in particular base 8 (called *octal*) and base 16 (called *hexadecimal*). We note this because of an oddity you might run into with integers: leading zeros are not allowed. Python assumes that if you precede a number with a 0 (zero), you mean to encode it in a base other than 10. A letter following the 0 indicates the base. If it is "o", base 8 (octal) is specified. An "x" specifies base 16 (hexadecimal) and a "b" specifies base 2 (binary). We illustrate this in a session:

```
In  [1]: 012 # leading zero without letter is invalid
Out [1]: SyntaxError: invalid token
```

```
In  [2]: 0o12 # "o" indicates octal, base 8
Out [2]: 10

In  [3]: 0x12 # "x" indicates hexadecimal, base 16
Out [3]: 18

In  [4]: 0b101 # "b" indicates binary, base 2
Out [4]: 5
```

Floating-Point Numbers

Floating-point or real numbers are designated in Python as type `float`. The floating-point type refers to non-integer numbers, numbers with decimal points. Floats are created either by typing the value, such as 25.678 or by using exponential notation, with the exponent represented by an "e". Thus, 2.99×10^8 is written as `2.99e8` and 9.109×10^{-31} can be written as `9.109e-31`. The operators are, like integers, +, −, *, and / (see Section 1.7 for more detail). Floats represent real numbers, but only approximately. For example, what is the exact decimal representation of the operation 2.0/3.0? As you know, there *is* no exact decimal equivalent because the result is an infinite series; that is $2.0/3.0 = 0.666\ldots$. Since a computer has a finite amount of memory, real numbers must be represented with approximations of their actual value. Look at the following session.

```
In  [1]: 2.0 / 3.0
Out [1]: 0.6666666666666666

In  [2]: 1.1 + 2.2
Out [2]: 3.3000000000000003

In  [3]: 0.1 + 0.1 + 0.1 - 0.3
Out [3]: 5.551115123125783e-17
```

If you were to do the calculations yourself, you would find that $1.1 + 2.2$ is equal to 3.3. However, the session shows it is 3.3000000000000003. The same applies for the last addition. The result should be 0 but Python returns a *very* small value instead. Approximations like this, if carried through multiple evaluations, can lead to significant differences than what is expected. Python does provide a module called the `decimal` module that provides more predictable, and controllable, results for floating-point numbers.

It is important to remember that floating-point values are approximate values, not exact, and that operations using floating-point values yield approximate values. Integers are exact, and operations on integers yield exact values.

Finally, unlike integers in Python, a leading 0 on a floating-point number carries no significance: 012. (notice the decimal point) is equivalent to 12.0.

Fractions

Python also provides the type *fraction* for rational numbers. A fraction consists of the obvious two parts: the numerator and the denominator. Fractions do not suffer from the conversion of a rational to a real number as discussed previously, and can be operated on without loss of precision using addition, subtraction, multiplication, and division. See Section 16.1.1 for more information.

1.6.2 Other Built-In Types

Python has more types that we will introduce in the coming chapters. We mention them briefly here as a preview.

Boolean

A Boolean value has a Python type *bool*. The Boolean type refers to the values `True` or `False` (note the capitalization). If an object is of type Boolean, it can be only one of those two values. In fact, the two Boolean objects are represented as integers: 0 is `False` and 1 is `True`. There are a number of Boolean operators, which we will examine in Chapter 2.

String

A string in Python has the type *str*. A string is our first *collection* type. A collection type contains multiple objects organized as a single object type. The string type is a *sequence*. It consists of a collection of characters in a sequence (order matters), delimited by single quotes (' ') or double quotes (" "). For example, "This is a string!" or 'here is another string' or even a very short string as "x". Some languages such as C and its derivatives consider single characters and strings as different types, but Python only has strings. Operations on strings are described in Chapter 4.

List

A list in Python is of type *list*. A list is also a sequence type, like a string, though it can have elements other than characters in the sequence. Because sequences are collections, a list is also a collection. Lists are indicated with square brackets ([and]), and its contents are separated by commas. Lists will be covered in Chapter 7. Here is a list:

[4, 3.57, 'abc']

Dictionary

A dictionary in Python is of type *dict*. A dictionary is a *map* type, a collection though not a sequence. A map type consists of a set of element pairs. The first element in the pair is the *key* and the second is the *value*. The key can be used to search for a value, much like a dictionary or phone book. If you want to look up the phone number (the value) or a person (the key), you can efficiently search for the name and find the number. Curly braces ({ and }) indicate dictionaries; a colon separates the key and value pair. Dictionaries will be covered in Chapter 9. Here is a dictionary:

```
{'Jones':3471124, 'Larson':3472289, 'Smith':3471288}
```

Set

A set in Python is of type *set*. A set is a collection of unique elements, similar to a set in mathematics. Sets, like dictionaries, use curly braces, but unlike dictionaries there are no colons. A set supports the mathematical set operations such as *union* and *intersection*. Sets will be covered in Chapter 9. Here is a set:

{1,3,5}

PROGRAMMING TIP

Be careful that you do not select a variable name that is already in use by Python as a built-in or module name. For example, you might run the following code—`str = "abc"`—assigning a value to the variable `str`. The only problem is the Python is using `str` as the name of the string type. However, Python is happy to oblige. During the remainder of your program, `str` is a variable and not a type. Pay attention to **colors** when creating variable names. SPYDER colors Python keywords. If a color pops up on your variable, perhaps you should look and see if it is a Python keyword. Finally, if you fix the problem (change the variable name), when you start Python up again, the problem will go away.

1.6.3 Object Types: Not Variable Types

As noted earlier, every object has a type in Python. Variables can freely change their object association during a program. A Python variable can refer to any object, and that object, and potentially its type, can change over time. For example, a variable could be associated with a string one moment and be reassigned to an integer later on. Consider this Python session:

```
In  [1]: my_var
Traceback (most recent call last):
  File "<stdin>", line 1, in <module>
NameError: name 'my_var' is not defined
In  [2]: my_var = 7 # create my_var as type int (integer)
In  [3]: my_var
Out [3]: 7

In  [4]: my_var = 7.77 # now associate my_var with a float (floating point)
In  [5]: my_var
Out [5]: 7.77

In  [6]: my_var = True # now type is bool (Boolean)
In  [7]: my_var
Out [7]: True
```

```
In  [8]: my_var = "7.77" # now type is str (string)
In  [9]: my_var
Out [9]: '7.77'

In  [10]: my_var = float(my_var) # convert string my_var to float (floating point)
In  [11]: my_var
Out [11]: 7.77
```

Initially, `my_var` is undefined as it has never had a value assigned to it (has no association with a value yet), so the Python interpreter complains when you ask for its associated object. Remember that to create a variable name in the namespace, we must assign (or otherwise define) the variable. Subsequently in the example, we assign an integer value (type int) to `my_var`, the integer 7. Next, we assign a floating-point value, 7.77, to `my_var`, so it is now associated with an object of type float. Next we assign a Boolean value to `my_var`, so it becomes associated with a type bool (Boolean) value. Finally, we assign a string to `my_var` (type str). For illustration purposes, the characters we chose for the string are the same ones used for the floating-point example. However, note the quotes! Because we put the characters in quotes, the Python interpreter considers the characters to be a string (a sequence of printable characters) rather than a number. To further illustrate that point, we then used the *`float`* function to convert the string value in `my_var` to a floating-point object and then assigned that floating-point object value back to `my_var`. Python's *`float`* could create the new floating-point object from the string object, because the string consisted of only numbers and a decimal point. If we had tried to convert a string of letters, *`float`* would have generated an error: *`float ("fred")`* is an error.

Because the computer has separate hardware for integers and floating-point arithmetic, the Python interpreter keeps careful track of types for use in expressions. Also, operators may perform different operations depending on the type of the operands. For example, with the plus (+) operator, if the operands are of type *`int`* or *`float`*, addition will be performed, but if the operands are of type *`str`* (that is, a string), concatenation will be performed. Here is an example showing the two interpretations of plus (+):

```
In  [1]: my_var = 2
In  [2]: my_var + my_var
Out [2]: 4

In  [3]: my_var = "Ni"
In  [4]: my_var + my_var
Out [4]: 'NiNi'
```

PROGRAMMING TIP

Because the type information is not part of the variable, it is often helpful to help keep track of types by affixing the type name to their variables, such as `my_int`, `b_float`, `phone_book_dict`. This style of naming is sometimes called "Hungarian notation."

Invented by Charles Simonyi, a programmer who worked at Xerox PARC, Hungarian notation puts the type of the value associated with the variable in front of the name (much as Hungarian puts the family name before the surname). We use a variation that places the type as a suffix.

1.6.4 Constructing New Values

We noted earlier that every object has a type and that the type determines both what is stored in the object and the kinds of operations that can be performed on that object.

There are also some operations associated with the type itself. One of the most useful of those operations is the *constructor*. A constructor is a special operation that is used to *make* a particular object of that type. For example, the operation `int` will create a new object that is of type integer.

Each type has an associated constructor: the constructor's name is the name of the type (`int`, `float`, `str`, . . .). If no value is provided within the parentheses, then a default value of that type is provided (for `int` it is 0; for `float` it is 0.0, for `str` it is ''). If a value *is* provided in the parentheses, then the constructor will *convert* that value to a new object of the specified type if it can. Thus, constructors can be used to convert one object to a new object of a different type. You have seen conversion in previous examples.

- `int(my_var)` returns an integer representation of the object associated with `my_var`.
  - Note `my_var` itself is unaffected. The object associated with `my_var` is provided to the function `int`, a new object is created, the conversion of the `my_var` object to an `int`, and that new converted object is returned.
  - If the object associated with `my_var` cannot be converted to an integer (say, the value `'a'`), then an error will occur.
- `float (my_var)` returns a floating-point representation of the object associated with `my_var`. As with `int`, if the object cannot be converted to a floating-point number, then an error will occur.
- `str(my_var)` returns a string representation of the object associated with `my_var`.

It is again important to note that 1 and `"1"` are very different.

- 1 is the integer 1.
- `"1"` is the character digit that gets typed on a keyboard.

Next is an example Python session that illustrates using constructors for conversion. The comments explain what is happening:

```
In  [1]: int("1") # convert string to integer
Out [1]: 1

In  [2]: int(1.7) # convert floating point to integer; note the truncation
Out [2]: 1
```

```
In [3]: int(True) # convert Boolean to integer
Out [3]: 1

In [4]: int('1.1') # can't go from a string, to a float, to an int. Too far!
Traceback (most recent call last):
  File "<stdin>", line 1, in <module>
ValueError: invalid literal for int() with base 10: '1.1'
In [5]: float("3.33") # convert string to floating point
Out [5]: 3.33

In [6]: float(42) # convert integer to floating point; note the .0
Out [6]: 42.0

In [7]: str(9.99) # convert floating point to string; note the quotes
Out [7]: '9.99'

In [8]: my_var = "2" # create a string
In [9]: my_var
Out [9]: '2'

In [10]: int(my_var) # show that conversion does not change my_var
Out [10]: 2

In [11]: my_var
Out [11]: '2'

In [12]: my_var = int(my_var) # need assignment to change my_var
In [13]: my_var
Out [13]: 2
```

Note what happens when you convert a floating-point value like 1.7 into an integer. No error occurs: the decimal portion is simply removed and the integer portion used as the value. When an integer is converted to a float, a decimal portion is added (that is, .0 is appended).

1.7 OPERATORS

As we noted in Section 1.6, for every type there is a set of operations that can be performed on that type. Given the limited number of symbols available, some symbols are used for different purposes for different types. This is called *operator overloading*, which is a term that indicates that a symbol might have multiple meanings depending on the types of the values. For example, we saw earlier that the plus (+) sign performs different operations depending on whether the operands are integers or strings.

1.7.1 Integer Operators

Most of the operators for integers work exactly as you learned in elementary arithmetic class. The plus (+) sign is used for addition, the minus (−) is for subtraction, and the asterisk (*) is for multiplication.

Division works as you would expect as well, but it is a little different from the other operators. In particular, the integers are not closed with respect to division. By closure, we mean that if you add two integers, the sum is an integer. The same is true for subtraction and multiplication. However, if you divide two integers, the result is not necessarily an integer. It could be an integer (say 4/2) or it could be a float (4/3). Mathematically it is a rational (also known as fraction), but Python represents it as a float. For consistency's sake *whenever* you do division, regardless of the types of the operands, the type yielded is a ***float***. The next session shows this behavior.

```
In  [1]: a_int=4
In  [1]: b_int=2
In  [1]: a_int + b_int
Out [1]: 6

In  [2]: a_int * b_int
Out [2]: 8

In  [3]: a_int - b_int
Out [3]: 2

In  [4]: a_int / b_int # note, 2.0 not 2. Result is always float
Out [4]: 2.0

In  [5]: result = a_int / b_int
In  [6]: type(result) # checking the type, yes it's a float
Out [6]: float

In  [7]: a_int / 3 # important that it be a float here
Out [7]: 1.3333333333333333
```

However, perhaps indeed you only want an integer result. Python provides an operator that when used with integers provides only the integer part of a division, that is, the quotient (what type is an interesting question, but keep reading). That operator is the // operator. Let us see how it works.

Consider how you did division in elementary school. For example, consider 5 divided by 3, as shown in Figure 1.3.

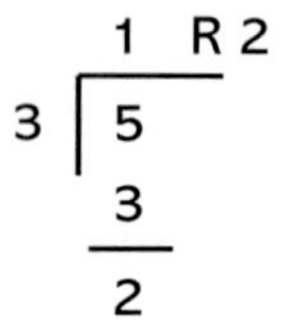

FIGURE 1.3 Long division example.

The *quotient* is 1 and the *remainder* is 2. Observe that both the quotient and remainder are integers, so the integers are closed under the quotient and remainder operations. Therefore, in Python (and many other programming languages), their there are separate operators for quotient, `//` and remainder `%`.[6] We can see these two operators in action by showing the same 5 divided by 3 equation from Figure 1.3 expressed with the two expressions for quotient and remainder.

```
In  [1]: 5 // 3 # integer quotient
Out [1]: 1

In  [2]: 5 % 3 # integer remainder
Out [2]: 2

In  [3]: 5.0 // 3.0 # integer quotient, but as a float
Out [3]: 1.0

In  [4]: 5.0 % 3.0 # integer remainder, but as a float
Out [4]: 2.0

In  [5]: 5.0 / 3.0 # regular division
Out [5]: 1.6666666666666667

In  [6]: 5 // 3.0 # when types are mixed, result is a float
Out [6]: 1.0
```

It is interesting to note the type of the results, though not the value, depends on the types of the operands. If the operation has integer operands, that is, `5 //3`, the quotient is 1, an `int`. If the operation has floating-point operands, that is, `5.0 //3.0`, the result is 1.0. This is the correct quotient, but its type is a `float`. When the types are mixed, i.e., `5 // 3.0`, the type is also a `float`. See Section 1.7.3 for more details as to why.

In that session it appears that the `//` operation works the same for both integers and floats, but there is a subtle difference. If the floating-point values have no fractional part, for example, 2.0, the operation is the same. However, fractional parts indicate that the floating-point operation is actually floating-point division followed by truncation.

Therefore, the full set of operators for integers is as follows:

+	addition
−	subtraction
*	multiplication
/	division
//	quotient
%	remainder
**	exponentiation

[6] The remainder operation is known in mathematics as the *modulo* operation.

1.7.2 Floating-Point Operators

Floating-point operators work as expected. Note that you may use both the quotient and remainder operators as well on floating-point numbers.

+	addition
−	subtraction
*	multiplication
/	division
//	quotient
%	remainder
**	exponentiation

As with integers, addition, subtraction, multiplication, and division perform as expected. As shown in the previous session, quotient and remainder work as well, giving the proper value but as a type *float*.

1.7.3 Mixed Operations

VideoNote 1.1
Simple Arithmetic

What is the difference between the number 42 and 42.0?[7] The answer is that they are different types. Same value, but different types! Therefore, when you perform operations with them, you might get different answers.

What happens when you mix types? For example, how does the computer handle dividing an integer by a floating-point number? The answer is, "it depends." In general, operations provided by each type dictate the rules of what can and cannot be mixed. For numbers, a computer has separate hardware for integer and floating-point arithmetic. Because of that hardware, the operation is best done in one type or the other, so the numbers must be of the same type. Those that are not of the same type must be converted. Given that, what is the correct conversion to perform: integer-to-float or float-to-integer?

Clearly no information is lost when converting an integer to a float, but conversion of a float to an integer would lose the fractional information in the float. Therefore, most programming languages, including Python, when presented with mixed types will "promote" an integer to be a floating point so that both operands are floats and the operation can be performed as floats.

```
In [1]: var_int = 42
In [2]: var_float = 42.0
In [3]: var_int * 5 # multiplication , int times int yields int
Out [3]: 210

In [4]: var_int * 5.0 # multiplication , int times float yields float
Out [4]: 210.0
```

[7] The answer to Life, the Universe, and Everything is 42 according to Douglas Adams's *The Hitchhiker's Guide to the Galaxy*.

```
In  [5]: var_float + 5 # addition, float plus int yields float
Out [5]: 47.0

In  [6]: var_int / 7 # division, int divide int yields float
Out [6]: 6.0                     # division always yields a float!
```

PROGRAMMING TIP

Normal division in Python always yields a float, even when working with only integer operands.

1.7.4 Order of Operations and Parentheses

The order of arithmetic operations in Python and most common programming languages is the same as you learned in arithmetic: multiplication and division before addition or subtraction. The term used to describe the ordering is *precedence*. In this case, we say that multiplication and division have greater precedence than addition or subtraction, so they are done first. Further, exponents have greater precedence than multiplication and division, also as in arithmetic. If operations have the same precedence—that is, multiplication and division—they are done left to right. Finally, as in arithmetic, parentheses can be used to override the precedence order and force some operations to be done before others, regardless of precedence. The precedence of arithmetic operations is shown in Table 1.4; the order in the table is from highest precedence (performed first) to lowest.

Operator	Description
()	Parenthesis (grouping)
**	Exponentiation
+x, -x	Positive, Negative
*, /, %, //	Multiplication, Division, Remainder, Quotient
+, -	Addition, Subtraction

TABLE 1.4 Precedence (order) of arithmetic operations: highest to lowest.

Here is a session to illustrate precedence and parentheses.

```
In  [1]: 2 + 3 - 4 # same precedence: left to right
Out [1]: 1

In  [2]: 4 / 2 * 5 # same precedence: left to right
Out [2]: 10

In  [3]: 2 + 3 * 5 # multiplication before addition
Out [3]: 17
```

```
In  [4]: (2 + 3) * 5 # parentheses force addition before multiplication
Out [4]: 25

In  [5]: 2 + 3 * 5**2 # exponents before multiplication before addition
Out [5]: 77

In  [6]: 2 + 3 * 5**2 - 1
Out [6]: 76

In  [7]: -4 + 2 # negation before addition and subtraction
Out [7]: -2
```

In Chapter 2, you will learn about Boolean operators and their precedence with respect to the arithmetic operators. The full table of all Python operator precedence is in Appendix G.

1.7.5 Augmented Assignment Operators: A Shortcut!

Operations—especially groups of operations—that are used repeatedly are often provided with a *shortcut*, a simpler way of typing. Python, like other languages, has such shortcuts. They are not required, but they do make typing easier and, at some point, make the code shorter and easier to read.

Our first short cut is the combination of an integer operation and the assignment (=) sign. Though you might not have noticed, they were listed in Table 1.2. They are a combination of one of the arithmetic operators such as `+`, `-`, `*`, `/` along with the assignment sign `=`. Some examples would be `+=`, `-=`, `/=`, `*=`. Note that the operation comes before the assignment sign, not after!

Shortcut	Equivalence
`my_int += 2`	`my_int = my_int + 2`
`my_int -= 2`	`my_int = my_int - 2`
`my_int /= 2`	`my_int = my_int / 2`
`my_int *= 2`	`my_int = my_int * 2`

TABLE 1.5 Augmented assignment.

What does `+=` mean? Let's look at an example, `my_int += 2`. The augmented operator, in general, means: "Perform the augmented operation (plus here) using the two operands, the value `2` (value on the rightside) and `my_int` (variable on the left side), and reassign the result to `my_int` (variable on the left side)." That is, the following two expressions are exactly equivalent: `my_int += 2` or `my_int = my_int + 2`. The first is a shortcut, the second the "long" way. Table 1.5 lists the most commonly used shortcuts. However, incrementing `my_int += 1` is by far the most commonly used shortcut.

PROGRAMMING TIP

If you are going to use an augmented assignment, it is important to note that the variable be defined already, meaning that at some point you have assigned it a value. That is, you cannot add 2 to `my_int` if `my_int` doesn't already have a value. Otherwise, you will get an error that `my_int` is undefined.

Check Yourself: Types and Operators

1. Give the values printed by the following program for each of the labeled lines and answer the associated questions.

```
a_float = 2.5
a_int = 7
b_int = 6

print(a_int / b_int)        # Line 1
print(a_int // a_float)     # Line 2
print(a_int %  b_int)       # Line 3
print(int(a_float))         # Line 4
print(float(a_int))         # Line 5
```

(a) `Line 1`: what is printed; what is its type?
(b) `Line 2`: what is printed; what is its type?
(c) `Line 3`: what is printed; what is its type?
(d) `Line 4`: what is printed; what is its type?
(e) `Line 5`: what is printed; what is its type?

2. Give the values printed by the following program for each of the labeled lines.

```
a_int = 10
b_int = 3
c_int = 2

print(a_int + b_int * c_int)        # Line 1
print( (a_int + b_int) * c_int )    # Line 2
print(b_int ** c_int)               # Line 3
print(0o10 + c_int)                 # Line 4
```

(a) What is printed by `Line 1`?
(b) What is printed by `Line 2`?
(c) What is printed by `Line 3`?
(d) What is printed by `Line 4`?

1.8 YOUR FIRST MODULE, MATH

Python has many strengths, but one of its best is the availability of the many *modules* for various tasks. If you take a look at the Python Package Index (`http://pypi.python.org/pypi`) you will see that there are hundreds[8] of packages provided as modules for you to use in Python—all for free! The Python community, part of the Open Source community, created those modules for everyone to use. As we described earlier, a module is a collection of instructions saved together as a whole. Those instructions can be loaded into our program using the ***import*** command. We did just that—we used the ***import*** command to import the math module in the program to determine the circumference of a circle in Section 1.2. Let's take a deeper look at the math module.

When we import that math module, all the code contained in the math module is made available to our program. The contents of the math module can be found in a couple of ways. The best way is to look online in the Python documentation. Go to the Python docs and take a look: `http://docs.python.org/library/math.html`. You could also import the math module in the iPython console, and do the following:

- Type ***import*** `math`
- Type `math.<TAB>`

When you type the tab character after "math.", a list will be created of all the code that was brought in during the import. Alternatively, you could type `help(math)`.

What is typically brought in is either a function (a piece of code we can call to perform some operation) or a variable. Either way, the *name* of the imported code is always preceded with `math.a_name` meaning "in the math module, the item a_name." Thus, in Section 1.2.1, we used the variable `math.pi`. The `math.` indicates the module name and the name after the "." is one of its elements, in this case the variable `pi`. More simply, "pi in the math module." All the code imported from the math module is referenced in this way. Although there are other ways to import a module, this is the preferred way.

Functions will be properly introduced in Chapter 8. A function has two parts: the *name* of the function, which hopefully indicates what operation it performs, and an *argument* list, which is a parenthetical list of values to be sent into the function as part of its operation. When the function completes its operation, a *return value* is returned from the function. A typical function is the `math.sin(a_float)` function. The name of the function is `math.sin` and the argument list follows: a parenthetical list of one value, which must be a floating-point number. When `math.sin(a_float)` completes, the sine of `a_float` (which would also be a float) is returned. The returned value can be captured with an assignment, printed, or otherwise used elsewhere in the program.

[8] There are 16,000 for Python 2.7 so we can expect many more.

Some useful functions in the math module include the following:

`math.sin` Takes one numeric argument, and returns the sine of that argument as a float.
`math.cos` Takes one numeric argument, and returns the cosine of that argument as a float.
`math.pow` Takes two numeric arguments, x and y, and returns x^y (x raised to the power y) as a float.
`math.sqrt` Takes one numeric argument, and returns the square root of that argument as a float.
`math.hypot` Takes two numeric arguments, x and y, and returns $\sqrt{x^2 + y^2}$, the Euclidean distance.
`math.fabs` Takes one numeric argument, and returns the absolute value of the argument.

At any time, you can type "help(object)" and Python will provide help on that object. For example:

```
In  [1]: import math
In  [2]: help(math.pow)
Help on built-in function pow in module math:

pow(...)
    pow(x,y)

    Return x**y (x to the power of y).
```

1.9 DEVELOPING AN ALGORITHM

You know a lot more than when we started this chapter about how to write programs, especially with numbers. Let's take a look at solving a simple problem to see how well you can do. Here's a question:

> How many gallons of water fall on an acre of land given the number of inches of rain which fell? For example, how many gallons for 1 inch, 2 inches, etc.?

This problem really has to do with the weather and how it is reported. When the weather person on television tells you that "one inch of rain" has fallen, what does that really mean? In case you didn't know, "one inch of rain" means pretty much what it says. Rain has accumulated to a depth of one inch over a certain area.

How do we attack this problem? Our goal is to develop an *algorithm* from which we can derive our program. What is an algorithm? It is one of those common words that can be hard to define precisely. One definition that works for what we need to do in this book is:

> **algorithm:** A method—a sequence of steps—that describes how to solve a problem or class of problems.

When we describe an algorithm, we are describing what we—as human problem solvers—need to do to solve a problem. We can provide a description in a variety of ways: English language, diagrams, flowcharts, whatever works for us. Having worked out a solution to a problem in our own best way, we can translate that algorithm into the code that realizes that algorithm.

For our rainfall problem, how can we develop our algorithm? First, we observe that the problem statement is a combination of linear measurement (inches) and square measurement (acres), but the desired result is in volume (gallons). We must find some intermediate unit for the conversion process. Representing volume in cubic feet is one way; metric units would work as well.

Our algorithm starts with these steps:

1. Prompt the user for the number of inches that have fallen.
2. Find the volume (in cubic feet) of water (where volume = depth * area).
3. Convert the volume (in cubic feet) to gallons.

The Internet can provide the conversion formulas:

```
1 acre = 43,560 square feet
1 cubic foot = 7.48051945 gallons
```

With this information, we can start on our algorithm. Let's begin parts two and three, assuming just one inch of rain on one acre:

1. Find the volume in cubic feet of water of one inch over one acre
   1 inch is equivalent to 1/12 foot
   volume = depth * area = (1/12)*43560 cubic feet
2. Convert the volume in cubic feet to gallons
   gallons = volume * 7.48051945

Now let's try this in Python. We can begin in the Python shell and try out the volume formula:

```
In  [1]: volume = (1/12) * 43560
In  [2]: volume
Out [2]: 3630.0
```

Note that the type of `volume` is floating point even though the arguments are integers. This is how division works in Python; it always yields a *`float`*.

Now let's include the conversion to gallons:

```
In  [1]: volume = (1/12) * 43560
In  [2]: volume
Out [2]: 3630.0
```

```
In  [3]: gallons = volume * 7.48051945
In  [4]: gallons
Out [4]: 27154.2856035
```

That looks reasonable. Now we should include part one and prompt the user for the number of inches that have fallen. To do this we need the `input` function, so let's add that to the previous program. We prompt the user for a value `inches` and divide that by 12 to obtain our volume. Let's take a look.

```
In  [1]: inches = input("How many inches of rain have fallen:")
How many inches of rain have fallen:1
In  [2]: volume = (inches/12) * 43560
Traceback (most recent call last):
  File "<stdin>", line 1, in <module>
TypeError: unsupported operand type(s) for /: 'str' and 'int'
```

Hmm, an error. What is the problem? If we look at the error, it gives us a hint: "unsupported operand type(s) for /: 'str' and 'int'". How did a *str* get in there?

Yes, that's right. If we do the `input` in isolation we can see the problem.

```
In  [1]: inches = input("How many inches of rain have fallen:")
How many inches of rain have fallen:1
In  [2]: inches
Out [2]: '1'
```

The `input` function returns what the user provides as a string (note the quotes around the 1). We need to convert it to a number to get the result we want. Let's take the value from the `input` function and convert it using the *int* function. Let's be smarter about naming our `inches` variable as well, so we can tell one type from another.

```
In  [1]: inches_str = input("How many inches of rain have fallen:")
How many inches of rain have fallen:1
In  [2]: inches_int = int(inches_str)
In  [3]: volume = (inches_int/12) * 43560
In  [4]: volume
Out [4]: 3630.0

In  [5]: gallons = volume * 7.48051945
In  [6]: gallons
Out [6]: 27154.2856035
```

That looks reasonable. Now let's put it together in a program (in SPYDER) and call it `rain.py`. We ran the program by selecting "Run ⇒ Run" (or F5). See Code Listing 1.2

Code Listing 1.2

```
# Calculate rainfall in gallons for some number of inches on 1 acre
inches_str = input("How many inches of rain have fallen: ")
inches_int = int(inches_str)
volume = (inches_int/12)*43560
gallons = volume * 7.48051945
print(inches_int," in. rain on 1 acre is", gallons, "gallons")
```

```
In [1]: runfile('/Users/user/python/file.py', wdir='/Users/user/python')

How many inches of rain have fallen: 1
1  in. rain on 1 acre is 27154.2856035 gallons


In [2]: runfile('/Users/user/python/file.py', wdir='/Users/user/python')

How many inches of rain have fallen: 2
2  in. rain on 1 acre is 54308.571207 gallons


In [3]: runfile('/Users/user/python/file.py', wdir='/Users/user/python')

How many inches of rain have fallen: 0.5
Traceback (most recent call last):
  File "/Users/enbody/Documents/book/tpocup/ch01/programs/program1-3.py", line
 3, in <module>
    inches_int = int(inches_str)
ValueError: invalid literal for int() with base 10: '0.5'
```

For 1 and 2 inches it worked great, but for a value of 1/2 an inch, 0.5, we got an error. Why? Again, the error message describes the problem: "invalid literal for int() with base 10: '0.5'." We entered a floating-point value in response to the inches prompt, and Python cannot convert the string `'0.5'` to an integer.

How can we fix this? If we are to allow floating-point input, and it seems reasonable to do so, then we should convert the user-provided value to a `float`, not an `int`, to avoid this problem.

Therefore, we change the conversion to be the `float` function, and to help readability we change the name of `inches_int` to `inches_float`. Then we test it again (see Code Listing 1.3).

Code Listing 1.3

```
# Calculate rainfall in gallons for some number of inches on 1 acre
inches_str = input("How many inches of rain have fallen: ")
inches_float = float(inches_str)
volume = (inches_float/12)*43560
gallons = volume * 7.48051945
print(inches_float," in. rain on 1 acre is", gallons, "gallons")
```

```
In  [1]: runfile('/Users/user/python/file.py', wdir='/Users/user/python')

How many inches of rain have fallen: 1
1.0  in. rain on 1 acre is 27154.2856035 gallons


In  [2]: runfile('/Users/user/python/file.py', wdir='/Users/user/python')

How many inches of rain have fallen: 2
2.0  in. rain on 1 acre is 54308.571207 gallons


In  [3]: runfile('/Users/user/python/file.py', wdir='/Users/user/python')

How many inches of rain have fallen: 0.5
0.5  in. rain on 1 acre is 13577.14280175 gallons
```

The result is fine, but the output isn't very pretty. Take a look ahead at Section 4.4 for ways to make the output prettier.

1.9.1 New Rule—Testing

VideoNote 1.2
Solving Your First Problem

One of the things you should learn from the development of the previous algorithm is the importance of testing. You need to test your approach at every point, in as many ways as you can imagine, to make sure your program does what it is supposed to do. This is such an important point that we are going to add a new programming rule:

> **Rule 5:** Test your code, often and thoroughly!

Testing is so important that a number of programming paradigms emphasize the development of tests before code is written. Look up the concepts of "test-driven development" and "extreme programming" on the Internet to get a feel for these approaches.

Remember, only in testing your code, all of it, can you be assured that it does what you intended it to do.

VISUAL VIGNETTE

1.10 TURTLE GRAPHICS

Python version 2.6 introduced a simple drawing tool known as Turtle Graphics. Appendix B provides an introduction and describes a few of the many commands that are available. The concept is that there is a turtle that you command to move forward, right, and, left combined with the ability to have the turtle's pen move up or down.

Let's draw a simple five-pointed star. We begin by importing the turtle module. By default, the turtle begins in the middle of the window pointing right with the pen down. We then have the turtle repeatedly turn and draw a line. See Code Listing 1.4.

Code Listing 1.4

```
# Draw a 5-pointed star
import turtle

turtle.forward(100)
turtle.right(144)
turtle.forward(100)
turtle.right(144)
turtle.forward(100)
turtle.right(144)
turtle.forward(100)
turtle.right(144)
turtle.forward(100)
```

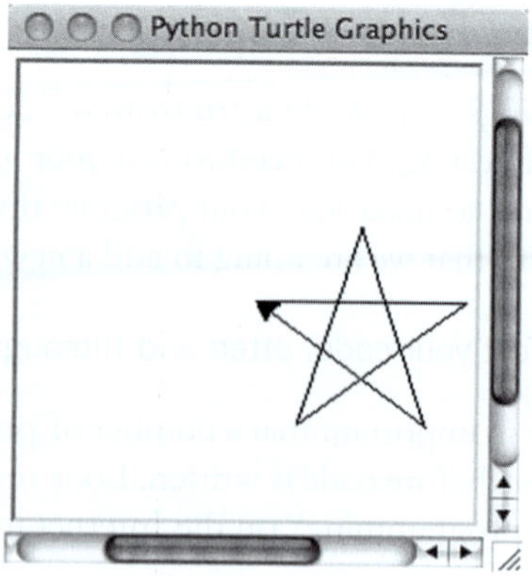

[Screenshot from Python Turtle Graphics. Copyright © by Python. Used by permission of Python.]

As with any problem, the hard part is the thinking that goes into figuring out the details. In this case, what are the angles that we need on each turn? Notice that the center of the star is a regular pentagon. A quick Internet check reveals that each internal angle is 108°. One can view the star as five (isosceles) triangles attached to the pentagon. Because a side of the pentagon extends into a side of a triangle, supplementary angles are formed so the base angle of each triangle is 72° (supplementary angles: 180° − 108°). The two base angles of an isosceles triangle are equal and combine to be 144° so the third angle must be 36° (a triangle has 180°: 180° − 144°). To make the sharp turn, at each point of the star we need to make a 144° turn (180° − 36°). That is why we have `turtle.right(144)` for each point.

1.11 WHAT'S WRONG WITH MY CODE?

Here are suggestions for finding problems with your code. Refer to Appendix C for details.

The most important thing to do is, "Read the Error message!." Learning to read error message helps tremendously when deciphering errors.

Error messages can appear in two places:

- **In the SPYDER editor:** An error flag appears to the left of line numbers. You can mouse over error marker to see the error. If not a syntax error, the error is likely a kind of `NameError` (see below).
- **In the shell:** Two types of errors

  Static Errors that SPYDER can also point out in the editor. These include syntax errors, missing modules, and misnamed variables.

  Run-time Errors that can only be found when running the program.

Types of Error messages that are likely to occur from topics in this chapter.

- **ValueError** These are often a conversion error, for example, *`float('abc')`*.
  `ValueError: could not convert string to float: 'abc'`
- **TypeError** These often result from trying to do an operation on two different types that are not permitted in Python. For example, mismatched types, for example, `'abc' - 2`.

  `TypeError: unsupported operand type(s) for -: 'str' and 'int'`. The Variable Explorer shows type so it is a good place to check for helpful information.

  Also, remember our naming conventions in Section 1.4.6. If you append type information to your variables, it is easier to track down this kind of error.
- **NameError** This error usually means that the name is not in the namespace. This often means that you never gave the identifier (name) an initial value. Since Variable Explorer shows your namespace you will see that the name isn't there. There are generally two reasons:

   – *Identifier not initialized*, for example, `x = y` # but y never initialized
     `NameError: name 'y' is not defined`
   – *Forgot import*, for example, you forgot to import math or forgot to prepend math
     `x = sqrt(y)`
     `NameError: name 'sqrt' is not defined`

- **Syntax Error** For example,
  `x === 3`
  `SyntaxError: invalid syntax`
  In the shell, the message will point to the error.
- **ZeroDivisionError:** self-explanatory

There are other errors which either do not generate an error or the error generated is not helpful. Watch for these!

- **Mismatched Parentheses** can occur for many reasons and can be hard to find. If you have many parentheses or wonder if you have them correct, the IDE such as SPYDER can help by matching corresponding pairs. One trick is to delete parenthesis at the end of a line or expression and watch the IDE highlight the corresponding one as you add parentheses back in one at a time. Also, SPYDER automatically fills in all matching parenthesis as you type. An important thing to keep in mind is that errors with parenthesis can be generated by Python a few lines *after* where the error actually occurred—Python got confused and finally gave up and generated an unhelpful error message.

Note, error messages indicate a line number for the error, but sometimes, especially with a `SyntaxError`, the error actually happens on an earlier line. This is because the interpreter tries hard to understand what was given to it, but gives up at some point, usually down the program from where the error initially occurred.

Finally, be careful that you do not select a variable name that is already in use by Python as a built-in or module name. For example, you might run the following code `str = ``abc''`, assigning a value to the variable `str`. The only problem is the Python is using `str` as the name of the string type. However, Python is happy to oblige. During the remainder of your program, `str` is a variable and not a type. Pay attention to **colors** when creating variable names. SPYDER colors Python keywords. If a color pops up on your variable, perhaps you should look and see if it is a Python keyword. Finally, if you fix the problem (change the variable name), when you start Python up again, the problem will go away.

Summary

In this chapter, we introduced a simple, but complete program followed by a description of expressions versus assignments, whitespace and indentation, and finally operators. Most importantly, we showed how to use the Python shell to practice programming.

Elements

- Keywords: Table 1.1 on page 79
- Operators: Table 1.2 on page 79
- Names
  – begin with a letter; otherwise letters, digits, and underscore
  – (beginning with an underscore has special meaning left for later)
- Namespace
  Association between a name and an object
- Expression
  Expression is similar to a mathematical expression: it returns a value
- Statement
  Statement performs a task (side effect); does not return a value
- Assignment LHS = RHS
  Steps
  – evaluate expression on RHS; return value
  – associate value from RHS with the name on the LHS
- Modules
  Code that can be imported

Built-in Types

- *int*
  – integers, of any length
  – operations: +, −, *, **, /, //, %
  note: // is quotient; % is remainder (mod)
- *float*
  – floating-point, also known as decimals
  – operations: +, −, *, **, /, //, %
- Others
  – Booleans: Chapter 2
  – Strings: Chapter 4
  – Lists: Chapter 7
  – Dictionaries and Sets: Chapter 9

Rules

- **RULE 1:** Think before you program!
- **RULE 2:** A program is a human-readable essay on problem solving that also happens to execute on a computer.
- **RULE 3:** The best way to improve your programming and problem skills is to practice!
- **RULE 4:** A foolish consistency is the hobgoblin of little minds.
- **RULE 5:** Test your code, often and thoroughly!

Exercises

1. What is a program?
2. Python is an interpreted language. What does "interpreted" mean in this context?
3. What is a Python *comment*? How do you indicate a comment? What purpose do they serve?
4. What is a *namespace* in Python?
5. Whitespace:
   (a) What is whitespace in Python?
   (b) When does whitespace matter?
   (c) When does whitespace not matter?
6. Explain the difference between a statement and an expression. Give an example of both, and explain what is meant by a statement having a *side effect*.
7. Mixed operations:
   (a) What type results when you divide an integer by a float? A float by an integer?
   (b) Explain why that resulting type makes sense (as opposed to some other type).
8. Consider integer values of a, b, and c, and the expression (a + b) * c. In mathematics, we can substitute square brackets, [ ], or curly braces, { }, for parentheses, ( ). Is that same substitution valid in Python? Try it.
9. Write a Python program that will assign values to three variables and print them. The first variable should contain the string "Python", the second should contain the integer 10, and the third should contain the floating point value 1000.0.
10. A nursery rhyme: *As I was going to St. Ives, I met a man with seven wives. Every wife had seven sacks, and every sack had seven cats, every cat had seven kittens. Kittens, cats, sacks, and wives, how many were going to St. Ives?* There are interesting aspects to this puzzle, such as who is actually going to St. Ives. For our purposes, assume that everyone and everything are headed to St. Ives. Write a program to calculate that total.

11. Assignment:

```
my_int = 5
my_int = my_int + 3
print(my_int)
```

(a) If you execute the three lines of code, what will be printed? Explain your answer using the rules of assignment.

(b) Rewrite `my_int = my_int + 3` using the += symbol.

12. Assignment:

```
my_var1 = 7.0
my_var2 = 5
print(my_var1 % my_var2)
```

If you execute these three lines of code, what will be printed?

13. Try to predict what will be printed by the following:

```
x = 4
y = 5
print(x//y)
```

14. Given the expression: 30 − 3 ** 2 + 8 // 3 ** 2 * 10

(a) What is the output of the expression? (You can check your answer in the Python shell.)

(b) Based on precedence and associativity of the operators in Python, correctly parenthesize the expression such that you get the same output as above.

15. (Order of operations) One example expression was 2 + 3 * 5, the value of which was 17. Using the same expression, include parentheses to arrive at a different value for the expression.

16. Predict the output (check your answer in the Python shell):

(a) 2**2**3
(b) 2**(2**3)
(c) (2**2)**3

Why do two of the expressions have the same output?
Rewrite expression (c) with one exponential operator (**) and one multiplication operator (*).

17. Prompt for input and then print the input as a string, an integer, and a float point value. What values can you input and print without errors being generated?

18. (Illegal expressions) In a Python shell, try some of the illegal expressions mentioned in the chapter and observe the error messages. For example, try assigning a value to a keyword, such as ***and*** `= 4`. Each error message begins with the name of the error and that name is useful in checking for errors. Generate at least five different error messages.

19. Table 1.2 lists Python operators, some of which may have been unfamiliar to you. Open up the Python shell and experiment with unfamiliar operators and see how many you can define.

20. We know from mathematics that parenthesis can change the order of operations. For example, consider a + b * c, (a + b) * c, and a + (b*c). In general, two of those expressions will be the same and one will be different. Through trial and error, find one set of integer values for a, b, and c so that all three expressions have the same value and a != b != c.

21. Write a Python program to swap two integer variables. Now try out the same program with strings and floating point variables. What happens?

22. Consider the numbers 15.789, 15.50, and 15.9999. These numbers when converted to integers return the same value. What is that value, and why are the values all the same?

23. Predict the outcomes of the following expressions given a = 30, b = 20, and c = 10.

(a) `a//c`
(b) `a%b`
(c) `b**c`
(d) `b*=c`

24. Write a Python program that accept an integer n and computes the value of $n + n * n + n * n * n + n * n * n * n$.

25. Write the following mathematical expressions in Python and then find the value of the expression using the provided value of x:

(a) $x = (2^4 + 7 - 3 * 4)/5$, the value of x = 2
(b) $x = (1 + 3^2) * (16 \bmod 7)/7$, the value of x = 2.85174

26. In Python, try to execute the statement x = 0 % 0. Explain what happens to the program when Python tries to execute this statement.

27. Given the following variable assignments:

```
var_1 = 10
var_2 = 1
var_3 = 10
var_4 = 10
var_5 = '10'
```

What is the output of each of the following print statements? If the statement does not run, write ERROR and explain why.

(a) `print(var_1)`
(b) `print(var_2)`
(c) `print("var_3")`
(d) `print((var_1+var_2)*var_3*var_4)`
(e) `print(((var_1+var_2)*var_3)/var_4)`
(f) `print(var_1+(var_2*var_5)/var_4)`

---

28. (Integer operators) One way to determine whether an integer is even is to divide the number by two and check the remainder. Write a three-line program that prompts for a number, converts the input to an integer, and prints a zero if the number is even and a one if the number is odd.

29. Write a three-line program that prompts for a number, converts the input to an integer, and calculates and prints its square root.

30. Using Turtle Graphics, draw a *six* pointed star.

31. A day has 86,400 secs (24*60*60). Given a number in the range 1–86,400, output the current time as hours, minutes, and seconds with a 24-hour clock. For example, 70,000 sec is 19 hours, 26 minutes, and 40 seconds.

32. A telephone directory has N lines on each page, and each page has exactly C columns. An entry in any column has a name with the corresponding telephone number. On which page, column, and line is the X*th* entry (name and number) present? (Assume that page, line, column numbers, and X all start from 1.)

33. If the lengths of the two parallel sides of a trapezoid are X meters and Y meters, respectively, and the height is H meters, what is the area of the trapezoid? Write Python code to output the area.

34. Simple interest is calculated by the product of the principal, number of years, and interest, all divided by 100. Write code to calculate the simple interest on a principal amount of $10,000 for a duration of 5 years with the rate of interest equal to 12.5%.

35. Consider a triangle with sides of length 3, 7, and 9. The law of cosines states that given three sides of a triangle (a, b, and c) and the angle C between sides a and b: $c^2 = a^2 + b^2 - 2 * a * b * cos(C)$. Write Python code to calculate the three angles in the triangle.

36. Checking the user input for errors is a vital part of programming. The following simple program attempts to take a string input and convert it into an integer. What will happen if the user enters "Hello World" at the prompt rather than a number? Can you think of a way that the program can be altered to handle this input (hint: think about adjusting how the program handles different types of input)?

```
Raw1 = input ('Please enter a number:')
Int1 = int (Raw1)
```

37. The radius and mass of the Earth are $r = 6378 \times 10^3$ meters and $m1 = 5.9742 \times 10^{24}$ kg, respectively. Mr. Jones has a mass of X kg. Prompt the user to input X and then calculate the gravitational force (F) and acceleration due to gravity (g) caused by the gravitational force exerted on him by the Earth. Remember, $F = G(m1)(m2)/(r^2)$ and $F = mg$. Let the universal gravitational constant $G = 6.67300 \times 10^{-11}$ (in units of $m^3\ kg^{-1}\ s^{-2}$ assuming the MKS [Meter-Kilogram-Second] system). Check that the resulting value of g is close to $9.8\ m/s^2$.

38. (Using modules) Python comes with hundreds of modules. Here is a challenge for you: find a module that you can import that will generate today's date so you can print it. Use your favorite search engine for help in finding which module you need and how to use it. In the end, your task is to do the following:

```
>>> print("Today's date is:", X )
Today's date is: 2009-05-22
```

39. In football, there is a statistic for quarterbacks called the *passer rating*. To calculate the passer rating, you need four inputs: pass completions, pass attempts, total passing yards, and interceptions. There are five steps in the algorithm. Write a program that asks for the five inputs and then prints the pass rating:

(a) C is the "completions per attempt" times 100 − 30 all divided by 20.
(b) Y is the "yards per attempt" − 3 all divided by 4.
(c) T is the "touchdowns per attempt" times 20.
(d) I is 2.375 minus ("interceptions per attempts" times 35).
(e) The pass rating is the sum of C, Y, T, and I all divided by 6 and then multiplied by 100.

40. Body Mass Index (BMI) is a number calculated from a person's weight and height. According to the Centers for Disease Control, the BMI is a fairly reliable indicator of body fatness for most people. BMI does not measure body fat directly, but research has shown that BMI correlates to direct measures of body fat, such as underwater weighing and dual energy X-ray absorptiometry. The formula for BMI is:

$$weight / height^2$$

where *weight* is in kilograms and *height* is in meters.

(a) Write a program that prompts for metric weight and height and outputs the BMI.
(b) Write a program that prompts for weight in pounds and height in inches, converts the values to metric, and then calculates the BMI.

41. A triangle has sides of 10 cm, 20 cm, and 25 cm. Calculate its area and perimeter.

42. Write a program that prompts the user to input an integer that represents cents. The program will then calculate the smallest combination of coins that the user has. For example, 27 cents is 1 quarter, 1 nickle, and 2 pennies.

43. Python comes with hundreds of modules. Find a module that will let you output calendars, and use it to display the calendar for any month.

44. Write a Python program that takes two dates as input and calculates the number of days, months, years between them.

45. The world record in the 100-meter dash is 9.58 seconds, set by Usain Bolt. Write a program that prompts for a runner's time in the 100 meter dash. Given that there are approximately 3.28 feet in a meter and 5280 feet in a mile, calculate and print the runner's average speed in miles per hour.

46. Write a program to calculate the time to run 5 miles, 10 miles, half marathon, and full marathon if you can run at a constant speed. The distance of a half marathon is 13.1 miles and that of a full marathon is 26.2 miles. Report the time in the format of hours and minutes. Your program will prompt for your running speed (mph) as an integer.

47. Using Turtle Graphics, draw a five-point star without lines inside.

48. Using pylab, graph five circles in the form of the Olympic rings. Assign each circle the appropriate color and make sure none is filled.

49. Use pylab to create subplots of the graph $y = cx^3$ for different values of c. There will be five subplots arranged in two rows and three columns. The values of c, reading from left to right for the subplots, are 0.1, 0.2, 0.5, 1, and 2.

Programming Projects

1. **The Great Lakes are how big?**
The Great Lakes in the United States contain roughly 22% of the world's fresh surface water (22,810 km^3). It is hard to conceive how much water that is. Write a program to calculate how deep it would be if all the water in the Great Lakes was spread evenly across the 48 contiguous U.S. states. You will need to do some Internet research to determine the area of that region.

2. **Where is Voyager 1?**
The Voyager 1 spacecraft, launched September 15, 1977, is the farthest traveling earth-made object. It is presently on the outer edges of our solar system. The NASA update page on September 25, 2009, reported it as being a distance of approximately 16,637,000,000 miles from the Sun, traveling away from the Sun at 38,241 miles/hour.

Write a program that will prompt the user for an integer number that indicates the number of days after 9/25/09. You will calculate the distance of Voyager from the Sun using the numbers from 9/25/09 (assume that velocity is constant) plus the entered number of days and report:

- Distance in miles
- Distance in kilometers (1.609344 kilometers/mile)
- Distance in Astronomical Units (AU, 92,955,887.6 miles/AU)
- Round trip time for radio communication in hours. Radio waves travel at the speed of light, listed at 299,792,458 meters/second.

3. Oil conversions and calculations

Write a program that will prompt the user for a floating-point number that stands for gallons of gasoline. You will reprint that value along with other information about gasoline and gasoline usage:

- Number of liters
- Number of barrels of oil required to make this amount of gasoline
- Number of pounds of CO_2 produced
- Equivalent energy amount of ethanol gallons
- Price in U.S. dollars

Here are some approximate conversion values:

- 1 barrel of oil produces 19.5 gallons of gasoline.
- 1 gallon of gasoline produces 20 pounds of CO_2 gas when burned.
- 1 gallon of gasoline contains 115,000 BTU (British Thermal Units) of energy.
- 1 gallon of ethanol contains 75,700 BTU of energy.
- 1 gallon of gasoline costs $3.00/gallon.

Look on the Internet for some interesting values for input such as the average number of gallons consumed per person per year, or consumed by the country per day, or consumed per year.

4. Population estimation

The U.S. Census provides information on its web page (`http://www.census.gov`) about the current U.S. population as well as approximate rates of change.
Three rates of change are provided:

- a birth every 7 seconds.
- a death every 13 seconds.
- a new immigrant every 35 seconds.

These are obviously approximations of birth, death, and immigration rates, but they can assist in providing population estimates in the near term.

Write a program that takes years as input (as an integer) and prints out an estimated population (as an integer). Assume that the current population is 307,357,870, and assume that there are exactly 365 days in a year.

Hint: Note that the rate units are in seconds.

CHAPTER 2

Control

> If you come to a fork in the road, take it.
>
> Yogi Berra

THE ABILITY TO MAKE BILLIONS OF DECISIONS PER SECOND AND MAKE THEM repeatedly is the source of computing's power. In this chapter, we introduce control in the form of selection (making decisions) and repetition (performing an operation over and over). These two kinds of control form the basis of all computer programming.

Our plan is to begin this chapter with a quick introduction to selection and repetition along with a couple of examples so that you can get a feel for the power of control constructs. The second half of the chapter will cover control in detail.

Up to this point, all we have been able to do is write Python code that is executed sequentially; that is, one statement after another, as shown in Figure 2.1. We have not yet shown a way to incorporate either decisions or repetition into our programs. So let's get into that now.

2.1 QUICKSTART CONTROL

2.1.1 Selection

The simplest decision presents a choice of doing one of two things: of doing one thing or the other. In programming, selection is the process of applying a decision to control: the choice of executing one part of a program or another. Representing the results of such a decision, do one thing or another, lends itself to a straightforward representation in computer hardware. That is, a *binary* decision is either (`False`) or (`True`), in hardware either zero(0) or one(1). It is important to note once you have learned about binary decisions, you have the ability create more complex kinds of decisions by simply assembling multiple binary decisions in the appropriate fashion.

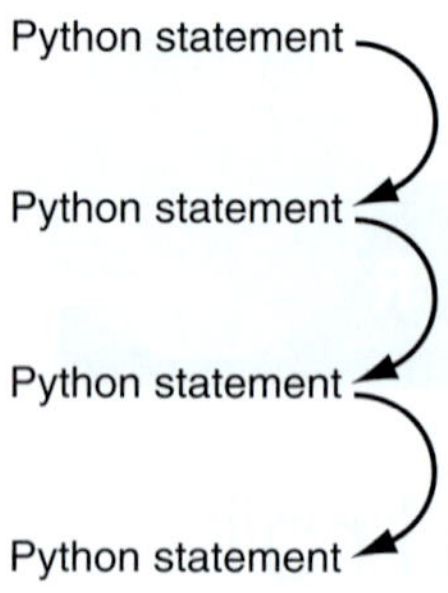

FIGURE 2.1 Sequential program flow.

Consider executing instructions one after another until a selection is reached. It is like a fork in the road: you must choose to go one way or the other. Associated with statements like a selection or repetition is a Boolean expression (an expression that is true or false) or more succinctly a *condition*. After evaluating the selection's Boolean expression (`True` or `False`, a Boolean result is returned to be used in selection. If the condition result is `True`, we take one fork and execute one set of statements; if it is `False`, we take the other fork and execute a different set of statements. Either way, after having finished with the selection, we continue on with the rest of the program, executing statements again in sequence. This selection control flow is shown in Figure 2.2.

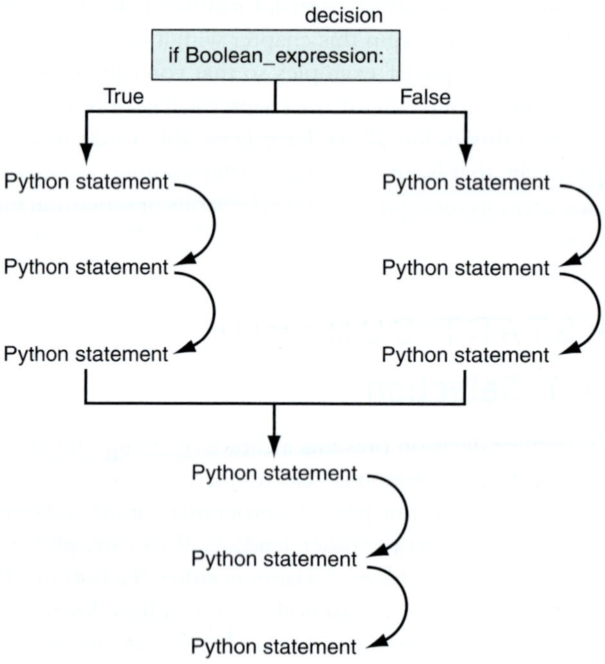

FIGURE 2.2 Decision making flow of control.

2.1.2 Booleans for Decisions

The choices in the Yogi Berra quote earlier are binary: go one way or the other. Python provides a type that represents binary decision values known as a *Boolean*. A Boolean type can take on only one of two values: `True` or `False`. A Boolean can be used as a condition as discussed. In a selection statement, if a condition expression evaluates to `True`, then selection will execute one part of the program; if the expression is `False`, selection will execute a different part of the program. Both selection and repetition require a condition expression that evaluates to `True` or `False` as part of their control.

An expression such as "x greater than 5" is a Boolean expression. The expression evaluates whether the value associated with `x` is greater than 5. The result of that evaluation is a Boolean; it is either `True` or `False`, hence it is a Boolean expression. In Python we write that expression in a familiar way: `x > 5`. If we want to express "x greater than or equal to 5," we use a *pair* of characters (>=), `x >= 5` because there is no single "greater-than-or-equal-to" key on our keyboards. Expressing equality in a Boolean expression is a bit of a challenge. We are used to using the `=` sign for equality in mathematics, but as you have seen, the `=` represents assignment, not equality, in Python. To xdeal with this problem, Python uses a *pair* of equal signs, `==`, to represent equality. For example, `x == 5` is a measure of equality: Is the value represented by `x` equal to 5? Based on the previous information, it is fairly easy to guess the remaining Boolean operators, but Table 2.1 lists them for you.

<	less than
>	greater than
<=	less than or equal to
>=	greater than or equal to
==	equal to
!=	not equal to

TABLE 2.1 Boolean operators.

2.1.3 The *if* Statement

The **if** statement expresses selective execution in Python. It is our first control statement and, simple as it is, it is quite powerful. Selective execution is one of the primary control mechanisms in general programming. It is a critical part of enabling computers to perform complex tasks.

The Basic *if* Statement

We begin with a basic **if** statement. It has a Boolean expression (or condition) that is evaluated, and the result of that Boolean expression dictates what happens next.

```
if boolean_expression:
    # if suite
```

The basic **`if`** statement does the following:

1. Evaluate `boolean_expression`, yielding either *`True`* or *`False`*.
2. If `boolean_expression` yields *`True`*,
   (a) Execute the Python suite of code *indented* under the **`if`**, the *if suite*.
   (b) Once the indented code is executed, continue with any Python code *after* the indented code (that is, any code following the **`if`** at the same indentation as the **`if`** itself).
3. If `boolean_expression` yields *`False`*,
   (a) Ignore any code indented under the **`if`**, (that is, do not execute it).
   (b) Continue with any Python code *after* the indented code (that is, any code following the **`if`** at the same indentation as the **`if`** itself).

Indentation and a Suite of Python Code

As mentioned earlier (Section 1.4.3), indentation in Python matters. Indentation is Python's method for associating or grouping statements. Indentation gets used in many Python statements, including the **`if`** statement. For **`if`**, the indentation indicates that the indented statements following the **`if`** are associated with that **`if`**. This group is called a *compound statement*, where the **`if`** *keyword* is part of the *header* and the set of indented statements is called the *suite*, see Figure 2.3. A compound statement is considered to be one logical statement.

A suite of statements is a set of statements that has the same indentation, and these statements are executed as a group. Other languages use explicit characters to mark compound statements, but because indentation makes compound statements easier to read, Python settles for the indentation alone. Therefore, indentation has a dual purpose: to indicate compound statements and to make compound statements easier to read. As we will soon see, one can have compound statements within compound statements, and the indentation indicates how they relate to each other.

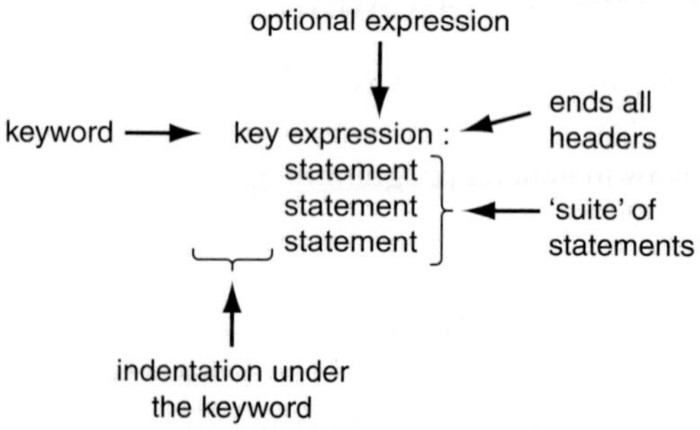

FIGURE 2.3 Control expression.

PROGRAMMING TIP

Pay *attention* to indenting in Python because the indentation indicates the structure of the code. Be *consistent* with indentation: four spaces is common. More importantly, do not mix tabs and spaces! Use spaces. That is the Python way.

Let's take a look at a short example. The **if** statement that follow checks to see whether a number is negative, and if so, it changes the number to zero.

```
In   [1]: my_int = -5
In   [2]: if my_int < 0:
...:        my_int = 0
...:        print(my_int)
0
```

In this example, the initial value of the variable `my_int` is −5. We begin by evaluating the Boolean expression `my_int < 0`. The "less-than" operator works on these two integer values just like in mathematics, comparing the two values and returning a value—a Boolean. In this case, the Boolean expression evaluates to *True*. As a result, the **if** suite `my_int = 0` is executed. Note the indentation on the second line of the **if** statement (done automatically after typing the colon (:) in SPYDER). Once execution finishes with the compound **if** statement, the next statement after the **if** (the **print** statement, in this case) is executed, and we see that the value of `my_int` has indeed been changed to 0.

The *if-else* Statement

A variation on the basic **if** statement adds the ability to execute one suite of statements if the decision Boolean is *True or* to execute a different suite of statements if the Boolean expression is *False*. Note that there are two statements and two suites here: the suite associated with the **if** and the suite associated with the **else**. Also, note that the **if** and **else** are at the same indentation; the **else** is not part of the **if** suite, but together they create an **if-else** compound statement.

```
if boolean_expression:
    # if suite
else:
    # else suite
```

The **if-else** statement operation is as follows:

1. Evaluate `boolean_expression` to yield *True* or *False*.
2. If `boolean_expression` yields *True*,

   (a) Execute the ***if*** suite, indented under the ***if***.
   (b) Continue with the rest of the Python program.
3. If `boolean_expression` yields *False*,
   (a) Execute the ***else*** suite, indented under the ***else***.
   (b) Continue with the rest of the Python program.

Let's see a short example. In this example, if the `first_int` variable is greater than the `second_int` variable, the program prints "The first int is bigger!"; if not, the program prints "The second int is bigger!"

```
In  [1]: first_int = 10
In  [2]: second_int = 20
In  [3]: if first_int > second_int:
...:     print("The first int is bigger!")
...: else:
...:     print("The second int is bigger!")

The second int is bigger!
```

In this example, the Boolean expression `first_int > second_int` evaluates to *False*, so the program skips to the ***else*** suite and executes the `print("The second int is bigger!")` statement. That output is shown at the bottom of the example.

2.1.4 Example: What Lead Is Safe in Basketball?

With our simple ***if-else*** construct, we can solve a very interesting problem. Basketball is a high-scoring game in which a lead can evaporate quickly. As a spectator, it would be nice to be able to figure out when a lead is insurmountable near the end of a game. Fans of the leading team would like to know when they can relax and be comfortable in the knowledge that victory is almost certain. Sports writer Bill James of the online magazine `www.slate.com` has pondered that problem and developed an algorithm for determining when a lead in basketball is insurmountable.[1]

James's algorithm, developed after many years of watching basketball, determines whether a lead is insurmountable: "safe" in his terminology. Of course, this algorithm does not guarantee that a lead is safe—anything can happen, but as a sports analyst this is when he feels a game is safe. Here is his algorithm, exactly as he wrote it:

1. Take the number of points one team is ahead.
2. Subtract three.
3. Add a half-point if the team that is ahead has the ball, and subtract a half-point if the other team has the ball. (Numbers less than zero become zero.)

[1] From "Slate," © 2008 The Slate Group. All rights reserved. Used by permission and protected by the Copyright Laws of the United States.

4. Square that result.
5. If the result is greater than the number of seconds left in the game, the lead is safe.

It took years of observation to come up with the algorithm, but with the algorithm in hand, we can easily convert it to a Python program. You will learn that coming up with the algorithm is the hardest part of programming.

Let's take these steps one at a time.

1. *Take the number of points one team is ahead.*

   We can ask a user to input the number of points using the `input` command. We remind ourselves that `input` yields a string that we can assign to an appropriate variable name. We then convert the input to an *`int`* so we may do arithmetic on the value. See Code Listing 2.1.

Code Listing 2.1

```
# 1. Take the number of points one team is ahead.
points_str = input("Enter the lead in points: ")
points_ahead_int = int(points_str)
```

Why convert the input string to an int? Basketball scores are integers.

2. *Subtract three.*

   That's simple arithmetic—we can do that. Remember that we use an assignment statement to capture the result of the arithmetic in a variable. See Code Listing 2.2.

Code Listing 2.2

```
# 2. Subtract three.
lead_calculation_float = float(points_ahead_int - 3)
```

We create a new variable `lead_calculation_float` to store our calculations as we go along. Why create that variable as *`float`*? Why not an *`int`*? Looking ahead a bit, we have to manipulate the variable by adding or subtracting 0.5. That means at some point we have to do floating-point arithmetic. Good to get ready for it now.

3. *Add a half-point* **if** the team that is ahead has the ball, and subtract a half-point **if** the other team has the ball. (Numbers less than zero become zero.)

   Here it gets interesting. Notice the two **if**s that we highlighted. That English statement needs to be converted to a Python ***`if-else`*** statement. However, first we need to know whether the leading team "has the ball" so we have to ask the user using `input`. In

Code Listing 2.3, note the use of the double-equal sign in the Boolean expression to check for equality: `==`. Further, note that if the user enters "No," the Boolean expression result will be `False`, resulting in the `else` suite (`lead_calculation_float = lead_calculation_float-0.5`) being executed. For the user response, notice that we are are comparing strings. That is, we are comparing whether two sequences of characters, the string "Yes" and the user response, are the same (more of that in Chapter 4).

Code Listing 2.3

```
# 3. Add a half-point if the team that is ahead has the ball,
#    and subtract a half-point if the other team has the ball.

has_ball_str = input("Does the lead team have the ball (Yes or No): ")

if has_ball_str == "Yes":
    lead_calculation_float = lead_calculation_float + 0.5
else:
    lead_calculation_float = lead_calculation_float - 0.5
```

We overlooked the statement in parentheses: numbers less than zero become zero. If `lead_calculation_float` is less than zero, we assign it a value of zero. See Code Listing 2.4.

Code Listing 2.4

```
# 3. Add a half-point if the team that is ahead has the ball,
#    and subtract a half-point if the other team has the ball.

has_ball_str = input("Does the lead team have the ball (Yes or No): ")

if has_ball_str == 'Yes':
    lead_calculation_float = lead_calculation_float + 0.5
else:
    lead_calculation_float = lead_calculation_float - 0.5

# (Numbers less than zero become zero)
if lead_calculation_float < 0:
    lead_calculation_float = 0
```

4. *Square that.*
Simple arithmetic—remember the exponentiation operator (**) (Section 1.2.1) and assignment (Code Listing 2.5):

Code Listing 2.5

```
# 4. Square that
lead_calculation_float = lead_calculation_float ** 2
```

5. *If the result is greater than the number of seconds left in the game, the lead is safe.*
Here we have another `if` statement nicely phrased by James. We'll also expand this algorithm to inform the user when the lead is *not* safe. That expansion requires an `else` clause. We also need to ask the user to input the number of seconds remaining and convert the input to an integer. Notice that we used the `input` *as an argument* to the `int` function. As discussed earlier (Section 1.7.4), we execute code *inside* the parentheses first, the `input`, and then that result is used by `int`. Combining these two lines of code may make it more readable (Code Listing 2.6).

Code Listing 2.6

```
# 5. If the result is greater than the number of seconds left in the game,
#    the lead is safe.
seconds_remaining_int = int(input("Enter the number of seconds remaining: "))

if lead_calculation_float > seconds_remaining_int:
    print("Lead is safe.")
else:
    print("Lead is not safe.")
```

Let's take a look at the whole program (Code Listing 2.7). Notice how we used comments to include James's original algorithm. The next time you watch a basketball game, try it out and see how well James did with his algorithm.

Code Listing 2.7

```
# Bill James' Safe Lead Calculator
# From http://www.slate.com/id/2185975/
```

```python
# 1. Take the number of points one team is ahead.
points_str = input("Enter the lead in points: ")
points_remaining_int = int(points_str)

# 2. Subtract three.
lead_calculation_float= float(points_remaining_int - 3)

# 3. Add a half-point if the team that is ahead has the ball,
#    and subtract a half-point if the other team has the ball.
has_ball_str = input("Does the lead team have the ball (Yes or No): ")

if has_ball_str == 'Yes':
    lead_calculation_float= lead_calculation_float+ 0.5
else:
    lead_calculation_float= lead_calculation_float- 0.5

# (Numbers less than zero become zero)
if lead_calculation_float< 0:
    lead_calculation_float= 0

# 4. Square that.
lead_calculation_float= lead_calculation_float** 2

# 5. If the result is greater than the number of seconds left in the game,
#    the lead is safe.
seconds_remaining_int = int(input("Enter the number of seconds remaining: "))

if lead_calculation_float> seconds_remaining_int:
    print("Lead is safe.")
else:
    print("Lead is not safe.")
```

With a working program in hand, it is useful to look back over it for refinements. For example, what if the user answers "YES" or "yes" instead of exactly "Yes" to the question of whether the leading team has the ball? It would be reasonable to accept all three. How can we do that? It will take some work on your part to manipulate the strings, something you will see in Chapter 4.

VideoNote 2.1
Simple Control

2.1.5 Repetition

The **if** statement provided selection as a way to make decisions. Next we consider ways to *repeat* statements. The ability to execute instructions—especially decisions—over and over is the source of considerable power in computing. That is, repeatedly making billions of simple (True/False) decisions per second allows the computer to make complex decisions to complete complex tasks.

Python offers two different styles of repetition: **`while`** and **`for`**. Here, we introduce the **`while`** loop and the **`for`** iterator to be described in more detail in Section 2.2.

The **`while`** statement introduces the concept of *repetition*. The **`while`** statement allows us to repeat a suite of Python code as long as some condition (Boolean expression) is `True`. When the condition becomes `False`, repetition ends and control moves on to the code following the repetition. The **`for`** statement implements *iteration*. Iteration is the process of examining all elements of a collection, one at a time, allowing us to perform some operations on each element. One characteristic of Python is that it provides powerful iterators so one frequently uses **`for`** in Python programs.

Finally, programmers often refer to any repeating construct as a "loop," because a diagram of the construct looks like a loop.

Basic *While*

We want to execute a set of instructions repeatedly and, most importantly, to control the condition that allows us to keep repeating those instructions. A **`while`** statement is structurally similar to an **`if`**. It consists of a header (which has the loop condition) and a suite of statements. We repeatedly execute the **`while`** suite as long as the associated condition is `True`. The condition is, as was true with selection, a Boolean expression. We evaluate the condition and, if the condition is `True`, we evaluate *all* of the **`while`** suite code. At the end of that suite, we again evaluate the condition. If it is again `True`, we execute the entire suite again. The process repeats until the condition evaluates to `False`.

The **`while`** loop contains a Boolean decision that can be expressed in English as:

"While the Boolean expression is `True`, keep looping—executing the suite."

Figure 2.4 is a diagram that shows the control flow of a **`while`** loop.

The Python syntax is:

```
while boolean_expression:
    # while suite
```

A **`while`** loop works as follows:

1. The program enters the **`while`** construct and evaluates the Boolean expression (condition).
2. If the Boolean expression is `True`, then the associated **`while`** suite is executed.
3. At the end of the suite, control flows back to the top of the **`while`** where the Boolean expression is re-evaluated.
4. If the Boolean expression yields `True`, the loop executes again. If the Boolean yields `False`, then the **`while`** suite is skipped and the code following the **`while`** loop is executed.

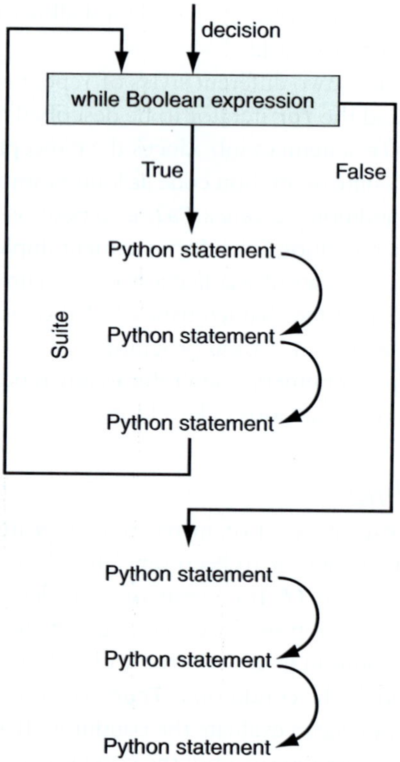

FIGURE 2.4 ***while*** **loop.**

Let's take a look at a simple example that prints out the numbers zero through nine. See Code Listing 2.8.

Code Listing 2.8

```
# simple while

x_int = 0     # initialize loop-control variable

# test loop-control variable at beginning of loop
while x_int < 10:
    print(x_int, end=' ')  # print the value of x_int each time through the
                           while loop
    x_int = x_int + 1  # change loop-control variable

print()
print("Final value of x_int: ", x_int)  # bigger than value printed in loop!
```

```
0 1 2 3 4 5 6 7 8 9
Final value of x_int:  10
```

Let's take a look at Code Listing 2.8 line by line:

Line 3: Before the loop begins, we initialize the variable `x_int = 0`. We call this our *loop-control* variable as its value will determine whether we continue to loop or not.

Line 6: Test the loop-control variable in the Boolean decision expression: `while x_int < 10:`. Because we initialized `x_int` to be zero, this Boolean expression will be `True` for `x_int` values of 0–9 but will be `False` for larger integer values.

Line 7: The `print (x_int, end=' ')` prints the value of the variable. The `end=' '` in the `print` statement indicates that the print ends with an empty string rather than the default new line. This means that the output from multiple calls to `print` will occur on the same output line.

Line 8: In the final instruction of the suite, we change the value associated with the loop-control variable. In this case, we increase its present value by 1 and reassign it (re-associate it) with the variable. Over the course of running the `while` loop, `x_int` will take on the integer values of 0–10 (but note that 10 is not printed in the loop).

Line 10: After the `while` suite, the code prints the value of `x_int`. This shows the conditions under which the `while` loop ended. The value printed is 10, meaning that when the loop ended, `x_int == 10`. This made the Boolean expression `False`, which is why the `while` loop ended.

Some things to note about how a `while` statement works. The condition is evaluated *before* the suite is executed. This means that if the condition starts out `False`, the loop will never run. Further, if the condition always remained `True`, the loop will never end. Imagine that we did not add 1 each time to `x_int` earlier. The condition would always be `True` (`x_int` started with a value of 0, which is less than 10, and never changes through each loop iteration) and the program loops "forever."

Iteration: The Basic *for* Statement

An iterator is an object associated with all the collection types in Python. As we briefly mentioned (Section 1.6.2), a *collection* in Python is a single object that contains multiple elements that are associated with the collection object. For example, a string is such a collection. It is a single object that has a group of individual characters, each associated with the string. In fact, a string is a particular kind of collection, called a *sequence*. A sequence is a collection where there is an order associated with the elements. A string is a sequence because the order of the characters is important. A *set* is a collection that is not a sequence, as membership, not order, is important for a set. However, for both a string and a set—in fact, for any Python collection—an iterator allows us to examine each individual element in that collection, one at a time. Such a collection is called an *iterable*, a collection that can be examined by a `for` loop. For a sequence, the iterable's access is ordered, so that when we iterate through a sequence, we iterate through each element in the sequence in order, from first to last. The **for** loop uses the collection's associated iterator to give us programmatic access to the individual elements of a collection.

The generic pattern of the **for** loop is shown in Code Listing 2.9. The variable an_element is a variable associated with the **for** loop that is assigned the value of an element in the collection. The variable an_element is assigned a different element during each pass of the **for** loop. Eventually, an_element will have been assigned to each element in the collection. The variable collection is a collection that has an associated iterator that acts as the source of elements. The keyword **in** precedes the collection. Like the **if** and **while** statement, the **for** statement has a header and an associated suite.

```
for element in collection:
    # for suite
```

A simple example of a **for** loop and its output is shown here:

```
In  [1]: for the_char in 'hi mom':
...     print(the_char)
...
h
i

m
o
m
```

Because the collection in this case is a string, the variable the_char is assigned, one at a time, to each character in the string. Since a string is also a sequence (i.e., an ordered collection) the variable the_char is assigned *in order* from the first character, "h", to the last, "m". We will talk much more about strings in Chapter 4. As with a **while** loop, the entire **for** suite is evaluated during each pass of the loop. One can therefore perform operations on each element of a collection in a very straightforward way. In this particular case, we print only the value of the_char each time the **for** loop iterates. The **for** loop completes when the last of the elements has been assigned to the_char. The result in this case will be a printout with six lines, each line printing out one character (including the blank space at the third position).

In general a **for** statement operates as shown in Figure 2.5.

2.1.6 Example: Finding Perfect Numbers

Numbers and number theory are an area of study that dates back to antiquity. Our ancestors were interested in what numbers were and how they behaved, to the extent that some ancient philosophers, such as Pythagoras, attributed mystical properties to numbers.

One class of integers created by the ancients is the *perfect number*. It dates back at least to Euclid and his *Elements* from around 300 B.C. A perfect number is an integer whose sum of

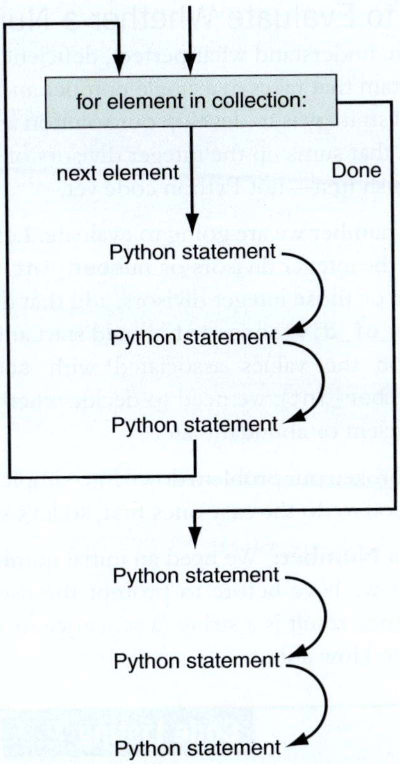

FIGURE 2.5 Operation of a ***for*** loop.

integer divisors (excluding the number itself) add up to the number. Following are the first four perfect numbers:

$$\begin{aligned}
6 &= 1+2+3 \\
28 &= 1+2+4+7+14 \\
496 &= 1+2+4+8+16+31+62+124+248 \\
8128 &= 1+2+4+8+16+32+64+127+254+508+1016+2032+4064
\end{aligned}$$

Numbers whose sum of divisors is larger than the number are called *abundant numbers*. Those whose sum is less than the number are called *deficient numbers*. Perfect numbers have other interesting properties,[2] but for now we are interested only in writing a program that classifies integers into one of three categories: perfect, abundant, or deficient.

[2] http://mathworld.wolfram.com/PerfectNumber.html

Program to Evaluate Whether a Number Is Perfect

Now that you understand what perfect, deficient, and abundant numbers are, how can you write a program that takes in a single number and properly classifies it?

A useful strategy is to develop our solution a little at a time. In this case, let's begin with an approach that sums up the integer divisors of a number. Furthermore, let's express our ideas in English first—not Python code yet.

1. Get the number we are going to evaluate. Let us call it `number_int`.
2. Find all the integer divisors of `number_int`.
3. For each of those integer divisors, add that divisor to a `sum_of_divisors_int` value. The `sum_of_divisors_int` should start at 0 (0 is the additive identity: $0 + x = x$).
4. Based on the values associated with `sum_of_divisors_int` and the number itself(`number_int`), we need to decide whether the number is perfect (we can classify it as deficient or abundant later).

Having broken our problem down into simpler pieces, let us attack each one individually. It's always good to do the easy ones first, so let's start with steps 1 and 4.

Step 1, Get a Number: We need an initial number to check. We can use Python function `input` as we have before to prompt the user for an integer to evaluate. Remember: the returned result is a string (a sequence of characters), not an integer, so we have to convert it. How about:

Code Listing 2.9

```
number_str = input("Please enter a number to check:")
number_int = int(number_str)
```

Step 4, Check Perfection: We need to see whether `sum_of_divisors_int` is equal to `number_int`. How about:

Code Listing 2.10

```
if number_int == sum_of_divisors_int:
    print(number_int,"is perfect")
else:
    print(number_int,"is not perfect")
```

Finally, we can attack steps 2 and 3.

Step 2, Find the Divisors: What is a divisor? For a number N, a divisor is a number that divides into N evenly. What does "divide evenly" mean? It means that the remainder is zero. That is, for a potential divisor *div*, we need to determine whether the remainder of the integer division N/div is 0. Expressed as Python, we need to determine `if N % divisor_int == 0`. If so, then *div* is a divisor of N.

Let's construct a trial piece of code to print the divisors of some number N. We'll have our potential divisors start at 1 (why is it bad in this case to start with zero?) and try each one (up to N). Because we listed the divisors of 28 earlier, we have those values to check against, so let's use $N = 28$:

```
In  [1]: N_int = 28
In  [2]: divisor_int = 1
In  [3]: while divisor_int < N_int:
           if N_int % divisor_int == 0:  # found a divisor
                print(divisor_int,end=' ')
           divisor_int = divisor_int + 1  # get next divisor candidate

1 2 4 7 14
```

A Note on Naming

At this point, you might feel a bit irritated with our naming convention that includes the type at the end of the name. In certain situations, it does become tedious to include the type information, when the type being used is clear from the context or the type of all the variables is really the same. Such is the case with this code. *All* of our numbers will be integers in this case, so it becomes redundant to add the type information to the end of each variable name. It would probably suffice to provide a comment at the top of such a program that indicates that, unless stated otherwise, the type of variables without type information is an `int` (or `float` or whatever is appropriate).

When readability suffers, it is important to do "what's right" to make the code more readable. Thus we invoke **RULE 4**, our "violate the rules" rule, and drop the `int` at the end of all the numbers in this example.

Step 3, Sum the Divisors: Now that we have a loop that generates divisors, we need to find the sum of those divisors. We can initialize `sum_of_divisors` to zero, and then every time we find a new divisor (we printed divisors earlier), we can add it to `sum_of_divisors`. Here is our code:

Code Listing 2.11

```
divisor = 1
sum_of_divisors = 0
while divisor < number:
    if number % divisor == 0:          # divisor evenly divides theNum
        sum_of_divisors = sum_of_divisors + divisor
    divisor = divisor + 1
```

Note a few things about this piece of code:

- We initialize `divisor = 1` and `sum_of_divisors = 0` before the loop begins.
- The decision condition of the loop is the Boolean expression: `divisor < number`.
- We increment `divisor` each time through the loop, making the condition `False` at some point and ending the loop.

Putting It All Together

We have all the pieces now; we just need to put it all together. There are still issues in doing the assembly, we can still get it wrong, but we have solved some of the subproblems. We just need to assemble them in a reasonable way. Remember what the parts were:

1. Prompt for the number to check.
2. Find all the divisors of that number, from 1 up to but not including the number.
3. Sum all those divisors.
4. Classify the number based on that sum.

Code Listing 2.12 assembles all the pieces together.

Code Listing 2.12

```
# perfect number checker
# unless otherwise stated, variables are assumed to be of type int. Rule 4

# get a number to check
number_str = input("Please enter a number to check:")
number = int(number_str)

# find and sum up the divisors
divisor = 1
sum_of_divisors = 0
while divisor < number:
    if number % divisor == 0:
        sum_of_divisors = sum_of_divisors + divisor
    divisor = divisor + 1

#classify the result
if number == sum_of_divisors:
    print(number,"is perfect")
else:
    print(number,"is not perfect")
```

If we run that code, we get the following results:

```
Please enter a number to check:100
100 is not perfect

In [1]: runfile('/Users/user/python/file.py', wdir='/Users/user/python')

Please enter a number to check:128
128 is not perfect

In [2]: runfile('/Users/user/python/file.py', wdir='/Users/user/python')

Please enter a number to check:496
496 is perfect
```

PROGRAMMING TIP

Inside every difficult problem is a simpler problem. Note how we broke this problem down into simpler pieces and solved each one individually. It is a very powerful problem-solving technique.

2.1.7 Example: Classifying Numbers

We can now take a particular number and classify it as to whether it is perfect or not. However, it would be more satisfying if we could check a whole range of numbers and decide what each number is: abundant, deficient, or perfect. Then we could look for more perfect numbers!

The Process of Changing a Program

As we have said before, a program is an object to be read and understood as well as an object that performs some function. This is especially true when we want to *extend* a program, add functionality that was not there previously. Our last version does much of what we want, but not all. If we were to describe what we would like to do *now*, it would be:

1. Check each number in a range of numbers as to their classification: abundant, deficient, or perfect. Previously, we checked only one number.
2. For each number, determine the sum of its divisors. This task is largely complete.
3. Classify the number based on the sum of the divisors. We only checked for perfect numbers in the previous version.

Therefore, we do have to change the first part and the last part of the previous program, but the main part, the summation of divisors, remains roughly the same. Because we wrote the program in a readable, understandable way, it is much easier to see what was done and what must be changed to extend the program.

Looking at a Range of Numbers

How can we check a whole range of numbers? A loop is a likely candidate. Instead of prompting for each number individually, it would be helpful to the user if they were only required to enter the *final* number in a range of numbers. Our assumption would be that we would check all the numbers from 2 up to that final number. Thus, we will ask the user to enter the highest number in a range of integers, and our program will then check every number up to that number for its classification. We start with the number 2 because by definition, the number 1 cannot be perfect. Code Listing 2.13 reflects this.

Code Listing 2.13

```
# classify a range of numbers with respect to perfect, adundant, or deficient
# unless otherwise stated, variables are assumed to be of type int. Rule 4

top_num_str = input("What is the upper number for the range:")
top_num = int(top_num_str)
number = 2
while number <= top_num:
    # sum the divisors of number
    # classify the number based on its divisor sum
    number += 1
```

Notice that we use the increment shortcut to add 1 to `number`. Remember that that statement is equivalent to `number = number + 1`.

We prompt for the upper range number, convert it to an int, then count from 2 to that number. For each number in the range, we must get the sum of divisors for the number and classify that number. Note that those last two parts are left unspecified in the code provided, but we used comments as markers, places where we must provide the code to do the job the comments indicate. We often call such a piece of incomplete code a *skeleton* of a program. We indicate what must be done, but not necessarily at the level of Python code. We add "meat" to the skeleton, the details of the code, as we go along, but we clearly indicate what must be added. Thus, the organization of our solution is clear, even though it will not run as a program—at least not yet!

Summing Divisors

Good news here. We can just take the entire section of code for divisor summing derived previously and stick it in at the comment of our skeleton code. Code Listing 2.14 shows the next version.

Code Listing 2.14

```
# classify a range of numbers with respect to perfect, adundant, or deficient
# unless otherwise stated, variables are assumed to be of type int. Rule 4

top_num_str = input("What is the upper number for the range:")
top_num = int(top_num_str)
number = 2
while number < top_num:
    # sum up the divisors
    divisor = 1
    sum_of_divisors = 0
    while divisor < number:
        if number % divisor == 0:
            sum_of_divisors = sum_of_divisors + divisor
        divisor = divisor + 1
    # classify the number based on its divisor sum
    number += 1
```

We must be careful with the indentation. The entire section of code that does the divisor summing is now within a **`while`** suite, as indicated by the indentation.

Classify the Numbers

We have three categories to check. If `sum_of_divisors` is greater than `number`, `number` is abundant. If `sum_of_divisors` is less than `number`, `number` is deficient. Otherwise, it must be perfect. We can extend the previous code to account for the three conditions as shown in Code Listing 2.15. Note that the last thing the loop does is increase the value associated with `number` by 1. Failure to do so will mean we have an infinite loop—a loop that will end only when we manually stop it.

Code Listing 2.15

```
# classify a range of numbers with respect to perfect, adundant or deficient
# unless otherwise stated, variables are assumed to be of type int. Rule 4

top_num_str = input("What is the upper number for the range:")
top_num = int(top_num_str)
number=2
while number <= top_num:
    # sum up the divisors
    divisor = 1
```

```
sum_of_divisors = 0
while divisor < number:
    if number % divisor == 0:
        sum_of_divisors = sum_of_divisors + divisor
    divisor = divisor + 1
# classify the number based on its divisor sum
if number == sum_of_divisors:
    print(number,"is perfect")
if number < sum_of_divisors:
    print(number,"is abundant")
if number > sum_of_divisors:
    print(number,"is deficient")
number += 1
```

The following is a session that shows the operation of the final program.

```
What is the upper number for the range:29
2 is deficient
3 is deficient
4 is deficient
5 is deficient
6 is perfect
7 is deficient
8 is deficient
9 is deficient
10 is deficient
11 is deficient
12 is abundant
13 is deficient
14 is deficient
15 is deficient
16 is deficient
17 is deficient
18 is abundant
19 is deficient
20 is abundant
21 is deficient
22 is deficient
23 is deficient
24 is abundant
25 is deficient
26 is deficient
27 is deficient
28 is perfect
29 is deficient
```

Check Yourself: Basic Control Check

1. What output occurs for the following program on the given input?

```
user_str = input("Enter a positive integer:") # Line 1
my_int = int(user_str)
count = 0

while my_int > 0:
    if my_int % 2 == 1:
        my_int = my_int//2
    else:
        my_int = my_int - 1
    count = count + 1          # Line 2

print(count)                   # Line 3
print(my_int)                  # Line 4
```

   (a) Given user input of 11, what value is output by Line 3 of the program?
   (b) Given user input of 12, what value is output by Line 4 of the program?
   (c) What type is referenced by (associated with) `user_str` in Line 1 of the program?
   (d) What is the purpose of the = (equal sign) on Line 2 of the program?
   (e) What is the purpose of the : (colon) at the end of the ***while*** statement?

2.2 IN-DEPTH CONTROL

As mentioned earlier, the intelligence that computers appear to have comes from their ability to make billions of tiny decisions every second. Each of those decisions is based on a choice between the truth or falsity of expressions. In this section, we begin with a closer look into the variables that can hold the logical values of *True* and *False*. Then we examine how to use them for control.

To consider truth and falsity we begin with a nineteenth-century school teacher: George Boole.

2.2.1 *True* and *False*: Booleans

George Boole was a mid-nineteenth-century school teacher who wrote a few articles that established an important branch of mathematics upon which the logic of computers is based. The title of one of his articles tells of his topic's importance: "An Investigation of the Laws of Thought, on Which are Founded the Mathematical Theories of Logic and

Probabilities."[3] The importance of his work was not realized until a century later (1940) when Claude Shannon learned of Boole's work in a philosophy class and demonstrated that electrical circuits could perform Boolean algebra to do arithmetic. Shannon's master's thesis[4] is considered a seminal work for computing.

2.2.2 Boolean Variables

Python and most other computing languages explicitly represent the values of `True` and `False`, and call that type a *Boolean*. In Python, the values of `True` and `False` are capitalized and the type is `bool`.

The type Boolean has a value of `True` or `False` (note capitalization).

Because computer hardware can store only ones and zeros, the Boolean value `True` is stored as 1 and `False` as 0. More generally, an object with value zero is considered to be the equivalent of a `False` Boolean value and any nonzero value is considered to be the equivalent of a `True` Boolean value. In addition, any empty object such as an empty string (`' '`) is considered to be `False`.

PROGRAMMING TIP

An *empty* object (0 for int, 0.0 for float, `''` for string) is considered to be `False`; all *non-empty* objects are considered to be `True`.

2.2.3 Relational Operators

As you saw earlier, Boolean expressions are composed of relational operators that yield results that are evaluated as `True` or `False`. The relational operators are well known: less than, equal to, and so on. Remember the unusual "equal to" sign: it has a *pair* of equal signs so that it can be differentiated from an assignment operator.

These operators are common across many currently popular programming languages. Remember Table 2.1, which lists the relational operators.

We will next explain these in detail with some examples.

```
In  [1]: 3 > 2
Out [1]: True

In  [2]: 5+3 < 3-2 # expressions evaluated first then comparison
Out [2]: False

In  [3]: 5 == 6 # equality test
Out [3]: False
```

[3] Boole, George. "An Investigation of the Laws of Thought, on Which Are Founded the Mathematical Theories of Logic and Probabilities." London: Walton and Maberly and Cambridge: Macmillan and Co, 1854.

[4] C. E. Shannon, "A Symbolic Analysis of Relay and Switching Circuits," Massachusetts Institute of Technology, Department of Electrical Engineering, 1940.

```
In  [4]: '1' < 2 # weird mixture of string and int: illegal!
Traceback (most recent call last):
  File "<pyshell#0>", line 1, in <module>
    '1'<2
TypeError: unorderable types: str() < int()
```

PROGRAMMING TIP

What happens when you forget to use "==" and use "=" instead? For example, what happens when you try to compare two numbers and accidentally use the "=" sign `print('0 and 0.0 are:', 0 = 0.0)` Python generates an error. Do you remember why? The "=" is the assignment statement and it has a side-effect (assign the right-hand side to the left-hand side), but it *doesn't return a value.* Python helps you avoid such an error.

Explanation:

- $3 > 2$: is 3 greater than 2? True
- $5 + 3 < 3 - 2$
  - Boolean operators have low precedence. That is, other operations are completed first before the Boolean operators are applied.
  - Here, we complete the addition and subtraction before we apply the Boolean relation '<'

    $5 + 3 < 3 - 2$
    $8 < 1$
    False
- '1' < 2 *# Illegal!*
  - Error
  - Comparison between numeric and non-numeric types, a string and an int in this case, is illegal in Python. It isn't clear what the comparison criteria should be across types, so rather than guess, Python simply throws an error.
  - Be careful to compare the appropriate type of values. Did you mean to convert the string to a number?:

    int('1') < 2
    True
  - Did you mean to convert the number to a string?

    '1' < str(2)
    True

What Does It Mean to be Equal?

Equality presents a special problem on a computer, especially in Python. There are really two different kinds of equality:

- Two different names are associated with objects that have the *same value.*
- Two different names are associated with the *same object* (i.e., objects with the same ID).

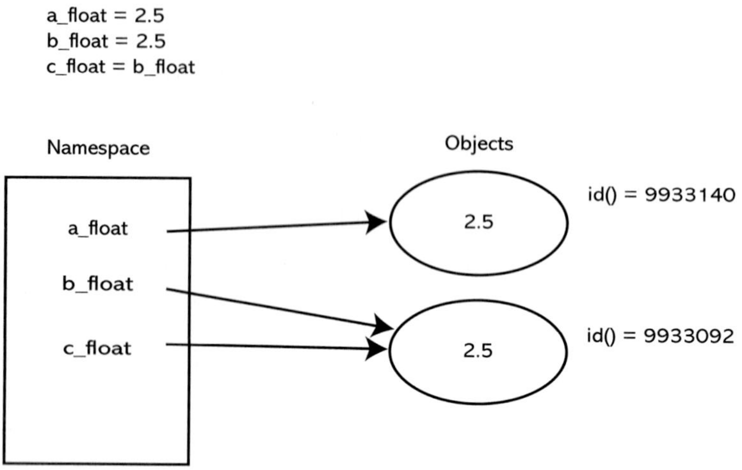

FIGURE 2.6 What is equality?

Do you remember our diagram on namespace in Section 1.5? Figure 1.1 showed the relationship between names and their associated objects? Consider the three lines of code and the namespace of Figure 2.6.

Both names `b_float` and `c_float` have been associated with the same object (because of the `c_float = b_float` assignment) so they also are both equal in value. The `a_float` name is associated with a different object whose value happens to be the same as the other two objects. Python provides a way to check each kind of equality:

== to check whether two names refer to objects that have the *same value*, **`is`** to check whether two names refer the *same object* (have same ID).

Here is the example of Figure 2.6 in the Python shell:

```
In  [1]: a_float = 2.5 # a_float and b_float are associated with different objects
In  [2]: b_float = 2.5
In  [3]: c_float = b_float # c_float and b_float are associated with the same object
In  [4]: a_float == b_float # values are the same
Out [4]: True
In  [5]: c_float == b_float
Out [5]: True

In  [6]: a_float is b_float # objects are different
Out [6]: False
```

```
In  [7]: c_float is b_float # objects are the same (so values are, too)
Out [7]: True
In  [8]: id(a_float) # look at id to understand "is"
Out [8]: 9933140

In  [9]: id(b_float)
Out [9]: 9933092

In  [10]: id(c_float)
Out [10]: 9933092
```

When you assign the same object to different variables using separate assignments, you create separate objects that happen to have the same value. Therefore, the equality check (==) returns *True*, but the sharing check (**is**) returns *False*.[5] However, when you assign two variables to the *same* object, then both == and **is** return *True*.

While we are on the subject of equality, let's discuss equality of floating-point values. Remember that floating points are approximations of Real numbers because of the problem of representing infinitely divisible Real values in a finite number of bits in computer memory. If one executes a series of computations, especially with floating-point values, some round off error is likely to occur. For example, in mathematics, the associative property of addition says that `(u + v) + w` is the same as `u + (v + w)`. However, with a computer, rounding off may give you a different result. Using the two previous expressions and the values `u = 11111113`, `v = -11111111`, and `w = 7.51111111`, one would expect both to yield the same value. It's close, but not exactly the same.

```
In  [1]: u = 11111113
In  [2]: v = -11111111
In  [3]: w = 7.51111111
In  [4]: (u + v) + w
Out [4]: 9.51111111

In  [5]: u + (v + w)
Out [5]: 9.511111110448837

In  [6]: (u + v) + w == u + (v + w)
Out [6]: False
```

How can we handle the rounding off of floating-point calculations? You can check to see if the difference is very small—you decide what "small" is. For example, let's take the previous example one step further.

[5] For efficiency, small integers work in an implementation dependent way. That is, it works differently on different systems. There is little value in applying "is" to system-defined objects such as integers.

```
In  [1]: u = 11111113
In  [2]: v = -11111111
In  [3]: w = 7.51111111
In  [4]: x = (u + v) + w
In  [5]: y = u + (v + w)
In  [6]: x == y
Out [6]: False

In  [7]: abs(x - y) < 0.0000001 # abs is absolute value
Out [7]: True
```

In the case of `x == y`, we are checking to see if `x` and `y` have *identical values*. In the case of `abs(x - y) < 0.0000001`, we are checking to see if `x` and `y` are "close enough." We use absolute value (abs) because if the difference `x - y` happens to be negative (as it is in this case), the expression will always be ***True*** even if the values are not close. When comparing for floating-point equality, the latter is the correct way to do it. The former will often result in incorrect results with floating-point values.

PROGRAMMING TIP

Instead of performing a strict equality test of two floating-point numbers

```
if x == y :
```

test whether they are close. Furthermore, use the absolute value of the difference (using `abs`) to get signs correct. That is, for some small delta of your choice, such as `delta = 0.0000001`,

```
if abs(x - y) < delta:
```

Chained Relational Operators

Chained relational expressions work just like they do in mathematics (which is not true for many programming languages):

```
In  [1]: a_int = 5
In  [2]: 0 <= a_int <= 5
Out [2]: True

In  [3]: 0 <= a_int <= 2
Out [3]: False
```

The two expressions represent:

- is `a_int` greater than or equal to 0 and less than or equal to 5.
- is `a_int` greater than or equal to 0 and less than or equal to 2.

The first expression yields ***True***, the second ***False***. One should be careful with such chaining however, as some odd results can occur (see the next section, Section 2.2.4)

2.2.4 Boolean Operators

The basic Boolean operators are: ***and***, ***or***, ***not***.[6] Many students learn the Boolean operators as part of a high school geometry course, but they are worth reviewing in the context of Python. A common way to describe Boolean operators is to list all the possible operands and results in a table. Traditionally, `p` and `q` are the names of the operands that represent a Boolean expression.

- ***not*** `p`
  - The ***not*** operator flips the value of the Boolean operand. That is, it converts *True* to *False*, and *False* to *True*.

p	***not*** p
True	*False*
False	*True*

- `p` ***and*** `q`
  - The ***and*** operator requires both `p` and `q` to be *True* for the whole expression to be *True*. Otherwise, the value of the expression is *False*. Observe that the four rows in the `p` and `q` columns represent all the possible combination values that the Booleans `p` and `q` can have. You should take a moment and convince yourself of that observation.

p	q	p ***and*** q
True	*True*	*True*
True	*False*	*False*
False	*True*	*False*
False	*False*	*False*

- `p` ***or*** `q`
  - The ***or*** operator only requires one of `p` or `q` to be *True* for the whole expression to be *True*. Therefore, the expression is *False* only when neither `p` nor `q` is *True*.

p	q	p ***or*** q
True	*True*	*True*
True	*False*	*True*
False	*True*	*True*
False	*False*	*False*

With Boolean operators in hand, we can revisit the chained expression mentioned previously:

```
a_int = 5
0 <= a_int <= 5
```

[6] There are other operators, such as "exclusive or," which is also known as XOR. Students who go on to build circuits as electrical and computer engineers will study them.

The chained expression is converted to an equivalent Boolean expression for evaluation. First the expression is converted into two relations (<=), which are ***and***'ed together. That is, the expression `0 <= a_int <= 5` means that you are evaluating the Boolean expression `0 <= a_int` *and* `a_int <= 5`. You can then evaluate each relational expression and combine the results referring to the ***and*** table. In the table, you can see that if `p == True` and `q == True`, then the value of the whole expression is `True`.

```
(0 <= a_int) and (a_int <= 5)
    (0 <= 5) and (5 <= 5)
       True and True
            True
```

We can evaluate other Boolean expressions similarly:

- Given X = 3, evaluate

```
(X > 2) or (X > 5)
 (3>2) or (3>5)
 True or False
     True
```

- Order of operations: ***and*** before ***or***

```
  True and False or True and False
(True and False) or (True and False)
        False or False
            False
```

However, you should be careful. Some chained expressions that "look good" do not provide the result you expect. Consider the following expression: `4 < 5 == True`.

What result is returned? Upon first glance, it would seem the `True` would be returned, but in fact `False` is returned. Why is that?

Remember that a chained expression is really the equivalent of two expressions that are ***and***'ed together. What is the equivalent ***and*** expression?

It is: `(4 < 5) and (5 == True)`. While the first expression is `True`, the second is `False` since 5 is not equal to `True`. Hence the whole expression is `False`. Be careful that you know what a chained expression really means!

2.2.5 Precedence

In Chapter 1, you learned the that precedence of arithmetic Python operators was the same as in arithmetic. In this chapter, we have introduced a number of new operators. Where do they fit in precedence with respect to the arithmetic operators? Table 2.2 shows the combined precedence. The full table of all Python operator precedence is in Appendix G.

Operator	*Description*
()	Parenthesis (grouping)
**	Exponentiation
+x, -x	Positive, Negative
*,/,%	Multiplication, Division, Remainder
+,-	Addition, Subtraction
<, <=, >, >=,! =, ==	Comparisons
not x	Boolean NOT
and	Boolean AND
or	Boolean OR

TABLE 2.2 Precedence of relational and arithmetic operators: highest to lowest.

2.2.6 Boolean Operators Example

Although the description of the Boolean operators might seem complicated, most of us use these operators nearly every day. Where? Why, search engines of course!

The interaction most users have with search engines is to provide a list of keywords. The search engine uses those keywords to find online documents that *contain* those words. However, we all know that finding the right combination of words that leads to a helpful search result can be quite difficult. To aid in writing a better search query, most engines provide an interface that uses Boolean operators to improve the search results. Google's advanced search interface is shown in Figure 2.7.

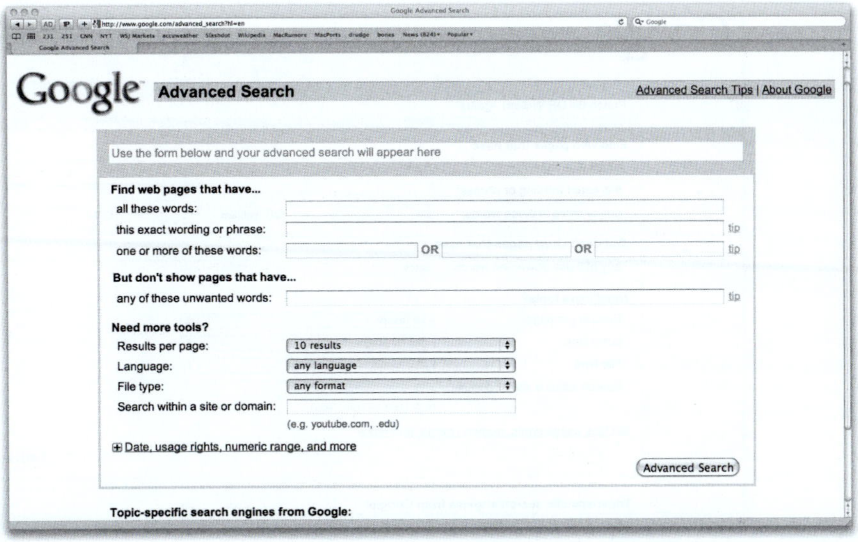

FIGURE 2.7 The Google advanced search page. [Screenshot from Google Chrome. Copyright © by Google Inc. Used by permission of Google Inc.]

The "all these words" text field is really an ***and*** of all the words: all the words listed *must* be in any document for this search. The "one or more of these words" text field is clearly an **or** of the words: one or more of the words should occur. Finally, the "any of these unwanted words" text field is a **not** condition: those words should not occur in any document of this search. In this way, we see the three Boolean operators (and, or, not) incorporated into the Google advanced search.

The standard Google search assumes an ***and*** of all the words listed. However, you can construct Boolean expressions in the Google search field. As mentioned, the default situation for a list of words is ***and***, to indicate **or** the phrase `OR` in all caps is required, and **not** is indicated by the minus (-) sign.

Let's do a little egosearch on Google (see Figure 2.8). The search expression for one of the authors is:

"Punch Bill OR William"
which translates to a normal Boolean expression as:
`'Punch' and ('Bill' or 'William')`

This expression generates some undesired search results, in particular some nasty pages about punching a certain former Microsoft executive. We clean it up by changing the search expression to:

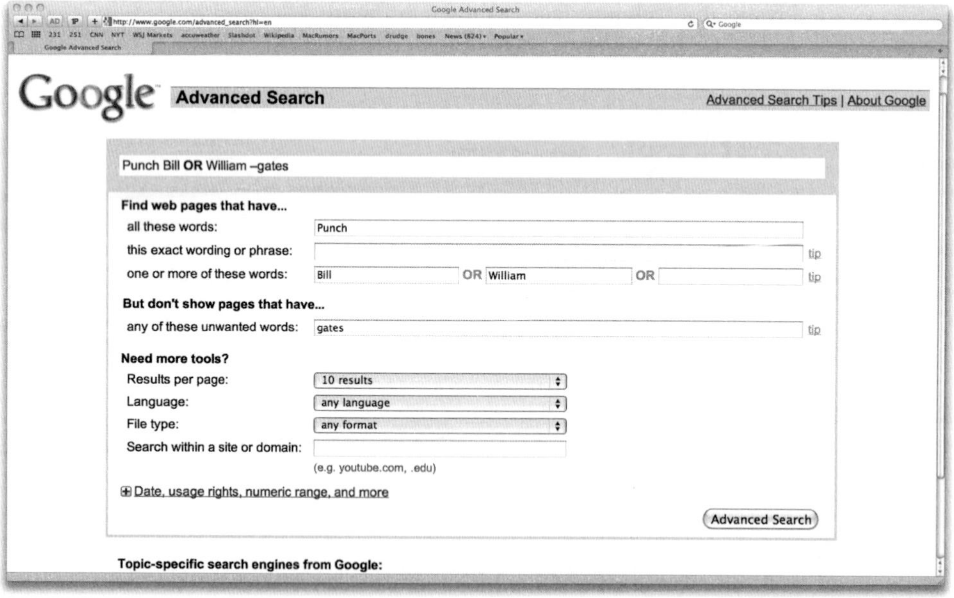

FIGURE 2.8 The Google advanced search page after our egosearch. [Screenshot from Google Chrome. Copyright © by Google Inc. Used by permission of Google Inc.]

"Punch Bill OR William -gates"
which translates to a normal Boolean expression as:
'Punch' ***and*** *('Bill'* ***or*** *'William')* ***and not*** *'gates'*

If we do the search and then go to the Advanced Search page after the search is completed, we see that the text fields were filled in as we described.

Check Yourself: Loop Control Check

1. What output occurs for the following program on the given input?

```
int_str = input("Please give me an integer:")
first_int = int(int_str)
int_str = input("Please give me a second integer:")
second_int = int(int_str)
tens_count = 0
loop_count = 0

while first_int > 10 and second_int < 20:
    if first_int == 10 or second_int == 10:
        tens_count += 1
    first_int -= 5
    second_int += 5
    loop_count += 1


print(tens_count)     # Line 1
print(loop_count)     # Line 2
print(first_int)      # Line 3
print(second_int)     # Line 4
```

(a) Given user input of 20 followed by an input of 10, what value is output by:
  i. Line 1 of the program?
  ii. Line 2 of the program?
  iii. Line 3 of the program?
  iv. Line 4 of the program?

(b) Given user input of 20 followed by an input of 20, what value is output by:
  i. Line 1 of the program?
  ii. Line 2 of the program?
  iii. Line 3 of the program?
  iv. Line 4 of the program?

(c) What input will cause both `first_int` and `second_int` to be equal to 10 at the end of the program?

2.2.7 Another Word on Assignments

Remember how assignment works:

LHS = RHS

Step 1: Evaluate the RHS (Right-Hand Side) to get a value.
Step 2: Associate that value with the variable named on the LHS (Left-Hand Side).

Multiple Assignment

In Python, we can do multiple assignments on the same line by separating corresponding LHS and RHS by commas. That is,

```
a_int, b_int, c_int = 15, 10, 17
```

is equivalent to

```
a_int = 15
b_int = 10
c_int = 17
```

The multiple assignments work in a natural way. The first name on the LHS gets the first value on the RHS, the second name on the LHS gets the second value on the RHS, and so on.

PROGRAMMING TIP

When doing multiple assignments, make sure that the number of variables on the LHS is the same as the number of values being returned by the RHS. If there is a mismatch, you will get errors like the following:

```
In [1]: a_int, b_int = 1,2 # exactly two objects on each side of "="
In [2]: print(a_int, b_int)
1 2
In [3]: a_int, b_int = 1, 2, 3 # different number of variables: Error

Traceback (most recent call last):
  File "<pyshell#10>", line 1, in <module>
    a_int, b_int = 1, 2, 3
ValueError: too many values to unpack

In [4]: a_int, b_int, c_int = 1, 2 # different number of objects: Error

Traceback (most recent call last):
  File "<pyshell#11>", line 1, in <module>
    a_int, b_int, c_int = 1, 2
ValueError: need more than 2 values to unpack
```

Swap

Swapping the values of two variables can be confusing when done on a computer. For example, suppose that `a_int = 2` and `b_int = 3` and that we would like to swap values so `a_int = 3` and `b_int = 2`. Consider the naïve way of doing it:

```
In  [1]: a_int = 2
In  [2]: b_int = 3
In  [3]: a_int = b_int
In  [4]: b_int = a_int
In  [5]: a_int
Out [5]: 3

In  [6]: b_int
Out [6]: 3

In  [7]: a_int is b_int
Out [7]: True
```

What happened? The problem came with the statement `a_int = b_int`. The last line illustrates the problem: that assignment associated the names `a_int` and `b_int` with the same object. A key point is that when the assignment was done, the original value of `a_int` was lost. Therefore, we need to keep `a_int`'s original value somewhere, if we are to swap correctly. We do this by introducing a third variable `temp_int` to temporarily store `a_int`'s initial value, which can later be assigned to `b_int`. Here is it again, but with `temp_int`:

```
In  [1]: a_int = 2
In  [2]: b_int = 3
In  [3]: temp_int = a_int # remember the original a_int
In  [4]: a_int = b_int
In  [5]: b_int = temp_int
In  [6]: a_int
Out [6]: 3

In  [7]: b_int
Out [7]: 2
```

Python's multiple assignment let us perform a swap in one line:

```
In  [1]: a_int = 2
In  [2]: b_int = 3
In  [3]: a_int, b_int = b_int, a_int
In  [4]: a_int
Out [4]: 3

In  [5]: b_int
Out [5]: 2
```

How is this done in one line in Python? Consider the way we described the assignment process, as having two steps: get the value(s) of the RHS and then assign the value(s) to the

LHS. The "get the value(s)" on the RHS stores those values in temporary memory locations. This means that implicitly we are using the equivalent of a `temp_int`—actually two `temp_int`'s in the case of swap—one temporary storage for each of the two values on the RHS of swap.

2.2.8 The Selection Statement for Decisions

We have shown ***if*** and ***if-else*** statements as a way to make decisions in Section 2.1.3. Let's review what we said there. The simplest decision presents a choice of doing one thing or another—of executing one suite or another. Such a simple choice fits nicely with computer hardware, as mentioned because the choice itself can be represented as a zero (*False*) or not-zero (*True*). We saw this behavior implemented as the ***if-else*** statement. More complex decisions can be built from combinations of simple ones.

2.2.9 More on Python Decision Statements

The ***if*** statement expresses selective execution in Python, but it comes in a number of variations. We examine these in this section.

You have seen the basic ***if*** and ***if-else*** statements in Section 2.1.1. Let's briefly restate them and then move on to the variations. First the basic ***if***:

```
if boolean_expression:
    # suite executed when True
```

The ***if-else*** statement has two compound statements with two headers: the ***if*** and the ***else***. Each also has a suite for its associated binary decision: one suite under the ***if*** for when the decision results in *True* and one under an ***else*** for when the decision results in *False*:

```
if boolean_expression:
    # suite executed when True
else:
    # suite executed when False
```

Pay particular attention to the indentation: the ***else*** and the ***if*** part of the expression are at the same indentation (they are part of the same overall statement). The ***if*** has an associated Boolean expression; the ***else*** does not. Take a moment and convince yourself why ***else*** alone does not need its own Boolean expression.

The *if-elif-else* Statement

A third kind of header available to us is the ***elif*** header. The ***elif*** is simply shorthand for "else if"—a shorthand that also exists in some other languages. The ***elif*** header has an associated condition, just like an ***if*** statement. It too has an associated suite. Again, note the indentation: the keywords (if, elif, else) are indented the same amount as they are part of the overall `if` statement. Further, each of the `if`, `elif`, and `else` statements can have an associated suite.

The basic idea of a set of `if-elif-else` statement is to find the *first* `True` condition in the set of `if` and `elif` headers and execute that associated suite. If no such `True` condition is found, the `else` is executed. The important point is that only *one* suite will be executed.

```
if boolean_expression1:
    # suite1
elif boolean_expression2:
    # suite2
elif boolean_expression3:
    # suite3
# as many elif statements as you like
else:
    # suite_last
```

The `if-elif-else` statement operation is as follows:

1. Evaluate `boolean_expression1` to yield `True` or `False`.
2. If `boolean_expression1` yields `True`,
   (a) Execute suite1.
   (b) Continue with the next statement after suite_last.
3. If `boolean_expression1` yields `False`, then evaluate `boolean_expression2`.
   If `boolean_expression2` yields `True`,
   (a) Execute suite2.
   (b) Continue with the next statement after suite_last.
4. If all preceding `boolean_expressions` yield `False`, evaluate `boolean_expression3`.
   If `boolean_expression3` yields `True`,
   (a) Execute suite3.
   (b) Continue with the next statement after suite_last.
5. If all preceding `boolean_expressions` yield `False`,
   (a) Execute the `else` part and suite_last.
   (b) Continue with the next statement after suite_last.

For each `elif`, statement, the associated suite will be executed if all preceding `boolean_expressions` are `False` and its `boolean_expression` is `True`. If all `if` and `elif` conditions are `False`, then the `else` clause is executed.

Mixing and Matching *elif and else*

In a selection statement, only the `if` header is required. Both `elif` and `else` are optional, which to include is up to the programmer. It is worth examining the flow of control in a little more detail, however, using the following program and session.

Code Listing 2.16

```
# determine a letter grade from a percentage input
# by the user

percent_float = float(input("What is your percentage? "))

if 90 <= percent_float < 100:
    print("you received an A")
elif 80 <= percent_float < 90:
    print("you received a B")
elif 70 <= percent_float < 80:
    print("you received a C")
elif 60 <= percent_float < 70:
    print("you received a D")
else:
    print("oops, not good")
```

```
What is your percentage? 95
you received an A

In [1]: runfile('/Users/user/python/file.py', wdir='/Users/user/python')

What is your percentage? 55
oops, not good
```

When the code is evaluated with `percent_float` set to 95, the ***if*** condition is evaluated, returning *True*. Note that *none* of the other conditions are evaluated. When the code is evaluated with `percent_float` set to 55, all of the ***if*** and ***elif*** conditions are evaluated, returning *False*, thus requiring the ***else*** suite to be executed.

Examine now the situation shown in the next program.

Code Listing 2.17

```
# determine a letter grade from a percentage input
# by the user. No elif version!

percent_float = float(input("What is your percentage? "))

if 90 <= percent_float < 100:
    print("you received an A")
if 80 <= percent_float < 90:
```

```
9       print("you received a B")
10  if 70 <= percent_float < 80:
11      print("you received a C")
12  if 60 <= percent_float < 70:
13      print("you received a D")
14  else:
15      print("oops, not good")
```

```
What is your percentage? 95
you received an A
oops, not good

In  [1]: runfile('/Users/user/python/file.py', wdir='/Users/user/python')

What is your percentage? 55
oops, not good
```

Note that all the ***elif*** headers are replaced with ***if*** headers. The suites are unchanged. There are two control flow differences in this code. Again, consider the example of having `percent_float` set to 95. First, how many conditions are evaluated now? The answer is *all 5 conditions are* evaluated, even though the first one returned is *True*. This is because, in the first program, there was only one ***if*** statement. In the second program, there are five. The combination of ***if***, ***elif***, and ***else*** constitutes one logical statement in the first program.

Second, with what statement is the final ***else*** associated? An ***else*** is associated with the *most recent* ***if*** statement at the same indentation level, in this case see line 12. Each ***if*** can have one ***else***, and each ***else*** must have an associated ***if***. It is for this reason that we get the "oops" output for the input of 95. Make sure you can follow the flow of control for this example.

You are free to mix and match, but make sure you understand how that combination works.

Updating Our Perfect Number Example

If we write our code so that we can read and understand what we have written, we are better able to update that code to take advantage of new constructs, more efficient approaches, improved algorithms, and so on. The process of taking existing code and modifying it such that its structure is somehow improved but the functionality of the code remains the same is called *refactoring*. Let's take a look at our perfect number example from Section 2.1.6 and see if we can improve it by refactoring.

The area of interest is the classification part of the code. Let's take a look at that part.

In this part of the solution, we observe that we checked for conditions that we know are not going to be *True*. For example, if the number is indeed perfect, it cannot be abundant or deficient, but we checked those conditions anyway. A better approach would be to rewrite this code so that as soon as a condition is found to be *True*, the associated suite is run and

Code Listing 2.18

```
# classify the number based on its divisor sum
if number == sum_of_divisors:
    print(number,"is perfect")
if number < sum_of_divisors:
    print(number,"is abundant")
if number > sum_of_divisors:
    print(number,"is deficient")
number += 1
```

the statement ends. Using an ***if-elif-else*** statement seems like a good choice. We can rewrite this part of the code, without changing its functionality for the rest of the solution, as shown in Code Listing 2.19.

Code Listing 2.19

```
# classify the number based on its divisor sum
if number == sum_of_divisors:
    print(number,"is perfect")
elif number < sum_of_divisors:
    print(number,"is abundant")
else:
    print(number,"is deficient")
number += 1
```

Notice that the final Boolean expression `number > sum_of_divisors` is no longer needed because if a number is neither perfect nor abundant it must be deficient.

There are two more things to note here. First, because the solution was written in a readable, logical way, it was relatively easy to modify. Second, the modification we made does not affect the answers provided by the solution, but it does make better sense, and is less wasteful, by using a more appropriate construct.

2.2.10 Repetition: the *while* Statement

Earlier we introduced the ***for*** iteration statement and the ***while*** repetition statement. The ***for*** statement makes use of iterators to move through a collection, one element at a time, allowing us to perform an operation on each element using the suite of the ***for*** statement. The ***while*** executes its suite of statements as long as its Boolean expression is *True*. It is important to keep the function of these two statements clear. The ***while*** statement is the most general statement for repetition and any repetition can be code in a **`while`** statement. However, when working with collections, which is very common in Python, the **`for`** statement is very convenient and faster.

Basic Repetition and the *while* Loop

The **`while`** loop is sometimes called a "top-tested loop" because there is a Boolean expression to be evaluated at the top of the loop. It is important to remember that the condition is evaluated first before the associated suite is ever executed. If the condition is never `True`, the loop never executes.

Loop Control and Initialization

The Boolean decision expression controls the loop, so care must be taken in designing it. Often, especially for novice programmers, there is one variable in the expression, so we'll consider that case. That variable is often called the *loop-control variable.* Our comments generalize naturally to more complex expressions.

There are usually three issues to consider when writing a **`while`** loop:

Initialization: Outside of the loop and before the loop is entered, the loop-control variable needs to be initialized. What value to initialize the variable requires some consideration. The initial value should (typically) allow the loop to begin (run through the first iteration). This variable's value will control when the loop ends so it is initialized with the condition statement in mind.

Control: The condition statement of the **`while`** loop needs to be written, and the Boolean expression is typically written in terms of the loop-control variable. The initial value and this condition are related and should be considered together.

Modification: Third, somewhere in the **`while`** loop suite, the loop-control variable is modified so that eventually the Boolean expression of the **`while`** becomes `False` so that the loop ends. This often means that the loop-control variable will have a different value in the suite during each iteration of the loop. It is the changing of value that allows the programmer to control when the loop will end.

Besides not solving the problem as intended, there are two undesired consequences that could occur when writing a **`while`** loop without full consideration of these three issues:

Loop never starts: Because the first action of a **`while`** loop is to evaluate the Boolean expression, if that expression yields `False`, the suite of instructions will not be executed.

Loop never stops: If the Boolean expression yields `True`, the loop will stop only if some instruction within the suite of instructions changes the loop-control variable so that the Boolean expression evaluates to `False` at some point. If the Boolean expression is always `True`, this situation is called an *infinite loop.*

How do I halt a program that has entered an infinite loop? The first thing to try with all programs is Ctl-C (hold down the Control key and type the letter C—it can be lower or upper case). An alternative in Anaconda's SPYDER is to *reset* the shell using the icon in the upper-right corner of the shell (Figure A.5).

PROGRAMMING TIP

Generic While Structure:

> Set an initial value for loop-control variable.
> ***while*** some Boolean tests the loop-control variable:
>   Perform tasks as part of the loop.
>   At the loop's end, update the loop-control variable.

Check Yourself: More Control Check

1. What output occurs for the following program on the given input?

```
number_str = input("Enter an int:")
number = int(number_str)
count = 0

while number > 0:
    if number % 2 == 0:
        number = number // 2
    elif number % 3 == 0:
        number = number // 3
    else:                       # Line 1
        number = number - 1     # Line 2
    count = count + 1

print("Count is: ",count)       # Line 3
print("Number is: ",number)     # Line 4
```

(a) Given user input of 9, what value does Line 3 of the program print?
(b) Given user input of 9, what value does Line 4 of the program print?
(c) Given user input of 7, what value does Line 3 of the program print?
(d) Given user input of 1, what value does Line 3 of the program print?
(e) If the ***else*** clause on Line 1 and Line 2 were removed, what effect would that have on the program with the input value 1?
  i. No effect, program would give the same results.
  ii. count would be larger.
  iii. count would be smaller.
  iv. The ***while*** loop would not end.
  v. None of the above.

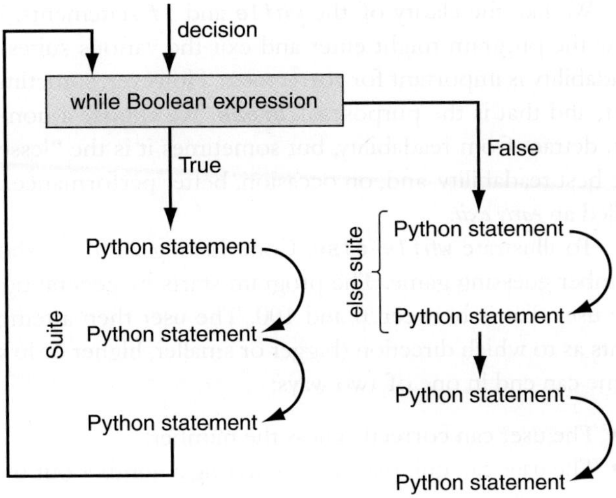

FIGURE 2.9 ***while-else***.

else and *break*

Similar to the ***if-else*** statement, you can have an ***else*** clause at the end of a ***while*** loop. The ***else*** is strictly optional, but it does have some very nice uses.

```
while boolean_expression:
    # suite1
else:
    # suite2
```

The ***else*** clause is entered after the ***while*** loop's Boolean expression becomes *False*. See Figure 2.9. This entry occurs even if the expression is initially *False* and the ***while*** loop never ran (its suite was never executed). As with other header statements, the ***else*** part of the ***while*** loop can have its own associated suite of statements. Think of the ***else*** statement on the ***while*** loop as "clean up" for the action performed as the loop ends normally.

The ***else*** clause is a handy way to perform some final task when the loop ends normally. Figure 2.9 shows how the ***else*** works.

Break Statement and Non-Normal Exit

The ***else*** clause is often used in conjunction with the ***break*** statement. The ***break*** statement can be used to *immediately* exit the execution of the *current* loop and skip past all the remaining parts of the loop suite. It is important to note that "skip past" means to skip the ***else*** suite (if it exists) as well. Remember, the ***else*** is only entered if the loop condition becomes *False*. The ***break*** statement is useful for stopping computation when the "answer" has been found or when continuing the computation is otherwise useless.

We like the clarity of the **`while`** and **`if`** statements. They make it clear to the reader how the program might enter and exit the various suites and, as we have said repeatedly, readability is important for correctness. However, sometimes we need to take a non-normal exit, and that is the purpose of **`break`**. We choose a non-normal exit sparingly because it can detract from readability, but sometimes it is the "lesser of two evils" and will provide the best readability, and, on occasion, better performance. A non-normal exit is sometimes called an *early exit*.

To illustrate **`while-else`**, Code Listing 2.20 is a short program that plays a "hi-lo" number guessing game. The program starts by generating a random number hidden from the user that is between 0 and 100. The user then attempts to guess the number, getting hints as to which direction (bigger or smaller, higher or lower) to go on the next guess. The game can end in one of two ways:

- The user can correctly guess the number.
- The user can quit playing by entering a number out of the range of 0–100.

Here is an algorithm for the game:

```
Choose a random number.
Prompt for a guess.
while guess is in range:
    Check whether the guess is correct;
        If it is a win, print a win message and exit.
        Otherwise, provide a hint and prompt for a new guess.
```

Code Listing 2.20

```python
# while-else
# Simple guessing game: start with a random number and
# guess with hints until:
#     guess is correct
#     the guess is out of range indicating the user is quitting
# All non-typed variables are integers: Rule 4

import random # get the random number module
number = random.randint(0,100) # get a random number
                               # between 0 and 100 inclusive
print("Hi-Lo Number Guessing Game: between 0 and 100 inclusive.")
print()

# get an initial guess
guess_str = input("Guess a number: ")
guess = int(guess_str) # convert string to number

```

```
18 # while guess is range, keep asking
19 while 0 <= guess <= 100:
20     if guess > number:
21         print("Guessed Too High.")
22     elif guess < number:
23         print("Guessed Too Low.")
24     else:                    # correct guess, exit with break
25         print("You guessed it. The number was:",number)
26         break
27     # keep going, get the next guess
28     guess_str = input("Guess a number: ")
29     guess = int(guess_str)
30 else:
31     print("You quit early, the number was:",number)
```

Here is a line-by-line look at the program in Code Listing 2.20:

Lines 8–9: To get a random number we first import the `random` module. The random module provides a number of useful functions, including functions to generate random numbers. One such function is named `randint` (read as "random integers"); it generates and returns a random integer. The full name—`random.randint`—indicates that the `randint` name is to be found in the `random` module (which we imported in the preceding line). The function takes two arguments: an integer lower value and the upper value. The function will then generate a random number within the range. For example, `random.randint(0,100)` will generate a random number between 0 and 100 (including both 0 and 100). See Section 16.1.5 for more information on random numbers.

Lines 15–16: You have seen `input` before. In this case, the string "Guess a number:" will be printed as a prompt to the user. The variable `guess_str` will be the string returned that needs to be converted to a number (integer) for further processing. At this point, we have a randomly chosen number to try to guess and a first guess. Notice how we need to get an initial guess before we check it in the Boolean expression in the ***`while`*** loop. What would happen if that were not true? Try it!

Line 19: This is the "normal" exit condition for the loop. As long as the guess is in the range 0–100 *inclusive*, the loop will continue. As soon as the expression becomes *`False`*, the loop will end and the associated ***`else`*** suite will be run.

Lines 20–23: If the guess is incorrect (either too high or too low), we provide a hint to the user so that they might improve their next guess.

Lines 24–26: If it wasn't high and it wasn't low, it must be the answer. Is that true—or could it have been a number not in the range we were looking for (0–100)? No, we checked that in the ***while*** Boolean expression. It must be the correct number. We print a winner message and then use the ***break*** statement to exit the loop. Remember, a ***break*** will skip the ***else*** suite of the ***while*** loop!

Lines 28–29: We prompt for another guess at the bottom of the ***while*** suite. Note the pattern:

> Prompt for a guess.
> ***while*** guess is not correct:
>   Do something (e.g. provide a hint).
>   Prompt for a new guess.

This is a common pattern: you prompt before the ***while*** starts so the loop may begin, and then prompt again at the end of the ***while*** suite so we may change the value associated with `guess`. This is the pattern noted earlier in the "Programming Tip." You need to have some information for the Boolean expression before you encounter it the first time, and then at the bottom of the suite you need to again get information for the Boolean expression before you encounter it again.

Lines 30–31: You get to this print statement only if the ***while*** loop terminated normally so that you know without further checking that `0 <= guess <= 100` is no longer *True* and the user quits. Note that the ***break*** statement skips this suite.

A sample interaction is shown in the following session:

```
In [1]: runfile('/Users/user/python/file.py', wdir='/Users/user/python')
Hi-Lo Number Guessing Game: between 0 and 100 inclusive.

Guess a number: 50
Guessed Too Low.
Guess a number: 75
Guessed Too Low.
Guess a number: 82
Guessed Too High.
Guess a number: 78
Guessed Too High.
Guess a number: 77
Guessed Too High.
Guess a number: 76
You guessed it. The number was: 76

In [2]: runfile('/Users/user/python/file.py', wdir='/Users/user/python')
Hi-Lo Number Guessing Game: between 0 and 100 inclusive.

Guess a number: 50
Guessed Too High.
Guess a number: 25
```

```
Guessed Too High.
Guess a number: 10
Guessed Too Low.
Guess a number: -100
```

More Control Inside of a *while* Loop

Continue

Sometimes we might want to simply skip some portion of the **`while`** suite we are executing and have control flow back to the beginning of the **`while`** loop. That is, exit early from *this iteration* of the loop (not the loop itself), and keep executing the **`while`** loop. In this way, the **`continue`** statement is less drastic than the **`break`**. Similar to the **`break`**, it can make the flow of control harder to follow, but there are times when it yields the more readable code.

Consider writing a program that continuously prompts a user for a series of even integers that the program will sum together. If the user makes an error and enters a non-even (odd) number, the program should indicate an error, ignore that input, and continue with the process. Given this process, we need a way to end the loop. Let's choose a special character to stop the looping. In our case, if the special character "." is entered, the program will print the final sum and end.

The basic algorithm will be:

1. Prompt the user for a number.
2. Convert the input string to an int.
3. If the input is even, add it to the running sum.
4. If the input is not even (odd), print an error message—don't add it into the sum, just continue on.
5. If the input is the special character ".", end and print the final sum.

Checking User Input for Errors

Remember, when we prompt the user for a value using `input`, we get a string back, not a number. We must convert that string to an integer to be able to process it. Next we check if the number is even or not, and include it in the sum only if it is even.

Code Listing 2.21 shows a solution to the problem.

Code Listing 2.21

```
# sum up a series of even numbers
# make sure user input is only even numbers
# variable names without types are integers. Rule 4
```

```
4
5 print ("Allow the user to enter a series of even integers. Sum them.")
6 print ("Ignore non-even input. End input with a '.'")
7 # initialize the input number and the sum
8 number_str = input("Number: ")
9 the_sum = 0
10
11 # Stop if a period (.) is entered.
12 # remember, number_str is a string  until we convert it
13 while number_str != "." :
14     number = int(number_str)
15     if number % 2 == 1:  # number is not even (it is odd)
16         print ("Error, only even numbers please.")
17         number_str = input("Number: ")
18         continue  # if the number is not even, ignore it
19     the_sum += number
20     number_str = input("Number: ")
21
22 print ("The sum is:",the_sum)
```

Details:

Lines 7–8: Initialize the variables. `number_str` is set to the result of a `input` request to the user. Note that if the user enters a "." here, the loop will end without running. We append "str" to the variable name so we may keep straight that it in fact is a string, not a number. `the_sum` is initially set to 0. We use the name `the_sum` because the name `sum` is a built-in function name that will be explained later.

Line 13: The period (.) is our special indicator that indicates the loop should end, so we loop until a period is input.

Line 14: Convert the input string to a number (int).

Lines 15–18: Here we check whether `number` is even or odd by finding the remainder when dividing by 2 (using the % operator). If it is odd, we print the error message and then re-prompt the user. We ***`continue`*** which means that we go to the top of the ***`while`*** loop and evaluate its Boolean expression, skipping over the rest of the suite.

Lines 19–20: If we get to Line 19, we know that the number is even so include it in the sum. We then prompt the user for a new number.

Line 22: After the loop ends, print the sum of the integers accumulated in the variable `the_sum`.

You might have noticed a few things about the example solution. In particular, it has two places in the loop for prompting the user. Can we do it more effectively, using only one? Let us try and refactor using **`if-else`**. A solution without continue is shown in Code Listing 2.22.

Code Listing 2.22

```python
# sum up a series of even numbers
# make sure user input is only even numbers

print ("Allow the user to enter a series of even integers. Sum them.")
print ("Ignore non-even input. End input with a '.'")
# initialize the input number and the sum
number_str = input("Number: ")
the_sum = 0

# Stop if a period (.) is entered
# remember, number_str is a string  until we convert it
while number_str != "." :
    number = int(number_str)
    if number % 2 == 1:  # odd number
        print ("Error, only even numbers please.")
    else:                # even number
        the_sum += number
    number_str = input("Number: ")

print ("The sum is:",the_sum)
```

The new example is improved in three ways:

1. **`continue`** is replaced with **`if-else`**. No non-normal control flow is required.
2. The `number_str` input line appears before the loop and at the end of the loop, in keeping with the pattern described previously.
3. Only one prompt of the user is required within the suite.

If you think you need a **`continue`** statement, consider adjusting your algorithm to eliminate it because you'll often find the resulting code is more readable.

The `pass` Statement

The **`pass`** statement is a rather curious statement. Directly from the Python documentation, it says:

> The pass statement does nothing. It can be used when a statement is required syntactically but the program requires no action.

That pretty much says it all. You use **pass** when you *have* to put something in a statement (syntactically, you cannot leave it blank or Python will complain) but what you really want is nothing. For example:

```
for my_int in range(10):
    pass # do nothing
```

This **for** statement will iterate through the fange values but do nothing with them.

Odd as it seems, **pass** has its uses. It can be used to test a statement (say, opening a file or iterating through a collection) just to see if it works. You don't want to do anything as a result, just see if the statement is correct. More interestingly, you can use **pass** as a place holder. You *need* to do something at this point, but you don't know what yet. You place a **pass** at that point and come back later to fill in the details.

2.2.11 Sentinel Loop

A *sentinel loop* is a loop that is controlled by a sentinel—a guard. A guard or sentinel is a particular value is used to terminate the loop. The Boolean expression will be in the form: **while not** sentinel_value:.

```
value = some_value
while value != sentinel_value:
    # process value
    # get another value
```

An example of a sentinel loop is the preceding example, where we stopped if a period was entered:

```
while number != ".":
```

2.2.12 Summary of Repetition

We can put all the variations of **while** into one generic pattern:

```
while boolean_expression1:
    # statement_suite1

    if boolean_expression2:
        break # Exit loop now; skip else.
    if boolean_expression3:
        continue # Go to top of loop now.

else:
    # statement_suite2
```

2.2.13 More on the *for* Statement

Code Listing 2.23

```
# simple for
# find the sum of the numbers from 1 to 100

the_sum = 0

for number in range(1,101):
    the_sum = the_sum + number

print("Sum is:", the_sum)
```

The **for** statement was introduced in an earlier section. Just like the **while** statement, the **for** statement can support a terminal **else** suite, as well as the control modifiers **continue** and **break**. Their roles are as previously described, that is:

1. The **else** suite is executed after the **for** loop exits normally.
2. The **break** statement provides an immediate exit of the **for** loop, skipping the **else** clause.
3. The **continue** statement immediately halts the present iteration of the loop, continuing with the rest of the iterations.

Its more general form is shown here:

```
for target in object:
    # statement_suite1
    if boolean_expression1:
        break # Exit loop now; skip else.
    if boolean_expression2:
        continue # Go to top of loop now.

else:
    # statement_suite2
```

Using *range* to Generate a Number Sequence

As we have mentioned, Python provides a number of collection data types that can be examined by iterating through the collection's elements using a **for** loop. However, it turns out that we can easily generate a sequence of numbers using a special function provided by Python: the *range* function.

Let's look at *range*. Its operation generates a sequence of integers, in which the size and values in the range are dictated by its arguments. It takes up to three arguments: the start value, the end value, and the step or separation between each value. The *range* function generates what is termed a *half open* range. Such a range does *not* include the end value in the sequence generated.

The start value is the first value included in the sequence and, if not provided, defaults to 0. The stop value is used to determine the final value of the sequence. Again, the stop value itself is *never* included in the sequence. The stop value is a required argument. The step value is the difference between each element generated in the sequence, and, if not provided, defaults to 1. If only one argument is provided, it is used as the stop value. In the case of one argument, constituting the stop value, the start value is assumed to be 0 and the step value assumed to be 1. If two arguments are provided, the first is the start and the second is the stop. There is a step argument only if three arguments are used.

A `range` sequence can be iterated through using a **`for`** loop. Here are some examples using `range`. Try some examples yourself in the Python shell to gain an understanding of how `range` works.

```
In  [1]: for i in range(5):
...:     print(i,end=' ')

0 1 2 3 4
In  [2]: for i in range(3,10):
...:     print(i,end=' ')

3 4 5 6 7 8 9
In  [3]: for i in range(1,20,4):
...:     print(i,end=' ')

1 5 9 13 17
In  [4]: for i in range(1,20,2): # print odd integers
...:     print(i,end=' ')

1 3 5 7 9 11 13 15 17 19
```

Code Listing 2.24 is a simple example of range in practice. This famous example is reputed to have been solved by the noted mathematician Gauss in primary school: the problem is to find the sum of the first 100 whole numbers. The teacher assigned it to keep the students busy, but Gauss solved it immediately.

Code Listing 2.24

```
# simple for
# find the sum of the numbers from 1 to 100

the_sum = 0

for number in range(1,101):
    the_sum = the_sum + number

print("Sum is:", the_sum)
```

The details are as follows:

Line 4: Initialize variable `the_sum` to 0 to provide a starting point for the addition in the `for` loop.
Line 6: The expression `range(1,101)` generates a sequence of numbers from 1 to 100. It is used by the `for` loop to associate the variable `number` with each value of the sequence, one value at a time.
Line 7: The suite of the `for` loop. It adds the present value associated with `number` to the value associated with `the_sum`, then assigning the sum back to `the_sum`.
Line 9: After the loop ends, print the value associated with `the_sum`.

The code shown prints the value 5050. Gauss is noted for taking a short cut and figuring out the formula: $n(n+1)/2$.

The *range* Function and Iterables

What happens if you just type a call to the `range` function into the Python interpreter? What is returned? Look at the following session.

```
In  [1]: range(1,10)
Out [1]: range(1, 10)

In  [2]: my_range = range(1,10)
In  [3]: type(my_range)
Out [3]: range

In  [4]: len(my_range)
Out [4]: 9

In  [5]: for i in my_range:
   ...:     print(i, end=' ')

1 2 3 4 5 6 7 8 9
```

What is printed is *not* the actual set of numbers, but something that *represents* those numbers. Thus you can create a `range` of as many numbers as you like, and they are represented by this single value. What type is it? It is a *range* type. Of what use is it? Well, we have seen the answer to that. We can iterate through a range and operate on each value in the range, one at a time, using a `for` loop. It is for this reason that the `range` type is also called an *iterable.* As we said before, an iterable represents a set of values that can be iterated over, say by a `for` loop. Note that an iterable can be used as an argument to the `len` function and return how many elements it contains, even if they have not been generated yet!

This is a rather convenient way to represent things. We can generate a very large range of numbers, but we don't have to create all the numbers at once (which could take a lot of memory and time). Rather, we can represent the range as a special type and generate the individual values in the range when needed. We will see other iterable types, types we can iterate through, as we move along with our Python experience.

PROGRAMMING TIP

One might be tempted to use the variable name `sum` in the code shown earlier. As it turns out, `sum` is a function predefined by Python! In fact, the sum in Code Listing 2.24 can be done with one Python expression: `sum(range(1,101))`. Most editors colorize pre-defined Python variables so that color can warn you about pre-defined identifiers.

Interestingly, if you assign a value to `sum` anyway, Python will happily comply, though now `sum` will no longer operate as a function! However, the change is not permanent. If you make such a mistake, simply restart Python and all default Python values will be returned to their normal values.

Equivalence of *while* and *for*

It is possible to write a `while` loop that behaves exactly like a `for` loop. However, not every `while` loop can be expressed as a `for` loop.

Consider this simple `for` loop using the sequence generated by `range(5)`:

```
for i in range(5):
    print(i)
```

We can write an equivalent `while` loop as:

```
i = 0
while i < 5:
    print(i)
    i += 1
```

The `for` loop is easier to read and understand, but it is useful only for moving through the elements of objects with iterators. Fortunately, in Python you will find so many objects with iterators that you will frequently use a `for` loop.

> **Pythonic Pointer:** How to decide which to use, `for` or `while`? The `while` loop is more general but the `for` loop is useful for moving through all the elements of a collection. Fortunately, many objects can be examined using iteration. Think `for` first!

Refactor Perfect Numbers Using *for*

With *for* in hand we can refactor the Perfect Number classifier code replacing *while* with *for*. In Code Listing 2.13, replace `while number <= top_num:` with `for number in range(top_num+1):` noting the use of `top_num+1` because we need to include `top_num`. Also, the increment statement `number += 1` at the bottom of the *while* loop is no longer needed.

2.2.14 Nesting

VideoNote 2.2
Nested Control

We have mentioned nesting and have used it multiple times in examples, but it is worth a little more discussion. Within the suite of any control construct (`if`, `while`, `for`) we can insert another control construct (`if`, `while`, `for`). Within the inserted control construct, we can insert yet another one. We can nest one within another with no limit (in reality there usually is a limit, but if you reach it, your code is unreadable and should be restructured). Each time we insert another control construct, its suite will be indented. The indentation aids readability, but if the code is nested too much, the indentation will be difficult to read. In that case, the code should be rewritten so that it can again be readable. One tool, which we will cover in Chapter 5, is a *function*, which allows us to improve readability by encapsulating some of the indentation within a function.

If you look back to Code Listing 2.16, you can see the following nested control structure:

```
while ...
    while ...
        if ...
```

Check Yourself: *for* and *range* Check

1. What output occurs for the following program with the given input?

```
the_max = int(input("Enter the upper limit:"))
the_sum = 0
extra = 0

for number in range(1,the_max):
    if number%2 and not number%3:
        the_sum = the_sum + number
    else:
        extra = extra + 1    # Line 1

print(the_sum)               # Line 2
print(extra)                 # Line 3
```

(a) Given the input 10, what output is produced by Line 2 of the program?
(b) Given the input 11, what output is produced by Line 3 of the program?
(c) Which of the following is a reasonable replacement for Line 1 of the program?
  i. extra++
  ii. ++extra
  iii. extra =+ 1
  iv. extra += 1
  v. None of the above
(d) If Line 1 were removed from the program, which of the following statements would be true?
  i. No runtime errors.
  ii. Line 3 would always print 1.
  iii. Error, would run past the end of the range.
  iv. All of the above.
  v. None of the above.

2.2.15 Hailstone Sequence Example

The Collatz conjecture is an unsolved mathematical conjecture from 1937 that makes for an interesting programming example. The conjecture is that given the following formula and a positive integer, the generated sequence *always* ends in 1. Although this has been shown to be true for large initial integers (approximately 2.7×10^{16}) it has not yet been proven true for all. It is an active research area with a new proof recently submitted for publication but later withdrawn. The sequence is also called the *hailstone sequence* because the numbers bounce up and down like hail until they converge to 1. Our task is to write a program to generate the hailstone sequence.

The hailstone formula is as follows:

- If the number is even, divide it by 2.
- If the number is odd, multiply by 3 and add 1.
- When the number reaches 1, quit.

The sequence is formed by applying the formula to the initial number and then repeatedly to each number generated by the formula. The result is a sequence of integers ending at 1 (if you don't stop at 1, what will happen?). For example, if you start with 5, you get the following sequence: 5, 16, 8, 4, 2, 1.

We will create a program so you can try your hand at it. We will also output the length of the sequence.

Determining whether a number is even or odd integer can be done using the remainder operator (%). If we divide a number by 2 and the remainder is 0, the number is even. Otherwise it is odd. In particular:

```
if number % 2 == 1:
    print(number, "is odd")
else:
    print(number, "is even")
```

Because 1 is considered to be `True` for a Boolean expression, the Boolean expression `number % 2 == 1` is often shortened to simply `number % 2` as in:

```
if number % 2:
    print(number, "is odd")
else:
    print(number, "is even")
```

With that notation in hand, let's apply the hailstone formula repeatedly to generate a sequence (Code Listing 2.25).

Code Listing 2.25

```
# Generate a hailstone sequence
number_str = input("Enter a positive integer:")
number = int(number_str)
count = 0

print("Starting with number:",number)
print("Sequence is: ", end=' ')

while number > 1:  # stop when the sequence reaches 1

    if number%2:          # number is odd
        number = number*3 + 1
    else:                 # number is even
        number = number/2
    print(number,",", end=' ')   # add number to sequence

    count +=1             # add to the count

else:
    print()     # blank line for nicer output
    print("Sequence is ",count," numbers long")
```

Copy this code and run it to try your hand at generating hailstone sequences; observe how they all end in 1. If you find one that does not end in 1, either there is an error in your program or you have made a fantastic discovery.

Some other interesting notes. Are there common subsequences for different initial numbers? What is the longest common subsequence? What is the longest sequence in some range of initial numbers? What does a plot of initial number and sequence length look like?

VISUAL VIGNETTE

2.3 PLOTTING DATA WITH PYLAB

In addition to drawing explicitly using tools like the `turtle` module, Python provides tools to plot data in both two and three dimensions. One of the most useful of those tools is the module pylab, which includes the plotting package matplotlib. Matplotlib is a plotting library, created in the image of the Matlab plotting library, for making publication-quality figures. Their motto is "matplotlib makes easy things easy and hard things possible." Matplotlib and pylab are described in more detail in Appendix D

(including how to get and install them), but we can provide a simple introductions here. More complicated examples will be provided throughout the book.

2.3.1 First Plot and Using a List

As with many things in Python, plotting requires that you use one of the collection data structures called the `list` data structure. Lists are covered in detail in Chapter 7, but we can teach you enough about lists here to do some simple plotting.

A list is just a sequence of objects. Lists are denoted with square brackets, and individual elements in a list are separated by commas. Thus `[1,2,3,4]` is a list of four integer values. The empty list is designated by `[]`, and a very useful method used in conjunction with lists is the `append` method. A useful function is `len` that returns the length of a list. A typical use is demonstrated in Code Listing 2.26.

Code Listing 2.26

```
list_of_ints = []
for counter in range(10):
    list_of_ints.append(counter*2)

print(list_of_ints)
print(len(list_of_ints))
```

```
[0, 2, 4, 6, 8, 10, 12, 14, 16, 18]
10
```

The variable `list_of_ints` starts out empty, as designated by a pair of brackets (`[]`), and we append ten integers to the list. At the end, the length of the list is 10.

To plot the list we just created, all we need to do is import pylab and add two lines to the program.

Code Listing 2.27

```
import pylab
list_of_ints = []
for counter in range(10):
    list_of_ints.append(counter*2)

print(list_of_ints)
print(len(list_of_ints))

# now plot the list
pylab.plot(list_of_ints)
pylab.show()
```

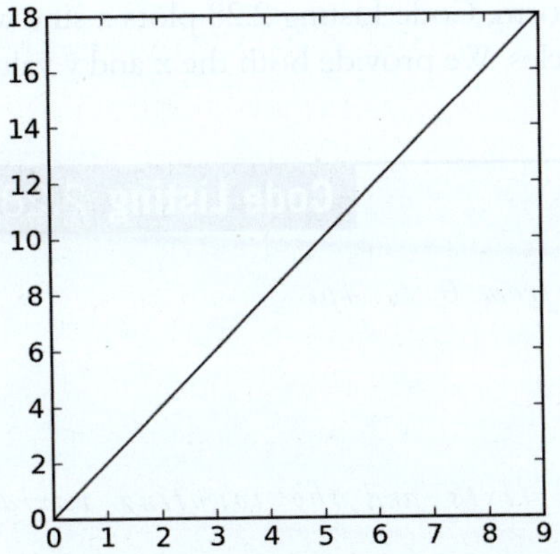

FIGURE 2.10 First plot with matplotlib.

The plot shown in Figure 2.10 will appear in the shell. The values in `list_of_ints` provide the values for the *y*-axis of the plot. The `pylab.plot` method provides the *x*-axis values as the sequence indices of the list. The first value in the list gets *x*-value 0, the second value gets *x*-value 1, and so on.

2.3.2 More Interesting Plot: A Sine Wave

As their motto indicates, matplotlib can do complicated things, but allows you to add complexity as necessary. There are an enormous number of options that you can use, but here are a couple of immediately useful ones.

Plotting Elements and Their Colors

You can plot using all kinds of "markers" for each point in the graph. Each "formatting string" consists of a two-character string:

Color: The first is a lowercase letter for the color. The mappings are fairly obvious: 'r' is red, 'b' is blue, 'g' is green. The only odd one is that 'k' is black.

Marker The second element is a single character indicating the type of marker. These are rather obscure—you simply have to learn them. For example: 'o' is for circles, '.' is for dots, 'x' is for an x marker, and '+' is for a plus marker. Look in Appendix C and the plot documentation for more details.

Putting them together, the formatting string 'ro' will print red circles, and 'bx' will print blue x's.

More Detailed Call of Plot

Using that information on markers, we can pass more than just a single list to `plot`. A more detailed invocation would be: `pylab.plot(x_values,y_values,format_string)`.

Using this form, Code Listing 2.28 plots a sine wave from 0 to $4 * \pi$ in increments of 0.1 with red circles. We provide both the x and y values.

Code Listing 2.28

```
# plot a sine wave from 0 to 4pi

import math
import pylab

#initialize the two lists and the counting variable num. Note is a float
y_values = []
x_values = []
number = 0.0

#collect both number and the sine of number in a list
while number < math.pi * 4:
    y_values.append(math.sin(number))
    x_values.append(number)
    number += 0.1

#plot the x and y values as red circles
pylab.plot(x_values,y_values,'ro')
pylab.show()
```

The resulting plot is shown Figure 2.11.

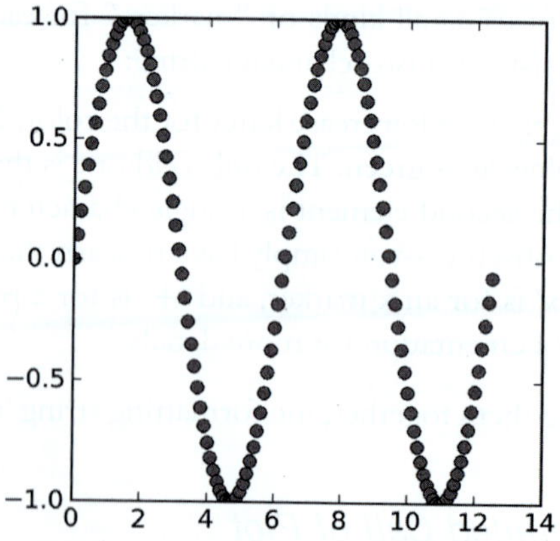

FIGURE 2.11 Sine plot with matplotlib.

2.4 COMPUTER SCIENCE PERSPECTIVES: MINIMAL UNIVERSAL COMPUTING

2.4.1 Minimal Universal Computing

An interesting question is:

How much language power do we need to be able to write any computer program?

Rephrased:

What is the minimal set of instructions that we need to compute any result that can be computed?

In the early days of computing, there was quite a competition to figure out the minimum. It turns out that theoretically, you do not need much. The answer is useful for us because it indicates how little is needed to write all programs, and it shows the importance of control.

The results are usually presented in assembly language. Assembly language is the somewhat English-like description of the ones and zeros of the computer's actual machine language. That is, assembly language is specifically matched to the CPU it runs on to generate commands for that CPU. The basic instructions involve manipulating memory—either an actual location or an "accumulator" register on the processor—and jumping to a specific instruction in a program. (You can think of the accumulator as what stores the result of your calculations when you use a calculator.) Accumulators were common on the first computers when hardware was expensive.

Here is a minimal instruction set[7]:

```
LOAD A     ; load contents at RAM address A into accumulator
STORE A    ; store accumulator contents into address A in RAM
CLR        ; clear accumulator
INC        ; increment accumulator
BRZ X      ; branch to address X in RAM if accumulator is zero
```

All computer programs can be written using just those five instructions. *All* programs, ever! That is a very significant result! Such a program might be nearly impossible to make sense of (i.e., not readable), but it can be done in theory.

Notice that a "branch" instruction is one of the necessary instructions. That branch instruction is the most primitive type of control, and it is closely related to the simple **`if`** statement introduced earlier. This branch instruction, the "BRZ" instruction, tests the accumulator value to see whether it is all zeros, and if it is, the next instruction to execute is at

[7] R. Rojas, "Conditional Branching Is Not Necessary for Universal Computation in von Neumann Computers", *Journal of Universal Computer Science*, Vol. 2, No. 11, 1996, pp. 756–767. Published by Springer Publishing, © 1996.

address X in memory. Otherwise, it executes the instruction that follows, that is, the instruction at the address immediately following this BRZ instruction. There are more powerful and more readable styles of control instruction, but the BRZ is the simplest.

This simple branch instruction allows us to repeatedly do the INC instruction so we can perform addition: if you want to add 5 to something, increment it 5 times. Once you can do addition, you can do all the other arithmetic. It will be messy to read, but it is possible.

What is the point? After all, assembly language is very different from a high-level language such as Python. The point is that a simple combination of `if`, the BRZ instruction, and the ability to repeat, in this case by branching back to the beginning of the program if one so chooses, is enough to write any program. Selection and repetition are two core parts of programming!

2.5 WHAT'S WRONG WITH MY CODE?

Here are suggestions for finding problems with control. Refer to Appendix C for details.

- **Conditional**:
  - *Boolean expression error*: test your Boolean expression in the shell.
  - *Value errors*: insert a breakpoint on the header line to examine the values in the Boolean expression.
  - *Incorrect indentation* is rare: inspection is the only solution.
- **Repetition**:
  - *Started wrong*: the initialization expression is wrong: insert a breakpoint (or print the value) right before your Boolean expression first checks it.
  - *Stopped wrong*: the Boolean expression is wrong: insert a breakpoint on the loop's header line and examine the loop-control variable (or print the loop-control variable as the first instruction in the suite). It may be useful to put a breakpoint immediately **after** the loop to examine the final value of the loop-control variable (or print it).
  - *Incremented wrong*: the change expression is wrong or in the wrong place. A breakpoint (or print) at the first instruction in the suite is helpful.
- **Problem with the loop variable:** Generally the way to isolate these problems is to observe the loop variable. When you see the values changing that is often a valuable clue to the problem. There are three things you can try:
  - *Print* the loop variable and watch it change.
  - *Set a Breakpoint:* An alternative to printing is to break at the beginning of the loop and examine the loop value in the Variable Explorer.
  - *Print range:* Printing the range values with your expression can help understand what your code is actually iterating over. However, you need to wrap `list(...)` around range to see the values. For example, `print(list(range(5)))`.

Here are some common causes:

– *Modified loop variable in for*: modifying the loop variable in a *for* loop can cause unexpected problems. That is, if you have `for i in range(5):` do not modify `i` within the loop suite.
– *Range value is wrong*: a common problem is to forget that `range` generates a half-open interval in that it doesn't include the final value. That is, `range(5)` generates 0, 1, 2, 3, and 4, but **not** 5.
– *Range value is zero*: sometimes `range(x)` will be a problem because `x` is either zero or None.

Summary

In this chapter, we have introduced two control constructs: decision and repetition. With these in hand, you now have sufficient programming power to write powerful programs (in fact, any program). Everything after this point makes programs easier to read and easier to write—powerful concepts in their own right.

Selection: if-elif-else

```
if boolean_expression1:
    # suite1
elif boolean_expression2:
    # suite2
elif boolean_expression3:
    # suite3
# as many elif statements as you like
else:
    # suite_last
```

Repetition: while

```
while boolean_expression1:
    # statement_suite1

    if boolean_expression2:
        break # Exit loop now; skip else.
    if boolean_expression3:
        continue # Go to top of loop now.

else:
    # statement_suite2
```

Iteration: for

```
for target in object:
    # statement_suite1
    if boolean_expression1:
        break # Exit loop now; skip else.
    if boolean_expression2:
        continue # Go to top of loop now.

else:
    # statement_suite2
```

Rules

- **Rule 1:** Think before you program!
- **Rule 2:** A program is a human-readable essay on problem solving that also happens to execute on a computer.
- **Rule 3:** The best way to improve your programming and problem skills is to practice!
- **Rule 4:** A foolish consistency is the hobgoblin of little minds.
- **Rule 5:** Test your code, often and thoroughly!

Exercises

1. How many three-digit numbers are divisible by 17? Write a program to print them.
2. In your own words, describe what the statements **continue** and **break** do in loops.
3. Explain the difference between "is" and "==". Give an example (different from that used in the chapter) that illustrates items that return False for "is" and True for "==".
4. Professors often provide scores on tests, which are converted to grades at the end of the year. Write a python program that uses multiple if-else statements to prompt for a score and print the respective grade.

Score	Grade
Above 80	A
60–80	B
40–60	C
Below 40	D

5. Control:

```
if my_var % 2:
    if my_var**3 != 27:
```

```
        my_var = my_var + 4 # Assignment 1
    else:
        my_var /= 1.5       # Assignment 2
else:
    if my_var <= 10:
        my_var *= 2         # Assignment 3
    else:
        my_var -= 2         # Assignment 4
print(my_var)
```

(a) Find four values of `my_var` so each of the four assignment statements will be executed: each value should cause one assignment statement to be executed.

(b) Find four ranges of `my_var` values that will cause each of the four assignment statements to be executed.

6. Write a program that will print the largest among three numbers.

7. Consider the Python function *range*`(a,b)`. Label these statements as True or False.

- Value "a" is included in the range.
- Value "b" is included in the range.

8. What is an *iterator*? Give two examples of iterators.

9. What is the difference in the logic of the following two sets of code:

(a)
```
if BooleanA:
    SuiteA
if BooleanB:
    SuiteB
```

(b)
```
if BooleanA:
    SuiteA
elif BooleanB:
    SuiteB
```

10. Predict the outcome given x = 0, y = 2, and z = 4.

(a) x or y
(b) x and y
(c) x or z
(d) (x and y) or (y and z)

11. Predict the outcome of each line:

```
i=1
j=0
while i<10:
```

```
        i+=1
        j+=2*2
    print(i) # Line 1
    print(j) # Line 2
```

12. Write a program that prints all the leap years from 1900 to 2020 (inclusive).

13. Write a program that prompts for a number and checks whether or not it is a positive number. If it is a negative number, print 'Negative', if it is a positive number, print 'Positive', and if the input is 0, then print 'Zero'.

14. Rewrite this following "for" loop as a "while" loop:

```
for i in range(1, X + 1):
    if X % i == 0:
        print(i)
```

15. Simplify the following code so that it does not use any breaks or continue statements, yet the logic is equivalent.

```
counter = 0
while True:
    if counter >= 100:
        break
    elif counter % 2 == 0:
        counter += 1
        continue
    else:
        counter *= 2;
        continue
```

---

16. In this exercise you will convert knuts to sickles and galleons (the currency of the Harry Potter novels). Perform the calculation, and print only non-zero values. That is, if there are not enough knuts for there to be one sickle, then "0 sickle" should not be printed. (There are 29 knuts in one sickle and 17 sickles in one galleon.)

17. Write a short program that will:

- prompt the user for a number
- print the absolute value of the number if it is not a positive number
- prompt the user for another number if the input was not positive

18. Sum of consecutive integers

(a) Write a program that prompts for an integer—let's call it X—and then finds the sum of X consecutive integers starting at 1. That is, if X = 5, you will find the sum of $1 + 2 + 3 + 4 + 5 = 15$.

(b) Modify your program by enclosing your loop in another loop so that you can find consecutive sums. For example, if 5 is entered, you will find five sums of consecutive numbers:

```
1          =  1
1+2        =  3
1+2+3      =  6
1+2+3+4    =  10
1+2+3+4+5  =  15
```

Print only each sum, not the arithmetic expression.

(c) Modify your program again to only print sums if the sum is divisible by the number of operands. For example, with the sum $1 + 2 + 3 + 4 + 5 = 15$, there are five operands and the sum, 15, is divisble by 5 so that sum will be printed. (Do you notice a pattern?)

19. (Perfect numbers). In this chapter is a program that checks for *perfect* numbers. If you wanted to check many numbers (a large range of numbers), to see if any were perfect, then the program we wrote might not be the best. What could we do to improve it? For example, how would we output only perfect numbers, but just keep count of the deficient and abundant numbers? Do we need to check every number from 2 to `number-1`?

20. Write a program that prompts for an integer and prints the integer, but if something other than an integer is input, the program keeps asking for an integer. Here is a sample session:

```
Input an integer: abc
Error: try again. Input an integer: 4a
Error: try again. Input an integer: 2.5
Error: try again. Input an integer: 123
The integer is: 123
```

Hint: The string `isdigit` method will be useful.

21. Write a program to generate the following arithmetic examples.
Hints:

(1) Divide-and-conquer: what simpler problem do you need to solve?
(2) Consider using strings to build numbers and then convert.
(3) The *range* iterator may be helpful.

```
1 * 8 + 1 = 9
12 * 8 + 2 = 98
123 * 8 + 3 = 987
1234 * 8 + 4 = 9876
12345 * 8 + 5 = 98765
123456 * 8 + 6 = 987654
1234567 * 8 + 7 = 9876543
12345678 * 8 + 8 = 98765432
123456789 * 8 + 9 = 987654321

1 * 9 + 2 = 11
12 * 9 + 3 = 111
123 * 9 + 4 = 1111
1234 * 9 + 5 = 11111
12345 * 9 + 6 = 111111
123456 * 9 + 7 = 1111111
1234567 * 9 + 8 = 11111111
12345678 * 9 + 9 = 111111111
123456789 * 9 + 10 = 1111111111

9 * 9 + 7 = 88
98 * 9 + 6 = 888
987 * 9 + 5 = 8888
9876 * 9 + 4 = 88888
98765 * 9 + 3 = 888888
987654 * 9 + 2 = 8888888
9876543 * 9 + 1 = 88888888
98765432 * 9 + 0 = 888888888

1 * 1 = 1
11 * 11 = 121
111 * 111 = 12321
1111 * 1111 = 1234321
11111 * 11111 = 123454321
111111 * 111111 = 12345654321
1111111 * 1111111 = 1234567654321
11111111 * 11111111 = 123456787654321
111111111 * 111111111 = 12345678987654321
```

22. Write a program that checks to see if a number N is prime. A simple approach checks all numbers from 2 up to N, but after some point numbers are checked that need not be checked. For example, numbers greater than $\sqrt{N}$ need not be checked. Write a program that checks for primality and avoids those unnecessary checks. Remember to import the `math` module.

23. The perfect number example in this chapter uses two ***while*** loops. Rewrite the program replacing the two ***while*** loops with two ***for*** loops and *range*.

24. Here is an example of a `while` loop. There is an error; can you find the error in the `while` loop? Try to figure out what could be wrong by thinking through the `while` loop. Referring to the flow-chart figures in the chapter should help. Check to see if you are right by using Python!

```
sentence= "that car was really fast"
i=1
while i>0:
    for character in sentence:
        if character == "t":
            print("found a 't' in sentence")
        else:
            print("maybe the next character?")
```

25. Fill in the following table with values *True* or *False*—one value in each empty box.

p	q	(not p) or q	(p and q) or q	(p or q) and p	(p or q) and (p and q)
True	True				
True	False				
False	True				
False	False				

26. If your `while` loop is controlled by "`while True:`", it will loop forever. How do you control your loop so that it will stop? Provide a brief example in Python code.

27. (Quadratic formula) The forumla that calculates roots for a quadratic equation $ax^2 + bx + c$ is the quadratic formula $x = -b \pm \sqrt{b^2 - 4ac}/2a$. Because the square root of a negative is imaginary, one can use the expression under the square root (known as the *discriminant*) to check for the type of root. If the discriminant is negative, the roots are imaginary. If the discriminant is zero, there is only one root. If the discriminant is positive, there are two roots.

(a) Write a program that uses the quadratic formula to generate real roots, that is, ignores the imaginary roots. Use the discriminant to determine whether there is one root or two roots and then prints the appropriate answer.

(b) Python uses the letter 'j' to represent the mathematical imaginary number 'i' (a convention used in electrical engineering). However, the Python 'j' must always be preceeded by a number. That is, '1j' is eqivalent to the mathematical 'i'. Add the ability to handle imaginary roots to your program.

28. In order to understand what a program tries to accomplish, it is essential to be able to follow the flow of control. In the following example, what happens when x = 4?

```
while True:
    for x in range (6):
        y = 2*x+1
        print(y)
        if y > 9:
            break
```

(a) The program breaks out of the **`while`** loop and stops running.
(b) The program breaks out of the **`for`** loop, but the **`while`** condition continues to be *`True`*, resulting in an infinite loop.
(c) The program does not break, but simply continues processing the **`for`** loop.

29. Create a program that prompts for a positive number greater than 2 (check this condition), then keeps taking the square root of this number until the square root is less than 2. Print the value each time the square root is taken, along with the number of times the operation has been completed. For example:

```
Enter an integer greater than 2: 20
1: 4.472
2: 2.115
3: 1.454
```

Extra: Look ahead to string formatting (Section 4.4) to print the values to only 3 decimal places as shown.

30. In the exercises for Chapter 1, an algorithm was given for calculating the pass rating for football quarterbacks. One can use the pass rating to determine whether a quarterback had a mediocre, good, or great year. A rating is poor if it is 85 or below, mediocre if above 85, good if above 90 and great if above 95. Add to the pass rating program to output "poor," "mediocre," "good," or "great."

To test your program, you can look up actual data on www.nfl.com or use the following information from 2007:

	Completions	Attempts	Yards	Touchdowns	Interceptions
Donovan McNabb	180	316	2647	18	6
Tom Brady	319	516	3529	24	12
Peyton Manning	362	557	4397	31	9

31. The NPR radio show "Car Talk" always offers a puzzle to solve. Occasionally, one can be solved with a program. Try this one: My car's odometer measures distance traveled in whole numbers—no tenths of miles—up to 999,999. Last week I was driving along on the freeway and noticed that the last four digits, but not the last five digits, formed a palindrome; that is, it read the same backwards as forwards (e.g., 1221). After one mile went by, though, the last five digits did form a palindrome; and, after one more mile, the middle four digits formed a palindrome. Finally, when the third mile rolled over, all six digits formed a palindrome. What was my mileage at the time I first noticed all these palindromes?

32. Find the two-digit number such that when you square it, the resulting three-digit number has its rightmost two digits the same as the original two-digit number. That is, for a number in the form AB, AB*AB = CAB for some C.

33. A famous puzzle follows.

```
 SEND
+MORE
-----
MONEY
```

What interger values can be substituted to make the addition correct? Write a program to solve this puzzle. *Hint:* Brute force works well—try all possibilities.

34. Write a program to find the five-digit number such that if we put the digit 1 at the beginning, the resulting six-digit number is 3 times smaller than if we put the digit at the end of the number.

35. Write a program that continually generates and sums up random numbers between 1 and 20 and stops when the sum exceeds 1000. Stop early if more than 100 numbers have been generated.

36. Write a program that prompts for a number and prints whether it is an Armstrong number or not. [*Hint:* An Armstrong number is a number that is equal to the sum of its digits when each digit is raised to the number of digits in the number.]

37. In golf, each hole is given a par rating for the number of shots it should take to get it in the hole. Pars for a hole range from 3 to 5. Based on the number of shots compared to par your score is given a name: albatross for 3 under the par, eagle for 2 under, birdie for 1 under, par if it is the same, bogey for 1 over, double bogey for 2 over, and triple bogey for 3 over. Write a program which prompts the user for the par of a hole and the user's score for the hole. Then use this to print out the name of the user's score. Print an error message for scores less than 3 under par and print "bad hole" for those more than 3 over par.

38. Write a program that prompts the user for an integer `n` and then prints the sum of the first `n` natural numbers. The program should check that `n` is a positive number.

39. Write a program that will prompt the user to enter the names of countries they've visited, and will build a list of countries they have travelled. Use a `list` data structure, and check that the input is a string of letters.

40. Write a program that allows you to play rock, paper, scissors against the computer. Import the random module to select the computer's choice.

41. Write a program that creates a spiraling star using Turtle graphics.

42. Use the pylab package to plot hailstone sequences.

Programming Projects

1. **What is the invention of chess worth?**

   There is a popular myth about the man who invented chess. The local ruler was so pleased with the invention that he offered the inventor a great reward in gold. The inventor suggested an alternative reward: he would get one grain of wheat on the first square of the chess board, two grains on the second square, four on the third, eight on the fourth, and so on, doubling the number of grains each time. The ruler saw that this must be a much better deal for him, and accepted. The board has 64 squares. Write a program to determine the following:

   (a) How many total grains of wheat did the ruler have to pay the inventor?
   (b) A wheat grain weighs approximately 50 mg. How much did the wheat weigh?
   (c) Pick a region (state, country, etc.) and determine how deeply that region would be covered with that quantity of wheat. Prompt for the area of the region and then output the depth including the units you use.

2. **How thick does paper folding get?**

   Take one sheet out of your newspaper, and fold it in half, then fold it in half again, and again, and again. Can you fold it 30 times? Pretending that you can (you probably can't fold it more than eight times), how thick would it be after 30 times? Assume the paper is 1/200 cm. thick. Write a program to solve this puzzle. Prompt for the number of folds and output the thickness in meters.

3. **Turtle polygons**

   Prompt for the desired number of sides for your polygon. Given that the interior angle of a regular polygon is (sides $-$ 2) $\times$ 180°)/sides, draw the polygon. *Optional:* Prompt for a color and color the interior of your polygon.

4. **Weird multiplication**

   For this assignment, you will be implementing the so-called "Russian Peasant" or "Ancient Egyptian" method for multiplication. It looks a little odd, but just think of it as an algorithm, a recipe for doing multiplication in a way other than what you learned in grade school.

   The algorithm is as follows. If A and B are the 2 integers (only integers) to be multiplied, we repeatedly multiply A by 2 and divide B by 2, until B cannot be divided any further, that is, until its value becomes 0 (remember, this is integer division). During each step, whenever B is an odd number, we add the corresponding A value to the product we are generating. In the end, the sum of the A values that had corresponding odd B values is the product. Get it?

Here is an example:

If the two integers to be multiplied are 34 and 19, the operations would be:

A	B	Comment
34	19	add A to the product, B is odd
68	9	add A to the product, B is odd
136	4	ignore this A value, B is even
272	2	ignore this A value, B is even
544	1	add A to the product, B is odd

Sum up all the A values that had odd B values and you get: 34+68+544 = 646 => Final product.

(a) Part 1: Write a program to find the product of two integers.
(b) Part 2: Modify your program so that it repeatedly asks whether you want to find another product.

CHAPTER 3

Algorithms and Program Development

> A computer will do what you tell it to do, but that may be much different from what you had in mind.
>
> Joseph Weizenbaum, computer science professor

PROBLEM SOLVING USING COMPUTATIONAL METHODS IS BASED ON ALGORITHMS AND the programs that implement them. We briefly introduced the concept of an algorithm earlier. In this chapter, we further develop the concept of an algorithm and show its role in creating programs to solve problems.

3.1 WHAT IS AN ALGORITHM?

You will hear the word *algorithm* frequently in computer science (as well as in the closely related fields of computer engineering and mathematics). What is an algorithm?

The formal definition of an algorithm from a dictionary is[1]:

algorithm: A process or a set of rules to be followed in calculations or other problem-solving operations.

Informally, an algorithm is sometimes described as follows:

algorithm: A recipe for solving a problem.

The origin of the word "algorithm" has an interesting pedigree, which is recounted in beautiful detail by Donald Knuth in his book "The Art of Computer Programming, Volume I", pg. 1. Essentially, algorithm is a recent addition to the language (late 50s), but is

[1] Formal Definition of an Algorithm from Dictionary.app, Mac OS X. Copyright © by Apple Inc. Used by permission of Apple Inc.

derived from an older word, "algorism," which Knuth describes as "doing arithmetic using Arabic numerals." The word algorithm is derived from the name of a famous Persian author, Abū'Abd Allāh Muhammad ibn Mūsā al-Khwārizmī (circa 825). He was a mathematician, astronomer, and geographer from the House of Wisdom, a library and translation institute in ancient Baghdad. He was the author of a famous book that studied linear and quadratic equations, so famous that the the word "algebra" was derived from the title.

3.1.1 Example Algorithms

Let's consider a couple of simple algorithms that you might find familiar. First, consider making a chocolate cake from scratch. Algorithms for preparing food are better known as *recipes* and have two components: objects (ingredients) and actions on those objects. If the ingredients are fresh and we follow the steps correctly, the result is a cake to eat. Here is the recipe.[2]

Chocolate Cake Recipe

- 1½ c. flour
- 1 c. sugar
- 1/2 tsp. salt
- 1 tsp. baking soda
- 2 tbsp. cocoa
- 1 tbsp. vinegar
- 6 tbsp. oil
- 1 tsp. vanilla
- 1 c. water

1. Sift first five ingredients together.
2. Add remaining ingredients and mix.
3. Pour into an 9-inch greased and floured square pan.
4. Bake at 350 degrees for 30 minutes.
5. Let it cool and frost with your favorite frosting.
6. Eat!!!

Recipes can be used not only to make food, but to make calculations as well. Consider a mathematical algorithm to calculate the square root of a number: the Babylonian square root algorithm. It is an ancient algorithm attributed to the Babylonians[3] and first described by the Greek mathematician Heron of Alexandria in the first century. It is a surprisingly fast and accurate way to find a square root, even if just using pencil and paper. The

[2] Chocolate Cake Recipe from William F. Punch, Richard J. Enbody.

[3] Whether the Babylonians knew this algorithm is disputed, nonetheless it is known as the "Babylonian method."

algorithm is sometimes called Newton's method, from Newton's generalization of the algorithm. It is:

> Babylonian Square Root Algorithm
>
> 1. Guess the square root of the number.
> 2. Divide the number by the guess.
> 3. Average the quotient (from step 2) and the guess.
> 4. Make the new guess the average from step 3.
> 5. If the new guess is different from the previous guess, go back to step 2; otherwise, stop.

The Babylonian square root algorithm has a characteristic in common with many algorithms you will encounter: the devil is in the details. For example, what do we mean by "different" in step 5? Maybe if the guesses differ by a few thousandths, we will be satisfied with the answer (and worn out, if calculating with pencil and paper).

There exist a number of algorithms with roots in computer science that are applicable in everyday life. For example, if there are multiple tellers or ATM machines, notice how people tend to form (or are forced to form) one line. Fifty years ago there would have been multiple lines, but now people naturally choose the optimal queuing algorithm: one line for multiple servers (tellers). Similarly, there are a pair of algorithms named "first fit" and "best fit," which can be applied for parking in a mall or similar venue: should you drive around and try to find a parking spot close to the entrance (best fit) or would you save more time by simply picking the first available spot and walk (first fit)? Someone compared those approaches and found that on average a first-fit algorithm will get you to the door quickest. Google was founded based on a page-rank algorithm, which provided better search results than competitors. The founders, Page and Brin, became billionaires by starting with a better algorithm.

3.2 ALGORITHM FEATURES

Calling an algorithm a recipe works as a first description of an algorithm, but from a computer science point of view, it is insufficient. In particular, computer scientists are interested in what makes a *good* algorithm. There are a number of characteristics that good algorithms share. However, before we examine those characteristics, let's try to clarify the difference between an algorithm and a program.

3.2.1 Algorithm versus Program

Algorithms and their associated programs are so tightly coupled that sometimes one is confused with the other, especially when first learning how to program.

There is a difference, and here it is:

- An *algorithm* is a description of how a problem can be solved.
- A *program* is an implementation of an algorithm in a particular language to run on a particular kind of computer.

Consider our algorithms for chocolate cake and square roots. The cake recipe leaves out necessary details for particular kitchens. For example, it doesn't say where to find a bowl for mixing. The recipe also doesn't tell us how to set the oven temperature on a particular stove: do we spin a dial or punch buttons? The square root algorithm will be implemented differently when using pencil and paper than using a computer or even an abacus. In all cases, the missing details are particular to the circumstances of implementing the algorithm. To a cook working in his or her own kitchen, the implementation details missing from the recipe are not a problem because the cook knows where the bowls are and knows how to operate the oven. In a similar way, a programmer familiar with a particular programming language, operating system, and computer will implement an algorithm as a program using those details.

Separating what we *want to do* from how we *actually did it* provides us with a couple of advantages:

- We have the opportunity to analyze the algorithm itself, independent of how it was implemented. This analysis is the "science" in the discipline of computer science. Separating the algorithm from the implementation allows us to focus on the properties of the algorithm. For example, analysis of the algorithm may suggest improvements that improve all implementations.
- We have the opportunity to see how well a programming language allows us to realize an implementation of the algorithm. Every language has strengths and weaknesses that make different aspects of an algorithm easier or harder to implement. The design of computer languages partly focuses on this idea.
- We have the opportunity to analyze the impact of a particular computer and language on the implementation. For example, there may be cost or power constraints on a particular problem, so development time may be important or hardware costs may be a constraint. A programming language choice would affect the former; a processor choice would affect the latter.

We have emphasized the difference between the algorithm and implementation, and when first learning, it is best to think of them in that way. However, they are not always as independent as we have implied. Often there are multiple algorithms that provide correct solutions for a particular problem. For example, if we want to solve a problem on a particular computer, we may want to use an algorithm that is well suited to that style of computing. Two examples come to mind. One involves the multicore processor that can run multiple pieces of a program at the same time. Some algorithms are more suitable for such an environment than others. Another example is an embedded processor, such as one that controls brakes on an automobile. That processor may have little computing power and memory, so an algorithm with low power and memory demands may be more appropriate.

3.2.2 Qualities of an Algorithm

In the sections that follow, we try to identify four features that help us understand the qualities we would like to have in a "good" algorithm. We would like our algorithms to have these qualities:

- Detailed
- Effective
- Specific as to its behavior
- General Purpose

Detailed

An algorithm has to be detailed enough to specify all that must be done to accomplish the goal. However, "detailed enough" is tricky to define precisely. An algorithm needs to have sufficient detail so that by following it exactly (be it on paper or in a program), the desired result is achieved. Consider the chocolate cake algorithm (recipe). Obviously, "mix some ingredients and cook" would be an insufficient level of detail, but describing how to stir with a spoon ("pick up spoon in right hand, hold bowl with left, stick spoon in mixture, ...") would be too much detail. Common sense and experience defines what "detailed enough" is for recipes, and even with recipes, the detail varies with the audience. A recipe for an inexperienced cook contains more detail than what might be needed by an experienced chef. Similarly, common sense, experience, and the audience also define "detailed enough" for computer algorithms. The practice of learning about algorithms and encoding them in programs is necessary to develop an understanding of the level of detail needed in an algorithm.

Effective

Every algorithm should effectively compute its result. That's obvious, but what does that really mean in the context of computing? By effectively computing its result, we mean:

- The algorithm should eventually finish. That is, it should stop at some point in time and deliver an answer, even if the answer is wrong, or if the answer is "no answer available."
- The algorithm should not merely finish "at some point in time"; it should stop in a "reasonable" amount of time.

It is interesting to note the ambiguities in those statements:

- What is "reasonable"?
- How do you measure a reasonable time without actually implementing an algorithm as a program and running it?

Be aware that an algorithm can be impossibly slow, even if implemented efficiently in a programming language, and even if it runs on the fastest computer available. Some seemingly simple problems have algorithms that take an unreasonably long time to solve. For example, there are hundreds of millions of mailing addresses in the United States: in what order should those individual pieces of mail be delivered such that the delivery process uses the least amount of energy? Finding a good solution can be done in a reasonable amount of time, but finding the *best* solution could literally take multiple lifetimes on the fastest computers. Most people would agree that finding the best solution in that case would not be a "reasonable" amount of time. In addition, the solution time is so long that the problem itself would have changed before the best solution for the original problem was found—many addresses would have changed!

Finally, to achieve completion in a reasonable time, the behavior of the algorithm may not be exact. That is, it gets an answer all the time, but it may not be the "best" answer every time. Sometimes we must be willing to accept "close answers" as a trade-off for getting results in a reasonable time. There are many problems with this characteristic. Consider weather prediction. Weather prediction is a particularly difficult problem that typically requires so-called "supercomputers" to solve the problem. However, weather prediction is not perfect (as we are all too often aware) because the time it takes to get "better" solutions is presently far too high. For example, it would not be very helpful to take longer than 24 hours to predict the next 24 hours of weather!

Specify Behavior

An algorithm must specify its behavior, that is, what it is supposed to do, and even what it cannot do. For example, an important part of the behavior of an algorithm is the input it requires and output it produces given appropriate (perhaps even inappropriate) input. In fact, the algorithm provides a description that *relates* the input to the output. That is, given this input, the algorithm should produce this output. The algorithm should indicate what inputs are required (including no input) and defaults that might be assumed. The algorithm should also describe the output that should be produced, including error conditions that might result.

The "correct behavior" of the algorithm should be made clear. For example, if the algorithm is addition, then the input of two integers should result in the output of a single integer that is the sum of the two input integers.

Specifying input is also critically important for security because most security breaches are related to incorrect input handling. Knowing what input is required and expected is necessary for correct handling of it.

General Purpose Algorithms

Most algorithms are, at least to some extent, general purpose. For example, a bread recipe should result in bread: different ingredients will result in different-flavored breads, but the basic recipe is the same. Similarly, a sort algorithm which orders elements according to some comparison results should sort appropriately regardless of whether the elements being sorted are words or numbers. The basic steps of the algorithm are the same.

Algorithms are general purpose by design because an algorithm is an idealized computational module. The implementation details (how to compare types, how to iterate through types) are the problems of the implementation, not the general approach. Although any solution you might devise to solve a problem might be deemed an algorithm by you, a really good algorithm that stands the test of time should be written in a way that can apply to any instance of the problem.

Remember, a program is an implementation of an algorithm! You formulated an algorithm in order to create the program, but the algorithm is not the program. The sharing of algorithms with others for analysis is important for both correctness and robustness.

3.2.3 Can We Really Do All That?

Our list of features is good to have. We want the algorithms we create to have every one of those qualities, but that may not be possible in every case. In particular, achieving all of them when writing one's first algorithms is particularly difficult. However, striving for detail, effectiveness, specification of behavior, and generality is a worthy goal.

In practice, especially at the beginning, you will find your algorithms to be very specific to a particular problem. Your first algorithms will not be efficient. Also, if the problem is challenging, your algorithm may not lead to an exact result. All of those characteristics are the reality for novice algorithm writers, so they are acceptable in a first course. Nonetheless, we encourage you to strive for good algorithms.

3.3 WHAT IS A PROGRAM?

If an algorithm is an idealized computational process, then a program is an actual implementation of that ideal. It exists in a particular language to be run on a specific computer. In the sense that an algorithm is an abstraction of a solution to a problem, the program is the actual solution. As such, it has a number of features that differ from an algorithm. We describe in the following sections three important features of a program:

- Readability
- Robustness
- Correctness

3.3.1 Readability

> Programs must be written for people to read, and only incidentally for machines to execute.
>
> Abelson & Sussman[4]

[4] Abelson, H., and Sussman, G., *Structure and Interpretation of Computer Programs*, 2nd ed. (Cambridge MA: MIT Press, 1996), ISBN-13 978-0-2620-1153-2.

When students are asked, "What is the most important feature of a program?" we often get the answer "The program should run and solve the problem." It is true that a program should *do* something, but that may not be its most important feature. To most novices' surprise, one of the most important features of a program is that it be *readable*—it is a document that describes to a reader how the writer is solving a problem. This is a reiteration of our previous **RULE 2**, a program should be a human readable essay. As an implementation of an algorithm, a program is a piece of your thoughts made concrete. That is a powerful statement and worth emphasizing. A program is your thoughts on a problem, made concrete so that not only can they be read, but also implemented and realized. This is one of the promises, and the hopes of computer programming, and it is a lofty one at that.

As such, for anyone else to understand what you were thinking, the code should be written clearly. Note that there are really two audiences for your document: the computer and the reader. Good enough to "run" may not be good enough to be "understandable" to a human.

Programs need to be read and understood to be useful. A successful program will be used more than once and possibly maintained or modified by others. In fact, a poorly written program will be incomprehensible even to the author after some time. As a test, six months after completing this course, come back and see whether you can make sense of all your code. Some of it will be incomprehensible, even to you. Imagine how it looks to others!

Someone who writes difficult-to-read programs will not be able to get effective help or advice from others. Also, such code is unlikely to be secure, and the brief history of computing has reinforced the idea that code that is examined by many eyes is more likely to do what it was supposed to do with fewer errors.

Consider the Obfuscated C Code Contest.[5] This contest challenges programmers to write code that accomplishes a specific goal while being as unreadable and obfuscated (meaning made purposefully obscure) as possible. In so doing, the contest provides examples of what you can do to make the code "just run," ignoring and even defying readability. Take a look at some of the examples online and see what you think.

The Simplest Thing: Good Names

There are a variety of good rules for readable programs, but the first and most common is *good naming*. Good names help with readability, and good naming is easy. Basically, be descriptive in your naming. Descriptive names can be aided by using the Google naming rules we discussed in Section 1.5. The phrase "lower with underline" should be familiar to you by now.

- For variables, names should reflect what their role is and, potentially, information about what they can hold, such as a type.
- For operations, names should reflect what they do and, potentially, what they return.

[5] Copyright © 2004–2009, Landon Curt Noll, Simon Cooper, Peter Seebach, and Leonid A. Broukhis. www.ioccc.org.

As an example, consider the Code Listing 3.1. What does this code do?

Code Listing 3.1

```
a = input("give a number: ")
b,c=1,0
while b<=a:
    c = c + b
    b = b + 1
print(a,b,c)
print("Result: ", c/b-1)
```

First, it is hard to tell what the program does. Part of the problem is that the variable names are not descriptive. We will see that there is a time and a place for single-character variables, but a readable program will have few. Second, there are no comments. What is the program supposed to be doing? Third, there are two errors in this program, and its lack of readability makes them difficult to find. If you run the code, the first error prevents the code from running. (What is it?). Second, if that first error is fixed, we end up with the wrong answer.

Here is a cleaned-up and easier-to-read version of Code Listing 3.2. Is it easier to understand? Can you find the changes that fix the errors in the previous example?

Code Listing 3.2

```
# Calculate the average of a sum of consecutive integers in a given range.

limit_str=input("Range is from 1 to your input:")

limit_int = int(limit_str)
count_int = 1
sum_int = 0
while count_int <= limit_int:
        sum_int = sum_int + count_int
        count_int = count_int + 1
average_float = sum_int/(count_int - 1)
print("Average of sum of integers from 1 to",limit_int,"is", average_float)
```

What were the errors?

- We didn't convert the string input value in variable `a` to an *int*. Python does not allow comparison of numbers and characters.

- The order of operations for the calculating the average used improper order of operation: the expression (b - 1) should be in parentheses.

You need to be able to read what was written to find problems like this; otherwise, the errors (your errors!) can be very difficult to find.

Comments

Comments are essential for readability. Even though code is precise, programming languages are not the best language for human understanding—even for experienced programmers. The necessity of comments, even for the author of the code, is something that novice programmers find hard to accept. It is not uncommon for experienced programmers to go back at some time to read their own old code and find it incomprehensible. Such experience helps them appreciate the importance of comments.

Like other aspects of readability, there are no well-defined rules for how much commenting is necessary. Too many comments can make the program hard to read; too few make parts of the code difficult to understand. Finding a balance comes with experience. However, over time, some guidelines have surfaced.

Place comments to indicate:

- The overall goal of the code. This is usually placed at the top as a summary.
- The purpose of objects that are not clear from their names.
- The purpose of other functions that are provided by the system, or, as you will learn, written by us. This includes the input required and the output expected.
- Where something "tricky" or "unusual" is going on: if it required thought on your part, it should be commented.

The last guideline is particularly important. Your comment on some line of code should not just reiterate the code itself. For example, is the Code Listing 3.3 updated version of the previous program better for all the comments?

Code Listing 3.3

```
# Calculate the average of a sum of consecutive integers in a given range.

# input the value
limit_str=input("Range is from 1 to your input:")
#convert the input string to an input
limit_int = int(limit_str)
# assign 1 to the counting variable
count_int = 1
# assign 0 to the sum
sum_int = 0
# while loop runs while the counting variable is smaller than the input value
```

```
while count_int <= limit_int:
        # add the count and the sum, reassign to sum
        sum_int = sum_int + count_int
        # add one to the count
        count_int = count_int + 1
# calculate the average
average_float = sum_int/(count_int - 1)
# print the result
print("Average of sum of integers from 1 to",limit_int,"is", average_float)
```

No, it isn't. The code is well enough written so that most of those comments are not needed. Reiterating in comments what is clear already in the code actually makes things *harder* to read. Only at places where the code itself is hard to read, or some particularly important aspect of the algorithm is being laid out, should comments be inserted. As a rule of thumb, If it was hard to write, it would likely be hard to read unless it is explained via comments.

That is important enough that we should add it as one of our rules.

Rule 6: If it was hard to write, it is probably hard to read. Add a comment.

An experience you will have: you write some code and provide a silly comment like "good luck here" or something similar. You come back in a month after you have forgotten what you were doing, and find yourself angry at the callousness of the idiot who wrote that comment (which, as you recall, was you)!

You are enhancing readability not only for others, but also for yourself!

Indenting Code

Indenting is an important ingredient of readability. Getting indentation correct to show what code belongs to what control statement is crucial for readability. Thankfully, you *must* get this correct because Python makes you do so. This is one of the nice aspects of Python: enforcing readability right from the start.

3.3.2 Robust

Programs should be as *robust* as possible in the face of unpredictability. Programs should be able to recover from inputs that are unanticipated. For example, if a program does division, and a zero divisor is provided (remember that division by zero is undefined in mathematics), the program should not halt unexpectedly. The program should be designed to deal with such erroneous input.

In an ideal world, all input should be predictable, but the reality is different—something unexpected will happen if a program is sufficiently popular, especially if it's used in situations not imagined by the designer. A program by design should know what input it expects but be sufficiently robust to handle everything else—especially inputs the designer couldn't imagine. Most security errors in software come from mishandling of unanticipated input. Often the unanticipated input comes from the software being used in ways not imagined by the designers.

Achieving robustness requires two actions:

- The program designer should account for error situations in the design of a program. In particular, the designer should know what input is expected and design in a way to handle situations if anything else occurs.
- The designer should devise tests to determine whether the program not only satisfies the original design, but also, as it evolves, continues to deal with all cases (including error cases), no matter how the program is changed.

We remember **RULE 5** and its call to test and test often. However, it may not be very obvious that it can be very difficult to "fully test" a program. The number of cases can be very large—too large to test all cases in a reasonable amount of time. It may not even be obvious how many cases there are. A very good example is the case of the first Intel Pentium processor in 1994. The processor had a bug in its division unit that caused *only* 1 in 9 billion floating-point divides to be incorrect. The rarity of this error evaded testing, but showed up quickly after the processor was in the public's hands. The error is even more interesting because it turned out that a software error in loading a table for manufacturing was the root of the problem—a small part of the table came out as all zeros.[6] Testing before manufacturing showed the division to be correct, but testing after manufacturing didn't find the newly introduced error.

Robust testing methods exist and are beyond the scope of this course.

3.3.3 Correctness

Obviously, correctness is essential. It seems equally obvious that if we design an algorithm and then implement that algorithm as a program, the program should be correct—that it does what it was supposed to do. If the program is supposed to sum two numbers, then it should produce correct sums. It seems so simple, doesn't it?

In fact, determining correctness is extremely difficult. For any program of even moderate size, it is very difficult to determine from the design of the program alone (that is, without running it on test cases) that it is correct. Combine that fact with the knowledge that sometimes it is not possible to test all cases, and you find that *proving* correctness is often not feasible.

[6] http://www.trnicely.net/pentbug/pentbug.html

Proving correctness is a vital and growing area in computer science, but designing provably correct programs is a task for the future. For now, the best we can do is design well, and to test as best as we can. When done with care, testing early in program development can help produce more correct programs.

3.4 STRATEGIES FOR PROGRAM DESIGN

> If you can't solve a problem, then there is an easier problem you can solve: find it.
>
> Pólya[7]

There are many strategies for solving problems in general, and these strategies also work for solving problems with a computer. Different strategies work for different problems, and some people find that one strategy fits their style of thinking better than other strategies. In the end, you need to look at various approaches and find the one that works for you for the problem at hand. There isn't a one-size-fits-all method for solving problems, but we can provide some general guidelines.

If you want reference on problem solving, consider the classic *How to Solve It* by Pólya.[8] It was written in the first half of the twentieth century, but it is still one of the best, and most libraries have a copy.

3.4.1 Engage and Commit

You need to be ready to work on the problem. Problem solving is an activity that requires a commitment of mental resources. Persistence helps, so don't give up easily. Put some time in, even if it seems difficult. Multitasking can be particularly distracting. For example, Dr. Thomas Jackson of Loughborough University, England, found that it takes an average of 64 seconds to recover your train of thought after interruption by e-mail.[9] So people who check their e-mail every five minutes waste $8\frac{1}{2}$ hours a week figuring out what they were doing moments before.

It is particularly important to find some uninterrupted quality time to do the work. Remember that time is not effort. Putting 10 hours into a program does not (necessarily) mean that you were actually programming for 10 hours. If you are wasting time, change strategies or take a break and come back to it. Of course, if you have left the problem to the last minute, these last options are not available—even though they are frequently the most valuable.

To engage with the problem, set the mood—whatever that means for you. For most people, setting the mood involves removing distractions. Music may do the trick, or perhaps you prefer quiet. Regardless, find what works for you and use it.

---

[7] Quote from "Mathematical Discovery on Understanding, Learning, and Teaching Problem Solving," Volume I by Sam Sloan and George Pólya. Published by Ishi Press, © 2009.

[8] Pólya, George, *How to Solve It*, (Princeton: Princeton University Press, 1945), ISBN 0-691-08097-6.

[9] "Breaking the Email Compulsion," Suw Charman-Anderson, 28 August 2008. Copyright Guardian News and Media Ltd., 2008.

3.4.2 Understand, Then Visualize

Now that you are in problem-solving mode, you have to get a handle on the problem. You cannot solve it until you understand it.

What Is the Actual Problem?

Often a problem starts as a simple statement: we want to create a "horseless carriage"—a mode of transportation that does not require a horse to get around. Designing an automobile (which is what a horseless carriage is) for the first time is difficult. No one has ever seen one before! We use strategies therefore to address the problem. For example, is our problem similar to other, hopefully solved, problems? That is, are there any similar problems that you can relate this problem to? Is the process of designing a "horsed" carriage helpful? We could use carriage wheels and perhaps a carriage body, but there are problems not yet addressed, such as the engine and transmission.

With computational problems, ask yourself whether there are any similar problems with known solutions (in software design those are called "patterns"). In a course, you may find example problems or earlier homework that are sufficiently similar to use as a starting point toward understanding the problem at hand.

If the problem is something *you* have posed, finding a way to phrase the problem exactly can help. With a computational problem, that means:

- What inputs are required?
- What tests on the input are needed?
- For each input, what is the expected or required output?
- What tests on the output are appropriate?
- As mentioned earlier, do you know a similar problem?

If the problem is given to you as in a homework assignment, there may be many parts to the description. Do you understand each one? Did you get all the requirements? As with the formulation any problem you need to consider the inputs and outputs, how they relate, and how they are tested.

If you have a problem to solve and are expected to write a program to solve it, you have to understand just what is required to a level of detail that you rarely do for other problems.

Making the Problem Real

Now that you have some understanding of the problem, can you make it "real" somehow? What that means is up to you, but the result is that you can "play around" with your understanding and see better what is entailed. For example, if the problem is to write a program that plays a card game, now is the time to pull out a deck of cards and give it a try.

Other options for different kinds problems include:

- Work some simple examples using pencil and paper.
- Work some examples using objects such as playing cards or toy cars.

- Draw some graphs.
- Create diagrams of the interaction.
- Do something!

Can you visualize the problem in some way to make it more real to you? If so, it may give you better insight into the problem. By making the problem real in some way, you can play with the problem, and get a better grasp on what you have to do to solve the problem. This activity can also help you later on, if you get stuck part way through the solution.

3.4.3 Think Before You Program

We've seen this before. Heck, this is our **RULE 1**. It is easier said than done, but it is still important that you understand the problem before you program. Often, programming while you are simultaneously trying to solve the problem leads to a condition known as "dung ball" programming. Remember the lowly dung beetle, a creature that slaps pieces of dung onto a growing ball into which it places its eggs. Programming before you "get" the problem leads to a similar approach. Pieces of program are "slapped on" to the overall solution without much view towards the overall goal. How could this approach work, if you don't fully understand the problem? Sadly, the result is the same—a ball of dung.

3.4.4 Experiment

Now you know the problem and you've played with it a bit. What's next?

Instead of trying to write the whole program from beginning to end, try out some strategies. Python allows you to type code directly in the IPython console. Using Python in this mode allows you to try some of your ideas without coding a whole program. This is really a variant of our **RULE 3**. We can test out our ideas easily in the Python interpreter and see what results.

Can you translate some of your ideas into code? Even something small can give you something concrete to work with. If nothing comes immediately to mind, can you look around (help, books, Internet) and get some ideas on how to write something small as a start? That is, simplify!

It is most important to try some things to see what happens. Experiment with code. Try something—it will be wrong at first, but as Edison famously observed: you now know one more thing that doesn't work. Novice programmers especially seem very reluctant to try things. They want to just solve the problem and move on. It is better to try a few ideas out and get rid of the bad ones before they become part of your solution.

3.4.5 Simplify

Of all the approaches, this is the best strategy! As observed by Pólya, if you cannot solve a problem directly, perhaps an easier (more restricted, focused on some particular aspect, etc.)

version of the problem exists, which you can solve. Look for those simpler aspects of the problem!

Think of your problem as a puzzle with multiple pieces, each has its own smaller problem to solve. The smaller problems will be more manageable and hence more easily solved by you. In fact, you may find the whole problem totally unsolvable, yet find each piece easy to solve. Having solved the smaller pieces, the assembly of those pieces into an overall solution is much easier than tackling the whole problem. Another name for this strategy comes from the military: divide and conquer.

To be successful with simplification, you must:

- Find the pieces. Can you find the subtasks in your problem?
- Solve each of the pieces.
- Put all the solved pieces back together as an overall solution.

The hardest part is the first step: find the pieces. The ability to find the smaller parts develops with experience, but there are few computational problems that cannot be broken down into smaller pieces. Try very hard to find the pieces.

By breaking the problem down into simpler problems, you accomplish two things. Psychologically, you make the overall problem more tractable. Rather than staring at the larger problem and lamenting that you don't know how to start, you can start by solving smaller, simpler pieces and moving on. Success breeds further success. Also, smaller pieces usually are simpler to approach. By solving the smaller problems in isolation, you can solve them better and more completely. Not only will you have broken down the problem into easier pieces, but you will also have better solutions to each piece when the time comes to put it all back together.

Persistence is important. Expect to be able to divide and conquer the problem.

Some of our longer examples illustrate the divide-and-conquer strategy. For example, look back at the perfect number example in Section 2.1.6 and observe how we broke the problem into smaller and simpler pieces to solve the larger problem.

The "Onion" Approach

One useful way to divide and conquer a problem is to write the larger solution as if the solutions to the pieces already exist. For example, if you were writing a program to control a robot to go someplace, you might start with "turn in the right direction." You likely don't know how to program the robot to do exactly that, but you can simply assume that you can figure it out later and concentrate now on the next task. When you come back to that problem piece, you will need to consider only "turn in the right direction" rather than the whole problem.

In this way, you will find it easier, to write programs that are essentially skeletons of what you think the final program will look like. Once the skeleton is created, you can go back and begin to slowly fill in pieces. You imagine tasks and, though you may not be able to solve them immediately, you can position the task in the code, perhaps only with comments about what the task does. Work through the problem with tasks that you imagine can be done. In this way, you bring the program to "life." With the pieces identified, you can now tackle them in isolation.

In this way, you tackle the problem layer by layer, adding more to the onion until you are satisfied. The example at the end of the chapter illustrates this approach.

3.4.6 Stop and Think

At some point in the middle of this process, you need to stop and look at what you have done so far and evaluate your results. It might be that your skeleton is not coming to life as you had hoped. You might have started down a problem-solving path that, now that you are further along, seems like a poor approach. You need to be willing to throw something out if it isn't working. Avoid the dung-beetle approach to programming: rolling a bigger ball of dung by adding more bad code onto existing bad code. Be brave and be willing to throw the bad part away and do it right. Don't be "stiff," and don't bang your head against the wall trying force a solution you thought was correct in the beginning and isn't working anymore.

That is, stop and think.

3.4.7 Relax: Give Yourself a Break

VideoNote 3.1
Algorithm Decomposition

If you work long enough at a difficult problem, you are likely to get stuck at some point. What do you do now? How do you unstick yourself ? One of the best approaches is to walk away, let it go for a while, take a breather, and come back when you are fresh. Letting a problem sit is a way to relax and look at it with fresh eyes later on. Having broken down the problem into smaller pieces makes this step easier—reconnecting with a smaller problem is easier than with a larger problem. Also, you may be able to work for a while on a different piece of the puzzle.

However, if you have left your problem to the last minute, you do not have this step available. Use your time well. Starting late on a program makes everything harder.

3.5 A SIMPLE EXAMPLE

Let's implement the Babylonian square root algorithm to illustrate how to apply some of the ideas presented so far.

First, note the subtle difference in this version when compared to the earlier version. Earlier, we observed that equality between two floating-point values was not precisely defined. In fact, we discussed that a "small enough" difference was good enough. Here we have addressed that issue by introducing a *tolerance*. That is, "different" means that the two values differ by less than some tolerance that we define as "good enough" for our algorithm.

We begin with the requirements:

1. The user provides three inputs: an integer number to find the square of, an integer initial guess, and a floating-point tolerance. All of these inputs are required. When the difference between two successive answers generated by the algorithm differ by a value less than the provided tolerance, the algorithm finishes.
2. Babylonian square root algorithm:
   (a) Guess the square root of the number.
   (b) Divide the number by the guess.
   (c) Average the quotient (from step b) and the guess.
   (d) Make the new guess the average from step (c).
   (e) If the new guess differs from the previous guess by more than the specified tolerance, go back to step (b); otherwise, stop.
3. When the algorithm reaches the finishing condition, output the original conditions (number, guess, tolerance), its square root, and the number of iterations (guesses) required to reach that result.

3.5.1 Build the Skeleton

Let's now try to put together an outline of the program in the form of a skeleton program. There are three parts to the description, so let's start with three parts of the skeleton. We express this skeleton first as comments in English:

```
# get three inputs from the user (two ints, 1 float)

# do the algorithm steps described above

# output the three original values, the number of
# iterations and the square root
```

See, that wasn't too hard. In fact, it was trivial, but that is the point. Start with something you can do. We now have three pieces that can be considered separately.

3.5.2 Output

Which piece should we solve first? Go for the easiest. Let's pick output. Here is an outline of what our code might be:

```
print("Square root of",number," is:",guess)
print("Took ",count," reps to get it to tolerance: ",tolerance)
print("Starting from a guess of:", original_guess)
```

Some of the variables we will use in other parts of the program are first defined here in these output statements. Of course, our program piece won't run yet because those variables have not yet been assigned values. Here is what our program looks like so far:

```
# get three inputs from the user (two ints, 1 float)

# do the algorithm steps described above

# output the three original values, the number of
# iterations and the square root
print("Square root of",number," is:",guess)
print("Took ",count," reps to get it to tolerance: ",tolerance)
print("Starting from a guess of:", original_guess)
```

Notice how we have left out the type suffix. We did that to illustrate a point: let's see what trouble we get into because of that omission.

3.5.3 Input

The input looks like the next easiest task. It will use some of the variables we have already defined, providing them with the values that they presently lack. Properly doing input will require checking whether we are getting the input we want, but we can begin by assuming the input is good initially. That assumption lets us get going and allows us to come back later and solve the input problems more fully. Filling in details later makes solving the problem easier now and allows us to focus better later when only details remain.

For our *first cut*, let's just work with one of the inputs, the number to find the square root of. We'll need to do something similar for the other two numbers, so let's keep it simple by doing one first. That is, simplify first, and then once we get that working, repeat it for the remaining numbers. What we have to do is:

- prompt the user
- turn the resulting string into the appropriate type (here, an integer)

```
number_str = input("Find the square root of integer: ")
number_int = int(number_str)
```

Is that good enough? Yes and no. As long as you expect the user to type only integers in response to the prompt, then it is good enough. However, what if the user mistypes, an "a" instead of a "1"? What will happen? (Try it in the IPython console.) Remember that our goal is to create a *robust* program, one that can respond to even incorrect input. What might we do to deal with this problem? Ultimately, it comes down to checking whether the input, a string in this case, has the kind of information within that we desire. Doing so at this stage is a little beyond our abilities, but it is important to be aware that we have a problem here, and that we will learn how to address it when we learn more about string. For now, we will assume that the user types an integer in response to the prompt. If they do not, the program will halt with an error.

We can repeat the process for the other input, giving good names to the new variables. Note that for the `tolerance_flt` value, we combined the `input` and conversion to *`float`* into one line. We did this by taking the return value of the `input` function and calling the *`float`* function on that return value. This looks like a "function within a function" in the code. It is shorter, but is it more readable? You be the judge. Code is shown in Code Listing 3.4.

Code Listing 3.4

```
# Newton's method to calculate square root

# get three inputs from the user (two ints, 1 float)
# note not robust on bad input
num_str = input("Find the square root of integer: ")
num_int = int(num_str)
guess_str = input("Initial guess: ")
guess_int = int(guess_str)
tolerance_float = float(input("What tolerance: "))

original_guess_int = guess_int # hang onto the original guess
count_int = 0                  # count the number of guesses

# do the algorithm steps as described above

# output the three original values, the number of
# iterations and the square root
print("Square root of",num_int," is: ",guess_int)
print("Took ",count_int," reps to get it to tolerance: ",tolerance_float)
print("Starting from a guess of: ", original_guess_int)
```

Testing the Input Routine

Ah, **Rule 5** again. We need to test what we have, even though it is incomplete. When run, the program should prompt for input and provide some output. No calculations are yet made, so the answers are wrong, but the existing parts do work. Having confirmed that the two provided parts work as required, we can move on to the next step:

```
Find the square root of integer: 16
Initial guess: 2
What tolerance :0.01
Square root of 16  is:  2
```

```
Took  0 reps to get it to tolerance:  0.01
Starting from a guess of:  2

In [1]: runfile('/Users/user/python/file.py', wdir='/Users/user/python')

Find the square root of integer: 16
Initial guess: a
Traceback (most recent call last):
  File "/Users/bill/tpocup/ch03/programs/program4-3.py", line 8, in <module>
    guess_int = int(guess_str)
ValueError: invalid literal for int() with base 10: 'a'
```

Even though our testing is not complete, it looks promising. Note the program does fail with incorrect input.

3.5.4 Doing the Calculation

Now we have two simple parts working: the input and output. Next we need to do the real work: the calculation. Here is the basic algorithm again:

Babylonian square root algorithm:

1. Guess the square root of the number.
2. Divide the number by the guess.
3. Average the quotient (from step 2) and the guess.
4. Make the new guess the average from step 3.
5. If the new guess differs from the previous guess by more than the specified tolerance, go back to step 2; otherwise, stop.

We already have the initial guess, so let's focus next on steps 2, 3, and 4. Those steps are simple enough to write directly from the English in the algorithm. Observe how steps 3 and 4 are combined into one Python statement. Step 3 is on the right-hand side and step 4 is the left-hand side of the statement.

```
quotient = number/guess
guess = (quotient+guess)/2
```

Step 5 tells us to repeat our steps, but how often? Step 5 tells us to keep going if the new guess differs from the old guess by a tolerance. Rephrased, step 5 tells us that while the difference is greater than the tolerance, we keep going. What difference? We calculate the difference between the previous guess and the current guess. The result is:

```
while (previous - guess) > tolerance:
    quotient = number/guess
    guess = (quotient+guess)/2
```

We now have a slight problem because the variable named `previous` does not have a value. We need to get the previous value of the variable named `guess`. In addition, `previous` needs to change every time there is a new guess. A good time to do that is before `guess` gets its new value. Finally, `previous` needs an initial value before we find the difference the first time. An initial value of zero works fine, as there is no "previous" value initially.

```
previous = 0
while (previous - guess) > tolerance:
    previous = guess
    quotient = number/guess
    guess = (quotient+guess)/2
```

Now let's stick that piece of code into the rest of the program. Let's clean up the names a bit as well and add their types to their names (so we can track things better). Note that we need to change `guess` from an *int* to a *float*, and subsequently other variables as well. Take a look at Code Listing 3.5 and see if you can tell why[10]?

Code Listing 3.5

```
# Newton's method to calculate square root

# get three inputs from the user (two ints, 1 float)
# note not robust on bad input
number_str = input("Find the square root of integer: ")
number_int = int(number_str)
guess_str = input("Initial guess: ")
guess_float = float(guess_str)
tolerance_float = float(input("What tolerance: "))

original_guess_float = guess_float # hang onto the original guess
count_int = 0                      # count the number of guesses
previous_float = 0                 # track the previous calculated value

while (previous_float - guess_float) > tolerance_float:
        previous_float = guess_float
        quotient_float = number_int/guess_float
        guess_float = (quotient_float + guess_float)/2
        count_int = count_int + 1

# output the three original values, the number of
# iterations and the square root
print("Square root of",number_int," is: ",guess_float)
print("Took ",count_int," reps to get it to tolerance: ",tolerance_float)
print("Starting from a guess of: ", original_guess_float)
```

[10] Reason:**guess** is going to be updated by division, which always returns a float.

Two output variables that we didn't discuss are handled in the previous code. The first is that we needed a value for the variable `original_guess_flt`. It needs to go right after the conversion of `guess_str` to `guess_flt` so it holds the original value of the guess. We also included `count_int`, which is a count of the number of times through the loop.

Now the program appears to have all the pieces, but does it give us the answers we want? Let's test it:

```
Find the square root of integer: 100
Initial guess: 5
What tolerance: 0.0000001
Square root of 100  is:  5
Took  0  reps to get it to tolerance:  1e-07
Starting from a guess of:  5
```

Hmmm, that isn't very good, is it. What's wrong?

We need to apply some of our debugging strategies discussed in Appendix C. We could set a breakpoint in SPYDER and step through the program, and this is a good strategy. However, perhaps we can solve this by inspection. Where did we go wrong?

Scanning the output for anomalies is a good start. "Took 0 reps to get it to tolerance" sticks out. That means that the main ***while*** loop was never entered. Hmmm.

Let's reason our way through the code one step at a time:

- The input used means that `num_int = 100`, `guess_flt = 5`, and `tolerance_flt = 0.0000001`. There are three reasons to believe that the input part is okay. First, it is simple; second, we output the input as a check; and third, it was tested. By having tested the code previously, we are confident it is correct.
- We can verify by reading that `previous_flt` correctly gets set to 0.
- When the loop is entered, the difference `previous_flt - guess_flt` is −5.0. Is −5.0 > .0000001? No, so the Boolean expression is ***False*** and we never entered our ***while*** loop.

We found a problem!

The negative value in the Boolean expression is causing us a problem. The variables `previous_flt` and `guess_flt` are 5 apart, but the difference is −5.0, which, as it turns out, is less than our tolerance. It would be better for the difference to always be positive. How can a difference always be positive? How about an absolute value function? Such a function would always yield a positive number. Fortunately, Python provides a `abs` function. Note that this issue is essentially the same as the Programming Tip on floating-point equality in Section 2.2.3.

The revised ***while*** loop is now:

```
while abs(previous_flt-guess_flt) > tolerance_flt:
```

Let's test it to see how we are doing.

```
Find the square root of integer: 100
Initial guess: 5
What tolerance: 0.0000001
Square root of 100 is:  10.0
Took  6  reps to get it to tolerance:  1e-07
Starting from a guess of:  5.0
```

That result looks promising. Let's try another:

```
Find the square root of integer: 2
Initial guess: 1
What tolerance :0.0000001
Square root of 2 is:  1.414213562373095
Took  5  reps to get it to tolerance:  1e-07
Starting from a guess of:  1.0
```

That looks good as well.

Here then is the final program (Code Listing 3.6).

Code Listing 3.6

```
# Newton's Method to calculate square root

# get three inputs from the user (two ints, 1 float)
# note not robust on bad input
number_str = input("Find the square root of integer: ")
number_int = int(number_str)
guess_str = input("Initial guess: ")
guess_float = float(guess_str)
tolerance_float = float(input("What tolerance: "))

original_guess_float = guess_float # hang onto the original guess
count_int = 0                      # count the number of guesses
previous_float = 0                 # track the previous calculated value

while abs(previous_float - guess_float) > tolerance_float:
        previous_float = guess_float
        quotient_float = number_int/guess_float
        guess_float = (quotient_float + guess_float)/2
        count_int = count_int + 1

# output the three original values, the number of
# iterations and the square root
```

```
print("Square root of",number_int," is: ",guess_float)
print("Took ",count_int," reps to get it to tolerance: ",tolerance_float)
print("Starting from a guess of: ", original_guess_float)
```

More tested might be needed, but we'll leave that as an exercise for the reader.

VideoNote 3.2
Algorithm Development

Summary

In this chapter, we introduced the concept of an algorithm, especially with respect to the implementation of algorithms in programs. We also discussed some problem-solving techniques. With these two concepts in hand, we can tackle more complex problems.

Algorithms

- An algorithm is a description of how a problem can be solved.
  A program is an implementation of an algorithm.
- An algorithm should be:
  - Detailed
  - Effective
  - Specific
  - General Purpose
- An program should be:
  - Readable
  - Robust
  - Correct

Rules

- **RULE 1:** Think before you program!
- **RULE 2:** A program is a human-readable essay on problem solving that also happens to execute on a computer.
- **RULE 3:** The best way to improve your programming and problem skills is to practice!
- **RULE 4:** A foolish consistency is the hobgoblin of little minds.
- **RULE 5:** Test your code, often and thoroughly!
- **RULE 6:** If it was hard to write, it is probably hard to read. Add a comment.

Exercises

1. Write an algorithm for frying an egg. Test it out with a friend: in a kitchen, read the algorithm and have the friend do *exactly* what you say. How did you do?

2. (Algorithms vs. programs)
   (a) Define algorithm and program.
   (b) In what ways are they the same?
   (c) In what ways are they different?

3. Write an algorithm that will find the sum of the digits in each number between 1 to 350.

4. We mentioned the first fit and best fit as applied to finding parking spaces at a mall.
   (a) Write a first-fit car parking algorithm.
   (b) Write a best-fit car parking algorithm.
   (c) In your own words, explain why first fit might be a better algorithm on average to minimize the time to get to the door of the mall.

5. When you are stuck on creating a program, it helps to stop and think. Can you see what is wrong with the following program? Why is it generating an error?

```
A_int = input('Enter an integer greater than 10: ')
    while A_int > 10:
    A_int = A_int - 1
    print(A_int)
```

PART 3

Data Structures and Functions

CHAPTER 4

Working with Strings

> The basic tool for the manipulation of reality is the manipulation of words.
>
> Phillip K. Dick, author

MUCH OF THE TIME SPENT ON COMPUTERS INVOLVES WORKING WITH WORDS. WE write e-mails and essays, we send text messages and instant messages, we post to blogs, we create Facebook pages, we Google for information, and we read web pages. In programming languages, any sequence of printable characters is referred to as a *string*. The origin of the word is unclear, but Dr. Don Weinshank notes:

> The 1971 OED (p. 3097) quotes an 1891 Century Dictionary on a source in the *Milwaukee Sentinel* of 11 Jan. 1898 (section 3, p. 1) to the effect that this is a compositor's term. Printers would paste up the text that they had generated in a long strip of characters. (Presumably, they were paid by the foot, not by the word!) The quote says that it was not unusual for compositors to create more than 1500 (characters?) per hour.[1]

A sequence of characters is not necessarily a word as we know it, that is, something that we might find in a dictionary. This distinction is particularly useful with computers because a short-cut such as `'brb'` used in instant messaging is a perfectly fine string, but does not appear in most dictionaries. Also, strings are independent of language so `'Gesundheit'` is a legal string. In fact, something nonsensical such as `'good4u2'` also counts as a string. A sequence of characters requires no underlying meaning; it is only a sequence. For us, that is all a string need be.

[1] Humanist Discussion Group, Vol. 5, No. 0883 by Don Weinshank. Published by Don Weinshank, © 1992.

4.1 THE STRING TYPE

The string type is one of the many collection types provided by Python. As first discussed in Section 2.1.5, a collection is a group of Python objects that can be treated as a single object. In particular, a string type is a special kind of collection called a *sequence*. A sequence type has its collection of objects organized in some order—a sequence of objects. A Python string is an object that has, as an attribute, a sequence of characters. A Python string object can be constructed either by using the string constructor `str` or, as a short cut, by encompassing a group of characters in either two single quotes (') or two double quotes (" ").

Examples of string objects are: `'a'`, `"brb"`, `'What is your name?'`. The only requirement is that the quotes on either end of the string match. That is, `'bad string"` is not a good string in Python because it uses a mixture of single and double quotes to create the string.

PROGRAMMING TIP

It is good to decide how you want to delimit strings and then stick with it. If you like double quotes, stick with that. In general, double quotes are a little less trouble, as you can encode possessives and contractions more easily, such as `"bill's"` or `"can't"`. If you try that with single quotes, you need to use the escape character ("\") in front of the apostrophe, such as `'bill\'s'`.

4.1.1 The Triple-Quote String

There is a special kind of string denoted by triple quotes, as in `'''Hello World'''`. This, too, is a string, but it has one special property. This string preserves all the format information of the string. If the string spans multiple lines, those carriage returns between lines are preserved. If there are quotes, tabs, any information at all, it is preserved. In this way, you can capture a whole paragraph as a single string. Here is an example from the "Bright Side of Life" song from the Monty Python movie, *Life of Brian*:

```
song_lyrics_str = '''When you're chewing on life's gristle
                  Don't grumble, give a whistle
                  And this'll help things turn out for the best...

                  And...always look on the bright side of life...
                  Always look on the light side of life...'''
```

The variable `song_lyrics_str`[2] is now associated with a string object with all the formatting of the paragraph preserved.

[2] Zen of Python, Python Software Foundation.

PROGRAMMING TIP

If you have a long, multiline comment that you want to insert, consider using a triple-quoted string. You need provide only the quotes at the beginning and the end of the comment, unlike using the # at the beginning of every line.

4.1.2 Nonprinting Characters

Some characters perform necessary operations, but show up as "whitespace" in the output. The two most common examples are the tab and the carriage return. We need to represent them, so the backslash character is combined with another character for that purpose. See Table 4.1. Here is a session illustrating the use of \n when printing a string.

```
In  [1]: print(" first line \n second line")
 first line
 second line
```

carriage return	\n
tab	\t

TABLE 4.1 Common nonprinting characters.

4.1.3 String Representation

What is the difference between a string and other Python types? For example, what is the difference between the integer 1 and the string `'1'`? One answer is obvious: they are different types! As we have discussed previously, the type of an object determines both the attributes of an object and the kinds of operations that can be performed on the object. A string is a collection type that has multiple parts. In contrast, an integer is the representation of a number. Integers are created with the constructor `int` or with a number (without decimal points); strings are created with the constructor `str` or by enclosing characters with a pair of quotes. Just as important as its creation, the type of an object determines much of what you can do with that object.

Single character strings, like all other data, are represented in a computer as numbers. When you type on your keyboard, the individual characters are stored in a special computer representation know as Unicode (UTF-8 is the Unicode default for Python 3). UTF-8, and any Unicode set in general, maps each character to an integer. By "map", we mean that in the UTF-8 set, each character is associated with a particular integer value. That integer is what gets stored in a computer, and Python labels its type as string. Because that integer is stored as a string type, Python knows how to map that integer to a particular character in the UTF-8 character set. Take a look at the UTF-8 character mapping shown in Appendix F.

Note that, at least within the groups of lowercase letters, uppercase letters and numbers, the *order* of the characters is as you would expect: `'a'` comes before `'b'`, `'1'` before `'2'` and so on. This ordering is useful for string comparison (see Section 4.2.3).

You can experiment with the mapping yourself. Python provides two special functions—`ord` and `chr`—to capture the relationship between UTF-8 and a character. The `ord` function shows the UTF-8 integer associated with a character. For example, `ord('a')` yields a value 97 because `'a'` is associated with 97 in the UTF-8 table. Similarly, the `chr` function takes an integer and yields the character associated with that integer in the UTF-8 table. Thus `chr(97)` yields the value `'a'` because `'a'` is associated with the integer 97 in the UTF-8 table.

4.1.4 Strings as a Sequence

We defined string objects as a sequence of characters. Therefore, `'Hello World'` is a sequence of 11 characters—remember that a space is a character. Because a sequence has an order, we can number the characters by their position in the sequence, as shown in Figure 4.1.

characters	H	e	l	l	o		W	o	r	l	d
index	0	1	2	3	4	5	6	7	8	9	10
									...	−2	−1

FIGURE 4.1 The index values for the string 'Hello World'.

This position is called the *index* of the character within the string. In Python, and other programming languages as well, the first index (the first position) in a sequence is index *0*. Starting the counting at zero feels strange at first, but you will get used to it.

Python lets us look at the individual characters in the string sequence using the *indexing* operator, represented by the square brackets operator [ ]. The integer in the brackets represents an index of the associated string, and returns the single character string at that index. An example of its use is `'Hello World'[0]`. The string associated with the square brackets is `'Hello World'`. The integer in between the square brackets, 0, indicating the single character string at index position 0, in this case `'H'`.

It is important to remember that indices start at 0. Thus `'Hello World'[4]` is the character at index position 4, which is the fifth element in the sequence: the single character string `'o'`.

Python also allows indexing from the back *end* of the sequence. Thus, if you want to index from the end of a string, Python can index the last character of the string with −1 and subtracts one from the index for each character to the left. Thus, the index numbers get smaller (-2, -3, -4) as you move towards the beginning of the string. Looking again at Figure 4.1, notice that −1 is the last character in the string, −2 is the second to last, and so forth.

The following session illustrates indexing. This session also shows how an index that is out of the range for the string generates an error:

```
In [1]: hello_str = "Hello World"
In [2]: hello_str
Out [2]: 'Hello World'

In [3]: hello_str[0] # counting starts at zero
Out [3]: 'H'

In [4]: hello_str[5]
Out [4]: ' '

In [5]: hello_str[-1] # negative index works back from the end
Out [5]: 'd'

In [6]: hello_str[10]
Out [6]: 'd'

In [7]: hello_str[11]
Traceback (most recent call last):
  File "<pyshell#19>", line 1, in <module>
    hello_str[11]
IndexError: string index out of range
```

PROGRAMMING TIP

What does "out of range" mean? A particular string is a fixed sequence of characters and thus has a fixed sequence of indicies. If the index provided within the square brackets operator is outside of this fixed range of indicies, Python generates an error as it is unclear what character the index represents. It is a very common error! Make sure the index you ask for exists in the string you are examining.

4.1.5 More Indexing and Slicing

Indexing in Python allows you to indicate more than just a single character string. You can also select *subsequences* of the string with the proper indicies. Python calls such a sub-sequence a *slice*. Remember, just like for a single index, a slice returns a new string and does not change the original string in any way (even though *slice* sounds like it would!).

To index a subsequence, you indicate a *range* of indicies within the square bracket by providing a pair of indices separated by a colon (:). The colon (:) within the index operator brackets indicates that instead of a single position being selected, a range of indices is being selected. Python uses a *half-open* range as we discussed in the context of the `range` function in

Section 2.2.13. A half-open range designates the beginning of the sequence that *is* included in the result along with an end of the sequence that *is not* included. For `hello_str[6:10]` the range indicates a subsequence consisting of the strings at indices 6, 7, 8, and 9. The string at index 10 is *not* included. The result returned is the string `'Worl'`, as shown in Figure 4.2 and displayed in the following section.

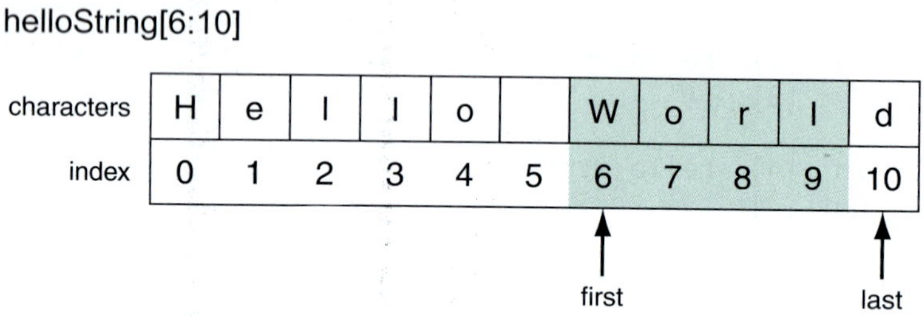

FIGURE 4.2 Indexing subsequences with slicing.

```
In  [1]: hello_str[6:10]
Out [1]: 'Worl'
```

Every range can be specified with two values: the beginning index of the range and end index of the range, separated by a colon (:). If a value on either side of the colon is missing, a *default* is used in place of the missing value. If the first index is missing, the index before the colon (:), Python assumes the start index is the beginning of the string, that is, index 0. If the last index is missing, the value after the colon (:), Python assumes the end of the sequence *including* the last character.

Look at the examples in Figure 4.3. The `hello_str[6:]` expression specifies a subsequence beginning at index 6 and continuing through the end of the string. In this case,

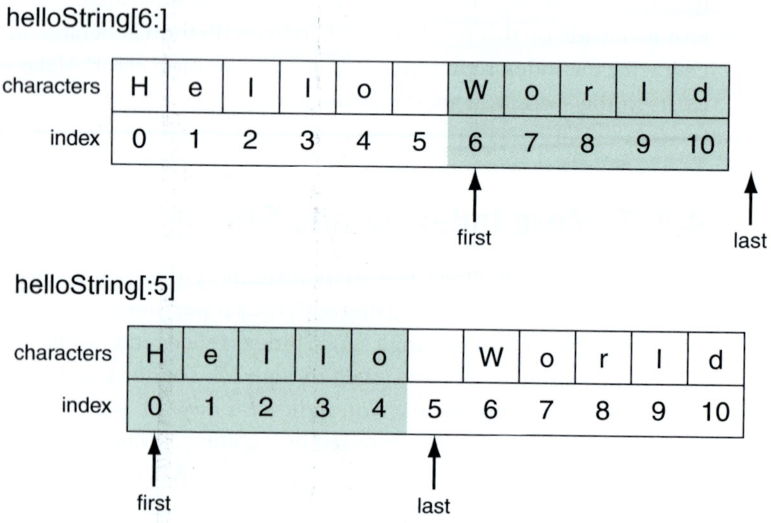

FIGURE 4.3 Two default slice examples.

the result is `'World'`. The same result can be achieved using `hello_str[6:11]`. The 11 is acceptable to specify the end of the sequence, as the second number indicates the index *after* the last element.

Similarly, in Figure 4.3, `hello_str[:5]` is the subsequence from the beginning of the string up to, but not including, the character at index 5. The same result is obtained with the expression `hello_str[0:5]`. Both expressions yield the subsequence `'Hello'`.

Knowing that the end of a sequence is specified as one *after* the end of the desired sequence helps make sense of the negative index. The negative index means that if the end marker is one more than the last index, the −1 (to the left) of that end marker is the last index, −2 the second to last, and so forth. Figure 4.4 shows the negative indices.

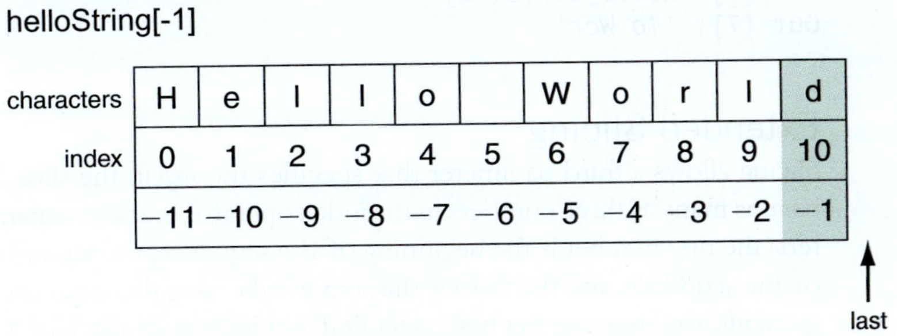

FIGURE 4.4 Negative indices.

Let's put this all together. Consider `hello_str[3:-2]`, which specifies the range starting at index 3 and ends three characters from the end resulting in the subsequence `'lo Wor'`. See Figure 4.5.

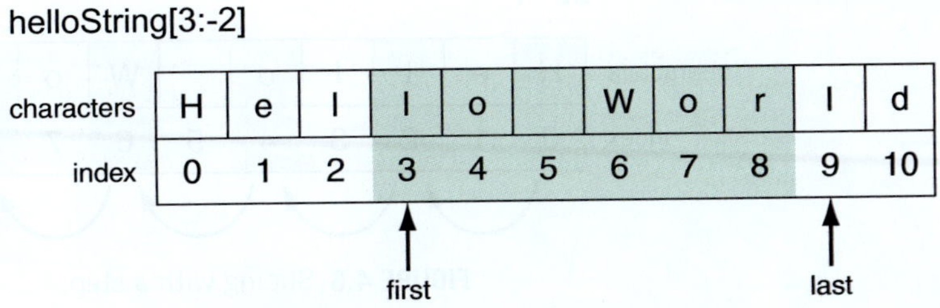

FIGURE 4.5 Another slice example.

In summary, here are the slicing operations we mentioned as they appear in the Python shell:

```
In  [1]: hello_str = "Hello World"
In  [2]: hello_str[6:11]
Out [2]: 'World'
```

```
In  [3]: hello_str[6:] # no ending value defaults to the end of string
Out [3]: 'World'

In  [4]: hello_str[:5] # no start value defaults to beginning of string
Out [4]: 'Hello'

In  [5]: hello_str[0:5]
Out [5]: 'Hello'

In  [6]: hello_str[-1] # negative index works back from the end
Out [6]: 'd'

In  [7]: hello_str[3:-2]
Out [7]: 'lo Wor'
```

Extended Slicing

Slicing allows a third parameter that specifies the *step* in the slice. This means that you can have as many as three numbers in the index operator brackets separated by two colon characters: the first number is the beginning of the sequence, the second number specifies the end of the sequence, and the third is the step to take *along* the sequence. As with the first two arguments, the step number has a default if not indicated: a step of 1. The step value indicates the step size through the sequence. For example, in the expression `'Hello World'[::2]`, we are indicating a subsequence from the beginning to the end of the sequence but, given a step size of 2, only every other character is specified. The expression would yield a new string `'HloWrd'`. Similarly, a step of 3 yields every third character. Figure 4.6 shows how a step of 2 works.

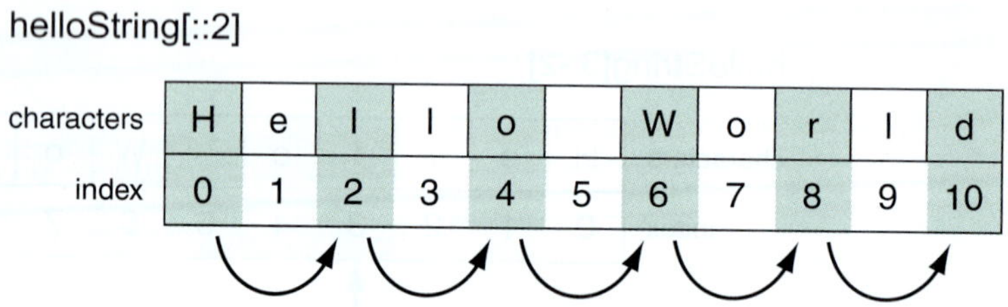

FIGURE 4.6 Slicing with a step.

One odd variation that is not immediately obvious is to use a step of −1. Python interprets a *negative* step number as stepping backwards. The following session demonstrates the use of a step:

```
In  [1]: hello_str = "Hello World"
In  [2]: hello_str[::2] # every other letter in the slice
Out [2]: 'HloWrd'
```

```
In  [3]: hello_str[::3] # every third letter
Out [3]: 'HlWl'

In  [4]: hello_str[::-1] # step backwards from the end to the beginning
Out [4]: 'dlroW olleH'

In  [5]: hello_str[::-2] # backwards, every other letter
Out [5]: 'drWolH'
```

An interesting application of the step can be seen by using a string of digits. Different steps and different starting points yield even, odd, or reversed digits, as shown in this session:

```
In  [1]: digits = "0123456789"
In  [2]: digits[::2] # even digits (default start at 0;skip every other)
Out [2]: '02468'

In  [3]: digits[1::2] # odd digits (start at 1; skip every other)
Out [3]: '13579'

In  [4]: digits[::-1] # reverse digits
Out [4]: '9876543210'

In  [5]: digits[::-2] # reverse odds
Out [5]: '97531'

In  [6]: digits[-2::-2] # reverse evens (start with 2nd last letter)
Out [6]: '86420'
```

Copy Slice

A common slicing application is the *copy slice*. If the programmer provides neither a beginning nor an end—that is, there is only a colon character in the square brackets([:])—a complete copy of the string is made. If you think about this, it is clear why. The [:] slice takes both defaults, from the beginning through the end of the string. This feature is illustrated in the following session:

```
In  [1]: name_one = 'Monty'
In  [2]: name_two = name_one[:]
In  [3]: name_two
Out [3]: 'Monty'
```

Remember, a new string is yielded as the result of a slice; the original string is not modified. Thus, a copy slice is indeed a new copy of the original string.

4.1.6 Strings Are Iterable

We saw the first discussion of what it means to be iterable in the context of the *range* function in Section 2.2.13. A data type that is iterable means that the individual elements can be "iterated through" using a ***for*** loop (or other methods). A string is indeed an iterable data type and you can iterate through the individual elements of a string using a ***for*** loop. Because strings are also a sequence, iteration through a string yields the elements of the string in the order in which they appear in the string. See the following session:

```
In  [1]: for char in 'Hi mom':
         print(char, type(char))

H <class 'str'>
i <class 'str'>
  <class 'str'>
m <class 'str'>
o <class 'str'>
m <class 'str'>
```

As with *range*, the ***for*** assigns each individual element of the string, one at a time, to the variable `char` and prints them out. In this session example, we also printed is the type of the object associated with `char`, which is of course type *str*.

Iterating through the elements of a collection (string in this case) is a very common operation in Python, one which you will see again and again.

Check Yourself: Slicing Check

1. Answer the questions for the following program.

```
user_str = "aabbcc"
sub_str1 = user_str[2:]
sub_str2 = user_str[1:4]
sub_str3 = user_str[1: :2]
sub_str4 = user_str[:-2]
print(sub_str1)     # Line 1
print(sub_str2)     # Line 2
print(sub_str3)     # Line 3
print(sub_str4)     # Line 4
index_int = 0
print(user_str[index_int],user_str[index_int+2]) # Line 5
```

(a) What output is produced by Line 1?
(b) What output is produced by Line 2?
(c) What output is produced by Line 3?
(d) What output is produced by Line 4?
(e) What output is produced by Line 5?

4.2 STRING OPERATIONS

Strings can utilize some of the same binary operators that integers and floating-point numbers use, though the functions these operators perform is quite different.

4.2.1 Concatenation (+) and Repetition (*)

The + and the * operators can be used with string objects. However, their meanings are not what you are used to with integers and floats:

+ : concatenate. The operator + requires two string objects and creates a new string object. The new string object is formed by concatenating copies of the two string objects together: the first string joined at its end to the beginning of the second string.

*** : repeat.** The * takes a string object and an integer and creates a new string object. The new string object has as many copies of the string as is indicated by the integer.

The following session shows some examples:

```
In  [1]: my_str = "Hello"
In  [2]: your_str = "World"
In  [3]: my_str + your_str # concatenation
Out [3]: 'HelloWorld'

In  [4]: your_str + my_str # order does matter in concatenation
Out [4]: 'WorldHello'
In  [5]: my_str + ' ' + your_str # add a space between
Out [5]: 'Hello World'

In  [6]: my_str * 3 # replication
Out [6]: 'HelloHelloHello'

In  [7]: 3 * my_str # order does not matter in replication
Out [7]: 'HelloHelloHello'

In  [8]: (my_str + ' ')*3 # parentheses force ordering
Out [8]: 'Hello Hello Hello '

In  [9]: my_str + ' ' * 3 # without parentheses: repeats 3 spaces
Out [9]: 'Hello   '

In  [10]: my_str
Out [10]: 'Hello'

In  [11]: your_str # original strings unchanged
Out [11]: 'World'
```

```
In [12]: 'hello' + 3 # wrong types for concatenation, requires two strings
Traceback (most recent call last):
  File "<stdin>", line 1, in <module>
TypeError: Can't convert 'int' object to str implicitly
In [13]: 'hello' * 'hello' # wrong types for replication: requires string and int
Traceback (most recent call last):
  File "<stdin>", line 1, in <module>
TypeError: can't multiply sequence by non-int of type 'str'
```

A couple of points of interest:

- Both the + and * create new string objects and do not affect the strings in the expression. That is, `a_str + 'a'` does not change the contents of `a_str`. Neither does `a_str * 3`.
- In concatenation, there is no space introduced between the end of the first and the beginning of the second string, unless you include it explicitly.
- The order of the two string objects *does* matter in concatenation. The first string shows up at the beginning of the new string object; the second string at the end. Changing the order changes the order the strings occur in the new string object.
- The order of the string and integer in replication *does not* matter.
- The types needed for each operator are very specific. For concatenation, you need two string objects. For replication, you need one string and one integer. No other combinations of types are allowed for each operator.

4.2.2 Determining When + Indicates Addition or Concatenation?

How does Python know whether to do concatenation or addition when it sees a + operator? The answer is that the *types* of the operands indicate the operation to be performed.

In general, the fact that a single operator can perform multiple tasks is called *operator overloading*. By overloading, we mean that a single operator, such as +, will perform different operations depending on the types of its operands.

When the Python interpreter sees a + operator, it examines the types of the operands. If the operands are numbers (integers or floating-point numbers), the interpreter will perform addition. If the operands are strings, the interpreter will perform concatenation. If the operands are a mixture of numbers and strings, the Python interpreter will generate an error. Python can dynamically (as it runs) examine the types of objects associated with variables. In this way, it knows the types of operands, and so it can determine which operation to perform. As a result, Python also knows what operations it can and cannot perform! If you give a Python operator a combination of types it does not have an operation for, it generates an error.

The `type` Function

You can also check the type of any object using the `type` function (as shown in Section 1.6). As we showed, the `type` function returns the type associated with any object. Like the *`int`* type for integers, a string has an associated type, *`str`*.

```
In [1]: my_str = 'Hello'
In [2]: type(my_str) # what type of object is associated with my_str
Out [2]: str

In [3]: my_str = 245 # bad variable name
In [4]: type(my_str)
Out [4]: int

In [5]: type(3.14159)
Out [5]: float
```

We can help the reader of a program keep track of types by including the type in the objects name, for example, `my_str` as we have been doing. By using that protocol, a human reader who sees `my_str + your_str` knows that `+` is supposed to mean concatenation.

4.2.3 Comparison Operators

Similarly, you can use the comparison operators we use with numbers to compare strings. However, the meaning of the comparison operators are, again, a little different from the operators with integers.

Single-Character String Compares

Let's first consider single-character strings. You can compare two, single-character strings using the equality operator ==, as in `'a' == 'a'`. If the two single characters are the same, the expression returns *`True`*. Note that the expression `'a' == 'A'` returns *`False`* as those are indeed two different strings.

What about the greater than (>) or less than (<) operators? The easy example would be `'a' > 'a'`, which is obviously *`False`*. What is the result of `'a' > 'A'`? If you type it into the shell, you will get the result *`True`*. Why? We introduced the functions `ord` and `chr` in Section 4.1.3. These two functions help us relate a character and its integer representation in the Unicode UTF-8 table. All comparisons between two single characters are done on the basis of their UTF-8 integer mapping. When we compare `'a' > 'A'`, Python fetches the associated UTF-8 number for both characters and compares those two numbers. Because `ord('a')` is 97 and `ord('A')` is 65, the question becomes whether `97 > 65`, which yields *`True`*. Conveniently, the lowercase letters are all sequentially ordered so that `'a' < 'b'`, `'b' < 'c'`, and so on. Similarly, the capital letters are sequentially ordered so that `'A' < 'B'`, `'B' < 'C'`, and so on. Finally, the numeric characters are also ordered so that `'0' < '1'`, `'1' < '2'`, and so on. However, only the run of lowercase, uppercase, and numeric strings follow the assumed order. It is also `True` that `'0' < 'a'` and `'A' < 'a'`. If you wonder about character ordering, the UTF-8 table (Appendix F) or the associated functions `ord` and `chr` should resolve the question.

Comparing Strings with More Than One Character

When strings with more than one character are compared, the process is slightly more complicated, though still based on the concept of a character's UTF-8 number.

String comparison—in fact, any sequence comparison—works as follows. The basic idea is to, in parallel, examine both string characters at some index and then walk through both strings until a difference in characters is found.

1. Start at index 0, the beginning of both strings.
2. Compare the two, single characters at the present index of each each string.
    - If the two characters are equal, increase the present index of both strings by 1 and go back to the beginning of step 2.
    - If the two characters are not equal, return the result of comparing those two characters as the result of the string comparison.
3. If both strings are equal up to some point but one is shorter than the other, then the longer string is always greater. For example, `'ab' < 'abc'` returns `True`.

The following session shows some examples:

```
In [1]: 'abc' < 'cde' # different at index 0, 'a' < 'c'
Out [1]: True

In [2]: 'abc' < 'abd' # different at index 2, 'c' < 'd'
Out [2]: True

In [3]: 'abc' < 'abcd' # 'abc' equal up to 'd' but shorter than 'abcd'
Out [3]: True

In [4]: '' < 'a' # the empty string's length is 0, always smaller
Out [4]: True
```

The empty string ('') is always less than any other string because it is the only string of length 0. It is an interesting challenge to write a string comparison algorithm using only single-character compares. See the exercises.

4.2.4 The *in* Operator

The `in` operator is useful for checking membership in a collection. An example of its use is: `'a' in 'abcd'`. The operator takes two arguments: the collection we are testing and the element for which we are looking for in the collection. As it applies to strings, the operator tests to see if a substring is an element of a string. As it is a membership check, it returns a Boolean value to indicate whether the first argument is a member of (can be found in) the second argument. For the previous example, the return value is `True`. The test string sequence must be found *exactly*. For example in `'ab' in 'acbd'`, the question being asked is whether the exact sequence `'ab'` occurs anywhere in the string. For this example, the return value is `False`. Like most of these operators, `in` can be used with other collections, in which the interpretation of membership depends on the collection type. Here is a session showing some ways to use the `in` operator:

```
In  [1]: vowels = 'aeiou'
In  [2]: 'a' in vowels
Out [2]: True

In  [3]: 'x' in vowels
Out [3]: False

In  [4]: 'eio' in vowels
Out [4]: True

In  [5]: 'aiu' in vowels
Out [5]: False

In  [6]: if 'e' in vowels:
        print("it's a vowel")

it's a vowel
```

4.2.5 String Collections Are Immutable

Given that a string is a collection—a sequence in fact—it is tempting to try the following kind of operation: create a string and then try to change a particular character in that string to a new character. In Python, that would look something like the following session:

```
In  [1]: my_str = 'Hello'
In  [2]: my_str[0] = 'J' # change 'H' to 'J', make the string 'Jello'
Traceback (most recent call last):
  File "<stdin>", line 1, in <module>
TypeError: 'str' object does not support item assignment
```

What is wrong? The problem is a special characteristic of some collections in Python. The string type, as well as some other types, are *immutable*. This means that once the object is created, usually by assignment, its contents cannot be modified. Having an index expression on the left side of an assignment statement is an attempt to do exactly that—change one of the elements of the string sequence. Such a modification is not allowed with the string type.

Check Yourself: String Comparison Check

1. Answer the questions for the following program:

```
my_str = input("Input a string: ")
index_int = 0
result_str = ''  # empty string
while index_int < (len(my_str) - 1):    # Line 1
    if my_str[index_int] > my_str[index_int + 1]:
        result_str = result_str + my_str[index_int]
    else:
        result_str = result_str * 2
    index_int += 1                      # Line 2
print(result_str)                       # Line 3
```

(a) What output is produced by Line 3 on the input 'abc' using the example program?
(b) What output is produce by Line 3 on the input 'cba' using the example program?
(c) What output is produce by Line 3 on the input 'cab' using the example program?
(d) What happens if Line 2 is removed?
(e) What happens if Line 1 is modified to `while index_int < len(my_str):`?

There are some efficiency reasons for this restriction. By making strings immutable, the Python interpreter is faster. However, immutable strings are an advantage for the programmer as well. No matter what you do to a string, you are guaranteed that the original string is *not* changed. By definition, it cannot be changed; it is immutable. As a result, all Python string operators must generate a *new* string. Once you create a string, you cannot change it. You must create a new string to reflect any changes you desire.

How, then, to solve the problem of "changing" a string? For example, how can I change the string `'Hello'` into the string `'Jello'`? The approach is to create a new string `'Jello'` from the existing string `my_str` (associated with the string object `'Hello'`). We do so by concatenating `'J'` to the front of a slice from `my_str`. The slice `my_str[:1]` is a new string object `'ello'`. If we concatenate the two strings, we get the desired result `'Jello'`.

For example, consider the following session:

```
In [1]: my_str = 'Hello'
In [2]: my_str = 'J' + my_str[1:] # create new string with 'J' and a slice
In [3]: my_str # my_str is now associated with the new string
Out [3]: 'Jello'
```

4.3 A PREVIEW OF FUNCTIONS AND METHODS

Here we take a brief look at **methods**, which are a variation on functions as used by Python data structures and, in particular, how they work with strings. For more information on functions, please visit Chapter 5.

4.3.1 A String Method

As mentioned, *method* is a variation on a function. A method shares a number of characteristics with a function. A method has a name and it has a list of arguments in parentheses. It differs, however, in the way it is invoked. Every method is called in *conjunction* with a particular object. The kinds of methods that can be used in conjunction with an object depends on the object's type. String objects have a set of methods suited for strings, they do not work with other objects. The invocation is done using what is called the *dot notation*. An example would be the string type `upper` method. An example invocation would be `'A String'.upper()`. In this case, the object, the string `'A String'` is calling the associated method `upper`. This method takes the associated object and creates a new string where all the letters are converted to uppercase, in this case the string object `'A STRING'`. The interpretation of this invocation, in plain English, would be something like: The object `'A String'` is calling the method `upper` on itself to create a new string, an uppercase version of the calling object. An example session for the method `upper` is shown here:

```
In  [1]: my_str = 'Python rules!'
In  [2]: my_str.upper()
Out [2]: 'PYTHON RULES!'
```

The calling object may be just an object, such as `'A STRING'` above, or a variable associated with an object such as `my_str`. There are reasons to have methods as separate from functions—concepts that we will cover in Chapter 11. In general, a method is invoked using "dot notation".

An example string method with arguments would be the `find` method. The `find` method's task is to locate a substring within the calling string (the object that invoked the method using the dot notation). The `find` method returns the index of the substring in the string where the substring *first* occurs (if there are multiple occurrences), but returns −1 if the substring is not found. As an example, let us try to find the character `'m'` in the string `'mellow yellow'`. We could do so by invoking the find method: `'mellow yellow'.find('m')`. In this method call, the object `'mellow yellow'` is invoking the `find` method, passing a single argument `'m'` as the search target. Note that the string object `'mellow yellow'` is the string to be searched by `find`, and is part of the invocation, the left part of the dot notation. The `'m'` character is first found is at index 0, which is the value returned by `find` (remember that indexing starts at zero). A search for `'ll'` returns 2, which is the position of the first (leftmost) substring `find` discovered (another is at index 9).

When find searches for 'z', that substring will not be found and find returns −1. Python offers an alternative method index that works like find, but returns an error if the argument is not in the string. Sometimes it is nice to get −1 returned; other times, it is useful to generate an error (see how to handle errors in Chapters 6 and 14).

```
In  [1]: my_str = 'mellow yellow'
In  [2]: my_str.find('m')
Out [2]: 0

In  [3]: my_str.find('ll')
Out [3]: 2

In  [4]: my_str.find('z')
Out [4]: -1

In  [5]: my_str.index('ll') # alternative method
Out [5]: 2

In  [6]: my_str.index('z')
Traceback (most recent call last):

  File "<ipython-input-13-dc1c379f4053>", line 1, in <module>
    my_str.index('z')

ValueError: substring not found
```

It is interesting to think about why the find method returns a −1 in the case of not finding the substring argument in the calling object. Why wouldn't it just return 0, which is synonymous with the value *False*? Look at the example above. A successful search *might* return a 0 as the location of a successful search, the first character of the calling object! For this reason, one must be careful when using find in a Boolean expression.

Chaining of Methods

A powerful feature of the Python language is that methods and functions can be *chained*, meaning there are a series of "dot notation" invocations such as 'A string'.upper().find('S'). The calls are chained in the sense that an object returned from one method can be used as the calling object in another method. The rule for the order of invocation is to proceed from left to right, using the resulting object of the previous method as the calling object in the next method. In our example, we first call the method'A string'.upper(), which produces the new string object 'A STRING'. That new object now becomes the calling object for the next method, the invocation 'A STRING'.find('S'). This expression yields the value 2, the index of the `'S'`. Another example is shown in the session below.

```
In  [1]: my_str = 'Python rules!'
In  [2]: my_str.upper()
Out [2]: 'PYTHON RULES!'

In  [3]: my_str.upper().find('O') # convert to uppercase and then 'find'
Out [3]: 4
```

Optional Arguments

Some methods have additional optional arguments. If the argument is not provided, a *default* for that argument is assumed. The default value depends on the method. However, you can choose to provide that argument and override the default. The `find` method is one with default arguments. You can start the find process from an index other than zero, the leftmost index. By default, `find` starts at index 0, but if you provide a second argument, that second argument is the index where the find process will begin.

Consider the assignment `a_str = 'He had the bat.'` in which you want to find `'t'`. The call `a_str.find('t')` will return 7, the index of the leftmost `'t'`. If you provide 8 as the second argument, you will start your search at index 8 and find the next `'t'`—that is, `a_str.find('t',8)` returns 13. The `find` method also has a third optional argument, the index where searching stops. The default is the end of the string, but if you provide the third argument, `find` will stop its search at that index. Thus, `a_str.find('t',1,6)` searches for `'t'` in the index range 1–6, which returns a −1 value (it is not found in the given range).

Nesting of Methods

You can also use method and function invocations as arguments to another method call. This kind of "method in a method" is called *nesting.* The rule for nested calls is that all invocations *inside* parentheses, such as those found in a function invocation, are done first. For example, how could you find the second occurrence of a substring. You do so by nesting one call of `find` as an argument of a `find` invocation in the following way. Suppose you wish to find the *second* `'t'`. The first step is to find the first `'t'`. The second step begins with a search (a second invocation of `find`) starting from one past the location where the first `'t'` is found. That is, find the index of the first `'t'`, add 1 to that index, and use that value as the starting point for a search for the second `'t'`. That is,

```
a_string.find('t', a_string.find('t')+1)
```

The nested method invocation is called first, yielding 7 + 1 = 8. The outer invocation then begins by searching for `'t'` starting at position 8. A session illustrating this process follows:

```
In  [1]: a_str = 'He had the bat.'
In  [2]: a_str.find('t') # look for 't' starting at beginning
Out [2]: 7

In  [3]: a_str.find('t',8) # start at index 8 = 7 + 1
Out [3]: 13

In  [4]: a_str.find('t',a_str.find('t')+1) # start at one after the first 't'
Out [4]: 13
```

4.3.2 Determining Method Names and Method Arguments

How can you determine the methods associated with a type, and once you find the name, how can you determine the arguments?

Your iPython console to the rescue!

You can ask iPython to show you all the potential methods for an object. Your iPython will show all the methods available for an object of that type if you type the object (or a variable of that type), the dot (.), and then a tab character. Your iPython will respond by providing a list of all the potential methods that can be invoked with an object of that type, as shown in Figure 4.7.

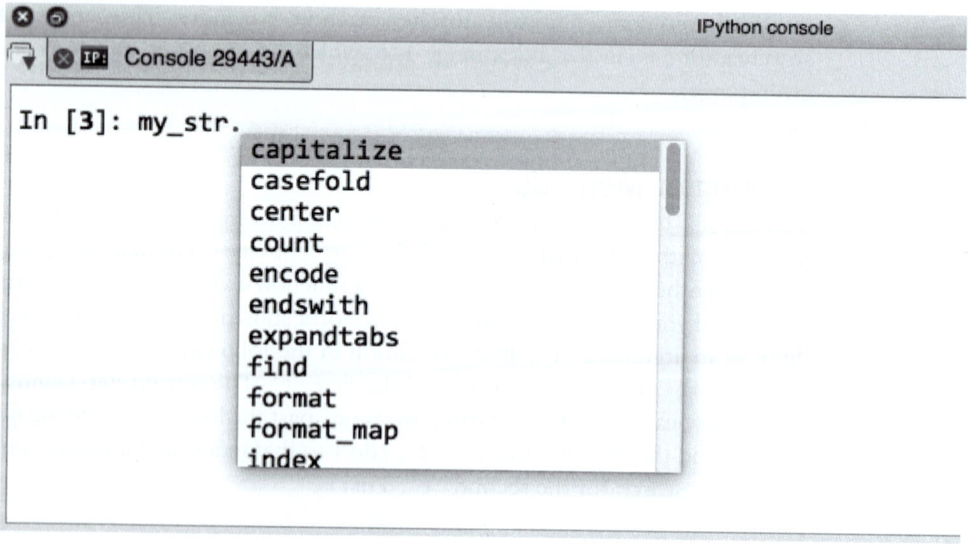

FIGURE 4.7 In your IDE, tab lists potential methods. [Screenshot from Python. Copyright © by Python. Used by permission of Python.]

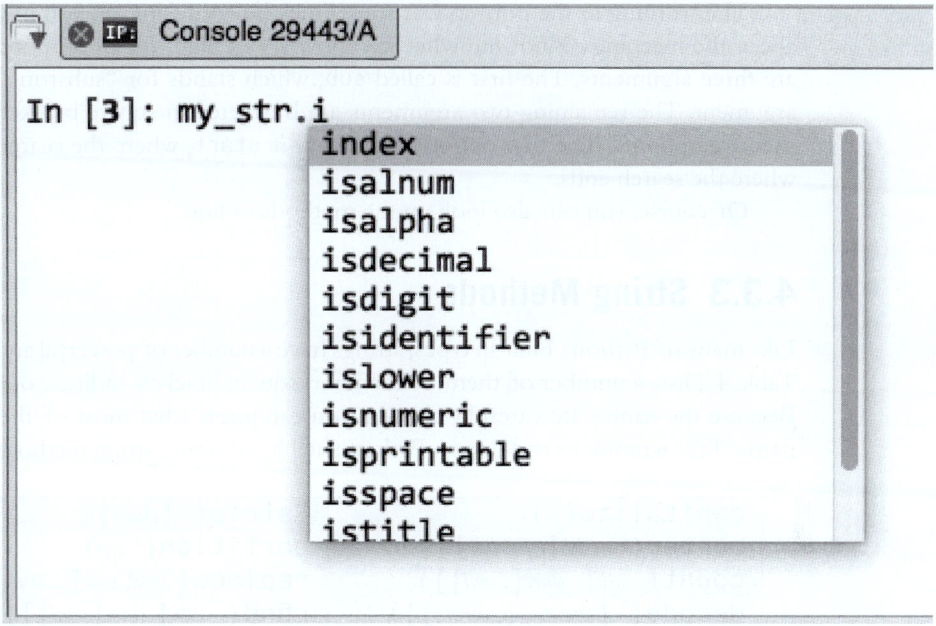

FIGURE 4.8 In iPython, tab lists potential methods, with leading letter. [Screenshot from Python. Copyright © by Python. Used by permission of Python.]

Because the variable `my_str` is associated with a string object, all the string methods are listed in alphabetical order. Note that `find` method is listed, as well as a number of other methods. If one provides the leading letter, for example `'i'`, before the tab is typed, then the list begins with the first method that begins with `'i'`, as shown Figure 4.8.

Once the `object.method_name` is typed, if you type the first parenthesis and wait just a moment, the list of arguments is also provided. The `find` function is shown in Figure 4.9.

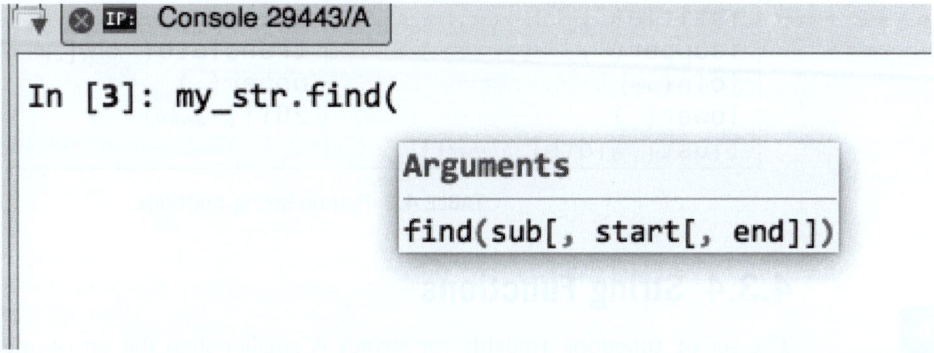

FIGURE 4.9 Your IDE pop-up provides help with function arguments. [Screenshot from Python. Copyright © by Python. Used by permission of Python.]

The wording in the pop-up can sometimes be confusing, so you might have to think about the meanings. Knowing what we know about find, the pop-up indicates that there are three arguments. The first is called sub, which stands for "substring." It is a required argument. The remaining two arguments are bracketed in square brackets, indicating that they are optional. The first optional argument is start, where the search starts, and end, where the search ends.

Of course, you can also look up the methods online.

4.3.3 String Methods

Like many of Python's built-in types, strings have a number of powerful and useful methods. Table 4.2 lists a number of them. Remember: square brackets indicate optional arguments. Because the names are carefully chosen, you can guess what most of them do from their name. Take a moment and open a Python shell to try some string methods. Experiment!

capitalize( )	lstrip([*chars*])
center(*width*[, *fillchar*])	partition(*sep*)
count(*sub*[, *start*[, *end*]])	replace(*old, new*[, *count*])
decode([*encoding*[, *errors*]])	rfind(*sub* [,*start*[,*end*]])
encode([*encoding*[,*errors*]])	rindex(*sub*[, *start*[, *end*]])
endswith(*suffix*[, *start*[, *end*]])	rjust(*width*[, *fillchar*])
expandtabs([*tabsize*])	rpartition(*sep*)
find(*sub*[, *start*[, *end*]])	rsplit([*sep* [,*maxsplit*]])
index(*sub*[, *start*[, *end*]])	rstrip([*chars*])
isalnum( )	split([*sep* [,*maxsplit*]])
isalpha( )	splitlines([*keepends*])
isdigit( )	startswith(*prefix*[, *start*[, *end*]])
islower( )	strip([*chars*])
isspace( )	swapcase( )
istitle( )	title( )
isupper( )	translate(*table*[, *deletechars*])
join(*seq*)	upper( )
lower( )	zfill(*width*)
ljust(width[, *fillchar*])	

TABLE 4.2 Python string methods.

4.3.4 String Functions

VideoNote 4.1
Playing with Strings

The set of functions available for strings is smaller than the set of methods, and those functions are generally common to other sequence types. You have seen only len so far, but you will see others later.

4.4 FORMATTED OUTPUT FOR STRINGS

Using the default ***print*** function is easy, but it provides no control of what is called the *format* of the output. By format, we mean a low-level kind of typesetting to better control how the output looks on the console. Python provides a finer level of control that gives us, the programmer, the option to provide "prettier," more readable, output. Conveniently, the control of console typesetting is done through the use of the string `format` method. The basic form of the `format` method is shown below.

```
"format string".format(data1, data2, ...)
```

The process of creating formatted output can be a bit complicated. In fact, there is enough detail to the formatting process that the Python 3 documentation refers to it as a "mini language" (Python 3 docs: 7.1.3.1. Format Specification Mini-Language). However, like many things in Python, we can learn a little about formatting and "grow into it" as we need more.

As with all strings, use of the `format` method creates a new string. The *format string*, the string that is used to call the `format` method, provides a normal, everyday string that is the "source" for the new string. Everything in that format string will be reproduced exactly in the new string (same spacing, same characters) with one important exception. The programmer can insert special character sequences, enclosed in braces ({}), in the format string that indicate a kind substitution that should occur at that position in the new string. The substitution is driven by the arguments provided in the `format` method. The objects in the arguments will be placed in the new string at the indicated position, as well as *how* it will be placed in the string at that position. After substituting the formatted data into the new string, the new string is returned. An example is shown in Figure 4.10.

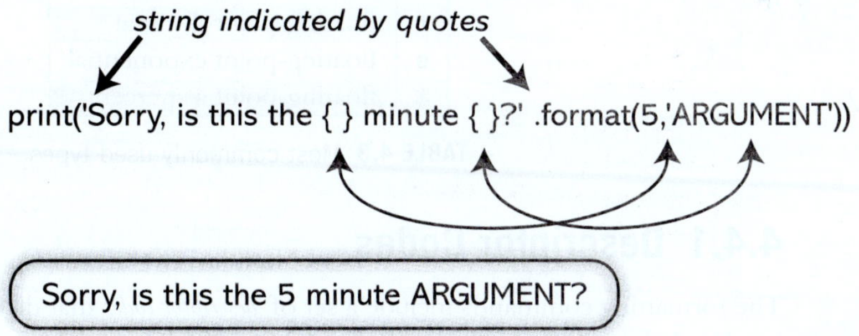

FIGURE 4.10 String formatting example.

In its simplest form, the formatting commands are just empty braces. The objects that will be substituted for each brace are determined by the order of both the braces and the arguments. The first brace will be replaced by the first argument, the second brace by the second argument, and so on. An example of this kind of formatting is shown in the following session:

```
In  [1]: "{} is {} years old".format("Bill",25)
Out [1]: 'Bill is 25 years old.'

In  [2]: import math
In  [3]: "{} is nice but {} is divine!".format(1, math.pi)
Out [3]: '1 is nice but 3.141592653589793 is divine!'
```

The way each object is formatted in the string is done by default based on its type, as was shown in the previous session. However, each brace can include *formatting commands* that provide directives about how a particular object is to be printed. The four pieces of information that one can provide for a particular object are: a *descriptor code*, an *alignment number*, a *width* number, and a *precision* descriptor. We will review each of those in the sections subseqently.

The general structure of the most commonly used parts of the format command is (more options are available):

```
{:[align] [minimum_width] [.precision] [descriptor]}
```

where the square brackets, `[ ]`, indicate optional arguments. It is important to note the placement of the colon. All the optional information comes after a colon in the braces.

The different types are described in Table 4.3. There are actually ten possible format commands—we will cover the others later.

s	string
d	decimal integer
f	floating-point decimal
e	floating-point exponential
%	floating-point as percent

TABLE 4.3 Most commonly used types.

4.4.1 Descriptor Codes

The formatting commands include a set of *descriptor codes* that dictate the type of object to be placed at that location in the string, and formatting operations that can be performed on that type. Table 4.3 shows the most commonly used descriptor codes. The descriptor can control how an individual object of that type is printed to the screen. For example, float descriptors can control the number of decimal points printed, and string descriptors can control leading or following spaces. However, each descriptor works only with its associated type. Associating an object of the wrong type with a descriptor will lead to a Python error. There are many more descriptor types, but this will suffice for most work. See the Python documentation if you need others.

<	left
>	right
^	center

TABLE 4.4 Width alignments.

4.4.2 Width and Alignment Descriptors

A field width can be specified for each data item. It specifies a printing-field width, counted as the number of spaces the object occupies. By default, formatted strings are left justified and formatted numbers are right justified. If the specification includes a less than (<), the data is placed left justified within the indicated width; a greater than (>) forces right justification. Centering can be done using "^"; see Table 4.4. In the following example, the string "*Bill*" is right justified in a width of 10 spaces, and the number 25 is left justified in a space of 10 spaces. Figure 4.11 displays an example.

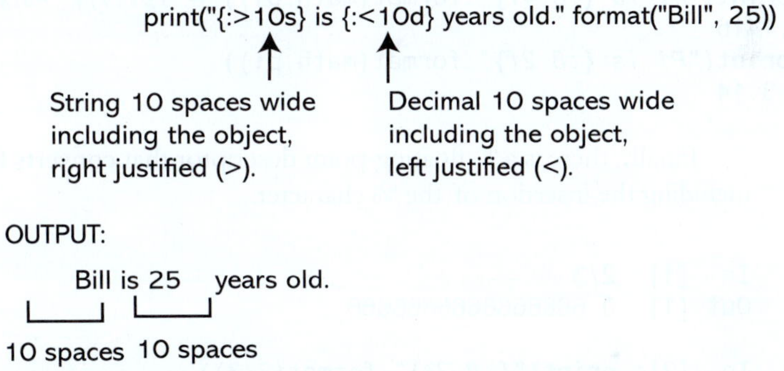

FIGURE 4.11 String formatting with width descriptors and alignment.

The following session illustrates printing both without a specified field width and with field width specified. Pay attention to how both spacing and justification is done.

```
In  [1]: print("{} is {} years old".format("Bill",25))
Bill is 25 years old.
In  [2]: print("{:>10s} is {:<10d} years old".format("Bill",25))
      Bill is 25         years old.
```

Formatting is useful for aligning values when printing tables as illustrated in the next session:

```
In  [1]: for i in range(5):
...:       print("{:10d} --> {:4d}".format(i,i**2))

         0 -->    0
         1 -->    1
         2 -->    4
         3 -->    9
         4 -->   16
```

4.4.3 Floating-Point Precision Descriptor

VideoNote 4.2
String Formatting

When printing floating-point values, it is desirable to control the number of digits to the right of the decimal point—that is, the precision. Precision is specified in the format descriptor using a decimal point followed by an integer to specify the precision. For example, {:.4f} specifies that the printed value will have only four digits to the right of the decimal point. Let's illustrate using the constant `pi` from the math module. We show unformatted printing, precision specified, and then both precision and width specified. Notice that rounding occurred.

```
In  [1]: import math
In  [2]: print(math.pi) # unformatted printing
3.141592653589793
In  [3]: print("Pi is {:.4f}".format(math.pi)) # floating-point precision 4
Pi is 3.1416
In  [4]: print("Pi is {:8.4f}".format(math.pi)) # specify both precision and width
Pi is   3.1416
In  [5]: print("Pi is {:8.2f}".format(math.pi))
Pi is     3.14
```

Finally, there is a % floating-point descriptor that converts from a decimal to a percent, including the insertion of the % character.

```
In  [1]: 2/3
Out [1]: 0.6666666666666666

In  [2]: print("{:8.2%}".format(2/3))
  66.67%
```

Check Yourself: More String Manipulation Check

1. What is the output of each ***print*** statement?

```
print("The word {} has {} letters.".format("Mississippi",11))
print("One number is {}; the other is {}.".format(4,3.5))
month = "June"
day = 5
year = 2011
print("The date is {} {}, {}.".format(month, day, year))
print("The interest rate is {:.2f} for you.".format(2.7))
print("{:>15s}: {:<8.1f}".format("Length",23.875))
```

4.5 CONTROL AND STRINGS

Let's write some code that manipulates strings. In particular, let's look at how the find method might be implemented. Let's begin with a string:

```
river = "Mississippi"
```

We can find the first letter 'p' using the find method:

```
In [1]: river = "Mississippi"
In [2]: river.find("p")
Out [2]: 8
```

How does the find method actually find a character and return its index? Let us see how we could reproduce the operation of that method using what we know about control and strings. Let's begin by experimenting with some features in the Python shell. First, let's find the length of the string using the len function:

```
In [1]: river = "Mississippi"
In [2]: len(river)
Out [2]: 11
```

Let's combine the length of the string with the *range* function to print out all the indices, one for each character in the word. Remember that the last argument to *range* is one more than the last value in the range. This is actually convenient. The length of the string is 11, but the active indices in the string are from 0 to 10. If we want a list of indices of the string, *range*(len(river)) does nicely as a nested call. The len(river) yields the value 11, which is used by *range* to generate the numbers 0–10. Very nice!

```
In [1]: river = "Mississippi"
In [2]: len(river)
Out [2]: 11

In [3]: for index in range(len(river)): # values of 0 upto, but not including 11
...:     print(index,end=' ')          # set end to a space to suppress new line

0 1 2 3 4 5 6 7 8 9 10
```

Now that we can print each index, we can use the same structure to print out each character in the word. Note that when we printed the indices above we used end=' ' (space); when we print the letters below we chose to use end='' (empty).

```
In [1]: for index in range(len(river)):
            print(river[index],end='')

Mississippi
```

We now have the ability to print each index, and each character associated with that index, in the string. We can now examine each character to see if it matches with the target character `'p'`. If it does, we print the index and ***break*** out of the loop, as we are only looking for the first match. If we do not find a match, the loop ends normally and any ***else*** clause of the ***for*** loop prints a failure message. The code and a session is shown in Code Listing 4.1.

Code Listing 4.1

```
# Our implementation of the find function. Prints the index where
# the target is found; a failure message, if it isn't found.
# This version only searches for a single character.

river = 'Mississippi'
target = input('Input a character to find: ')
for index in range(len(river)):                  # for each index
    if river[index] == target:                   # check if the target is found
        print("Letter found at index: ", index)  # if so, print the index
        break                                    # stop searching
else:
    print('Letter',target,'not found in',river)
```

```
In  [1]: runfile('/Users/user/python/file.py', wdir='/Users/user/python')

Input a character to find: s
Letter found at index:  2


In  [2]: runfile('/Users/user/python/file.py', wdir='/Users/user/python')

Input a character to find: a
Letter a not found in Mississippi
```

We frequently look for both an index and the character, so Python provides the `enumerate` iterator, which provides *both* the index of the character and the character itself as it steps through the string. Let's try it:

```
In  [1]: for index, letter in enumerate(river):
    ...:     print(index,letter)

0 M
1 i
2 s
3 s
```

```
4 i
5 s
6 s
7 i
8 p
9 p
10 i
```

Interestingly, notice that the ***for*** statement has *two* variables. This is because the `enumerate` statement yields two values each time: the index and the character. As in double assignment, we can capture both of those values by providing those two iterator variables.

Now that you've seen how `enumerate` works, let's refactor our code (Section 2.2.9). You may find it to be more readable. See Code Listing 4.2.

Code Listing 4.2

```
# Our implementation of the find function. Prints the index where
# the target is found; a failure message, if it isn't found.
# This version only searches for a single character.

river = 'Mississippi'
target = input('Input a character to find: ')
for index,letter in enumerate(river):          # for each index
    if letter == target:                        # check if the target is found
        print("Letter found at index: ", index) # if so, print the index
        break                                   # stop searching
else:
    print('Letter',target,'not found in',river)
```

Finally, what if we want to list *all* the occurrences of a letter? We can try by removing the ***break*** statement and see if we can find all occurrences of the target. See Code Listing 4.3.

Code Listing 4.3

```
# Our implementation of the find function. Prints the index where
# the target is found; a failure message, if it isn't found.
# This version only searches for a single character.

river = 'Mississippi'
target = input('Input a character to find: ')
for index,letter in enumerate(river):          # for each index
```

```
    if letter == target:                        # check if the target is found
        print("Letter found at index: ", index) # if so, print the index
        # break
else:
    print('Letter',target,'not found in',river)
```

```
Input a character to find: s
Letter found at index:  2
Letter found at index:  3
Letter found at index:  5
Letter found at index:  6
Letter s not found in Mississippi
```

Something is not quite right. Our program found all the examples of the `'s'` string but then *also* printed the failure message. What went wrong? In our previous two examples, we used the **`break`** statement to exit the loop which bypasses the **`else`**. We would execute the **`else`** only when the search failed. However, in this case, we did not break, meaning we *always* entered the **`else`** clause. What to do?

We leave fixing this problem as an exercise.

4.6 WORKING WITH STRINGS

Here are some short examples that show how to work with some of the common string methods to solve some simple problems.

4.6.1 Example: Reordering a Person's Name

Let's use a few string methods and try to do something useful. Here is our problem:

Transform a name from the order of `'First Middle Last'` to the order of `'Last, First Middle'`.

For example, if the name provided is `'John M. Cleese'` it would be transformed into `'Cleese, John M.'`

The string `split` method is very useful for this problem. The `split` method takes the calling string and creates substrings of that string, where substring creation occurs at a particular character(s). The invocation to split on spaces is `.split(' ')`; at every comma is `.split(',')`. For example, the invocation `'The Spanish Inquisition'.split()` would produce three strings: `'The'`,`'Spanish'`, and `'Inquisition'` using a split character of space (`' '`). The default is to split on whitespace, so commonly we simply use `split()` with no arguments.

Remember, strings are immutable, so we do not literally remove any part of the original string. Instead, `split` makes copies of parts that are created.

How could we use this to solve our problem? First, we can use the `split` method to break the string object associated with `name` into parts, where the split character is any white space character. We can then combine those results with Python's ability to do multiple assignments in the same line. For example,

```
In  [1]: name = 'John Marwood Cleese'
In  [2]: first, middle, last = name.split()
In  [3]: transformed = last + ', ' + first + ' ' + middle
In  [4]: print(transformed)
Cleese, John Marwood
```

The `split` method returns the three substrings from `name` when splitting at whitespace. We know this because our name is formatted as three, space-separated strings. The multiple assignment assigns the first substring to `first`, the second substring to `middle`, and the final substring to `last`. The next line assigns a rearrangement via concatenation to `transformed`, which is then printed.

Two things should be noted. This multiple-assignment approach has a problem if `split` does not return exactly three items to match the three variables on the left-hand side. You will learn later how to handle that problem using lists. Second, notice that the original string associated with `name` is not changed by the `split` method.

Here is a session that illustrates this transformation. The session also shows the error if the number of objects returned by the `split` method does not match the number of variables on the left-hand side. It also shows that `name` is not changed by these operations.

```
In  [1]: name = 'John Marwood Cleese'
In  [2]: first, middle, last = name.split()
In  [3]: transformed = last + ', ' + first + ' ' + middle
In  [4]: print(transformed)
Cleese, John Marwood
In  [5]: print(name)
John Marwood Cleese
In  [6]: print(first)
John
In  [7]: print(middle)
Marwood
In  [8]: print(last)
Cleese
In  [9]: first, middle = name.split() # error: not enough pieces

Traceback (most recent call last):
  File "<pyshell#71>", line 1, in <module>
    first, middle = name.split()
ValueError: too many values to unpack
In  [10]: first, middle, last = name.split(' ') # split on space ' '
In  [11]: print(first, middle, last)
John Marwood Cleese
```

The `split` method can be useful for comma-separated data such as those generated by spreadsheets and databases. The following example shows a string split based on a comma. You can `split` using any string, so `'+'` can be used to separate operands from operators as shown in the following code. We also illustrate how methods can be used with string literals rather than only variables. Finally, if a split character is not specified, splitting will be done with whitespace; that is, with spaces, tabs, or returns.

```
In  [1]: line = 'bob,carol,ted,alice'
In  [2]: first, second, third, fourth = line.split(',')
In  [3]: print(first, second, third, fourth)
bob carol ted alice
In  [4]: op1, op2 = "A+B".split('+')
In  [5]: print(op1, op2)
A B
```

4.6.2 Palindromes

Let's try to do something a little more complicated: determining whether a string is a palindrome. A palindrome is a string that reads the same forwards as backwards. Classic examples of a palindrome string are: "Madam, I'm Adam" or "A man, a plan, a canal, Panama".

If you look carefully though, those strings are not exactly the same forwards and backwards. We can easily show this with Python's help. We can print the string forwards and then, backwards, by simply reversing the string. Remember, string reversal is a slice from beginning to end with a −1 step. The following session shows both of the examples:

```
In  [1]: pal_1 = "Madam, I'm Adam"
In  [2]: pal_2 = "A man, a plan, a canal, Panama"
In  [3]: print("Forward: {} \nBackward: {}".format(pal_1,pal_1[::-1]))
Forward:  Madam, I'm Adam
Backward: madA m'I ,madaM
In  [4]: print("Forward: {} \nBackward: {}".format(pal_2,pal_2[::-1]))
Forward:  A man, a plan, a canal, Panama
Backward: amanaP ,lanac a ,nalp a ,nam A
```

We did a few things in that session. We had to use double quotes for the first palindrome so we could capture the apostrophe in the phrase `I'm`, and we did a little string formatting so that we could easily compare the two strings.

These palindromes are, in fact, not exactly the same forward and backward: for example, `pal_1[0] != pal_1[-1]` because of case issues and and `pal_1[4] != pal_1[-5]` as they aren't even the same character! Why are these called palindromes again?

In fact, the rules are relaxed in terms of character comparisons when talking about palindromes. Typically, we ignore the case of the individual characters, so that the first instance we noted previously is handled, and we completely discount nonalphabetic and nondigit characters, which takes care of the second instance. So to evaluate for palindromes, we really have two tasks:

1. Modify the input string so that:
   - The case of all the characters is the same.
   - Only letters and digits are in the string.
2. Once modified, compare the string forward and backward to see whether it is the same string.

The second task is easy, so let's concentrate on the first.

Changing Case

You have already seen the solution for this, but here is a quick reminder. Python provides a number of string methods that create a new string where something like case is modified. In the table in Section 4.3.3, there are two methods that look helpful: `lower` and `upper`. It doesn't matter which one we choose, as long as we apply it to the string and make all the characters in the string of one case. Let's use `lower`.

Only Letters and Digits

To accomplish the second subgoal of having the string contain only alphabetic and digit characters, there are a couple of options. However, there are two string concepts that are helpful no matter the approach.

The first is the ***in*** operator that we introduced in Section 4.2.4 for checking membership in a collection. We can use the ***in*** operator to query whether certain characters are in the string. Conveniently, Python provides another module that stores various groups of characters as a string for exactly this purpose. If we import the `string` module, you will see that it contains a number of predefined strings, including:

string.punctuation: '!"# $%&\'()*+,-./:;<=>?@[\\]^_`\{\}~' |
string.digits: '0123456789'
string.ascii_lowercase: 'abcdefghijklmnopqrstuvwxyz'
string.whitespace: '\t\n\x0b\x0c\r '

The last looks a bit odd, but it contains a representation using the backslash (\) prefix for the control characters, such as tab, carriage return, and space (which we couldn't see otherwise). We can use these predefined strings to do membership tests. For our palindrome, we want to test only lowercase letters or digits and exclude punctuation and whitespace. Once we find a character we do not want, what can we do?

Python provides another very useful string method: `replace`. The `replace` method takes two arguments: the first is the string we are looking for, and the second is the replacement string if the first string is found. For example, `'abbc'.replace('b','z')` would search through the string `'abbc'` looking for any `'b'` and, if found, replacing the `'b'` with a `'z'`. It would return the new string `'azzc'` (leaving `'abbc'` unchanged). One way to *remove* a character from a string is to `replace` with the empty string(''). This will be our strategy.

Putting It All Together

Code Listing 4.4 shows the solution. Examine it and then we'll discuss the parts.

Code Listing 4.4

```
1 # Palindrome tester
2 import string
3
4 original_str = input('Input a string:')
5 modified_str = original_str.lower()
6
7 bad_chars = string.whitespace + string.punctuation
8
9 for char in modified_str:
10     if char in bad_chars:  # remove bad characters
11         modified_str = modified_str.replace(char,'')
12
13 if modified_str == modified_str[::-1]: # it is a palindrome
14     print(\
15 'The original string is:   {}\n\
16  the modified string is: {}\n\
17  the reversal is:         {}\n\
18  String is a palindrome'.format(original_str, modified_str, modified_str[::-1]))
19 else:
20     print(\
21 'The original string is:   {}\n\
22  the modified string is: {}\n\
23  the reversal is:         {}\n\
24  String is not a palindrome'.format(original_str,modified_str,modified_str[::-1]))
```

Line 2: We import the `string` module to get the pre-defined Python strings.

Line 4: We prompt for a string to test.

Line 5: We lowercase the original string to get the case uniform throughout the string. We hold onto the original string.

Line 7: We create a new string, `bad_chars`, which is a concatenation of all the characters we *don't* want in our modified string, namely the punctuation and whitespace characters.

Lines 9–11: The ***for*** loop is short and simple. We iterate through each character in the modified string. If the character is in the string of unwanted characters, we remove it. We do so by replacing all occurrences of that bad character with an empty string, `''`, effectively deleting that character.

Line 13: This is the reversal test: is it or is it not a palindrome? That is, are the modified string and the reversal of it the same?

Lines 14–18: This is a pretty-printed line broken into multiple continuations—the backslash (\) at the end of the lines—to get the strings to line up and produce a nicely formatted output. The backslash (\) characters force carriage returns in the output.

Most of the work we had to do was in modifying the original string so that we could do our simple reversal test. Using `replace` to remove the bad characters is not the only way to do the palindrome. We leave as an exercise how to do palindromes without using `replace`.

4.7 MORE STRING FORMATTING

Earlier in Section 4.4, we introduced basic string formatting. The basic formatting we presented earlier was:

{:[align] [minimum_width] [.precision] [descriptor]}

Here we will describe more of the capabilities of string formatting.

{arg:[[fill]align][sign][*#*][*0*][*minimum_width*][*,*][*.precision*][*descriptor*]}

In our previous formatting examples we did not specify positional arguments so we relied on the default: match formatting to data by position in order. That is, the first format specifier applies to the first data item, then the second, and so on. The optional "arg" argument that appears *before* the colon allows one to specify *which* of the particular arguments to use. By so doing, format can mix arguments in a programmer determined way, even reusing an argument in multiple places. As usual, the numbering of arguments starts at zero so {1} specifies data argument 1 in the format list, that is, the second argument of the `format` statement.

Also, notice how formatting can be done on any string and it need not appear within a print statement.

```
In  [1]: print('{} is {}'.format('Bill',25)) # using defaults
Bill is 25
In  [2]: s = '{} is {}'.format('Bill',25) # print is not needed
In  [3]: s
Out [3]: 'Bill is 25'

In  [4]: print('{0} is {2} and {0} is also {1}'.format('Bill',25,'tall'))
Bill is tall and Bill is also 25
```

<	left (default for most objects)
>	right (default for numbers)
^	center
=	force fill between sign and digits (numeric only)

TABLE 4.5 Alignments format.

The align signs have been mentioned earlier (See Table 4.5): less than (<) left aligns, greater than (>) right aligns and "^" centers. However, there is a fourth, "=", that forces the "fill" to be placed after the numeric sign and before the digits (it only works with numeric data). The fill is a character that occupies any blank space in the formatted output. The "sign" specification controls the numeric sign: "+" forces a sign for both positive and negative values, "-" is the default and only display a sign for negatives, " " (space) puts a space for positives and a negative sign for negatives (allows easier alignment). (See Table 4.6). The next session illustrates their use.

+	sign for positive and negative
-	sign for negative only (default)
space	space for positive; minus for negative

TABLE 4.6 Sign format.

```
In  [1]: print('{0:.>12s} | {1:0=+10d} | {2:->5d}'.format('abc',35,22))
.........abc | +000000035 | ---22
```

The "#" sign specifies the use of an alternative form—more detail than we will get into here. However, one alternative form that may be useful to novices is when using # with floats: it forces a decimal point even if there are no digits to the right of the decimal point. The next session illustrates it use. Notice the difference between zero precision and no precision.

```
In  [1]: print('{:6.2f}'.format(3.4567))
  3.46
In  [2]: print('{:6.1f}'.format(3))
   3.0
In  [3]: print('{:6.0f}'.format(3)) # zero precision
     3
In  [4]: print('{:6f}'.format(3)) # no precision (default precision)
3.000000
In  [5]: print('{:#6.0f}'.format(3)) # decimal point forced
    3.
```

If the width field is preceded by a zero ("0") character, zero-padding is enabled. This is equivalent to an alignment type of "=" and a fill character of "0." The "," option signals the use of a comma as a thousands separator (the American standard). The next session illustrates their use.

```
In  [1]: print('{:04d}'.format(4)) # zero preceeds width
0004
In  [2]: print('{:,d}'.format(1234567890))
1,234,567,890
```

Finally, it is possible to specify names for arguments. In the session below, we named the data arguments “lat” and “long” (we should have used the full words, but the page wasn’t wide enough). Interestingly, it is also possible to specify various fields with data argument. It can be quite useful to specify width as a parameter. These concepts are illustrated in the following session:

```
In  [1]: 'Coordinates: {lat}, {long}'.format(long='-112.41E',lat='32.18N')
Out [1]: 'Coordinates: 32.18N, -112.41E'

In  [2]: print('{:{width}d}'.format(31,width=10))
        31
```

You will find formatted output most useful for creating tables and for displaying floating-point values.

For example, consider making a table of polygon sides, total interior degrees, the degrees of each interior angle, and the degrees for each exterior angle. The following session shows unformatted output. The leftmost number causes misalignment when it reaches 10, and the floating-point value for a septagon makes the table difficult to read.

```
In  [1]: for n in range(3,11):
...:     print(n,180*(n-2),180*(n-2)/n,360/n)

3 180 60.0 120.0
4 360 90.0 90.0
5 540 108.0 72.0
6 720 120.0 60.0
7 900 128.57142857142858 51.42857142857143
8 1080 135.0 45.0
9 1260 140.0 40.0
10 1440 144.0 36.0
```

Adding formatting we get the more readable

```
In  [1]: for n in range(3,11):
    print('{:4}-sides:{:6}{:10.2f}{:10.2f}'.format(n,180*(n-2),180*(n-2)/n,360/n))

   3-sides:   180     60.00    120.00
   4-sides:   360     90.00     90.00
```

```
 5-sides:   540    108.00     72.00
 6-sides:   720    120.00     60.00
 7-sides:   900    128.57     51.43
 8-sides:  1080    135.00     45.00
 9-sides:  1260    140.00     40.00
10-sides:  1440    144.00     36.00
```

4.8 UNICODE

We briefly mentioned Unicode in Chapter 0, but now that we have strings it is worth spending more time on the subject of encoding characters. Since the initial rapid growth of computing was dominated by English-speaking countries, the encoding of characters was initially dominated by English with the ASCII encoding (defined in 1963). However, the 128 ASCII characters were too limiting even for the European languages, let alone huge languages such as Chinese. A broader character set called Unicode was defined in the late 1980s to handle over 1 million characters across 93 scripts (alphabets). Each Unicode character then needs to be encoded into binary for use in the computer. There are a number of encodings, but a popular one is UTF-8 (defined in 1993). One reason for its popularity is that the well-entrenched ASCII encoding is a subset of UTF-8 so backwards compatibility issues are eased. A language needs to choose some encoding as its default and Python 3's default is UTF-8. Because ASCII is a subset of UTF-8, by default Python 3 can handily read existing ASCII text files. In addition, at the time of writing this text most pages on the World Wide Web (85%) are encoded in UTF-8.

A Unicode character maps to something called a *code point*, which is a theoretical concept. How that code point gets represented in a file is separate—that is the encoding. It is similar to Plato's *Theory of Forms* where there is an ideal, abstract representation of an object, for example, the theoretically perfect circle, and then there is the circle that you draw on paper which is not the *perfect* circle. With Unicode the *code point* is the abstract ideal, and the encoding is the actual representation in the computer. There is one ideal "A," but there are multiple ways to encode it in binary and UTF-8 is one of those ways. Fortunately, Python 3 hides most of the complexity of dealing with Unicode and its encoding from the programmer when dealing with text files. Life can get very complicated with other types of files.

We say that Python "mostly" hides the complexity because there are times when a programmer needs to consider encodings. For example, UTF-8 was defined before the Euro existed so it doesn't have a code for the Euro. If you are reading files, say from a spreadsheet (e.g., CSV), that discuss Euros, you will want to read the file using the Latin-1 encoding which understands the Euro symbol. Later we will see how Microsoft generates CSV files from its Excel spreadsheet using a particular encoding (Windows-1252)—a superset of ASCII, but different from UTF-8 so unreadable characters can creep in. In Section 14.1.7, we will describe how to specify the `encoding` when reading a file in those rare times when it will make a difference.

We mentioned earlier that you can use the `ord` function to get the encoding for any character. Since the default in Python 3 is UTF-8, the `ord` function provides the UTF-8 encoding (which for English characters is the same encoding as ASCII). The following session shows some encodings of uppercase and lowercase characters as well as some symbols. Notice that even the space character has an encoding; as does the "carriage return." Also, notice how the encoding of uppercase and lowercase each use a contiguous slice of numbers so the encoding can be used to sort characters.

```
In  [1]: chr(97)
Out [1]: 'a'

In  [2]: ord('A')
Out [2]: 65

In  [3]: chr(65)
Out [3]: 'A'

In  [4]: ord('a')
Out [4]: 97

In  [5]: chr(97)
Out [5]: 'a'

In  [6]: ord('b')
Out [6]: 98

In  [7]: ord('1')
Out [7]: 49

In  [8]: ord('2')
Out [8]: 50

In  [9]: ord('=')
Out [9]: 61

In  [10]: ord(' ')
Out [10]: 32

In  [11]: ord('\n')
Out [11]: 10
```

Using Unicode for Special Characters

The set of Unicode characters is vast. Almost any character you would like to print is available. If you seek a particular character, search for its Unicode specification online. For example, if you search for the Greek small letter 'pi', that is, π, you will likely find it specified as "U+03C0". Here is how you print it: `print('\u03C0')`. To print an exponent such as x^2 you can combine the string "x" with an exponent 2 as `print("x"+'\u00B2')`. Similarly, x_1 is achieved with `print('x'+'\u2081')`. Even nontext characters are available such as printing playing card symbols: `print('\u2660')` will print the spade symbol, ♠.

4.9 A GUI TO CHECK A PALINDROME

One way to build a GUI is to use an existing example and adapt it. That is what we are going to do here. We are going to work with the sine example of Appendix Section E.4.2 and modify it to serve our needs: build a Palindrome checker. Using that example as a template allows you to build a GUI in Python without understanding details of the underlying code. One nice thing about following this example is that you are using your browser for your GUI. For a more thorough understanding of how to build a GUI in Python using Flask, take a look at Appendix E.

PROGRAMMING TIP

As indicated in E.4.1, you need to use either the `conda` package manager or the `pip` package manager to download the package `flask-wtf`.

Figure 4.12 is a template based on a simple program that takes in one float as input and displays its sine value. In the figure we highlight the parts: you need to modify to create a GUI for our palindrome program from Section 4.6.2.

The template is divided into three main parts: the Model, the View, and the Controller, as noted in the comments. The "Model" at the top is a function where we will plug in our palindrome program from Section 4.6.2. The "View" in the middle contains the HTML description of what our GUI will look like in the browser. In browser terminology this is a "form", with input fields that need to be specified. At the bottom is the "Controller" that ties the "View" to the "Model". There are five elements we need to change for our new GUI:

- What GUI form fields to include.
- A function Model (our palindrome code from Section 4.6.2).
- Any specific text we want to display in our GUI, also known as the HTML View.
- Creating the `InputForm` with the GUI fields and naming those fields in the Controller, and using them in the View.
- Change some variable names in the Controller.

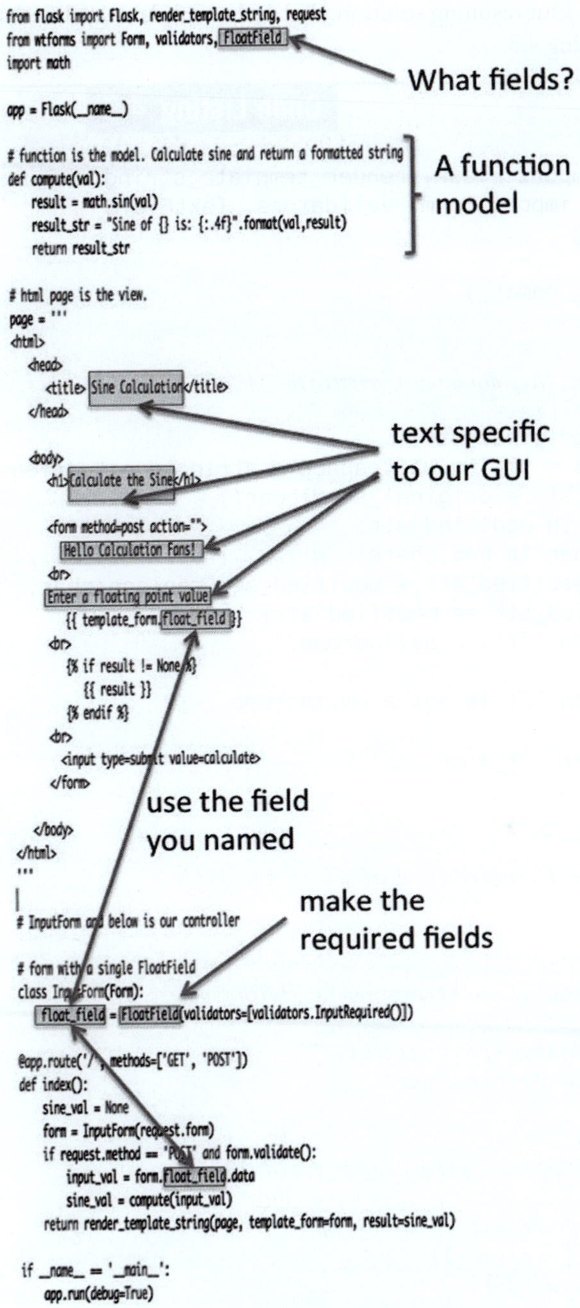

FIGURE 4.12 The GUI template.

Our resulting solution, that is, the template modified to be a palindrome GUI, is in Code Listing 4.5.

Code Listing 4.5

```
from flask import Flask, render_template_string, request
from wtforms import Form, validators, TextField
import string

app = Flask(__name__)


# function is the model. Calculate if original_str is a palindrome
# return a string
def compute(original_str):
    bad_chars = string.whitespace + string.punctuation
    modified_str = original_str.lower()
    for char in modified_str:
        if char in bad_chars:  # remove bad characters
            modified_str = modified_str.replace(char,'')
    if modified_str == modified_str[::-1]:
        return "It's a palindrome!"
    else:
        return "It is not a palindrome :-("

# html page is the view.
page = '''
<html>
   <head>
      <title> Palindrome Calculation</title>
   </head>

   <body>
      <h1>Check if a String is a Palindrome</h1>

      <form method=post action="">
         Hello String Fans!
      <br>
      Enter a string
         {{ template_form.text_field }}
      <br>
         {% if result != None %}
            {{ result }}
         {% endif %}
      <br>
        <input type=submit value=calculate>
```

```
42          </form>
43
44        </body>
45    </html>
46    '''
47
48    # InputForm and below is our controller
49
50    # form with a single TextField
51    class InputForm(Form):
52        text_field = TextField(validators=[validators.InputRequired()])
53
54    @app.route('/', methods=['GET', 'POST'])
55    def index():
56        palindrome_result = None
57        form = InputForm(request.form)
58        if request.method == 'POST' and form.validate():
59            input_val = form.text_field.data
60            palindrome_result = compute(input_val)
61        return render_template_string(page, template_form=form, result =
62                                      palindrome_result)
63
64    if __name__ == '__main__':
65        app.run(debug=True)
```

Form Fields: A variety of form input fields can be used, depending on one's needs (see Section E.4.3). For the sine example (our template), we used a `FloatField` because we needed a float input. For the palindrome we need text input so we use a `TextField` as shown on **Lines 2** and **51** of our Code Listing 4.5.

Function Model: The function is your program, the palindrome code in this case. For this style GUI the Model should **return a string** because that is what our template assumes.

For the palindrome problem, we took the code from Section 4.6.2 and turned it into a function that returned a string indicating if the provided argument was a palindrome. See **Lines 10–19**. (For more details on functions see Chapter 5.)

View Specific Changes: The HTML View, **Lines 23–45** need to be modified to suit our particular problem. We change **Lines 25, 29, 32, 34** to have text reflecting the new problem, palindromes. Any text can be inserted here so feel free to create new text, add HTML tags and more to make it more interesting!

InputForm: We need to instantiate the forms we want in our `InputForm` part of the Controller. We can add as many input forms as we like, and then display them in the View. We name each instantiation in the Controller and use it in the View.

In our example, we create a `TextField` that we name `text_field` on **Line 52** of the Controller and then execute that field in the View on **Line 35** using the same name, `text_field`, with `template_form` prepended with a dot (".") to indicate that `text_field` is part of a `template_form`.

Controller Variables: Technically, we don't **have** to change any variable names, but for readability we adhere to **RULE 2**. Therefore, on **Lines 56, 60, and 61** we update our variable name to `palindrome_result`.

Note how **Line 60** ties the Model (your program) to the Controller through the call to `compute`. The View is tied to the Controller through the `text_field`.

The output from our new program is shown in Figure 4.13, which is quite similar to the sine example in Section E.4.2. For details on how to run your GUI and tie it to your browser see Appendix E Section E.2.

a) Startup

b) String submitted is a palindrome

c) String submitted is not a palindrome

FIGURE 4.13 The Palindrome GUI Example. [William F. Punch, Richard J. Enbody.]

4.10 WHAT'S WRONG WITH MY CODE?

Here are suggestions for finding problems with your code. Refer to Appendix C for details.

With strings the error message itself is more useful than the type of error message generated. Two types of error messages dominate string errors: `IndexError` and `TypeError`.

Many string errors manifest themselves as `TypeError` so it is the error message itself that is most useful.

The two most common error messages are as follows:

- **IndexError: string index out of range** clearly describes the problem. For example, `s='hello'` and you try `s[15]` whose index is beyond the end of the string `s` (indices 0:4).
- **TypeError: 'str' object does not support item assignment** occurs when indexing appears on the LHS of an assignment statement, for example, `s[0]='x'`. Since a string is immutable, individual characters cannot be modified and this is the resulting error message.

Less common errors are these; both are `TypeErrors`.

- **TypeError: replace() takes at least 2 arguments (1 given)** or something similar occurs when the wrong number of arguments are used for the method. In this case, `replace` expects at least two arguments, but only one was provided: `s.replace('e')`. A similar error can occur for other string methods, or for a function with the wrong number of arguments such as `len()`, that is, providing no arguments when one is expected.
- **TypeError: unorderable types: str() < int()** occurs when two different types are compared, but such a comparison is not permitted in Python, for example, `'x'<5`. The problem is obvious in that example, but less obvious when comparing two identifiers, for example, `x<y` unless you know the types. Observing the types in SPYDER's variable explorer can help, as can the naming practices we have described (appending type info to the variable name, see Section 1.4.6).

Other errors which are less likely are as follows:

- **String arithmetic errors:** string arithmetic allows some operations, but not others. For example `'hello'*2` is fine; it results in `'hellohello'`. However, the following cause problems:
  - `'hello'*'a'` generates the error: `TypeError: Can't multiply sequence by non-int of type 'str'`. While multiplication by an integer is allowed, multiplying a string by another string is not permitted by Python.
  - `'hello'+2` generates the error: `TypeError: Can't convert 'int' object to str implicitly`. While multiplication is allowed, there is no corresponding operation for adding a string and a number. In this case, the interpreter thinks you might be trying to add two strings together (something it understands) and that the second argument, a number, should be converted to a string. However, as the error message indicates, there isn't a rule for automatically converting a number to a string. If your intent is to convert the number to a string, then you must do so explicitly: `'hello'+ str(2)`.

- **String formatting errors** come from a missmatch of either types or number of items to be formatted.
  - **Type missmatch** occurs when the format specifier type doesn't match the provided item, for example, specifying an integer format (`"{:d}"`) while providing a string argument, that is, `"{:d}".format("abc")`. The resulting error message is: `ValueError: Unknown format code 'd' for object of type 'str'`, which effectively says that the 'd' format isn't defined for use with a string (it is for use with an integer).
  - **Wrong number of arguments** occurs when you specify say two items to format, but there is a mismatch in the number of format elements and arguments, for example, `"{}{}".format("a")`. The resulting error message seems unrelated: `IndexError: tuple index out of range`. We don't describe 'tuples' until a later chapter, but the argument to the format method is implicitly a tuple and this message is saying that two items were expected, but only one was found, hence "out of range."
- **Missing Parenthesis in Method:** Some string methods such as `lower()` and `upper()` take no arguments so it is easy to forget the parenthesis. If you type such an expression into the interpreter you don't get an error message. Instead you get unexpected output such as `<function str.upper>` or `<built-in method upper of str object at 0x106e85998>`. Effectively you are not asking Python to **run** the method, which would require the parentheses, but instead asking Python to **report** what "lower" **is**, which Python dutifully reports.

  Even worse would be the following code: `f = "abc".lower`. Again, no error occurs but what is assigned to the variable `f` is the **function** "lower", not the result of **running** lower. Probably not what you wanted.

Summary

In this chapter, we introduced the string type and the variety of methods and functions that work on them. In isolation, these tools may not yet appear to be very useful or powerful. However, when combined with the ability to make decisions and repeat instructions, these tools will be heavily used.

Strings

- Strings are immutable.
- Strings are sequences.
- Strings have many methods. See Table 4.2.
- Standard operations:
  - length function: `len(s)`
  - membership: *`in`*

Indexing and Slicing

Given: s = 'Mississippi'

- Indexing starts at zero: s[0] is 'M'.
- Negative indices work backwards from the end: s[-1] is 'i'.
- Slicing selects a subset up to but not including the final index: s[3:6] is 'sis'.
- Slicing default start is the beginning so s[:4] is 'Miss'.
- Slicing default end is the end so s[7:] is 'ippi'.
- Using both defaults makes a copy: s[:].
- Slicing's optional third argument indicates step: s[:6:2] is 'Msi'.
- The idiom to reverse a string: s[::-1] is 'ippississiM'

Formatting

`{arg:[[fill]align][sign][#][0][ minimum_width ][,][. precision ] type }`

For example: `print('X{:<10.3f}Y'.format(12.345678))`
prints
```
X12.346     Y
```

Iteration: for, enumerate

- `for` walks through each character in a string:
  `for ch in 'Mississippi':`
- `enumerate` generates both the index and the character:
  `for index, ch in enumerate('Mississippi'):`

Rules

- **RULE 1:** Think before you program!
- **RULE 2:** A program is a human-readable essay on problem solving that also happens to execute on a computer.
- **RULE 3:** The best way to improve your programming and problem skills is to practice!
- **RULE 4:** A foolish consistency is the hobgoblin of little minds.
- **RULE 5:** Test your code, often and thoroughly!
- **RULE 6:** If it was hard to write, it is probably hard to read. Add a comment.

Exercises

1. Given the string "*Monty Python*":

(a) Write an expression to print the first character.
(b) Write an expression to print the last character.
(c) Write an expression inculding `len` to print the last character.
(d) Write an expression that prints "Monty".

2. Given the string "*homebody*":

(a) Write an expression using slicing to print "*home*".
(b) Write an expression using slicing to print "*body*".

3. Given a string `S` with even length:

(a) Write an expression to print out the first half of the string.
(b) Write an expression to print out the second half of the string.

4. Given a string `S` with odd length:

(a) Write an expression to print the middle character.
(b) Write an expression to print the string up to but not including the middle character (i.e., the first half of the string).
(c) Write an expression to print the string from the middle character to the end (not including the middle character).

5. Given `s = 'Earth'`, what is returned by `s.strip()`, `s.lstrip()`, and `s.rstrip()`?

6. Given the string `S = "What is your name?"`:

(a) What is returned by `S[::2]`?
(b) What is returned by `S[2:8:-1]`?

7. Write a program that accepts a sequence of whitespace-separated words as input and outputs the string after removing all repeated words.

8. Write a program that will print "It's a Yes!" if the user inputs 'yes', 'Yes', or 'YES', and will print "It's a No!" otherwise. Use string methods.

9. What will be printed by the following?

```
x = 'This is a test.'
print(x * 3)
```

10. In the following program, replace the `for` with a `while` loop.

```
S="I had a cat named amanda when I was little"
count = 0
for i in S:
    if i == "a":
        count += 1
print(count)
```

11. (String operators) The Monty Python comedy troupe has a famous skit set in a restaurant whose menu is predominately Spam®—a canned meat mixture of ham and pork. One menu entry was "Spam, Spam, Spam, Spam, Spam, baked beans, Spam, Spam, Spam, and Spam." Write a Python string expression using both the concatenation (+) and repetition (*) string operators to form that menu entry.

12. The following Python statement generates this error: "ValueError: too many values to unpack". Why?

```
first ,second = input('two space-separated numbers:')
```

13. We know that writing the following code:

```
print("I like writing in Python.")
print("It is so much fun.")
```

will result in:

```
I like writing in Python.
It is so much fun.
```

when executed. However, can you manage to do this same task with only one line of code?

14. Five string methods manipulate case: `capitalize`, `title`, `swapcase`, `upper`, and `lower`. Consider the strings: `s1 = "concord"`, `s2 = "sioux city"`, `s3 = " HONOLULU"`, and `s4 = "TopHat"`.

(a) Describe what `capitalize` does.
(b) Describe what `swapcase` does.
(c) Describe what `upper` does.
(d) Describe what `lower` does.
(e) Describe what `title` does.

15. Write a program that will take a string of words as input from the user and return the words sorted in alphabetical order.

16. Two string methods left and right justify strings within a specified width. In addition, they default by filling in with spaces, but can be specified to fill in with a character. Consider `s = "Topkapi"` and `s.rjust(20,".")` or `s.ljust(15)`. Experiment with right and left justification. Describe the rules for what `ljust` and `rjust` do.

17. Two string methods find where a character is in a string: `find` and `index`.

(a) Both work the same if a character is found, but behave differently if the character is not found. Describe the difference in how they behave when the character is not found.
(b) The `find` and `index` methods are not limited to finding single characters. They can search for substrings. Given `s = "Topkapi"`, what does `s.find("kap")` print? Describe the rule for what `find` prints.

18. Write a program to calculate the number of uppercase and lowercase letters in a string.

19. Using the `input` command, prompt for input, and then capitalize every alternate letter in the input.

20. Experiment with the `count` method. What does it count?
For example,

```
some_string = "Hello world!"
some_string.count("o")
```

21. Write a program that will accept a string containing special characters as input from the user, strip out all the special characters, and then print the remaining string.

22. The string methods that start with "is" all return either "True" or "False". Experiment with them to figure out how they work, that is, what causes them to return "True" and what causes them to return "False".

23. (String operators)
   (a) Suppose you want to print a line full of `'#'` characters. For simplicity, let's say that a line can have only 80 characters. One way is to create a long string to be printed. How would you do it more elegantly in Python using the plus operation (+) of strings?
   (b) Suppose you want to print a column full of `'#'` characters. For simplicity, let's say that a column could have only 30 characters. Similar to (a), how would you do it more elegantly in Python using the mulitply operation (*) of strings?

   Hint: Use the newline character ('\n').

24. Write a program that prompts the user to enter a string, and the percentage of the string they want to print. Print the corresponding slice of the string.

25. In British English, there is a word 'flavour'. The American spelling is 'flavor'. Suppose you have a string in Python called brit_word = 'flavour' and you want to convert it into the American variant and store it in a string called amer_word. How would you do it?

26. Which of the following works without any error?
   (a) `var = 'xyz' * 10.5`
   (b) `var = 'xyz' * '5'`
   (c) `var = 'xyz' * 5`
   (d) `var = 'xyz' * 5.0`

27. (Reversing a string) Given a string, say X = 'Alan Turing', write an expression to reverse it to get a string, Y = 'gniruT nalA'.

28. Suppose you have a string `ab_string = 'abababababababab'`. Write an expression to remove all the 'b's and create a string, `a_string = 'aaaaaaa'`.

29. Given the string `'abcdefghij'`, write a single line of code that will print the following (*Hint*: Slicing is your friend):

(a) `'jihgfedcba'`
(b) `'adgj'`
(c) `'igeca'`

30. Using the `find` method, write a short program that will print out the index of both 'o's when given the input "Who's on first?".

31. Write a program that given a name in the form of `''Chapman, Graham Arthur''` will convert it to the form `''Graham Arthur Chapman''`.

32. The expression `'dog' + 's'` will return `'dogs'`. What is returned by the expression 'dog' – 'g' ? Explain.

33. Without using division, write a one-line program that stores the last integer of an integer number as the variable `last_digit_int`. Be careful that the value returned is the correct type.

34. Using the following variable assignments below:

```
string1 = 'toY'
string2 = 'box'
string3 = "cAr"
string4 = 'to'
integer1 = 2
```

What is the result of the following print statements below? If the statement results in creating an error, write ERROR and explain why.

(a) print(string2.upper())
(b) print(len(string4))
(c) print(str(integer1).join(string3.swapcase()))
(d) print(string4.index(string1))
(e) print(string1.index(string4))
(f) print("string4" in string1)

35. Write a short program that will prompt for a string and then print the ASCII value of each character in the string.

36. Write a single line of code whose value is True if `a_string` contains only decimal values.

37. Write a program that prompts for two words. Print the longer one in all capitals and capitalize the first letter of the second word.

38. Similar to `.lower`: write a program that prompts for a string and prints the string in lowercase without using the string.lower method.

39. In the palindrome example we used `replace` to remove bad characters. Refactor that program to **keep** the good characters rather than remove the bad characters.

40. Given the following code:

```
x=input("Enter a string: ")
y=0
for i in x:
    print(y,i)
    y+=1
```

(a) What will be printed, if `"hello"` is entered?
(b) Refactor the code using enumerate.

41. Although Python's formatted printing can be cumbersome, it can often drastically improve the readability of output. Try creating a table out of the following values:

Melting and Boiling Points of Alkanes

Name	Melting Point (deg C)	Boiling Point (deg C)
Methane	−162	−183
Ethane	−89	−172
Propane	−42	−188
Butane	−0.5	−135

42. Write a program to prompt the user to input a string, and then count the number of digits, letters, and special characters present in the given string. Format the output into a table.

43. Write a program that plays the game of hangman. Use characters to print the hangman's status. Triple-quoted strings will be useful.
Hint: Draw the entire hangman status as a string picture with a full picture for each partial hangman status.

44. Write a program that prompts for a sentence and calculates the number of uppercase letters, lowercase letters, digits, and punctuation. Output the results neatly formatted and labeled in columns.

45. Write a program that returns True if the sentence string `sentence_str` contains every letter of the alphabet. If the sentence does not contain each letter, print which ones are missing. The results should not depend on capitalization.

46. Jacob has been passing notes in class without a problem until his teacher intercepted one today. In order to prevent future embarrassment, he wants a way to encode his notes so his teacher cannot read them. Help him by writing a program that encrypts a string by switching every letter with alphabetical position i with the letter with alphabetical position 26-i. It should be: letter `12 = 'm'` becomes the letter `26-12 = 14 = 'o'`.

47. You are creating a new account and need to provide a password. The password has the following requirements:

(a) The password must be at least 6 characters and at most 20 characters.
(b) It must contain at least one lowercase letter, one uppercase letter, and one number.

Write a program that prompts the user to input a password and checks if the password is valid. If the password is valid, print a confirmation statement. If it is not, print a statement that the password is not valid.

48. Write a program that prints a multiplication table for the numbers from 0 to 12. Do not do any of your calculations by hand. Format the output into a table.

49. Using the incredible power of the human mind, according to research at Cambridge University, it doesn't matter in what order the letters in a word are, the only important thing is that the first and last letter be in the right place. The rest can be total mess and you can still read it without a problem. This is because the human mind does not read every letter by itself, but the word as a whole. Amazing, huh? Yeah and I always thought spelling was important! Write a program that prompts for a word and prints the scrambled version (with first and last fixed).

Hint: The random module helps scramble words.

50. Develop a Python program that will: (1) prompt for input, (2) extract all the vowels in the input string and make them lowercase, (3) add all the nonduplicate vowels you found into a temporary string, and (4) stop the code when you have collected all five vowels (aeiou) and print the number of trials that you did to collect all five vowel characters.

51. Write a program that prompts for the user to input a sentence. Then check this sentence to make sure the first word of the sentence is capitalized and the sentence ends with a punctuation mark. If it is not properly written, fix the sentence, print the type of error, and print the fixed sentence.

52. Write a program that prompts the user to enter a three-digit number such that the digits are in order, for example, 123789. The program loops until a correct value is entered.

Programming Projects

1. **Mastermind**

Mastermind is a code-breaking game for two players; play can be simulated in text on a computer. Online versions exist and are useful for understanding how the game is played, but if you can get a hold of the actual board game, that is even better. The game is played using the following:

- A decoding board, with a shield at one end covering a row of four large holes, and twelve additional rows containing four large holes next to a set of four small holes;

- Code pegs of six different colors (we'll use "colors" ABCDEF), with round heads, which will be placed in the large holes on the board; and
- Scoring pegs, some black, some white, that are flat-headed and smaller than the code pegs; they will be placed in the small holes on the board. Only the quantity of black and white scoring pegs in each row matter in the game.

One player, the codemaker, selects four colors that are shielded from the other player, the codebreaker. In our version, colors cannot repeat, that is, AABB is illegal. The goal of the game is for the codebreaker to correctly determine both the four colors selected by the codemaker and their position in the code.

The codebreaker tries to guess the pattern, in both order and color, within 12 turns. Each guess is made by placing a row of code pegs on the decoding board. Once placed, the codemaker provides feedback by placing from zero to four scoring pegs in the small holes of the row with the guess. A black scoring peg is placed for each code peg from the guess that is correct in both color and position. A white peg indicates the existence of a correct color peg placed in the wrong position.

Once feedback is provided, another guess is made; guesses and feedback continue to alternate until either the codebreaker guesses correctly, or 12 incorrect guesses are made.

Write a program that simulates the game by providing the feedback. The codebreaker will input each guess by entering a string of 'colors'. Your simulation will ensure that guessing rules are followed: the guess consists of exacly four colors from 'ABCDEF'. Feedback will be a count of black pegs and a count of white pegs. Your program will determine the feedback and print it. The program will declare a win if the guess is correct or a loss after 12 incorrect guesses. In addition, the program should print the complete board state so the codebreaker can more easily view the history of guesses made.

Hints:

- Play the game using paper and pencil to understand how the game is played before designing your game playing algorithm.
- Use strings for the code and guesses.
- Use a string `'ABCDEF'` for the set of allowable colors so you can check membership using "in".
- The `isalpha` string method is useful for checking input.
- The history can be built as a long string using concatenation. The end-of-line character `'\n'` will be useful for readable output.

(a) The first version of the program should prompt for the codemaker's code. Such a game program isn't much fun to play, but it is easier to test.

(b) The final version should use the random module to create the codemaker's code so it can be kept shielded from the codebreaker.

   i. Use the `index = random.randint(start,end)` function (from Section 2.2.10) to generate random indices, $start \leq index \leq end$, to select code characters from `'ABCDEF'`.

ii. Or, use `random.sample(population,k)` that returns a sample of length k from a specified population. The `join` expression (that we will learn the meaning of later in Chapter 7) converts to a string what is returned by the `sample` function:

```
code = ''.join(random.sample('ABCDEF',4))
```

2. Mad Libs

Mad Libs (madlibs.com) is an old word game for children. (If you have never played Mad Libs, try it at eduplace.com/tales/) You are prompted for categories of words (color, girl's name, place, etc.) and then those words are inserted into a predefined story. The predefined story has place holders for those words which get replaced by the values prompted for. For example, Suppose you are prompted for a verb and a noun and respond with "giggle" and "spark". If the predefined string was the first line of Hamlet in this form:

To VERB or not to VERB: that is the NOUN:

The revised version will be:

To giggle or not to giggle: that is the spark:

Create your own predefined story with parts of speech replaced with their description in all capitals: VERB, NOUN, ADJECTIVE, and so on. Your story will be more interesting if you augment your words to be replaced with others appropriate for your story: BOYS_NAME, COLOR, ACTIVE_VERB, and so on. Be creative. If you are at a loss for ideas, begin with a fairy tale. For example, here is the beginning of "Little Red Riding Hood" (Note the backslash continuation character \):

```
story = "Once upon a time in the middle of a ADJECTIVE_ONE NOUN_ONE stood a \
        ADJECTIVE_TWO NOUN_TWO, the home of a ADJECTIVE_ONE ADJECTIVE_THREE \
        NOUN_THREE known to everyone as GIRLS_NAME."
```

Prompt the user for strings to replace the various parts of speech that you have specified. Print out the revised story.

Hint: The string method `replace(old,new)` will be helpful.

3. Pig Latin

Pig Latin is a game of alterations played on words. To make the Pig Latin form of an English word the initial consonant sound is transposed to the end of the word and an "ay" is affixed. Specifically there are two rules:

(a) If a word begins with a vowel, append "yay" to the end of the word.

(b) If a word begins with a consonant, remove all the consonants from the beginning up to the first vowel and append them to the end of the word. Finally, append "ay" to the end of the word.

For example:

- dog ⇒ ogday
- scratch ⇒ atchscray
- is ⇒ isyay
- apple ⇒ appleyay

Write a program that repeatedly prompts for an English word to translate into Pig Latin and prints the translated word. If the user enters a period, halt the program.

Hints:

- Slicing is your friend: it can pick off the first character for checking, and you can slice off pieces and concatenate to yield the new word.
- Making a string of vowels allows use of the "in" operator: `vowels = 'aeiou'`.

CHAPTER 5

Functions—QuickStart

> Function, the exercise, or executing of some office or charge.
>
> T. Blount, Glossographia, 1656 Earliest definition of function in the *Oxford English Dictionary*

YOU HAVE HAVE SEEN EXAMPLES OF USING PYTHON FUNCTIONS. IN THIS CHAPTER, you'll learn how to create your own functions.

The concept of a function should be familiar from its use in mathematics. Functions in programming languages share many of the characteristics of mathematical functions, but add some unique features as well that make them more useful for programming.

One of the main advantages for using functions is that they support divide-and-conquer problem solving. This technique encourages you to break a problem down into simpler subproblems, solve those subproblems, and then assemble the smaller solutions into the overall solutions. Functions are a way to directly encode the "smaller subproblem" solution. You'll see more about this as we work through this chapter.

5.1 WHAT IS A FUNCTION?

In mathematics, a function defines the relationship between values. Consider the function $f(x) \Rightarrow \sqrt{x}$. If you provide a particular value of x, for example, $x = 4$, the function will perform a calculation (here the square root operation) and return the associated value, for example, 2. Mathematicians term the variable x the *argument* to the function and say that the function *returns* the value 2.

It is possible for a function to have multiple arguments, for example a function that calculates multiplication requires two arguments: $f(x, y) \Rightarrow x * y$. However, a mathematical function returns only one object. Note that the returned object can be a *compound* object; an object with multiple elements. For example, when working with graph paper, each point is represented by by its x and y coordinates, an ordered pair (x, y). A function that returns an ordered pair object does indeed return a single value, but it is a value with multiple elements, the x and the y values. An example of such a function would be the *mirror* function. The *mirror* function swaps the x and y values of the ordered pair: $f(x, y) \Rightarrow (y, x)$. The notion that the object a function returns can be a compound object is very useful, including in Python.

Python functions share many of the characteristics of mathematical functions. In particular, a Python function:

- represents a single operation to be performed
- takes zero or more arguments as input
- returns one value (potentially a compound object) as output

A function is also important because it represents an *encapsulation*. By encapsulation, we mean that the details of an operation can be hidden, providing coarser operations that we as programmers can use without having to understand the function's internal details. A function can represent the performance of an operation without making the reader plow through the details of *how* the operation is actually performed.

Consider the square root (`sqrt`) function with respect to encapsulation. There are many ways to calculate a square root that vary in accuracy and speed. For example, we wrote a square root function in Section 3.5, and as you might guess there are other, more efficient approaches to solving the square root problem. However, each implementation performs the "square root" operation. Each implementation takes in an argument and returns its square root. As long as the result is correct, we need not be concerned with the details of how the operation is performed. That is encapsulation.

5.1.1 Why Have Functions?

As you progress in learning to program, you'll move from essential programming elements to important programming elements. In Chapter 2, selection (***`if`***) and repetition (***`while`***) are essential programming constructs. It is difficult to write any program without using these two essential features. Functions, on the other hand, allow us to write *better* code. Also, because functions allow us to divide programs into smaller pieces, they assist in divide-and-conquer problem solving. In that way, functions make programs *easier* to write. Finally, once a function is written, it can be *shared* and used by other programmers (including ourselves). Thus, functions provide a powerful construct that we can use to make our programs easier to read, write, and maintain.

From this point on, many of the programming elements we introduce will make some tasks easier and will subsequently make writing and understanding (i.e., reading) the program easier. You could write programs without them, but those programs would be more difficult to read, write, and maintain.

In more detail, functions provide the following features which help in programming:

- **Divide-and-Conquer Problem Solving**: As we have already mentioned, functions divide programs into smaller pieces, an approach that corresponds nicely to a divide-and-conquer approach to problem solving (introduced in Chapter 3).
- **Abstraction**: Functions provide a higher-level interface to operation that the function implements. By encapsulating details, functions provide a programmer with a high-level view of the function's operation that could be implemented in multiple ways—possibly by someone else. By analogy, consider how you drive a car. It has a simple interface that hides considerable complexity. Your car has many options, for example fuel-injected, turbocharged, or many others. Does the existence of these options change that basic interface you have to the car—that is turn the wheel, hit the gas, press the brake? Do you understand how fuel injection provides better performance for your car than a carburetor does? Do you care? You don't have to know the difference: you simply drive the car. Abstraction means that the operation the function represents (drive the car) can be implemented in many ways that does not affect the basic car interface. The underlying operations can also be changed (upgrade the engine) without changing the interface.
- **Reuse**: Once a function has been created, it can be reused. If you write a function that locates strings in a database, then anywhere that functionality is required can reuse that function. The more such a function is needed, the "simpler" the code that uses it.
- **Sharing**: Once your function is well tested, you can distribute it for use by other programmers. Those programmers can further test the function, refine its capabilities, and through improvement provide a service to everyone in the field. Useful functions can be collected into modules for sharing. Sharing of modules is one of Python's strengths, as programmers generously share modules in many diverse areas.
- **Security**: You hear again and again of security breaches in code: phone companies, computer distributors, software companies, and so on. One way to battle security issues is the use of functions. Small pieces of code can be more easily vetted, and security (and other issues) be more easily addressed. Once they have been approved, they can be used to construct other secure components, which can also be reused, and so on. Building securely from the "bottom up" is one approach to writing secure code.
- **Simplification and Readability** (duplication removal): Because a function provides an encapsulation, it can be used to simplify a program and make it more readable. Anywhere that multiple lines of code might be needed to address a problem, a function can replace those lines. If the replacement can be done in multiple places, the result is simpler code.

5.2 PYTHON FUNCTIONS

There are two parts to a Python function, and they correspond to the two parts found in mathematical functions[1]: the *definition* and the *invocation*. The definition defines (creates)

[1] Some languages, such as those derived from C (C++, Java, C#), have a third part—the declaration.

the function; the invocation is the application, the running or calling, of the function in a program. A function definition is the *second* way we have seen to create a name associated with an object in Python, the first being an assignment statement.

Consider an example function that converts Celsius temperatures to Fahrenheit.

- First we need a conversion formula: $C * 1.8 + 32$
- Mathematics has a function *invocation*:

$$fahrenheit = f(C)$$

where the *definition* of the function is:

$$f(C) = C * 1.8 + 32$$

- Python has a function *invocation* that looks very much like the mathematical one:

```
fahrenheit = f(C)
```

but the Python *definition* looks quite different:

```
def f(celsius_float):
    return celsius_float*1.8 + 32
```

As in mathematics, C is called an *argument* of the function. The `celsius_float` variable is termed a *parameter* of the function. Upon invoking the function, the argument C's value is passed to the parameter value `celsius_float` for use in the calculation.[2] More detail on the passing of values between arguments and parameters can be found in Section 8.1.1.

A function definition begins with the keyword **def**. The Python definition works similarly to an assignment statement. By executing a **def** statement, a new name is created in the namespace and a new object, a function object, is associated with that name. As we have observed elsewhere in Python, everything is an object, and functions are no different.

def is a compound statement, meaning that it provides a suite of other Python statements and expressions that are part of the function. The suite of statements are what will constitute the calculation done by the function object. One of the special keywords that can be used in functions is the **return** statement. The **return** indicates a value that is returned as output from the function invocation. A function's operation ends after a **return** statement is executed. A function may have more than one **return** statement, but the first one that is executed will end the function's operation. (We have used the phrase "to *invoke* a function," but an equivalent and frequently used phrase is "to *call* a function.") The general form of a function is shown in Figure 5.1.

Let's create a function to do our temperature conversion (Code Listing 5.1) and use it in a session. Note the parts of the function: the **def** and **return** keywords as well as the parameter (`celsius_float`). Finally, notice the indentation for the suite of statements, which is a part of the function definition. We will discuss the special comment with triple quotes (""")

[2] Note that to adhere to our naming convention, the argument C should have been named better such as `celsius_float`, but we left it as plain C so that it looked more like the mathematical function.

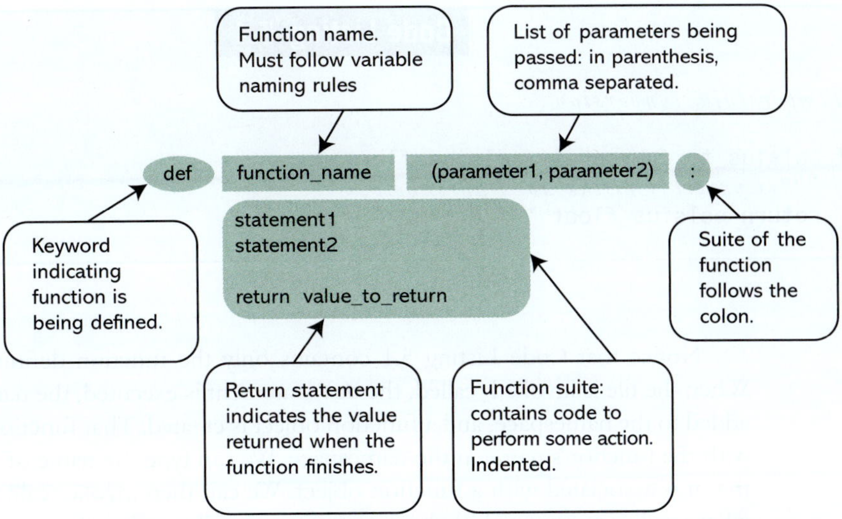

FIGURE 5.1 Function parts.

later, but a comment just after the header of a function is called a *docstring*. It is a convenient place to describe the function, its inputs and outputs, what it does, and so on, and it has some special properties, which we will discuss further in Section 8.3.2. Putting a docstring in a function is **always** a good idea.

```
In  [1]: runfile('/Users/user/python/file.py', wdir='/Users/user/python')

In  [2]: celsius_to_fahrenheit
Out [2]: <function celsius_to_fahrenheit at 0xcc22f0>

In  [3]: celsius_to_fahrenheit(100)
Out [3]: 212.0

In  [4]: celsius_to_fahrenheit(0)
Out [4]: 32.0

In  [5]: new_fn()
Traceback (most recent call last):
  File "<stdin>", line 1, in <module>
NameError: name 'new_fn' is not defined
In  [6]: new_fn = "a string object"
In  [7]: new_fn
Out [7]: 'a string object'

In  [8]: new_fn()
Traceback (most recent call last):
  File "<stdin>", line 1, in <module>
TypeError: 'str' object is not callable
```

Code Listing 5.1

```
# Temperature conversion

def celsius_to_fahrenheit(celsius_float):
    """ Convert Celsius to Fahrenheit."""
    return celsius_float * 1.8 + 32
```

Notice that Code Listing 5.1 contains only the function definition—no invocation. When the file is invoked/called, the ***def*** statement is executed, the name of the function is added to the namespace, and a function object is created. That function object is associated with the function's name in the namespace. We can type the name of the function and see that it is associated with a function object. We can then invoke (call) the function and see what results are returned. Python recognizes to call/invoke a function when a name is followed by parentheses. The parenthesis may or may not contain a list of arguments. It is the parentheses that mark the invocation, and the name adjacent to the parentheses is the function invoked. In the session, we converted 100°C to 212°F and 0°C to 32°F. If the function is not defined, or if the object associated with a name is not a function object, then an error occurs as is shown in the session.

5.3 FLOW OF CONTROL WITH FUNCTIONS

Functions introduce a new flow of control model. Up to this point, a program has essentially been a series of statements and expressions that are executed in the order they appear in the file. Some of the statements introduced local control paths within those statements, such as with selection or repetition, but the flow remained sequential in the file. With functions, we create a set of small, independent subprograms that can be used to construct a larger program.

In short, the flow of control with functions is to flow from the invocation (call) in the calling program, to the function itself, and then back to the calling program with the function's return value being made available to the calling program. Control *within* a function remains sequential: one statement after another along with local control statements.

For every program, there is usually one "main" part where execution begins. After that, the flow of control is based on the order of both statements and functions. In particular for functions, operation of a function is determined by when it is invoked, not when it is defined. Functions can be defined anywhere in the program file, as long as they are defined *before* they are invoked. Functions must be defined before use because the function name must be placed in the namespace before it can be called.

Figure 5.2 shows an example of function control flow.

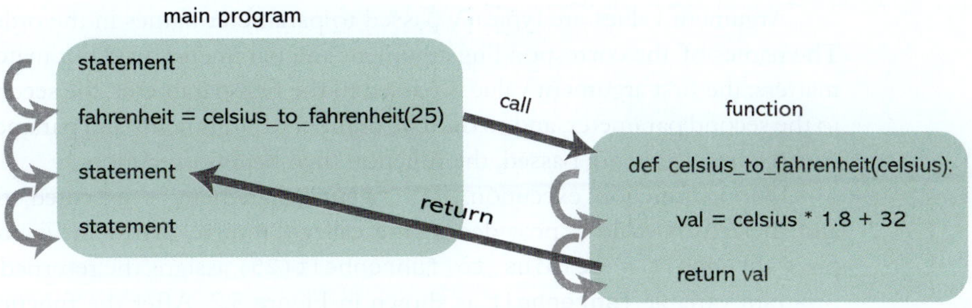

FIGURE 5.2 Function flow of control.

5.3.1 Function Flow in Detail

Consider two programs: the *caller,* the program presently executing, and the function. In this example, the caller is the main program, the program where execution begins. A caller executes its statements until it encounters a function invocation, `celsius_to_fahrenheit (25)` in Figure 5.2. At that point, the caller temporarily suspends, and the function begins. Thus, one program is suspended (the caller) waiting for a result from the now executing function. When the function finishes execution, the suspended caller receives the return value from the function and the main program (caller) resumes execution from that point.

Because the function is essentially a new program, the function gets its own namespace when it begins execution. Any object that gets created and given a name (by assignment, by a ***def***, etc.) *within* the function is placed in the function's separate namespace, *not* the main program's (caller's) namespace. If a new name is created in the function that is the same as a name that existed in the caller's namespace, the newly created association is used in the function. This protocol has some interesting consequences, which we will explore in Section 8.1.1.

5.3.2 Parameter Passing

VideoNote 5.1
Simple Functions

Parameter passing is the passing of values from a calling program to a function, so that the function can perform its operation. You will remember that the function `celsius_to_fahrenheit` had a single argument, called C. The function had a single parameter called `celsius_float`. Parameter passing is the passing of values from argument to parameter.

Parameter passing is done just before the calling program suspends. The caller associates its argument values to the corresponding function parameter in the function object. In Figure 5.2, the argument value 25 is associated with the parameter `celsius`. The parameter is then defined in the function's namespace and associated with the value of its corresponding argument. After that, function operation begins.

Argument values are typically passed to parameter names in the order they are listed.[3] The names of the corresponding argument and parameter need not match. Only the order matters: the first argument value is passed to the first parameter, the second argument value to the second parameter, and so on. The number of arguments and parameters must match.[4] Again, after values are passed, the function then begins execution.

During function execution, if a ***return*** statement is executed, the function ends and the return value is provided to the caller ("return" arrow in Figure 5.2). For example, `fahrenheit = celsius_to_fahrenheit(25)` assigns the returned value to the main program variable `fahrenheit` as shown in Figure 5.2. After the function ends, the caller continues.

Code Listing 5.2

```
# Conversion program

def celsius_to_fahrenheit(celsius_float):
    """ Convert Celsius to Fahrenheit."""
    return celsius_float * 1.8 + 32

# main part of the program
print("Convert Celsius to Fahrenheit.")
celsius_float = float(input("Enter a Celsius temp: "))
# call the conversion function
fahrenheit_float = celsius_to_fahrenheit(celsius_float)
# print the returned value
print(celsius_float," converts to ",fahrenheit_float," Fahrenheit")
```

Code Listing 5.2 is a sample program with a function that takes in a Celsius temperature to convert to Fahrenheit.

```
In  [1]: runfile('/Users/user/python/file.py', wdir='/Users/user/python')

Convert Celsius to Fahrenheit.
Enter a Celsius temp: 100
100.0  converts to  212.0  Fahrenheit


In  [2]: runfile('/Users/user/python/file.py', wdir='/Users/user/python')

Convert Celsius to Fahrenheit.
Enter a Celsius temp: 0
0.0  converts to  32.0  Fahrenheit
```

[3] Python also has other ways to pass argument values to parameters. See Chapter 8.

[4] In Chapter 8, you will learn about *default* values, which allow fewer arguments than parameters.

Lines 3–5 define the function. Notice ***def*** beginning the compound statement, the parameter (`celsius_float`), and the ***return*** with its associated expression within the function suite. To repeat, the ***def*** statement is executed by Python and creates the function. Once created, it can be called (invoked) by another program. Remember, a function must be defined (the ***def*** statement must be executed) before a program can call the function.

Lines 7–13 are the "main" program:

Line 9 prompts the user for input.

Line 11 invokes (calls) the function. The value in the argument `celsius_float` is passed to the parameter `celsius_float`. Then control passes to the function. When the function ends, it returns a value that the main program assigns to `fahrenheit_float`.

Line 13. The main program continues with Line 13 and prints the results.

Check Yourself: Simple Functions Check

1. Give the output of these calls to the following function:

```
def make_odd(n):
    return 2*n + 1

print(make_odd(2))
print(make_odd('2'))
n = 3
print(make_odd(n))
print(1 + make_odd(3))
```

2. Write a function `make_even(n)`.
   What happens if you use a string, such as `"24"`, as an argument?
   Why is the behavior different then with `make_odd(n)`?

5.3.3 Another Function Example

It is often useful to extract a digit from a particular location in a number—an *`int`*. A tradition for numbers is that the rightmost digit is named the *units* position, the next to the left is the *tens*, the next is *hundreds* and so on. Those positions are powers of 10, for example, the *tens* is 10^1, the *hundreds* is 10^2, and so on, with the *units* being 10^0. We then represent positions by the exponents so the rightmost is at position 0, the next at position 1, and so on. This numbering scheme is different from what we see in Chapter 4 where strings are numbered with position 0 as the leftmost, that is, just the opposite.

Let's write a function that takes two arguments: a number and its position (represented as an exponent, that is, rightmost digit is at position 0). It will return the digit in that position in the number. Extracting digits can be done with a combination of the integer quotient (`//`) and remainder (`%`) operators. Play with them in the IPython console and you will find the quotient operator with powers of ten for the denominator will remove digits from the right of an integer and that taking a remainder with ten as the denominator will yield the rightmost digit.

For example, if $n = 12345$, the operation `n//100` returns 123. If you take dividend 123 and take the remainder of that number when divided by 10, that is, `123%10`, the result is digit 3. Thus the digit in position 2 from the right (the hundreds position starting with position 0 as rightmost) is 3. If you represent 100 as 10^2 the combined expression is `n//10**2%10` and returns the digit in position 2. If p represents position, the expression is `n//10**p%10`. Including parenthesis makes the expression more readable: `n//(10**p)%10`.

We can now define a function to extract a digit in a specified position. We need two arguments, `number` and `position`, and our function will return the digit in that position. Code Listing 5.3 shows the function.

Code Listing 5.3

```
def get_digit(number,position):
    '''return digit in position in number counting from right'''
    return number//(10**position)%10
```

5.3.4 Function Example: Area of a Triangle

Let's consider the following problem:

> Given three vertices of a triangle, calculate its area.

First, we begin by exploring some mathematics to get the formulas we need. The classic formula for calculating the area of a triangle given the length of the three sides a, b, and c is Heron's Formula:

$$s = \frac{1}{2}(a + b + c)$$

$$area = \sqrt{s(s - a)(s - b)(s - c)}$$

If we begin with vertices, we need to find the length of each side using Euclidean distance (which is simply derived from the Pythagorean Theorem). The distance between two points (x_1, y_1) and (x_2, y_2) is

$$length = \sqrt{(x_1 - x_2)^2 + (y_1 - y_2)^2}$$

With the mathematical formulas in hand, we can consider how to solve the problem. Taking a divide-and-conquer approach, we can consider the overall problem as a series of smaller problems, which we will use functions to solve. The problem breaks down into these steps:

1. Prompt for the three vertices of the triangle.
2. Find the length of each side (Euclidean distance).
3. Find the area (Heron's Formula).

We have some design decisions to make.

- Since we have to input a vertex three times, let's have a function `get_vertex` that returns the *x* and *y* coordinates of a vertex.
- Continuing with our divide-and-conquer approach, let's have a function `get_triangle` that will call `get_vertex` three times, once for each vertex. It will return the *x* and *y* coordinates of all three vertices.
- Since we need to find the side length three times, it makes sense to have a function `side_length` that takes as arguments the vertices of two points and returns the length of the side.
- Finally, let's have a function `calculate_area`.
  - We need to decide if we want to call `side_length` within our `calculate_are` function or outside the function. Either makes sense, but we will call within to illustrate how that is done.

Let's now develop each function, one at a time. Input is always a good place to start because you cannot do much if you do not have some values to work with. Also, input problems tend to be easy to solve and give us a sense of moving forward!

Input

Since we decided to have `get_vertex` called by `get_triangle`, let's begin with `get_vertex`. It is quite simple. It takes no arguments and prompts for the *x* and *y* coordinates of a vertex. We will also convert the input to numbers; we will use *float*. We will return the two values: *x* and *y*. The resulting function is in Code Listing 5.4.

Code Listing 5.4

```
def get_vertex():
    x = float(input("    Please enter x: "))
    y = float(input("    Please enter y: "))
    return x,y
```

For `get_triangle` we simply need to call `get_vertex` three times adding a ***print*** to differentiate each call. Each call to `get_vertex` returns a pair of numbers, which we capture by using two identifiers separated by commas. Later, we will learn that we can add parentheses to make the return more readable—the parenthesis create tuples, for example, ***return*** (x1,y1),(x2,y2),(x3,y3) but that would be getting ahead of ourselves. You can look ahead to Section 7.7 if you are curious but the point is this: a tuple is a single Python data structure with multiple elements. This meets our requirements for a function. Further, if a function returns a tuple we can grab the individual elements with multiple assignments as we saw in Section 2.2.7. The resulting function is in Code Listing 5.5.

Code Listing 5.5

```
def get_triangle():
    print("First vertex")
    x1,y1 = get_vertex()
    print("Second vertex")
    x2,y2 = get_vertex()
    print("Third vertex")
    x3,y3 = get_vertex()
    return x1, y1, x2, y2, x3, y3
```

Find Side Length

We next tackle side length using the formula described earlier. Since we need to calculate the square root we need to include the math module. Since we need two points/coordinates for the calculation we have four parameters to capture (x_1, y_1) and (x_2, y_2). We include a docstring to describe the function. The resulting function is in Code Listing 5.6.

Code Listing 5.6

```
def side_length(x1,y1,x2,y2):
    '''return length of a side (Euclidean distance)'''
    return math.sqrt((x1-x2)**2 + (y1-y2)**2)
```

The function is simply one line long so one may ask: "Why bother with a function?" The answer is *readability*. We believe that, in this case, the program is easier to read. For example, we are able to explain in the docstring that we are using the Euclidean distance. Also, when reading the calling function, calculate_area, it is clear from the name of this function that you are calculating the length—something that may not be apparent from the formula alone. This choice, as with all readability choices, is personal.

With the function written it can be tested independently. Within the Spyder IDE highlight the function, and under the "Run" drop-down select "Run Selection or current line" to run the highlighted function. You can now test the function by itself, especially with arguments for which you know the answer. For example, side_length(0,0,1,1) should return $\sqrt{2} \approx 1.414$.

Calculate Area

With a function in hand to calculate the length of sides we can now apply Heron's Formula. In our design we decided to call `side_length` from within this function, so we begin with three calls to `side_length` to get the lengths of the three sides. After that we simply apply Heron's Formula. Add a docstring to describe what we are doing and the resulting function is in Code Listing 5.7.

Code Listing 5.7

```
def calculate_area(x1,y1,x2,y2,x3,y3):
    '''return area using Heron's forumula'''
    a = side_length(x1,y1,x2,y2)
    b = side_length(x2,y2,x3,y3)
    c = side_length(x3,y3,x1,y1)
    s = (1/2)*(a + b + c)
    return math.sqrt(s*(s-a)*(s-b)*(s-c))
```

Whole Program

All we need now is the main part of our program, which is simply:

- Get coordinates of the triangle's three vertices.
- Calculate the area of the triangle.
- Print the area.

The final program is in Code Listing 5.8.

Code Listing 5.8

```
# Calculate the area of a triangle given its vertices
import math

def get_vertex():
    x = float(input("    Please enter x: "))
    y = float(input("    Please enter y: "))
    return x,y

def get_triangle():
    print("First vertex")
    x1,y1 = get_vertex()
    print("Second vertex")
    x2,y2 = get_vertex()
```

```
    print("Third vertex")
    x3,y3 = get_vertex()
    return x1, y1, x2, y2, x3, y3

def side_length(x1,y1,x2,y2):
    '''return length of a side (Euclidean distance)'''
    return math.sqrt((x1-x2)**2 + (y1-y2)**2)

def calculate_area(x1,y1,x2,y2,x3,y3):
    '''return area using Heron's forumula'''
    a = side_length(x1,y1,x2,y2)
    b = side_length(x2,y2,x3,y3)
    c = side_length(x3,y3,x1,y1)
    s = (1/2)*(a + b + c)
    return math.sqrt(s*(s-a)*(s-b)*(s-c))

x1, y1, x2, y2, x3, y3 = get_triangle()
area = calculate_area(x1,y1,x2,y2,x3,y3)
print("Area is",area)
```

There are a few points that are worth noting about the example.

- The use of functions made our problem-solving task easier. The functions allowed us to consider the problem in smaller pieces—the divide-and-conquer technique introduced in Chapter 3.
- The main program is very readable. Even if we did not know the implementation of the functions, we could guess what they (likely) did and understand what the program was trying to do.
- Note the reuse of identifiers such as `x1` and `y1` in the both the main program and in functions. Because each function gets its own namespace, these identifiers are associated with different objects. More on this in Section 8.1.

5.3.5 Functions Calling Functions

There is no limitation to when a function can be called, except that it must be defined before it is called (the ***def*** must occur in the code before the calls). It is often the case that a function will call another function. This extension does not change the process described previously, though it does make the flow of control slightly more complicated for us to follow. More on this in Chapter 8. In fact, a function can call itself—a complicated control flow to which we devote Chapter 15.

5.3.6 When to Use a Function

There are no hard or fast rules about when to write something as a function or when to leave code as part of a larger program. However, here are some guidelines that may prove helpful.

Do One Thing: A function should be the encapsulation of a single, identifiable operation. A function should do one thing, and of course, do it well. Functions that try to do too many things are candidates to be broken into multiple functions (i.e., refactored).

Readable: A function should be readable. This is a reiteration of our venerable **RULE 2**.

Not Too Long: A function shouldn't be too long. What is "too long" depends on many things, but the idea is that if a function does one thing, a person should be able to read it easily and understand its purpose. If the function is too long, difficult to follow somehow, it might need to be broken into multiple functions.

Reusable: A function should be reusable in contexts other than the program it was written for originally. If possible, the function should be self-contained and not dependent on some nuance of the calling program. If it has dependencies, then those dependencies should be made clear so that others can use it more easily.

Complete: A function should be complete, in that it works in all potential situations. If you write a function to perform one thing, you should make sure that *all the cases* where it might be used are taken into account. It is often the case that the core of the function is very straightforward, but handling all the cases it might encounter requires supporting code.

Refactoring: We first mentioned the term refactoring in Section 2.9. Again, refactoring is the process of taking existing code and modifying it such that its structure is somehow improved but the functionality of the code remains the same. Functions can play a prominent role in this process, as they allow you to take long, difficult-to-follow code and break it into smaller, more manageable, pieces. If you need to "fix" some code, consider refactoring it into functions.

The idea that a function should "do one thing" is important enough that we will make it a rule.

> **Rule 8:** A function should do one thing.

PROGRAMMING TIP

A useful rule of thumb for novices is to keep each function small enough to fit on the screen. Like all rules of thumb, there are many reasons to break the rule, but you should ask yourself if there is a good reason to make a function longer than that.

5.3.7 What If There Is No Return Statement?

Sometimes we write functions without a **return** statement. Functions that do not return a value are often called *procedures*.

In that case, what, if anything, is returned? The answer is that a special Python value None is returned by default if the programmer does not provide a **return** statement. None is a kind of odd Python value—a value to represent nothing. Kind of cosmic!

There are some good reasons to use a procedure. One that often comes up is specially formatted output. Formatting output to look "pretty" can be laborious and potentially complicated. A print procedure is therefore a good place to do such output. The procedure isolates all the printing format but does not return a value. Other instances might require a change of state to the program, something like turning a graphics mode on or off, or changing the network connection to a different mode. Each of these elements is best isolated as a process, but as a function they do not need to return a value.

To see this process in action, let's write a trivial function that simply prints its parameter. We will then assign the result of the function to a variable. When we print the value of the variable, we see that None was printed.

```
In  [1]: def formatted_output(my_str, my_int):
...: print('The result of the processing for',my_str, 'was', my_int)
    # no return statement
...
In  [2]: formatted_output('Bill',100)
Out [2]: The result of the processing for Bill was 100

In  [3]: result = formatted_output('Fred',75) # capture the implicit return
The result of the processing for Fred was 75
In  [4]: print(result)
None                                          # return value was None
```

5.3.8 What If There Are Multiple Return Statements?

If there are multiple **return** statements, the first **return** encountered during the operation of the function stops the function at that point and returns that value. Consider the following example function, which returns "positive," "negative," or "zero," depending on the value of the argument.

```
In  [1]: def positive_negative_zero(number):
...:     if number > 0:
...:             return "positive"
...:     if number < 0:
...:             return "negative"
...:     else: #  number == 0
...:             return "zero"
```

```
In  [2]: positive_negative_zero(5) # test all three possible cases
Out [2]: 'positive'

In  [3]: positive_negative_zero(-2.5)
Out [3]: 'negative'

In  [4]: positive_negative_zero(0)
Out [4]: 'zero'
```

Note that the function works correctly whether the argument passed in is an `int` or a `float`. For that reason neither suffix is used in the name. Multiple return values can make following the flow of control in the function more difficult for the reader to follow. If possible, it is best to have as few returns as possible so the reader can more clearly follow the function.

VISUAL VIGNETTE

5.4 TURTLE FLAG

The first official United States flag was established by the Continental Congress on June 14, 1777, with first Flag Act: "Resolved, That the flag of the United States be made of thirteen stripes, alternate red and white; that the union be thirteen stars, white in a blue field, representing a new Constellation." The arrangement of the stars was not specified: Betsy Ross used a circle, others used rows.

Drawing a flag is an excellent illustration of the practicality of functions. In abstraction, the United States flag is a composition of two shapes: stars and stripes (rectangles). It is impractical to draw the 13 (or 50!) stars individually when a function can encapsulate the multiple steps required for each star. The same can be said for drawing the 13 stripes—they are simply rectangles. Even the blue field behind the stars is a rectangle, as is the overall shape. Therefore, to draw the flag using Python's Turtle graphics, one will

VideoNote 5.2
Problem Design Using Functions

want at least two functions: `draw_star` and `draw_rectangle`. The program is left as an exercise.

5.5 WHAT'S WRONG WITH MY CODE?

Here are suggestions for finding problems with functions. Refer to Appendix C for details.

- **Test Functions Independently:** A particularly useful trick is the ability to run individual functions within Spyder. This allows us to test functions independently. Within the Spyder IDE highlight the function, and under the "Run" drop-down select "Run Selection or current line" to run the highlighted function. After it has been "run" you can now call the function from within the shell. Run the function with sample arguments and see if it produces the results you expect. *Testing functions independently is one of the most important approaches to programming you can learn!*
- **Examine the Function's Namespace:** Setting a breakpoint within a function allows you to examine the function's namespace within the Variable Explorer window of Spyder (upper right of IDE). Knowing the value of variables, particularly the provided arguments, is useful for finding problems.
- **Stepping through a Function:** Set a breakpoint at the beginning of the function and then step through the function, one instruction at a time. This is useful for observing what the function is actually doing. Pay particular attention to which parts of control (loops or selection) that you step through. Often there is a problem with a Boolean expression or the values of variables within the expression.
- **Mismatched arguments and parameters:** This kind of error message is self-explanatory and helpful with its information. Here is an example.
  `TypeError: square() missing 1 required positional argument: 'x'`
- **None:** When a variable has an unexpected value, for example, `None`, it is often due to that variable being incorrectly assigned a value from a function call in one of two ways: First, mistakenly assigning the result of a function call that **has no return**, that is, `result = [1,3,2].sort()`. Such non-return functions are usually associated with mutable data structures such as lists. The other is forgetting the parenthesis in the function call, that is, `f = ''ABC''.lower`. The function was never **run**, and you don't get the result you expected.

  When you see such an error, walk the code back to find the function that provided a value to that variable. It likely is missing a ***return*** statement.
- **TypeError:** Sometimes you get a `TypeError` when there is mismatch of types between the provided argument and how that argument is used in the function. For example, maybe you passed a string to a function that is performing integer arithmetic that is not defined for strings. Again, either the Variable Explorer or proper naming can help sort out this problem.

Summary

In this chapter, we introduced the concept of functions in a programming language and showed how functions work in Python. Of particular importance is that functions aid us in the divide-and-conquer approach to problem solving. After covering the list data structure in a subsequent chapter, we will revisit functions to examine the complexities of passing mutable objects to functions.

Functions

- Working with functions requires two elements: a function *definition* and a function *invocation* (call).
- Control transfers from the calling point to the function.
- Caller's arguments map to the function's parameters in order from left to right.
- A function has its own namespace.
- Parameters are in the function's namespace.
- A function must be defined before it is called.
- Defining a function puts its name in the caller's namespace.
- Syntax: function definition:

```
def function_name(parameter_list):
    # statement_suite
    return # something
```

Rules

- **RULE 1:** Think before you program!
- **RULE 2:** A program is a human-readable essay on problem solving that also happens to execute on a computer.
- **RULE 3:** The best way to improve your programming and problem skills is to practice!
- **RULE 4:** A foolish consistency is the hobgoblin of little minds.
- **RULE 5:** Test your code, often and thoroughly!
- **RULE 6:** If it was hard to write, it is probably hard to read. Add a comment.
- **RULE 7:** All input is evil, until proven otherwise.
- **RULE 8:** A function should do one thing.

Exercises

1. Draw the parts of a function and label the parts. Write a brief definition for each part.
2. What are three guidelines used to determine whether creating a separate function is the sensible thing to do?
3. What does this function do? What does it return for num = 5?

```
def Func(number):
    total = 0
    while number > 0:
        total = total + number*(number-1)
        number = number - 1
    return total
```

4. What does this function do? What does it return if x = 5?

```
def Func(x):
    total = 0
    for i in range(x):
        total += i * (i-1)
    return total
```

5. What does this function do? What number is returned by this function?

```
def Func():
    number = 1.0
    total = 0

    while number < 100:
        total = 1//number
        number+=1

    return total
```

6. Write a function that takes mass as input and returns its energy equivalent. ($E = mc^2$). The units should be in the meter-kilogram-second system.
7. Menu Writing:
   (a) A common task while writing any software is to display a menu and ask the user for a choice. One such example is the menu on your cellphone. It has messaging, contacts, games, settings, media, and web (and possibly others) as options. Write a function called `display_menu` that displays the menu to the user and allows the user to make a choice (using `input`).
   (b) Write a function that takes the choice of the user and makes calls to the other functions that correspond to the operation to be performed. (Give meaningful names to the functions. You *don't* have to write the other function definitions.)

8. Write a function that takes in the lower and upper limits of a range, and prints all the prime numbers in that range. The function returns the sum of all primes in that range.

---

9. Write a function that takes as input an English sentence (a string) and prints the total number of vowels and the total number of consonants in the sentence. The function returns nothing. Note that the sentence could have special characters such as dots, dashes, and so on.

10. The Fibonacci sequence is: 1, 1, 2, 3, 5, 8, 13 ... You can see that the first and second numbers are both 1. Thereafter, each number is the sum of the previous two numbers.
    (a) Write a function to print the first N numbers of the Fibonacci sequence.
    (b) Write a function to print the Nth number of the sequence.

11. Suppose you are purchasing something online on the Internet. At the website, you get a 10% discount if you are a member. Additionally, you are also getting a discount of 5% on the item because its Father's Day.

    Write a function that takes as input the cost of the item that you are purchasing and a Boolean variable indicating whether you are a member (or not), applies the discounts appropriately, and returns the final discounted value of the item.

    Note: The cost of the item need not be an integer.

12. A leap year in the Gregorian calendar system is a year that's divisible by 4 but not by 100, unless it is also divisible by 400. For example, 1896, 1904, and 2000 were leap years but 1900 was not. Write a function that takes in a year as input and prints whether it's a leap year (or not).

13. Error checking with meaningful error messages is an important part of programming. Consider the following scenario: A customer has to pay his monthly credit card bill. The credit limit on the card is $1000. The minimum payment due is always $20. Let the payment on the credit card be $P. Write a function called `make_payment(P)` that takes as an argument the total payment on the credit card ($P) and prints "Success" or "Retry". Try to think of all the errors that should be taken care of and implement those in the function. One example would be that if the payment is less than $20, the program should remind the user that it's less than the minimum payment due.

14. You've decided to program a simple calculator. Your calculator can perform the following operations:
    (a) It can add two numbers.
    (b) It can subtract one number from another.
    (c) It can multiply two numbers.
    (d) It can divide one number by another.

Write a function that asks the user for two numbers, and the operation they wish to perform on these two integers, and return the result. *Note:* Choices should be entered as strings.

15. Chat:

(a) In certain chat programs or messaging applications, there is a limit on the number of characters that you can send in a message. Write a function that takes as input the message (a string) and checks whether the number of characters is less than 160 (or not). If the length of the message is less than 160, the message should be returned. If the length of the message is greater than 160, a string consisting of only the first 160 characters should be returned.

(b) How would you check if the restriction is on number of words rather than characters? Write a function that allows a message with only 20 words.

16. The highest common factor of two numbers is the product of the common prime factors of both numbers. Write a function to find the highest common factor of two input numbers.

17. (Refactoring) In Chapters 1 and 2, there were exercises to calculate football quarterback pass ratings and then to output the quality of the quarterback.

(a) Write the pass rating as a function. Have the main program prompt for the five inputs and then use those inputs as arguments to the function.

(b) Write the quality rating as a function and add it to the existing program.

18. In an exercise in Chapter 2, we wrote a program to check whether a number is an Armstrong number or not. Refactor your solution by writing a function to check for an Armstrong number, and using that in your solution, print all the Armstrong numbers between a range given by the user.

19. Write a function that takes as input a string that stores date and time (24-hour clock) in the following format:
"MM/DD/YYYY HR:MIN:SEC" and prints the following:

- DD/MM/YYYY
- HR:MIN:SEC
- MM/YYYY
- Whether the time is "AM" or "PM".

Validation of the input in the function is necessary. For example, if the user gives an input of "122/04/1990 13:12:12", the given string is invalid, as there can be only 12 months in a year. Think of all possible erroneous inputs and write code to handle them. The function doesn't return anything.

20. Write a function that takes as input a string that stores date and time in the format, "MM/DD/YYYY HR:MIN:SEC" and prints the number of seconds elapsed since "01/01/YYYY 00:00:00".

21. Write a function that prints all numbers in the range A to B (inclusive) that have all digits belonging to the set {1,3,4,8,9}. Check whether A is less than or equal to B; otherwise, swap them before proceeding. The function takes two integer arguments: A and B.

22. Given a string of length three representing a set (i.e., surrounded by curly braces) such as `"{ABC}"`, write a function that takes the string as an argument and returns a string of its permutations in comma separated form, such as `"{ABC, ACB, BAC, BCA, CAB, CBA}"`. *Hint*: Use multiple **`for`** loops.

23. Implement a textual progress bar in Python. In any progress bar, the space occupied by it is finite. Let's say, the textual progress bar could show only 10 Xs. So, you have to divide the total time by 10, and after those many seconds, you have to print an X on the output.

For example, if the time is 100 seconds:

At 0 secs :
At 10 secs : X
At 20 secs : XX
...
At 100 secs : XXXXXXXXXX

Write a function that takes the number of seconds as input and implements the progress bar. This task is easier if you look up Python's `time` module either in the documentation or online.

24. Write a function that accepts a list of strings and sorts them alphabetically.

25. Create a function `digit_count` that takes in an integer or float and returns the number of even digits, odd digits, and digits 0 before the decimal point. Return the three numbers in a tuple.

26. Write a function that takes in a string and rotates is such that it moves each character one space to the right, with the last character moving to the beginning. Return the rotated string.

27. A hapax legomenon (often abbreviated to hapax) is a word which occurs only once in a document. In the fields of computational linguistics and natural language processing, it is common to disregard hapax legomena (and sometimes other infrequent words), as they are likely to have little value for computational techniques. This disregard has the added benefit of significantly reducing the memory use of an application. Define a function that given the file name of a text will return all its hapaxes. Make sure your program ignores capitalization.

28. Suppose you are a manager of a smartphone company, and you want to determine the price of a new smartphone in an isolated market. The relationship between demand and price can be simplified as $Demand = -12 * Price + 600$. The cost of making each phone is $50, and you know that you will not sell the phone for more than $100. Write a function to determine the price at which you will get the maximum profit.

Programming Projects

1. **U.S. Flag in Turtle Graphics:**
Draw the United States flag using at least four functions. The regular polygons in the US flag are natural candidates for functions.

(a) Draw the flag shown earlier in the chapter with 13 stars arranged in rows. Add color for maximum effect.
(b) Draw the flag with the 13 stars arranged in a circle. (*Hint*: Is it really a circle, or is it some other *regular* figure?)
(c) Rewrite your program so it takes as input one positive Real number that specifies a scale factor. That is, 0.5 will cause a half-size flag to be drawn and 2.8 will draw a flag that is 2.8 times larger.

2. **DNA Sequencing:**
The term *DNA sequencing* refers to methods for determining the order of the nucleotide bases, adenine, thymine, cytosine, and guanine, in a molecule of DNA. The standard representation of the bases is to use their first letters, ATCG, so that DNA is represented as a string using only those four characters. However, DNA strings are millions of bases (characters) long.

Substring matching is the process of determining whether a shorter string (the substring) is contained within a longer string. Substring matching plays important roles in the reconstruction of an unknown DNA string from pieces, and in searching for interesting substrings within a known DNA string.

Python provides a `find(substring, start, end)` string method that returns the lowest index (integer) where the *substring* is found in the index range `start` ≤ `index < end`. The `start` and `end` arguments are optional, but for this exercise we will make them required (you will learn later how to handle optional arguments). If the substring is not found, −1 is returned.

(a) Without using the `find` string method, write a function that behaves exactly like the `find` string method. As your function is not a string method, the string to search must be an argument—let's make it the first one. The resulting format of your function will be:

```
find(some_string, substring, start, end)
```

(b) Biology researchers frequently want to find *all* the locations where a substring is found, not simply the first one. Write a function named `multi_find(some_string, substring, start, end)` that, instead of returning one integer index, returns a string that contains zero or more indices separated by commas. In this case, the string will contain digits representing the integer indices. If the substring is not found, an empty string is returned. You may use the `find` method that you wrote earlier.

(c) A nice feature of our `multi_find` function is that if the substring is not found, an empty string is returned. In particular, if the substring is not found, the returned empty string resolves to be `False` in a Boolean expression. The returned value will be `True` otherwise. That feature allows one to use `multi_find` in an `if` statement such as `if multi_find(S,substring,0,20)`: the Python `find` string method does not share that characteristic (why?). Write a program that exercises both your `find` and your `multi_find` functions including their use in Boolean expressions. Create some strings using only the base letters, ATCG, and search for substrings within them.

3. Heap of Beans:

We are going to play a game called *the heap of beans*. You start with a heap of beans (we will start with 16 beans) and two players. Each player can remove 1, 2, or 3 beans from the pile of 16. Each player is required to take some number of beans from the pile during each turn. The players take turns removing beans, and the player who takes the last bean from the pile is the loser. You can try this game with a partner using 16 pieces of paper as beans.

Each player is to be represented by a function, so we will have two functions. Each function takes a single argument, representing the present number of beans, and returns the number of beans remaining after the player function takes its turn. During the operation of the player function, the function reports (prints) how many beans were removed. Note that the function decides how many beans to remove. It takes no input from the user.

You also need a main program. The main program initializes the heap of beans to 16, and then alternately calls the first player function and the second player function until one of them gets the last bean. The main then reports who the loser is and exits.

(a) Write a simple player function such as one that always takes exactly one bean. It isn't very interesting, but it lets you test your program.

(b) Now for the fun part. Write a "smart player" function and test it against other students' functions in your class. A class tournament would be best—who has the best strategy?

CHAPTER 6

Files and Exceptions I

> Exceptio probat regulam in casibus non exceptis.
> Exception confirms the rule in the cases not excepted.
>
> 17th-Century English Law

NOW THAT WE UNDERSTAND STRINGS, LET US LOOK AT THE CONCEPT OF A FILE. FILES are an important part of working with computers, and in this section we will introduce the basics of file handling using Python.

6.1 WHAT IS A FILE?

A file is a collection of bytes of information that usually resides permanently on a disk. Files fall into two broad categories: text files and binary files. Text files were originally organized as ASCII data but now include Unicode data that can handle a greater variety of characters that are required by many languages (see Appendix F for the Python default encoding). In either case, text files are human-readable (when displayed in a text editor or browser, they will be readable). Binary files are all other files—they use some other coding scheme. A classic example is the format that Microsoft uses for Word documents. If you open a Word document in a text editor, it appears as random characters—not human-readable characters. For the rest of this chapter, we will focus on text files.

6.2 ACCESSING FILES: READING TEXT FILES

To access a file from Python you must open a connection between the Python shell and the file residing on a disk. Thus, we are creating a kind of "pipe" between the information on the disk and the program that will use it. This "pipe" will be the conduit for the file contents to pass back and forth between the disk where the file resides and the program.

The pipe in Python is a *file object* that is created when the connection is established. The file object uses the main memory of the computer to store data as they are moved between the disk and program. The Python `open` command sets up that connection and returns the file object that represents the connection. All subsequent actions we perform on a file are done through this file object, also sometimes called a *file descriptor* or *stream*. A file can be opened for reading or writing (or both) through this file object.

Let's assume that a text file named `temp.txt` exists and is in the same folder (directory) as our program (see Section 14.3.1 for a discussion of where the file needs to be). Here are the contents of the file `temp.txt`:

```
First line
Second line
Third line
```

Let's examine a Python shell session that opens the file for reading, reads the contents of the file, and then closes the file. The first line calls the `open` function with arguments specifying the file name and whether it is being opened for reading (`'r'`) or writing (`'w'`). The connection to the file is created as a file object named `temp_file`. Using `temp_file` we can iterate through the file contents line by line using a **`for`** statement, as we have done before. Remember, when iterating through a file object, we are iterating one *line* at a time. At the end we *close* the file with `temp_file.close()`, tearing down the connection between the shell and the file. If we forget to close the file, the Python shell will close it when the shell exits or is restarted.

```
In  [1]: temp_file = open("temp.txt","r") # open the file for reading
In  [2]: for line_str in temp_file: # iterate through the file via the file object
       print(line_str,end='') # use end=''; line_str already has a carriage return

First Line
Second Line
Third Line
In  [3]: temp_file.close() # close the file when done
```

6.2.1 What's Really Happening?

VideoNote 6.1
Reading Files

When you set up a connection between your Python program and a file, you are creating what is called a "stream" of data. Data flows from the file (on disk) to your program, as in Figure 6.1. An important part of the stream is the *buffer* that is in main memory where the data is stored on its way between the file on the disk and your program. The stream is managed by the operating system, which tries to ensure that when your **`for`** loop needs the next line, that line will already be in the buffer in memory. A buffer is needed because disk

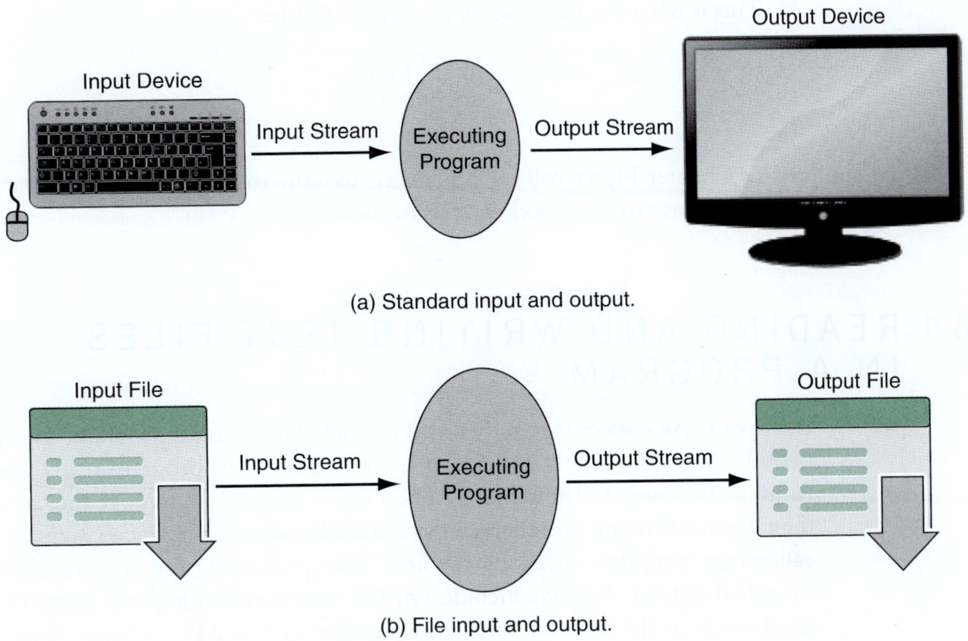

FIGURE 6.1 Input-output streams.

access is slow, so the computer, when it isn't busy, stores a lot of the file's contents in memory. If everything is working well, the whole process will be invisible to the programmer.

6.3 ACCESSING FILES: WRITING TEXT FILES

Writing files requires first creating a file object connection as we did for reading a file. The only difference is that one specifies "w" rather than "r" in the *open* command. If the file doesn't exist for writing, it will be created.

Once a file is open, you can print to the file by adding the `file=` argument to the ***print*** command. In the following session, we write to the file "temp.txt" using its file descriptor: `file=temp_file`.

```
# open file for writing:
#     creates file if it does not exist
#     overwrites file if it exists
In  [1]: temp_file = open("temp.txt","w")
In  [2]: print("first line", file=temp_file)
In  [3]: print("second line", file=temp_file)
In  [4]: temp_file.close()
```

This is what the file looks like when we finish:

```
first line
second line
```

In Chapter 14, we will see other ways to write to a file, but this approach is very simple and easy to use so it is good enough for now.

6.4 READING AND WRITING TEXT FILES IN A PROGRAM

Let's put these concepts together into a simple line-reversal program. This program opens two files: one for reading and the other for writing. The program reads, one line at a time, from the file named "`input.txt`." The `line` is stripped (to remove the carriage return) and then iterated through one character at a time. We add each character *to the left* of a new string called `new_str`, thus reversing the line. After processing the line, we write `new_str` to a file called `output.txt`. We include a ***`print`*** statement (with a little formatting to get things lined up correctly) to make sure we know what we should be getting. The program is Code Listing 6.1.

Code Listing 6.1

```
# reverse each line of the input file in the output file

input_file = open("input.txt", "r")
output_file = open("output.txt", "w")

for line_str in input_file:
    new_str = ''
    line_str = line_str.strip()      # remove the carriage return
    for char in line_str:
        new_str = char + new_str     # concat at the left (reverse)
    print(new_str,file=output_file)  # print to output_file

    # include a print to shell so we can observe progress
    print('Line: {:12s} reversed is: {:s}'.format(line_str, new_str))
input_file.close()
output_file.close()
```

We need to create the `input.txt` for the program to work on. Using a text editor, the following is the content of `input.txt`:

```
First Line
Second Line
Third Line
```

Applying our program to `input.txt`, the session below shows the result, followed by the contents of `ouput.txt`.

```
Line: First Line   reversed is: eniL tsriF
Line: Second Line  reversed is: eniL dnoceS
Line: Third Line   reversed is: eniL drihT
```

```
eniL tsriF
eniL dnoceS
eniL drihT
```

6.5 FILE CREATION AND OVERWRITING

When one opens a file for reading and the file doesn't exist on the disk (or the operating system cannot find the file), an error is generated. If the file exists, the file object connection is created and we can read values from the file.

When one opens a file for writing and the file doesn't exist, a file will be created in the folder where the program is running (see Section 14.3 on how to change that behavior). If the file already exists, its contents will be cleared; that is, the file contents will be lost, and any new material is added to the now-empty file. The program looks for the file in the folder that the program is running in.

The modes in which you can open a file and the effects they have on existing (or non-existing) files are shown in Table 6.1.

Mode	How opened	File Exists	File Does Not Exist
'r'	read-only	Opens that file	Error
'w'	write-only	Clears the file contents	Creates and opens a new file
'a'	write-only	File contents left intact and new data appended at file's end	Creates and opens a new file
'r+'	read and write	Reads and overwrites from the file's beginning	Error
'w+'	read and write	Clears the file contents	Creates and opens a new file
'a+'	read and write	File contents left intact and read and write at file's end	Creates and opens a new file

TABLE 6.1 File modes.

Check Yourself: File Check

1. Consider a file named *input.txt*.

   Which of the following is the proper way to read the file?

   (a)
   ```
   in_file = open('input.txt','r')
   for ln in in_file:
     # do something
   ```
   (b)
   ```
   in_file = open('input.txt')
   for ln in in_file:
     # do something
   in_file.close()
   ```
   (c)
   ```
   in_file = open('input.txt','r')
   for ln in in_file:
     # do something
   in_file.close()
   ```
   (d)
   ```
   in_file = open('input.txt','r')
   while ln in in_file:
     # do something
   in_file.close()
   ```
   (e) None of the above.

6.5.1 Files and Functions Example: Word Puzzle

Let's use strings and functions to solve a word puzzle.

> Find a word that contains the vowels `'a'`, `'e'`, `'i'`, `'o'`, and `'u'` in that order in a string.

To solve a word puzzle, we need a list of words.

Reading a File of Words

To read through the file, one line at a time, we can do the following:

- open the file for reading
- read through the file one line at a time

A Python program that reads through the whole file `dictionary.txt`, and simply prints each line of the file is shown in Code Listing 6.2.

Code Listing 6.2

```
# Print all words in a dictionary file that has one word per line

# open file named "dictionary.txt" for reading ('r')
data_file = open("dictionary.txt", 'r')

# iterate through the file one line at a time
for line_str in data_file:
    print(line_str)
```

Interestingly, this program prints the lines of the file in double-space format. Why is that[1]?

Searching a File of Words

Now that you have reviewed how to read through a file of words, let's try to solve our puzzle.

First, we need to handle a common feature of file's strings: there are often some characters that we don't want to deal with. In this case, the dictionary file contains a carriage-return character at the end of each line, and it may contain stray characters such as spaces or tabs. We can eliminate such characters using the `strip` string method, one of the methods listed in Section 4.3.3. If no arguments are provided to `strip`, then a new string is returned with whitespace removed from *either end* of the calling string. The calling string is not modified. If a string argument is provided to `strip`, only those characters in the argument string are removed. An example of its use is `a_str.strip('., ')`, which returns a new string that strips commas, periods, and the space character from the beginning and end of `a_str`. In particular, `'', this.''.strip('., ')` and `''this,,.''.strip('., ')` both return the new string object `'this'`. The blank character in the argument string is hard to see (after all, it is a blank) but it is there!

PROGRAMMING TIP

The `strip` method works only on the beginning and end of a string. For example, `'this string'.strip()` returns the string `'this string'`. Because no arguments are provided, the default behavior is to return a new string where whitespace (tabs, carriage returns, space characters, etc.) are removed from the ends, but the space in the *middle* of the string is unaffected. Note that *all* the whitespace characters are removed from the beginning and the end.

[1] Each line already has a carriage-return in the line. The print function adds another, hence double-spaced.

For every line we fetch from the file, we strip that line to remove whitespace at the beginning and end of the line. In addition, word puzzles are often easier if all characters are known to be only lower case (or only upper case). The string method `lower` is useful for that. Let's create a function that strips out whitespace characters and makes all of the remaining characters lowercase: Code Listing 6.3.

Code Listing 6.3

```
def clean_word(word):
    """Return word in lower case stripped of whitespace."""
    return word.strip().lower()
```

Notice the use of chained method invocation in the function as described in Section 4.3.1.

As our word puzzle requires a word with all five vowels in order, the word must be at least six characters long, so there is no reason to consider shorter words. We can add that check and the `clean_word` function to our file-reading program: Code Listing 6.4.

Code Listing 6.4

```
# Find a word with a single example of the vowels a, e, i, o, u in that order

data_file = open("dictionary.txt", "r")

def clean_word(word):
    """Return word in lower case stripped of whitespace."""
    return word.strip().lower()

# main program
for word in data_file:        # for each word in the file
    word = clean_word(word) # clean the word
    if len(word) <= 6:       # skip word if too small to have all vowels
        continue
    print(word)
```

Our program still does nothing to solve our puzzle, but we now have a framework to work in: a program that reads a file of words and and returns each word stripped of extraneous characters.

Solving the Puzzle

To solve this puzzle, we want to determine the vowels and their order in a word. Let's write a function that returns the vowels found in a word in the order in which they were found. A function lets us consider each word in isolation. For any word, we can check each character to see whether it is a vowel and collect the vowels into a string in the order in which they were found. To begin, we create a variable that is associated with the empty string, with the intent that we will add discovered vowels to that string. Our algorithm is:

- create an empty string, let's call it `vowels_in_word`
- for each character `char` in the word
  - if `char` is a vowel, add it to the string `vowels_in_word`

How do we check whether a character is a vowel? We can create a string of vowels `vowels_str` and associate it with `'aeiou'` and check to see whether each character in the dictionary entry `word` is ***in*** (is a member of) `vowels_str`.

Code Listing 6.5 is our algorithm implemented as a function.

Code Listing 6.5

```
def get_vowels_in_word(word):
    """Return vowels in string word—include repeats."""
    vowel_str = "aeiou"
    vowels_in_word = ""
    for char in word:
        if char in vowel_str:
            vowels_in_word += char
    return vowels_in_word
```

Let's try the function out in a session to find the vowels in the word `'create'`. The vowels in `'create'` in order are `'eae'`.

```
In  [1]: word = "create"
In  [2]: get_vowels_in_word(word)
Out [2]: 'eae'
```

Our function appears to be working. Of course, we need to check it more thoroughly, but as always we will leave that as an exercise for you to try on your own.

Now that we have a function that extracts the vowels in a word, we can consider our puzzle again. The puzzle requires a word with exactly the five vowels in order. That is, if our get_vowels_in_word function returns exactly *'aeiou'*, we have found our puzzle answer. Our refined algorithm to solve the puzzle is:

- open the file
- for each word in the file
  – strip the word
  – if the word is too small, skip it
  – get the vowels in the word
  – if the vowels returned is exactly *'aeiou'*, print the original word

Using that algorithm as the main part of our program, let's put it all together in Code Listing 6.6.

Code Listing 6.6

```
# Find a word with a single example of the vowels a, e, i, o, u in that order

data_file = open("dictionary.txt", "r")

def clean_word(word):
    """Return word in lower case stripped of whitespace."""
    return word.strip().lower()

def get_vowels_in_word(word):
    """Return vowels in string word—include repeats."""
    vowel_str = "aeiou"
    vowels_in_word = ""
    for char in word:
        if char in vowel_str:
            vowels_in_word += char
    return vowels_in_word

# main program
print("Find words containing vowels 'aeiou' in that order:")
for word in data_file:          # for each word in the file
    word = clean_word(word) # clean the word
    if len(word) <= 6:          # if word is too small, skip it
        continue
    vowel_str = get_vowels_in_word(word)  # get vowels in word
    if vowel_str == 'aeiou':              # check if you have exactly all vowels in order
        print(word)
```

```
Find words containing vowels 'aeiou' in that order:
facetious
```

Check Yourself: Function Practice with Strings

1. Give the output provided by the following program on the indicated input values.

```
def func1 (str1, str2):
    if str1 > str2:
        result_str = str1[1:]
    else:
        result_str = str2[:-1]
    return result_str

# main program}
response1_str = input("Enter a string:")
response2_str = input("Enter a second string:")

print(func1(response1_str, response2_str))     # Line 1
print(func1(response2_str, response1_str))     # Line 2
```

(a) Given the two input values (in order), `abc123` and then `bcd456`, what output is produced by Line 1?

(b) Given the two input values (in order), `abc123` and then `bcd456`, what output is produced by Line 2?

(c) Given the two input values (in order), `aaabbc` and then `aaabbcd`, what output is produced by Line 1?

(d) Given the two input values (in order), `aaabbc` and then `aaabbcd`, what output is produced by Line 2?

The `dictionary.txt` file we used for the example contained almost 40,000 words, and our puzzle-solving program found only one that satisfied the criteria of having the vowels *'aeiou'* in that order: facetious. A larger dictionary (we found one with over 234,000 words) returned a longer list as shown in the following session.

```
Find words containing vowels 'aeiou' in that order:
abstemious
abstemiously
abstentious
acheilous
acheirous
acleistous
affectious
annelidous
arsenious
arterious
bacterious
caesious
facetious
```

```
facetiously
fracedinous
majestious
```

There are a couple of points that are worth noting about the example.

- The use of functions made our problem-solving task easier. The functions allowed us to consider the problem in smaller pieces—the divide-and-conquer technique introduced in Chapter 3.
- The main program is very readable. Even if we did not know the implementation of the functions `clean_word` and `get_vowels_in_word`, we could guess what they (likely) did and understand what the program was trying to do.
- Note the reuse of the identifier `vowel_str` in the both the main program and in the function `get_vowels_in_word`. Because the function gets its own namespace, these identifiers are associated different objects. More on this in Section 8.1.

6.6 FIRST CUT, HANDLING ERRORS

We have been programming long enough now to know that errors occur in programs. Upon some reflection, these errors come in two broad categories: syntax errors and runtime errors.

Syntax errors are those where the code is malformed by the programmer. Somehow the code does not follow the rules of Python. Perhaps we forgot a colon at the end of a ***for*** statement or did not provide an end parenthesis for a ***print*** statement. Whatever the error might be, we as programmers must correct the problem and write the code so that it follows the rules.

Runtime errors are errors, not of syntax but of application. For example, we can write a Python program that is syntactically correct and tries to divide an integer by zero. There is no rule of the Python language that prevents this, but application of this incorrect program leads to an error. There are many examples of this: dividing by zero, accessing a character past the end of a string, a ***while*** loop that never ends, and so on. In particular, when we programmers interact with users, errors can occur. The user can provide a string of characters where an integer is needed, the file name string provided does not exist, and so on. What are we to do, as programmers, to try and deal with runtime errors when they occur?

Up to this point, our approach has been to ignore these issues. If the user provides a file that we cannot open (it doesn't exist, it is in the wrong directory, etc.), then the program quits at that point. This is not a very helpful solution since both the user is frustrated ("What the heck does *that* mean?"), and the programmer is frustrated because of a simple error. We need a way to handle these types of errors as programmers, if we can.

Python, and other programming languages, provides a way to deal with errors, the *Exception* system. We will deal with exceptions in more detail in Chapter 14, but for now, exceptions are how we can deal with user input errors.

6.6.1 Error Names

Though we haven't really paid much attention to it, Python provides very specific error names to the various situations that occur when something goes wrong. Look at the session below.

```
In  [1]: input_file = open("no_such_file.txt", "r")
Traceback (most recent call last):
  File "<stdin>", line 1, in <module>
FileNotFoundError: [Errno 2] No such file or directory: 'no_such_file.txt'
In  [2]: my_int = int('a string')
Traceback (most recent call last):
  File "<pyshell#1>", line 1, in <module>
    my_int = int('a string')
ValueError: invalid literal for int() with base 10: 'a string'
```

The last line of each error message explicitly names the error that Python has encountered. When we try to open a file that doesn't exist, Python stops the program with a `FileNotFoundError`. Note the capitalization. The name of the error is exact, including capitalization. When we try to convert a string of letters to an integer, Python stops the program with a `ValueError`. Python is not only giving us hints as to what is wrong, it is giving the error a very specific name, something we can take advantage of!

PROGRAMMING TIP

Typing code with a specific error in the shell is a very easy way to figure out what name Python gives the error. There are many names Python has for the various errors Python encounters, but rather than remember them all (and their spelling), just type an example of the error into the shell and see what name Python gives it!

6.6.2 The `try-except` Construct

Python provides a construct called the ***try-except*** construct that allows a programmer to capture a runtime error and give the programmer the option to handle that error. This construct has two suites named (not surprisingly) the ***try*** suite and some number of ***except*** suites. Their functions are as follows:

- The ***try*** suite contains code that we, as programmers, want to "watch over" for possible runtime errors. That is, we as programmers are concerned about a suite of code that might cause a runtime error.

- Each ***except*** clause has associated with it a particular Python error name,[2] and a suite of code that will run, if that particular error occurs.

In general, the construct looks like the following:

```
try:
    # suite of code to watch here
except ParticularErrorName:
    # suite of code to handle the named error, if it occurs
```

Marking a suite of code with a ***try*** might seem a bit odd at first. How can a programmer know what to watch? It is not as difficult as it might seem. The places where the user provides input to a program are, again, a prime example. We know what errors might occur if the user provides incorrect input. We should watch that code to make sure the user gets it right, and help the user correct his input if possible, reducing everyones frustration.

Failure to enforce correct input is a common source of security errors. In fact, this is an opportunity for a rule. This is a quote from Michael Howard and David LeBlanc from their book *Writing Secure Code*:

Rule 7: All input is evil, until proven otherwise.

Adherence to this rule would eliminate the majority of security errors.

6.6.3 try-except Flow of Control

The flow of control in a ***try-except*** is a little complicated as control can skip around a bit when an error occurs. The idea is something akin to an ***if*** statement. The conditions in an ***if*** are the equivalent of the names of the errors associated with the ***except***. Whichever error name matches the present error, that associated suite is executed. If no such match occurs, then the error suites are skipped.

Here is the flow of control in detail.

1. Normal flow of Python control enters a ***try*** suite.
2. If an error occurs within the ***try*** suite, stop executing the suite at the point where the error occurred and abandon the rest of the suite. If unexecuted lines of the ***try*** suite remain, they will be ignored.
3. *Raise* (let it be known that) the particular exception for that error that was encountered.
4. Look for an ***except*** suite that can handle that exception. That is, an ***except*** associated with the particular error name that occurred.
5. If such an ***except*** suite is found, move control from the error in the ***try*** suite to the beginning of the appropriate ***except*** suite. When the ***except*** suite finishes, skip to the end of the ***try-except*** construct and continue normal Python execution.

[2] In fact, an ***except*** can have no or multiple errors, see Chapter 14.

6. If an error occurs and no appropriate ***except*** suite is found (no ***except*** is associated with the present error) let Python handle it. This is the normal error process: print the type of error encountered, stop the program, and go back to the interpreter.
7. If no error occurs in the ***try*** suite, that suite finishes, the ***except*** suites are skipped, and Python continues with normal execution after the ***try-except*** construct.

6.6.4 Exception Example

VideoNote 6.2
Simple Exception Handling

Code Listing 6.7 shows a simple example of using a ***try-except*** construct, especially in the context of user interaction. The goal of the program is simple: to read a particular line, indicated by a line number, from a file. The user is required to provide both the file name and the line number. Take a look at this code, and we will examine it in detail next.

Code Listing 6.7

```
# read a particular line from a file. User provides both the line
# number and the file name

file_str = input("Open what file:")
find_line_str = input("Which line (integer):")

try:
    input_file = open(file_str)                # potential user error
    find_line_int = int(find_line_str)   # potential user error
    line_count_int = 1
    for line_str in input_file:
        if line_count_int == find_line_int:
            print("Line {} of file {} is {}".format(find_line_int, file_str,
line_str))
            break
        line_count_int += 1
    else:
        # get here if line sought doesn't exist
        print("Line {} of file {} not found".format(find_line_int, file_str))
    input_file.close()

except FileNotFoundError:
    print("The file",file_str,"doesn't exist.")

except ValueError:
    print("Line",find_line_str,"isn't a legal line number.")

print("End of the program")
```

Lines 4–5: The user is asked for the file name and the line number. Both are potential sources of user input error.

Lines 7–19: The ***try*** suite. Errors within this suite can potentially be handled by ***except*** suites.

Lines 8–9: The opening of the file and the conversion of the line number are the two errors we are interested in handling so we put them in the ***try*** suite.

Lines 10–11: The variable `line_count_int` will represent the number of lines read while `line_str` will represent the content of the line just read. Note that we don't actually look at the content of the line; we only count lines.

Lines 12–15: This is the heart of the example. We read each line, and if that line has as its line number the line number we seek, we print out a message. After we find the line we seek and print it, we ***break*** out of the ***for*** loop.

Lines 16–17: If we get to the ***else*** part of the ***for*** loop, then we have gone through the file and not found our line (we didn't ***break*** out of the loop). So we print a message.

Lines 21–22: The first ***except*** suite catches a file opening error. We print a message if the program cannot open the provided file.

Lines 24–25: The second ***except*** suite catches an *`int`* conversion error for the line number. We print a message if the program cannot convert the provided string to an integer.

Line 27: This is a ***print*** statement after the entire ***try-except*** construct. It gives us an opportunity to see that the Python program continues even after an error occurs.

We run a session under various circumstances to test this code. We provide a file, `input.txt` with the same contents as before, namely:

```
First Line
Second Line
Third Line
```

Second, we run the code with various user input errors, namely:

1. With proper input.
2. With a bad file name.
3. With a bad line number (a string).
4. With a line number not in the file.

```
Open what file:input.txt
Which line (integer):2
Line 2 of the file input.txt is Second Line

End of the program
```

```
In  [1]: runfile('/Users/user/python/file.py', wdir='/Users/user/python')

Open what file:badFileName.txt
Which line (integer):2
The file badFileName.txt doesn't exist
End of the program


In  [2]: runfile('/Users/user/python/file.py', wdir='/Users/user/python')

Open what file:input.txt
Which line (integer):abc
Line abc isn't a legal line number
End of the program


In  [3]: runfile('/Users/user/python/file.py', wdir='/Users/user/python')

Open what file:input.txt
Which line (integer):27
Line 27 of the file input.txt not found
End of the program
```

First, notice that even under the error conditions described, the code finishes with the final print statement. The errors were handled by the provided **except** suites. Second, follow the control under each user input error. If the code finishes without error (tests 1 and 4), the **except** suites are skipped and the program finishes. If an error occurs (tests 2 and 3), the **try** code halts at the error, the appropriate **except** suite is started, the final print statement is executed and then the program finishes.

For test case (2) when we enter a bad file name notice that we also must enter a line number before the error happens. It seems wasteful to enter a line number, if the file cannot be opened. How can we fix that? We could keep asking for file-name input until it is correct. That is, keep asking for a file's name until it could be opened (*hint:* loop and break). After getting a correct file name, we could then move on to keep asking for a line number until a correct line number was provided. We leave those as exercises.

PROGRAMMING TIP

If you look more closely, the non-error (first) part of the session above has an extra carriage return in its output. Why is that? By default, **print** ends with a carriage return. However, the line still contained its original carriage return, so an extra carriage return was printed. Including `end=''` in the **print** statement will suppress **print's** default (extra) carriage return.

Check Yourself: Exception Check

1. Given:

```
number_str = input("Input a floating-point number: ")
while True:
    # Line 1
print("Number is",number_float)
```

We want code that will keep prompting until a correctly formated floating-point value is entered so it can be printed at the bottom. Which is the correct replacement for Line 1?

(a)
```
try:
    number_float = int(number_str)
    break
except ValueError:
    number_str = input("Try again: input a floating-point number:")
```
(b)
```
try:
    number_float = float(number_str)
except ValueError:
    number_str = input("Try again: input a floating-point number:")
```
(c)
```
try:
    number_float = float(number_str)
    break
except ValueError:
    number_str = input("Try again: input a floating-point number:")
```
(d)
```
try:
    number_float = float(number_str)
    break
except FloatError:
    number_str = input("Try again: input a floating-point number:")
```

6.7 EXAMPLE: COUNTING POKER HANDS

The game of poker is a card game that emerged in its current form from New Orleans in the mid-nineteenth century. In its simplest form, a hand of five cards is dealt from a 52-card English deck, and the combinations within those five cards determine the value of the hand. Poker is a gambling game, so knowing the probabilities of the various combinations of hands is important. Using the mathematics of combinatorics, it is possible to calculate the probabilities, but with the computer we can also simply count the possibilities to determine probabilities.

In the 52-card English deck, each card has a rank (also known as value), for example, 9, as well as one of four suits (hearts, spades, diamonds, clubs). Therefore, a card's value is represented by a pair value:suit, for example, nine of clubs. In poker, card values proceed from ace (the highest), to king, then queen, all the way down to 2, the lowest. For poker,

Rank	Name	Description
9	Royal flush	{Ace, king, queen, jack, ten} + flush
8	Straight flush	Straight + flush
7	Four of a kind	Four equal ranks within five cards
6	Full house	Pair + different rank three of a kind
5	Flush	Five cards with the same suit
4	Straight	Five cards, sequentially ranked with no gaps
3	Three of a kind	Three equal ranks within five cards
2	Two pairs	Two pairs of equal ranks within five cards
1	One pair	One pair of equal ranks within five cards
0	Nothing in hand	

TABLE 6.2 Poker hand rankings.

players receive five cards, which constitutes a hand, and it is the rank of the hand that is used to determine winners in a game. Both card value and card suit can figure in ranking overall card hands. For example, a *flush* is a hand in which all five cards have the same suit. The rankings of hands (in contrast to ranking of individual cards) are shown in a tabular form in Table 6.2 and in pictorial examples in Figure 6.2.[3] Within the same hand rank, the hand with higher ranked card values wins, for example, a pair of tens wins over a pair of twos.

What are the chances of getting any particular hand? One way to determine the chances is to make a list of all 311,875,200 possibilities, count each type of hand, and divide each count by 311,875,200. One could approximate the exact probabilities by doing the same calculation with a smaller sample of 1,000,000 possibilities. If the smaller sample is representative, you will get a good approximation. Generating a good list of 1 million possibilities is an interesting problem in itself that is beyond your abilities at this point, but should be possible by the end of the book.

Fortunately, a good list of possible poker hands exists on the Internet.[4] The data file has 1 million lines, each containing the rank and suit of each of five cards along with the hand ranking, using the ranks in Table 6.2. The format is described in Table 6.3 with seven lines shown in Figure 6.3.[5] Each pair of values on each line represents a card. For example, the first three cards in the first line are the ten of diamonds, the seven of hearts, and the queen of spades. The number in the last (rightmost) column is the hand rank as specified in Table 6.2. Therefore, the first two hands have rank 0, which means that they have nothing of value. The third line represents a hand with rank 3 which is "three-of-a-kind"—there are three cards of rank 2 in the hand: two of diamonds, two of spades, and two of clubs. The

[3] The picture has one fewer hand because the "royal flush" is simply a special case of a "straight flush."

[4] It is available at the Machine Learning Repository at the University of California, Irvine, http://archive.ics.uci.edu/ml/datasets/Poker+Hand

[5] This seven-line slice was formatted into more readable columns—the original has no spaces.

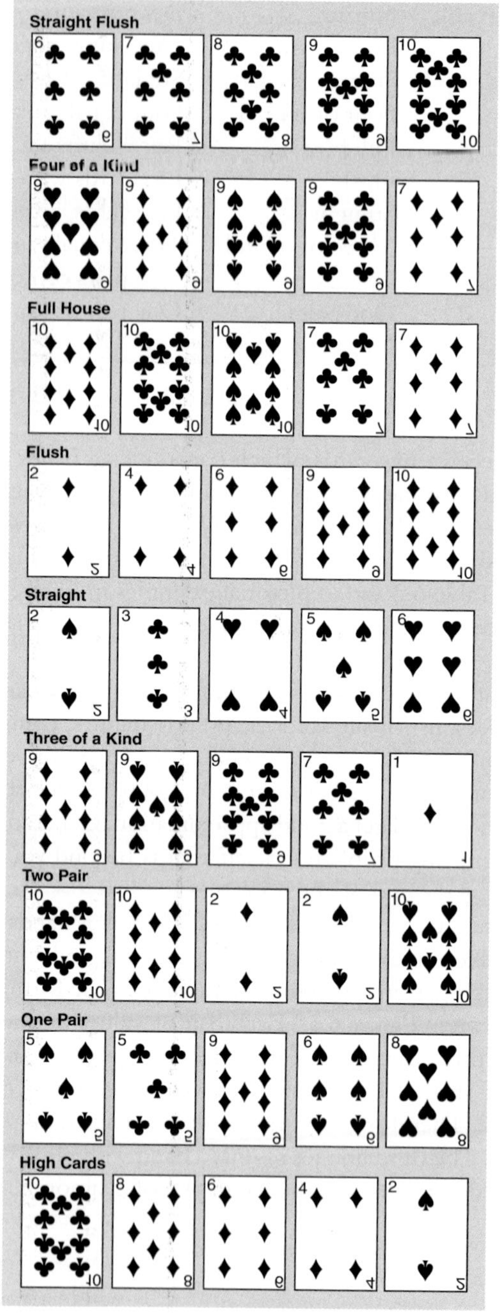

FIGURE 6.2 Poker hand rankings.

```
C1-suit, C1-rank, C2-suit, C2-rank, C3-suit, C3-rank, C4-suit, C4-rank, C5-suit, C5-rank, Hand Rank
```

TABLE 6.3 Poker file format.

```
3, 10, 1, 7, 2, 12, 4, 2, 2, 1, 0
4, 9, 4, 12, 4, 13, 2, 6, 3, 4, 0
3, 2, 2, 2, 3, 12, 3, 1, 4, 2, 3
4, 11, 2, 8, 1, 13, 4, 7, 1, 7, 1
4, 8, 3, 8, 1, 3, 1, 4, 3, 7, 1
2, 7, 2, 5, 3, 10, 4, 13, 3, 7, 1
1, 4, 3, 4, 3, 5, 4, 10, 2, 10, 2
```

FIGURE 6.3 Poker file—seven lines out of 1 million.

next three hands each have one pair (hand rank 1): sevens, eights, and then sevens again. The final hand has two pairs (hand rank 2): fours and tens.

6.7.1 Program to Count Poker Hands

Now that we have covered the file format and the game rules, how will we count hands? First, observe that all we care about is the last column of the line of the file, which indicates that hand's rank. Someone has already determined hand rank for us (something you will be able to do yourself by the end of the book). Remember that the eleventh column is index number 10, as we start indexing at zero.

Program to Count the Total Hands in the File

As always, a useful strategy is to develop a program a little at a time. In this case, let's begin with a program that counts the number of hands in the file. We know that there should be 1 million—let's see if we get that. Here is our algorithm:

1. Open the file for reading.
2. Create a variable to hold our count and initialize it to zero.
3. Loop through the file, adding one to our counter each time we get a line.
4. Print the value of the counter.

Let's name the variable to hold our count `total_count_int`. We create a file object `poker_file` by using the *open* function, giving a file name as an argument. As we have seen, the ***for*** iterates through all the lines of the file, and we add one to `total_count_int` for each line. The program counts the number of lines in the file. See Code Listing 6.8. In the output, we see that we indeed have 1 million hands.

```
Total hands in file:  1000000
```

Code Listing 6.8

```
# count poker hands

# 1. open the poker data file for reading
poker_file = open("poker-hand-testing.data",'r')

total_count_int = 0 # 2. create variable to hold the count— initialized it

# 3. step through each line of the file
for line_str in poker_file:
    total_count_int = total_count_int + 1 # at each line increment the counter

print("Total hands in file:", total_count_int)
```

Program to Count the Hands with One Pair

Now that we can loop through the file examining every line, let's take another step toward our goal. Using a **for** loop, we read each line of the file into the variable `line_str`. Using this line, let's count the number of hands with exactly one pair. Such a hand has a rank 1, so we need to examine the last (rightmost) item in each line to determine that hand's rank. Remember, each line represents a hand of poker. The line is formatted in a common text format known as *comma-separated value* (CSV) format. A CSV format separates multiple fields in a single line of data by commas as you saw in Table 6.3. To access each individual field in a line, we can `split` the line on a comma character and then examine the last field. The `split` method returns a data structure we have not yet discussed, a *`list`* (see Chapter 7), but for now all we need to know is that `split` separates the string into individual string elements. For this example, the separation character is a comma (','), so we get 11 different string fields for each line, and we store those fields in the `fields` variable. Because a *`list`* indexes in the same way as a string, we can use an index of -1 to reference the last field. Remember that `split` returns each individual field as type *`str`*, so we must convert any field element to an *`int`* if we wish to do arithmetic on it. We also need a variable to hold our count of pairs, `pair_count_int`, and remember to initialize it to zero.

Let's update our algorithm with these changes highlighted in italics. Remember that at this point we are only counting pairs.

1. Open the file for reading.
2. Create *variables* to hold our *counts* and initialize them to zero.
3. Loop through the file reading one line at a time,
   (a) add 1 to our total counter each time we read a line.
   (b) *get the hand rank: split on comma and get the last item (index -1).*

(c) *if handRank is 1, then add one to our pair counter.*

4. Print the *values* of the counter.

```
Total hands in file:  1000000
Count of pair hands:  422498
```

Our code is Code Listing 6.9. The ***for*** loop assigns each line from the file to the `line_str` variable. The `line_str` is a string of 11 comma separated field. We use the `split` function, `line_str.split(',')`, to split the line at the commas and store the 11 resulting strings in the `fields` variable, and then we grab the last item, `fields[-1]`, which is the hand rank. However, the resulting `hand_rank_str` is still a string so we must convert it to an integer using `int(hand_rank_str)`. We can now check to see whether the converted `hand_rank_int` has a value of 1—remember that checking equality in Python uses a double-equal sign (==). If its value is 1; that is, `if hand_rank_int == 1:`, that hand contains one pair, so we increment the pair count: `pair_count_int = pair_count_int + 1`.

Code Listing 6.9

```
# count poker hands

# 1. open the poker data file for reading
poker_file = open("poker-hand-testing.data",'r')

total_count_int = 0 # 2. create and initialize variable to hold the total count
pair_count_int = 0 # create and initialize variable to hold pair count

# 3. Loop through each line of the file
for line_str in poker_file:
    total_count_int = total_count_int + 1      # (a). add one total for each hand

    fields = line_str.split(',')               # (b). split on a comma
    hand_rank_str = fields[-1]                 #      and get the last field
    hand_rank_int = int(hand_rank_str)

    if hand_rank_int == 1:                     #(c) if handRank is 1 (it is a pair
)
        pair_count_int = pair_count_int + 1 #    add one to pair count

print("Total hands in file: ", total_count_int) # 4. print the values
print("Count of pair hands: ", pair_count_int)
```

Program to Calculate the Probability of One Pair

An astute reader will have noticed that we wanted a probability, but only did a count. Calculating such a probability is straightforward: the count of pairs divided by the total number of hands in the file. Simply including the expression `pair_count_int/total_count_int` provides the probability. Python division yields the appropriate floating point, and we convert the result to a percentage using the "%" formatting command in the format statement.

Let us experiment with these calculations and printing the results in a session. After running the program in the console, the values for `pair_count_int` and `total_count_int` are still available, so we can play with them in the Python shell. Here is a session showing how the Python shell can be used to develop expressions to put into the program. We want nicely aligned output, so we use right justification, limit the number of decimal points, and automatically convert to percentages:

```
In  [1]: runfile('/Users/user/python/file.py', wdir='/Users/user/python')

Total hands in file:  1000000
Count of pair hands:  422498
In  [2]: pair_count_int/total_count_int
Out [2]: 0.422498

In  [3]: print("result:{}".format(pair_count_int/total_count_int))
result:0.422498
In  [4]: print("result:{:%}".format(pair_count_int/total_count_int))
result:42.249800%
In  [5]: print("result:{:5.2%}".format(pair_count_int/total_count_int))
result:42.25%
In  [6]: print("result:{:>9.4%}".format(pair_count_int/total_count_int))
result: 42.2498%
```

Code Listing 6.10

```
# count poker hands

# 1. open the poker data file for reading
poker_file = open("poker-hand-testing.data",'r')

total_count_int = 0  # 2. create and initialize variable to hold the total count
pair_count_int = 0   #    create and initialize variable to hold pair count

# 3. Loop through each line of the file
for line_str in poker_file:
    total_count_int = total_count_int + 1     # (a). add one total for each hand
```

```
    fields = line_str.split(',')                    # (b). split on a comma
    hand_rank_str = fields[-1]                      #      and get the last field
    hand_rank_int = int(hand_rank_str)

    if hand_rank_int == 1:                          #(c) if handRank is 1 (it is a pair)
        pair_count_int = pair_count_int + 1         #    add one to pair count

print("Total hands in file: ", total_count_int)  # 4. print the values
print("Count of pair hands: ", pair_count_int)
print("Probability of a pair:  {:>9.4%}".format(pair_count_int/total_count_int))
```

We can now put that expression into our code (Code Listing 6.10) and try it out:

```
Total hands in file:  1000000
Count of pair hands:  422498
Probability of a pair:    42.2498%
```

Error Checking

Now that we have the basic code working, let's add error checking; that is, apply **RULE 7**. Our initial code had a fixed file for input. A more general approach would be to prompt for a file name and then ensure that it opened correctly before proceeding. We can do that by putting a ***try-except*** block into a ***while True*** infinite loop and then ***break*** out of the loop if the file is opened successfully. A file that fails to open will raise a FileNotFoundError exception, so that is the exception name we catch. Once we break out of the file opening loop, we know that the file has opened and we can move on. A second error check can be made where we read the hand type from the file. There we convert the input to an *int*, and we can check if that conversion was successful. If it fails, we have chosen to ignore the line as bad input, and not count it. Code Listing 6.11 is the revised code to count pairs.

Code Listing 6.11

```
# count poker hands

# 1. open the poker data file for reading
file_str = input("Enter a file name: ")
while True:   # loop until you break
    try:
```

```
        poker_file = open(file_str,'r')
        break                    # success! so move on to rest of program
    except IOError:
        print("Error opening file:",file_str)
        file_str = input("Enter a file name: ")


total_count_int = 0  # 2. create and initialize variable to hold the total count
pair_count_int = 0   #    create and initialize variable to hold pair count

# 3. Loop through each line of the file
for line_str in poker_file:
    total_count_int = total_count_int + 1      # (a). add one total for each hand

    fields = line_str.split(',')               # (b). split on a comma
    hand_rank_str = fields[-1]                 #      and get the last field
    try:
        hand_rank_int = int(hand_rank_str)
    except ValueError:
        continue                    # bad line: quietly skip this line of the file

    if hand_rank_int == 1:                     #(c) if handRank is 1 (it is a pair)
        pair_count_int = pair_count_int + 1 #  add one to pair count

print("Total hands in file: ", total_count_int) # 4. print the values
print("Count of pair hands: ", pair_count_int)
print("Probability of a pair: {:>9.4%}".format(pair_count_int/total_count_int))
```

The Rest of the Program

We now have a partial program that calculates the probability of getting a poker hand with just one pair. To complete the program, we must include a counter for each type of hand, and we need to increment that counter each time that type of hand is encountered. The resulting program, Code Listing 6.12, is quite a bit longer, but if you examine it carefully, you will see that we simply duplicated the counter initialization and increment statements. (Later, you will learn how to write a more compact program with one compound counter as a list to accommodate all 10 types of hands.)

Also, some details need to be decided upon—a common issue in problem solving: the devil is in the details. In this case, when we count the number of flush-type hands, do we include straight flushes, or is the flush count really "flushes that are not straight flushes?" For simplicity, we have chosen the latter, but either would be reasonable.

Code Listing 6.12

```
# count poker hands

# 1. open the poker data file for reading
file_str = input("Enter a file name: ")
while True:  # loop until you break
    try:
        poker_file = open(file_str,'r')
        break                    # success! so move on to rest of program
    except IOError:
        print("Error opening file:",file_str)
        file_str = input("Enter a file name: ")

# all counts are ints, so count as a suffix is enough
total_count          = 0
nothing_count        = 0
pair_count           = 0
two_pair_count       = 0
three_of_a_kind_count= 0
straight_count       = 0
flush_count          = 0
full_house_count     = 0
four_of_a_kind_count = 0
straight_flush_count = 0
royal_flush_count    = 0

for line_str in poker_file:
    total_count = total_count + 1
    fields = line_str.split(',')           # split on a comma
    hand_rank_str = fields[-1]             # and get the last field
    try:
        hand_rank_int = int(hand_rank_str)
    except ValueError:
        continue          # bad line: quietly skip this line of the file
    if hand_rank_int == 1:
        pair_count = pair_count + 1
    elif hand_rank_int == 2:
        two_pair_count = two_pair_count + 1
    elif hand_rank_int == 3:
        three_of_a_kind_count = three_of_a_kind_count + 1
    elif hand_rank_int == 4:
        straight_count = straight_count + 1
    elif hand_rank_int == 5:
        flush_count = flush_count + 1
```

```
    elif hand_rank_int == 6:
        full_house_count = full_house_count + 1
    elif hand_rank_int == 7:
        four_of_a_kind_count = four_of_a_kind_count + 1
    elif hand_rank_int == 8:
        straight_flush_count = straight_flush_count + 1
    elif hand_rank_int == 9:
        royal_flush_count = royal_flush_count + 1
    else:
        nothing_count = nothing_count + 1

print("Total hands in file: ", total_count)
print("Hand counts by rank number: ", nothing_count, pair_count, two_pair_count, \
      three_of_a_kind_count, straight_count, flush_count, full_house_count, \
      four_of_a_kind_count, straight_flush_count,  royal_flush_count)

print("Probability:")
print(" of nothing:          {:>9.4%} ".format(nothing_count/total_count))
print(" of one pair:         {:>9.4%} ".format(pair_count/total_count))
print(" of two pairs:        {:>9.4%} ".format(two_pair_count/total_count))
print(" of three of a kind:  {:>9.4%} ".format(three_of_a_kind_count/total_count))
print(" of a straight:       {:>9.4%} ".format(straight_count/total_count))
print(" of a flush:          {:>9.4%} ".format(flush_count/total_count))
print(" of a full house:     {:>9.4%} ".format(full_house_count/total_count))
print(" of four of a kind:   {:>9.4%} ".format(four_of_a_kind_count/total_count))
print(" of a straight flush: {:>9.4%} ".format(straight_flush_count/total_count))
print(" of a royal flush:    {:>9.4%} ".format(royal_flush_count/total_count))
```

Finally, *a note on naming*. Remember **RULE 4**, we can modify rules if it helps in readability. Every count in the program is an integer, and it seems, at least for this program, that "count" and "int" are redundant. So we modify our names to make them a bit more compact, but add a comment to notify the reader that every count variable is an `int`.

```
Enter a file name: poker-hand-testing.data
Total hands in file:  1000000
Hand counts by rank number:  501209 422498 47622 21121 3885 1996 1424 230 12 3
Probability:
 of nothing:          50.1209%
 of one pair:         42.2498%
 of two pairs:         4.7622%
```

```
of three of a kind:    2.1121%
of a straight:         0.3885%
of a flush:            0.1996%
of a full house:       0.1424%
of four of a kind:     0.0230%
of a straight flush:   0.0012%
of a royal flush:      0.0003%
```

Notice how spacing was used to make both the program and the output more readable. Also, in the statement that prints the counts, notice a backslash (\). Remember, the backslash indicates that the statement continues onto the next line—usually a newline or carriage return indicates the end of a statement. This improves the readability of the code, which is important, but does not affect running the code.

Observations on the Output

The final output is interesting. Notice that slightly more than half the possible hands have no value, and that a hand with only one pair makes up almost all the remaining possibilities—very useful information, if you play poker.

6.8 GUI TO COUNT POKER HANDS

We have done all the work to figure out how to calculate the probability of a particular poker hand occurring using a file of some large number of hands. We would like to wrap that in a GUI for the same calculation, only this time as a web page.

We continue the development we did in Section 4.9 to develop our new interface. We have the same five elements to modify as we did then, but to help us remember here they are again:

1. What GUI form fields to include?
2. A function Model for our problem (our poker probability program).
3. Any specific text we want to occur in HTML View.
4. Creating the `InputForm` with the GUI fields and naming those fields in the Controller, using them in the View.
5. Change some variable names in the Controller.

If you would like a visualization of where these elements are in code, please look at Figure 4.12 in Section 4.9. Of those five elements, the only real changes have to do with number 2, our function Model.

6.8.1 Count Hands Function

Let's look at the new Model in Code Listing 6.13.

Code Listing 6.13

```
def compute(file_str):
    while True:   # loop until you break
        try:
            poker_file = open(file_str,'r')
            break                    # success! so move on to rest of program
        except IOError:
            print("Error opening file:",file_str)
            file_str = input("Enter a file name: ")

    # all counts are ints, so count as a suffix is enough
    total_count             = 0
    nothing_count           = 0
    pair_count              = 0
    two_pair_count          = 0
    three_of_a_kind_count= 0
    straight_count          = 0
    flush_count             = 0
    full_house_count        = 0
    four_of_a_kind_count = 0
    straight_flush_count = 0
    royal_flush_count       = 0

    for line_str in poker_file:
        total_count = total_count + 1
        fields = line_str.split(',')                # split on a comma
        hand_rank_str = fields[-1]                  # and get the last field
        try:
            hand_rank_int = int(hand_rank_str)
        except ValueError:
            continue            # bad line: quietly skip this line of the file
        if hand_rank_int == 1:
            pair_count = pair_count + 1
        elif hand_rank_int == 2:
            two_pair_count = two_pair_count + 1
        elif hand_rank_int == 3:
            three_of_a_kind_count = three_of_a_kind_count + 1
        elif hand_rank_int == 4:
            straight_count = straight_count + 1
        elif hand_rank_int == 5:
            flush_count = flush_count + 1
```

```
        elif hand_rank_int == 6:
            full_house_count = full_house_count + 1
        elif hand_rank_int == 7:
            four_of_a_kind_count = four_of_a_kind_count + 1
        elif hand_rank_int == 8:
            straight_flush_count = straight_flush_count + 1
        elif hand_rank_int == 9:
            royal_flush_count = royal_flush_count + 1
        else:
            nothing_count = nothing_count + 1

    result_str = "<pre>"
    result_str +='Total hands in file:    {:<10d}\n'.format(total_count)
    result_str += "Probability:\n"
    result_str += " of nothing:             {:>9.4%}\n".format(nothing_count/
                                                   total_count)
    result_str += " of one pair:            {:>9.4%}\n".format(pair_count/total_count)
    result_str += " of two pairs:           {:>9.4%}\n".format(two_pair_count/
                                                   total_count)
    result_str += " of three of a kind:     {:>9.4%}\n".format(three_of_a_kind_count/
                                                   total_count)
    result_str += " of a straight:          {:>9.4%}\n".format(straight_count/
                                                   total_count)
    result_str += " of a flush:             {:>9.4%}\n".format(flush_count/total_count)
    result_str += " of a full house:        {:>9.4%}\n".format(full_house_count/
                                                   total_count)
    result_str += " of four of a kind:      {:>9.4%}\n".format(four_of_a_kind_count/
                                                   total_count)
    result_str += " of a straight flush:    {:>9.4%}\n".format(straight_flush_count/
                                                   total_count)
    result_str += " of a royal flush:       {:>9.4%}\n".format(royal_flush_count/
                                                   total_count)
    result_str += "</pre>"


    return result_str
```

We start by taking the program from Section 6.11 and turning it into a function. We remove the file prompt and replace it by passing the file to open as the only argument to the new function.

The biggest change comes at the end of the function. Remember that our advice is to return a string as that makes things easiest for our template. So now we create a large string, with each line separated by a "\n" (new line character) using concatenation.

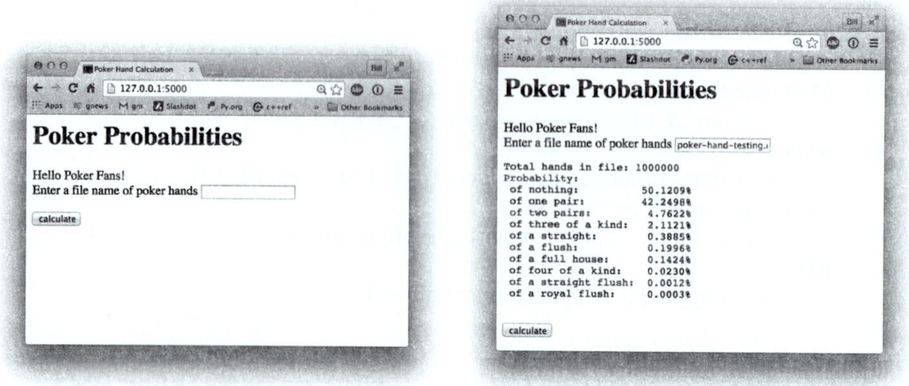

(a) Startup (b) Successful Count

FIGURE 6.4 The poker hand count GUI example. [William F. Punch, Richard J. Enbody.]

However, there are two odd elements on **Lines 52, 65**, the <pre> and <\pre> HTML tags. When we return our string it would be wonderful if the formatting could be preserved. However, the flask process does not always respect the new lines and spacing that we added so carefully. However, anything in between the <pre> ... <\pre> tags are rendered **exactly** in the HTML. Thus, the string we return gets rendered with all the formatting information on the HTML page.

6.8.2 The Rest of the GUI Code

The rest of the GUI portion of the code in Code Listing 6.14 is nearly the same as the template; the differences are our own changes of variable names and HTML text appropriate for this problem, with the exception of the Model code. Because the Model code is so much larger, we have chosen to have the Model stored in a separate file and import it into our code. This change occurs on **Line 6** where we import the compute function from the file named `program5_pokerCount.py` in the same directory. The change makes the code more readable. The GUI is shown in Figure 6.4.

Code Listing 6.14

```
1 from flask import Flask, render_template_string, request
2 from wtforms import Form, validators, TextField
3 import string
4
5 # function model in a separae file
6 from program5_pokerCount import compute
7
8 app = Flask(__name__)
9
```

```
# html page is the view.
page = '''
<html>
    <head>
        <title> Poker Hand Calculation</title>
    </head>

    <body>
        <h1>Poker Probabilities</h1>

        <form method=post action="">
            Hello Poker Fans!
        <br>
         Enter a file name of poker hands
            {{ template_form.text_field }}
        <br>
          {% if result != None %}
              {{ result }}
          {% endif %}
        <br>
          <input type=submit value=calculate>
        </form>

    </body>
</html>
'''

# InputForm and below is our controller

# form with a single TextField
class InputForm(Form):
    text_field = TextField(validators=[validators.InputRequired()])

@app.route('/', methods=['GET', 'POST'])
def index():
    poker_result = None
    form = InputForm(request.form)
    if request.method == 'POST' and form.validate():
        input_val = form.text_field.data
        poker_result = compute(input_val)
    return render_template_string(page, template_form=form, result = poker_result)

if __name__ == '__main__':
    app.run(debug=True)
```

6.9 ERROR CHECK FLOAT INPUT

When you want an *int* input you can check the input using the string `isdigit()` method. However, there is no comparable check for *float*. The solution is to use try-except to check for floats by trying to convert the input string to a *float* and if it fails (ValueError), we can reprompt for input. The resulting code is similar to the ***try-except*** we used previously to check for *int* in the poker-probability code. See Code Listing 6.15.

Code Listing 6.15

```
# Error check float input
num_str = input("Enter a float: ")

while True:
    try:
        num_float = float(num_str)
        break
    except ValueError:
        num_str = input("Error, Enter a float: ")
print("Success:",num_float)
```

6.10 WHAT'S WRONG WITH MY CODE?

Here are suggestions for finding problems with files. Refer to Appendix C for details.

Here are three common errors or problems you will find when opening and writing to files:

- **FileNotFoundError:** The error message describes the problem, but not what caused it. Here are the two most common causes:
  - **Misspelled file name:** If you misspelled the file name, Python cannot find it.
  - **File not in the same folder as the program:** By default a program looks for a file in the same directory as the program. If it isn't there, Python cannot find it. If the file is in another directory by choice, you must give a fully qualified path to that file, that is, "/Users/bill/Documents/file.txt"
  - Remember that the ipython console can help with the previous two errors in two ways:
    - In the console itself, when you **Run** your edited file a line shows up in the console of the form: `runfile('/Users/user/python/file.py', wdir='/Users/user/python')` where the `wdir` is the working directory, the assumed location of any files you are trying to open. Is that the correction working directory?

* You can use the ipython history commands (the up and down arrow on your keyboard) to get the previous command back and fix any misspellings of the file name.

- **Empty or partially written file:** If you forget to `close` a file, some of what you wrote to the file might be missing. Python tries to deal with this, but it is not always successful. *Always remember to close files!*
- **Accidentally overwriting a file:** Python does not warn you if you are about to overwrite a file. For example, if you open a file with "w" as the modifier, the contents of the file, if it already exists, will be lost.

Here are some errors you might run into when reading the contents of a file, especially when iterating through the file's contents line by line.

- **TypeError**: Remember that what is returned by iterating through a file is a string. Even if that file's contents contains a number on that particular line, that number is returned as a **string**, not an integer (or a float, or anything else). You must explicitly convert the numeric-string to its appropriate arithmetic value before you can use it in an arithmetic calculation.
- **Extra Line**: Not a Python error per se, but if you print out your lines of input and get an extra line (like double spacing), what happened? Did you remember to `strip` your line when you got it? Otherwise it is carrying a extra `''n''`.
- **IndexError**: Remember that some of the file lines may only have a `''n''`, basically a blank line in the file. When you `strip` such a line you are left with an empty string. You cannot index any character in an empty string as it has none, thus leading to the `IndexError`.

Summary

In this chapter, we introduced file reading and writing with more detail to come in a later chapter. We also introduced exceptions as a way to handle errors, again with more details to come in a later chapter.

Files

- Text files contain Unicode characters.
  All other files are called binary files.
- Files need to be opened for reading:
```
file_handle = open("file_name","r")
for line_str in file_handle:
```
- Files need to be opened for writing:
```
file_handle = open("file_name","w")
print(string,file=file_handle)
```
- When done, files are closed using: `file_handle.close()`

Exceptions

- Exceptions handle exceptional events such as errors.
- Errors raise exceptions with particular names. Two of the most common are:
  – ValueError: errors when converting strings to numbers
  – FileNotFoundError: errors when opening files
- Exception syntax:

```
try:
    # suite
except ErrorName:
    # suite
```

Rules

- **RULE 1:** Think before you program!
- **RULE 2:** A program is a human-readable essay on problem solving that also happens to execute on a computer.
- **RULE 3:** The best way to improve your programming and problem skills is to practice!
- **RULE 4:** A foolish consistency is the hobgoblin of little minds.
- **RULE 5:** Test your code, often and thoroughly!
- **RULE 6:** If it was hard to write, it is probably hard to read. Add a comment.
- **RULE 7:** All input is evil, until proven otherwise.

Exercises

1. Why is closing a file important? Be specific.
2. In the exception example of Section 6.6.4 when error "(2) bad file name" occurred the user had to enter a line number before the error occurred. Rewrite the code so that if a bad file name is entered, the error will be handled before a line number is requested.
3. In the exception example of Section 6.6.4 rewrite the code so that if error "(2) bad file name" occurs the program keeps asking for input until the user gets it right.
4. In the exception example of Section 6.6.4 rewrite the code so that if error "(3) bad line number (string)" occurs the program keeps asking for input until the user gets it right.
5. In the exception example of Section 6.6.4 rewrite the code so that if error "(4) line number not in file" occurs the program keeps asking for input until the user gets it right.

6. File manipulations:

(a) Write a Python program that will open a file named "thisFile.txt" and write every occurrence of a word input by the user into the file "thatFile.txt."

(b) Extend your program using the `os` module to save your file to a different directory (folder).

7. Create a file "jumble.txt" that contains a long string of letters, numbers, whitespaces and special characters (approximately 5000 characters long). Next, create a program that prompts for the file name, and then counts the frequency of each whitespace (spaces, tabs, returns) and stores the values in a dictionary. Print a histogram of the count of whitespaces.

8. Create a test file with a paragraph containing more than 20 lowercased sentences. Read the file, capitalize the first word of every sentence, and write the text to a new text file that will contain one sentence on each line.

---

9. In the exercises for Chapters 1 and 2 the football quarterback pass rating was developed into a program. Go to `http://nfl.com`, find the quarterback data, and copy that data into a file. It is easiest to grab the data of the "qualified" quarterbacks, as they fit on only one web page. Write a program that reads your file, uses your pass rating function to calculate the pass ratings of the quarterbacks, and prints the players from best to worst.

10. Write a program that prompts for three numbers. Divide the first number by the second number and add that result to the third number. Using exceptions check for the following errors: ValueError and ZeroDivisionError.

11. Write a function named `safe_input(prompt,type)` that works like the Python `input` function, except that it only accepts the specified type of input. The function takes two arguments:

- `prompt`: *`str`*
- `type`: *`int`*, *`float`*, *`str`*

The function will keep prompting for input until correct input of the specified type is entered.

The function returns the input. If the input was specified to be a number (*`float`* or *`int`*), the value returned will be of the correct type; that is, the function will perform the conversion.

The default for a prompt is the empty string. The default for the type is string.

12. Write a function to prompt for a file name, sorts all words in the file alphabetically, and then prints the results to the console. The program should repeatedly attempt to read the specified file until a correctly specified file has been entered.

13. Find a text file online that contains the English dictionary. Write a program that cycles through this text file to find compound words. Your program should return these compound words along with the two words that compose it. For example, a "raincoat" is a compound word so your program should return raincoat = rain + coat.

14. Two words that end in the same portion of letters but sound different are said to eye rhyme. Write a program that prompts the user for an input and prints all words that eye rhyme with the input; that is, words with the same last three letters (we cannot test if they sound the same!). [*Hint:* Use the dictionary file.]

15. Write a program that prompts the user for an equation of a line and a circle and calculates the point(s) of intersection between the two. If the two do not intersect, return The two do not intersect. Be careful of the case where the discriminant is negative—**`try-except`** is handy here. [*Hint:* First calculate the points on paper by setting the general equations of a line and of a circle equal and solve for x.]

16. Write a program that prompts for a file name and reverses each line of the file. Your program should be sufficiently robust that if a file doesn't exist, the program will reprompt.

17. Create a test file containing at least 100 lines of text. Then write a program that prompts the user to enter a list of numbers, remove the lines at those numbers, and save the output to a new text file.

Programming Projects

1. Scrambled Words.
Read the following paragraph as quickly as you can, and see if you encounter any difficulties.

> Aoccdrnig to rscheearch at an Elingsh uinervtisy, it deosn't mttaer in waht oredr the ltteers in a wrod are, the olny iprmoetnt tihng is taht the frist and lsat ltteer is at the rghit pclae. The rset can be a toatl mses and you can sitll raed it wouthit a porbelm. Tihs is bcuseae we do not raed ervey lteter by itslef but the wrod as a wlohe.

This has been presented as an example of a principle of human reading comprehension. If you keep the first letter and the last letter of a word in their correct positions, then scramble the letters in between, the word is still quite readable in the context of an accompanying paragraph. However, it seems that this is a bit of a myth and not truly based on solid research.[6] In short, for longer words the task is much more difficult. Nonetheless, we are going to imitate the process on some English text.
The task will be to read in a paragraph from a file, scramble the internal letters of each word, and then write the result to a file.

[6] http://www.balancedreading.com/cambridge.html

Handling punctuation is tricky. You are required to deal with punctuation that comes at the end of a word (period, question mark, exclamation, etc.); that is, punctuation is left untouched and does not count as the final unscrambled letter. Optionally, one can deal with the more difficult task of handling all punctuation such as apostrophes for possessives or hyphenated words.

Truely randomizing the order of letters is a task for later in the text, but we can do some reasonable approximations now.

Attacking this problem in a divide-and-conquer way should begin by writing code to scramble the letters in a word. Here are three different approaches you might take, in increasing order of difficulty:

(a) **Easiest:** Rotate letters by 13 (known as ROT13). That is, 'a' becomes 'n', 'b' becomes 'l', ..., 'n' becomes 'a', ... The `chr` and its inverse, `ord`, functions will be useful.

(b) **Harder:** For each letter choose a random number and rotate that letter by the random amount. Import `random` and use the `random.randint(a,b)` function where 'a' and 'b' define the range of random numbers returned.

(c) **Hardest:** Improve on the preceding techniques by scrambling the letters by a method of your choice.

CHAPTER 7

Lists and Tuples

> List, a Scrowl of the Names of several Persons of the same Quality with whom we have Business.
>
> E. Phillips, *New World of Words*, 1696

7.1 WHAT IS A LIST?

Python's built-in *list* type is also a collection type. In fact, like strings, lists are a sequence type and are an iterable type. They therefore share some of the characteristics of strings. However, a list differs from a string in two fundamental ways:

- A list can contain elements other than strings. In fact, a list can contain a sequence of elements of *any* type, even different typed elements mixed together in the same list.
- A list is a *mutable* type. This means that, unlike a string object, a list object can be changed after it is initially created.

If we keep these differences in mind, we can use our knowledge of the string type to work with lists.

Making Python Lists

Lists can be created with the `list` constructor or with square brackets ([ ]). This capability can be a little confusing, as the same square brackets are also used as the index operator. One way to tell the difference is the presence of the comma character: each element of a list is separated by a comma. Thus, if you see square brackets with multiple elements separated by commas, you know it is a list. Otherwise, you will have to use the context to determine what the brackets mean.

Here are a few examples of making a list in a Python session:

```
In  [1]: a_list = [1,2,'a',3.14159]
In  [2]: week_days_list = ['Monday', 'Tuesday', 'Wednesday', 'Thursday', 'Friday']
In  [3]: list_of_lists = [ [1,2,3], ['a','b','c']]
In  [4]: list_from_collection = list('Hello')
In  [5]: a_list
Out [5]: [1, 2, 'a', 3.1415899999999999]

In  [6]: week_days_list
Out [6]: ['Monday', 'Tuesday', 'Wednesday', 'Thursday', 'Friday']

In  [7]: list_of_lists
Out [7]: [[1, 2, 3], ['a', 'b', 'c']]

In  [8]: list_from_collection
Out [8]: ['H', 'e', 'l', 'l', 'o']

In  [9]: []
Out [9]: []
```

Here are a few things to notice about these lists.

- `a_list` is a sequence of four elements (two integers, a character, and a floating-point number). Any Python type can be a list element and different types can be in the same list. Again, this differs from a string, which *requires* its elements to all be characters.
- As previously noted, each element of the list is separated from the next by a comma. The comma indicates elements of a collection, and the square brackets indicate that collection is a list.
- The `list_of_lists` is a list of only two elements. The first element is a list as is the second. Again, a list can be a sequence of any typed element—even another list!
- The `list_from_collection` is a list built using the constructor `list`. The resulting list is `['H', 'e', 'l', 'l', 'o']`, containing five elements, each a single character string. This constructor takes a single argument and that argument must an iterable. The `list` constructor takes each element of the argument iterable and adds that element to the new list. Non-iterable types (integers, floats, Booleans, etc.) cannot be used as an argument to the `list` constructor since they do not contain multiple elements (are not iterable).
- The special list with no elements, designated as `[ ]`, is called the *empty list*. Like other "empty" elements, it is equivalent to a `False` value in Python.

Note the naming convention for lists. As with other collections we append the collection type to the end of the name, "list" for lists. This protocol is similar to our naming convention we have used for other types. As per RULE 4, we will violate this convention when a more meaningful name is appropriate such as the `list_of_lists`.

List of Lists

Lists that contain lists as elements such as `list_of_lists` in the previous session are useful for representing many types of data. An organization that has a list within a list is often called a *nested* list. Consider a couple of two-dimensional data sets, such as a spreadsheet (rows vs. columns) or the Cartesian plane (*x* vs. *y*). These 2D data sets can be represented as a list of lists. For a spreadsheet, the elements of the list can be the rows (lists) and the elements of those nested lists can be the column values. To index an individual element, we use two pairs of brackets: the first one selects the row list, and the second one selects the column value within the list. Here is a session to illustrate that concept:

```
In  [1]: spreadsheet_list = [ ['Name','Age','GPA'], ['Bill', 25, 3.55],
                              ['Rich', 26 , 4.00]]
In  [2]: row = spreadsheet_list[1]
In  [3]: row
Out [3]: ['Bill', 25, 3.55]

In  [4]: column = row[2]
In  [5]: column
Out [5]: 3.55

In  [6]: spreadsheet_list[1][2]
Out [6]: 3.55
```

Some observations:

- `spreadsheet_list[1]` selects row 1 of the list—the second list—and assigns it to the variable `row`. We then print the value of `row`, display the list `['Bill', 25, 3.55]`.
- `row[2]` selects the third column of that row and assigns it to the variable `column`. We then print the value of `column`, 3.55.
- We then show the equivalent single expression to access the value in `column`, `spreadsheet_list[1][2]`.

This concept generalizes to any level of nesting of lists. For example, to represent the *xyz* 3D plane, how would we approach it? This would be a list of lists of lists. The outermost list would represent a 2D plane, the list within that list would represent all the values in a particular row (say *x*), and then a particular value would be the index into that row (say *y*).

7.2 WHAT YOU ALREADY KNOW HOW TO DO WITH LISTS

Because lists are sequences and iterable, many things that you learned to do with strings also work for lists. Let's take a look and refresh your memory.

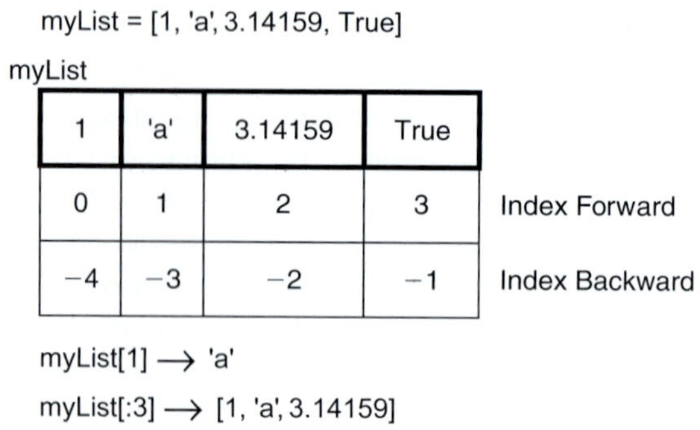

FIGURE 7.1 The structure of a list.

7.2.1 Indexing and Slicing

Indexing and slicing work *exactly* the same with lists and strings. To remind yourself, look at Figure 7.1.

- Each element of the list has an associated index. The index values begin at 0 on the left and get larger, or they can begin with −1 on the right and get smaller.
- The index operator is a set of square brackets with either a single integer or a slice. If it contains a single integer, that integer is the index of the element within the list.
- Accessing an element at an index that does not exist in the list is an error.
- The slice operation is the same as with strings. Within square brackets, you may have one or two colons (:). The number before the first colon is the start index, the number after the first colon is the end index, and the number after the second colon is the step. The defaults for all three are (in order): the beginning of the list, the end of the list, and a step of 1.
- A slice uses a half-open range, meaning that the end index is not included in the slice.

The following session shows these operations:

```
In  [1]: my_list = [1,'a',3.14159,True]
In  [2]: my_list[1]
Out [2]: 'a'

In  [3]: my_list[-1]
Out [3]: True

In  [4]: my_list[:] # copy slice
Out [4]: [1, 'a', 3.1415899999999999, True]

In  [5]: my_list[:3:2]
Out [5]: [1, 3.1415899999999999]
```

```
In  [6]: my_list[::2]
Out [6]: [1, 3.1415899999999999]

In  [7]: my_list[2:]
Out [7]: [3.1415899999999999, True]

In  [8]: my_list[:3]
Out [8]: [1, 'a', 3.1415899999999999]

In  [9]: my_list[10]
Traceback (most recent call last):
  File "<stdin>", line 1, in <module>
IndexError: list index out of range
In  [10]: [1,2,3,4,5][2] # ugly: first [] indicates a list , the second an index
Out [10]: 3
```

There is nothing here that is new to you except the very last expression. It is a little ugly to have both a list creation operation and a index operation together, but if you can understand what it means, you are well on your way to understanding lists. We read the expression left to right, noting that the first `[ ]` is creating a list (notice the commas) and then, having made the list, we are indexing into that list.

7.2.2 Operators

You can use both the addition (+) and multiplication (*) operators with lists with results similar to that of strings. The addition operator takes two lists as operands and concatenates the two lists together, making a new list whose contents are the first list joined at its end to the beginning of the second list. The multiplication operator takes a list and an integer as operands and replicates the list the size of the integer number of times.

As with strings, the types are fixed for this operation. You can concatenate only two lists (not a list and a string, not a list and an integer, etc.). You can replicate a list only in combination with an integer. No other combination of types will do. This is again an example of addition and multiplication being overloaded. When the addition operator (+) has two string operands, it makes a string. When it has two list operands, it makes a list. Two different types, two different operations, one symbol.

Comparison works as it did with strings, so you can use the >,<,==,<=,>=, and != signs as operators between two list operands. As with strings, comparison begins by comparing the first element of each list. If the first elements are equal, the comparison process moves to the second element of each list. The process continues in this way, comparing corresponding elements, until the process finds two elements are different. At that point, the comparison between the two different elements determines the result of the operation. If one list is equal to but shorter than the other list, the longer list is considered greater.

Finally, the ***in*** operator for membership testing works as it did in strings. The expression `'a' in ['a','b','c']` is a query, testing whether the first operand exists in the second operand. In this case it does, returning *True*.

The following session demonstrates these operations on lists:

```
In  [1]: my_list = [1,2,3]
In  [2]: your_list = ['a','b','c']
In  [3]: concat_list = my_list + your_list # concat 2 lists , operand lists
                                             unchanged
In  [4]: concat_list
Out [4]: [1, 2, 3, 'a', 'b', 'c']

In  [5]: my_list
Out [5]: [1, 2, 3]

In  [6]: your_list
Out [6]: ['a', 'b', 'c']

In  [7]: rep_list = my_list * 3 # replicate my_list, my_list is unchanged
In  [8]: rep_list
Out [8]: [1, 2, 3, 1, 2, 3, 1, 2, 3]

In  [9]: my_list
Out [9]: [1, 2, 3]

In  [10]: [1,2,3,4] < [1,2,3,0] # first difference at index 3, is 4 < 0?
Out [10]: False

In  [11]: [1,2,3,4] < [1,2,3,4,0] # second list longer, always greater
Out [11]: True

In  [12]: 1 in my_list # membership operation in
Out [12]: True

In  [13]: 1 in your_list
Out [13]: False

In  [14]: [1,2,'one','two'] < [3,4,5,6] # no error, difference occurs on same
                                          type 1 and 3
Out [14]: True

In  [15]: [1,2,'one','two'] < [1,2,5,6] # error, comparison of 5 and 'one'
Traceback (most recent call last):
  File "<pyshell#13>", line 1, in <module>
    [1,2,'one','two'] < [1,2,5,6]
TypeError: unorderable types: str() < int()
```

PROGRAMMING TIP

Because lists are containers that can hold anything, you will sometimes find that in comparing lists that you are comparing elements of different types—effectively comparing something such as `'a' > 1`. You should avoid such comparisons because Python 3 will generate an error.

Finally, comparisons underly other operations that depend on order, such as the sorting, maximizing, and minimizing operations discussed later in this chapter.

7.2.3 Functions

There are a number of functions that work with any collection. In particular, you have seen the `len` function. With strings, the `len` function returns the number of characters in a string. With lists, the `len` function returns the number of comma separated elements in the list. Again, remember that a list can have as an element another list and that list still counts as one element. Thus the result of `len([1,[1,2,3],3])` is 3. The second element, the element at index 1, is another list `[1,2,3]`. Here are some functions that work on collections, including lists:

`len(C)`: Returns the length of collection C, that is, the number of elements.

`min(C)`: Returns the minimum element in collection C. If the argument is a list of lists, only the first element in each list is considered for the purposes of comparison.

`max(C)`: Returns the maximum element in collection C. If the argument is a list of lists, only the first element in each list is considered for the purposes of comparison

`sum(L)`: Returns the sum of elements in list L. The particular function *requires* the the list elements be numbers.

As we have stated previously, you must be careful when using comparison operators on lists. Comparing elements of different types generates an error.

A session demonstrating these functions is shown subsequently.

```
In  [1]: int_list = [1,2,3,4,5]
In  [2]: float_list = [1.0, 2.0, 3.0, 4.0, 5.0]
In  [3]: str_list = ['a', 'b', 'c', 'd', 'e']
In  [4]: nested_list = [int_list, float_list, str_list]
In  [5]: len(int_list)
Out [5]: 5

In  [6]: len(nested_list)
Out [6]: 3

In  [7]: min(float_list)
Out [7]: 1.0
```

```
In  [8]: min(str_list)
Out [8]: 'a'

In  [9]: max(str_list)
Out [9]: 'e'

In  [10]: sum(int_list)
Out [10]: 15

In  [11]: sum(str_list) # elements must be numbers
Traceback (most recent call last):
  File "<pyshell#25>", line 1, in <module>
    sum(str_list)
TypeError: unsupported operand type(s) for +: 'int' and 'str'

In  [12]: min(nested_list) # comparing different types: 1 and 'a'
Traceback (most recent call last):
  File "<pyshell#26>", line 1, in <module>
    min(nested_list)
TypeError: unorderable types: str() < int()
```

7.2.4 List Iteration

We can iterate through all the elements of a list, in order, using the ***for*** operator. This action is similar to what we saw for strings.

```
In  [1]: my_list = [1,3,4,8]
In  [2]: for element in my_list: # iterate through list elements
...:     print(element ,end=' ') # prints on one line

1 3 4 8
```

In this example, the variable `element` is assigned the values 1, 3, 4, and 8, one at a time, and then the statement(s) in the suite are executed using that value for `element`. In this trivial example, the print statement will execute with each value of `element` and print it.

PROGRAMMING TIP

Never modify the list you are iterating through. For example, if you have `for i in L:` do not modify L in the suite of the loop. Try printing "i" followed by `L.remove(i)` and you will find that you don't print all items in the list—likely you will print every other one.

7.3 LISTS ARE DIFFERENT THAN STRINGS

We've seen what's the same about lists and strings, so let's look a bit more at what's different.

7.3.1 Lists Are Mutable

When we covered strings, we emphasized that they are immutable. In particular, we noted that you could not have a string index operator on the left-hand side of an assignment statement. In other words, you could not change a character of the string at some index within an existing string to a different character. Once created, the string cannot be changed.

Lists, on the other hand, are *mutable*; the element at some index in a list can be changed. This is called *index assignment*. You can even change an entire slice of the list to be different! This is called *slice assignment*. These two operations show both the power and one of the dangers of mutable objects. They are very flexible and very useful; however, you must take care in using them because you can accidentally change a list in ways you did not intend.

Let's see how mutability works in a session:

```
In  [1]: my_list = [1, 2, 'a', 'z']
In  [2]: my_list[0]
Out [2]: 1

In  [3]: my_list[0] = True # change the first element
In  [4]: my_list
Out [4]: [True, 2, 'a', 'z']

In  [5]: my_list[-1] = 7 # change the last element
In  [6]: my_list
Out [6]: [True, 2, 'a', 7]

In  [7]: my_list[:2] = [27] # change the first two elements to one element
In  [8]: my_list
Out [8]: [27, 'a', 7]

In  [9]: my_list[:] = [1,2,3,4] # change the whole list
In  [10]: my_list
Out [10]: [1, 2, 3, 4]

In  [11]: my_list[2:] = 'abc' # change the last two elements
In  [12]: my_list
Out [12]: [1, 2, 'a', 'b', 'c']

In  [13]: my_list[:2]=15 # only an iterable
Traceback (most recent call last):
  File "<stdin>", line 1, in <module>
TypeError: can only assign an iterable
```

Let's note a few things about this session:

- A list in combination with the index operator can occur on the left-hand side of the assignment statement. This means that, after the assignment occurs, the value at that index is changed to be the value of the right-hand side of the assignment statement. This is index assignment.
- As a result of *every* operation in that session, the list is changed. This means that every time we perform one of these operations, the changed list is carried forward to the next line in the session. In other words, the list elements associated with `my_list` at the end of the session are the cumulative result of all the operations that came before, in the order they were performed.
- Because the assignment operator does not return a value, we have to type the name of the variable associated with the list to see what was changed as a result. This is not new, but it is useful to note that the change occurred and we were not "notified" in anyway what the change was until we actively looked.
- You can change not only a single element, but also an entire slice of the list (multiple elements) at a single time. This is slice assignment. The only caveat is that the values being assigned must be a *collection*. Each individual element of assigned collection is added to the list at the slice indices. You cannot slice assign an individual value to a list, though the session shows assigning a list with a single value is acceptable. Only assigning a collection makes some sense if you consider it for a moment. A slice is in fact a collection (a subsequence of the original), so to replace it implies that we need another collection. The collection replacing the slice can be bigger, smaller, or the same size.

7.3.2 List Methods

As we mentioned previously, a method is a function that works with a particular type of Python object. The string type had a large number of methods that could be applied to strings, but those methods can be applied *only* to strings. Lists have their own associated methods that work only with lists. The number of list methods is quite a bit smaller—only nine. They come in two different categories:

- Those that change the list.
- Those that do ***not*** change the list.

It is important that we keep those two categories straight, so we know whether our list is changed as a result of using the method.

PROGRAMMING TIP

Remember that you can use the tab key in IPython to help you remember what the methods of a list are. See Section A.2.3.

Nonmodifying Methods

These methods do *not* change the list, but they return a value as a result of their processing. They are:

`index(x)`: Returns the index of the first element in the list whose value is equal to *x*. Python throws an error if there is no such value in the list.

`count(x)`: Returns the number of times *x* appears in the list. Returns 0 if *x* does not appear in the list.

Methods That Modify the List

There are two things to note about these methods. First, the list that calls the method will be modified as a result of the operation of the method. Second, none of the methods except the `pop` method returns a value. This fact may seem odd, but taking a closer look may help. In our previous experience, every string method returned a value: a new string object. Remember, though, that strings are immutable. They *had* to return a value, typically a string, so that the change could be captured. These list methods do not need to return a list object for the change, as the list itself is changed (it is mutable).

`append(x)`: Appends an element to the *end* of the list. The length of the list is increased by one. The element is appended exactly, so a collection is added as a single element.

`pop()`: Removes the element at the end of the list and return that element. The list is shortened by one element. If an index is specified, `a.pop(an_index)` removes the element at that position and returns that item.

`extend(C)`: Requires a collection C as an argument. The list is extended by adding *each individual* element of the argument collection C to the end of the list.

`insert(i, x)`: Inserts an element at a given position. The first argument is the index *before* which to insert in the list. Thus `my_list.insert(1, 'a')` inserts the `'a'` into position 1 of the list, sliding all the rest of the list elements down one (the element at index 1 moves to index 2, the element at index 2 moves to index 3, and so on).

`remove(x)`: Removes the first element from the list whose value is *x*. An error results, if there is no such item. The length of the list is decreased by one if successful.

`sort()`: Sorts the elements of the list, in place. If sorting a list of lists, only the first element in each list is considered in the comparison operations. Only the order of the list elements is modified (unless already sorted).[1]

`reverse()`: Reverses the elements of the list, in place. Only the order of the list elements is modified.

Let's use our IPython shell to demonstrate each method. Remember the *dot* format for methods, in which you provide a list object (an object of type `list`), followed by a dot (.), followed by the method name:

[1] Contrast this list method with the function `sorted`, mentioned later, that returns a sorted list while leaving the original unchanged.

```
In  [1]: a_list = [1, 12, 5, 8]
In  [2]: a_list
Out [2]: [1, 12, 5, 8]

In  [3]: a_list.append(17) # append to the end
In  [4]: a_list
Out [4]: [1, 12, 5, 8, 17]

In  [5]: a_list.append([40,50,60]) # append a list rather than simply one item
In  [6]: a_list
Out [6]: [1, 12, 5, 8, 17, [40, 50, 60]]

In  [7]: another_list = [20, 2]
In  [8]: a_list.extend(another_list) # append another_list's elements to end
                                       of a_list
In  [9]: a_list
Out [9]: [1, 12, 5, 8, 17, [40, 50, 60], 20, 2]

In  [10]: a_list.insert(3,30) # insert 30 at position 3
In  [11]: a_list
Out [11]: [1, 12, 5, 30, 8, 17, [40, 50, 60], 20, 2]

In  [12]: a_list.remove(8)
In  [13]: a_list
Out [13]: [1, 12, 5, 30, 17, [40, 50, 60], 20, 2]

In  [14]: a_list.pop() # pop last element off a_list, and return it
Out [14]: 2

In  [15]: a_list
Out [15]: [1, 12, 5, 30, 17, [40, 50, 60], 20]

In  [16]: a_list.index(17) # find index (remember counting starts at 0)
Out [16]: 4

In  [17]: a_list.count(5)
Out [17]: 1

In  [18]: a_list.remove([40,50,60])  # remove the list so we can sort
In  [19]: a_list.sort() # sort the list

In  [20]: a_list
Out [20]: [1, 5, 12, 17, 20, 30]

In  [21]: a_list.reverse() # reverse the list
In  [22]: a_list
Out [22]: [30, 20, 17, 12, 5, 1]
```

Some notes:

- The `append` and `insert` methods are similar: `append` adds to the end of the list; `insert` puts an element into an existing list at a particular position that must be provided. If you `append` or `insert` a list as an argument, the list (including brackets) will be added as a single element to the list.
- If you want to add the *contents* of another collection to the end, use `extend`. The `extend` method adds each of the individual elements of the argument collection to the list, one at a time. The addition begins at the end of the list. The argument must be a collection.
- The `remove` method searches for and removes a particular element, but only removes the first occurrence of that element. If that element is not in the list, Python throws an error. Because of this behavior, its use is usually preceded by a check for that element's existence using the ***`in`*** operator. The `index` method, which returns the index of the first occurrence of an element, throws a similar error if the index is not found. It is also often used in conjunction with an ***`in`*** check.
- The `pop` method gets its name from its association with a classic data structure called a *stack*. We will talk more about stacks in Chapter 15. Python will throw an error if you try to `pop` an empty list.
- The `sort` method only works with homogeneous lists—those containing all elements of the same type due to difficulties in the comparison of different types that we have discussed. We remove the list `[40, 50, 60]` so our list is all numbers as opposed to being a mixed list of numbers and a list.

PROGRAMMING TIP

`Ordering`: when dealing with functions, methods, or operations that depend on ordering (such as `sort`, `sorted`, `reverse`, `min`, `max`, `<`, `>`, `==`) use only homogeneous elements, for example, all numbers or all strings. Mixed elements do not have a natural ordering and will generate an error in Python.

More on Sorting

Sorting a list of lists will sort on the first item in each list. One can create lists with the desired items to sort on first, but Python also has tools to sort on values other than the first. There is a module named `operator` that contains the useful `itemgetter` for sorting on values other than the first and allows sorting on multiple values.

To illustrate, we will use the `sorted` function, which returns a new sorted list *without changing* the original list (see Section 7.4.3). Arguments are the same as the `sort` method so everything illustrated here works with sort. We begin by importing `itemgetter` from the `operator` module. Then we create a list of lists. The default sorts on the first item in each list. Using `key=itemgetter(1)` we can sort on index 1 in each list. Two arguments, such as `key=itemgetter(1,2)`, will sort first on index 1 and then on index 2.

```
In  [1]: from operator import itemgetter

In  [2]: L = [['sarah', 'Jr', 30], ['rich', 'So', 10], ['bill', 'Jr', 20]]

In  [3]: sorted(L) # default search on index 0
Out [3]: [['bill', 'Jr', 20], ['rich', 'So', 10], ['sarah', 'Jr', 30]]

In  [4]: sorted(L,key=itemgetter(1)) # sort on index 1
Out [4]: [['sarah', 'Jr', 30], ['bill', 'Jr', 20], ['rich', 'So', 10]]

In  [5]: sorted(L,key=itemgetter(2))
Out [5]: [['rich', 'So', 10], ['bill', 'Jr', 20], ['sarah', 'Jr', 30]]

In  [6]: sorted(L,key=itemgetter(1,2)) # sort on index 1 first then 2
Out [6]: [['bill', 'Jr', 20], ['sarah', 'Jr', 30], ['rich', 'So', 10]]
```

Check Yourself: Basic Lists Check

1. Answer the following questions using the example program.

```
str_list = ['hi','mom','dad']
num_list = [1,57,15]

num_list[-1] = 25
print(str_list + num_list)          # Line 1
print([str_list[0],num_list[-1]]) # Line 2
print(str_list.append(num_list))  # Line 3
print(str_list)                     # Line 4
print(str_list.sort())              # Line 5
print(str_list)                     # Line 6
print(str_list.extend([127,256])) # Line 7
print(str_list)                     # Line 8
print(str_list.pop())               # Line 9
print(str_list)                     # Line 10
```

(a) What output is produced by Line 1 when the program is executed?
(b) What output is produced by Line 2 when the program is executed?
(c) What output is produced by Line 3 when the program is executed?
(d) What output is produced by Line 4 when the program is executed?
(e) What output is produced by Line 5 when the program is executed?
(f) What output is produced by Line 6 when the program is executed?
(g) What output is produced by Line 7 when the program is executed?
(h) What output is produced by Line 8 when the program is executed?
(i) What output is produced by Line 9 when the program is executed?
(j) What output is produced by Line 10 when the program is executed?

7.4 OLD AND NEW FRIENDS: SPLIT AND OTHER FUNCTIONS AND METHODS

7.4.1 Split and Multiple Assignment

We have used the string method `split`, but we have done so without talking about it in the context of lists. What is particularly applicable is that `split` returns a list. We have avoided talking about this characteristic by using multiple assignment from the returned lists, but now that we know about lists, you can see how these operations work.

When a string calls `split`, it creates a list of substrings from the calling string by splitting the calling string at a specific argument string (such as a comma or blank). As we have seen, if no such argument string is provided, `split` uses any whitespace to split the calling string into substrings.

If we *know* the number of substrings that will be split from the string, then we can use multiple assignment to assign each of the substrings to a variable (as we did in the name reversal example in Section 4.6.1). In general, we can assign every element of a list to a variable using multiple assignment if we know the number of elements and match each element to its corresponding variable.

The following session shows some of this behavior:

```
In  [1]: result = 'this is a test'.split() # split on whitespace
In  [2]: result
Out [2]: ['this', 'is', 'a', 'test']

In  [3]: result = 'field1,field2,field3,field4'.split(',') # split on commas
In  [4]: result
Out [4]: ['field1', 'field2', 'field3', 'field4']

In  [5]: element1,element2,element3=[1,2,3] # multiple assignment from a list
In  [5]: element1
Out [5]: 1

In  [6]: element2
Out [6]: 2

In  [7]: element3
Out [7]: 3

# multiple assignment from returned list
In  [8]: field1,field2,field3 = 'Python is great'.split()
In  [9]: field1
Out [9]: 'Python'

In  [10]: field2
Out [10]: 'is'
```

```
In  [11]: field3
Out [11]: 'great'

In  [12]: element1, element2 = [1, 2, 3] # number of vars and elements must match
Traceback (most recent call last):
  File "<pyshell#36>", line 1, in <module>
    element1, element2 = [1, 2, 3]
ValueError: too many values to unpack (expected 2)

In  [13]: element1, element2, element3 = [1, 2]
Traceback (most recent call last):
  File "<pyshell#37>", line 1, in <module>
    element1, element2, element3 = [1, 2]
ValueError: need more than 2 values to unpack
```

7.4.2 List to String and Back Again, Using `join`

It is sometimes very helpful to convert back and forth between a list and a string. Some operations are better performed, even only performed, in one type or the other, so you will find it important to understand how to do this. One useful method for this is the string `join` method. The `join` method takes a list of strings as an argument and concatenates (in order) each of those string into a new string. What is odd about this method is that the *calling* string is the string that is placed between each string as they are concatenated together. That is, the calling string is used as a separator. For example, the call `':'.join(['a','b','c'])` concatenates all the elements of the list together using a colon (`:`) as a separator, generating the string `'a:b:c'`. Note that `join` does not use the separator in front of the first element nor behind the last.

You can use `join` to recreate a string after you have done some processing on string elements.

The following session takes a string, splits it on whitespace, reverses each string element, then recreates the string of reversed elements.

```
In  [1]: my_str = 'This is a test'
In  [2]: string_elements = my_str.split() # split on whitespace, get words
In  [3]: string_elements
Out [3]: ['This', 'is', 'a', 'test']

In  [4]: reversed_elements = []
In  [5]: for element in string_elements: # for each element
...:     reversed_elements.append(element[::-1]) # reverse string and append
...:
In  [6]: reversed_elements
Out [6]: ['sihT', 'si', 'a', 'tset']

In  [7]: new_str = ' '.join(reversed_elements) # join using space as a separator
In  [8]: new_str
Out [8]: 'sihT si a tset'                   # new string with each word reversed
```

When we do the final `join`, we use a space (a two quotes with a space between) to join the elements back together.

7.4.3 The Sorted Function

VideoNote 7.1
List Operations

Unfortunately, the `sort` method works only with lists. What if we want to sort a string? We could:

- Turn a string into a list of individual characters using the `list` constructor.
- Sort the list.
- Use the `join` method of strings to put the string back together.

While this would work, there is an easier way. The `sorted` function (not a method, a function) will sort any collection. It will:

- Separate the collection into individual elements.
- Sort those elements.
- Return the elements in sorted order as a list.

The argument provided to `sorted` is *not* modified by the action of the function.

The following session demonstrates the `sorted` function:

```
In  [1]: my_list = [27,56,4,18]
In  [2]: sorted(my_list)
Out [2]: [4, 18, 27, 56]

In  [3]: my_str = 'Hi mom'
In  [4]: sorted(my_str)
Out [4]: [' ', 'H', 'i', 'm', 'm', 'o']
```

Note the difference between the function `sorted` and the list method `sort`. The function `sorted` returns a list, whereas the list method `sort` changes the list itself (a side effect). The difference is illustrated in the following session.

```
In  [1]: my_list = [27,56,4,18]
In  [2]: sorted_list = sorted(my_list) # my_list is not changed
In  [3]: sorted_list
Out [3]: [4, 18, 27, 56]

In  [4]: my_list
Out [4]: [27, 56, 4, 18]

In  [5]: my_list.sort() # my_list IS changed
In  [6]: my_list
Out [6]: [4, 18, 27, 56]
```

Check Yourself: Lists and Strings Check

1. Answer the following questions using this program.

```
my_list = [1.6, 2.7, 3.8, 4.9]
new_list = []
a_list = []

for val in my_list:
    temp = str(val)
    a_list.append(temp.split('.'))

for val in a_list:
    new_list.append(int(val[0]))

my_str = ':'.join(val)

print(my_list)          # Line 1
print(a_list)           # Line 2
print(new_list)         # Line 3
print(val)              # Line 4
print(my_str)           # Line 5
```

(a) What output is produced by Line 1 when the program is executed?
(b) What output is produced by Line 2 when the program is executed?
(c) What output is produced by Line 3 when the program is executed?
(d) What output is produced by Line 4 when the program is executed?
(e) What output is produced by Line 5 when the program is executed?

7.5 WORKING WITH SOME EXAMPLES

You know a lot about lists now, so let's see if you can use them to solve a few problems.

7.5.1 Anagrams

Two (or more) words are *anagrams* if they use a different arrangement of the same set of letters to form words. For example, *cinema* and *iceman* are anagrams, forming different words by re-ordering the same set of letters.

In this example, we will design a program that tests two words to check whether they are anagrams. How to do this? Our approach is to find some common representation that only two anagram words would share. One canonical representation would be the sorted letters of a word. Consider our example. If we take the two anagrams, *cinema* and *iceman*, and sort the letters of each word, they both form the string *aceimn*. Think about what this means.

The sorted list is just another ordering of the same set of letters used to form both *cinema* and *iceman*. Sorting a word gives us a representation that any anagram of a particular word would share. That is, every anagram should have the same sorted letter string.

Here are the main steps for our algorithm:

1. Input the two words to examine.
2. Sort the letters of each word into a new string.
3. Compare the resulting sorted strings.

The first step is "input the two words," so let's prompt the user for two space-separated words. If the user does as asked, `input` will return the two words in one string separated by a space, for example, `'cinema'` and `'iceman'`. Therefore, we can use `split` to recover each individual word as an element in a list. Once we have a list of words, we need to extract the two words. We can do that extraction using indexing—remembering that indexing starts at zero. Let's try it out in a Python shell:

```
In  [1]: two_words = input("Input two space-separated words: ")
Input two words: cinema iceman
In  [2]: two_words # check the string that was input
Out [2]: 'cinema iceman'

In  [3]: two_words.split() # split the string into a list of words
Out [3]: ['cinema', 'iceman']

In  [4]: two_words_list = two_words.split() # give the list a name
In  [5]: two_words_list
Out [5]: ['cinema', 'iceman']

In  [6]: word1 = two_words_list[0] # extract first word (indexing starts at 0)
In  [7]: word2 = two_words_list[1]
In  [8]: word1 # check on values of words
Out [8]: 'cinema'

In  [9]: word2
Out [9]: 'iceman'
```

Now that we have two words, `word1` and `word2`, we can move on to sort the elements of the two strings. We use the `sorted` function to make a list of single character strings in sorted order. In our example, `word1`, which is `'cinema'`, gets sorted into `['a', 'c', 'e', 'i', 'm', 'n']`.

```
In  [1]: word1
Out [1]: 'cinema'

In  [2]: word2
Out [2]: 'iceman'
```

```
In  [3]: word1_sorted = sorted(word1) # sorted returns a sorted list
In  [4]: word2_sorted = sorted(word2)
In  [5]: word1_sorted
Out [5]: ['a', 'c', 'e', 'i', 'm', 'n']

In  [6]: word2_sorted
Out [6]: ['a', 'c', 'e', 'i', 'm', 'n']
```

The words are sorted; now we need to check to see whether they are identical.

```
In  [1]: if word1_sorted == word2_sorted:
             print("The words are anagrams.")
         else:
             print("The words are not anagrams.")

The words are anagrams.
```

We've developed our ideas within the Python shell. Let's put them together into a program. First, let's create a function that checks if two words are anagrams, returning `True` if they are anagrams and `False` if not. Within that function, we will sort the words and then compare the sorted lists of characters as we did in the sessions. See Code Listing 7.1.

Code Listing 7.1

```
def are_anagrams(word1, word2):
    """Return True, if words are anagrams."""
    #2. Sort the characters in the words
    word1_sorted = sorted(word1)    # sorted returns a sorted list
    word2_sorted = sorted(word2)

    #3. Check that the sorted words are identical.
    if word1_sorted == word2_sorted:  # compare sorted lists
        return True
    else:
        return False
```

```
In  [1]: runfile('/Users/user/python/file.py', wdir='/Users/user/python')

In  [2]: are_anagrams('cinema','iceman')
Out [2]: True

In  [3]: are_anagrams('soap','soup')
Out [3]: False
```

With the `are_anagrams` function in hand, we can take two words from input, use them as arguments in the `are_anagrams` function, and then print an appropriate message based on whether the function returns *True* or *False*. See Code Listing 7.2.

Code Listing 7.2

```
# Anagram test

def are_anagrams(word1, word2):
    """Return True, if words are anagrams."""
    #2. Sort the characters of the words
    word1_sorted = sorted(word1)       # sorted returns a sorted list
    word2_sorted = sorted(word2)

    #3. Check that the sorted words are identical.
    if word1_sorted == word2_sorted:  # compare sorted lists
        return True
    else:
        return False

print("Anagram Test")

# 1. Input two words.
two_words = input("Enter two space separated words: ")
two_word_list = two_words.split() # split the input string into a list
                                    of words
word1 = two_word_list[0]            # extract first word
word2 = two_word_list[1]            # extract second word

if are_anagrams(word1, word2):      # function returned True or False
    print("The words are anagrams.")
else:
    print("The words are not anagrams.")
```

```
Anagram Test
Enter two words: cinema iceman
The words are anagrams.
```

Refactoring

With a working program in hand, we should look at it so see if we can refactor it, that is, keep the functionality but make the program "better." Three modifications are worth considering simply to illustrate alternatives.

First, the ***return*** statement in the function can directly return the value of the comparison rather than run an ***if*** test at the end. This is because the comparison will already result in a value of *True* or *False*, so let's simply return that, as in:

```
return word1_sorted == word2_sorted
```

A second alternative code sequence is to use multiple assignment when we split `two_words` into `word1` and `word2`. By using multiple assignment, we can skip the `two_word_list` entirely:

```
word1, word2 = two_words.split()
```

Let's incorporate those alternatives into our code. The result is terse, and possibly more readable. See Code Listing 7.3.

Code Listing 7.3

```
# Anagram test

def are_anagrams(word1, word2):
    """Return True, if words are anagrams."""
    #2. Sort the characters of the words.
    word1_sorted = sorted(word1)    # sorted returns a sorted list
    word2_sorted = sorted(word2)

    #3. Check that the sorted words are identical.
    return word1_sorted == word2_sorted

print("Anagram Test")

# 1. Input two words.
two_words = input("Enter two space separated words: ")
word1,word2 = two_words.split()  # split the input string into a list of words

if are_anagrams(word1, word2):   # function returned True or False
    print("The words are anagrams.")
else:
    print("The words are not anagrams.")
```

Finally, what about errors? Remember **RULE 7**, we should check the input provided by the user. What if they get the input wrong? Well, what could go wrong? The problem will likely be in the multiple assignment and `split` method combination. If more or less than two, space-separated words are provided by the user, we will get an error, a `ValueError`.

We can certainly catch such an error when it occurs, but it would be nice to re-ask the user to fix their mistake so that the program can continue its processing, rather than just stop. The following is an outline of, in general, how to reprompt the user for a response.

- Set a boolean sentinel just before a ***while*** loop to *False*.
- Write the ***while*** to loop based on the Boolean sentinel being *False*. The following operations are then part of the ***while*** loop
  - Inside of a ***try*** suite, prompt the user
  - Perform any required operations on the user response (multiple assignment, `split`, `(len)`, etc.)
  - If the operation is successful, that is there are no errors, set the Boolean sentinel to *True*. This will end the ***while*** loop.
  - Catch any error using an ***except*** suite. Here you can ***print*** an error message to inform the user. If the flow of control gets to the ***except***, then the Boolean sentinel will remain *False* and the ***while*** loop will continue

The following program will reprompt the user if they do not provide a response that can be split into two elements. The ***except*** suite catches the `ValueError` if the `split` fails. The error suite prints an error message, and the loop starts again since the sentinel variable `valid_input_bool` remains *False*. If the `split` succeeds, the Boolean `valid_input_bool` is set to *True* and the loop ends. Once the proper input is set, the rest of the program will run. See Code Listing 7.4.

Code Listing 7.4

```
# Anagram test

def are_anagrams(word1, word2):
    """Return True, if words are anagrams."""
    #2. Sort the characters of the words.
    word1_sorted = sorted(word1)    # sorted returns a sorted list
    word2_sorted = sorted(word2)

    #3. Check that the sorted words are identical.
    return word1_sorted == word2_sorted

print("Anagram Test")

# 1. Input two words, checking for errors now
valid_input_bool = False
while not valid_input_bool:
    try:
        two_words = input("Enter two space separated words: ")
        word1,word2 = two_words.split()  # split the input string into a
                                           list of words
        valid_input_bool = True
    except ValueError:
```

```
        print("Bad Input")

if are_anagrams(word1, word2):    # function returned True or False
    print("The words {} and {} are anagrams.".format(word1, word2))
else:
    print("The words {} and {} are not anagrams.".format(word1, word2))
```

The next session shows the reprompting in action. As soon as a user response passes the `split` without error, the program finishes. Until the user provides such a response, the program will continue to prompt.

```
Anagram Test
Enter two space separated words: fred
Bad Input
Enter two space separated words: fred joe maria
Bad Input
Enter two space separated words: cinema iceman
The words cinema and iceman are anagrams.
```

7.5.2 Example: File Analysis

Programmers are often required to take a file of text and analyze it in various ways. Let's use our knowledge of lists to analyze a file. Specifically, we will:

- Determine a file's length, in words.
- Count the number of unique words in a file.

We will use as sample input President Abraham Lincoln's Gettysburg Address (1863). This address is famous for many reasons, but in particular, it is very short. Let's use Python to do some simple analysis of the address.

Length of Gettysburg Address

You have seen the `len` function that returns the length of a list, so let's put all the words of the address into a list and find the list's (and therefore the file's) length.

We downloaded the address from the Internet, put it in a file we named "*gettysburg.txt*", and put that file in the same folder (directory) as our program. We then develop the following strategy:

1. Open the file for reading
2. Initialize the speech list to be empty
3. For each line in the file:
   (a) Extract words from the line into a list (`split`)
   (b) Add that list of words onto the speech list (`extend`)
4. Find the length of the speech list

Separating a file into a list of individual words sounds like something we can apply **RULE 8** to, a function to do one thing. Let's call that function `make_word_list`, and incorporate it into a main program that opens a file, calls our function, and then prints the resulting list. See Code Listing 7.5.

Code Listing 7.5

```
# Gettysburg address analysis
# count words, unique words

def make_word_list(a_file):
    """Create a list of words from a file."""
    word_list = []        # 2. list of speech words: initialized to be empty

    for line_str in a_file:              # 3. read file line by line
        line_list= line_str.split() # 3a. split each line to a list of words
        word_list.extend(line_list)    # 3b. add words to list of speech words
    return word_list

##############################################

gba_file = open("gettysburg.txt", "r") # 1. open file for reading
speech_list = make_word_list(gba_file)

# 4. print the speech and its lengths
print(speech_list)
print("Length: ", len(speech_list))
```

```
['Four', 'score', 'and', 'seven', 'years', 'ago', 'our', 'fathers',
'brought', 'forth', 'on', 'this', 'continent', 'a', 'new', 'nation,'

# many lines deleted

'freedom', '--', 'and', 'that', 'government', 'of', 'the', 'people,', 'by',
'the', 'people,', 'for', 'the', 'people,', 'shall', 'not', 'perish', 'from',
'the', 'earth.']
Length:  278
```

The output is quite long, so in the session, we cut out the middle, so you can see the entire output.

In the `speech_list`, the list returned by `make_word_list`, we see some non-words: `'--'` in particular. We should update the function to eliminate that non-word before adding to the `word_list`, the local variable that stores the list of words. However, that means that we need to examine words one at a time before adding them to that list. Rather than using `extend` to add to the `word_list`, lets walk through the `line_list` one word at a time and use `append` method to add words one at a time to the `word_list`. The construct ***for*** `word` ***in*** `line_list:` iterates through the words in `line_list` one at a time and assigns them to `word`. Then we can `append` each `word` to `word_list` one at a time. However, before appending `word`, we can check whether it is the non-word `'--'`. Only if it is not do we append it. Code Listing 7.6 shows the program with the modified function:

Code Listing 7.6

```
# Gettysburg address analysis
# count words, unique words

def make_word_list(a_file):
    """Create a list of words from the file."""
    word_list = []       # list of speech words: initialized to be empty

    for line_str in a_file:                 # read file line by line
        line_list = line_str.split()  # split each line into a list of words
        for word in line_list:              # get words one at a time from list
            if word != "--":                # if the word is not "—"
                word_list.append(word)   # add the word to the speech list
    return word_list

##########################################

gba_file = open("gettysburg.txt", "r")
speech_list = make_word_list(gba_file)

# print the speech and its lengths
print(speech_list)
print("Speech Length: ", len(speech_list))
```

```
['Four', 'score', 'and', 'seven', 'years', 'ago', 'our', 'fathers',
'brought', 'forth', 'on', 'this', 'continent', 'a', 'new', 'nation,',

# many lines deleted

'freedom', 'and', 'that', 'government', 'of', 'the', 'people,', 'by',
'the', 'people,', 'for', 'the', 'people,', 'shall', 'not', 'perish', 'from',
'the', 'earth.']
Length:  271
```

Now when we examine the output (again with many lines deleted), we see that the `'--'` non-word is gone, and we have a more accurate count: 271 words.

Unique Words in Gettysburg Address

The address is known not only for its content, but also for its brevity. We now know how many words, but how many *unique* words are in it? How might we determine that? Again, it sounds like **RULE 8** applies and a function to do one thing is in order. Let us call the function `make_unique`. Since we already have a list of words from the file, we will provide that list as the argument to the function and have the function return a list of the unique words.

How should the function work? Let's make a list of unique words and then find the length of that list. The hard part of that is how to we create a list of only unique words? The process is fairly similar to what we have already done. We can start with an empty list of unique words (notice the pattern here!). We will walk through each word of the argument list, words one word at a time, but before we add a word to the unique list, we check whether it is already in the unique list using the ***in*** operator. If it is not there, we add it. Here is an algorithm:

1. Initialize our unique list to empty
2. For each word in the argument list:
   (a) If a word is not already in unique list,
   (b) Add word to unique list

Here is the implementation of `make_unique`, along with the updated main code and corresponding session. The count of words is now 153. See Code Listing 7.7.

Code Listing 7.7

```
# Gettysburg address analysis
# count words, unique words

def make_word_list(a_file):
    """Create a list of words from the file."""
    word_list = []        # list of speech words: initialized to be empty

    for line_str in a_file:                # read file line by line
        line_list = line_str.split()  # split each line into a list of words
        for word in line_list:             # get words one at a time from list
            if word != "--":               # if the word is not "—"
                word_list.append(word)  # add the word to the speech list
    return word_list

def make_unique(word_list):
    """Create a list of unique words."""
    unique_list = [] # list of unique words: initialized to be empty

    for word in word_list:            # get words one at a time from speech
```

```
        if word not in unique_list: # if word is not already in unique list ,
            unique_list.append(word)# add word to unique list

    return unique_list


##########################################

gba_file = open("gettysburg.txt", "r")
speech_list = make_word_list(gba_file)

# print the speech and its lengths
print(speech_list)
print("Speech Length: ", len(speech_list))
print("Unique Length: ", len(make_unique(speech_list)))
```

```
['Four', 'score', 'and', 'seven', 'years', 'ago', 'our', 'fathers',
'brought', 'forth', 'on', 'this', 'continent', 'a', 'new', 'nation,',

# many lines deleted

'freedom', 'and', 'that', 'government', 'of', 'the', 'people,', 'by',
'the', 'people,', 'for', 'the', 'people,', 'shall', 'not', 'perish', 'from',
'the', 'earth.']
Speech Length:  271
Unique Length:  153
```

Better Idea of Unique

There are some adjustments we can make based on the idea of "unique word".

- A word should not be unique if it exists in the provided word list with different types of capitalization, for example, "we" and "We".
- A word should not be unique if it exists in the provided word list with different surrounding punctuation, for example, "here.", "here,", and "here".

We previously described the string method `strip`, which strips specified characters from the beginning and end of strings, as well as the `lower` method, which converts a string to lowercase. These will be useful methods for implementing these changes. The appropriate place for the adjustments is in the `make_word_list` function, where we are already doing some filtering, that is, removing the `'--'` string. The strategy will be to `lower` every word to make sure all the letters are lowercase, and to `strip` every word of the punctuation marks period(.) and comma(,). By filtering words through those functions, we reduce the unique count from 153 to an accurate 138. Here is the program with both functions. We removed printing of the original speech, and added printing of the list of unique words. See Code Listing 7.8.

Code Listing 7.8

```
# Gettysburg address analysis
# count words, unique words

def make_word_list(a_file):
    """Create a list of words from the file."""
    word_list = []       # list of speech words: initialized to be empty

    for line_str in a_file:              # read file line by line
        line_list = line_str.split()  # split each line into a list of words
        for word in line_list:           # get words one at a time from list
            word = word.lower()          # make words lowercase
            word = word.strip('.,')      # strip off commas and periods
            if word != "--":             # if the word is not "—"
                word_list.append(word)    # add the word to the speech list
    return word_list

def make_unique(word_list):
    """Create a list of unique words."""
    unique_list = [] # list of unique words: initialized to be empty

    for word in word_list:           # get words one at a time from speech
        if word not in unique_list: # if word is not already in unique list,
            unique_list.append(word)# add word to unique list

    return unique_list


#########################################

gba_file = open("gettysburg.txt", "r")
speech_list = make_word_list(gba_file)
print("Speech Length: ", len(speech_list))
unique_list = make_unique(speech_list)
# print the speech and its lengths
print(unique_list)
print("Unique Length: ", len(make_unique(unique_list)))
```

```
Speech Length:  271
['four', 'score', 'and', 'seven', 'years', 'ago', 'our', 'fathers',
```

```
# many lines deleted

'highly', 'resolve', 'shall', 'died', 'vain', 'under', 'god', 'birth',
'freedom', 'government', 'people', 'by', 'perish', 'earth']
Unique Length:  138
```

As before, we removed some of the output to save space. Now we have an accurate count of the length of the speech (271 words) and the unique words in the speech (138 unique words).

What an accomplishment to create such a noteworthy speech from only 138 different words!

7.6 MUTABLE OBJECTS AND REFERENCES

Lists are mutable—the values in a list can be changed. We briefly considered mutability earlier, but it is worth closer examination. To understand what mutable means in the context of Python, we need to review how variables and their values are structured. In Chapter1 we discussed how variables work in Python. Let's review a few facts:

- A variable name comes into existence when it is associated with a value, for example, *x* = 5.
- A variable name has no specific type associated with it.
- Once made, a variable is associated with a particular Python object (and that object has a type).
- Python maintains a *namespace* that keeps track of variables and the objects they are associated with.

Computer scientists often refer to this association as a *reference*. That is, a variable name "references" an object. Programming languages handle referencing in different ways. In Python, references are maintained in the namespace. A namespace maintains the association or reference between a variable name and an object.

We will diagram some examples to review those concepts and then examine mutability in detail. The code in Figure 7.2 creates an initial set of associations.

Let's modify one of the variables, `your_int`. Notice how the association changes. Figure 7.3 shows the effect. Remember that `your_int` is referencing an `int` which is immutable.

Every operation on an immutable object creates a reference to a *new* object as shown in Figure 7.3. Let's consider some similar operation on lists. We'll begin with an initial association as shown in Figure 7.4.

When two names reference the same mutable object, there are some interesting consequences. The key issue is this: If two or more variables reference the same object, and through one variable the object is modified (because it is mutable), then *all* variables that reference that object will reflect that change.

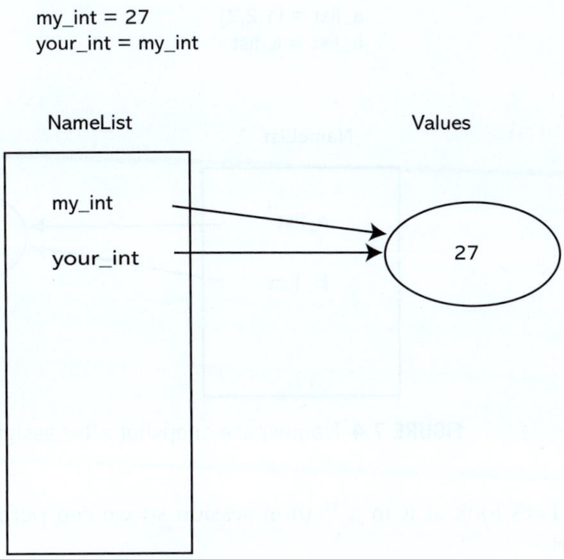

FIGURE 7.2 Namespace snapshot #1.

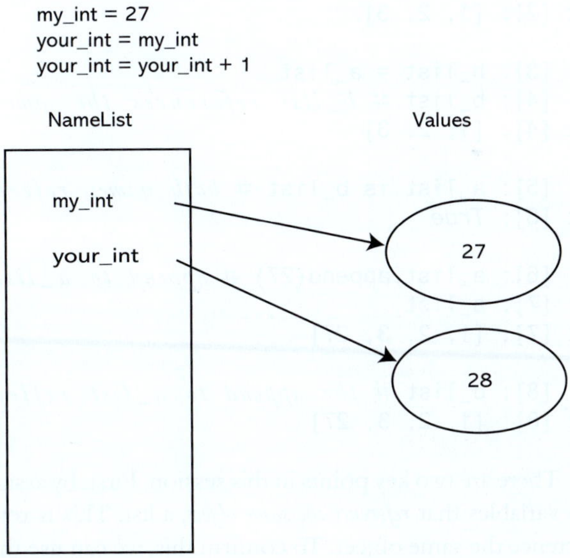

FIGURE 7.3 Modification of a reference to an immutable object.

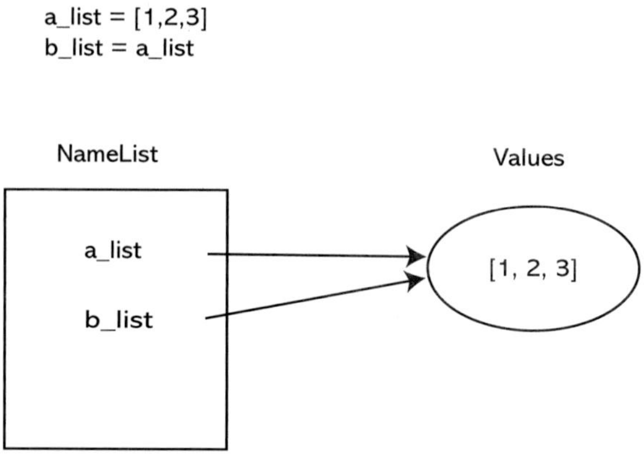

FIGURE 7.4 Namespace snapshot after assigning mutable objects.

Let's look at it in a Python session so we can perhaps see this concept a little more clearly.

```
In  [1]: a_list = [1,2,3]
In  [2]: a_list
Out [2]: [1, 2, 3]

In  [3]: b_list = a_list
In  [4]: b_list # b_list references the same object as a_list
Out [4]: [1, 2, 3]

In  [5]: a_list is b_list # both names reference the same object? True.
Out [5]: True

In  [6]: a_list.append(27) # append to a_list
In  [7]: a_list
Out [7]: [1, 2, 3, 27]

In  [8]: b_list # the append to a_list reflect in b_list
Out [8]: [1, 2, 3, 27]
```

There are two key points in this session. First, by assigning `b_list` to `a_list`, we create two variables that *reference the same object*, a list. This is reflected in Figure 7.4—both names reference the same object. To confirm this, we can use the ***is*** operator which is *True* if the variables reference the same object.

Second, if we perform an operation such as `append` to the referenced list through one of the variables, in this case `a_list`, then the list is modified. Again, this is because the list is mutable and `append` is a method that modifies the list. However, `b_list` references the

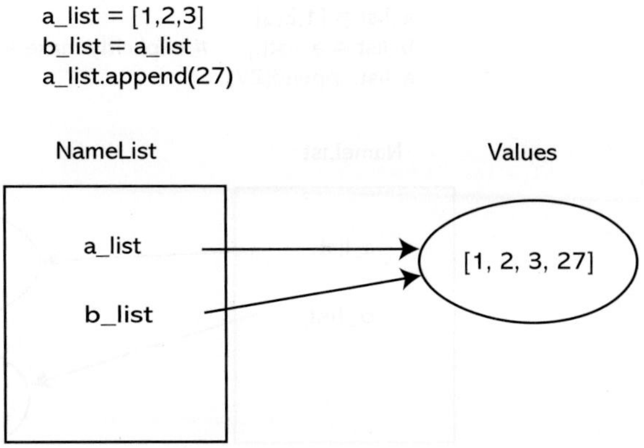

FIGURE 7.5 Modification of shared, mutable objects.

same object so when we print `b_list`, that associated list is changed even though we did not directly modify `b_list`. See Figure 7.5.

There are ways to *copy* a list before assigning to a variable. For example, we could make a copy slice (`[:]`) (from beginning to end) that we introduced with strings in Section 4.1.5. The copy slice creates a new list and copies the elements in the first list to the copied list. Since the result is a new list, that list is different from the old. As a result, application of the ***is*** operator shows that the variables do not reference the same object. This situation is shown in the session that follows and in Figure 7.6. While a copy slice is a simple way to copy a list, it too has its drawbacks which we discuss in Section 7.6.1.

```
In  [1]: a_list = [1,2,3]
In  [2]: a_list
Out [2]: [1, 2, 3]

In  [3]: b_list = a_list[:] # explicitly make a distinct copy
In  [4]: a_list is b_list # Both names reference same object? False.
Out [4]: False

In  [5]: b_list
Out [5]: [1, 2, 3]

In  [6]: a_list.append(27) # append now only modifies a_list
In  [7]: a_list
Out [7]: [1, 2, 3, 27]

In  [8]: b_list # b_list is unchanged
Out [8]: [1, 2, 3]
```

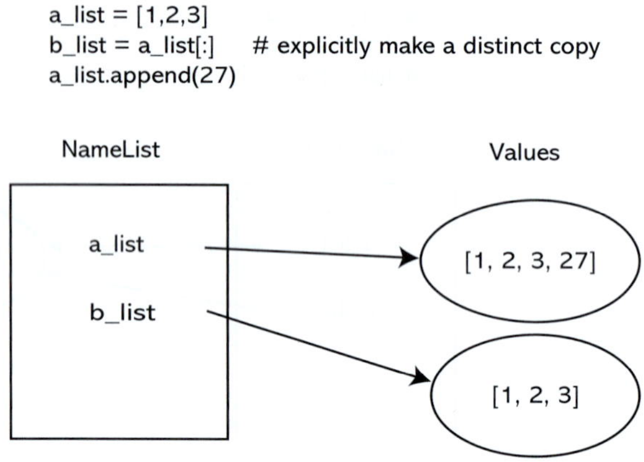

FIGURE 7.6 Making a distinct copy of a mutable object.

Figure 7.6 illustrates the creation of a distinct copy of a mutable object using slicing. What happens when you do the following?

```
In  [1]: a_list = [1,2,3]
In  [2]: a_list.append(a_list)
In  [3]: a_list
Out [3]: [1, 2, 3, [...]]
```

When a list appends *itself* as an element, an infinite regress occurs. That is, the list has as an element itself which has as its element itself which has as an element itself .... To avoid any issues, a new reference is inserted into the list as shown in Figure 7.7. When the list is printed, an element that has square brackets containing ... is printed, indicating a self-reference.

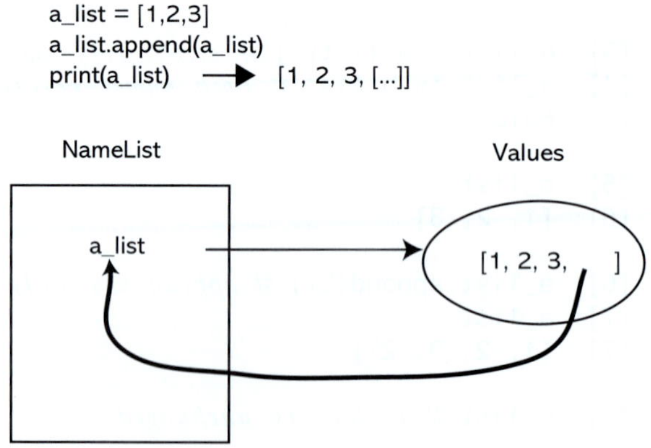

FIGURE 7.7 Self-referencing.

7.6.1 Shallow versus Deep Copy

What does it mean to make a copy? In Python, it is important to understand what elements are stored in a list, particularly when one of the list elements is, itself, a list. To see how this works, consider this session:

```
In  [1]: a_list = [1,2,3]
In  [2]: b_list = [5,6,7]
In  [3]: a_list.append(b_list)
In  [4]: a_list # append stuck b_list into a_list as expected
Out [4]: [1, 2, 3, [5, 6, 7]]

In  [5]: c_list = b_list # we just gave the object another name
In  [6]: c_list # c_list looks like b_list: different names for same object
Out [6]: [5, 6, 7]

In  [7]: b_list is c_list # Both names reference same object? True.
Out [7]: True

In  [8]: c_list[2] = 88
In  [9]: c_list # as expected: we changed the item at index 2 to 88
Out [9]: [5, 6, 88]

In  [10]: b_list # b_list changed: c_list and b_list name the same object
Out [10]: [5, 6, 88]

In  [11]: a_list # whoa! what happened here? we didn't touch a_list!
Out [11]: [1, 2, 3, [5, 6, 88]]
```

To aid in understanding what is going on let's draw some pictures. Figure 7.8 shows the layout after we create `a_list` and `b_list`.

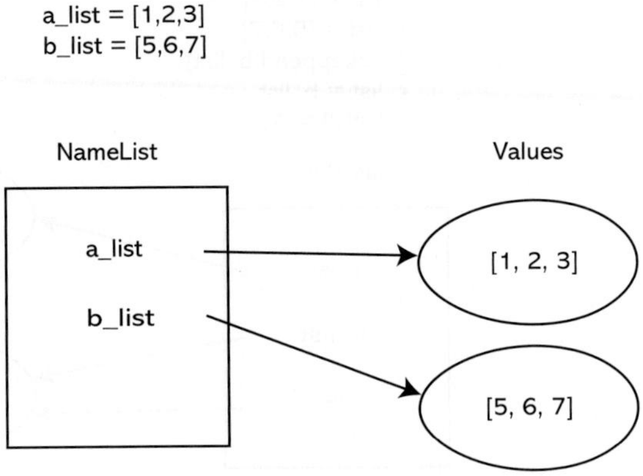

FIGURE 7.8 Simple lists before append.

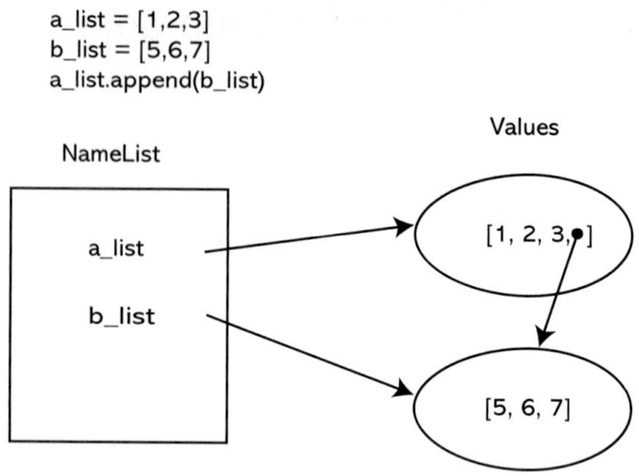

FIGURE 7.9 Lists after append.

Figure 7.9 illustrates the namespace after the `a_list.append(b_list)` call. Notice how `a_list` now has a *reference* to the object that `b_list` named as an element, not a copy of that object. That point is worth emphasizing. Variable `a_list` has four elements: three integers and one *reference* to a list. This is not unexpected given that we have seen the same behavior when assigning a list object to another variable. What is assigned is the reference. As a result, we get similar, perhaps unexpected, results. When we change `b_list`, we expect to see the change reflected in `a_list`. However, a change to `c_list` also changes the last element of `a_list`, since they both refer to the same object. Figure 7.10 shows the effect of `c_list[2] = 88`.

Can't we just make a copy using the copy slice operation? The answer is yes, but it again raises the question as to what gets copied. There was a key phrase we used with we talked about using copy slice. We said that it "copies the elements" from one list to the new

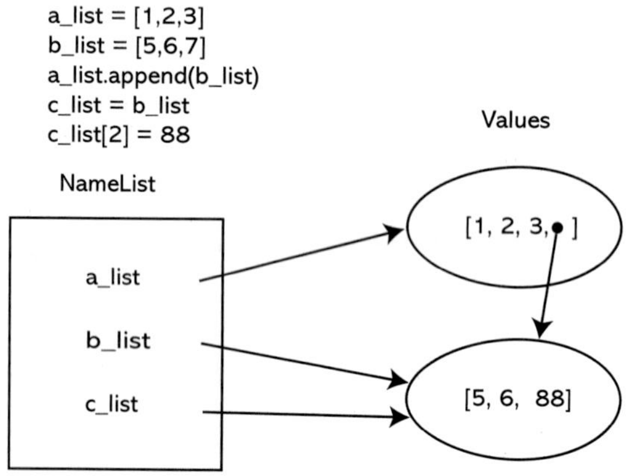

FIGURE 7.10 Final state of copying example.

list. However, as we just saw, sometimes the elements are themselves references. Let's take a look at an example.

```
In  [1]: a_list = [1, 2, 3]
In  [2]: b_list = [5, 6, 7]
In  [3]: a_list.append(b_list)
In  [4]: a_list
Out [4]: [1, 2, 3, [5, 6, 7]]

In  [5]: c_list = a_list[:] # c_list is a copy slice of a_list
In  [6]: c_list
Out [6]: [1, 2, 3, [5, 6, 7]]

In  [7]: b_list[0]=1000 # this should affect a_list
In  [7]: a_list
Out [7]: [1, 2, 3, [1000, 6, 7]]        # it does affect a_list

In  [8]: c_list
Out [8]: [1, 2, 3, [1000, 6, 7]]        # it affects c_list as well
```

Figure 7.11 shows the situation.

We create the same situation we had before: `a_list` has as an element a reference to `b_list`. We then create a copy of `a_list` using copy slice and store it in `c_list`. However, that phrase "copy the elements" is shown clearly in Figure 7.11. A new list was created for `c_list`, but it was created by copying the elements of `a_list`. Because `a_list` had as an element a reference, the reference (not a new copy of the object) was copied. Thus a change to `b_list` was still reflected in `c_list` even though we made a copy!

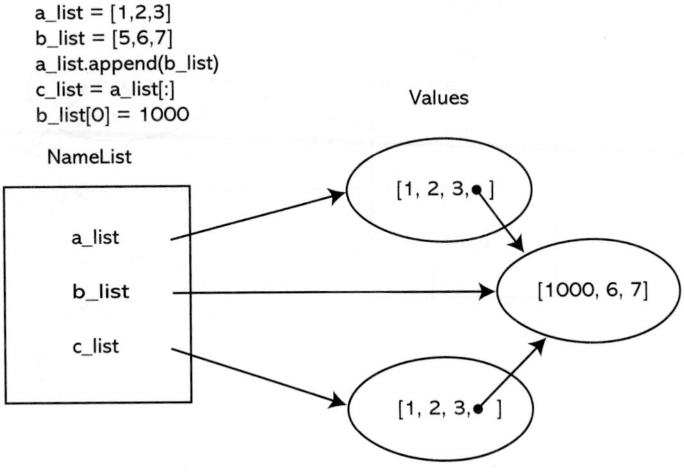

FIGURE 7.11 Effects of copy slice (a shallow copy).

The case in which only the references, not the objects themselves, are copied is called a *shallow copy*. By now it should be clear that a copy slice is just a shallow copy. It copies the elements in a list, even if the elements are references. If what you desire is to copy the *contents* rather than simply the reference, you need to perform what is called a *deep copy*. A deep copy will copy any object, even it if means it must follow a reference to find the object. Such a copy could be very slow if there are many references, but it will provide a true copy of the object.

There is a `copy` module that has a `deepcopy` function which is guaranteed to follow all references and create a true copy. The next session shows the use of `deepcopy`, and Figure 7.12 shows the result of a deep copy operation.

```
In  [1]: a_list = [1, 2, 3]
In  [2]: b_list = [5, 6, 7]
In  [3]: a_list.append(b_list)
In  [4]: import copy
In  [5]: c_list = copy.deepcopy(a_list)
In  [6]: b_list[0]=1000
In  [6]: a_list
Out [6]: [1, 2, 3, [1000, 6, 7]]

In  [7]: c_list
Out [7]: [1, 2, 3, [5, 6, 7]]
```

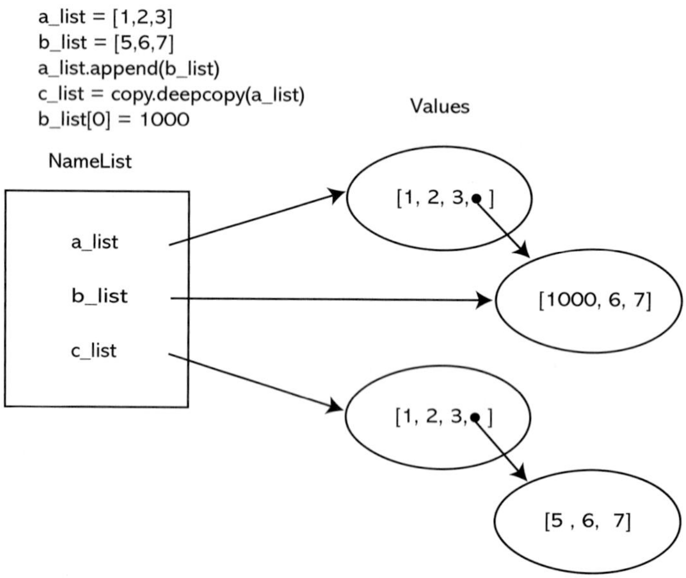

FIGURE 7.12 Using the copy module for a deep copy.

Even though the last element of `a_list` was a reference, the `deepcopy` function created a copy of the referenced object and then placed the reference as the last element of `c_list`. Now `c_list` is truly a copy, a deep copy.

7.6.2 Mutable versus Immutable

VideoNote 7.2
List Application

It is worth taking a moment to revisit the consequences of working with mutable objects. When a variable references an immutable object, any operation that uses that object (concatenation, replace, strip, etc.) creates a new object; it does not change the referenced object. In contrast, a variable that references a mutable object can either create a new object *or* change the referenced object itself, depending upon the operation.

PROGRAMMING TIP

Operations on variables that reference mutable objects may change the object itself or create a new object. When making a copy of a mutable object, be sure you know what you are getting. If you are in doubt, do a deep copy using `deepcopy` from the `copy` module.

Check Yourself: Mutable List Check

1. Show the output for the following program. To make it easier, draw a diagram similar to the ones above to keep straight the connections between the three lists.

```
str_list = ['hi','mom','dad',['grandma','grandpa']]
new_list = str_list
copy_list = str_list[:]

str_list[0] = 'bye'
new_list[1] = 'mother'
copy_list[2] = 'father'
copy_list[-1][0] = 'nanna'

print(str_list)        # Line 1
print(new_list)        # Line 2
print(copy_list)       # Line 3
```

(a) What output is produced by Line 1 when the program is executed?
(b) What output is produced by Line 2 when the program is executed?
(c) What output is produced by Line 3 when the program is executed?

7.7 TUPLES

Here is the quick definition of a *tuple*. Tuples are essentially immutable lists. A tuple shares all the characteristics of a list except those that violate immutability. That is, any function or method that can change a list is *not* available for tuples.

Because it is immutable, a tuple has some similarity to a string. However, as with its cousin the list, a tuple can contain elements of any type. Tuples are delimited by parentheses when printed, and like a list its elements are separated by commas. To make a tuple, use this syntax:

```
my_tuple = (1,2,3)
```

It is important to note that the *comma*, not the parentheses, is the operator that creates the tuple. The expression `1,2,3`, no parentheses, yields the tuple `(1,2,3)`. To create a single-element tuple one *cannot* create it with the expression `(1)`, which simply yields 1 in the interpreter. The expression `(1),` *does* create a single-element tuple. The confusion is due to the overloaded nature of the parentheses. In most situations, parentheses indicate grouping and Python will interpret them as such. The inclusion of the comma indicates that the parentheses are being used as part of tuple creation, not grouping. The bottom line is that commas are the operators that make a tuple. The following session emphasizes these facts:

```
In  [1]: 10,12 # Python creats a tuple
Out [1]: (10, 12)

In  [2]: tup = 2,3 # assigning a tuple to a variable
In  [3]: tup
Out [3]: (2, 3)

In  [4]: (1) # not a tuple, a grouping
Out [4]: 1

In  [5]: (1,) # comma makes it a tuple
Out [5]: (1,)

In  [6]: x,y = 'a',3.14159 # tuple creation on right, multiple assignment from it
In  [7]: x
Out [7]: 'a'

In  [8]: y
Out [8]: 3.14159

In  [9]: x,y # create a tuple
Out [9]: ('a', 3.14159)
```

The operations familiar from other sequences (lists and strings) are available, except, of course, those operators that violate immutability.

- Operators such as + (concatenate) and * (repeat) work as before.
- Slicing also works as before.
- Membership (`in`) and `for` iteration also work on tuples.
- `len`, `min`, `max`, greater-than (>), less-than (<), `sum`, and others work the same way. In particular, any comparison operation has the same restrictions for mixed types.

None of the operations that change lists are available for tuples. For example, `append`, `extend`, `insert`, `remove`, `pop`, `reverse`, and `sort` do not work on tuples. Here is a session demonstrating the various operators working with tuples:

```
In  [1]: my_tuple = 1,2,3,4,5
In  [2]: my_tuple
Out [2]: (1, 2, 3, 4, 5)

In  [3]: my_tuple + my_tuple # concatenation (addition)
Out [3]: (1, 2, 3, 4, 5, 1, 2, 3, 4, 5)

In  [4]: my_tuple * 3 # multiplication
Out [4]: (1, 2, 3, 4, 5, 1, 2, 3, 4, 5, 1, 2, 3, 4, 5)

In  [5]: my_tuple[1] # indexing
Out [5]: 2

In  [6]: my_tuple[:3] # slicing
Out [6]: (1, 2, 3)

In  [7]: my_tuple[1:3]
Out [7]: (2, 3)

In  [8]: my_tuple[-1]
Out [8]: 5

In  [9]: 2 in my_tuple # membership (in)
Out [9]: True

In  [10]: 10 in my_tuple
Out [10]: False

In  [11]: for x in my_tuple: # for
...:      print(x,end=' ')

1 2 3 4 5
In  [12]: len(my_tuple) # length
Out [12]: 5
```

```
In  [13]: min(my_tuple) # min and max
Out [13]: 1

In  [14]: max(my_tuple)
Out [14]: 5

In  [15]: sum(my_tuple)
Out [15]: 15

In  [16]: 1,2,3 > 3,2,1
Out [16]: False
```

7.7.1 Tuples from Lists

It is easy to convert a list to a tuple and vice versa using the available data structure constructors. That is, you can convert a tuple to a list using the *list* constructor and a list to a tuple using the *tuple* constructor. In the following session, we show how you might sort a tuple. First, we turn a list into a tuple using the *tuple* constructor. Second, we try to sort the tuple with the sort method, but that approach fails because of the immutability of the tuple. We then apply the sorted function to the tuple, which returns a new sorted list. We confirm the returned object is in fact a list with the type function. Finally, we turn the sorted list into a tuple using the *tuple* constructor.

Here is a session that illustrates these points:

```
In  [1]: a_list = [6,1,3,4]
In  [2]: a_tuple = tuple(a_list) # convert from list to tuple
In  [3]: a_tuple
Out [3]: (6, 1, 3, 4)   # note the parentheses: indicates a tuple

In  [4]: a_tuple.sort() # cannot sort an immutable object

Traceback (most recent call last):
  File "<pyshell#37>", line 1, in <module>
    a_tuple.sort()
AttributeError: 'tuple' object has no attribute 'sort'

In  [5]: sorted_list = sorted(a_tuple) # sorted creates a new object, a list
In  [6]: type(sorted_list)
Out [6]: <class 'list'>

In  [7]: sorted_list
Out [7]: [1, 3, 4, 6]

In  [8]: new_tuple = tuple(sorted_list)
In  [9]: new_tuple
Out [9]: (1, 3, 4, 6)
```

7.7.2 Why Tuples?

The question is, why have an immutable list, a tuple, as a separate type? The reason is that an immutable list provides a data structure with some integrity and some persistence. It is not possible to accidentally change a tuple.

Also, because tuples are immutable, they can be used in a few places where mutable objects are not allowed.

7.8 LISTS: THE DATA STRUCTURE

Python comes with a number of built-in data structures. So far we have looked at *strings*, *lists*, and *tuples*.

What is a data structure? In Section 1.6, we covered the type of an object and what that entailed. We observed that a type described what was stored in an object of a particular type and the operations we can perform on an object of that particular type. More generally, we consider the concept of a *data structure*. A data structure is related to a data type, in that a data type is the realization (implementation) of a data structure in a program. Thus, a data structure is a more abstract concept, indicating what a programmer would like to be done as opposed to how the programmer actually implements the concept in code (the data type). In particular, a data structure focuses on the *organization of data* and the operations that can act on the data—often with an emphasis on *efficiency*. For example, a Google search potentially examines the content of the whole Internet. How must one organize this vast amount of data so that searches can be both accurate and fast? Part of the answer is in how the data is organized and manipulated, that is, what data structures are used. The company founders, Larry Page and Sergey Brin, became very rich by coming up with a more efficient data structure and algorithm for Internet data search (they named it MapReduce).

When we speak of efficiency we could mean one of a few things:

1. **Efficient with respect to an *algorithm*.** Data structures are tightly linked with the algorithms that work on them. Thus, it might be efficient to perform some operations (sorting, storing, inserting) on a particular organization of the data. However, making one operation efficient might make another operation inefficient on the same data structure.
2. **Efficient with respect to *space*.** One way to organize the data is to be efficient in memory usage. If the data being stored is very large (say, all the text in the Library of Congress), storage efficiency might be very important. Again, how data gets stored might well affect what we can efficiently do with the data.
3. **Efficient with respect to *time*.** Another important consideration is time. If our algorithm is tasked with controlling flaps on an airplane in flight, then determining proper settings quickly is crucial. Many variables come to play in that decision and data organization (the data structure) is critical.

Not surprisingly, those three meanings of efficiency are not necessarily independent. For example, Google's data organization is tightly tied to their algorithm, storage is critical because of the immense amount of data, and time is important because a slow search is not useful to people. Entire courses are devoted to the theory of data structures and the algorithms that work well with them.

We have seen that algorithms can be described abstractly, and the same is true for data structures. The abstract data structure is an abstraction of the data organization and that organization's implications towards efficiency, however defined. When we define a data structure, we will also define a set of operations that can be done on the data structure. Various trade-offs will result: some algorithms may run slowly, certain data examples will occupy too much space, and so on. We design the data structure to solve the main problems at hand. For example, Google provides a search operation to search the Internet, but it would be odd to provide a print operation that printed the Internet.

7.8.1 Example Data Structure

You have already seen three Python data types: strings, lists, and tuples. Let's consider a string as a data structure. We first learned that a string was a sequence of characters. A sequence is a way of organizing data—characters, in the case of strings; anything, in the case of lists. One of the properties of a sequence is that it has an order. Other data structures do not share such a property; for example, a `set` is a data structure that is an unordered collection of items (covered in Chapter 9). We chose a sequence for strings because the order of characters is important. It wouldn't be useful if the characters of English (or any language) words were rearranged to some arbitrary order just to be more "efficient."

As a data structure, we saw that strings had a set of operations. There were functions (`len`), methods (`split`), and operators (addition), all with specific meanings for a string. There were also things missing from strings: no way to sort a string, no way to index assign in a string.

As an abstraction, there are implementation details that are hidden from you, the user. We conceive of the string as a sequence, but don't really know (or care) about its implementation details, for example, how it is stored and manipulated in memory. We manipulate a string using the methods and operations provided. The details don't matter as long as the methods and operators work correctly (and efficiently).

Like most data structures, a string data structure does some things efficiently and other things inefficiently (or not at all).

What does a string do efficiently?

- Holds a sequence of characters efficiently in memory
- Maintains information about the size of the string
- Allows quick access to any individual element

What does a string *not* do efficiently (or not do at all)?

- Cannot modify a string element: strings are immutable, so you must make a copy to change anything
- Cannot efficiently manipulate elements for tasks like:
  - Find the largest element (have to look at all the elements)
  - Store elements other than characters
  - Other things (you will see shortly)

7.8.2 Other Example Data Structures

We can imagine some other data structures that might be handy to have around. In fact, the possibilities are endless. Here is a sampling of some common data structures:

- A *queue* is a sequence of data elements that "stand in a line," in which the data can only be removed from the front of the line and new elements can only be added to the back of the line (as in the British English: "queue up for the bus"). Elements enter the queue and wait, typically in order, until they come to the front of the queue for removal. Queues are useful for modeling how cars move through intersections or data flows through nodes on the Internet. Associated operations check to see if the queue is empty, add to the back, and remove from the front.
- A *dictionary* data structure is one in which we can look up a key (like a word in the dictionary) and access some value (like the definition of the word). A phone book could be implemented as a dictionary. Operations would include: look up a value associated with key, add key-value pairs, remove key-value pairs, and so on.
- A *set* of unordered elements, which would allow us to access and modify individual elements. Operations would include: insertion, removal, union, intersection, and so on.
- A *matrix* of numbers is a common mathematical data structure that is extensively used in science and engineering. Associated operations would include: multiplication, find determinant, invert, transpose, and so on.

Some data structures are built into languages (Python has dictionaries and sets); others must be created by the programmer (Python does not have built-in matrix or queue data structures, though they are available in modules). Ideally, it will be good to define our own data structures to solve special problems. You will learn later how to combine the data structures provided by Python into structures tailored to our needs.

7.9 ALGORITHM EXAMPLE: U.S. EPA AUTOMOBILE MILEAGE DATA

The U.S. Environmental Protection Agency (EPA) gathers data on cars and trucks. It is best known for its mileage data, but they also gather information on car type (van, pickup, sport car, etc.), engine type, luggage capacity, seating, and so on. This data is available online[2] in CSV-format (CSV = comma-separated values). We can download the data file and analyze it to answer any questions we might have. For instance, if we are interested in mileage data, we must sift through the data and extract those values. Take a look at the data file to get a feel for what is there.

Here are some questions we might ask:

- What are the maximum and minimum mileage ratings for cars in this file?
- Which car(s) get the maximum mileage in this file?
- Which car(s) get the minimum mileage in this file?

As is often the case when working with real data, we often have to refine the question we are asking. Which year are we interested in? The website organizes its data by year. For this program, we choose to download the file for 2015 and store it in the same directory as our program. We named the file "*epaData.csv*". What defines a car? It turns out that the file contains data for vehicles other than cars, including pickup trucks, vans, and SUVs. Examination of the data file reveals that there is a column that labels vehicles as "Car," "Truck," and so on. The file records many different types of mileage; we choose to use the highway mileage for conventional fuel.

Given our refined question, here is our general algorithm:

1. Open the EPA data file for the year 2015.
2. Extract from the file the highway mileage data for cars and store those values in a list.
3. Find the minimum and maximum values in the list.

The EPA website has a file describing how the data is arranged (bottom of the web page, downloads as a Readme.txt). Each line in the file represents a vehicle, and each line contains over 150 different pieces of data. Though somewhat cryptic, at the top of the file is a "header" line, which describes the data associated with each column.

Here are the first few column labels of that first header line of the 2015 data file:

['Model Year', 'Mfr Name', 'Division', 'Carline', 'Verify Mfr Cd', 'Index (Model Type Index)', 'Eng Displ', '# Cyl', 'Transmission', 'City FE (Guide) - Conventional Fuel', 'Hwy FE (Guide) - Conventional Fuel', …

The first thing to notice is that "Hwy FE" ("FE" is for Fuel Economy) is the eleventh element in the header (at index 10). Also, the manufacturer's division ("Division") is the third element and type ("Carline") is the fourth. Finally, far down the list, well beyond the few headers we show, in column 71 is "Car/Truck Category" that indicates the category of vehicle, for example, "Car", "Van", which will be useful to eliminate "Van" and "Truck" from consideration. Note that there are a number of classifications, and we will only consider "Car." Now that we understand how the data in the file is structured, let's begin the

[2] http://www.fueleconomy.gov/FEG/download.shtml

process of developing a program. First, let's begin by opening the file and printing some information from it. As a first cut at working with this data, let's print out every line that mentions "CORVETTE." Because each line in the file is very long, we'll print out only the first characters. See Code Listing 7.9.

Code Listing 7.9

```
# highest mileage data
# from http://www.fueleconomy.gov/FEG/download.shtml

# 1. open EPA data file
epa_file = open("epaData.csv", "r")

for line in epa_file:          # get each line one at a time from the file
    if 'CORVETTE' in line:     # if 'CORVETTE' is anywhere in the line print it
        print(line[:75])       # only print first 75 characters
```

```
2015,General Motors,Chevrolet,CORVETTE,GMX,59,6.2,8,Auto(S8),16,29,20,20,40
2015,General Motors,Chevrolet,CORVETTE,GMX,67,6.2,8,Auto(S8),13,21,16,16.4,
2015,General Motors,Chevrolet,CORVETTE,GMX,60,6.2,8,Manual(M7),17,29,21,21.
2015,General Motors,Chevrolet,CORVETTE,GMX,68,6.2,8,Manual(M7),15,22,18,18.
```

The output isn't very interesting, but we demonstrated that we can open and read data from the data file we had downloaded and look for particular data within that file.

The next step in the algorithm is to gather the highway mileage data and store it in a way that we can more easily examine/manipulate. Our first cut at the program reads lines one at a time from the file, so for each of those lines we need to extract the highway data. Already we've noted that the highway mileage data is in column 11 (index 10, counting from 0). Since each line has its data separated by commas (remember the file is in comma-separated value format), we can gather the highway mileage data from each line using the `split(',')` method. From the list generated by `split`, we can extract the highway mileage data with index 10. We need to store all the highway mileage values, so we choose to `append` each value into a list.

Here are those steps in algorithmic form. Note that this algorithmic segment expands the detail of step 2 in the previous algorithm:

1. initialize a mileage list to be empty
2. for each line in the file:
   (a) split the line at commas into a list
   (b) append list element 10 onto a list of mileage values

The processing of each line is definitely a "do one thing" operation, so following **Rule 8**, create a function named `create_mileage_list` to process the file information and return a list of mileage values. The main program will open the file, call function `create_mileage_list` and print the results. Because the list is long, we show an abbreviated print out of the 1250 mileage values. See Code Listing 7.10.

Code Listing 7.10

```
# highest mileage data
# from http://www.fueleconomy.gov/FEG/download.shtml

def create_mileage_list(epa_file):
    """Create a list of cars and mileage from epa_file."""
    # 2a create a mileage list and initialize it to empty
    mileage_list = []

    for line in epa_file:                      # 2b. get each line from the file
        line_list = line.split(',')            # 2bI.  csv => split on comma
        mileage_list.append(line_list[10])  # 2bII. append highway mileage
    return mileage_list

##########################################

# 1. open EPA data file
epa_file = open("epaData.csv", "r")
mileage_list = create_mileage_list(epa_file)

print(mileage_list)
```

```
['Hwy FE (Guide) - Conventional Fuel', '34', '18', '21', '19', '21', '19', ...
```

The first element of the list is the header text information for column 10 (index 9), the remainder of the list contains the highway mileage for all the vehicles in the file. The good news is that, as a confirmation of getting the right thing, the header is "Hwy FE," which is exactly the column we want. The bad news is that the header information is not an integer string, which is what we are looking for. We can safely ignore that header value, giving us a uniform list of mileage values, which we can more easily convert to integer numbers. Let's clean up our code to reflect these two changes: ignore the header and convert the integer strings to integer numbers.

We want to clean up our code with the following:

- ignore the header line
- convert mileage data to integers before appending to `mileage_list`

Converting the mileage data is easy. We apply the `int` constructor on the highway mileage string before appending:

```
mileage_list.append(int(line_list[10]))
```

There are a number of ways to ignore a line. One easy way is `readline()` that reads and returns one line. We can read one line before the loop so our loop handles the remaining lines. In our code we assign the returned line to `header` and then never use that variable—effectively ignoring it. An alternative to use the **`continue`** control construct. Remember how a **`continue`** works. When executed, it ends that particular iteration of a loop, ignoring any code that comes after the **`continue`** and continues with subsequent iterations. From our examination of the header line, we know that the header line begins with "Model Year" so we know that we are looking at the header line if the first ten characters are "Model Year". We can skip processing the header line with `if line[:10] == 'Model Year': continue`.

Let's add that code to our program and see what we have. Again, the output shown is only the beginning of the `mileage_list` output. See Code Listing 7.11.

Code Listing 7.11

```
# highest mileage data
# from http://www.fueleconomy.gov/FEG/download.shtml

def create_mileage_list(epa_file):
    """Create a list of cars and mileage from epa_file."""
    # 2a create a mileage list and initialize it to empty
    mileage_list = []
    header=epa_file.readline()  # skip header line
    for line in epa_file:                    # 2b. get each line from the file
        line_list = line.split(',')          # 2bI.  csv => split on comma
        if 'Car' in line_list[70]:           # 2bII. append highway mileage
            mileage_list.append(int(line_list[10]))
    return mileage_list

########################################

# 1. open EPA data file
epa_file = open("epaData.csv", "r")
mileage_list = create_mileage_list(epa_file)

print(mileage_list)
```

```
[19, 21, 23, 23, 32, 34, 34, 40, 32, 34, 24, 22, 22, 22,...
```

Now we have a list of integers from the highway mileage column. Let's find the minimum and maximum. Conveniently Python has built-in functions for just those two problems: `max` and `min` (we leave writing your own `max` or `min` function as an exercise). We can apply those to `mileage_list`. If there is more than one maximum or minimum, then only one will be selected.

While we are at it, we specified that we only want to include cars, not other vehicle types such as trucks. We can look at the raw data and see that cars are called just that so we can only include data from rows with "Car" at index 70. See Code Listing 7.12.

Code Listing 7.12

```python
# highest mileage data
# from http://www.fueleconomy.gov/FEG/download.shtml

def create_mileage_list(epa_file):
    """Create a list of cars and mileage from epa_file."""
    # 2a create a mileage list and initialize it to empty
    mileage_list = []
    epa_file.readline()
    for line in epa_file:                   # 2b. get each line from the file
        line_list = line.split(',')         # 2bI.  csv => split on comma
        if 'Car' in line_list[70]:          # 2bII. append highway mileage
            mileage_list.append(int(line_list[10]))

    return mileage_list

##########################################

# 1. open EPA data file
epa_file = open("epaData.csv", "rU")
mileage_list = create_mileage_list(epa_file)

# 3. find max and min mileage
max_mileage = max(mileage_list)
min_mileage = min(mileage_list)

print("Max and Min Mileage: ", max_mileage, min_mileage)
```

```
Max and Min Mileage:  48 18
```

We now have the maximum and minimum mileage for cars. That begs the question: which cars are those?

There are many ways to find out which cars have the max or min mileage, but here are two. Currently, the first pass through the file finds that the maximum mileage is 48. To find all the cars with that mileage, we would have to make a second pass through the file from the beginning looking for cars with that value and print them out.

Here is another approach. Instead of appending only mileage, let's also append the name of the car so we have a name with each data point. We can group name and mileage together by placing them in a list. Better still, since such a list will never change, we could wrap the values in a tuple. Now our `mileage_list` will no longer be a list of integers; instead, it will be a list of tuples. Each tuple will have a name and a mileage.

Here it is in algorithmic form:

1. get mileage data
2. get name (make and model, e.g., `'CHEVROLET' 'MALIBU'`)
3. put mileage and name in a tuple, e.g., `(30, 'CHEVROLET', 'MALIBU')`
4. append tuple to `mileage_list`

From the description of the data, we can see that the make of the car ("Division" in EPA nomenclature) is in element 2 and that the model ("Carline") is in element 3. Both are probably important for determining the type of car so we should record both. We also need to record the mileage. What order should these values come in the tuple? Mileage should come first because of the way Python does comparisons of collections. Both `max` and `min` use the first element to compare collections. If we want to organize by mileage, then mileage must come first in each tuple we record. The make and model can be placed at index 2 and index 3 in the tuple. Let's see what this looks like in Code Listing 7.13.

Code Listing 7.13

```python
# highest mileage data
# from http://www.fueleconomy.gov/FEG/download.shtml

def create_mileage_list(epa_file):
    """Create a list of cars and mileage from epa_file."""
    # 2a create a mileage list and initialize it to empty
    mileage_list = []
    epa_file.readline() # skip header line
    for line in epa_file:                  # 2b. get each line from the file
        line_list = line.split(',')    # 2bI.  csv => split on comma
        if 'Car' in line_list[70]:     # 2bII. append highway mileage
          mileage_list.append((int(line_list[10]), line_list[2], line_list[3]))
     return mileage_list

###########################################

```

```python
# 1. open EPA data file
epa_file = open("epaData.csv", "r")
mileage_list = create_mileage_list(epa_file)

# 3. find max and min mileage
max_mileage = max(mileage_list)
min_mileage = min(mileage_list)

print("Max and Min Mileage: ", max_mileage, min_mileage)
```

```
Max and Min Mileage: (48, 'Volkswagen', 'Jetta Hybrid') (18, 'Bentley', 'Mulsanne')
```

That is a better solution, but it is not yet as nice as we'd like. There is only one name associated with the minimum and maximum mileage values. What if multiple cars have the same mileage values? As we have said, `min` (and similarly `max`) returns the first minimum value, not all minimum values. In this case, we want all. How can we do that?

Observe that our `mileage_list` has the information we want—all cars with maximum and minimum mileage values. That is, let's create a list of maximum mileage cars and a separate list of minimum mileage cars. Here is an algorithm that can create those lists:

1. create and initialize separate lists for minimum and maximum mileage cars
2. find the min and max mileage
3. for each car in `mileage_list`:
   (a) if a car has maximum mileage, append it to the maximum mileage list
   (b) if a car has minimum mileage, append it to the minimum mileage list

In step 2, let's return to having `max_mileage` and `min_mileage` only be the integer for mileage, not the car tuple. We can do that by extracting the mileage from the tuple that `min(mileage_list)` returns. Since mileage is the first item in the tuple we can use the following: `min(mileage_list)[0]`. This expression works because `min (mileage_list)` is a tuple, and we can directly index that tuple with `[0]`. In the previous example, we saw that `min(mileage_list)` was the tuple `(18, 'Bentley','Mulsanne')` so using the index `min(mileage_list)[0]` yields the integer 18. Here are the two lines to find the max and min:

```python
max_mileage = max(mileage_list)[0]
min_mileage = min(mileage_list)[0]
```

Steps 1 and 3 can be placed in a function named find_max_min_mileage that returns lists of all the maximum and minimum mileage cars. Let's add that code to our program. Code Listing 7.14 shows the function and the program output:

Code Listing 7.14

```
def find_max_min_mileage(mileage_list, max_mileage, min_mileage):
    """Make a list of cars with max and min mileage: list of car tuples."""
    max_mileage_list = []
    min_mileage_list = []

    # 5. find max and min mileage cars; append them to the appropriate list
    #    car_tuple[0] is item 0 of the tuple which is the mileage
    for car_tuple in mileage_list:
        if car_tuple[0] == max_mileage:
            max_mileage_list.append(car_tuple)
        if car_tuple[0] == min_mileage:
            min_mileage_list.append(car_tuple)

    return max_mileage_list, min_mileage_list
```

```
Max and Min Mileage:  48 18

Maximum Mileage Cars: [(48, 'Volkswagen', 'Jetta Hybrid'), (48, 'TOYOTA', 'PRIUS')]
Minimum Mileage Cars: [(18, 'Chevrolet', 'CAMARO'), (18, 'Bentley', 'Mulsanne'),
                       (18, 'Cadillac', 'CTS')]
```

The output is not pretty, so let's walk through the list of tuples and print only the make and model. With that modification and a few more comments, Code Listing 7.15 shows the final program and output:

Code Listing 7.15

```
# highest mileage data
# from http://www.fueleconomy.gov/FEG/download.shtml
def create_mileage_list(epa_file):
    """Create a list of cars and mileage from epa_file."""
    # 2a create a mileage list and initialize it to empty
    mileage_list = []
    epa_file.readline()  # skip header line
```

```
    for line in epa_file:                # 2b. get each line from the file
        line_list = line.split(',')      # 2bI.  csv => split on comma
        if 'Car' in line_list[70]:       # 2bII. append highway mileage
            # create tuple: (mileage, make, model)
            car_tuple = (int(line_list[10]), line_list[2], line_list[3])
            mileage_list.append(car_tuple) # 2bII. append tuple
    return mileage_list



def find_max_min_mileage(mileage_list, max_mileage, min_mileage):
    """Make a list of cars with max and min mileage: list of car tuples."""
    max_mileage_list = []
    min_mileage_list = []

    # 5. find max and min mileage cars; append them to the appropriate list
    #     car_tuple[0] is item 0 of the tuple which is the mileage
    for car_tuple in mileage_list:
        if car_tuple[0] == max_mileage:
            max_mileage_list.append(car_tuple)
        if car_tuple[0] == min_mileage:
            min_mileage_list.append(car_tuple)

    return max_mileage_list, min_mileage_list

##############################################################
# 1. open EPA data file
epa_file = open("epaData.csv", "r")

print("EPA Car Mileage")
print() # blank line

# 2a create a mileage list
mileage_list = create_mileage_list(epa_file)

# 3. find max and min mileage
#     mileage_list is a list of tuples (mileage, make, model)
#     max(mileage_list)[0] finds the max mileage tuple and extracts the mileage
max_mileage = max(mileage_list)[0]
min_mileage = min(mileage_list)[0]

print("Max and Min Mileage: ", max_mileage, min_mileage)
print()  # print blank line

#4. create a list of all cars with max and min mileage: list of car tuples
```

```
max_mileage_list, min_mileage_list = \
                find_max_min_mileage(mileage_list,max_mileage,min_mileage)

print("Maximum Mileage Cars:")
for car_tuple in max_mileage_list:
    print("   ", car_tuple[1], car_tuple[2])
print("Minimum Mileage Cars: ")
for car_tuple in min_mileage_list:
    print("   ", car_tuple[1], car_tuple[2])
```

```
EPA Car Mileage

Max and Min Mileage:  48 18

Maximum Mileage Cars:
   Volkswagen Jetta Hybrid
   TOYOTA PRIUS
Minimum Mileage Cars:
   Chevrolet CAMARO
   Bentley Mulsanne
   Cadillac CTS
```

Notice how we developed this program incrementally, especially, that we tested the code as we developed it. Also, notice how we developed the algorithm in stages.

One final step: does the output make sense? We see that two hybrid cars had the highest mileage and that two luxury cars and a performance car had the lowest mileage; however, what happened to those high-performance Corvettes? If you look at where we printed out the Corvette values earlier, you can count over elements and see that their highway mileage is 21 or greater. Why? At highway speeds, aerodynamic design has a dramatic impact on mileage; therefore, our results look reasonable.

7.9.1 csv Module

Python has a very useful module named `csv` that makes reading messy CSV files easier (details in Section 14.2). For example, if a spreadsheet has commas *within* fields, simply splitting rows on commas doesn't work because some rows will yield extra elements. In fact, the EPA example had two problematic entries: "Ferrari North America, Inc." and "Volvo Cars of North America, LLC" in the "Division" column. For the previous example, we edited the file to remove the commas. A better solution would be to `import csv` and add `reader = csv.reader(epa_file)` to the `create_mileage_list` function.

Code Listing 7.16 shows the function using `csv`. Since one generally wants to split lines into a list when reading `csv` files the split is built into the `reader` so no `split` call is needed. Unfortunately, the `csv` module has no `readline` method so if one wants to skip header lines, one must use ***continue*** as mentioned earlier. Finally, some especially complex spreadsheets have features that make simple splitting of rows difficult, but the `csv` module handles them easily.

Code Listing 7.16

```
# highest mileage data
import csv

def create_mileage_list(epa_file):
    """Create a list of cars and mileage from epa_file."""
    mileage_list = []
    reader = csv.reader(epa_file) # create csv reader
    for line_list in reader:       # no split needed
        mileage_list.append(line_list[10])
    return mileage_list

#############################################

# 1. open EPA data file
epa_file = open("epaData_2.csv", "r")
mileage_list = create_mileage_list(epa_file)

print(mileage_list)
```

VISUAL VIGNETTE

7.10 PLOTTING EPA DATA

Let's plot the EPA highway mileage data over time from its beginning in 1975 using data from the same source. Here is what the first two lines of the data file looks like. Note that it is a space-separated file with no heading:

```
1975 13.4 18.7 15.3 12.0 14.6 13.1
1976 14.6 20.2 16.7 13.2 15.7 14.2
```

The unadjusted highway MPG is in the third column (index 2). If we gather years from index 0 into a list of x values and the highway mileage from index 2 into a list of y values, we can plot the values with `pylab.plot(x_values,y_values)`. The plot is shown in

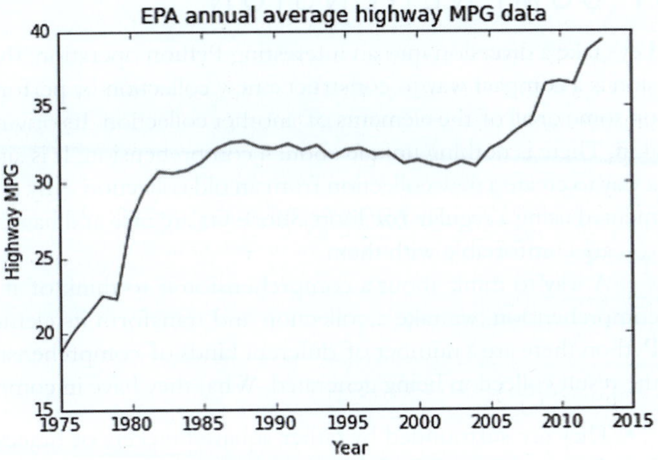

FIGURE 7.13 Plot of EPA highway mileage from 1975.

Figure 7.13. The code showing how the labels were added is shown in Code Listing 7.17. Displayed in this way one can see a dramatic improvement in the highway mileage of new cars over time as well as a large flat spot in the plot.

Code Listing 7.17

```
import pylab

fp = open("epa_data.txt")
x,y = [],[]
for line in fp:
    line_lst = line.strip().split()
    x.append(int(line_lst[0]))  # year
    y.append(float(line_lst[2])) # unadjusted highway MPG
fp.close()

pylab.plot(x,y)
pylab.ylabel("Highway MPG")
pylab.xlabel("Year")
pylab.title("EPA annual average highway MPG data")
#pylab.show()
pylab.savefig("epa_plot.png")
```

7.11 LIST COMPREHENSION

Let's take a diversion into an interesting Python operation: the *comprehension*. A comprehension is a compact way to construct a new collection by performing some simple operations on some or all of the elements of another collection. Its origins lie in mathematical set notation. There is nothing unique about a comprehension. It is simply a shortcut for expressing a way to create a new collection from an old collection. Any comprehension could be implemented using a regular **`for`** loop. Shortcuts are nice and have their place. Use them if/when you are comfortable with them.

A way to think about a comprehension is to think of it as a *transformation*. By using a comprehension, we take a collection and transform its elements into a new collection. In Python there are a number of different kinds of comprehensions depending on the type of the result collection being generated. What they have in common is the following:

- They are surrounded by either square brackets or braces, which indicates the type of the comprehension and thus the type of the result collection.
- They have as their first element an *expression*. This expression is run on every element of the collection being processing and the result of that expression is added as an element to the new collection.
- They have as their second element a **`for`** expression that indicates the collection being processed.
- They have an optional third element that indicates a *condition* under which an element from the collection being processed should be run through the expression. If the condition is *`False`* for a particular element, it is not processed and not added to the result collection. The default is that all elements should be processed.

A list comprehension would look like the following:

[*expression* **`for`**`-clause` *condition*]

Let's take a look at an example.

```
In  [1]: [i for i in range(20) if i%2 == 0]
[0, 2, 4, 6, 8, 10, 12, 14, 16, 18]
```

This is a list comprehension. It is surrounded by square brackets, indicating it will generate a list. The many uses of square brackets in Python can be a bit confusing, but the context of its contents should help to make it clear. Here, we have the three elements of a comprehension:

- The first element, the expression, in this case is the variable `i`. We will collect `i` and place it in a new list whenever the condition (third element) is true
- The second element, the for clause is **`for`** `i` ***`in`*** *`range`*`(20)`. This will iterate through the integers from 0 to 19 and each time set `i` to that value. This is the old collection.
- The third element, the condition is ***`if`*** `i%2 == 0`. We will only collect `i` if it is even.

What does this comprehension do? It creates a list of all the even numbers between 0 and 19. Note that the variable of the ***for*** loop is used in both the expression and the condition of the comprehension. This must be true since we need to create each new element based on each old element and we determine when to collect an element based on some condition of the old element.

One can write more complicated expressions to transform the numbers. Look at the next session:

```
In  [1]: [(i, i**2, i**3) for i in range(20) if i%2 == 0]
[(0, 0, 0), (2, 4, 8), (4, 16, 64), (6, 36, 216), (8, 64, 512), (10, 100, 1000),
    (12, 144, 1728), (14, 196, 2744), (16, 256, 4096), (18, 324, 5832)]
```

Here we collect a tuple of each even number that contains the number, the square of the number and the cube of the number. The result is a list of tuples.

Of course, the technique isn't limited to numbers. Let's process a string (a collection) and create a list of all the vowels in the string.

```
In  [1]: word = "solidarity"
In  [2]: vowels = "aeiou"
In  [3]: [v for v in word if v in vowels]
['o', 'i', 'a', 'i']
```

One can work from multiple sequences and can have complicated conditionals. For example, suppose you wanted to generate pairs of numbers (think of Cartesian coordinate pairs) with x in the range from zero up to three and y in the range from zero up to four. Notice, however, that this multiple sequence is *nested*. That is, when `x` has the value 0, `y` iterates through all the values 0–4. Then when `x` has the value 1, `y` again iterates through all the values 0–4. Comprehensions on multiple sequences are nested from left to right. One could limit the pairs by requiring x to be even and x>y.

```
In  [1]: [(x,y) for x in range(3) for y in range(4)]
[(0, 0), (0, 1), (0, 2), (0, 3), (1, 0), (1, 1), (1, 2), (1, 3), (2, 0), (2, 1),
    (2, 2), (2, 3)]
In  [2]: [(x,y) for x in range(3) for y in range(4) if x > y and x%2 == 0]
[(2, 0), (2, 1)]
```

List comprehension is also useful for doing conversions. For example, consider a string of letters and digits. In this example we extract only the digits and convert them to `int`s.

```
In  [1]: some_string="John Doe, 874 Main St., East Lansing, MI, 48823"
In  [1]: [int(c) for c in some_string if c.isdigit()]
Out [1]: [8, 7, 4, 4, 8, 8, 2, 3]
```

For those who enjoy puzzles, comprehension can be addicting. Once you get a feel for them, you will frequently use them for creating readable, compact code. Fortunately, they often execute quickly, so they are efficient to use.

7.11.1 Comprehensions, Expressions, and the Ternary Operator

One of the restrictions on the expression part of the comprehension is that it must, indeed, be an expression. It must return a value. One cannot use a statement such as ***if***, ***while***, or other control statements as the first part of a comprehension. You can write your own function as the expression, as long as it takes the ***for***-clause variable as an argument and returns a value.

There is, however, an interesting statement we have not discussed yet called the *ternary* operator, which works well in comprehensions. The ternary operator is a kind of abbreviated ***if*** statement that returns one of two values depending on some condition. It is called ternary ("composed of three parts") because it has those three parts: the two potential return values and a condition. A ternary operator has the following general form:

True-expression **if** *condition* **else** *False-expression*

The meaning is: "Return the result of the True expression if the condition is *True*, else return the result of the False expression."

The ternary operator allows the return of only the True-expression or the False-expression, hence its description as a limited if statement. The session that follows shows an example

```
In  [1]: age = 20
In  [2]: 'Hi Mommy' if age < 10 else 'Hi Mother'
'Hi Mother'
In  [3]: [i**2 if i%2 else i**3 for i in range(10)]
[0, 1, 8, 9, 64, 25, 216, 49, 512, 81]
```

The first part of the example returns either the string "Hi Mommy" or "Hi Mother" depending on the value of the variable `age`. The second uses a ternary operator in a list comprehension. It squares every odd number and cubes every even number. What does the condition `i % 2` represent. It is a test of being odd as it returns 1 (stand-in for *True*) when a number is odd, 0 (stand-in for *False*) when it is even.

When a simple binary choice is desired, a ternary operator can be very useful.

VISUAL VIGNETTE

7.12 MORE PLOTTING

You saw in Section 2.3 that most of the plotting done with `matplotlib` is done using lists. You were not familiar with lists then, but you are now. Let's do some more plotting now that you know about lists.

As we said, the `plot` command imported from the `pylab` module takes a minimum of a single list, the list of *y*-values to be plotted. If two lists are provided, the first is assumed to be a list of *x*-values, and the second the list of *y*-values. It is *required* that the length of the two lists be the same: one *x*-value for each *y*-value and vice versa.

7.12.1 Pylab Arrays

An important component of the `pylab` module is another Python module called `numpy`, short for "numeric Python." It provides the following capabilities:

- A new data type, the *array* object.
- Support for floating-point data types to interact with arrays.
- Support functions for floating-point values interacting with arrays.

The array datatype and its associated methods and functions is particularly useful. In fact, `pylab` works not with lists, but `pylab` arrays. If you provide a list as an argument, `pylab` converts it to an array.

Arrays and `range`

An array is similar to a list. It is a sequence data structure with indexing and slicing. It is also a mutable data structure and responds to index assignment. The big difference is that a `pylab` array can contain only the same data type, by default a floating-point number. It is type restricted so that floating-point operations can be done more efficiently on the array. There are a number of ways to make an array. The `array` constructor can take a list object and convert it to an array. The elements of the list must consist only of numbers. The resulting array object will consist of numbers all of the same type. If mixed types exist (`floats` and `ints`), then all numbers will be converted to floats. When printed, an array has the string "array" printed as part of the object. One can append onto the end of an existing array using the `pylab` function `append`.

Very much like the *`range`* function, the `pylab arange` function generates a range of values. The difference is that the values are floating-point values instead of integers. The `arange` takes three arguments: the begin value (*`float`*), the end value (*`float`*), and an increment (*`float`*). The following session demonstrates the use of `pylab` arrays and `arange`. As mentioned in Appendix D an alternative to `arange` is the `pylab` method `linspace`. The main difference is that with `arange` you specify how far apart you want the values, whereas in `linspace` you specify how many values you want. Which is best depends on your needs.

```
In  [1]: import pylab
In  [2]: my_array = pylab.array([1,2,3,4])
In  [3]: my_array
Out [3]: array([1, 2, 3, 4])                    # all integers

In  [4]: pylab.append(my_array,50.0)
array([  1.,   2.,   3.,   4.,  50.])     # append a float, now all floats
In  [5]: new_array = pylab.arange(0,2,0.1) # new array using arange
# new_array2 = pylab.linspace(0,2,20,endpoint=False)  # alternative
In  [6]: new_array
Out [6]: array([ 0. ,  0.1,  0.2,  0.3,  0.4,  0.5,  0.6,  0.7,  0.8,  0.9,  1. ,

      1.1,  1.2,  1.3,  1.4,  1.5,  1.6,  1.7,  1.8,  1.9])
```

Broadcasting

One of the best aspects of using arrays is the ability to perform operations between two arrays using standard arithmetic operators. This means that the operators are overloaded for arrays. For example, if you were to multiply an array by a floating-point number, then *every* element of the array will be multiplied by that number, yielding a new array. The same will occur if you apply a function to an array. *Every* element of the array has the function applied, yielding a new array.

```
In  [1]: import pylab
In  [2]: my_array = pylab.arange(0,6.3,0.1)
In  [3]: my_array
Out [3]: array([ 0. ,  0.1,  0.2,  0.3,  0.4,  0.5,  0.6,  0.7,  0.8,  0.9,  1. ,

        1.1,  1.2,  1.3,  1.4,  1.5,  1.6,  1.7,  1.8,  1.9,  2. ,  2.1,
        2.2,  2.3,  2.4,  2.5,  2.6,  2.7,  2.8,  2.9,  3. ,  3.1,  3.2,
        3.3,  3.4,  3.5,  3.6,  3.7,  3.8,  3.9,  4. ,  4.1,  4.2,  4.3,
        4.4,  4.5,  4.6,  4.7,  4.8,  4.9,  5. ,  5.1,  5.2,  5.3,  5.4,
        5.5,  5.6,  5.7,  5.8,  5.9,  6. ,  6.1,  6.2])
In  [4]: new_array = my_array * 2
In  [5]: new_array
Out [5]: array([  0. ,   0.2,   0.4,   0.6,   0.8,   1. ,   1.2,   1.4,   1.6,

         1.8,   2. ,   2.2,   2.4,   2.6,   2.8,   3. ,   3.2,   3.4,
         3.6,   3.8,   4. ,   4.2,   4.4,   4.6,   4.8,   5. ,   5.2,
         5.4,   5.6,   5.8,   6. ,   6.2,   6.4,   6.6,   6.8,   7. ,
         7.2,   7.4,   7.6,   7.8,   8. ,   8.2,   8.4,   8.6,   8.8,
         9. ,   9.2,   9.4,   9.6,   9.8,  10. ,  10.2,  10.4,  10.6,
        10.8,  11. ,  11.2,  11.4,  11.6,  11.8,  12. ,  12.2,  12.4])
In  [6]: new_array = pylab.sin(my_array)
In  [7]: new_array
Out [7]: array([ 0.        ,  0.09983342,  0.19866933,  0.29552021,  0.38941834,

        0.47942554,  0.56464247,  0.64421769,  0.71735609,  0.78332691,
        0.84147098,  0.89120736,  0.93203909,  0.96355819,  0.98544973,
        0.99749499,  0.9995736 ,  0.99166481,  0.97384763,  0.94630009,
        0.90929743,  0.86320937,  0.8084964 ,  0.74570521,  0.67546318,
        0.59847214,  0.51550137,  0.42737988,  0.33498815,  0.23924933,
        0.14112001,  0.04158066, -0.05837414, -0.15774569, -0.2555411 ,
       -0.35078323, -0.44252044, -0.52983614, -0.61185789, -0.68776616,
       -0.7568025 , -0.81827711, -0.87157577, -0.91616594, -0.95160207,
       -0.97753012, -0.993691  , -0.99992326, -0.99616461, -0.98245261,
       -0.95892427, -0.92581468, -0.88345466, -0.83226744, -0.77276449,
       -0.70554033, -0.63126664, -0.55068554, -0.46460218, -0.37387666,
       -0.2794155 , -0.1821625 , -0.0830894 ])
```

7.12.2 Plotting Trigonometric Functions

Knowing about `pylab` arrays makes it a lot easier to create graphs. Consider Code Listing 7.18, which generates sine and cosine curves in the same graph; the plot is shown in Figure 7.14.

Code Listing 7.18

```
import pylab

# Generate lists of points for both sine and cosine
x_values = pylab.linspace(0, 4*pylab.pi,100)
y1_values = pylab.sin(x_values)
y2_values = pylab.cos(x_values)

# Plot two curves on the same graph
pylab.title('Sine and Cosine Plot')
pylab.plot(x_values,y1_values,'b')
pylab.plot(x_values,y2_values, 'r')
pylab.show()
```

Notice that we can place as many plots as we like in the figure before we show it.

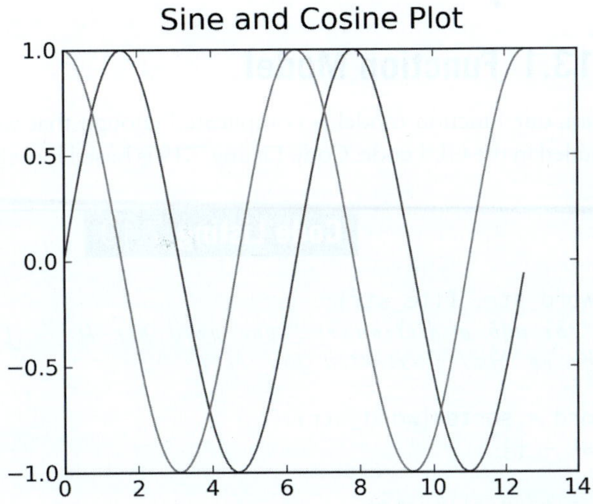

FIGURE 7.14 A graph of sine and cosine from 0 to about 4π.

7.13 GUI TO FIND ANAGRAMS

Building off of our previous examples in Section 4.9 and Section 6.8, here we will create a GUI program to find all the anagrams of a particular word in a file of words. An example of the final GUI is shown in Figure 7.15.

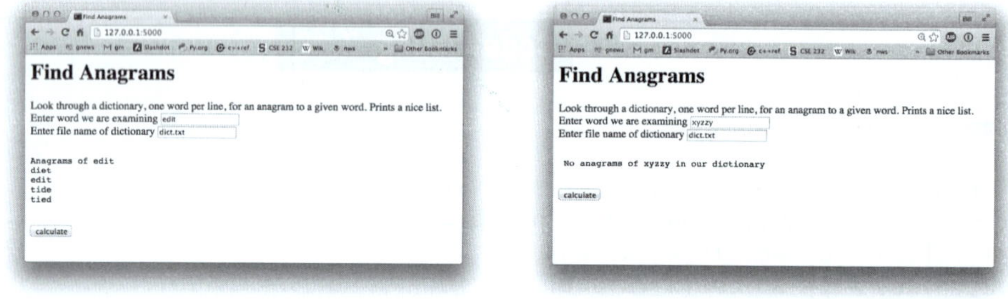

FIGURE 7.15 The anagram GUI example. [William F. Punch, Richard J. Enbody.]

Again, let's remember what we have to do to change our template based on previous examples:

- What GUI form fields to include?
- A function Model for our problem (our program).
- Any specific text we want to occur in HTML View.
- Creating the `InputForm` with the GUI fields and naming those fields in the Controller, using them in the View.
- Change some variable names in the Controller.

7.13.1 Function Model

Again, our function model is complicated enough that we place it in a separate file to be included in the GUI code. Code Listing 7.19 is based loosely on the code from Section 7.5.1.

Code Listing 7.19

```python
def compute(word_str, file_str):
    ''' Look through a dictionary, one word per line, for anagrams of word
        return an html formatted pre list
    '''
    sorted_word = sorted(word_str)
    result_lst = []

    file_obj = open(file_str)
    for line in file_obj:
```

```
10         new_word = line.strip()
11         new_word = new_word.lower()
12         sorted_new_word = sorted(new_word)
13         if sorted_word == sorted_new_word:
14             result_lst.append(new_word)
15     if not result_lst:
16         result_str = "<pre> \n No anagrams of " + word_str + " in our
17                                     dictionary </pre>"
18     else:
19         result_str = "<pre> \n"
20         result_str += "Anagrams of " + word_str + "\n"
21         for w in result_lst:
22             result_str += w + "\n"
23         result_str += "</pre>"
24 
25     return result_str
```

The function (still named compute) takes in two arguments: the word to check, word_str, and the file of words to check against, file_str. We assume that the file file_str refers to is a list of words: one word per line in the file.

On **Line 5** we sort the letters of the word into sorted_word.

Lines 9–14 grab each line, strip off any extraneous characters from either end, lowercase the word, and create a sorted list of those letters called sorted_new_word.

Anytime sorted_word == new_sorted_word we have a new anagram and append it to a list of anagram words result_lst.

Finally, as we did in Section 6.8 we return a single string. If we find some anagrams, the string is a list of words, with "\n" between each word and enclosed between <pre> ... <//pre> tags to maintain our formatting. If there are no anagrams, an appropriate message is produced.

7.13.2 Controller

The Controller, in Code Listing 7.20, is a little different this time since we are going to be working with **two** input fields.

Code Listing 7.20

```
from flask import Flask, render_template_string, request
from wtforms import Form, validators, TextField
import string
```

```

# function model in a separae file
from program6_checkAnagrams import compute

app = Flask(__name__)

# html page is the view.
page = '''
<html>
    <head>
        <title> Find Anagrams</title>
    </head>

    <body>
        <h1>Find Anagrams</h1>

        <form method=post action="">
            Look through a dictionary, one word per line, for an anagram to a given word. Prints a nice list.
        <br>
        Enter word we are examining
            {{ template_form.word_field }}
        <br>
        Enter file name of dictionary
            {{ template_form.dict_field }}
        <br>
          {% if result != None %}
              {{ result }}
          {% endif %}
        <br>
          <input type=submit value=calculate>
        </form>

    </body>
</html>
'''

# InputForm and below is our controller

# form with a single TextField
class InputForm(Form):
    word_field = TextField(validators=[validators.InputRequired()])
    dict_field = TextField(validators=[validators.InputRequired()])

@app.route('/', methods=['GET', 'POST'])
```

```
48 def index():
49     anagram_result = None
50     form = InputForm(request.form)
51     if request.method == 'POST' and form.validate():
52         word_to_check = form.word_field.data
53         dict_file = form.dict_field.data
54         anagram_result = compute(word_to_check, dict_file)
55     return render_template_string(page, template_form=form,
56                                   result = anagram_result)
57
58 if __name__ == '__main__':
59     app.run(debug=True)
```

As in Section 6.8, on **Line 6** we import our function model.

On **Lines 44 and 45** we add **two** fields to our `InputForm` called `word_field` to grab the word we wish to check and `dict_field` for the name of the dictionary file.

We enter those two fields on **Lines 24 and 27** on the View separated by a
 (break) tag to keep the fields on separate lines of the View.

Lines 52 and 53 access the results of those two fields and feed them as arguments to `compute` on **Line 54**, resulting in the answer being stored in `anagram_result`.

7.14 WHAT'S WRONG WITH MY CODE?

Here are suggestions for finding problems with lists. Refer to Appendix C for details.

As a sequence, lists have similar issues with ranges as we saw in strings. Tuples, being immutable, cannot have their elements changed, as we also saw in strings. Lists do not have as many methods (11) as strings (44) so there are fewer errors associated with method use. However, there are some errors that tend to happen with lists that are really control problems.

- **None:** a common way to end up with `None` with lists is to combine assignment with append, for example, `x=my_list.append(y)`. Since append has a side effect of updating the end of the string and **no return**, the value of x will be `None`. A similar thing happens by mixing up the `sorted` function (which returns a sorted list) vs. the `sort` method (with has a side effect of sorting the list and no return). The problem manifests itself with `x=my_list.sort(y)`, which results in x having a value of `None`.
- **[ ]:** an unexpected empty list is usually a control error—your `append` statement was never executed. Usually that is a problem with the Boolean expression or its values. Set a breakpoint and check Variable Explorer for errant values.

- **IndexError:** as with other collections such as strings an `IndexError` comes from two sources:
  - The list has a different length than expected. Often the list is empty, but another common problem is "off by one", that is, the list is one element smaller or larger than expected. Remember, indices in lists begin with 0 and the last index is at length −1. This is often a control problem so set a breakpoint and examine your Boolean expression.
  - The index variable is wrong—again, "off by one" is common.
- **Tuples are immutable** so item assignment is not allowed. This problem is similar to what happens with strings, the other immutable collection. For example, `my_tuple[2]=5` will generate this error: `TypeError: 'tuple' object does not support item assignment`.
- **IndexError**: Finally, there is a way to generate an `IndexError` other than "off by one" error or the like. Unlike other sequences, Lists are mutable. Thus, as you iterate through a list it is possible to modify the list as you iterate. However, **never modify a mutable during iteration**. We mentioned this as a programming tip in Section 7.2.4 but `IndexError` is one way this manifests itself.
- **TypeError**: If you mistakenly add parentheses to a list name such as `my_list()` you will get: TypeError: 'list' object is not callable.

Summary

In this chapter, we developed the list data structure in detail and introduced tuples. Our final example showed the incremental development of a program—an important problem-solving technique.

Lists and Tuples

- Lists are mutable; tuples are immutable.
- Lists and tuples are sequences.
- Lists allow assignment: L[3] = 7
  Tuples do not.
- Standard operations:
  - length function: `len(L)`
  - membership: *`in`*
  - max and min: `max(L)` and `min(L)`
  - sum: `sum(L)`

Indexing and Slicing

Given: L = `['a', 7, 6, 5, [2, 9, 1], 3.4]`
Tuples work the same with indexing and slicing.

- Indexing starts at zero: L`[0]` is `'a'`.
- Negative indices work backwards from the end: L`[-1]` is `3.4`.

- Slicing selects a subset up to but not including the final index: L[1:4] is [7, 6, 5].
- Slicing default start is the beginning so L[:3] is ['a', 7, 6].
- Slicing default end is the end so L[4:] is [[2, 9, 1], 3.4].
- Using both defaults makes a copy: L[:].
- Slicing's optional third argument indicates step: L[:6:2] is ['a', 6, [2, 9, 1]].
- The idiom to reverse a list: L[::-1] is [3.4, [2, 9, 1], 5, 6, 7, 'a'].

List Methods (Partial List)

Given: L1 = [1, 3, 2] and L2 = [7, 8]

- `L1.append(0)` changes L1 to be `[1, 3, 2, 0]`
- `L1.append(L2)` changes L1 to be `[1, 3, 2, [7, 8]]`
- `L1.extend(L2)` changes L1 to be `[1, 3, 2, 7, 8]`
- `L1.sort()` changes L1 to be `[1, 2, 3]`
- `L1.insert(2, 11)` inserts 11 before index 2 so L1 becomes `[1, 3, 11, 2]`
- `L1.remove(3)` removes 3 so L1 becomes `[1, 2]`
- `L1.reverse()` changes L1 to be `[2, 3, 1]`
- `L1.pop()` pops 2 off so L1 becomes `[1, 3]` and returns 2

Methods Shared by Lists and Tuples (Partial List)

Given: L1 = [1, 3, 2] and L2 = [7, 8]

- `L1.index(3)` returns the index of item 3, which is 1
- `L1.count(1)` counts the number of 1's in L1: 1 in this case

Iteration: for, Enumerate

- *for* walks through each item in a list or tuple:
  `for i in L1:`
- `enumerate` generates both the index and the item:
  `for index, value in enumerate(L1):`

Rules

- **RULE 1:** Think before you program!
- **RULE 2:** A program is a human-readable essay on problem solving that also happens to execute on a computer.

- **RULE 3:** The best way to improve your programming and problem skills is to practice!
- **RULE 4:** A foolish consistency is the hobgoblin of little minds.
- **RULE 5:** Test your code, often and thoroughly!
- **RULE 6:** If it was hard to write, it is probably hard to read. Add a comment.
- **RULE 7:** All input is evil, until proven otherwise.
- **RULE 8:** A function should do one thing.

Exercises

1. Compare and contrast strings, lists, and tuples. For example, consider what they can hold and what operations can be done on the data structures.
2. Create a list of the squares of all numbers between 1 and 20.
3. Create a list of 100 integers whose value and index are the same, for example, L[5]=5.
4. A list shares characteristics with string, but there are some things that can be done with a list that cannot be done with a string. Describe them.
5. What happens when you add two tuples together? What happens when you multiply an integer and a tuple?
6. Consider the following code:

```
list1=[1,2,99]
list2=list1
list3=list2
list1=list1.remove(1)
print(list3)
```

   (a) What is printed?
   (b) How can you change the code so `list3` is unchanged?

7. Consider:

```
ListA = [1,2,3,4,5]
ListB = ListA
ListA[2] = 10
```

   What is the value of `ListB[2]`?

8. Consider:

```
ListA = [1,2,3,4,5]
ListB = []
for num in ListA:
    ListB.append(num)
ListA[2] = 10
```

(a) What is the value of `ListB[2]`?
(b) What is the value of `ListB`?

9. Given `a = [1,2,3,4,5]` and `b = [3,4,5,6,7]`, what is the result of

(a) `2 in a`
(b) `a + b`

10. Consider the following code:

```
langs = ["Python", "C++", "Perl", "C", "Java"]
print (langs)        # Line 1
del langs[1]
print (langs)        # Line 2
del langs[:]
print (langs)        # Line 3
```

(a) What is printed by Line 1?
(b) What is printed by Line 2?
(c) What is printed by Line 3?

11. Given `x = [1,2,3]`, write the Python code to:

(a) create a list y such that changing x also changes y.
(b) create a list y such that changing x does not change y.

12. Given the following program what will be printed?

```
numList = [1,2,3]
x = 'Hello There!'

for i in x:
    print(numList)
    x.append(numList)
```

13. Transform the tuple `(1,2,3,4,5,6)` into the list `['One',2,'III','hello',5, 'III*2']`. (Note that there are many possible different answers.)

14. Given a list `L = [1,2,3,4]`, we want to convert the list to the string `'1234'`. We tried `''.join([i for i in L])`, but it doesn't work. Fix it.

15. Come up with three different ways to create a list of 25 1's without simply typing the 25 1's.

16. Tuples and Lists (try this in the Python shell).

(a) Is is possible to have a tuple in a list? Why or why not?
(b) Is it possible to have a list in a tuple? Why or why not?

17. What differentiates a tuple from a list? Be specific.

18. Write a program to combine two lists in such a way that duplicate entries are removed only from the second list, and not from the first.

19. If a tuple is immutable, why are we able to modify `x=[1, (2,3),4]` into `x=[1,(5,6),4]`? Are we changing the tuple or changing the list?

20. What is the result of this expression: `sorted(['7','q','e','3','m','n'])`? Explain.

21. What does the command `len` do to the following inputs? Try counting it by hand, and then input it into your Python shell. It is important to understand how the `len` function deals with different inputs.

(a) `List1 = ["this", "is", "just", "an", "example",1,2,3,4]`
(b) `X = "I know that sometimes things look difficult, but don't worry you'll get it"`
(c) `Y = "I", "know", "that", "sometimes", "things", "look", "difficult", "but", "don't", "worry", "you'll", "get", "it"`
(d) `Z = "I know you can do it!"`

22. Given a list of integers, write Python code to create a new list with same number of elements as the original list such that each integer in the new list is the sum of its neighbors and itself in the original list. For example, if `listA = [10, 20, 30, 40, 50]`, `listB = [30, 60, 90, 120, 90]`.

23. Write a function that takes a list and an integer as arguments, and returns how many times the integer in present in the list.

24. Make a list of the words in a sentence. No punctuation should be attached to a "word" in your list, for example, "end." is not a correct word, but "end" is.

(a) Use a `while` loop.
(b) Use a `for` loop.

25. Make a list of the unique letters used in a sentence. That is, if the letter "x" is used twice in a sentence, it should only appear once in your list. No punctuation should appear in your list. For the purpose of simplicity, consider the following characters as punctuation: `.,;?!-`

(a) Use a `while` loop.
(b) Use a `for` loop.

26. Create a list of 20 numbers and

(a) Sort the list
(b) Print the reverse of the sorted list

27. Given the code:

```
myList = ['1','2','3','4','5']
for z in range(0,len(myList)):
    text = ''.join(myList[z])
    text.center(10)
```

(a) If this code is run in the shell, what is the output?
(b) If this code is a program that is then run in the shell, what is the output?
(c) Why is the output different?
(d) Fix the program to run the same in both environments.

28. Given a list of items, write a program that generates a list of lists of the following form:

`[a,b,c,...,z]` ⇒ `[[z], [y,z], [x,y,z], ... , [a,b, ... ,y,z]]`

Hint: Slicing is your friend.

29. Indexable and iterable:

(a) Give two examples of types that are indexable.
(b) Give two examples of types that are iterable.
(c) Does membership in one category imply membership in the other? Explain.

30. Consider two lists, A and B, such that A returns `[1,2,3]` and B returns `[1,2,3]`.

(a) Create A and B so `A is B` returns *True*.
(b) Create A and B so `A is B` returns *False*.

31. How will these lists be sorted by the `sorted(L)` function? *Hint:* Consider their ASCII values.

(a) `L = ['1','2','3','h','E','l','L','o','W','o','R','l','d']`
(b) `L = ['A','a','B','b','1','2','3']`

32. Pop vs. Remove:

(a) What is the difference between `pop` and `remove`?
(b) Which built-in data types of Python can use each?

33. Write a program that takes a list as an argument, and moves all elements divisible by 13 to a new list.

34. Given a list `[4,8,9,6,5,4,8,7,8]` and using the `len` and `sum` functions, determine the average value of the integers in the list.

35. Write a function using a ***for*** loop that takes a string S as an argument and returns S in reversed order. For example, if S="stressed", it should return "desserts."

36. Write a function using a ***for*** loop that takes a sentence S as an argument and returns the words in S in reversed order. For example, if S="What is your quest," it should return "quest your is What".

37. Given a list L of words such as the following and assignment to List1:

```
L = ['Always', 'look', 'on', 'the', 'bright', 'side', 'of', 'life.']
List1=[[i.upper(), i.lower(), len(i)] for i in L ]
```

(a) What is the value of List1?
(b) Write a list comprehension that uses List1 to create a list of words of length 4.

38. Using list comprehension create an expression that sums up all the factors of a number that you input. (*Hint:* If you input 6, it should print 12 (i.e., $1 + 2 + 3 + 6 = 12$).)

39. Given a list of integers L, use list comprehension to:
(a) find the sum of the even integers in list L
(b) find the sum of the odd integers in list L.

40. What will the following list return?

```
[ (n*n) for n in range(13) if (n*n)%2==0 ]
```

41. Given `x='January 1, 2000'`:
(a) Using list comprehension, create a list of all the letters used in x.
(b) In one line, add to your list comprehension so the resulting list is sorted.

42. Tuples resemble lists in many ways. However, as an immutable type, the ways in which they can be interacted with are limited. Take the following statements. What will happen if you try to add to the tuple in the manner shown? How can you rewrite the code to achieve the intended result?

```
Tuple = ()
for i in range (10):
    Tuple += i
```

43. Predict the outcomes of the following expressions:
(a) `3*[25]`
(b) `3*list("25")`
(c) `3*list(range(3))`

44. Given L1=`[1,3,5,5,2]`. Write a program that:
(a) Sorts the list.
(b) Adds 4.
(c) Removes one duplicate.
(d) Inserts 6.
(e) Prints the number of items in the list.

45. Write a function that takes a list of email addresses as an argument, and returns a list of tuples of usernames and domains.

46. Write a program that generates two lists of random numbers, sorts them, and then merges them.

---

47. Write a function that takes a string as an argument, converts the string to a list of characters, sorts the list, converts the list back to a string, and returns the resulting string.

48. Write a function that takes a string as an argument and returns a list of the words in the string.

49. Print the interesting words in the Gettysburg Address in order from most used to least used.

50. Write a program that keeps accepting input from the user and adding it to a list, until the user enters `-1`.

51. Write your own versions of the Python built-in functions `min` and `max`. They should take a list as an argument and return the minimum or maximum element. *Hint:* Pick the first element as the minimum (maximum) and then loop through the elements to find a smaller (larger) element. Each time you find a smaller (larger) element, update your minimum (maximum).

52. Create a program that uses the Gettysburg Address as input and outputs a list of tuples for every two words. For example: `[('Four', 'score'),('and', 'seven'), ...]`.

53. Fractions:
You can express a fraction as a tuple: (numerator, denominator).

(a) Write a function that adds two fractions that are passed as tuples.
(b) Write a function that multiplies two fractions that are passed as tuples.

54. It is often times advantageous to be able to transfer data between multiple lists while rearranging their order. For instance, say that `list1 = [1,2,3,4,5,6,7,8,9]` and you wish to add the numbers in the index range 4:7 of `list1` to another list, `list2`, in reverse order while simultaneously removing them from `list1`. If `list2 = [100,200]`, the result will be `list2 = [100,200,7,6,5]`. Write a function named `transform` that takes as arguments `list1`, `list2`, `r1`, and `r2`, that removes items from list1 in the slice `r1:r2`, appends them onto `list2` in reverse order, and returns the resulting list. For example, in this case, the function call will be `transform(list1, list2, 4,7)`.

55. A matrix can be represented in Python using a list of lists. The elements of the list would be the row values, and the elements of the nested lists would be the column values. Write a function that accepts a list of lists `matrix` and transposes it by switching around the row and column values.

56. Given a list of N numbers, write a function to shift the numbers circularly by some integer k (where $k < N$). The function should take a list and k as a arguments and return the shifted list.

(a) Write a function that assumes shifting is to the left.
(b) Write a function that takes a third argument that specifies shifting left or right.

57. The letters a, b, d, e, g, o, p, and q all have something in common: a hole. If you imagine that the letters were made of stretchy material such as rubber, you could transform one letter into another while preserving the hole. If tearing or gluing are not allowed, no other letter (without a hole) could be transformed by stretching into one of these letters with holes. Mathemeticans say that these letters are topologically similar: one set has a hole, the rest do not.

(a) Write a function that takes as an argument a lowercase string and finds the counts of letters in the string with holes and and a count of letters without holes.
(b) Write a function that searches a word list and prints all the words that have two or more letters with holes.
(c) The set of uppercase letters with holes is different from the set of lowercase letters, e.g., lowercase "e" belongs to the set of letters with a hole, but its capital "E" does not. Refactor your functions to consider uppercase letters.

58. Sally invited 17 guests to a dance party. She assigned each guest a number from 2 to 18, keeping 1 for herself. The sum of each couple's numbers was a perfect square. Write a program to find the number of Sally's partner.

59. Using the Python int operators +, −, *, /, ** (not %), and the numbers, 2, 3, 4, and 5, find an expression using all four numbers exactly once and any three of the operators exactly once that evaluates to 26. *Hint:* Build strings and then use the Python `eval` function, which takes a string as an argument, evaluates the string, and returns its value, for example, `eval('2*3+4')` returns the integer 10.

60. 123456789 = 100. Of course, it doesn't, but:

(a) Using only the addition operator +, can you insert some addition operators between those successive digits so that it does sum to 99?
(b) Similarly, but more complicated: using the four standard integer arithmetic operators +, −, *, and / (not %), how many different solutions can you find (there are more than 100)?

61. Jim Loy poses this puzzle: I have before me three numeric palindromes (numbers that read the same backwards and forwards, like 838). The first is two digits long, the second is three digits long, and when we add those two numbers together, we get the third number, which is four digits long. What are the three numbers? (*Hint 1:* Numeric palidromes can be easily created by making strings of digits first. *Hint 2:* There is a reason that this exercise is in this chapter.)

62. Program: Work with Census Data
Use this file: http://www.census.gov/population/www/censusdata/files/urpop0090.txt

The census file is a text file with data for the 10-year census from 1900 to 1990 (e.g., 1900, 1910, 1920, …). It has population data for each state as well as regional and overall data. Each state is on its own line, but the data are grouped so that only three decades of data is on each line—complicating the task of extracting the data. In addition, the data is further broken down into total, urban, rural, and percentages.

Write a program that for any census year input (e.g., 1970) the program will print the state and its total population with the minimum and maximum. For example:

```
Enter census year 1900 to 1990: 1970
Minimum: (302853, 'Alaska')
Maximum: (19971069, 'California')
```

We had the output display a tuple as a hint to assist with solving the problem rather than illustrating readable output. Some points to consider:

(a) Begin by generating clean data: there are footnotes that need to be eliminated, numbers contain commas, some rows (lines) have data you are not interested in (e.g., region data), you are not interested in all columns (e.g., percentages), and so on. Simply printing the lines with extraneous data removed is a good start.
(b) You will likely want to combine multiple state name strings into one, for example, "New" "York" becomes "New York."
(c) A tuple (population, state) provides a way to tag population data with a state in a way that allows a list of tuples to be sorted (remember that by default, sorting uses the first value).

63. Using only list comprehensions (no loops) how would you change a list of positive integers such as [2, 3, 4, 5] and [9, 9, 1, 9] into their actual numbers 2345 and 9919?

64. Create a program that constantly prompts a user for new integers which are then added to a list until it gets to a length of 25 or if the user types "exit" into the input.

65. An earlier exercise scrambled the inner letters of a word, leaving the first and last letter unchanged. Expand that exercise to read in a text file and scramble all words. It be useful to take the earlier exercise and make that into a function for use by this solution. Can you read the resulting scrambled words?

66. Write a function translate() that will translate a text into "rövarspråket" (Swedish for "robber's language"). That is, double every consonant and place an occurrence of "o" in between. For example, translate ("this is fun") should return the string "tothohisos isos fofunon".

67. Write a function that takes a list of integers as an argument and returns a list of three of the integers whose sum is zero. Return an empty list if no such integers exist.

68. Write a function named "change" that takes a list and an two integers as arguments and returns a list that changes each matching value of list (without changing the structure of the list). For example, if L = `[3, 2, [3, [[3], 4]]]`, then change `(L,3,5)` will return `[5, 2, [5, [[5], 4]]]`.

69. Using pylab draw a graph of equation $y = sin(x)/x$ from -6π to 6π.

70. Write a function whose argument is a list of numbers that returns the standard deviation.

71. Write a program that prompts for two sentences and prints the combined words in alphabetical order. Ignore case and discard punctuation.

72. Write a program that prompts for a file name and prints the number of words in the file as well as the average word length. Ignore punctuation and numbers. Format your output.

Programming Projects

1. **Word Puzzles.**

Will Shortz is a noted puzzlemaster for the *New York Times* and National Public Radio who frequently posts challenging word puzzles. Many word puzzles can be solved by iterating through a list of words while checking for characteristics specified by the puzzle. Many word lists exist on the Web and we provide one on the text's website—any sufficiently large one will suffice. We have not covered file reading in detail yet, so here we provide a function that reads a file named "wordList.txt" and returns a list of words in lowercase. The file has one word per line. For each puzzle, copy this program and write your solution as the `puzzle` function. Note that the `puzzle` function has one parameter—the `wordList`.

Code Listing 7.21

```
# Word puzzle driver
# Assumes word_list.txt file of one word per line

def get_word_list():
    """Return a list of words from a word_list.txt file."""
    data_file = open("word_list.txt","r")
    word_list = []              # start with an empty word list
    for word in data_file:    # for every word (line) in the file
        # strip off end-of-line characters and make each word lowercase
        # then append the word to the word_list
        word_list.append(word.strip().lower())
    return word_list
```

```
def puzzle(word_list):
    """Puzzle solution goes here."""
    pass    # filler that does nothing except put something in the suite

word_list = get_word_list()
puzzle(word_list)
```

(a) The comparative form of the adjective "big" is *bigger*, and the superlative form is *biggest*. All three forms (big, bigger, and biggest) are related; however, there exists a root word that is not an adjective that when "er" is appended and "est" is appended, the result is a set of three words whose meanings are unrelated. Write a puzzle function that prints out all such triples (root, root + "er", root + "est"). Scan through your list to find a set of triples that are unrelated to each other.

(b) Find an uncapitalized, unhyphenated word that contains all but one of the letters of the alphabet from "l" to "v" ("lmnopqrstuv").

(c) What word consists of two consecutive pronouns? This list of pronouns will be helpful.

```
pronouns = ['thou', 'thee', 'thine', 'thy', 'i', 'me',
'mine', 'my', 'we', 'us', 'ours', 'our', 'you', 'yours',
'your','he','him','his', 'she', 'her', 'hers', 'it',
'its', 'they', 'them','theirs', 'their']
```

(d) What six-letter word has its meaning reversed when its first letter is changed from "c" to "h"? Print out the candidates and then select by hand.

(e) Find an uncapitalized, seven-letter word, containing just a single vowel that does not have the letter "s" anywhere within it.

(f) The word "mimeographs" contains all the letters of "memphis" at least once. Find other words that also contain all the letters of "memphis".

(g) Find a word that contains the string "tantan."

(h) The word "marine" consists of five consecutive, overlapping state postal abbreviations: Massachusetts (MA), Arkansas (AR), Rhode Island (RI), Indiana (IN), and Nebraska (NE). Find a seven-letter word that thas the same property.

(i) When you are writing in script, there are four letters of the alphabet that cannot be completed in one stroke: "i" and "j" (which require dots) and "t" and "x" (which require crosses). Find a word that uses each of these letters exactly once.

(j) There are four words that contain the consecutive letters "nacl". Find them.

(k) Find a word that contains the vowels "a," "e," "i," "o," and "u" in that order.

(l) Consider the word "sure". If we asked you to add two pairs of doubled letters to it to make an eight-letter word, you would add p's and s's to make "suppress". Find an eight-letter word resulting from adding two pairs of doubled letters to "rate".

(m) Find three words that are spelled the same except for their first two letters, which can be "sw," "tw," or "wh."

(n) Two US state capitals have a prefix that is the name of a month. Find them.

2. Pascal's Triangle:

Pascal's triangle is a geometric arrangement of sums that have interesting mathematical properties—most famously, the binomial coefficients.

The rows of Pascal's triangle are conventionally enumerated starting with row 0, and the numbers in each row are usually staggered relative to the numbers in the adjacent rows. A simple construction of the triangle proceeds in the following manner. On row 0, write only the number 1. Then, to construct the elements of following rows, add the number directly above and to the left with the number directly above and to the right to find the new value. If either the number to the right or left is not present, substitute a zero in its place. For example, the first number in the first row is $0 + 1 = 1$, whereas the numbers 1 and 3 in the third row are added to produce the number 4 in the fourth row. Here are the first six rows of Pascal's triangle:

```
          1
        1   1
      1   2   1
    1   3   3   1
  1   4   6   4   1
1   5  10  10   5   1
```

Write a program that prompts for the height of Pascal's triangle and then generates the triangle in the same style as previous example.

Hint: Use a list for each row, and use a list of row lists to hold the whole triangle.

3. Scrambled English:

Read the following paragraph as quickly as you can and see if you encounter any difficulties.

> Aoccdrnig to rscheearch at an Elingsh uinervtisy, it deosn't mttaer in waht oredr the ltteers in a wrod are, the olny iprmoetnt tihng is taht the frist and lsat ltteer is at the rghit pclae. The rset can be a toatl mses and you can sitll raed it wouthit a porbelm. Tihs is bcuseae we do not raed ervey lteter by itslef but the wrod as a wlohe.

This paragraph was published as an example of a principle of human reading comprehension. If you keep the first letter and the last letter of a word in their correct positions and scramble the letters in between, the word is still quite readable in the context of a surrounding paragraph. However, it seems that this is a bit of a myth and not truly based on solid research. It turns out that for longer words, the task is much more difficult. Nonetheless, we are going to imitate the process on some English text.

Handling punctuation is tricky. You need to deal with punctuation that comes at the end of a word: comma, period, question mark, exclamation, and so on. For example, in the previous sample, the word "university" ends with a comma, so you need to ensure that you do not treat the comma as the "last letter of the word" when you scramble all but the first and last letters.

Hints:

- Don't bother trying to scramble words fewer than four characters long.
- The string `split` method is useful to create a list of words from a string of words.
- The string `strip` method is useful to remove end-of-line characters and other whitespace.
- To scramble a string, convert it to a list, use `random.shuffle` from the `random` module to scramble the string, and then use the `join` string method to convert back to a string: `''.join(list)`

(a) A simple way to get some text to work with is to simply put it in a long string. (Note the backslash continuation character: \)

```
text = "Four score and seven years ago \
        our fathers brought forth \
        on this continent a new nation,"
```

(b) Alternatively, you could use a modification of the wordlist driver from the preceding word puzzle programming project to read a file. To read a file named "someFile.txt" into one long string:

```
def getWordString():
    dataFile = open("someFile.txt","r")
    wordString = ''          # start with an empty string of words
    for line in dataFile:
        wordString += line   # add each line of words to the word string
    return wordString
```

(c) Optionally, add the capability to handle punctuation in the middle of words, for example, a hyphen in a word. Scramble on either side of the hyphen.

4. Code Breaking:

In this exercise we will break the code of an encrypted message using the technique of frequency analysis. If a substitution cipher such as the well-known Caesar cipher is used, it can be broken using that technique. First, you need to make a program that can encrypt and decrypt Caesar ciphers. Then we'll see how to break them.

(a) The Caesar cipher is named after Julius Caesar, who used this type of encryption to keep his military communications secret. A Caesar cipher replaces each plain-text letter with one that is a fixed number of places down the alphabet. The plain text is your original message; the cipher text is the encrypted message. The following example employs a shift of three so that "B" in the plain-text becomes "E" in the cipher-text, a "C" becomes "F" and so on. The mapping wraps around so that "X" maps to "A" and so on.

Here is the complete mapping for a shift of three:

```
Plain: ABCDEFGHIJKLMNOPQRSTUVWXYZ
Cipher: DEFGHIJKLMNOPQRSTUVWXYZABC
```

To encrypt a message, substitute the plain-text letters with the corresponding cipher-text letter. For example, here is an encryption of "the quick brown fox jumps over the lazy dog" using our shift-three cipher (case is ignored):

```
Plain text: the quick brown fox jumps over the lazy dog
Cipher text: WKH TXLFN EURZQ IRA MXPSV RYHU WKH ODCB GRJ
```

To decrypt the message, reverse the process.

Write a program that prompts for a shift value (such as the 3 in our example) and then prompts for plain text to encode. Output the encrypted cipher text, and then decrypt the cipher text and output that. If your program is correct, the decrypted ciper text should match the original plain text.

Hints:

i. Create the cipher by starting with an alphabet string. Use slicing and concatenating to accomplish the shift.

ii. If you plan to allow spaces in your plain text, you need to add a space character into your "Plain" alphabet string.

iii. If you have two strings like the "Plain" and "Cipher" shown earlier, notice that the letter to substitute is at the same index in both strings. You can use that fact for both encryption and decryption.

iv. Use pencil and paper to encrypt and decrypt before designing your algorithm.

v. Optional: one way to find indices is with modular arithmetic:

```
cipherTextIndex = (plainTextIndex + 3) % 26
```

(b) Now the fun part—code breaking. If we know that we are breaking a Caesar cipher, our goal is to find the shift. From the program in the previous exercise, we can see that if we know the shift, we can decrypt the message. One fact is important: to make code breaking more difficult, neither spaces nor capitalization is used. Frequency analysis is based on the concept that some letters are used more often than others. For example, in English the most common letter is "e", which occurs nearly 13% of the time. Knowing that we are dealing with a simple Caesar cipher, we need to find only the most common letter, guess that it encodes to "e", and figure out the appropriate shift. However, we need a large message to have confidence that we have actually found the most frequent letter. Note that, in general, if spaces are allowed, that will always be the most frequent character, by a lot—allowing spaces makes code breaking too easy.

Write a program that takes in a cipher text, determines the shift, decodes it, and outputs the decoded message.

Hints:

i. Make a list of counters, one for each letter.
ii. There is a maximum function for lists: `max(someList)`.
iii. An easy way to input a large cipher text is to use the `getWordString` function from the previous exercise.
iv. You can create a cipher text by using the encrpytion program you created.
v. Remember, no spaces.

CHAPTER 8

More on Functions

> We are thinking beings, and we cannot exclude the intellect from participating in any of our functions.
>
> William James, psychologist/philosopher

WE INTRODUCED FUNCTIONS IN CHAPTER 5 AND SHOWED YOU HOW THEY ARE important for the divide-and-conquer problem solving introduced in Chapter 3. In this chapter, we introduce more capabilities of functions and some subtleties involved in their use. For example, now that you know the difference between mutable and immutable objects, we can observe how these two types of objects behave differently when passed as arguments to functions. To understand this process, we first investigate the concept of *scope*.

8.1 SCOPE

The details of how arguments' values are passed to function parameters can be confusing, so we will examine the process in more detail here. An important concept in programming languages is *scope*. We will examine the concept of scope in more detail in Section 9.6, but for now, know that scope means:

The set of program statements over which a variable exists, that is, can be referred to.

We bring up scope here because a function is the first place where we can easily see the effect of different scopes. As we noted earlier, when a function is executed, it creates its own namespace. Any variable that comes into existence (for example, when a variable gets assigned a value) within the suite of that function gets entered in the *function's* namespace. We say that a function's variables are *local* to the scope of the function. "Local scope" means that the variable can only be referenced, its associated object accessed, within the suite of the function because that is the active namespace. Variables defined locally within a function (within the scope of the function) are not accessible outside of the function because when a call to a function ends, its namespace is hidden.

Every program and function has a namespace that defines a scope within which variables are defined and are available for use. Only variables within the current, active namespaces (note the plural), can be referred to during execution. Consider Code Listing 8.1.

Code Listing 8.1

```
# a function with a local variable
def scope_function (a_int):
    new_int = a_int    # local variable created
    print('new_int value (in function) is: ',new_int)

# main program
scope_function(27)
print('new_int value is:',new_int)  # ERROR! (scope)
```

```
new_int value (in function) is:  27
Traceback (most recent call last):
  File "program7-2.py", line 8, in <module>
    print('new_int value is:',new_int)  # ERROR! (scope)
NameError: name 'new_int' is not defined
```

This program generates an error because `new_int` is defined in the local scope of `scope_function` so it cannot be referenced outside of the suite of the function.

The scope determined by `scope_function` is the function's suite (indented under the ***def*** statement). Besides the suite, the namespace also includes the function's parameters as part of the function's local scope. The function's namespace becomes active when function execution begins and ends when function execution ends. The function's namespace doesn't exist outside of the function's execution of the suite, so the request in the *main* program for the object associated with `new_int` cannot be found. Literally, the variable does not exist, as the namespace that defines it is not presently active.

PROGRAMMING TIP

A function name is just another name in the namespace. As we have mentioned, the ***def*** statement creates an entry in the namespace, associating the function name with the executable code of the function. You can reassign a function name to be associated with a different value. For example, the predefined `len` is initially associated with a function object. However, we are free to reassign it and associate it with anything we like, for example `len = 12`. At this point, `len` can no longer be called as a function because the name `len` is now associated with the integer 12.

Don't worry. If you restart Python, everything will go back to normal. However, be careful with your variable names! Don't step on existing names, or odd things can happen.

8.1.1 Arguments, Parameters, and Namespaces

Let's take a closer look at passing information from arguments to parameters and the role of namespaces.

Before we begin, remember that a namespace contains a set of pairs: a name and a Python object associated with that name. The association is called a *reference* and we can say that the name *references* the object. Also, from the scope discussion earlier, remember that the main program and function each have their own separate namespaces.

Here's the big question. When we call a function, what gets copied between the argument and its corresponding parameter? The answer is that the association, the reference, gets copied, not a new copy of the object itself. That is worth saying again. The association (reference) is copied, not the object itself. This means that after passing the argument to the parameter, both the parameter and argument will now be associated with the *same* object, as shown in Figure 8.1. The argument name in the calling namespace is `arg`, the parameter name in the function namespace is `param`, and they both are associated with the same object, 25. Figure 8.1 shows the situation as the function begins execution.

Following is the example from Figure 8.1 in the Python shell. We begin by defining the function. Within the function, we print `param` and its `id`. Remember, the `id` function prints a unique identification number for each object. No two objects have the same ID. When we

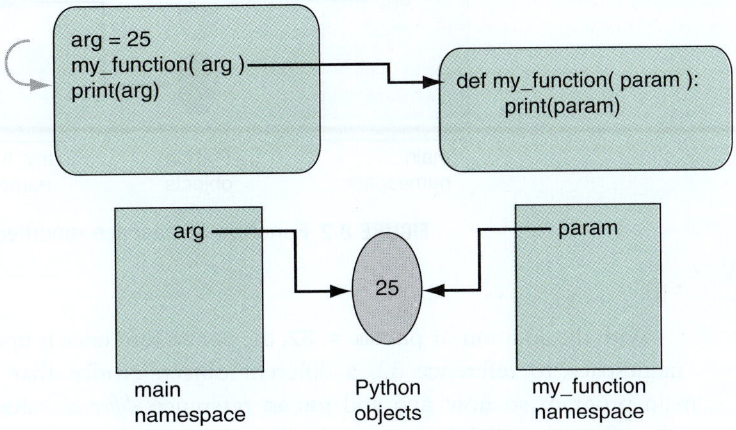

FIGURE 8.1 Function namespace: at function start.

executed the ***def*** statement, the function is created and made available for invocation. We create the variable arg by assigning it the value 25. We also print the ID of the integer 25. We then use arg as an argument in a function call. Within the function we print the value and ID of the parameter param. In this case, both arg and param have an association with the same object.

```
In  [1]: def my_function(param): # print value and id
...      print('parameter value is:{}, its id is:{}'.format(param,id(param)))
...
In  [2]: arg = 25
In  [3]: id(arg) # id of int object 25
Out [3]: 4296849472

In  [4]: my_function(arg)
parameter value is:25, its id is:4296849472  # arg and param objects the same
```

What if my_function now changes the value associated with param? Let's add a line to my_function: param = 32. The change is diagrammed in Figure 8.2.

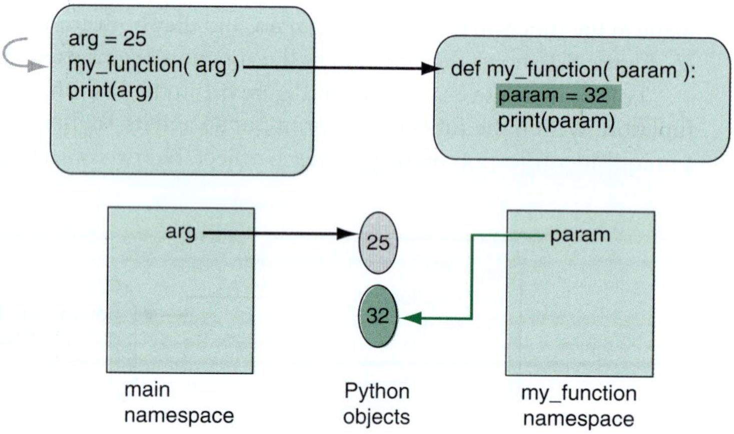

FIGURE 8.2 Function namespace modified.

With the addition of param = 32, the param reference is updated in the my_function namespace to reference 32, a different object. Notice that arg is unaffected in the main program so now arg and param reference *different* values. The results of the id calls reflect that. While param initially references the same object as arg as shown in

Figure 8.1, the assignment *changes the reference to a different object*, namely the integer 32, as shown in Figure 8.2. This change is illustrated in the following session.

```
In  [1]: def my_function(param):
...     param = 32
...     print('parameter value is:{}, its id is:{}'.format(param,id(param)))
...
In  [2]: arg = 25
In  [3]: id(arg)
Out [3]: 4296849472

In  [4]: my_function(arg)
parameter value is:32, its id is:4296849696

In  [5]: arg
Out [5]: 25

In  [6]: id(arg)
Out [6]: 4296849472                    # arg object is unchanged
```

8.1.2 Passing Mutable Objects

We discussed the concept of a shallow copy of mutable objects in Section 7.6.1. A similar problem arises when passing mutable arguments.

In the previous example, the argument and parameter of the function make reference to an immutable object. If the object being referenced is immutable, such as a number, string, or tuple, it is not possible to change anything about that object. Whenever we assign a new object to a parameter, we *break* the association of both argument and parameter to the same object.

What about mutable objects? We can change the value(s) of a mutable object. How does that affect parameter passing?

In Figure 8.3, we pass a list—a mutable object. As with the previous example, an argument *reference* (to `arg_list` in this example) is passed to the parameter name (`param_list`) so both become associated with that object. The figure shows the state of the namespaces before the statement `param_list[0] = 100` is executed. Note the similarity to Figure 8.1.

The assignment statement `param_list[0] = 100` in the function does not assign a new object to `param_list`; it *changes the object* itself. Remember, index assignment is a modification to an existing object. The variable `param_list` remains associated with the same list object, but that object's contents are changed to `[100,2,3]` as shown in Figure 8.4. Because `arg_list` references the same object, `arg_list` also reflects the modification. Such a change to the object would not be possible with an immutable object since we cannot change an immutable object.

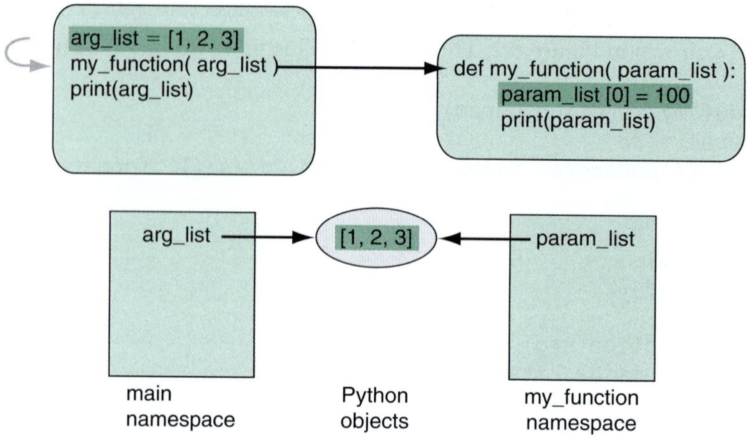

FIGURE 8.3 Function namespace with mutable objects: at function start.

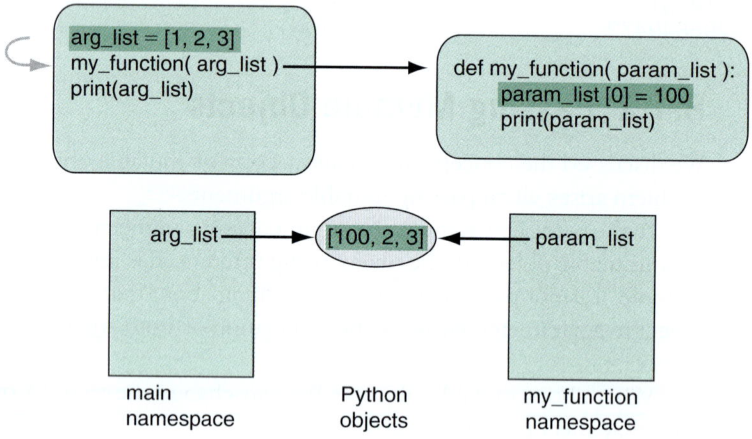

FIGURE 8.4 Function namespace with mutable objects after `paramList[0]=100`.

Here is the example from Figures 8.3 and 8.4 shown in the Python shell. An additional ***print*** statement is added to the function so we can see the object associated with `param_list` before and after it is modified. Note how `arg_list`, associated with the same object, reflects the change to that object.

```
In  [1]: def my_function(param_list):
   ...:     # print object as passed in
   ...:     print("param_list before modification:", param_list)
   ...:     # modify param_list
   ...:     param_list[0] = 100
   ...:     # print modified object
   ...:     print("param_list after modification:", param_list)
```

```
In  [2]: arg_list = [1,2,3]
In  [3]: my_function(arg_list)
param_list before modification: [1, 2, 3]

param_list after modification: [100, 2, 3]
In  [4]: arg_list # arg_list is changed too!
Out [4]: [100, 2, 3]
```

PROGRAMMING TIP

Passing mutable objects allows a function to change values in the calling program.

Handling mutable vs. immutable parameters is complicated by the fact that Python doesn't specify parameter *types*. Remember that we cannot tell the type of a variable unless we examine what object is associated with that variable. Python allows flexibility on this point, but the flexibility affects readability. Having the type as part of the name improves that readability.

8.1.3 Returning a Complex Object

As we mentioned previously, a function returns one object. However, now that we know about collections (e.g., lists), we can now return a single object such as a collection that has multiple parts. The following is an example of returning a list. The session defines a function `evens`. The function takes a single integer argument n, indicating the quantity of even numbers to generate, constructs a list of the first n even numbers, and then returns those numbers as a list. In the first part of the session, we invoke `evens` and the returned value is printed by Python. In the second part of the session, we invoked `evens` and assigned the returned value it to a variable `num_list`. A single object is returned by `evens`, but that single list object contains multiple objects. Note that this function does not check the validity of its input. Checking is left as an exercise at the end of the chapter.

```
In  [1]: def evens(n):
...:     evens_list = []              # initialize list to empty
...:       # to get "n" numbers starting at 1, range must go to "n+1"
...:     for i in range(1,n+1):
...:         evens_list.append(2*i)   # 2*i is always even; add it to the list
...:     return evens_list            # return the list of evens

In  [2]: evens(5) # executing the function (return is printed)
Out [2]: [2, 4, 6, 8, 10]
```

```
In  [3]: num_list = evens(3) # executing the function with assignment to num_list
In  [4]: num_list # let's see the value of num_list
Out [4]: [2, 4, 6]
```

If you return a series of results separated by commas, Python will build a single tuple containing those values (in order) and return the tuple. Consider the function `mirror` in the following session. The function takes a single collection argument with at least two elements and returns the first two elements as a tuple in reverse order. In the first invocation of `mirror`, we pass a tuple of two integers and a tuple of those two integers is returned and printed by Python. In the second invocation, we do multiple assignment on the returned value and the elements of the returned tuple are assigned in order to the variables `first` and `second`. If single assignment is used, then the assigned object is a tuple as shown associated with the variable `a_tuple`.

```
In  [1]: def mirror(pair):
      '''reverses first two elements;
        assumes "pair" is as a collection with at least two elements'''
...: return pair[1], pair[0]

In  [2]: mirror((2,3))
Out [2]: (3, 2)        # the return was comma separated: implicitly
                         handled as a tuple

In  [3]: first,second = mirror((2,3)) # comma separated works on the
                                        left-hand side also

In  [4]: first
Out [4]: 3

In  [5]: second
Out [5]: 2

In  [6]: first,second # reconstruct the tuple
Out [6]: (3, 2)

In  [7]: a_tuple = mirror((2,3)) # if we return and assign to one name,
                                   we get a tuple!

In  [8]: a_tuple
Out [8]: (3, 2)
```

An astute reader will notice that the `mirror` function is not very robust. That is, one can pass it a variety of values that will cause an error. Enter the function into a Python shell and try to break it (cause errors) in multiple ways. We leave as an exercise modifying this function to avoid such errors.

Check Yourself: Passing Mutables Check

1. Give the output indicated for the following program. It will be helpful to draw diagrams to indicate the relationships among arguments, parameters, and their objects. Think about which arguments are mutable and which are immutable.

```
def func1 (list1, list2, str1):
    if len(list1) > 3:
        list1 = list1[:3]
    list2[0] = 'goodbye'
    str1 = ''.join(list2)

arg1_list = ['a','b','c','d']
arg2_list = ['hello','mother','and','father']
arg_str = 'sister'

func1(arg1_list, arg2_list, arg_str)

print(arg1_list)        # Line 1
print(arg2_list)        # Line 2
print(arg_str)          # Line 3
```

(a) What output is produced by Line 1 when the program is executed?
(b) What output is produced by Line 2 when the program is executed?
(c) What output is produced by Line 3 when the program is executed?

8.1.4 Refactoring evens

The `evens` function offers an opportunity to illustrate refactoring. In Section 7.11, we introduced list comprehension as a way to build lists. Because `evens` builds a list, let's refactor the function using a list comprehension. In fact, the whole suite of the function can be replaced with one line:

```
return [2*i for i in range(1, n+1)]
```

Note how the ***for*** header is the same, and that the expression from the append appears just after the left bracket. The exercises ask for yet another refactoring of the function by using the step argument of *range*.

When refactoring you should ask yourself two questions: (1) is the code more readable and (2) is the code "better"—usually more efficient? It turns out that a list comprehension is very efficient, so this version is certainly more efficient. Whether list comprehension is more readable is in the eyes of the reader.

8.2 DEFAULT VALUES AND PARAMETERS AS KEYWORDS

Two additional characteristics of parameter passing we will now examine are the ability to have *default values* and the ability to *pass parameters by name.*

A default parameter value is pretty much just that: a value assigned to a function parameter by default in the event that the user did not provide a value. We have seen defaults before, for example, in slicing; there is a default for each of the three values in a slice if the user does not provide one. However, when the user does provide a value that provided value *always* overrides the default value.

A default parameter is created in the parameter list of a function definition. A default parameter looks like an assignment statement in the parameter list, something like `param_name = value`. The `value` on the right-hand side of the assignment is the default value for parameter `param_name`. The user of the function is free not to provide a value for that parameter, and the default will be used. If a parameter is listed without the assignment, it is a *required* parameter. The user *must* provide an argument for the parameter or Python will signal an error.

Arguments are mapped to parameters as before in a left-to-right positional matching. That is, the leftmost argument maps to the leftmost parameter, then the next leftmost argument is mapped to the next leftmost parameter, and so on. If there are more parameters then arguments, any unmatched parameters get their default values. Therefore, default values can only be used on the rightmost parameters.

Consider an example function `func1`, shown as follows, where the rightmost parameter, `param_default`, is assigned a default value. When the function is called with two arguments, the arguments are matched to parameters, from left to right as before, and the default value is ignored. However, when only one argument is used, `func1(5)`, the 5 is mapped to the leftmost parameter, `param_required`, and as there is no second argument, the parameter `param_default` gets its default value of 2.

```
In  [1]: def func1(param_required, param_default = 2): # note default value
...:     print(param_required, param_default)

In  [2]: func1(5,6) # both specified so default is ignored
5 6

In  [3]: func1(5) # only param_required, default used for param_default
5 2
```

Python also allows you to use the names of the parameters as keywords in the function *invocation*. That is, in the invocation you may also use an assignment statement of the form `param_name = value`. This feature means that you wish to provide `value` as the argument value for the parameter named `param_name`. In this way you can, with some care, ignore the standard order of argument-to-parameter names by specifically indicating which argument-to-parameter match your wish. For example, using the same function `func1` from the session above, we change the function invocation to indicate which argument value should go with which parameter name using the invocation `func1(param_default=4, param_required=3)`.

```
In  [1]: def func1(param_required, param_default = 2):
...:      print(param_required, param_default)

      # arg order doesn't matter: passing by name
In  [2]: func1(param_default = 4, param_required = 3)
3 4
```

Use of parameter names as keywords in a function invocation is particularly useful when there are many parameters and many have default values. The programmer can then easily specify a few desired arguments they wish to change, without regard to order, and accept the default values for the rest.

8.2.1 Example: Default Values and Parameter Keywords

VideoNote 8.1
More on Parameters

Let's create a simple function that uses default values and parameter names as keywords. The `rhyme` function prints variations of the classic "Roses are red" poem. Let's parameterize the flower and color from the first two lines and leave the closing lines unchanged. We will assign each parameter a default value so that if no parameters are specified, the original poem is printed. In the second invocation, we specify the first two arguments and leave the remaining two to the default values. In the final invocation, we name the parameters so that the second flower and color are specified leaving the first two to their default values. Here is the session:

```
In  [1]: def rhyme(flower1="Roses",color1="red",flower2="Violets",color2="blue"):
...:     print(flower1, "are", color1)
...:     print(flower2, "are", color2)
...:     print("Sugar is sweet")
...:     print("And so are you")

In  [2]: rhyme() # use all defaults
Roses are red
Violets are blue
Sugar is sweet
And so are you

In  [3]: rhyme("Daises", "white") # use default values for right-most parameters
Daises are white
Violets are blue
Sugar is sweet
And so are you

In  [4]: rhyme(flower2="Irises") # pass 1 parameter by name, the rest by default
Roses are red
Irises are blue
Sugar is sweet
And so are you
```

PROGRAMMING TIP

Because any parameter name can be used as a keyword during function invocation, you should name your parameters in a meaningful way. In a sense, the parameter names you use provide more documentation about the function. Sensible naming allows the function user to assign non-default values to known parameters more easily.

Issues with Default Values

Argument-to-parameter order can be a bit tricky when mixing standard invocation (i.e., without parameter keyword names) and parameter keywords. In general, you should stick with one style or the other (either invoke with all the parameters named or no parameters named), but if you do mix, make sure that:

- No argument is provided twice, for example first as normal argument and second as a parameter named argument.
- All the required arguments are provided.

A nastier problem can arise, if you use a parameter default value that is mutable, such as a list. Don't do it, but let's explain why. Default parameter values are only evaluated once, when **`def`** is evaluated, and that association is preserved between invocations. This persistence means that changes to the default object associated with the parameter name persists between calls. We illustrate this phenomenon in the following example. We create a function `func2` whose parameter `param_list` has as a default value the empty list. The default value is evaluated when the function is defined and the association between `param_list` and its object is created in the function's local namespace. The first invocation `func2(1)` uses the default for `param_list` and appends a 1 onto the *default* list: `[1]` is returned. That is worth repeating. The value 1 is appended onto the default list. When we make a second call, again using a default argument for `param_list`, `func2(2)`, the 2 gets appended on to the default object as well. However, since that object was modified in the previous call, that change remains and the returned value is now `[1, 2]`. Any change to the default object, if that object is mutable and modified, will be preserved across invocations. At the end of the session we make a final call that doesn't use defaults. This shows that 4 is appended to the end of the provided list argument `[7,8,9]` as expected.

```
In  [1]: def func2(element, param_list=[]):
   ...:     param_list.append(element)
   ...:     return param_list
In  [2]: func2(1) # uses the default for param_list
Out [2]: [1]

In  [3]: func2(2) # again uses default, but that object was modified previously
Out [3]: [1, 2]

In  [4]: func2(3) # again, the default object associated with param_list persists
Out [4]: [1, 2, 3]
```

```
In  [5]: func2(4,[7,8,9]) # no defaults , works as expected
Out [5]: [7, 8, 9, 4]

In  [6]: func2(5) # use defaults; default modifications still persist
Out [6]: [1, 2, 3, 5]
```

Such problems do not occur with immutable defaults because those objects cannot be modified.

PROGRAMMING TIP

You should *never* use a default value that is a mutable. If a default mutable is required, it is better to provide a value such as `None` as the default value in the function definition, and then check for that default value in the function code itself. At that point in the code, you can make a new object and perform the required task.

Check Yourself: More on Functions Check

1. Answer the questions for the following program.

```
def func1(multiplier=5,reps=3):
    result_list=[]
    for i in range(1,reps+1):
        result_list.append(i*multiplier)
    return multiplier,result_list

print(func1(10))          # Line 1
print(func1(reps=4))      # Line 2
print(func1(multiplier=3))# Line 3
print(func1(7,5))         # Line 4
```

(a) What output is produced by Line 1?
(b) What output is produced by Line 2?
(c) What output is produced by Line 3?
(d) What output is produced by Line 4?
(e) What is the length of every returned value from `func1`?

8.3 FUNCTIONS AS OBJECTS

As we observed earlier, defining a function creates an object in Python. As with any other object, there are methods and variables associated with function objects. To see what those methods and variables are, you can type in a known function name, followed by a dot (.) and the Tab character in the Python shell to see what the associated methods and variables are.

Of particular interest are those properties that begin and end with double underscores (_). These are names reserved by Python and serve special purposes. Some of the names associated with functions include:

1. *__name__* The name associated with the function.
2. *__str__* The function used to construct a string from the function. This is the function that **`print`** uses to represent a function.
3. *__dict__* The namespace of the function (it is a dictionary—Chapter 9).
4. *__doc__* The docstring, which contains information about the function provided by the programmer.

We will cover some of these (and other) methods and properties when we investigate objects, but annotations and docstrings are particularly interesting, so we cover them in more detail next.

8.3.1 Function Annotations

Python allows you to indicate an *annotation* for both the parameters of a function and the return value of the function. An annotation is an arbitrary piece of information that can be associated with a parameter or return value that can be used by either the function writer or user as they see fit (including ignoring that information). That is, the function writer can associate any kind of information with some or all of the parameters or the return value of the function, but Python does nothing with this annotation. It is up to the user or writer to take advantage of that information.

Annotations are associated as pairs in the parameter list, in the form `param_name : annotation`. Annotations on the return value are done using the special symbols `->` *after* the parameter list but before the ":" symbol, in the form: `def fn_name(param_name) -> annotation:`.

The session below shows such an example

```
def my_func (param1 : int, param2 : float) -> None :
...: print('Result is:', param1 + param2)

In  [1]: my_func(1, 2.0)
Result is: 3.0

In  [2]: my_func(1, 2)
Result is: 3

In  [3]: my_func('a', 'b')
Result is: ab
```

In this session, `param1` is associated with the type `int`, `param2` is associated with the type `float`, and the return value is associated with `None`. However, these values are not used in the function itself, and are ignored.

So what is the point then? The function writer can provide annotations as suggestions to the function user. In this case, the suggestion is the types that are *expected* for the parameters and return value, even if the expectations are not enforced. Note we passed in `str` type parameters without a problem in the previous session. However, these annotations are available within the function if the writer wishes to use them. The annotations are made into a a Python data structure (a dictionary) at function definition time and provided in a special variable as part of the function object called `__annotations__`. This data structure is part of the function object itself and so is accessed by `func_name.__annotations__`.

The following session shows this dictionary.

```
def my_func (param1 : int, param2 : float) -> None :
    print('Result is:', param1 + param2)

In  [1]: my_func.__annotations__
Out [1]: {'return': None, 'param2': <class 'float'>, 'param1': <class 'int'>}
```

Later in Chapter 9, we will learn how to make use of dictionaries. For now it suffices to observe that a record of the annotations is available in a Python data structure. The function writer could choose to use this information in the function, or just use it as "more documentation" for the user.

If you are interested in more uses for annotations, please see the Python documentation.

8.3.2 Docstrings

Python has a nice feature for documenting functions that can be accessed by other Python tools. By following this convention it is possible for a user to retrieve information about a function, for example, how to invoke it, what is returned, its purpose, and so on.

Suppose you wanted to know what was in the `math` module. There is a `dir` function that lists the names in the module. If you want to know more about a particular function, you can use `__doc__` with double underscores to inquire about a function. For example, after using `dir` to get the names in the math module, you might wonder what the `ceil` and `pow` functions do. Here is a session in the Python shell illustrating these concepts:

```
In  [1]: import math
In  [2]: dir(math)
Out [2]: ['__doc__', '__file__', '__name__', 'acos', 'asin', 'atan', 'atan2',
          'ceil', 'cos', 'cosh', 'degrees', 'e', 'exp', 'fabs', 'floor', 'fmod',
          'frexp', 'hypot', 'ldexp', 'log', 'log10', 'modf', 'pi', 'pow',
          'radians', 'sin', 'sinh', 'sqrt', 'tan', 'tanh']

In  [3]: math.ceil.__doc__
Out [3]: 'ceil(x)\n\nReturn the ceiling of x as a float.\nThis is the smallest
         integral value >= x.'

In  [4]: math.pow.__doc__
Out [4]: 'pow(x,y)\n\nReturn x**y (x to the power of y).'
```

Minimal information about each function is returned in the docstring, but if the protocol is followed, something useful can always be found. In addition, development environments such as SPYDER automatically display the docstring when you type the function name into the shell.

A docstring is included in a function using triple quotes to delimit the string. It must appear after the header line (just after the **def**). A docstring should either be one brief line or a brief line followed by a blank line, followed by a lengthier description. We include one-line docstrings in most of our function examples. It is good practice.

8.4 EXAMPLE: DETERMINING A FINAL GRADE

For this example, we want to process a file that contains a list of scores and the owner of those scores, and determine the final grade. The scores will be weighted; that is, some scores are worth more to the overall final grade than others. In the end, our program will nicely print out the name, in order: first name, last name, and the final grade.

8.4.1 The Data

We make some assumptions about the file of scores:

- Each line of the file contains five comma-separated fields.
  - The first field is the last name.
  - The second field is the first name.
  - The last three fields are the exam1, exam2, and final exam scores.
- Each score is an integer between 0 and 100.
- There are no empty fields.

Those are very specific assumptions, and it would take some work to ensure that the code we write enforces those assumptions. For this example, we will assume all files are in the correct format. Developing a properly error-checked version is left as an exercise.

8.4.2 The Design

Here is a first pass at an outline of our algorithm design:

1. Read each line of the file.
2. For each line, extract the name and scores; then calculate that grade based on provided weights.
3. Create a nice printout of the form: `first_name last_name final_grade`.

We can refine that design as follows:

1. Prompt for a file to open.
2. For each line in the file:
   (a) Extract the name and scores.

(b) Calculate the grade.
(c) Print out each grade in a nice format.

Remember that each function should "do one thing." The three actions taken on each line are good candidates for functions. However, printing can be done in one line so we have chosen to not make it a function.

- `parse_line`: Parse the line to extract names and scores.
- `weighted_grade`: Calculate the weighted grade.
- Print out each name and grade in a nice format.

A third function could be a `main` driving function. Let's tackle them one at a time.

8.4.3 Function: *weighted_grade*

This function needs to take in a list of scores (*ints* or *floats*) and return a weighted grade (*float*). As part of the calculation we need a list of weights. We could fix them within the function or take them as a parameter. To illustrate use of defaults we will take them in as a parameter. Because the weights are usually fixed by the course, we will give them default values. To avoid issues with mutable data structures as defaults, we will use a tuple as a default with three weights. See, tuples really are handy!

The processing then is to multiply each score by its weight and to sum those products together into a final grade. We then return that value. See Code Listing 8.2.

Code Listing 8.2

```
1 def weighted_grade(score_list, weights_tuple=(0.3,0.3,0.4)):
2     '''Expects 3 elements in score_list. Multiples each grade
3     by its weight. Returns the sum.'''
4     grade_float = \
5         (score_list[0]*weights_tuple[0]) +\
6         (score_list[1]*weights_tuple[1]) +\
7         (score_list[2]*weights_tuple[2])
8     return grade_float
```

The continuations on lines 4–7, as well as the parentheses, are not necessary but make the process more readable. Note that there is a docstring for the function on lines 2–3.

8.4.4 Function: *parse_line*

The `parse_line` function receives a single parameter, a line from the file of scores. It should extract the two name parts: reverse the order of the names and then collect the scores into a list. The reordered name and the score list are returned as a tuple (implicitly). See Code Listing 8.3.

Code Listing 8.3

```python
1 def parse_line(line_str):
2     '''Expects a line of form last, first, exam1, exam2, final.
3     returns a tuple containing first+last and list of scores.'''
4     field_list = line_str.strip().split(',')
5     name_str = field_list[1] + ' ' + field_list[0]
6     score_list = []
7     # gather the scores, now strings, as a list of ints
8     for element in field_list[2:]:
9         score_list.append(int(element))
10    return name_str,score_list
```

Lines 2–3: Docstring description of the function.

Line 4: Extracts the five fields by splitting on the comma, creating a list of five strings. We first strip off any whitespace characters such as carriage returns.

Line 5: Takes the first two fields (`last_name` is field 0, `first_name` is field 1), and concatenates them together into `first_name last_name` with a space in-between.

Lines 8–9: Create a list of scores from the remaining three fields.

Lines 10: Returns the new name and score list as a tuple. Note that the comma is enough to create a tuple on the return.

8.4.5 Function: *main*

The main program itself can be made into a function as well. This has some advantages. When the program is loaded, it does not begin running until the user invokes the function directly. It is also useful for creating stand-alone scripts in Python. In any event, we will create the function `main` to process the file. The code is in Code Listing 8.4.

Code Listing 8.4

```python
def main ():
    '''Get a line_str from the file, print the final grade nicely.'''
    file_name = input('Open what file:')
    grade_file = open(file_name, 'r')
    print('{:>13s}  {:>15s}'.format('Name','Grade'))
    print('-'*30)
```

```
7       for line_str in grade_file:
8           name_str,score_list = parse_line(line_str)
9           grade_float = weighted_grade(score_list)
10          print('{:>15s} {:14.2f} '.format(name_str, grade_float))
```

Line 2: Docstring.

Lines 3–4: Prompt for a file name, and open the file for reading.

Lines 5–6: Print a header for our output. Note the use of the replication operator on line 6.

Lines 7–10: For each line, call a function to parse the line into a name and a list of scores. Next call another function to calculated the weighted grade. Finally, print out the name and grade. Note the multiple assignment of line 8 which implicitly is a tuple.

8.4.6 Example Use

Given a file such as:

```
Smith, John,      100,0,0
CableGuy, Larry, 0,100,0
Harder, Try,      0,0,100
Python, Monty,    100,100,100
Frost, Jack,      50,50,50
Jones, Terry,     75,75,75
```

An example of using our program on that file is shown in the session below.

```
In  [1]: main()
Open what file:grades.txt

           Name             Grade
------------------------------
     John Smith             30.00
 Larry CableGuy             30.00
     Try Harder             40.00
   Monty Python            100.00
     Jack Frost             50.00
    Terry Jones             75.00
```

8.5 PASS ''BY VALUE'' OR ''BY REFERENCE''

Languages that trace their roots to procedural languages such as C++, Java, and C#, differentiate between parameters that are passed "by value" vs. "by reference." A common question is: which does Python use? The useful answer for novice programmers is "neither," in the sense the concept applies to those languages. It would take too long to both define those concepts precisely, and to explain why "neither" is the useful answer, but if you go on to study one of those languages, it is useful to know that Python programmers do not need to think in those terms.

The best answer is to say that Python passes *object references*. Everything in Python is an object, so every value passed is a reference to an object. Therefore, an object is not copied in this process. Python passes a reference to that object as illustrated in Figures 8.1–8.4. If the object is mutable, then a change made in the function is reflected in the outer scope of the object, for example, where function was called. If it is not mutable, a new object is referenced when the reference is updated.

8.6 WHAT'S WRONG WITH MY CODE?

The problems we encounter here all center on the use of mutable parameter objects such as lists.

- If you pass a mutable, such as a list, to a function, then a change in that mutable is preserved across the call. That is, the mutable **argument** in the calling program will be changed by any change to that mutable **parameter** in the function. You can check for this by setting a breakpoint before and after the function call in SPYDER and watching how the mutable value is updated.
- Another problem discussed in some detail in Section 8.2.1 is using a mutable, such as a list, as a default parameter value. The short answer is **don't**. A default value is created once, and only once, when the function is defined. If the default is modified in the function, then as a mutable that change persists and you get changing default values. As mentioned, if you need a mutable default value, assign a value of `None` as the default and check for it in the function code.

Summary

In this chapter, we further developed the concept of functions in a programming language and showed how functions work in Python. As you will see in later chapters, functions aid us in the divide-and-conquer approach to problem solving. Finally, we examined the role of refactoring with respect to functions.

Functions

- Scope is the set of program statements over which an object exists
- Passing mutable objects allows a function to change values in the calling program.
- Default paramaters are specified with assignment (=), for example, `param = value`.
- Don't use a mutable object as a default parameter value.

- Optionally, parameters can be specified in an invocation using the name of the parameter, for example, `fun(param=4)`.
- Docstrings describe a function's purpose and appear in the line after the function header.

Rules

- **RULE 1:** Think before you program!
- **RULE 2:** A program is a human-readable essay on problem solving that also happens to execute on a computer.
- **RULE 3:** The best way to improve your programming and problem skills is to practice!
- **RULE 4:** A foolish consistency is the hobgoblin of little minds.
- **RULE 5:** Test your code, often and thoroughly!
- **RULE 6:** If it was hard to write, it is probably hard to read. Add a comment.
- **RULE 7:** All input is evil, until proven otherwise.
- **RULE 8:** A function should do one thing.

Exercises

1. What is the difference between an argument and a parameter?
2. What does the following code print? Explain.

```
def my_function(message, times = 1):
    print(message * times)

fun('Hello')
fun('World', 5)
```

3. What does the following code print? Explain.

```
number = 50
def func(number):
    print(number)
    number = 2
    print(number)
func(number)
print(number)
```

4. Consider the following code. The "print(x)" statement generates an error. Provide two different ways to print "x" properly. You will need to make assumptions about what is reasonable to print.

```
def add_one(number):
    x=1
    number = number + x
    print(number)

add_one(3)
    print(x)
```

5. Write a function `my_function` that takes a list, an index value, and either `pop` or `insert` as arguments, and pops or inserts an element from or into the specified index location.

6. Understanding scope is important when working with functions. The value of x was defined to be 1 (below), so why do we get an error when we inquired about its value?

```
def add_one(number):
    x=1
    number=number+x
    print(number)

>>> add_one(5)
6

>>> x
NameError: name 'x' not defined
```

7. Write a function that takes three integers as its input and returns whether a triangle with those side lengths is a right triangle or not. *Hint:* sort is your friend.

8. Write a function `merge_lists` that takes two lists as arguments, merges them into an ordered third list, and returns the third list after removing duplicates from it.

9. Write a function that takes a string of letters and digits as an argument and returns a list that has digits in a tuple and the letters in a list.

10. Write a function that takes a list of integers as an argument and returns a tuple with the smallest and largest integers in the list. In case of a tie, either value is acceptable.

---

11. In Section 8.1.3, we defined a function called `evens(n)` that generated a list of "n" even numbers. The `range()` function takes a third argument that is the "step"—the step between numbers in the range. Rewrite the function using the third argument in the range. Note that you will also need to change the second argument so that the correct number of even numbers is generated.

12. Refactor the Gettysburg Address Analysis program from Section 7.5.2 using at least four functions.

13. The `mirror()` function example is not robust.

    (a) Determine function arguments that will generate errors.

    (b) Rewrite the function so those errors will be checked and avoided.

14. Anagrams. In an earlier chapter we created a program that tested whether two strings were anagrams. (We sorted the strings and then compared them.)

    (a) Write a function that returns True, if two strings are anagrams, and False otherwise. (Starting hint: how many parameters do you need?)

(b) Write a program that uses your function. The program should prompt for the two strings, call the function, and then print results (something other than "True" or "False").

15. Palindromes. A palindrome is a word that is the same backwards as forwards. The word "rotor" is an example of a palindrome.

(a) Write a function which returns True, if two strings are palindromes. (*Hints:* You can create a list from a string using the `list()` function. Lists are handy because there is a `reverse()` method.)

(b) Write a program that uses your function. The program should prompt for the two strings, call the function, and then print results (something other than "True" or "False").

(c) Some palindrome rules ignore spaces and capitalization so "Never odd or even" is an acceptable palindrome. Improve your function to ignore spaces and capitalization. (*Hints:* Lists have a `remove()` method, and strings have a `lower()` method.)

16. Write a function that takes a list as an argument and verifies whether the list is sorted. Return True if sorted; False if not.

17. Remove Odds or Evens:

(a) Write a function that takes a list of integers as an argument, removes even numbers from the list, and returns the modified list.

(b) Write a function that takes a list of integers as an argument, removes odd numbers from the list, and returns the modified list.

(c) Write a function that takes a list of integers and a Boolean as arguments. If the Boolean is *`True`* the function removes odd numbers from the list; otherwise, evens are removed. The function returns the modified list.

18. Starting in 1999 the U.S. Government Mint released state-specific quarters at a rate of five states per year. Find the release year for each state's quarters online, for example, www.usmint.gov. Copy that information into a Python program (as a string, or a list, or tuples, or list of lists, etc.) Write functions that do the following:

(a) Print the names of the states in the order of release of their quarters. Also, print the years, along with the names.

(b) Print the names of the states in increasing order of the length of their names. Also print the years along with the names.

(c) Prompt for a year and print all the quarters issued that year.

19. In the earlier chapter on functions there was an exercise based on DNA searching to make a `multi_find()` function. That function had two constraints that we can now remove: (i) it returned the indices in a string, and (ii) it couldn't handle default arguments. In this exercise we will fix both.

(a) Write a string function `multi_find(some_string, sub_string [,start] [,end])` where *start* and *end* are optional arguments with default values for the start and end of *some_string*. The *start* and *end* are interpreted as they are in slicing, that is:

$$0 = \text{start} \leq \text{index} < \text{end} = \text{len(some\_string)}$$

The function should return a list of indices of occurrences of *sub_string* in *some_string*. If the substring is not found, return an empty list.

(b) Demonstrate that your string function works and that you can use it in a Boolean expression.

20. In the chapter on strings there was an example that counted poker hands. Refactor that program with two goals: (i) break the program down into functions and (ii) use a list of counters rather than individual counter variables.

Programming Projects

1. **Data mining stock prices**

Data mining is the process of sorting through large amounts of data and picking out relevant information. It is usually used by business intelligence organizations, and financial analysts, but is increasingly being used in the sciences to extract information from the enormous data sets generated by modern experimental and observational methods.

In this project, we want to do some preliminary data mining to the prices of some company's stock. So that we can speak in specifics, let's look at Google. Your program will calculate the monthly average prices of Google stock from 2004 to 2008, and tell us the 6 best and 6 worst months for Google. We provide the data reading function; you write the next two and a main that calls the functions.

(a) First you need a history of stock prices. Go to finance.yahoo.com, enter Google in the search field, select "Historical Prices" (currently on the left of the page), and find the "download to spreadsheet" option. Choose to save the file in the folder where your Python program will be saved. The default name is "table.csv" so we will use that name. The file format is indicated by the first few lines:

```
Date,Open,High,Low,Close,Volume,Adj Close
2008-09-19,461.00,462.07,443.28,449.15,10006000,449.15
2008-09-18,422.64,439.18,410.50,439.08,8589400,439.08
```

(b) `get_data_list(file_name)`

The "csv" file is a "comma-separated file", so we can split the data on commas. The following function will read a file, split the lines in the file on commas, and put the data in to a list that is returned. The result is a list of lists where each line is a list. Also, every item is a string. To read our file, call it using our file name:

`get_data_list('table.csv')`. Experiment with this function in the shell to get a sense of what is returned.

```
>def get_data_list(file_name):
    data_file = open(file_name,"r")
    data_list = [ ]           # start with an empty list
    for line_str in data_file:
        # strip end-of-line, split on commas, and append items to
        list data_list.append(line_str.strip().split(','))
    return data_list
```

(c) `get_monthly_averages(data_list)`
In this function, you will use the data_list generated by the get_data_list function as the parameter. Use the Date, Volume, and Adj Close fields to calculate the average monthly prices. Here is a formula for the average price for a month, where Vi is the volume and Ci is the day i's adjusted close price (Adj Close).

$$\text{average\_price} = (V1 * C1 + V2 * C2 + \cdots + Vn * Cn)/(V1 + V2 + \cdots + Vn)$$

For each month create a tuple with two items: the average for that month, and the date (you need only the month and year). Append the tuple for each month to a list (e.g., monthly_averages_list), and after calculating all the monthly averages, return this list. We use tuples here because once these values are calculated we don't want to accidentally change them!

(d) `print_info(monthly_averages_list)`
In this function, you need to use the list of monthly averages calculated in the get_monthly_averages function. Here you will need to find and print the 6 best (highest average price) and 6 worst (lowest average price) months for Google's stock. Print them in order from highest to lowest and print to 2 decimal places. Format the output so that it looks good and include informative headers. This function does not return anything.

(e) If you don't call these functions, they are useless. Thus, you should write code to call them.

Hints:

(a) The list `sort()` and `reverse()` methods will be useful. Experiment with how they sort a list of tuples—notice how they sort on the first item.

(b) To create a tuple, put items in a comma-separated list with parentheses: (x,y).

(c) When working with a list-of-lists (or a list-of-tuples), the first item in the first list is `some_list[0][0]` and the second item in that same first list is `some_list[0][1]`.

2. Who was the Best NBA Basketball Player?

The National Basketball Association (NBA) is the North America's professional men's basketball league. You are going to write a program to find the best players in NBA history. You are to get the raw NBA stats from the Web, compute the efficiency of nearly 4000 players, and output the 50 most efficient players, as well as some other interesting statistics.

Efficiency
How do many NBA coaches quickly evaluate a player's game performance? They check his efficiency. NBA.com evaluates all players based on the efficiency formula indicated below (and shown on the aboutstats.htm page) In this project, we will use this efficiency formula. Since we are not evaluating a player based on one game, we need to divide the total efficiency by the number of games the player played. So the formula is:

$$Efficiency = \frac{(pts + reb + asts + stl + blk) - ((fga - fgm) + (fta - ftm) + turnover)}{gp}$$

The abbreviations are described as follows:

Other Stats Besides efficiency, also collect:

- The player who played the most minutes.
- The player who played the most games.
- The player who scored the most points.
- The player who got the most rebounds.
- The player who got the most penalties.
- The player who made the most free throws.

(a) `Get Data`
Go to `http://www.databasebasketball.com/stats_download.htm` and download the database (currently named databaseBasketball2.1.zip). Double-click on the file to unpack the zip file. We will use the file "player_regular_season_career.txt" so move that file into the folder where you will be writing your Python program. The first line of the file has headers for the columns, but they are abbreviated. At the bottom of the stats page is a link to a page describing the abbreviations (`http://www.databasebasketball.com/about/aboutstats.htm`).

(b) `Read Data`
To read the data we can use the `get_data_list()` function from the previous problem, but we need to make one important modification. Since the basketball data file separates the fields using vertical bars `('|')`, we must replace the comma in the split function with a vertical bar: `split('|')`. The function will return a list-of-lists that has one list for each player.

(c) `Process Data`

Calculate the statistics mentioned earlier and then output them. For the efficiency, find the top 50 and then order them from best to worst. For calculating the "other" statistics, you could write one function for each, but you should notice a pattern after writing one or two that will indicate how to write one function that you can call for each statistic.

(d) `Output`

Format your output to make it readable and good-looking. Remember to print the 50 top in efficiency in order from best to worst. Printing should be a function.

CHAPTER 9

Dictionaries and Sets

> A set is a gathering together into a whole of definite, distinct objects of our perception and of our thought—which are called elements of the set.
>
> Georg Cantor, the founder of set theory, 1884

WHEN WE INTRODUCED LISTS, WE ALSO INTRODUCED THE CONCEPT OF A DATA structure and the important role that data structures play in computer science. Understanding data structures means understanding how data is organized and the kind of algorithms that can work on data organized in that fashion. Lists and strings were examples of data structures that come with Python. In this chapter, we will add *dictionaries* and *sets*, data structures also included in Python. Dictionaries in particular are a very powerful data structure that are useful for solving many problems. In fact, Python relies heavily on dictionaries in its underlying organization.

9.1 DICTIONARIES

What is the dictionary data structure? A dictionary is a collection, but it is *not* a sequence. A dictionary is often referred to as a *map* collection, also sometimes as an *associative array*. You can think of a dictionary as a list of pairs, where the first element of each pair is the *key* and the second element of each pair is the *value*. A dictionary is designed so that a search for a key, and subsequently its associated value, is very efficient. The word "map" comes from this association: the key maps to the value.

All operations on dictionaries are built to work through keys. The data structure is called a "dictionary" because of its similarity to a real dictionary, such as Webster's dictionary. Think of the keys as the words in Webster's dictionary. It is easy to look up a word (the key) because of the organization of Webster's dictionary (alphabetical). Once the key is found, the associated value, the definition, is clearly indicated. Note that the opposite search, a search for the the value (i.e., the definition), is not easily done. Imagine trying to find a definition without the associated word (key) in Webster's dictionary. It is only possible by examining every definition in the whole dictionary from beginning to end—not very efficient![1] Dictionaries, both the data structure and Webster's, are optimized to work with keys. However, the dictionary data structure and Webster's are different in one important way: Webster's key organization is based on an alphabetical (sequential) ordering of the keys. In a Python dictionary, keys are arranged to make searching go quickly, not necessarily sequentially. Furthermore, the arrangement is hidden from the user. As a result, you cannot print a dictionary collection and count on a particular order. As new key-value pairs are added, the dictionary is modified to make key searching efficient for Python.

9.1.1 Dictionary Example

A contact list such as is found in a cell phone could be implemented as a Python dictionary. Imagine that we have three people in our phone contact list, "bill," "rich," and "jane" and assume that we have a phone number for each one. Figure 9.1 diagrams the data structure. Each name is a *key*, and for each key there is an associated *value*, a phone number as a string. If you want the phone number for "bill," you simply look up his name (the *key*) in the contacts and get the associated phone number (the *value*). Note that order of the names (keys) does not matter; only the association between a key and its value matters.

You will notice that the figure for the dictionary looks just like the figures for namespaces. That is not by accident: namespaces are implemented as dictionaries in Python. When Python wants the value of a variable it refers to the namespace dictionary using the variable name as the key and the associated object as the value.

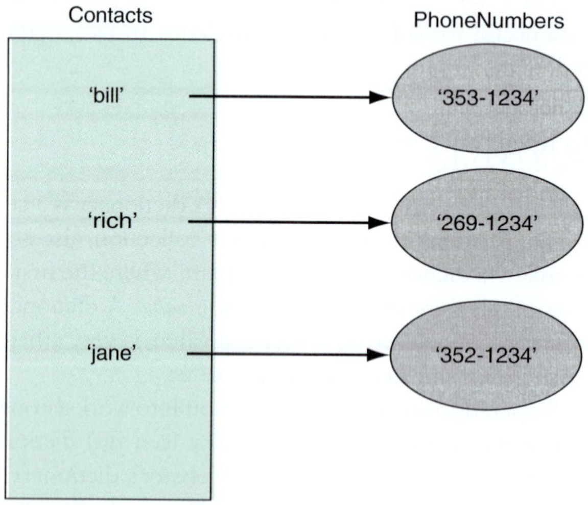

FIGURE 9.1 Phone contact list: names and phone numbers.

[1] Such an approach is often called a *brute force* approach, as it requires examining all possibilities.

9.1.2 Python Dictionaries

Let's implement the dictionary of "contacts" shown in Figure 9.1. As we have seen, a list can be created by either the constructor `list` or a shortcut, the square brackets ([ ]). Dictionaries also have a constructor, called `dict` and have a shortcut, curly braces: { }. Like lists, curly braces are often used, although, as with lists, there are applications for the `dict` constructor. When designating the contents of a dictionary, the individual key-value pairs are separated by a colon (:). Values may be anything, but *keys can only be immutable objects* such as integers, strings, or tuples. In this session, we create a contacts dictionary, display it, get a number for "bill," and add a contact for "barb." Note the unordered nature of a dictionary when printed: it is not kept in any apparent order—not even the order of the key-value pair's creation.

```
# create contacts
In  [1]: contacts = {'bill': '353-1234', 'rich': '269-1234', 'jane':'352-1234'}
In  [2]: contacts # display contacts: note order
Out [2]: {'jane': '352-1234', 'bill': '353-1234', 'rich': '269-1234'}

In  [3]: contacts['bill'] # get contact info for "bill"
Out [3]: '353-1234'

In  [4]: contacts['barb'] = '271-1234' # add contact info for "barb"
In  [5]: contacts # observe change in contacts
Out [5]: {'jane':'352-1234', 'bill':'353-1234', 'barb':'271-1234', 'rich':'269-1234'}
```

9.1.3 Dictionary Indexing and Assignment

Dictionaries are collections that respond to the index operator: [ ]. However, we do not use a sequence number (0 for the first element, −1 for the last, etc.) as we did with other collections. Instead, we use the *key as the index value*. Thus, `contacts['bill']` is an index into the dictionary, using the key `'bill'` to retrieve its associated value `'353-1234'`. If no such key presently exists in the dictionary, Python throws an error—a `KeyError`. To add a key-value pair to a dictionary, we can do so by index assignment. That is, `contacts['barb']='271-1234'` is an assignment of `'271-1234'` to the key `'barb'` in the dictionary `contacts`. If the key does not yet exist, it is created and then associated with the value. If the key already exists, the new value is associated with the key.

Dictionaries Are Mutable

Because we can do index assignment in a dictionary, a dictionary is our second example of a mutable data structure (the first was a list). In addition to index assignment, dictionaries have a number of methods that change the dictionary in place. As with lists, there are potential consequences to passing a mutable object to functions. If a dictionary is modified in a function, it is modified in the calling program. You will see examples of mutable methods later in this chapter.

Dictionaries with Different Key Types

The power of dictionaries is a combination of its indexing speed and the fact that the value can be any data structure, even another dictionary. Furthermore, different types of keys can be used in the same dictionary as long as they are immutable types. In the next session, we create a dictionary with keys that are `int`s, `tuple`s, and `str`s. Of particular note is that the values are `list`s, `int`s, and `dict`s. We then show access using each key, followed at the end by accessing an element of the dictionary value contained in our dictionary. As with previous chained expressions, they proceed from left to right.

```
# values as list, int, dict
In  [1]: demo = {2:['a','b','c'], (2,4): 27, 'x':{1:2.5, 'a':3}}
In  [2]: demo # kept in "arbitrary" order
Out [2]: {'x': {'a': 3, 1: 2.5}, 2: ['a', 'b', 'c'], (2, 4): 27}

In  [3]: demo[2] # access dictionary with each key
Out [3]: ['a', 'b', 'c']

In  [4]: demo[(2,4)] # key is a tuple!
Out [4]: 27

In  [5]: demo['x'] # value is a dictionary
Out [5]: {'a': 3, 1: 2.5}

In  [6]: demo['x'][1] # access item "1" in the dictionary value
Out [6]: 2.5
```

The expression `demo['x']` yields a dictionary as a value, and that yielded dictionary is further referenced by the index `[1]`, yielding the value 2.5.

As with other data structures we have used, such as strings and lists, we often want to initialize a dictionary to be empty. A pair of curly brackets creates an empty dictionary. Alternately, one can use `dict` with no argument.

```
some_dict = {}
another_dict = dict()
```

9.1.4 Operators

Familiar Collection Operations

Most of the collection operations you have become familiar with work with dictionaries. However, keep two things in mind: dictionaries are optimized for operations on *keys* and that dictionaries are mutable.

`[ ]`: indexing using the key as the index value.
`len()`: the "length" is the number of key-value pairs in the dictionary.
`in`: Boolean test of membership, is the *key* in the dictionary (not the value)?
`for`: iteration through *keys* in the dictionary.

In the following session, we illustrate the use of the standard operations. Things to note, especially given the focus of dictionary operations on keys:

- The length operator measures the number of key-value pairs (or, if you prefer, the number of keys).
- The membership operation is an operation on keys, not values.
- Iteration yields the keys in the dictionary.

To discover the values associated with the keys, we must index the dictionary with that key (or use one of the iterators in the next section).

```
In  [1]: my_dict = {'a':2, 3:['x','y'], 'joe': 'smith'} # create a dictionary
In  [2]: my_dict # display it
Out [2]: {'a': 2, 3: ['x', 'y'], 'joe': 'smith'}

In  [3]: my_dict['a'] # use square brackets to index
Out [3]: 2

In  [4]: len(my_dict) # lenth is the number of key:value pairs
Out [4]: 3

In  [5]: 'a' in my_dict # membership test
Out [5]: True

In  [6]: 2 in my_dict # "in" only looks at keys, not values
Out [6]: False

In  [7]: for key in my_dict: # iteration is through the keys, not the values
...:     print(key)

a
3
joe
In  [8]: for key in my_dict: # if you want values, include indexing []
...:     print(key, my_dict[key])

a 2
3 ['x', 'y']
joe smith
```

Given the above description, it should not be surprising that in the context of a dictionary, the functions `min`, `max`, and `sum` are also operations on keys.

Some Dictionary Methods

Given the default behavior of dictionary iteration on keys, Python provides a number of other methods that allow the programmer to iterate through other dictionary elements:

`items()`: all the key-value pairs as a list of tuples
`keys()`: all the keys as a list
`values()`: all the values as a list

Check out their use in a session:

```
In  [1]: my_dict = {'a':2, 3:['x','y'], 'joe':'smith'}
In  [2]: for key,val in my_dict.items(): # iterate over key,value
...:    print("Key: {:7}, Value:{}".format(key,val))
...
Key: a      , Value:2
Key: joe    , Value:smith
Key:       3, Value:['x', 'y']

In  [3]: for key in my_dict.keys(): # iterate over keys
...:    print(key)
...
a
joe
3
In  [4]: dict_value_view = my_dict.values()
In  [5]: dict_value_view # a view
Out [5]: dict_values([2, 'smith', ['x', 'y']])

In  [6]: type(dict_value_view) # of type view
Out [6]: dict_values

In  [7]: for val in dict_value_view: # iterate over view
...:    print(val)
...
2
smith
['x', 'y']

In  [8]: my_dict['new_key'] = 'new_value'
In  [9]: dict_value_view # view updated
Out [9]: dict_values([2, 'smith', ['x', 'y'], 'new_value'])

In  [10]: dict_key_view = my_dict.keys()
In  [11]: dict_value_view
Out [11]: dict_values([2, 'smith', ['x', 'y'], 'new_value'])

In  [12]: dict_key_view
Out [12]: dict_keys(['a', 'joe', 3, 'new_key'])
```

These three methods allow us to iterate through the dictionary yielding key-value pairs (each as a separate item), only keys, or only values. If you type an invocation of one of these methods you get an unusual type back: a `dict_values` or `dict_keys` type. Python calls these types *view objects*. View objects have a couple of interesting properties.

- A view object is iterable. Thus we can use the in a ***for*** loop.
- Though the order of keys and values in a dictionary cannot be determined, views of keys and values will correspond. That is, whatever the order of the key view is, the value

view will have the same order (the elements of the key view and the value view match as found in the dictionary).

- View objects are dynamic. Once assigned, if the dictionary is updated in some way the view object reflects that update.

Because the `items` iterator generates tuples, we can assign two values for every iteration of the **for** loop: the first element is the key of the pair and the second is the value (similar to `enumerate`).

Dictionaries have a `copy` method. The `copy` method makes a shallow copy of the dictionary values. This means that keys are copied properly (as they must be immutable), but if the values are mutable, problems such as we have seen before can arise. See the following session.

```
In  [1]: my_dict = {'a':2, 3:['x','y'], 'joe':'smith'}
In  [2]: new_dict = my_dict.copy() # shallow copy
In  [3]: new_dict['a'] = 'new_value'
In  [4]: my_dict
Out [4]: {'a': 2, 3: ['x', 'y'], 'joe': 'smith'}

In  [5]: new_dict
Out [5]: {'a': 'new_value', 3: ['x', 'y'], 'joe': 'smith'} # updated immutable
                                                             value works

In  [6]: a_value = new_dict[3] # a mutable list
In  [7]: a_value
Out [7]: ['x', 'y']

In  [8]: a_value[0] = 'new_element' # update list
In  [9]: new_dict # copy is changed
Out [9]: {'a': 'new_value', 3: ['new_element', 'y'], 'joe': 'smith'}

In  [10]: my_dict # original is changed
Out [10]: {'a': 2, 3: ['new_element', 'y'], 'joe': 'smith'}
```

When a copy of `my_dict` is created and assigned to `my_dict`, copies of all the references are made, a shallow copy (see Section 7.6.1). If index assignment is made to the list value in `new_dict`, the change is also shown in `my_dict`.

Dictionaries are a very powerful data structure that are useful for many tasks. Here is a simple example. Imagine you are trying to count the frequency of word occurrence in a list of words (perhaps gathered from a text file). We can represent that data using a dictionary, with the words as the keys and the values as the frequency of occurrence. There are two operations you need to perform in the process of updating a dictionary with a word from the list. You can add a word to the dictionary if it doesn't exist (with a frequency of one in that case) or you can add one to the frequency of an existing word already in the dictionary. The first method is shown later. It uses the ***in*** method to check for the existence of the word in the dictionary. Remember, this membership is a check of keys, so this is a check to see if the word is already in the dictionary. If so, then one is added to the frequency (the value associated with the word is updated by one). If not, the word is assigned as a key to the dictionary with a frequency of one.

```
count_dict = {}
for word in word_list:
    if word in count_dict:
        count_dict[word] += 1
    else:
        count_dict[word] = 1
```

An alternative to membership checking is to use exceptions. In this case, the **try** suite assumes that the key exists in the dictionary (the word is already a key) and tries to add one to its frequency value. If this assumption is incorrect (the word is not a key), the KeyError exception is raised. The KeyError exception suite then adds the key to the dictionary (solves the exception condition) with a frequency value of 1. Here is the same code with exceptions.

```
count_dict = {}
for word in word_list:
    try:
        count_dict[word] += 1
    except KeyError:
        count_dict[word] = 1
```

It is an interesting question as to which is the "better" way. From an efficiency (faster running times) standpoint, no difference would be noticed until the dictionaries got very large, at which point the membership test is probably faster. Which is more readable is somewhat debatable, though the exception does focus on "what you wanted to do" and leaves the error problems to a different clause entirely.

Since we are playing this game, there is indeed a third approach which uses a dictionary method, the get method. This method takes two arguments: a key and a default value. The behavior of get is to provide normal dictionary operations when the key exists (return the associated value), but if the key does not exists, it returns the default as the value for that key (no error). Here is the same code using get:

```
count_dict = {}
for word in word_list:
    count_dict[word] = count_dict.get(word,0) + 1
```

The get approach is the most concise, but possibly the least readable.

Check Yourself: Dictionary Check

1. Indicate the requested output for the following program:

```
def f1 (my_dict):
    temp = 0
    for value in my_dict.values():
        temp = temp + value
    return temp

def f2 (my_dict):
    temp = ''
    for key in my_dict:
        if temp < key:
            temp = key
    return temp

def f3(my_dict,k,v):
    if k in my_dict:
        my_dict[k]=v

a_dict={'bill':1,'rich':2,'fred':10,'walter':20}

print(f1(a_dict))                          # Line 1
print(f2(a_dict))                          # Line 2
print(None == f3(a_dict,'bill',-1))        # Line 3
print(a_dict)                              # Line 4
```

(a) What output is produced by Line 1 of the program?

(b) What output is produced by Line 2 of the program?

(c) What output is produced by Line 3 of the program?

(d) What output is produced by Line 4 of the program?

9.1.5 Ordered Dictionaries

Standard Python dictionaries have no order which is by design for efficiency. However, sorted collections are useful so the `collections` module has an `OrderedDict` type. The operations and methods we have described for regular dictionaries work with ordered dictionaries. However, when you add items to an ordered dictionary order is not preserved: new items are simply appended to the end of the dictionary. That maintains effeciency, but if you want order, you must resort the ordered dictionary. That characteristic limits its usefulness so we will not cover it in any detail.

9.2 WORD COUNT EXAMPLE

In Section 7.5.2, we introduced text analysis using the Gettysburg Address. In that section, we showed how to count the number of words in a text file and how to count the number of unique words in the text.

With dictionaries, we can now do more analysis. In particular, we can determine the word frequency of a file with the aid of a dictionary. As we did in the previous example, we use each word as a key and use as a value the number of occurrences of that word. For every word in the file, we check to see whether that word is already in the dictionary. If the word is in fact already there, we increase its associated count (value) by 1. If the word is not yet in the dictionary, we insert it with a count (value) of 1.

9.2.1 Count Words in a String

Let's warm up by first counting the frequency of words in a string. Our algorithm will be:

- Initialize our `word_count_dict` dictionary to be empty.
- Split the string `speech` into a list `speech_list`.
- For every word in a `speech_list`:
  - If the word is ***in*** `word_count_dict`:
    - Add 1 to its value.
  - Else:
    - Insert the word into `word_count_dict` with a value of 1.

We can check whether a word (the key) is in the dictionary using the ***in*** operator, the first of the three options we mentioned earlier. If a word is already in the dictionary, we can access its value using the word (key) as an index and increment its associated value. If the word (key) is not present, we can use index assignment to create the key and set its associated value to 1. Code Listing 9.1 is the Python code followed by a session. The output is just the dictionary, no nice output formatting yet. Using the words in the famous Shakespearean quote "to be or not to be," the result is "be" and "to" with counts of 2 and the other words with counts of 1.

Code Listing 9.1

```
# Count words in string

speech = "to be or not to be"
speech_list = speech.split()

word_count_dict = {}

```

```
for word in speech_list:
    if word in word_count_dict:
        word_count_dict[word] += 1
    else:
        word_count_dict[word] = 1

print(word_count_dict)
```

```
{'not': 1, 'to': 2, 'or': 1, 'be': 2}
```

9.2.2 Word Frequency for Gettysburg Address

Now that we have an understanding of how to use dictionaries to get word frequencies, let's apply them to the original problem: word frequency in a text file. As always, let's break the problem down:

- Open the file and process each line.
- Either add each word to the dictionary with a frequency of one or update the word's count by one
- Nicely print the output, in this case from high to low frequency.

Again, we want to achieve each major goal with a function, in keeping with **RULE 8** (one function, one action). We can find four functions in the goals stated (perhaps you can find more):

add_word: Add each word to the dictionary. Parameters are the word and a dictionary. No return value.

process_line: There is some work to be done to process the line: strip off various characters, split out the words, and so on. Parameters are a line and the dictionary. It calls `add_word` with each processed word. No return value.

pretty_print: Because formatted printing can be messy and often particular to each situation (meaning that we might need to modify it later), we separated out the printing function. The parameter is a dictionary. No return value.

main: We will use a main function as the main program. As usual, it will open the file and call `process_line` on each line. When finished, it will call `pretty_print` to print the dictionary.

Now let's examine each function in detail.

add_word

This function is fairly straightforward and follows from the previous example on word counting. For each word, we check to see whether the word (key) is in the dictionary using the *in* operator. If it is, we increment the associated value count. If not, we add the new word to the dictionary as a key with an associated value of 1. The code is shown in Code Listing 9.2.

Code Listing 9.2

```
def add_word(word, word_count_dict):
    '''Update the word frequency: word is the key, frequency is the value.'''
    if word in word_count_dict:
        word_count_dict[word] += 1
    else:
        word_count_dict[word] = 1
```

Note that there is no return value. Because a dictionary is mutable and because the operations use index assignment, we modify the existing object and that change is reflected in the calling function (`process_line` in this case). Returning the dictionary might seem to be a reasonable design decision, but the copy created could be large and the shallow copy could hide problems related to the sharing of mutable items.

process_line

The function receives both the line and the dictionary as parameters. We need the dictionary because we need to pass it as a parameter to the `add_word` function. From the line, we need to extract each word. The code is shown in Code Listing 9.3.

Code Listing 9.3

```
import string
def process_line(line, word_count_dict):
    '''Process the line to get lowercase words to add to the dictionary.'''
    line = line.strip()
    word_list = line.split()
    for word in word_list:
        # ignore the '--' that is in the file
        if word != '--':
            word = word.lower()
            word = word.strip()
            # get commas, periods and other punctuation out as well
            word = word.strip(string.punctuation)
            add_word(word, word_count_dict)
```

We've seen much of this code before in Code Listing 6.7, but briefly:

Lines 4–5: Strip whitespace from the front and back of the line, then split the line to get a list of words. Remember that the default argument to `split` splits at any whitespace character. These lines could be chained together as:

```
word_list = line.strip().split()
```

Lines 6–8: Iterate through each word in `word_list`. Skip the special string `'--'` that we found in the file (see Section 7.5.2).

Lines 9–10: Make each word all lowercase and strip off whitespace characters from either end. Lowercase allows us to get a better count so that `'Nation'` is not different from `'nation'`. If case matters, we need to fix that here. Also, these lines could be chained together as we showed earlier.

Line 12: This is the only really "different" line of code. Why do we strip the word twice? The first time stripped out whitespace, what `strip` uses when the default is provided. However, there are situations in the file where a punctuation mark follows a word. For example, if you look at the file, you will see `'nation,'` and `'nation'`. The default `strip` does not remove punctuation, but it seems reasonable that the two strings above should be equivalent. So we strip each line again using the variable `string.punctuation` as an argument to `strip`. That variable contains a string with all the normal punctuation characters. Using it as an argument to `strip` will remove punctuation marks at the beginning or end of a word (but not the middle!). To do so, we must first import the `string` module, which we do in line 1. Remember **RULE 6**. We need to add a comment here.

Line 13: Call `add_word` with the processed word and the dictionary that was provided as a parameter.

Again, the function does not return a value. All modifications made are made to a mutable data structure (a dictionary) using index assignments. Any change will be reflected in the calling function (`main` in this case).

pretty_print

Printing the dictionary is a little more complicated than one might think at first. What we would like to do is print the dictionary in sorted order, sorting on the values (the frequencies) from largest to smallest. However, dictionaries are by definition un-ordered. We can sort dictionaries using the `sorted` function, but it sorts by keys, giving us the list in alphabetical order, but not frequency order. The only way around this is to turn the dictionary into a list of reversed (value-key) pairs and sort that list. The question is, how to do that? The code is shown in Code Listing 9.4.

Code Listing 9.4

```
1  def pretty_print(word_count_dict):
2      '''Print nicely from highest to lowest frequency.'''
3      # create a list of tuples, (value, key)
4      # value_key_list = [(val,key) for key,val in d.items()]
5      value_key_list=[]
6      for key,val in word_count_dict.items():
7          value_key_list.append((val,key))
8      # sort method sorts on list's first element, the frequency.
9      # Reverse to get biggest first
10     value_key_list.sort(reverse=True)
11     # value_key_list = sorted([(v,k) for k,v in value_key_list.items()],
       reverse=True)
12     print('{:11s}{:11s}'.format('Word', 'Count'))
13     print('_'*21)
14     for val,key in value_key_list:
15         print('{:12s} {:<3d}'.format(key,val))
```

Lines 5–7: do the hard work. We iterate through the dictionary using the `items` method. Remember that `items` returns a tuple in the form of `(key, value)` for each dictionary entry. We do multiple assignment to assign the key and value from the returned tuple, and then append them onto the list as a new tuple in `(value, key)`order, the reverse of what `items` provides. Why? The `sort` method compares list elements on their first value if the element is a compound object. Because we want to sort on the frequencies, we need them to be first in the tuple.

Line 4: is commented out: it is a list comprehension that performs all the tasks of Lines 5–7. We show it as an example of alternative ways you can accomplish a task as you become more familiar with Python.

Line 10: then sorts the list using the keyword argument `reverse = True` (note the lowercase first letter `'r'` of reverse). This gives us an order of largest to smallest (the default is smallest to largest, hence the reverse) The remaining code prints out the frequency-word pairs in columns.

Line 11: is commented out. Again, this is a list comprehension that performs all the operations of lines 6–10. Short but a little hard to read.

main

After all that, `main` is pretty straight forward. It initializes the dictionary `word_count_dict`, which gets passed to all the other functions. It opens the predetermined filename, grabs each line and processes that line. It then prints the dictionary. The code is shown in Code Listing 9.5.

Code Listing 9.5

```
def main ():
    word_count_dict={}
    gba_file = open('gettysburg.txt','r')
    for line in gba_file:
        process_line(line, word_count_dict)
    print('Length of the dictionary:',len(word_count_dict))
    pretty_print(word_count_dict)
```

9.2.3 Output and Comments

VideoNote 9.1
Using a Dictionary

An abbreviated output of our code on the Gettysburg Address follows. It has 138 entries, as we discovered in Section 7.5.2, most of which have frequencies of 1. To again reflect the number of unique words, `main` prints the length of the dictionary, which is, in fact, the number of unique words.

```
>>> main()
Length of the dictionary: 138
Word              Count
_______________________
that               13
the                11
we                 10
to                  8
here                8
a                   7
and                 6
of                  5
not                 5
nation              5
it                  5
have                5
...
altogether          1
all                 1
ago                 1
advanced            1
add                 1
above               1
>>>
```

A few things are worth noting:

- The `sort` method will use other elements of a compound object to order objects when the first element is equivalent. Thus all the words with a frequency of 1 are listed in reverse alphabetical order.
- We can easily exclude any word with a frequency of 2 or less in our output. If we do so, the number of words is reduced to only 27. Where would this change be made?
- We could also exclude from the list common, non-meaningful words such as articles (and, the, in, it, etc.). These are often called *stop words* and lists of stop words can be found online. More easily, one can exclude any word with three or fewer letters (which are typically stop words). Where would this change be made?

If we print under the conditions we just listed, frequency greater than 2 and key length greater than 3, we get the following 11 entries:

```
>>> main()
Length of the dictionary: 138
Word               Count
_____________________
that                13
here                 8
nation               5
have                 5
this                 4
dedicated            4
they                 3
shall                3
people               3
great                3
dead                 3
>>>
```

The results here are more interesting. We see that "nation" is used five times, "dedicated" is used four times, and "great", "dead", and "people" are each used three times. Because the Gettysburg Address was given at a dedication of a cemetery for the historic Battle of Gettysburg, the words "dedicated", "great", "dead," and "people" would be expected. The frequent use of "nation" is interesting and indicates that the speech was about more than dedicating the cemetery. Look what our analysis revealed!

9.3 PERIODIC TABLE EXAMPLE

Using a dictionary requires that you first identify the key and value elements to be used. Consider the example of the periodic table of the elements. We can use an element's atomic symbol as a key and store any interesting data as another data structure associated with that key. For example, the symbol for silicon is "Si" and if our dictionary is named "periodic_table," we can access the data on silicon using `periodic_table["Si"]`.

9.3.1 Working with CSV Files

We'll need a periodic table for our data. There are many online, but the particular one we are using here was found as a spreadsheet.[2] Spreadsheets and other application formats often store data in a proprietary format, one developed by the company. However, many can also save the data in the "comma-separated values" (CSV) format that we saw earlier. CSV files are text files and more portable than an application's proprietary format. Typically a CSV file has a single line for each row (in this case, the row with data about a particular element) where each value in the row is separated from the other values by a comma (hence the name). The row information for the periodic table is listed in Figure 9.2. We are particularly interested in the fields that contain the atomic symbol and the atomic mass (rounded).

```
'atomic #','atomic symbol','NewGroup','OldGroup','Period','name', 'atomic mass',...
'1', 'H', '1', 'I A', '1', 'hydrogen', '1.008','±1',...
```

FIGURE 9.2 Periodic table CSV file showing column headers and one row.

However, there is a problem reading the file that is illustrated in the next session. We use ***pass***, the "do nothing" statement (Section 2.2.10), as the suite of this loop as we are testing the loop, not what we get from it.

```
In  [1]: periodic_file = open("Periodic-Table.csv", "r")
In  [2]: for line in periodic_file:
...:     pass

Traceback (most recent call last):
  File "<stdin>", line 1, in <module>
  File "/Library/Frameworks/Python.framework/Versions/3.2/lib/python3.2/codecs.py",
        line 300, in decode
    (result, consumed) = self._buffer_decode(data, self.errors, final)
UnicodeDecodeError: 'utf8' codec can't decode byte 0xb1 in position 461: invalid
                    start byte
```

What happened? First notice the error: "UnicodeDecodeError: `'utf8'` codec can't decode byte 0xb1." The offending symbol can be seen in Figure 9.2 as ± (plus/minus symbol) near the end of the second line. That mathematical symbol doesn't exist in the translation of numbers to characters using the UTF-8 character set. Thus when the file reading routine encounters that symbol, it cannot translate it to text and throws an error. It turns out that this CSV file was generated by Microsoft's Excel spreadsheet software. Microsoft, especially for some of their older products, used a different encoding of numbers to characters that is called in **windows-1252**, the ± (plus/minus).[3] The official name in Python is cp1252 but

[2] http://www.jeffbigler.org/documents/Periodic-Table.xls

[3] https://msdn.microsoft.com/en-us/goglobal/cc305145.aspx

windows-1252 is an alias and more descriptive, so we use it here. We cover this topic in more detail in Section 14.1.7.

If you look at the Microsoft Web page in the footnote, you can see the the ± (plus/minus) symbol is represented by number 177 (in hexadecimal, 0xb1) which is the symbol reported as causing the problem in the error message).

We need to indicate that the file was created with a different encoding to get around this problem. The code to do this is:

```
periodic_file = open("Periodic-Table.csv", "r",encoding="windows-1252")
```

However, setting the correct encoding does not necessarily solve all of our problems. As simple as a CSV format seems, and that was the point after all, to create a simple format, there are small variations in the details of how a CSV file can be created. These small differences in the actual CSV format used can make reading such a file difficult.

Python to the rescue! As we did in Section 7.9.1, we import the `csv` module and then open a file in the normal way, creating a file object. We then create a special `reader` object by calling the function `csv.reader` with an argument of the file. The reader object can be used with **`for`** to iterate through the CSV file. Each iteration yields a row of the file as a list of strings where each element of the list is one of the comma-separated fields in that row.

```
In  [1]: import csv
In  [2]: periodic_file = open("Periodic-Table.csv", "r",encoding="windows-1252")
In  [3]: reader = csv.reader(periodic_file)
In  [4]: for row in reader:
...:         print(row)

# some of the output data
['2', 'He', '18', 'VIII A', '1', 'helium', '4.003', '0', '', '', ...]
['3', 'Li', '1', 'I A', '2', 'lithium', '6.941', '+1', '', '', ... ]
['4', 'Be', '2', 'II A', '2', 'beryllium', '9.012', '+2', '', '', ...]
['5', 'B', '13', 'III A', '2', 'boron', '10.81', '+3', '', '', ...]
# etc. etc.
```

Note a couple of things.

- We opened the file for reading with a different encoding than the default UTF-8, Microsoft's Windows-1252. If you work with enough files, you will run into many file encodings (Mandarin Chinese, Thai, Arabic, etc.) so it is good to remember how to change an encoding.
- We used the `csv` module to help us read the file. Though it is possible to read such a file without the `csv` module, it is useful to know that we can use the module to get through format issues of various files.

You can look at Section 14.1.7 for more detail.

9.3.2 Algorithm Overview

For this example, we will store some general data about each element (extracted from the CSV periodic table) in our dictionary and use the atomic mass of each element to determine a chemical compound's atomic weight. That is, if someone enters the formula for a compound such as sulfuric acid (H_2SO_4) as "H2-S-O4", we can look up the mass of each element, multiply that mass by the count of that element in the compound (e.g., H2 means two hydrogen atoms), then add all the masses together. One challenge will be to parse the compound formula, for example, to separate the atomic symbol of the element and the element count (H2, O4, etc.).

Let's begin with an algorithm:

1. Read in the contents of the periodic table CSV file.
2. Create a dictionary of the periodic table using each element symbol as a key and the remaining CSV file information (shown in Figure 9.2) as the value.
3. Prompt for a compound string and convert it into a list of elements.
4. Parse the compound into symbol-quantity pairs, for example, "H2" becomes ("H", 2).
5. Print the name of each element in the compound.
6. Add each component's atomic mass to the total mass using the information in the dictionary.

9.3.3 Functions for Divide and Conquer

Let's take the top two actions listed previously and create two functions to achieve those goals:

`read_table(file_object)` takes a file object as input and returns a dictionary where the key is the atomic symbol and the values are the remaining information for each element found in the CSV file.

`parse_element(element_string)` takes in a string of the form `'symbol_count'`, such as `'H2'`, and returns a pair in the form `(symbol,count)` such as `('H',2)`.

read_table

The `read_table(data_file)` function takes arguments: an opened file object and a dictionary. Its processing should:

1. Create a `csv.reader` (from the `csv` module) to read the file.
2. Go through every row of the file and extract the atomic symbol (to use as the key) and the remaining values.
3. Place them in the dictionary provided as an argument.

Again, there is no return from the function as the dictionary, a mutable object, is updated in the function. This is shown in Code Listing 9.6.

Code Listing 9.6

```
1  def read_table(a_file, a_dict):
2      """Read Periodic Table file into a dict. with element symbol as key.
3          periodic_file is a file object opened for reading """
4      data_reader = csv.reader(a_file)
5
6      for row in data_reader:
7          # ignore header rows: elements begin with a number
8          if row[0].isdigit():
9              symbol_str = row[1]
10             a_dict[symbol_str] = row[:8]  # ignore end of row
```

Some things to note:

Line 4: We begin with an empty dictionary: `periodic_table = {}`.

Lines 6–10: The ***for*** loop processes each data row. We get the element's symbol: `symbol_str = row[1]`, and then add the element to the dictionary using the symbol as the key. For the dictionary's value, only the first seven fields of the row are used because the rest of the row happens to have extraneous data (the fields are not filled in). The file has quite a few header rows that we wish to discard (they are descriptive of the data that follows). Because every data row begins with a number (the element's atomic number), we can discard any line that does not begin with a number (line 5). Grabbing the first seven fields includes the symbol in the dictionary's value, but it is neither a problem nor an advantage.

parse_element(element_str)

The function `parse_element(element_str)` takes a single string, such as `'H2'`, and converts it to a tuple of symbol and quantity, `('H',2)`. Note a couple of tricky issues:

- `'H2'` should return `('H',2)`
- A singleton, such as `'H'`, should have a quantity 1
- Some symbols have two letters, so `'Si4'` should return `('Si',4)`

The *pattern* is one or more letters followed by zero or more digits.

The function should:

- Gather all the characters at the beginning of the string. These constitute the symbol.

- Gather all the digit characters (which we assume to be digits) after the last character. These constitute the quantity.
- Make the quantity an integer and return the tuple of (symbol, quantity).

The function is shown in Code Listing 9.7.

Code Listing 9.7

```
1 def parse_element(element_str):
2     """Parse element string into symbol and quantity,
3        e.g. Si2 returns ('Si',2)"""
4     symbol_str=""
5     quantity_str = ""
6     for ch in element_str:
7         if ch.isalpha():
8             symbol_str = symbol_str + ch
9         else:
10            quantity_str = quantity_str + ch
11    if quantity_str == "":  # if no number, default is 1
12        quantity_str = "1"
13    return symbol_str, int(quantity_str)
```

Some things to note:

Lines 7–10: The ***if*** statement is used to separate characters from numbers using the `isalpha` method.

Lines 11–12: This ***if*** statement sets the quantity to “1”, if no quantity is found.

assumption: Note that this code assumes a well-formed string of the format indicated. A string with the wrong format will not return the proper value. We'll leave input checking as an exercise for the reader.

With those two functions in hand, we can now write the complete program. We open the file and create an empty dictionary. We call the function with the file and the dictionary. The provided dictionary is updated with the information from the file. We prompt for a hyphen-separated compound and split the compound into a list using `split("-")` to split on hyphens. For each of the now element-number strings (H2, O4), we call `parse_element` function, returning a tuple of (atomic-symbol, element-count). Now we have a symbol that we can use to access the row values stored in `periodic_table[symbol_str]`. We access the name (at index 5) and print it. Then we use the atomic mass (at index 6), convert it to a float, and multiply by the `quantity_int` to calculate the mass that we add onto our total. Here is the program and output using sulfuric acid, H2-S-O4. See Code Listing 9.8.

Code Listing 9.8

```
import csv

def read_table(a_file, a_dict):
    """ '''Read Periodic Table file into a dict. with element symbol as key.
        periodic_file is a file object opened for reading """
    data_reader = csv.reader(a_file)

    for row in data_reader:
        # ignore header rows: elements begin with a number
        if row[0].isdigit():
            symbol_str = row[1]
            a_dict[symbol_str] = row[:8]  # ignore end of row

def parse_element(element_str):
    """Parse element string into symbol and quantity,
       e.g. Si2 returns ('Si',2)"""
    symbol_str=""
    quantity_str = ""
    for ch in element_str:
        if ch.isalpha():
            symbol_str = symbol_str + ch
        else:
            quantity_str = quantity_str + ch
    if quantity_str == "":                  # if no number, default is 1
        quantity_str = "1"
    return symbol_str, int(quantity_str)

# 1. Read File
periodic_file = open("Periodic-Table.csv", "r",encoding="windows-1252")

# 2. Create Dictionary of Periodic Table using element symbols as keys
periodic_dict={}
read_table(periodic_file, periodic_dict)

# 3. Prompt for input and convert compound into a list of elements
compound_str = input("Input a chemical compound, hyphenated, e.g. C-O2: ")
compound_list = compound_str.split("-")

# 4. Initialize atomic mass
mass_float = 0.0
print("The compound is composed of: ", end=' ')

# 5. Parse compound list into symbol-quantity pairs, print name, and add mass
```

```
for c in compound_list:
    symbol_str, quantity_int = parse_element(c)
    print(periodic_dict[symbol_str][5], end=' ') # print element name
    mass_float = mass_float + quantity_int *\
                 float(periodic_dict[symbol_str][6]) # add atomic mass

print("\n\nThe atomic mass of the compound is", mass_float)

periodic_file.close()
```

```
Input a chemical compound, hyphenated, e.g. C-O2: H2-S-O4
The compound is composed of:  hydrogen sulfur oxygen

The atomic weight of the compound is 98.086
```

Notice how convenient it was in this example to access the periodic table using the element's symbol. That is the power of the dictionary data structure.

9.4 SETS

The next built-in data structure we consider is the *set*. Sets should be familiar to you from either elementary or middle school mathematics. Sets in Python are similar to those sets.

9.4.1 History

Sets were invented by Georg Cantor, a German mathematician, in the late 1800s. Though not old by the standards of math, sets have become an integral part of mathematical theory and used to revolutionize many aspects of mathematics. In spite of their power, the main concepts are so simple that they can be taught at an early age.

Let's review the set theory we all learned in elementary and middle school as we learn about Python's sets.

9.4.2 What's in a Set?

A *set* is a collection of objects, regardless of the objects' types. These are the *elements* or *members* of the set. Only *one copy* of any element may exist in the set—a useful characteristic. There is no order to the elements in the set, thus it is, like a dictionary, not a sequence. A set with no elements is the "empty set," also known as the "null set." A set is an iterable, as are all the collections we have seen.

9.4.3 Python Sets

A set is created by calling the `set` constructor or using curly braces and commas. The use of curly braces as a way to construct a set can be a bit confusing as it looks much like the way to construct a dictionary. How to tell them apart? When making a dictionary, the elements are of the form `key:value`, where the colon (`:`) separates the key from the value. In a set, there is only a list of comma separated elements. That is how you may tell the two data structure constructors apart, by the form of their elements.

Furthermore, since empty curly braces are used to create an empty dictionary, you *must* use the `set` constructor to specify an empty set: `set()`. The `set` constructor requires an iterable argument must like the list constructor, e.g. `set('abcd')`. The result is a set with each element of the iterable as a member `'a', 'c', 'b', 'd'`. Again, there is no order to the elements of a set. The order can change as elements are added.

Like a list or a dictionary, a Python set can contain a mixture of types. We illustrate these concepts in the following session:

```
In  [1]: null_set = set() # set() creates the empty set
In  [2]: null_set
Out [2]: set()

In  [3]: a_set = {1,2,3,4} # set constructor. No colons, must be a set
In  [4]: a_set
Out [4]: {1, 2, 3, 4}

In  [5]: b_set = {1,1,2,2,2} # duplicates are ignored
In  [6]: b_set
Out [6]: {1, 2}

In  [7]: c_set = {'a', 1, 2.5, (5,6)} # set of different types is OK
In  [8]: c_set
Out [8]: {(5, 6), 1, 2.5, 'a'}

In  [9]: a_set = set("abcd") # set constructor with iterable argument: a string
In  [10]: a_set
Out [10]: {'a', 'c', 'b', 'd'}                # order not maintained!
```

If duplicate values are added to a Python set, only one such element is actually placed in the set. This means that you can add an element as many times as you wish to a set and only one example of the element will appear.

Python Sets are Mutable

Like lists and dictionaries, sets are a mutable data structure. Though index assignment is not possible on a set (it isn't a sequence), various methods of the set (such as `add` or `remove`) change the elements of a set.

9.4.4 Methods, Operators, and Functions for Python Sets

Typical Operations

`len()` Like all collections, you can determine the number of elements in a set using the `len` function.

`in` Is an element in the set? The *`in`* operator tests membership and returns a Boolean, *`True`* or *`False`*, depending on whether the element is or is not a member of the set.

`for` Like all collections, you can iterate through the elements of a set using the *`for`* statement. The order of the iteration through the objects is not known as sets have no order.

These operations are shown in the following session.

```
In  [1]: my_set = {'a', 'c', 'b', 1, 3, 2}
In  [2]: len(my_set)
Out [2]: 6

In  [3]: 'a' in my_set
Out [3]: True

In  [4]: 'z' in my_set
Out [4]: False

In  [5]: for element in my_set:
...:     print(element,end = ' ')

a 1 2 3 c b
```

9.4.5 Set Methods

Python implements the typical mathematical set operations. There are two ways to call each of these operations: using a method or using a binary operator. The results of either approach are the same, though there is some difference in the way they are used. We note in the explanation of each operation that some are commutative and some are not, that is the order of the operation may or may not matter. The binary operators for set operations are `&, |, -, ^, <=, >=`. Each binary operator takes two sets with an intervening operator such as `a_set & b_set`. The methods available are `intersection, union, difference and symmetric_difference, issubset`, and `issuperset`. For these methods, a set calls the method (using the dot notation) with another collection as the argument. One difference between the binary operators and methods are that the methods approach allows the argument to be *any* iterable collection. The binary operators require both arguments to be sets. Readability is an issue as well. The methods approach makes it clear what operation is being performed though the method names are rather long. The binary operator approach is short but can be difficult to read if you are not clear on the meaning of the binary operator symbols. We will tend to use the methods approach because of the clarity of the method names.

Intersection

Intersection is done using the `&` operator or the `intersection` method. This operation creates a new set of the elements that are common to both sets (Figure 9.3). The order of the sets does not matter.

```
In  [1]: a_set = {'a','b','c','d'}
In  [2]: b_set = {'c','d','e','f'}
In  [3]: a_set & b_set # elements in both a_set and b_set
Out [3]: {'c', 'd'}

In  [4]: b_set & a_set # commutative, order doesn't matter
Out [4]: {'c', 'd'}

In  [5]: a_set.intersection(b_set) # same thing with a method
Out [5]: {'c', 'd'}

In  [6]: a_set.intersection('cdef') # string iterable as an argument
Out [6]: {'c', 'd'}
```

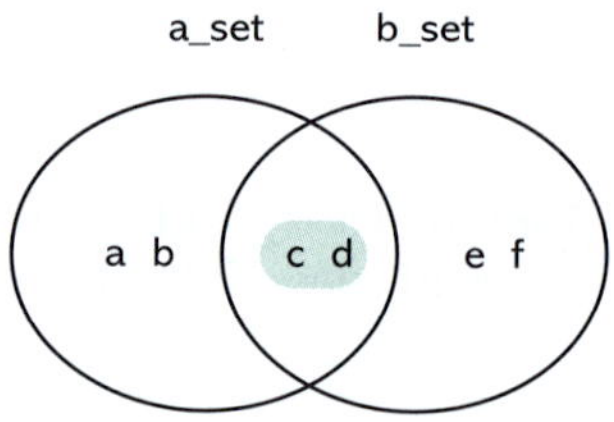

FIGURE 9.3 Intersection of `{'a', 'b', 'c', 'd'}` and `{'c', 'd', 'e', 'f'}`.

Union

Union is done using the `|` operator or the `union` method. Union creates a new set that contains all the elements in both sets (Figure 9.4). The order of the sets does not matter.

```
In  [1]: a_set = {'a','b','c','d'}
In  [2]: b_set = {'c','d','e','f'}
In  [3]: a_set | b_set # union of all elements
Out [3]: {'a', 'c', 'b', 'e', 'd', 'f'}

In  [4]: b_set | a_set # commutative, order doesn't matter
Out [4]: {'a', 'c', 'b', 'e', 'd', 'f'}

In  [5]: a_set.union(b_set) # method approach
Out [5]: {'a', 'c', 'b', 'e', 'd', 'f'}

In  [6]: a_set.union(['c', 'd', 'e', 'f']) # list iterable as an argument
Out [6]: {'a', 'c', 'b', 'e', 'd', 'f'}
```

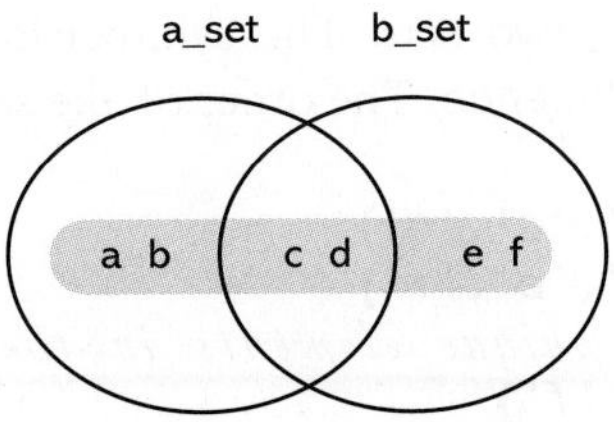

FIGURE 9.4 Union of {'a', 'b', 'c', 'd'} and {'c', 'd', 'e', 'f'}.

Difference

Difference is done using the – operator or the `difference` method. Difference creates a new set whose elements are in the first(calling) set and *not* in the second(argument) set (Figure 9.5). Unlike the other set operators, the difference operator is *not commutative* (much in the same way that integer subtraction is not commutative: 5 − 2 is not the same as 2 − 5).

```
In  [1]: a_set = {'a','b','c','d'}
In  [2]: b_set = {'c','d','e','f'}
In  [3]: a_set - b_set # elements of a_set that are not in b_set
Out [3]: {'a', 'b'}

In  [4]: b_set - a_set # order matters!
Out [4]: {'e', 'f'}

In  [5]: a_set.difference(b_set) # method approach
Out [5]: {'a', 'b'}

In  [6]: b_set.difference(a_set)
Out [6]: {'e', 'f'}

In  [7]: a_set.difference('cdef') # string interable as an argument
Out [7]: {'a', 'b'}
```

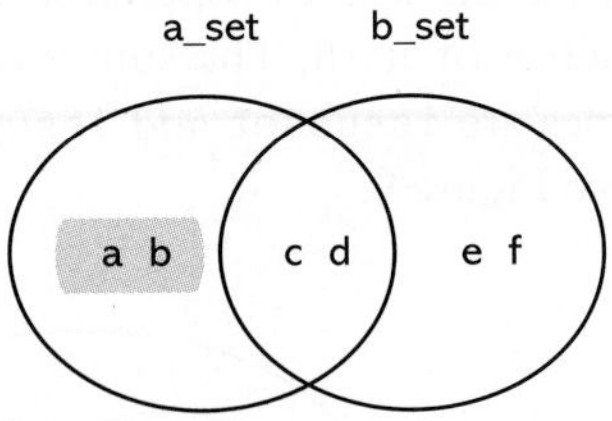

FIGURE 9.5 Difference of {'a', 'b', 'c', 'd'} and {'c', 'd', 'e', 'f'}.

Symmetric Difference

This symmetric difference operation might be new to you. Essentially, symmetric difference is the opposite of intersection. It creates a new set of values that are *different*, not in either, of the two sets. The symmetric difference operator is ^ and the method is `symmetric_difference`. The order of the sets does not matter.

```
In  [1]: a_set = {'a','b','c','d'}
In  [2]: b_set = {'c','d','e','f'}
In  [3]: a_set ^ b_set # unique elements in the sets
Out [3]: {'a', 'b', 'e', 'f'}

In  [4]: b_set ^ a_set # commutative, order doesn't matter
Out [4]: {'a', 'b', 'e', 'f'}

In  [5]: a_set.symmetric_difference(b_set) # method approach
Out [5]: {'a', 'b', 'e', 'f'}

In  [6]: a_set.symmetric_difference('cdef') # string iterable as an argument
Out [6]: {'a', 'b', 'e', 'f'}
```

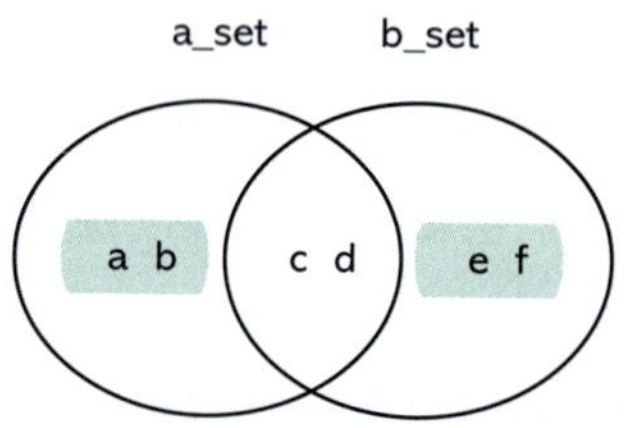

FIGURE 9.6 Symmetric difference of {'a', 'b', 'c', 'd'} and {'c', 'd', 'e', 'f'}.

Subset and Superset

The concept of *subset* and *superset* should be familiar. A set is a subset of another set only if *every* element of the first set is an element of the second set. Superset is the reversed concept: set A is a superset of set B only if set B is a subset of set A. Clearly, the order of set operation matters in these operations; that is, it is not commutative. A set is both a subset and a superset of itself. The subset operator is <= and the superset operator is >=. The method names are `issubset` and `issuperset`. All four of these operations return a Boolean value. See Figure 9.7.

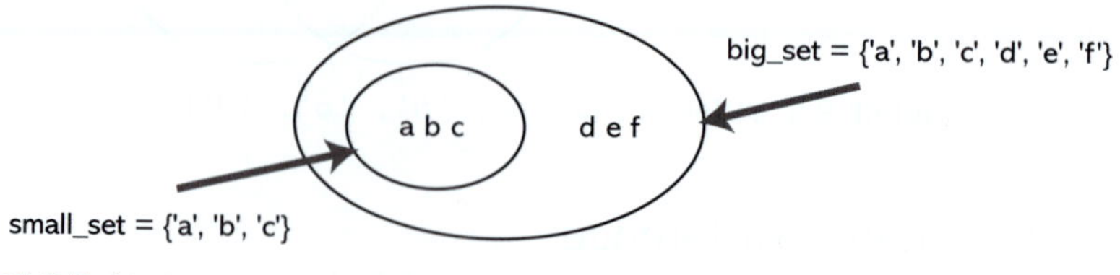

FIGURE 9.7 {'a', 'b', 'c'} is a subset of {'a', 'b', 'c', 'd', 'e', 'f'}.

```
In  [1]: small_set = {'a', 'b', 'c'}
In  [2]: big_set = set('abcedf')
In  [3]: small_set <= big_set # subset
Out [3]: True

In  [4]: big_set >= small_set # superset
Out [4]: True

In  [5]: big_set <= big_set # each set is a sub of itself
Out [5]: True

In  [6]: small_set >= small_set # each set is a super of itself
Out [6]: True

In  [7]: small_set >= big_set
Out [7]: False

In  [8]: small_set.issubset('abcdef') # string iterable as argument
Out [8]: True

In  [9]: small_set.issuperset('abcdef') # string iterable as argument
Out [9]: False
```

Check Yourself: Set Check

1. Indicate the requested output for the following program.

```
def f1 (s1,s2,op=4):
    if op == 1:
        temp = s1.intersection(s2)
    elif op == 2:
        temp = s1.difference(s2)
    else:
        temp = s1.union(s2)
    return temp

set1 = {'ab'}
set2 = {'cd'}

print(f1(set1,set2))          # Line 1
print(f1(set1,set2,1))        # Line 2
print(f1(set1,set2,2))        # Line 3
```

(a) What output is produced by Line 1 of the program?
(b) What output is produced by Line 2 of the program?
(c) What output is produced by Line 3 of the program?

Other Set methods

There are a few other set methods that you might find useful;

`add(element)` adds the element to the set. There is no effect if the element is already in the set (remember, only one copy of an element in a set). It modifies the set, so there is no return value.

`clear()` Removes all the elements of the set (making it empty).

`remove(element)` and `discard(element)` Both methods remove the element if it exists. The difference is that `remove` will cause an error if the element being removed is not part of the set. In contrast, `discard` will not give an error even if the argument being removed does not exist in the set. There is no value returned.

`copy()` Returns a *shallow* copy of the set.

9.5 SET APPLICATIONS

There are many applications that can make use of sets. However, two general categories are worth mentioning:

- Finding the unique elements (of a list, file, etc.). It is relatively simple to accomplish with a set. Just add each element to the set and let the set deal with multiples copies.
- Finding various combinations of elements using the set operators.

9.5.1 Relationship between Words of Different Documents

Earlier in this chapter (Section 9.2.2), we counted the frequency of words in a file using the Gettysburg Address as an example. Let's build on this work to do even more file analysis, by comparing the words used in two different files to see what that might tell us about the documents. We will use sets to discover properties such as the common words, the number of unique words used by both, and the number of unique words used in each document. For this example, we will continue to use the Gettysburg Address and compare its contents to the Declaration of Independence.

The good news is that the outline of work from Section 9.2.2—even some of the code itself—can be reused or only slightly modified to solve this new problem. Code reuse is one of the advantages of good, modular design. Functions that solve a problem well can be used in other contexts with little or no change required.

Here is a list of functions we will reuse. Modifications are described as well.

add_word: Add each word to the set. Parameters are the word and a set. No return value. This function must be modified from its previous definition to use the appropriate set methods.

process_line: There is some work to be done to process the line: strip off various characters, split out the words, and so on. Parameters are a line and the set. It calls `add_word` with each processed word. No return value. Happily, this function can be used as is! Though the parameter names are inappropriate for this context, the code functions perfectly.

pretty_print: The parameters are the two file sets. No return value. *As the output required is quite different, this function will have to be rewritten.*

main: We will use a main function as the main program. As before it will open each file and call `process_line` on each line. When finished, it will call `pretty_print` and print the results for the two sets. *This function requires some slight modifications.*

Let's take a look at the functions in detail.

add_word

We are working with sets, so we must use different methods—in particular the `add` method. Again, it is useful to note that this change is isolated in this function. We need not change other parts of the code to deal with changing the set. The code is shown in Code Listing 9.9.

Code Listing 9.9

```
1 def add_word(word, word_set):
2     '''Add the word to the set. No word smaller than length 3.'''
3     if len(word) > 3:
4         word_set.add(word)
```

As we hinted at in Section 9.2.2, it is useful to treat any word of length 3 or less as a stopword. The `if` statement on line 3 does this.

process_line

This code is untouched from the previous version except to use an appropriate parameter name for this context. The code is shown in Code Listing 9.10.

Code Listing 9.10

```
import string
def process_line(line, word_set):
    '''Process the line to get lowercase words to be added to the set.'''
    line = line.strip()
    word_list = line.split()
    for word in word_list:
        # ignore the '--' that is in the file
```

```
    if word != '--':
        word = word.strip()
        # get commas, periods and other punctuation out as well
        word = word.strip(string.punctuation)
        word = word.lower()
        add_word(word, word_set)
```

main

The main program is modified slightly. We must now open two files to do the comparison, and for each we must create a set for processing and then process all the lines of the file using `process_line`. After both sets are created, we call `pretty_print` with the two sets to print out the information. The code is shown in Code Listing 9.11.

Code Listing 9.11

```
def main ():
    '''Compare the Gettysburg Address and the Declaration of Independence.'''
    gettysburg_address_set = set()
    declaration_of_independence_set = set()
    gettysburg_file = open('gettysburg.txt')
    declaration_independence_file = open('declOfInd.txt')
    for line in gettysburg_file:
        process_line(line, gettysburg_address_set)
    for line in declaration_independence_file:
        process_line(line,declaration_of_independence_set)
    pretty_print(gettysburg_address_set, declaration_of_independence_set)
```

pretty_print

The main differences of the programs are here. The function takes the two sets as parameters and then prints out various pieces of information about the documents. At the end, we print out the common words in a nice format as well. As is often the case with print-oriented code, it appears complicated, but each element is straight forward. The code is shown in Code Listing 9.12.

Some comments.

Line 4: We print the lengths of the two sets. These lengths represent the number of unique words (no duplicates in a set, remember) for each document. Because of the change we made to `add_word`, these are only the words of length four or greater.

Code Listing 9.12

```
1 def pretty_print(ga_set, doi_set):
2     # print some stats about the two sets
3     print('Count of unique words of length 4 or greater')
4     print('Gettysburg Addr: {}, Decl of Ind: {}\n'.format(len(ga_set),len(doi_set)))
5     print('{:15s} {:15s}'.format('Operation', 'Count'))
6     print('-'*35)
7     print('{:15s} {:15d}'.format('Union', len(ga_set.union(doi_set))))
8     print('{:15s} {:15d}'.format('Intersection', len(ga_set.intersection(doi_set))))
9     print('{:15s} {:15d}'.format('Sym Diff', len(ga_set.symmetric_difference(doi_set))))
10    print('{:15s} {:15d}'.format('GA-DoI', len(ga_set.difference(doi_set))))
11    print('{:15s} {:15d}'.format('DoI-GA', len(doi_set.difference(ga_set))))
12
13    # list the intersection words, 5 to a line, alphabetical order
14    intersection_set = ga_set.intersection(doi_set)
15    word_list = list(intersection_set)
16    word_list.sort()
17    print('\n Common words to both')
18    print('-'*20)
19    count = 0
20    for w in word_list:
21        if count % 5 == 0:
22            print()
23        print('{:13s}'.format(w), end=' ')
24        count += 1
```

Lines 7–12: Here we print out the lengths, not the contents, of the sets that result from various set operations. We format the results in two columns.

Lines 14–16: The only contents we'll print are the intersection result, as it is the smallest. We create the intersection set, then turn the contents into a list. We do this because it would be nice to list the common words in alphabetical order and sets are unordered. Once converted to a list, we sort the list. Alternatively, we could have used the function `sorted`.

Line 20–24: All of this code is to print the list of sorted words in a five-column format. We iterate through the list and print each word one at a time. That print statement on line 23 has `end=' '` so that no new line character is printed. All the words will print to the same line. However, we keep a variable `count` to track how many words are printed. Every fifth word triggers the ***if*** statement on line 21, which prints a blank line. The result is that the code prints five columns of words.

9.5.2 Output and Comments

The session below show the output of the program on the two files.

```
In  [1]: main()
Count of unique words of length 4 or greater

Gettysburg Addr: 100, Decl of Ind: 487

      Operation          Result
-----------------------------------
          Union             556
   Intersection              31
       Sym Diff             525
         GA-DoI              69
         DoI-GA             456

 Common words to both
--------------------

        cause        civil      created        earth        equal
         from         full   government        great         have
         here      liberty        lives         long       nation
       people        power    remaining        shall       should
         that        their        these         they         this
        those         thus        under        which         will
        world
```

We can confirm that these numbers make sense. The sum of the two sets is 587, but the intersection has 31 words, meaning that the union should have a count of $587 - 31 = 556$. Good so far. The `Gettysburg_addr - Decl_of_Independence` should be the difference of the first set size minus the common set size, $100 - 31 = 69$. Also good. The symmetric difference should be the difference between the union size and the intersection size, $556 - 31 = 525$. All good.

As for the common (intersection) words, they are interesting to see. Words appear that you would expect such as "nation", "liberty", "government," "people," and so on.

9.6 SCOPE: THE FULL STORY

In Section 8.1, we defined the term "scope," mostly as it applies to functions. Now that we have dictionaries, we can provide a more complete explanation. A novice programmer can get by without a complete understanding of scope, but a greater understanding is useful as you advance in Python (or another programming language). Also, a better understanding of scope can help interpret some error messages.

9.6.1 Namespaces and Scope

Remember, a namespace is a relation between names and objects. We use a namespace to determine what object is associated with a variable. It is easy to think of a namespace as a dictionary, where the keys are the names and the values are the objects.[4] In Python, there can be multiple namespaces. These namespaces do not share names. A name in one namespace can have as a value any Python object, and the same name in different namespaces can be associated with a different object. However, multiple namespaces can work together to resolve a name if a name-resolution protocol exists. That is, if there are multiple namespaces (and there always are), we can define an order of search to look through different namespaces to find a name (or find that the name does not exist in any recognized namespace). That process defines scope in Python.

In Python, we resolve names by defining a search rule that defines the order that Python looks through multiple namespaces to find a name (or find that the name is not yet defined).

9.6.2 Search Rule for Scope

In the book *Learning Python*,[5] the authors define a lovely acronym that summarizes the Python rule for scope. He calls it the *LEGB* rule, where the letters stand for:

- **L**ocal
- **E**nclosing
- **G**lobal
- **B**uilt-in

This *LEGB* rule defines the sequence of namespaces examined when looking for a name (variable name, function name, etc.). If the entire sequence is examined and the name is not found, then Python returns an error. Let's take a look at each of the namespaces searched.

9.6.3 Local

The local namespace is the namespace that we discussed in Section 8.1 in the context of a function. It is the namespace within a function that comes into being when the function is invoked and becomes inactive when the function invocation ends. While the local namespace is active, it is the first namespace that is checked for the existence of a name. If the name is

---

[4] The Python documentation notes that, although namespaces are currently implemented as dictionaries, it would be dangerous to count on that fact, as the implementation might change!

[5] *Learning Python*, 3rd Edition, by: Mark Lutz, Published by O'Reilly Media, Inc., ©2007 Mark Lutz, All rights reserved. Used by Permission of O'Reilly Media, Inc.

found in the local namespace, then the associated object (or an error if the name exists but no value is yet associated) is returned. Look at Code Listing 9.13 and session.

Code Listing 9.13

```
global_X = 27

def my_function(param1=123, param2='hi mom'):
    local_X = 654.321
    print('\n=== local namespace ===')
    for key,val in locals().items():
        print('key:{}, object:{}'.format(key, str(val)))
    print('local_X:',local_X)
    print('global_X:',global_X)

my_function()
```

```
=== local namespace ===
key:local_X, object:654.321
key:param1, object:123
key:param2, object:hi mom
local_X: 654.321
global_X: 27
```

The special function `locals` takes no arguments and returns a dictionary of the local namespace—in this case, the namespace found in the function `my_function` while it is running. Notice that there are three entries: the two parameters `param1` and `param2` and the variable created by assignment in the function suite, `local_X`. Further, notice that the variable `global_X` assigned outside of the function is not found in the local namespace of the function. Yet, as evidenced by the print statement, it is available and can be printed in the function.

Python is able to resolve `global_X` because `global_X` is in the global namespace. The search rule, LEGB, says to look first in the local space (then in the Enclosing space—described later), and then in the global space. Let's look at the global namespace.

9.6.4 Global

One place where a namespace is maintained is in a module. Modules are Python files, and they contain objects such as functions that can be imported and used by other programs. The `math` module is the one we've discussed the most. When a module such as `math` is imported, that module brings with it a namespace that relates all the names of the module to objects. This namespace can be observed by looking at the dictionary stored in `__dict__` in each module. This dictionary is the namespace for the module.

If we want to reference one of the objects in a module such as `math`, we precede the associated name with the module name using dot notation. When we do so, we are asking for the object associated with a name in that module. For example, `math.pi` is a request for the object (in this case, a floating-point number) associated with the name `pi` in the `math` module.

When the Python interpreter starts up, it loads two default modules without requiring an import: the module `__main__` and the module `__builtins__`. The `__main__` is the default, global module in which all new objects are stored. The dictionary of that namespace can be accessed by using the function `globals`. Like the previously observed `locals` function, `globals` returns a dictionary representing the global namespace. When we type interactively to the Python interpreter, `globals` is the active namespace.

Look at Code Listing 9.14 and resulting session. The function `my_function` is identical to the function in the previous example.

Code Listing 9.14

```python
import math
global_X = 27

def my_function(param1=123, param2='hi mom'):
    local_X = 654.321
    print('\n=== local namespace ===')
    for key,val in locals().items():
        print('key: {}, object: {}'.format(key, str(val)))
    print('local_X:',local_X)
    print('global_X:',global_X)

my_function()

key,val = 0,0 # add to the global namespace. Used below
print('\n--- global namespace ---')
for key,val in globals().items():
    print('key: {:15s} object: {}'.format(key, str(val)))

print('\n-----------------------')
#print 'Local_X:', local_X
print('Global_X:', global_X)
print('Math.pi:',math.pi)
print('Pi:',pi)
```

```
=== local namespace ===
key: local_X, object: 654.321
key: param1, object: 123
key: param2, object: hi mom
local_X: 654.321
global_X: 27

--- global namespace ---
key: my_function     object: <function my_function at 0xe15a30>
key: __builtins__    object: <module '__builtin__' (built-in)>
key: __package__     object: None
key: global_X        object: 27
key: __name__        object: __main__
key: __doc__         object: None
key: math            object: <module 'math' from '/Library/Frameworks/Python.
framework/Versions/2.6/lib/python2.6/lib-dynload/math.so'>

----------------------
Global_X: 27
Math.pi: 3.14159265359
Pi:

Traceback (most recent call last):
  File "/Volumes/Admin/Book/chapterDictionaries/localsAndGlobals.py", line 22, in
<module>
    print('Pi:',pi)
NameError: name 'pi' is not defined
```

The `local` function results are exactly as in the previous example, but we now also print the global values. Notice a few things. First, `global_X` is indeed in the global namespace, which is why the print statement in `my_function` does work. Python first looks in the local namespace, fails, and moves on to look in the global namespace as it follows the LEGB rule.

Second, `my_function` is itself a name in the global namespace! Finally, the variable `local_X` is not in the global namespace. If we try to print its value, we get an error. There is an error, because at that point in the program, outside of the running function, the function's namespace is unavailable. The function's namespace is active only while the suite of the function is actually executing.

Third, `math` is now a name in the global namespace due to the import of the math module, so we can use `math` as a prefix to names in that module. When we print `math.pi`, we get a value, but when we print `pi` by itself, we get an error. That name `pi` is not in the global namespace!

The Local Assignment Rule

One interesting effect of Python's approach is something we call the *local assignment rule.* If anywhere in a function an assignment is made, then that assignment is assumed to create a name *only in the presently active namespace*. This has the sometimes painful side effect shown in Code Listing 9.15.

Code Listing 9.15

```

my_var = 27

def my_function(param1=123, param2='Python'):
    for key,val in locals().items():
        print('key {}: {}'.format(key, str(val)))
    my_var = my_var + 1      # causes an error!

my_function(123456, 765432.0)
```

```
key param2: 765432.0
key param1: 123456
Traceback (most recent call last):
  File "localAssignment1.py", line 9, in <module>
    my_function(123456, 765432.0)
  File "localAssignment1.py", line 7, in my_function
    my_var = my_var + 1      # causes an error!
UnboundLocalError: local variable 'my_var' referenced before assignment
```

We first create the variable `my_var` by assignment in the global namespace. The natural expectation is that, when we try to add 1 to that value within the function, the function looks in the local namespace, cannot find it, and moves on to the name in the global namespace. Sadly, that is not how it works.

Python makes the following assumption. If an assignment of a variable takes place *anywhere* in the suite of a function, Python adds the name to the local namespace. The statement `my_var = my_var + 1` has an assignment of the name `my_var`. Python assumes, no matter where the assignment occurs, that `my_var` is part of the local namespace of the function `my_function`. When Python tries to add 1 to `my_var`, the name is in the local namespace but has no value (yet), so Python generates an error.

The problem is *when* Python decides to make `my_var` local. It does so *before* the code is run, that is, when Python encounters the function definition. As the local namespace is created (before the code actually runs), Python examines the code and populates its local namespace. Before it runs the offending line, it sees the assignment to `my_var` and adds it to the local namespace. When the function is executed, the Python interpreter finds that `my_var` is in the local namespace but has no value yet—generating an error.

The global Statement

There is a way around this conundrum. If, within a function suite, a variable is declared to be a global variable using the **global** statement, then Python will not create a local name in the namespace for that variable. The following session shows the change in the new function better_function while keeping the old code around for comparison. The updated code is shown in Code Listing 9.16.

Code Listing 9.16

```python

my_var = 27

def my_function(param1=123, param2='Python'):
    for key,val in locals().items():
        print('key {}: {}'.format(key, str(val)))
    my_var = my_var + 1          # causes an error!

def better_function(param1=123, param2='Python'):
    global my_var
    for key,val in locals().items():
        print('key {}: {}'.format(key, str(val)))
    my_var = my_var + 1
    print('my_var:',my_var)



# my_function(123456, 765432.0)
better_function()
```

```
key param2: Python
key param1: 123
my_var: 28
```

9.6.5 Built-Ins

As we mentioned earlier, there are two namespaces that are created when Python starts: __main__ and __builtins__. The latter is a link to all the regular Python programs and data types that are provided by default. Following the LEGB search rule, if Python cannot find a name in first the local namespace, then the global namespace, it looks for a Python built-in name.

The builtin module, like other modules, has a __dict__ attribute, which is the module's namespace. The following code will print out the key-value pairs in that namespace. The output from Code Listing 9.17 is too long to include here.

Code Listing 9.17

```

builtin_dict = __builtins__.__dict__
print('Builtin dictionary has {} entries\n'.format(len(builtin_dict)))

for key,val in builtin_dict.items():
    print('key:: {:20s} val:: {}'.format(key,str(val)))
```

9.6.6 Enclosed

An astute reader will note that we skipped one letter: what about the "E" in the LEGB rule, the "Enclosed" namespace? A beginning programmer may not encounter this situation, but we include it for completeness.

The "Enclosed" scope rule applies when a function defines a function; that is, within a function's suite, a new function is defined. Take a look at the code and output in Code Listing 9.18.

Code Listing 9.18

```

global_var = 27

def outer_function(param_outer = 123):
    outer_var = global_var + param_outer

    def inner_function(param_inner = 0):
        # get inner, enclosed and global
        inner_var = param_inner + outer_var + global_var
        # print inner namespace
        print('\n--- inner local namespace ---')
        for key,val in locals().items():
            print('{}:{}'.format(key,str(val)))
        return inner_var

    result = inner_function(outer_var)
    # print outer namespace
    print('\n--- outer local namespace ---')
    for key,val in locals().items():
        print('{}:{}'.format(key,str(val)))
    return result

result  = outer_function(7)
print('\n--- result ---')
print('Result:',result)
```

```
--- inner local namespace ---
outer_var:34
inner_var:95
param_Inner:34

--- outer local namespace ---
outer_var:34
param_Outer:7
result:95
inner_function:<function inner_function at 0xe2ba30>

--- result ---
Result: 95
```

The `inner_function` is defined within the suite of `outer_function`. In the session output, you can see that `inner_function` is part of the local namespace of `outer_function`, meaning that *only* code within the suite of the `outer_function` can call `inner_function`. Said another way, the `inner_function` is available for execution only during the execution of `outer_function`. The full LEGB rule is to check the local namespace, then any functions that enclose our local namespace, as `outer_function` encloses `inner_function`, then the global namespace, and ending with the built-ins. The output shows the dependencies of the various pieces.

For the beginning programmer, this kind of "nested" function is uncommon. Still, it does show fairly clearly how the scope search rule of Python works.

9.7 USING ZIP TO CREATE DICTIONARIES

An interesting and very useful operator is `zip`, which creates pairs from two parallel sequences. The `zip` operator works like a zipper to merge multiple sequences into a list of tuples. It is not special to dictionaries, but when combined with the *dict* constructor, it provides a useful way to create dictionaries from sequences.

```
In  [1]: keys = ["red","white","blue"]
In  [2]: values = [100, 300, 500]
In  [3]: d = dict(zip(keys,values))
In  [4]: d
Out [4]: {'blue': 500, 'white': 300, 'red': 100}
```

The `zip` function provides another way to reverse key-value pairs, but it is possible only if values are immutable so that they are allowable as keys. Here is a session that reverses the key-value pairs of the previous session:

```
In  [1]: d
Out [1]: {'blue': 500, 'white': 300, 'red': 100}

In  [2]: d2 = dict(zip(d.values(), d.keys()))
```

```
In  [3]: d2
Out [3]: {300: 'white', 500: 'blue', 100: 'red'}
```

9.8 DICTIONARY AND SET COMPREHENSIONS

VideoNote 9.2
More Dictionaries

In Section 7.11, we introduced the idea of a comprehension and, in the context of the list collection, the list comprehension. Because we know about two more collections, it turns out there are two more comprehensions we can work with: the dictionary and set comprehension. The general format is as with lists, but the brackets are different:

{expression ***for***-clause condition}

Dictionary and set comprehensions both use curly braces, but dictionaries are differentiated by the colon used to separate the elements of the expression part of the comprehension. The set comprehension returns a set and the dictionary comprehension returns a dictionary. In the following session, we create a dictionary, reverse its key-value pairs, and then create a list for sorting.

```
In  [1]: a_dict = {k:v for k,v in enumerate('abcdefg')}
In  [2]: a_dict
Out [2]: {0: 'a', 1: 'b', 2: 'c', 3: 'd', 4: 'e', 5: 'f', 6: 'g'}

In  [3]: b_dict = {v:k for k,v in a_dict.items()} # reverse key—value pairs
In  [4]: b_dict
Out [4]: {'a': 0, 'c': 2, 'b': 1, 'e': 4, 'd': 3, 'g': 6, 'f': 5}

In  [5]: sorted(b_dict) # only sorts keys
Out [5]: ['a', 'b', 'c', 'd', 'e', 'f', 'g']

In  [6]: b_list = [(v,k) for v,k in b_dict.items()] # create list
In  [7]: sorted(b_list) # then sort
Out [7]: [('a', 0), ('b', 1), ('c', 2), ('d', 3), ('e', 4), ('f', 5), ('g', 6)]
```

Set comprehension is similar. Again note that we can differentiate the set from the dictionary comprehension by the lack of colon in the expression part of the comprehension. Note how when building the set we end up with unique items.

```
In  [1]: a_set = {ch for ch in 'to be or not to be'}
In  [2]: a_set
Out [2]: {' ', 'b', 'e', 'o', 'n', 'r', 't'}  # set of unique characters

In  [3]: sorted(a_set)
Out [3]: [' ', 'b', 'e', 'n', 'o', 'r', 't']
```

VISUAL VIGNETTE

9.9 BAR GRAPH OF WORD FREQUENCY

Having constructed the dictionary of word-frequency pairs, it would be interesting to plot the words versus their frequency to visualize the results. Pylab provides a `bar` command to plot bar charts, so that is a natural choice.

There are three general steps to make the bar chart in this case. The first is to set up the *x*-axis to use the words as the labels. The second is to get the dictionary data gathered together in the appropriate format for plotting (that will be the *y*-data). The third is to actually make the plot. Let's see some code, then go through these issues one at a time. We add a new function, the `bar_graph` function, that takes as a parameter our `word_count_dict` from Section 9.2.2 and plots a bar graph of word versus frequency. The code is shown in Code Listing 9.19.

Code Listing 9.19

```python
def bar_graph(word_count_dict):
    '''bar graph of word—frequency, xaxis labeled with words'''
    # collect key and value list for plotting
    word_list = []
    for key,val in word_count_dict.items():
        if val>2 and len(key)>3:
            word_list.append((key,val))
    word_list.sort()
    key_list = [key for key,val in word_list]
    value_list = [val for key,val in word_list]
    # get ticks as the keys/words
    bar_width=0.5
    number_of_keys = len(key_list)
    x_values = pylab.linspace(0, number_of_keys-1, number_of_keys)
    pylab.xticks(x_values+bar_width/2, key_list, rotation=45)
    # create the bar graph
    pylab.bar(x_values, value_list, width=bar_width, color='r')
    pylab.show()
```

9.9.1 Getting the Data Right

Ultimately, what we want are two lists: a list of the keys in alphabetical order (*x*-values) and another corresponding list of values (*y*-values). "Corresponding" means that we want the index of the key list to "line up" with its associated value in the value list. Let's take a look:

Lines 4–7: We make a list `word_list` and append onto it all the key-value pairs as tuples from `word_count_dict`. As we did in Section 9.2.2, we take only those words that appear to be important: frequencies greater than 2 and word length greater than 3. We order the tuples in (key,value) order, actually (word,frequency) in our case because we want to then sort the list into alphabetical order on the words. Thus, we need the key to be first in each tuple.

Lines 9–10: We then create the two lists, `key_list` and `value_list`, that contain the keys and the values, respectively. The index of the keys and values are aligned, that is, the key at index 0 corresponds to the value at index 0 and so forth. We use a list comprehension in both cases.

9.9.2 Labels and the `xticks` Command

Pylab provides a command to orient and label each x-axis entry. These entries are often called "ticks," so the commands to label them are called `xticks` and `yticks`. If you do not provide such a command, ticks will be labeled with the x-values used. However, you have the option to say what each tick label should be and where it should be located. Let's look.

Line 12: We set a width `bar_width` for the width of our bars in the graph.

Line 13: We set `number_of_keys` to make the expression in the next line easier to read.

Line 14: We create a list with numbers from 0 to the `number_of_keys-1`. We use the pylab function `linspace`, to generate the list (see Appendix D). These `x_values` will be the domain of the plot and will also be the number of xticks on our graph.

Line 15: The `xticks` command takes three arguments. The first argument is a list of locations of the ticks. To each element of the list we center the label by adding an offset to each tick position using the `bar_width` divided by 2. The addition-division is done to each element of the `x_values` list (see Appendix D for more details). The second argument is the list of labels, the `key_list`. The third argument is optional and specifies to rotate each label 45 degrees.

9.9.3 Plotting

Lines 17–18 do the plotting. The `bar` command takes four arguments here. The first is the list of xtick locations. The labels were set previously by the `xticks` command. The second is the list of values to plot, the `value_list`. The last two are plot options, the bar width and the bar color. The `show` command then draws the plot.

The plot is shown in Figure 9.8.

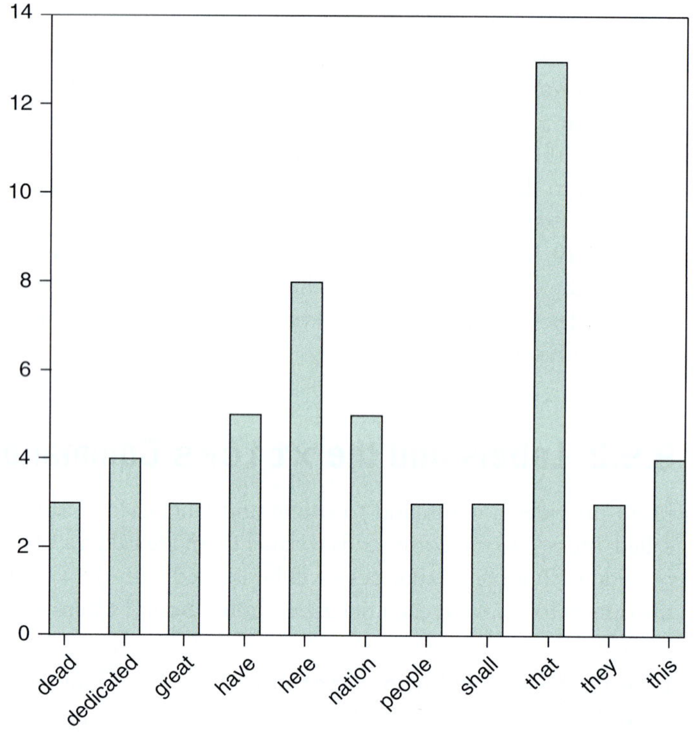

FIGURE 9.8 Bar graph of the Gettysburg Address "important" word frequencies.

9.10 GUI TO COMPARE FILES

We are going to develop a GUI based on the comparison of two files problem in Section 9.5.1. As before, we have our five issues to worry about in our template solution:

1. What GUI form fields to include.
2. A function Model for our problem (our program).
3. Any specific text we want to occur in HTML View .
4. Creating the `InputForm` with the GUI fields and naming those fields in the Controller, using them in the View.
5. Change some variable names in the Controller.

Before we dive in this time, let's take a look at what we are trying to build: see Figure 9.9.

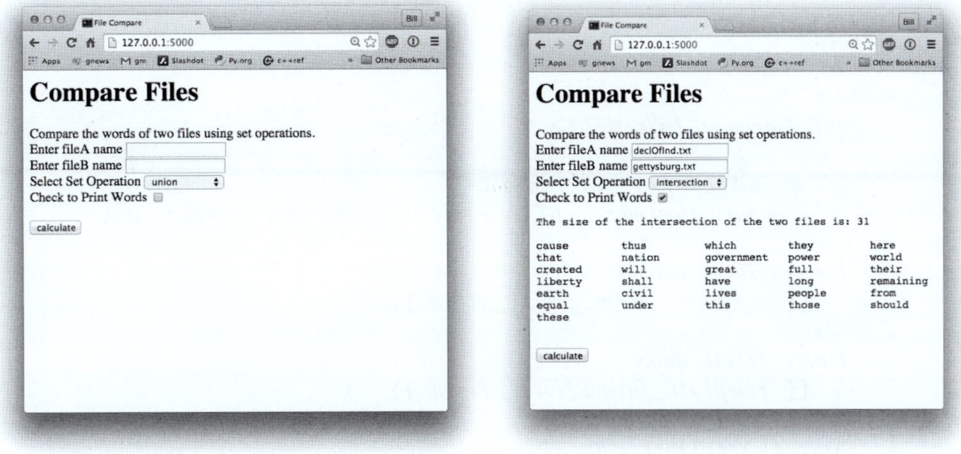

(a) Startup (b) Successful Comparison

FIGURE 9.9 The file comparison GUI example. [William F. Punch, Richard J. Enbody.]

We are generalizing the work done in Section 9.5.1 so that we can:

- Select the two text files to compare.
- Select the set operation to perform on the file words.
- Display the resulting words if we like.

9.10.1 Controller and View

Let's start with the controller and view. Consider Code Listing 9.20.

Code Listing 9.20

```
from flask import Flask, render_template_string, request
from wtforms import Form,  SelectField, TextField, BooleanField, validators
from program9_compute import compute

app = Flask(__name__)

# html page is the view.
page = '''
<html>
    <head>
        <title> File Compare</title>
```

```
  </head>

  <body>
    <h1>Compare Files</h1>

    <form method=post action="">
        Compare the words of two files using set operations.
    <br>
     Enter fileA name
        {{ template_form.fileA_field }}
    <br>
     Enter fileB name
        {{ template_form.fileB_field }}
    <br>
     Select Set Operation
        {{ template_form.select_field }}
    <br>
     Check to Print Words
        {{ template_form.boolean_field }}
    <br>
      {% if result != None %}
          {{ result }}
      {% endif %}
    <br>
      <input type=submit value=calculate>
    </form>
  </body>
</html>
'''

# InputForm and below is our controller
class InputForm(Form):
    fileA_field = TextField(validators=[validators.InputRequired()])
    fileB_field = TextField(validators=[validators.InputRequired()])
    select_field = SelectField(
        choices=[('union','union'),('intersection','intersection'),
                 ('a-b', 'a-b'), ('b-a', 'b-a')],
        validators=[validators.InputRequired()])
    boolean_field = BooleanField()

@app.route('/', methods=['GET', 'POST'])
def index():
    result_str = None
    form = InputForm(request.form)
    if request.method == 'POST' and form.validate():
```

```
57         fileA_val = form.fileA_field.data
58         fileB_val = form.fileB_field.data
59         select_val = form.select_field.data
60         boolean_val = form.boolean_field.data
61         result_str = compute(fileA_val, fileB_val, select_val, boolean_val)
62     return render_template_string(page, template_form=form, result=result_str)
63 
64 if __name__ == '__main__':
65     app.run(debug=True)
```

Our `InputForm`, **Lines 44–49**, is a little more complicated as we are using more fields here; 4 in fact. We have used the `TextField` in earlier examples, but the `SelectField` and `BooleanField` are new, though they were covered briefly in Section E.4.3.

The `SelectField`, **Line 46**, is for a pull-down menu. It takes two arguments: a list of tuples assigned to `choices` and the typical validator we have added to each field. Each tuple represents a pull-down menu label (the first element) and a value returned by the field if the menu label is selected (the second element). For our pull-down, we use the same two strings for both the label and the return value.

The `BooleanField`, **Line 50**, is for a check box which returns either *`True`* if the box is checked or *`False`*. We **do not** put a validator on this field because doing so would **require** the box to be checked, which we have chosen to not require.

We place those fields in the View section, as we have done previously, in **Lines 20-31** with `<br>` tags separating them.

We gather the results of filling out the fields in **Lines 57-60** and provide them as arguments to the `compute` function in **Line 61**.

9.10.2 Function Model

As we did previously, we have separated the code for the function Model into its own separate file. The code being used is very similar to the code in Section 9.5.1. In fact, both the `add_word` and `process_word` are exactly the same. Hurray for function reuse! Thus, we only show the modified `compute` and `pretty_print` functions in Code Listing 9.21.

Code Listing 9.21

```
def pretty_print(the_set, op_str, bool_val):
    ''' return a <pre> ... </pre> string with the size, and potentially the
    contents, of the set
    '''
```

```
    sz = len(the_set)
    result_str = "<pre>\n"
    result_str += "The size of the {:s} of the two files is:
                   {:d}\n".format(op_str, sz)
    if bool_val:
        count = 0
        for w in the_set:
            if count % 5 == 0:
                result_str += "\n"
            result_str += '{:13s}'.format(w)
            count += 1
    result_str += "</pre>"
    return result_str

def compute (fileA_str, fileB_str, select_str, boolean_val):
    '''Compare two files using a set operation'''
    fileA_set = set()
    fileB_set = set()
    fileA_obj = open(fileA_str)
    fileB_obj = open(fileB_str)
    for line in fileA_obj:
        process_line(line, fileA_set)
    for line in fileB_obj:
        process_line(line, fileB_set)
    if select_str == "union":
        result_set = fileA_set | fileB_set
    elif select_str == "intersection":
        result_set = fileA_set & fileB_set
    elif select_str == "a-b":
        result_set = fileA_set - fileB_set
    else:
        result_set = fileB_set - fileA_set

    return pretty_print(result_set, select_str, boolean_val)
```

The `compute` function is similar to the `main` function in Section 9.5.1 with the following exceptions:

- `compute` takes in two arguments which are the files to compare.
- `compute` takes in the set operation to perform in the argument `select_str`, generated by the pull-down menu field. The ***if*** structure performs the requested operation generating the new set `result_set`.
- `compute` returns a string generated by the `pretty_print` function.

The `pretty_print` function takes in:

- `the_set`, the resulting set from the set operations.
- `select_str`, the operation performed.
- `bool_val`, the Boolean result of the check box. If the box was checked, we will add the words in `the_set` to the output.

As we did previously, we are generating a string bracketed by `<pre> ... </pre>` tags to preserve vertical and horizontal spacing. If the words are to be included, we choose to print five words to a line with a max of 13 spaces for each word.

The `pretty_print` function returns the string, which in turn is returned by `compute` as the result to be displayed on the web page.

9.11 WHAT'S WRONG WITH MY CODE?

Here are suggestions for finding problems with dictionaries, sets, and scope. Refer to Appendix C for details.

- **Dictionaries**
  - **TypeError: 'builtin_function_or_method' object is not iterable:** happens when you forget the parenthesis in `for k,v in D.items():`. Similarly for the `keys()` or `values()` methods. You must invoke the method (use parentheses) to generate the results you require.
  - **KeyError** occurs when the key doesn't exist in the dictionary, similar to "out of range" for lists and strings. The error message prints the errant key.
  - **Empty dictionary:** When you unexpectedly find that your dictionary has no values, that is a *control* error. Suggestions include setting a breakpoint and examining your control Boolean expression and values.
  - **Unexpected value:** If you find unexpected values in a dictionary, you may have overwritten an existing key,value pair by reusing a key with a new value. Remember, dictionaries are mutable and the key can be updated with a new value.
  - **TypeError: unhashable type: 'list':** happens when you use a mutable for a key. Remember, you cannot use mutable items as a key in a dictionary. As in this example error, you cannot use a List as a key.
- **Sets**
  - **AttributeError: 'dict' object has no attribute 'add':** happens when you initialized a set with `s={}` instead of `s=set()`, that is, you created a dictionary when you wanted a set. You can observe the type in the Variable Explorer.
- **Scope**
  - **Global:** The most common "error" with respect to scope is using global variable references. A global variable is set in the outermost scope of the program and available to all other program elements. While not specifically an error, resolving why a global variable is being properly set can be difficult to debug. It is better to pass arguments to

functions specifically to indicate the values being operated on by the function, making debugging easer. Setting a breakpoint at the end of a function lets you observe a function's namespace in Variable Explorer.

More difficult is the **shadowing problem** discussed in Section 9.6. You can have the same name in different namespaces, and the **LEGB** rule is used to resolve the value. Thus you may try to refer to a variable's value and not get the expected result because **LEGB** resolved the value in an unexpected way. In particular, if you assign a variable inside of a function, that variable is now **local to the function namespace**. Again, passing arguments explicitly to functions can help make debugging the problem easier.

– **NameError** for a name you know exists usually occurs because the name is in a different namespace. Variable Explorer is helpful for seeing what names are in the current namespace.
– **UnboundLocalError** can occur when you unintentionally reference a global variable within a function. In this case you get a helpful error message: *UnboundLocalError: local variable 'i' referenced before assignment.* How did this happen? Consider the following code. In the `test()` function the `i + 1` on the RHS refers to `i` which is local to the function because `i` first occurs on the LHS, but the local name has not been initialized.

```
def test():
  i = i + 1

i = 0
test()
```

Summary

In this chapter, we introduced the powerful and useful dictionary and set data structures. We also more fully developed the idea of scope.

Dictionaries

- Dictionaries are unordered collections specified by curly braces: `{}`.
- Each dictionary item is a key:value pair (specified with a colon).
- Key must be immutable.
- Example: `{ 'a':5, 6:[1,2], (3,4):'abc'}`
- Assignment: D[2] = `'xyz'` creates entry 2:`'xyz'`

- Iterating through a dictionary D:
  - for k in D: # iterate by key
  - for k,v in D.items(): # iterate by key,value pairs
  - for v in D.values(): # iterate by value
  - for k in D.keys(): # iterate by key

Sets

- Sets are unordered collections of *unique* items–just like mathematical sets.
- Sets are specified by curly braces–like dictionaries, but there are no colons.
- Common mathematical set operations are supported.
  For A = `{'a','b','c','d'}` and B = `{'c','d','e','f'}`:
  - A.intersection(B) is `{'c','d'}`; shorthand: `A & B`
  - A.union(B) is `{'a','b','c','d','e','f'}`; shorthand: `A | B`
  - A.difference(B) is `{'a','b'}`; shorthand: `A - B`
  - A.symmetric_difference(B) is `{'a','b','e','f'}`; shorthand: `A^B`
  - A.issubset(B) is False; shorthand: `A <= B`
  - A.issuperset(B) is False; shorthand: `A >= B`

Scope

- Practically, scope is a search through various namespaces to find a reference to an object
- The rule is **LEGB**:
  - *L*ocal (local namespace)
  - *E*nclosing (any enclosing functions)
  - *G*lobal (global namespace)
  - *B*uilt-in, the Python built-ins

Rules

- **RULE 1:** Think before you program!
- **RULE 2:** A program is a human-readable essay on problem solving that also happens to execute on a computer.
- **RULE 3:** The best way to improve your programming and problem skills is to practice!
- **RULE 4:** A foolish consistency is the hobgoblin of little minds.
- **RULE 5:** Test your code, often and thoroughly!

- **RULE 6:** If it was hard to write, it is probably hard to read. Add a comment.
- **RULE 7:** All input is evil, until proven otherwise.
- **RULE 8:** A function should do one thing.

Exercises

1. What are the characteristics and limitations of sets?
2. What does the set operator "in" return? Give an example.
3. Why is it important for a *key* of a dictionary to be immutable, even though the dictionary itself is mutable?
4. Given `D = {'a':3, 'x':7, 'r':5}`:
   (a) Write Python code that returns the value at key `'x'`.
   (b) Write Python code that returns the key given value `'7'`.
5. A dictionary that Refers to Itself.
   Consider this code:

```
other_hash = {}
other_hash[2] = 10

self_hash = {}
self_hash[2] = other_hash
self_hash[3] = 4
self_hash["2"] = self_hash
```

   Whats the output of `self_hash["2"]["2"]["2"]["2"][2][2]`?
   Try it!
6. Create a dictionary from two strings `'Jack Jim Jose'` and `'Guitar Drums Bass'`, with the names as keys and the instruments as values.
7. Given two dictionaries, `my_dict` and `your_dict`
   (a) Write a function to merge the two into a new dictionary
   (b) Write a function to add `your_dict` to `my_dict`.
8. If `my_dict = {'a':15, 'c':35, 'b':20}`, write Python code
   (a) to print all the keys.
   (b) to print all the values.
   (c) to print all the keys and values pairs.
   (d) to print all the keys and values pairs in order of key.
   (e) to print all the keys and values pairs in order of value.

9. Given the following sets, predict the outputs and then check them in your shell. (*Hint:* Remember which is independent of the order, that is, when it matters that a_set is first versus b_set being first.)

```
a_set="the", "coat", "had", "many", "colors", "red", "blue", "yellow"
b_set="my", "coat", "had", "two", "main", "colors", "red", "blue"
x= a_set.intersection(b_set)
y= b_set.intersection(a_set)
print(x)
print(y)
w= a_set.union(b_set)
v= a_set.union(a_set)
print(w)
print(v)
t= a_set.difference(b_set)
u= b_set.difference(a_set)
print(t)
print(u)
r= a_set.symmetric_difference(b_set)
s= b_set.symmetric_difference(a_set)
print(r)
print(s)
```

10. Write a function that will take a dictionary, a key, and a value as arguments, and will update the specified key with the value provided. If the key does not exist, then it should be created with the provided value.

11. A Caesar cipher encrypts a message by shifting letters in the alphabet. For example, a shift of 4 maps `'a'` to `'e'` and maps `'p'` to `'t'` Here is a famous line from Shakespeare encrypted with a shift of 4: 'vq dg qt pqv vq dg: vjcv ku vjg swguvkqp.'

(a) Write a program that takes as input a string to be encrypted and an integer encrpytion shift (such as 4 mentioned earlier), and prints the encrypted string. [*Hint:* `zip()` is helpful in building a dictionary. Also, remember to handle space–it doesn't shift].

(b) Extend your program to take an additional input that indicates if your program is to encrypt or decrypt the string.

12. Texting on portable devices has developed a set of abbreviations due to the necessary brevity of text messages. Create a dictionary of texting abbreviations, and use it to write functions that can translate to and from English. Of course, your dictionary cannot be complete. For example: "y r u l8?" translates to "Why are you late?"

13. Write a program to show how searches can be done in a dictionary. Create a dictionary with names of people and their age. Prompt the user for a name, and display the age of that person. If the person is not in the dictionary, then ask the user for their age and insert it into the dictionary.

14. Letter Counts Using Dictionaries
Remember to consider spaces as a special case.

(a) Write a function that takes as input a string and returns the most common letter in the string.

(b) Write a function that takes as input a string and returns a dictionary of letter counts.
(c) Write a function that takes as input a string and prints a histogram of letter counts. A histogram can be done with matplotlib or using different length strings of characters.

15. Write a function that takes a person's first and last names as input and
(a) uses lists to return a list of the common letters in the first and last names (the intersection).
(b) uses sets to return a set that is the intersection of the characters in the first and last names.
(c) uses sets to return the set that is the symmetric difference between the first and last names.

16. Create a dictionary that maps countries to their capitals. You may start with an empty dictionary. Ask the user to input the name of the country and its capital and add them to the dictionary.

For example, Capitals = { 'Argentina':'Buenos Aires', 'France':'Paris', 'US':'Washington D.C.'}

Once the dictionary is created, print the capitals in alphabetical order.

17. Consider a file in which every line is of the format: City, Country. Read the file, record the information in a dictionary, and report the number of cities in each country. For example, if the file contains

```
London, UK
Chicago, US
Detroit, US
```

The output will be:

```
UK : 1
US : 2
```

18. A book could be written by a single author or multiple authors. Consider the organization of a dictionary, for example, what should be used as the key in the dictionary?
(a) What should the organization of the dictionary be, if we want to find the names of all the books written by a given author?
(b) What should the organization of the dictionary be, if we want to find the names of all the authors of a given book?
(c) Find a list of books and authors on the Internet (there are many). Put the list in a file. Write a program to read the books and authors in the file and put them in a dictionary. Output the books organized by author.

19. Create a dictionary with some key-value pairs. Try using the `pop` and `popitem` operations on the dictionary. What happens with each?

20. Write a function that takes a list as an argument and returns a dictionary with the elements of the list as keys, with a default value set randomly for each key.

21. Write a function that takes a string as an argument and returns a list of unique characters in the string. Ignore case.

22. Write a function that takes as an argument an unordered list of integers and returns a dictionary of the three integers with the highest count and their counts. That is, key is integer; value is its count. In case of a tie, either value can be returned.

---

23. A person can have more than one credit card, but a credit card can belong to only person. Create a hypothetical file that contains the name and credit card number of a person on each line. Read the file and organize a dictionary to return all the credit cards associated with a person. Your program should behave as follows:

```
Input : Name of person
Output : List of credit cards.
```

24. In an earlier set of exercises, we provided a code framework for solving word puzzles. Using that framework, solve this puzzle: find an uncapitalized seven-letter word in which six of the seven letters use the same number on a telephone key pad. For example, the word "cabbala" on a telephone would be 222-2252.

25. Morse Code uses a series of short and long pulses called dots and dashes respectively to encode letters and digits. For example, the letter "A" is "dot-dash", "B" is "dash-dot-dot-dot". Find a table of Morse Code on the Internet to create a dictionary for mapping characters and digits to Morse Code. Use the dictionary to create a program that can translate between Morse Code and characters and digits.

26. Use a dictionary to create a program that prompts for an integer and prints out the integer using words. For example: 138 will print "one three eight."

27. Say the last letter in a word is missing. For example, let the word be "fantasti." Could you find out the original word ("fantastic") from a word list? Write a function to retrieve the original word and print it. In some cases, a set of words might have to be returned, for example, if the word is "bas", the original word could have been "bask" or "bass". So far in this problem, you have not needed to use a Python dictionary. Rather than linearly scanning through the input word list and checking for the original word, how could you store the words so you can search faster?

28. Write a program that reads a word list and prints out all the anagrams in the word list. In earlier exercises you saw how to read a word list. Also, in earlier examples we saw how the sorted characters of a word are a useful canonical representation of an anagram (*Hint:* Therefore, useful as a key).

29. Find two historic documents to compare—similar to the example in this chapter. For example, use the preamble to the U.S. Constitution and compare it to the Declaration of Independence. Find the most common, meaningful words, and output them in alphabetical order.

30. In Chapter 10 we mentioned the Machine Learning Repository `http://archive.ics.uci.edu/ml`. One of their most popular databases is the Iris database. Irises come in three different species: setosa, virginica, and versicolor. Each entry in the data set has five values: sepal length, sepal width, petal length, petal width, and the species name (setosa, virginica, and versicolor). Read in the data and create a dictionary with the key as the species name and the values as the averages of each of the four characteristic values: sepal length, sepal width, petal length, petal width. That is, the size of the dictionary will be three. Write functions to create the dictionary and display the contents of the dictionary.

31. Time magazine[6] created a list of the 50 worst cars ever made. Create a dictionary with keys as the car manufacturer with values a tuple for the (year, model). Note that in some cases, the model might be absent. Then, write a function to find the company that has made the maximum number of worst cars.

32. Create a test file `'test.txt'`, print each line, and create a set from the contents of the file. Each line of the file will be an element of the set.

33. Write a function given a telephone number as an argument returns a list of all the combinations of letters that the numbers could represent. What would be a useful dictionary to make this problem easier?

Programming Projects

1. Data mining the Internet Movie Data Base

Websites like the Internet Movie DataBase (www.imdb.com) maintain extensive information about movies and actors. If you search for a movie on the website, a web page showing information about the movie is displayed. It also shows all the actors in the movie. If you click on the link for an actor, you are taken to an actor's page, where you can find information about him or her, including the movies they are in. This assignment should give you some insight into the working of such websites.

Here is what we'd like to do with the data:

(a) Given two titles of a movie, each representing the set of actors in that movie:
  i. Find all the actors in those movies: That is, A union B (A & B).

[6] http://content.time.com/time/specials/packages/completelist/0,29569,1658545,00.html

ii. Find the common actors in the two movies: That is, A intersection B (A | B).
iii. Find the actors who are in either of the movies but not both: symmetric difference (A - B).

(b) Given an actor's name, find all the actors with whom he or she has acted.

The data is available as a huge, compressed text file (at www.imdb.com/interfaces) that lists each actor followed by their movies and the year the movie was made. Here is a small sample (also available on the text website) that you can work with for this exercise:

```
Brad Pitt, Meet Joe Black (1998), Oceans Eleven (2001), Se7en (1995), Mr &
Mrs Smith (2005) Tom Hanks, Sleepless in Seattle (1993), Catch Me If You Can (2002),
You've got mail (1998) Meg Ryan, You've Got Mail (1998), Sleepless in Seattle (1993),
When Harry Met Sally (1989) Anthony Hopkins, Hannibal (2001), The Edge (1997), Meet
Joe Black (1998), Proof (2005) Alec Baldwin, The Edge (1997), Pearl Harbor (2001)
Angelina Jolie, Bone Collector (1999), Lara Croft Tomb Raider (2001), Mr &
Mrs Smith (2005) Denzel Washington, Bone Collector (1999), American Gangster (2007)
Julia Roberts, Pretty Woman (1990), Oceans Eleven (2001), Runaway Bride (1999)
Gwyneth Paltrow, Shakespeare in Love (1998), Bounce (2000), Proof (2005)
Russell Crowe, Gladiator (2000), Cinderella Man (2005), American Gangster (2007)
Leonardo Di Caprio, Titanic (1997), The Departed (2006), Catch Me If You Can (2002)
Tom Cruise, Mission Impossible (1996), Jerry Maguire (1996), A Few Good Men (1992)
George Clooney, Oceans Eleven (2001), Intolerable Cruelty (2003)
Matt Damon, Good Will Hunting (1997), The Departed (2006), Oceans Eleven (2001)
Ben Affleck, Bounce (2000), Good Will Hunting (1997), Pearl Harbor (2001)
Morgan Freeman, Bone Collector (1999), Se7en (1995), Million Dollar Baby (2004)
Julianne Moore, Assassins (1995), Hannibal (2001)
Salma Hayek, Desperado (1995), Wild Wild West (1999)
Will Smith, Wild Wild West (1999), Hitch (2005), Men in Black (1997)
Renee Zellweger, Me-Myself & Irene (2000), Jerry Maguire (1996), Cinderella Man
(2005)
```

What is an appropriate data structure? A dictionary is suggested, as we want to access the movies and actors efficiently, but what should be the key? A key needs to be unique, which rules out actors' names—they are unique in our sample, but not in the whole database. On the other hand, movie titles and production dates form a unique identity that suggests an immutable tuple—perfect as keys. We can arrange our dictionary with (title, year) pairs as keys and have a collection of actors in each movie as the dictionary values. As we will be looking at the intersection and union of actor combinations, that suggests using sets for the collection of actor's names in each movie. Read in the data and add the data to a dictionary that is structured as described.

Repeatedly prompt the user until some sentinel is entered. If two movies are entered, they should be separated by the appropriate operator: &, |, - to indicate the appropriate set operation to be performed (union, intersection, symmetric difference). If an actor is entered, find all the actors that he or she has been in movies with.

2. Metadata: Organizing your iTunes.

Digitized music such as that managed by iTunes has metadata such as the name, artist, and so on. Internally, iTunes uses the XML format to manage its metadata, and Python has modules to work with XML, but XML has more complexity than we can deal with in a problem (or even a few chapters). However, using copy-and-paste you can copy your iTunes metadata from the text "list" view of your playlist into your favorite text editor such as TextEdit or WordPad. The result is a file that is tab-separated, that is, fields are separated by the tab character. Because the `split()` method can take an argument of what to split on, we can split the lines of your text file using `line.split("\t")`. Remember that we can specify the tab character with `"\t"`.

What is an appropriate data structure? It is natural to organize music around the artist and an artist's name is immutable, so a dictionary is suggested with the artist as the key. The remaining metadata becomes the value of each record. You can read in your metatdata and place it in a dictionary.

Write a program that does the following:

(a) Reads the metadata from a file into a dictionary.

(b) Loops to repeatedly prompt for:

i. Name: list all tunes by the specified artist.
ii. Album: list all tunes on the specified album.
iii. Genre: list all tunes in a specified genre.
iv. Add: add a tune.
v. Delete: delete a specified tune (specify its name).
vi. Popular: finds the artist with the most tunes in your collection.
vii. Longest: finds the longest tune in your collection and prints its metadata.

[*Hint:* To sort to find the most popular or longest, you need to convert your dictionary into a data structure that you can sort, such as a list or tuple. Remember that the Python sort will sort on the first item in each list (or tuple), so you will need to arrange your lists appropriately.]

CHAPTER 10

More Program Development

> The ability to simplify means to eliminate the unnecessary so that the necessary may speak.
>
> Hans Hofmann, artist

10.1 INTRODUCTION

In Chapter 3, we covered designing algorithms and subsequently building programs. We introduced strategies to help with that task.

Now that you have functions and new data structures such as lists and dictionaries in your repertoire, you can do an even better job of breaking larger problems into smaller, more manageable, pieces.

10.2 DIVIDE AND CONQUER

We have developed a number of programs, but these programs tended to be relatively small. As programs get bigger, designing those programs so they can be easily read, implemented and tested becomes more important. We described simplification as one strategy available for writing programs in Chapter 3, especially *divide and conquer*. Divide and conquer is a general strategy for problem solving: breaking a problem down into smaller, interacting pieces that can be addressed more easily individually than the problem as a whole. Functions can be particularly useful in a divide-and-conquer approach as parts of the program can be broken off into functions that can be refined later.

10.2.1 Top-Down Refinement

As we have done with previous development, we will use divide and conquer and the principle of *top-down refinement* to guide our development of a program.

Approaching design from the top down begins with a description of a solution at a very high level—not in Python. Having done so, we then refine that description into more detail. Where we identify an appropriate piece of the solution description, we create a function to fulfill the role identified.

In the initial (top-level) design, we worry about the "big picture" approach to solving the problem. We describe what data structures we need and what "big" processing steps we might take along the way.

To make this process concrete, we will use a complicated example that will require more development on our part.

10.3 THE BREAST CANCER CLASSIFIER

Scientists make data sets available for use by other researchers in the hopes that the data itself will be helpful in solving important problems. Various repositories exist around the world that distribute such data sets, made freely available to everyone. One such repository is the University of California-Irvine Machine Learning Repository (`http://archive.ics.uci.edu/ml`). As of this writing, this repository houses 177 datasets on topics from character recognition to flower identification. One of the datasets describes tumors removed from breast cancer patients. The data was provided by Dr. William H. Wolberg at the University of Wisconsin Hospitals in Madison. Each of the patients had a tumor *biopsy*—a small needle was inserted into the tumor to remove some tissue. That tissue was examined by oncologists (physicians who specialize in cancer) to describe various features of the tissue. Subsequent to that examination, they determine if the tumor was *benign* or *malignant*. A malignant cancer is the bad one: that means that the cancer is spreading. Benign means that the cancer is isolated to the tumor itself so it is much less of a threat to the patient.

10.3.1 The Problem

The problem is to determine, based on the the tumor attributes, whether the tumor is malignant or benign. We do so by examining the data provided by Dr. Wolberg. The data lists 699 patients, each with nine tumor attributes provided by oncologist who examined the biopsy, as well as whether that patient was ultimately diagnosed as having a benign or malignant cancer. That is, the "solution" (malignant or benign) is included in the data set. Therefore, every patient has a set of eleven values: a patient ID, the nine tumor attribute values, and the ultimate diagnosis. By examining this data, we hope to discover patterns that *predict* based on the tumor attributes alone whether the tumor is malignant or benign. That is, for a patient we have not yet seen (and do not yet know her diagnosis), we wish to predict whether the tumor is malignant or benign based on the tumor attributes.

How are we going to do that?

10.3.2 The Approach: Classification

It turns out that there are a number of approaches we could take to solve this problem. In fact, there is an entire research area, "data mining," that works on ways to solve such problems. Most of those approaches share some high-level concepts that we will use to solve our problem. The approach we will use is to create a *classifier*—a program that takes in a new example (patient, in our case) and determines what "class" the new example belongs to simply on the basis of previous examples that it has observed.

For this problem, we consider patients, along with their associated tumor attributes, as our examples and separate each into one of two classes: benign or malignant.

Now that we have identified a broad approach to solving this problem, how do we create a classifier? We begin with a look at training and testing.

10.3.3 Training and Testing the Classifier

A classifier begins by *training* on examples with known solutions. In training, the classifier looks for patterns that indicate classifications (e.g., malignant or benign). After patterns have been identified, they are *tested* against "new" examples with known solutions. By testing with known solutions, we can determine the accuracy of the classifier.

In our case, we provide patients' tumor attributes to the classifier that have a known result (benign or malignant). Each patient contributes towards building an *internal model* of what patterns are used to distinguish between our two classes. Once we have trained the classifier, we must test the effectiveness of our classifier. We do this by providing "new" patients, or patients who were not used as data for the training process, to see what class the classifier predicts each new patient belongs to.

We have to take our data and split it into two parts: data we will use to "train" the classifier, and data we will use to "test" the classifier. In practice, we will create two separate files with most of the data in the training file and the remainder in the testing file.

Now the issue is this: how do we write a program that can find patterns in the training data?

10.3.4 Building the Classifier

There are many interesting internal models that a classifier could use to predict the class label of a new example. We will use a simple one, but as you will see, it can be quite effective.

The model we choose is itself a result of divide and conquer and problem solving. The approach is as follows. Look at a tumor attribute for each individual, and then combine the observations on that attribute into a decision value used to classify an individual for that particular attribute. For example, one attribute is tumor thickness measured on a scale of 1–10. A good decision value for this attribute might be 7. For a value of 7 or greater (i.e., a thick tumor) our classifier will predict malignant. For a value of less than 7, our classifier will predict benign. We can use these values to predict a patient's class.

How do we find these decision values? For each of the nine tumor attributes, let us develop two averages. The first average for each attribute will represent the average value over all the training data for women with *benign* tumors. The second average for that attribute will represent that average value over all the training data for women with *malignant* tumors. After training on the nine attributes, we should end up with eighteen averages: nine averages for benign tumors and nine averages for malignant tumors.

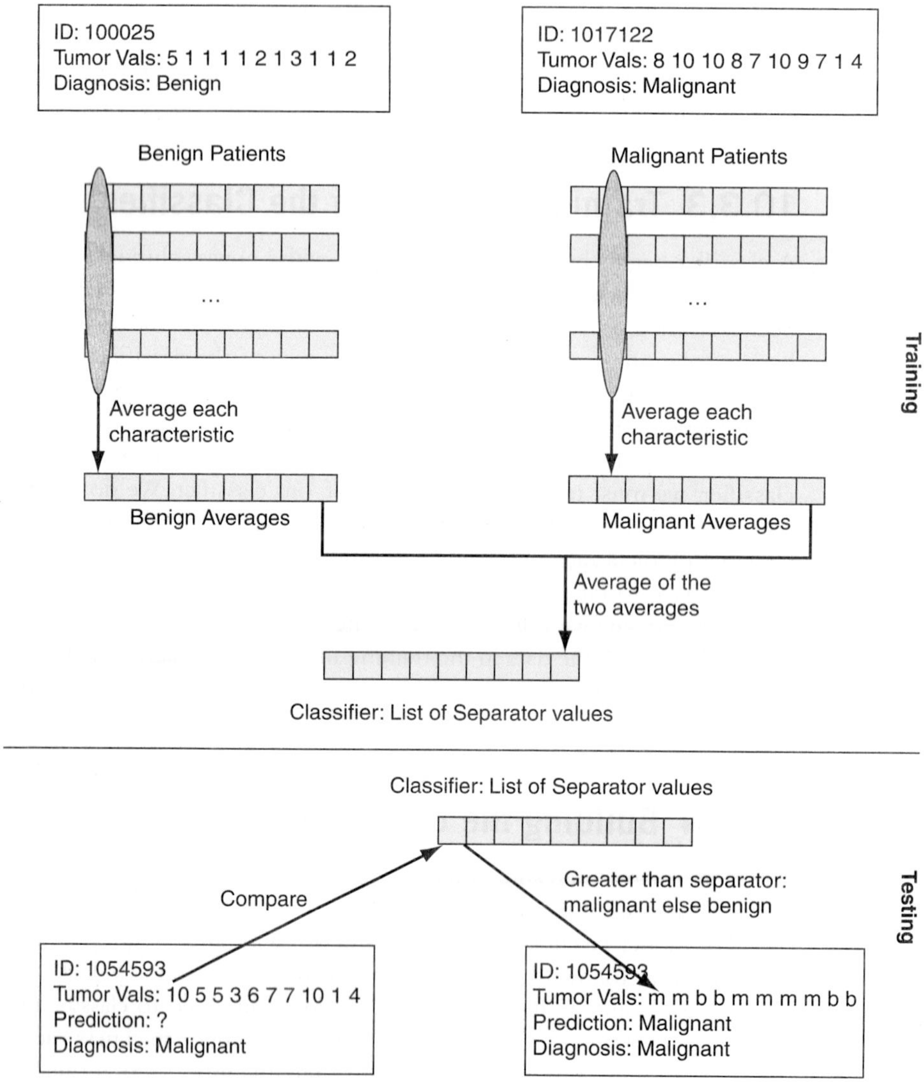

FIGURE 10.1 Overview of classifier approach.

Our classifier will be constructed as follows: for each attribute, we will find the midpoint between the benign average and the malignant average. This midpoint of averages will be our decision value, which is better termed the *class separation value*. Our classifier will consist of nine separation values, one for each attribute. If a new sample comes along with a value less than the separation value of an attribute, we will predict that this patient is benign, at least on that attribute. If the sample is greater than the separation value, we predict that it is malignant.

To select which overall class that we predict the patient belongs to, we compare each of the nine tumor attributes for that patient to attribute's classifier separation value. We label that attribute based on whether it is larger or smaller than the separator value. Remember, in this case, smaller indicates benign and greater indicates malignant. For the overall patient, we let the majority rule. Whichever class label predominates over the nine attributes, we use that label for the patient overall.

Figure 10.1 shows an overview of the process.

10.4 DESIGNING THE CLASSIFIER ALGORITHM

That's a lot of description for what we have to do. Let's see if we can use our top-down refinement to get started. Here is our first cut of an algorithm in English:

1. Create a training set from a training file.
2. Create a classifier by using the training set to determine separator values for each attribute.
3. Create a test set from a test file.
4. Use the classifier (separator values) to classify data in the test set while keeping score of the accuracy of those decisions.

Code Listing 10.1 is a Python version of that algoritm. It shows the overall structure of the program, including both the names of the function and the arguments of those functions.

Code Listing 10.1

```
def main():

    print("Reading in training data...")
    training_file_name = "breast-cancer-training.data"
    training_set_list = make_training_set(training_file_name)
    print("Done reading training data.\n")

    print("Training classifier...")
    classifier_list = train_classifier(training_set_list)
```

```
10      print("Done training classifier.\n")
11
12      print("Reading in test data...")
13      test_file_name = "breast-cancer-test.data"
14      test_set_list = make_test_set(test_file_name)
15      print("Done reading test data.\n")
16
17      print("Classifying records...")
18      result_list = classify_test_set_list(test_set_list, classifier_list)
19      print("Done classifying.\n")
20
21      report_results(result_list)
22
23      print("Program finished.")
```

Notice that the code listing has all the essential elements of the algorithm we described earlier, even though it lacks most of the details. For example:

- **Line 1** defines a `main` function, a function to be called by the user to run the rest of the program.
- **Line 5** calls a function called `make_training_set` that takes the name of a file (training data) and returns a `training_set_list` data structure (not yet defined).
- **Line 9** calls a function called `train_classifier` that takes the `training_set_list` as an argument and returns a `classifier_list` data structure (not yet defined).
- **Line 14** calls a function called `make_test_set` that takes the name of a file (test data) and returns a `test_set_list` data structure (not yet defined).
- **Line 18** returns a `result_list` data structure from the function `classify_test_set`, which take both the `test_set_list` and `classifier_list` as arguments.
- **Line 21** calls the `report_results` function, which takes the `result_list` as an argument.

This is not code that will presently run, as there are five undefined functions. However, it does show us a couple of things we need to do:

- Define the four data structures: `test_set_list`, `training_set_list`, `classifier_list`, `result_list`
- Define five functions: `make_training_set`, `train_classifier`, `make_test_set`, `classify_test_set`, `report_results`

We can fix up our main program to run by defining skeleton versions of all the functions. Again, by "skeleton," we mean that the function is defined, the argument numbers are correct, and the function returns a value. Otherwise, the function definitions are empty. By doing so, we create a running program with all the requisite parts. Sadly, it doesn't *do* anything, but that is something we can work on. Code Listing 10.2 is a second version with skeleton functions. Remember that the functions *must* be defined before they are called.

Code Listing 10.2

```
def make_training_set(training_file_name):
    return []

def train_classifier(training_set_list):
    return []

def make_test_set(test_file_name):
    return []

def classify_test_set_list(test_set_list, classifier_list):
    return []

def report_results(result_list):
    print("Reported the results")

def main():

    print("Reading in training data...")
    training_file_name = "breast-cancer-training.data"
    training_set_list = make_training_set(training_file_name)
    print("Done reading training data.\n")

    print("Training classifier..."  )
    classifier_list = train_classifier(training_set_list)
    print("Done training classifier.\n")

    print("Reading in test data...")
    test_file_name = "breast-cancer-test.data"
    test_set_list = make_test_set(test_file_name)
    print("Done reading test data.\n")

    print("Classifying records...")
```

```
    result_list = classify_test_set_list(test_set_list, classifier_list)
    print("Done classifying.\n")

    report_results(result_list)

    print("Program finished.")
```

Following is a test of that code. The important thing to notice is that it works! Of course, it doesn't do anything useful, but it is a working program that we can continue to develop. Most importantly though, it gives an outline for the entire program.

```
In  [1]: import second_cug
In  [2]: second_cut.main()
Reading in training data...

Done reading training data.

Training classifier...
Done training classifier.

Reading in test data...
Done reading test data.

Classifying records...
Done classifying.

Reported the results
Program finished.
```

This session illustrates a useful technique when developing larger code incrementally in Python. Here we ***import*** our program into the iPython console, rather than using SPYDER's "run" command. The ***import*** command takes the name of the Python program file without the ".py" extension. For example, in this session the program file name is "second_cut.py." Similar to when we imported modules such as math, we must preface function calls by the name of the file. Therefore, to call our `main` function we must use "second_cut.main()". Once we import our program file the functions in the file become available for our use. We will use this style of development in the sessions of this chapter. Alternatively, one could run the program within SPYDER and the call the functions (without the "second_cut" prefix).

10.4.1 Divided, now Conquer

By designing the program as we did, we have in fact divided the program into smaller pieces, tied together by the overall design. Of course, there are many ways we could have divided up the program. Our job now is to decide about the required data structures and further apply our divide-and-conquer strategy to each of the functions.

10.4.2 Data Structures

We need to make some decisions about our data structures—this is what design is all about. Again, there are many valid possibilities—we show only one. Other choices are left for exercises.

- `training_set_list`, `test_set_list`: The data structures `training_set_list` and `test_set_list` contain information about each individual patient. Because the data on each patient is never modified, each patient's data could be stored as a tuple of values. A list of tuples would then hold all patient data. Therefore, a list of tuples will serve for the training and test data structures. The tuple format will be:
  – First position: patient ID. String.
  – Second position: patient diagnosis. String (single letter, `'m'` or `'b'`).
  – Positions 3–12: tumor attributes 1–9 in order. Integer.
- `classifier_list`: The classifier is simply a sequence of nine values, the separation values. A tuple of values will suffice, as these values also do not change. It will consist of nine floating-point values: the average of each benign and malignant attribute average (the midpoint between each of the two averages).
- `results_list`: For the results, we need a list of tuples again, but what to put in each tuple? The classifier provides the number of attributes for each patient that indicate malignant and benign. We also need the actual diagnosis for the patient. Therefore, we need to store:
  – The patient ID: String
  – The number of attributes which indicate malignant: Integer
  – The number of attributes which indicate benign: Integer
  – The actual diagnosis: String (either `'m'` or `'b'`).

10.4.3 File Format

We have not yet discussed the actual data. The file format as provided by Dr. Wolberg through the ML Repository is shown in Table 10.1.

The "id number" can be interpreted as a string; the "Class" at the end of the file line is the known diagnosis: 2 for benign, 4 for the malignant. The values in between are the attributes as integers between 1 and 10. Figure 10.2 is an example of the first few file lines.

Note that on a file line, each attribute is separated by a comma. We could either use the `csv` module discussed previously in Section 14.2 or do the parsing by hand. In this case, we can do the parsing by hand because parsing the file happens to be well behaved.

#	Attribute	Domain
1	Sample code number	id number
2	Clump Thickness	1 - 10
3	Uniformity of Cell Size	1 - 10
4	Uniformity of Cell Shape	1 - 10
5	Marginal Adhesion	1 - 10
6	Single Epithelial Cell Size	1 - 10
7	Bare Nuclei	1 - 10
8	Bland Chromatin	1 - 10
9	Normal Nucleoli	1 - 10
10	Mitoses	1 - 10
11	Class	(2 for benign, 4 for malignant)

TABLE 10.1 File format.

```
1000025,5,1,1,1,2,1,3,1,1,2
1002945,5,4,4,5,7,10,3,2,1,2
1015425,3,1,1,1,2,2,3,1,1,2
1016277,6,8,8,1,3,4,3,7,1,2
1017023,4,1,1,3,2,1,3,1,1,2
1017122,8,10,10,8,7,10,9,7,1,4
```

FIGURE 10.2 A small part of the data file.

10.4.4 The `make_training_set` Function

With our main program defined, we must now work on the functions. Which one should we do first?

One way to choose is by doing the easiest, or at least the most obvious, first. We have a working program, so by filling in an existing empty function with a working function, we maintain a working program, and the program does more of what it is supposed to do.

The input and output are often easy and the input will be needed by other functions. Therefore, let's begin with the `make_training_set` function. According to our main function, `make_training_set` takes as an argument the name of the file that has the patient data for training. It returns the filled-in data structure `training_set_list` whose format was described earlier. We need to further refine what the function will accomplish—more divide and conquer. Here are some of the things the function must do:

- Open the file. Optionally, we should also have some tests to make sure the file exists and help the user if the file name does not exist. We will focus on just the opening for now and refine it to have error checking later.
- Initialize the training set list to be empty.
- For each line in the file.

  – Parse the line into its constituent parts as described earlier.
  – Create a tuple for the patient.
  – Append the tuple to the training set list.
- Return the training set list.

We can write the function as a series of comments, reflecting what we need to do in the function, and then fill each one in. Remember, if any piece gets too complex, we should think about breaking that piece out as a function. Code Listing 10.3 is that first cut.

Code Listing 10.3

```
1 def make_training_set(file_name):
2 # open file
3
4 # initialize training_set list
5
6 # for each line in the file
7
8     # parse the line into its 11 parts
9
10    # create a tuple for the patient
11
12    # append to the end of the training_set list
13
14 # return the training_set list
```

As expected, some of those elements are fairly easy to fill in.

- **Line 2**: `open` the file (no error checking, something we need to fix later).
- **Line 4**: We need to make an empty list to hold the training set (called `training_set_list`).
- **Line 6**: Get each line from the `training_file` descriptor using a ***for*** iterator.
- **Line 8**: Extract each of the fields with a `split` method on the `line_str` using the comma (,) as the separation element. We can do multiple assignment to create 11 new variables: `id`, `diag`, and attributes `a1`–`a9`. Remember, they are all strings initially! We could have used a list, but decided this was more readable.
- **Line 14**: When we are all done, we return the resulting `training_set_list`. Note the nesting: the indentation of the return is at the same level as the statements of the function, *not* at the level of the ***for*** iterator.

Our second cut is shown in Code Listing 10.4. Note that at some point the comments start to interfere with the readability of the program. We can clean up the comments as we fill in the code.

Code Listing 10.4

```
def make_training_set(file_name):
    training_set_list = []
# open file
    training_file = open(file_name)
# read in a line of the file
    for line_str in training_file:
# parse the line into its 11 parts
        id_str,a1,a2,a3,a4,a5,a6,a7,a8,a9,diagnosis_str = line_str.split(',')

# create a new training_set element

# append to the end of the training_set list

# return the training set
    return training_set_list
```

We did the easy and obvious coding. Now let's finish it. The next pass is shown in Code Listing 10.5.

Code Listing 10.5

```
def make_training_set(file_name):
    """Reads a training set from the specified file.
       return list of tuples in format: id, diagnosis, 9 attributes."""
    training_set_list = []

  # open file. Fix the error checking
    training_file = open(file_name)

    for line_str in training_file:
        id_str,a1,a2,a3,a4,a5,a6,a7,a8,a9,diagnosis_str = line_str.split(',')
        patient_tuple=id_str,diagnosis_str,int(a1),int(a2),int(a3),int(a4),\
            int(a5),int(a6),int(a7),int(a8),int(a9)
        training_set_list.append(patient_tuple)
    return training_set_list
```

In this version, we did the following:

- We removed comments that were no longer really needed. However, we did keep some, including a note that we need to clean up the error checking on file opening.
- We added a docstring for the function.
- **Line 9**: Created the newly formatted patient as a tuple, called `patient_tuple`. We need to take those 11 new variables, rearrange them to go with our specified data structure format (`id_str`, `diagnosis_str`, `a1`, ..., `a9`). We specified that the attributes would be integers, and everything we brought in from the file is a string, so the attributes have to be converted to integers using the *`int`* constructor. The comma operator (,) is used to make a tuple. Note the use of the line continuation character (\) because the line is so long.
- **Line 11**: Once `patient_tuple` is created, we simply use the `append` method to append it to the end of the `training_set_list` list and return it.

How did we do? We should test this little piece of code to make sure that it works (remember **RULE 5**). We need to do it now while we are freshly working on it. Once it's tested, we can set it aside and move on to the other parts of the program. How do we go about testing it? We *could* open the training data set, but that is a pretty big file making the results hard to visualize easily. Instead, let's create a small file in the same format. We'll call the file "*test_data.txt*," and use the data shown in Figure 10.2—just has a few lines from the original file.

Here is a test session using the function and the small input file. We'll be honest: we did find a few typing bugs at this point (not shown previously, of course!). Testing at this level is a good idea!

```
In  [1]: import fileInputThirdCut
In  [2]: fileInputThirdCut.make_training_set('testData.txt')
Out [2]: [('1000025', '2\n', 5, 1, 1, 1, 2, 1, 3, 1, 1), ('1002945', '2\n',
          5, 4, 4, 5, 7,
10, 3, 2, 1), ('1015425', '2\n', 3, 1, 1, 1, 2, 2, 3, 1, 1), ('1016277', '2\n', 6,
8, 8, 1, 3, 4, 3, 7, 1), ('1017023', '2\n', 4, 1, 1, 3, 2, 1, 3, 1, 1), ('1017122',
'4\n', 8, 10, 10, 8, 7, 10, 9, 7, 1)]
```

How well did we do? Well, it is close to what we want. We did get a list of tuples, and the tuples have the correct information in the correct order. The attributes are all integers and the id is a string. However, there are a couple of problems. Look at the the first tuple and its second element. It has the value `'2\n'`. According to the earlier specifications, it should be a string, either `'m'` or `'b'`. Furthermore, where did that `'\n'` come from?

What we did to fix these issues:

- **Line 10**: `'\n'` is the linefeed or end-of-line character. It exists on every line. Remember in our line format that the diagnosis was originally the last character on every line. We can use the `strip` method to remove them.

- **Lines 12–15**: Convert the `'2'` and `'4'` to `'m'` or `'b'`, respectively. A simple `if` statement will do, with the creation of a new variable `diagnosis_str`.

The final cut is shown in Code Listing 10.6, along with the session output.

Code Listing 10.6

```
1  def make_training_set(file_name):
2      """Reads a training set from the specified file.
3      return list of tuples in format: id, diagnosis, 9 attributes."""
4      training_set_list = []
5
6  # open file. Fix the error checking
7      training_file = open(file_name)
8
9      for line_str in training_file:
10         line_str = line_str.strip() # strip off end-of-line character "\n"
11         id_str,a1,a2,a3,a4,a5,a6,a7,a8,a9,diagnosis_str = line_str.split(',')
12         if diagnosis_str == '4': # diagnosis is "malignant"
13             diagnosis_str = 'm'
14         else:
15             diagnosis_str = 'b' # diagnosis is "benign"
16         patient_tuple=id_str,diagnosis_str,int(a1),int(a2),int(a3),int(a4),\
17             int(a5),int(a6),int(a7),int(a8),int(a9)
18         training_set_list.append(patient_tuple)
19     return training_set_list
```

```
In  [1]: import fileInputFourthCut
In  [2]: fileInputFourthCut.make_training_set('testData.txt')
Out [2]: [('1000025', 'b', 5, 1, 1, 1, 2, 1, 3, 1, 1), ('1002945', 'b', 5, 4, 4,
          5, 7, 10,  3, 2, 1), ('1015425', 'b', 3, 1, 1, 1, 2, 2, 3, 1, 1),
          ('1016277', 'b', 6, 8, 8, 1, 3, 4, 3, 7, 1), ('1017023', 'b', 4, 1, 1,
          3, 2, 1, 3, 1, 1), ('1017122', 'm', 8, 10, 10, 8, 7, 10, 9, 7, 1)]
```

We hope you get the idea of how to slowly break the problem down, first as functions, then as pieces within the functions, to solve the problem. Remember that testing each piece is important to make sure they do what they are required! Testing each function as you write it allows you to fix problems while your design is fresh in your head. Let's take a look at the remaining functions.

10.4.5 The `make_test_set` Function

There is good news with the `make_test_set` function. If you look closely, the `make_training_set` and `make_test_set` functions perform similar tasks. They take in a file name and return the same data structure format. The only real difference is that they read from two different files: the test data and the training data, both of which have the same file format.

Thus, we can *reuse* our code from `make_training_set` to accomplish the same task in the `make_test_set` function. To reflect this, we will rename the function to `make_data_set` and use it in for both operations in the `main` function.

10.4.6 The `train_classifier` Function

The `train_classifier` function is the heart of the program. Based on Figure 10.1, let's outline what this function needs to do:

- The function takes the training set as an argument. The training set is a list of patient tuples where the tuples are in the format described earlier.
- For each patient tuple in the training set:
  - If the tuple represents a benign tumor, add each patient attribute to the running sum of benign attributes. Keep a count of the number of benign patients as well.
  - If the tuple represents a malignant tumor, add each patient attribute to the running sum of malignant attributes. Keep a count of the number of malignant patients as well.
  - In the end, we have 18 sums, the sum of every benign patient's attributes and the sum of every malignant patient's attributes. We also end up with two counts, the number of benign patients and the number of malignant patients.
- For each of the nine benign attributes and each of the nine malignant attributes, find the average attribute value (sum/count).
- For each of the nine attributes find the average of its benign average and its malignant average, that is, an average of averages. These nine separator values specify the mid-point, the separation value, between a malignant diagnosis and a benign diagnosis for that attribute. These nine values are the classifier.
- Return the classifier: a list of 9 separator values.

As before, let's implement the function, beginning with comments and obvious structure. We can fill in the details later. Code Listing 10.7 is the first cut.

Code Listing 10.7

```
def train_classifier(training_set_list):

    for patient_tuple in training_set_list:
#   if patient_tuple is benign:
#       add attributes from patient_tuple to corresponding benign_sums_list
#       attribute
```

```
#       increase the benign_count by 1
#   else:
#       add attributes from patient_tuple to corresponding malignant_sums_list
#       attribute
#       increase the malignant_count by 1
#   create benign_averages_list by dividing each benign_sums_list by the
#   benign_count
#   create malignant_averages_list by dividing each malignant_sums_list by the
#   malignant_count

#   create classifier_list by dividing the sum of each attribute from
#   benign_averages_list and malignantAvg by 2

    return classifier_list
```

Some Utility Functions for Manipulating Lists

In looking at the first cut for `train_classifier`, it seems we have to keep track of a lot of individual sums and averages. The 18 sums and averages are a lot of variables, so let's organize the variables into lists. For example, a list of the `benign_sums_list`, a list of the `benign_averages_list` and so on. If we use lists instead of individual variables, we have to write code to add two lists. Because we have to find this sum multiple times, a function will make this task easier. We also need to turn a list of sums into a list of averages. As we have to find averages multiple times, it makes sense to break this out as a function, too.

Let us call these two functions `sum_lists` and `make_averages`. These functions are *utility functions*—general-purpose functions that help with the work to be done.

The `sum_lists` Function

The `sum_lists` function takes two arguments, two lists of the same size, and returns a new list that contains the sums of the elements from the two argument lists. That is, we take the first element from the first argument list and add it to the first element from the second argument list, and store that sum as the first element in the sum list. The code for this function is shown in Code Listing 10.8.

Code Listing 10.8

```
def sum_lists(list1,list2):
    """Element-by-element sums of two lists of 9 items."""
    sums_list = []
    for index in range(9):
        sums_list.append(list1[index]+list2[index])
    return sums_list
```

Some things to note:

- **Line 3**: We create a new list called `sums_list` that will hold the nine sums; initialized to empty.
- **Lines 4–5**: We create a variable called `index` that can be used as an index into `list1` and `list2` so we can walk through the two lists at the same time. We iterate through the indices, adding the two argument list elements at `index` and appending the sum onto `sums_list`.
- **Line 6**: Return `sums_list`.

Note that the size of the lists are all fixed at 9. This fixed size is fine for our present application, but is limiting if this function is to be used in other applications. How could you make the function more general? Also, this function could be written using list comprehension. (See the exercises.)

The `make_averages` Function

The function `make_averages` is not much different from the `sum_lists` function earlier. It takes in a list and a total, and divides each element in the list by the total, collecting the results in a list to be returned. The code for this function is shown in Code Listing 10.9.

Code Listing 10.9

```
1 def make_averages(sums_list,total_int):
2     """Convert each list element into an average by dividing by the total."""
3     averages_list = []
4     for value_int in sums_list:
5         averages_list.append(value_int/total_int)
6     return averages_list
```

Some things to note:

- **Line 3**: Initialize `averages_list` to be empty.
- **Lines 4–5**: Iterate through the `sums_list`, finding the average at each element in the list and appending the result onto the `averages_list`.
- **Line 6**: Return `averages_list`.

As with the `sum_lists` function, this function could be written using list comprehension and is left for an exercise.

10.4.7 `train_classifier`, Round 2

Using our utility functions and the `train_classifier` function outline, we can fill in the details for the `train_classifier` function. See Code Listing 10.10.

Code Listing 10.10

```
def sum_lists(list1,list2):
    """Element—by—element sums of two lists of 9 items."""
    sums_list = []
    for index in range(9):
        sums_list.append(list1[index]+list2[index])
    return sums_list

def make_averages(sums_list,total_int):
    """Convert each list element into an average by dividing by the total."""
    averages_list = []
    for value_int in sums_list:
        averages_list.append(value_int/total_int)
    return averages_list


def train_classifier(training_set_list):
    """Build a classifier using the training set."""
    benign_sums_list=[0]*9    # list of sums of benign attributes
    benign_count=0            # count of benign patients
    malignant_sums_list=[0]*9 # list of sums of malignant attributes
    malignant_count=0         # count of malignant patients

    for patient_tuple in training_set_list:
        if patient_tuple[1]=='b':   # if benign diagnosis
          # add benign attributes to benign total
          benign_sums_list=sum_lists(benign_sums_list,patient_tuple[2:])
          benign_count += 1
        else:                       # else malignant diagnosis
          # add malignant attributes to malignant total
          malignant_sums_list=sum_lists(malignant_sums_list,patient_tuple[2:])
          malignant_count += 1

    # find averages of each set of benign or malignant attributes
    benign_averages_list=make_averages(benign_sums_list,benign_count)
    malignant_averages_list=make_averages(malignant_sums_list,malignant_count)

    # separator values for each attribute averages benign and malignant
    classifier_list=make_averages(\
                    sum_lists(benign_averages_list,malignant_averages_list),2)

    return classifier_list
```

Some things to note:

- **Lines 18–21**: These lines establish and initialize the two nine-value lists: `benign_sums_list` and `malignant_sums_list` and the two count variables: `benign_count` and `malignant_count`.
- **Line 24**: We can determine if the patient tuple represents either a malignant or benign tumor based on the diagnosis at position 2 (index 1).
- **Lines 26 and 30**: Calls the `sum_lists` function to add the patient tuple to the appropriate sum list.
- **Lines 27 and 31**: When the tuple is added to the sum, the appropriate count is incremented by 1.
- **Line 34 and 35**: Once the sums and counts are calculated, we can calculate the benign and malignant averages by calling the `make_averages` function with the appropriate sum list and count.
- **Lines 38 and 39**: Finally, we create the classifier. We use *both* of the utility functions we wrote. We use the `sum_lists` function to add the two averages and then pass the resulting list to the `make_averages` function to divide each sum by 2.

A Little Testing

We need to test to ensure that we are on the right track. We can load the code we have written so far and test how well the classifier works on the simple data file we created, which was shown in Figure 10.2. Following is that session:

```
In  [1]: import make_data_set
In  [2]: import train_classifier
In  [3]: training_set_list = make_data_set.make_data_set('testData.txt')
In  [4]: for patient_tuple in training_set_list:
...     print(patient_tuple)
...
('1000025', 'b', 5, 1, 1, 1, 2, 1, 3, 1, 1)
('1002945', 'b', 5, 4, 4, 5, 7, 10, 3, 2, 1)
('1015425', 'b', 3, 1, 1, 1, 2, 2, 3, 1, 1)
('1016277', 'b', 6, 8, 8, 1, 3, 4, 3, 7, 1)
('1017023', 'b', 4, 1, 1, 3, 2, 1, 3, 1, 1)
('1017122', 'm', 8, 10, 10, 8, 7, 10, 9, 7, 1)
In  [5]: classifier_list = train_classifier.train_classifier(training_set_list)
In  [6]: for average in classifier_list:
...     print("{:.3f}".format(average))
...
6.300
6.500
6.500
5.100
5.100
6.800
6.000
4.700
1.000
```

In the session, we first imported the "make_data_set" file, then the "train_classifier" file. The "train_classifier" file has both the two utility functions and the train_ classifier function. We read in the test set to create a test set. We then printed out the data set in a nice format so we could verify that the file was read correctly. We then used the created data set to create a classifier, and printed out the classifier values. To make the classifier values easier to read, we used string formatting.

Using a calculator, we can check the averages of the data set and verify that they match the classifier.

10.4.8 Testing the Classifier on New Data

Now we need to see whether the classifier we have created will properly predict the patient diagnosis based only on the patient's tumor attributes. This testing is done with the classify_test_set function.

Let's remember what this function has to do. It takes in a set of test data, consisting of patient tumor data along with the determined diagnosis. We compare each attribute in the patient with the corresponding classifier average. If the attribute is larger than the classifier average, that attribute is considered to be evidence of malignancy. If it is smaller, then that attribute indicates benignity. For each of those patients, we count the number of benign and malignant attributes, and the majority rules. That is, whichever type of attribute is in the majority, that is the classifier's predicted diagnosis.

Code Listing 10.11 is an outline of our code in our typical way, listing comments and obvious pieces of code.

Code Listing 10.11

```
1 def classify_test_set_list(test_set_list, classifier_list):
2
3 # for each patient in the set
4     for patient_tuple in test_set_list:
5       # for each attribute of the patient
6           # if attribute is greater than the classifier corresponding attribute
7           # increase the count of attributes indicating malignancy, otherwise
8           # increase the count of attributes indicating benignity
9       # create result tuple: (id,benign_count,malignant_count,diagnosis)
10      # append the result tuple to the list of result tuples
11 # return the list of result tuples
```

Some notes about this example code:

- **Line 5**: A loop to go through each tuple in the test_set_list list, that is, each patient.

- **Line 6**: This is a loop nested within the outer, patient loop. This inner loop iterates through each attribute in the patient tuple.
- **Line 10**: Once the two counts are set, we create a result tuple in the format indicated earlier, that is (`patient_ID`, `benign_count`, `malignant_count`, `actual_diagnosis`).

The nested loop is an important concept. There are two parts: an outer loop and an inner loop. Nested loops work as follows: for every iteration of the outer loop, the inner loop runs through a complete loop (all iterations). Thus, if the outer loop runs five iterations and the inner loop runs four iterations, a total of 20 iterations are run.

Code Listing 10.12 is a final version of the `classify_test_set` function.

Code Listing 10.12

```
1  def classify_test_set_list(test_set_list, classifier_list):
2      '''Given test set and classifier, classisfy each patient in test set; return
3         list of result tuples: (id,benign_count,malignant_count,diagnosis)'''
4      result_list = []
5      # for each patient
6      for patient_tuple in test_set_list:
7          benign_count = 0
8          malignant_count = 0
9          id_str, diagnosis_str = patient_tuple[:2]
10         # for each attribute of the patient
11         for index in range(9):
12             # if actual patient attribute is greater than separator value
13             if patient_tuple[index] > classifier_list[index]:
14                 malignant_count += 1
15             else:
16                 benign_count += 1
17         result_tuple = (id_str,benign_count,malignant_count,diagnosis_str)
18         result_list.append(result_tuple)
19     return result_list
```

Notes about this code:

- **Line 7 and 8**: We need to reset the two counts, `benign_count` and `malignant_count`, at the beginning of the inner loop because we maintain the counts for each patient. After the inner loop runs, the two counts contain the respective counts for that patient. When the outer loop runs again, it has moved on to the next patient, and we need to reset those counts to 0 so we can get an accurate count for the next patient.

- **Line 11**: Again, we need to use an index so we can access the same element in the two lists.
- **Line 17**: Create the result tuple by using the patient ID (from the first element of the patient), the two counts, and then the actual diagnosis (from the second element of the patient list).
- **Line 18**: Append the tuple to the end of the complete set of results.

Testing the `classify_test_set` Function

We continue by testing using our small `"testData"` set. Following is the session.

```
In [1]: import make_data_set
In [2]: import train_classifier
In [3]: import classify_test_set
In [4]: training_set_list = make_data_set.make_data_set('testData.txt')
In [5]: classifier_list = train_classifier.train_classifier(training_set_list)
In [6]: results_list = classify_test_set.classify_test_set(training_set_list,
        classifier_list)
In [7]: for patient_tuple in training_set_list:
...     print(patient_tuple)
...
('1000025', 'b', 5, 1, 1, 1, 2, 1, 3, 1, 1)
('1002945', 'b', 5, 4, 4, 5, 7, 10, 3, 2, 1)
('1015425', 'b', 3, 1, 1, 1, 2, 2, 3, 1, 1)
('1016277', 'b', 6, 8, 8, 1, 3, 4, 3, 7, 1)
('1017023', 'b', 4, 1, 1, 3, 2, 1, 3, 1, 1)
('1017122', 'm', 8, 10, 10, 8, 7, 10, 9, 7, 1)
In [8]: for average in classifier_list:
...     print("{:.3f}".format(average),end=' '),
...
6.300 6.500 6.500 5.100 5.100 6.800 6.000 4.700 1.000
In [9]: for result_tuple in results_list:
...     print(result_tuple)
...
('1000025', 6, 3, 'b')
('1002945', 4, 5, 'b')
('1015425', 6, 3, 'b')
('1016277', 4, 5, 'b')
('1017023', 6, 3, 'b')
('1017122', 0, 9, 'm')
```

How are we doing? Something is wrong. Look at the first patient, the counts are wrong. From our earlier testing, the classifier appeared to be working (though that isn't a guarantee;

it is an indication), so something we did with the `classify_test_set` function is wrong. Let's look at the first patient (ID 1000025), their attributes, and the classifier values. We'll print them again so they are easier to examine:

```
patient_tuple:          ('1000025', 'b', 5, 1, 1, 1, 2, 1, 3, 1, 1)
classifier averages: 6.300 6.500 6.500 5.100 5.100 6.800 6.000 4.700 1.000
result_tuple:           ('1000025', 6, 3, 'b')
```

Looking at the patient attributes and the classifier cutoffs, the counts are indeed wrong. For example, by examining the values from the first patient number 1000025 and the classifier, we should have come out with all nine predictions benign. That is, count values of "9, 0" instead of the "6, 3" in the output. What did we do wrong?

The indexing is off. The problem is in Line 10. We compared the first element (index 0) of `patient` against the first element (index 0) of `classifier_list`. But what is the format of the patient tuple? The first two values are the ID and the diagnosis, respectively. In fact, we want to compare the *third* element of `patient` with the first of `classifier_list`. We can solve this issue by adding 2 to each index for the patient tuple (line 13), so we skip over the first two values.

Code Listing 10.13 shows the working version and session.

Code Listing 10.13

```
1  def classify_test_set_list(test_set_list, classifier_list):
2      '''Given test set and classifier, classisfy each patient in test set; return
3         list of result tuples: (id,benign_count,malignant_count,diagnosis)'''
4      result_list = []
5      # for each patient
6      for patient_tuple in test_set_list:
7          benign_count = 0
8          malignant_count = 0
9          id_str, diagnosis_str = patient_tuple[:2]
10         # for each attribute of the patient
11         for index in range(9):
12             # if actual patient attribute is greater than separator value
13             # Note: the patient tuple has two extra elements at the beginning
14             # so we add 2 to each patient index to only index attributes.
15             if patient_tuple[index+2] > classifier_list[index]:
16                 malignant_count += 1
17             else:
18                 benign_count += 1
19         result_tuple = (id_str,benign_count,malignant_count,diagnosis_str)
20         result_list.append(result_tuple)
21     return result_list
```

```
In  [1]: import make_data_set
In  [2]: import train_classifier
In  [3]: import classify_test_set
In  [4]: training_set_list = make_data_set.make_data_set('testData.txt')
In  [5]: classifier_list = train_classifier.train_classifier(training_set_list)
In  [6]: results_list = classify_test_set.classify_test_set(training_set_list,
classifier)
In  [7]: for patient_tuple in training_set_list:
...     print(patient_tuple)
...
('1000025', 'b', 5, 1, 1, 1, 2, 1, 3, 1, 1)
('1002945', 'b', 5, 4, 4, 5, 7, 10, 3, 2, 1)
('1015425', 'b', 3, 1, 1, 1, 2, 2, 3, 1, 1)
('1016277', 'b', 6, 8, 8, 1, 3, 4, 3, 7, 1)
('1017023', 'b', 4, 1, 1, 3, 2, 1, 3, 1, 1)
('1017122', 'm', 8, 10, 10, 8, 7, 10, 9, 7, 1)
In  [8]: for average in classifier_list:
...     print("{:.3f}".format(average),end=' ')
...
6.300 6.500 6.500 5.100 5.100 6.800 6.000 4.700 1.000
In  [9]: for result_tuple in results_list:
...     print(result_tuple)
...
('1000025', 9, 0, 'b')
('1002945', 7, 2, 'b')
('1015425', 9, 0, 'b')
('1016277', 6, 3, 'b')
('1017023', 9, 0, 'b')
('1017122', 1, 8, 'm')
```

10.4.9 The `report_results` Function

Finally, we need to report the results. You might think that this would be pretty straightforward and not really require a function, but what should be reported? The accuracy would be nice, but one could imagine reporting how many 9/0 votes, how many close votes, and so on. Therefore, we write a function because we want to isolate potential future changes.

For now, we'll just report the accuracy. Remember that the results data structure is a list with four elements, in order: `id`, `benign_count`, `malignant_count`, `diagnosis`. Also, remember that the diagnosis in the results is the *actual* patient's diagnosis, not our classifier prediction.

What do we mean by accuracy? "Majority Rules" means that if the `benign_count > malignant_count`, our prediction is benign `'b'` and similarly for malignant. Does our predictor correctly predict the actual diagnosis?

The function is shown in Code Listing 10.14:

Code Listing 10.14

```
1 def report_results(result_list):
2     '''Check results and report count of inaccurate classifications.'''
3     total_count=0
4     inaccurate_count = 0
5     for result_tuple in result_list:
6         benign_count, malignant_count, diagnosis_str = result_tuple[1:4]
7         total_count += 1
8         if (benign_count > malignant_count) and (diagnosis_str == 'm'):
9             # oops! wrong classification
10            inaccurate_count += 1
11        elif diagnosis_str == 'b':  # and (benign_count < malignant_count)
12            # oops! wrong classification
13            inaccurate_count += 1
14    print("Of ",total_count," patients, there were ",\
15          inaccurate_count," inaccuracies")
```

Notes on this function:

- **Lines 3** and **4**: Initialize the total and inaccurate counts.
- **Line 8**: If the `benign count > malignant count` and actual diagnosis is `'m'` for malignant, there is an inaccuracy.
- **Line 11**: Similar logic for the malignant count. Note that since the number of attributes is odd (nine), it isn't possible for the counts to be equal.
- **Line 14**: Print the results.

The following session shows a test of the code.

```
In [1]: import make_data_set
In [2]: import train_classifier
In [3]: import classify_test_set
In [4]: training_set_list = make_data_set.make_data_set('testData.txt')
In [5]: classifier_list = train_classifier.train_classifier(training_set_list)
In [6]: results_list = classify_test_set.classify_test_set(training_set_list,
        classifier)
In [7]: for result_tuple in results_list:
...     print(result_tuple)
...
('1000025', 9, 0, 'b')
('1002945', 7, 2, 'b')
('1015425', 9, 0, 'b')
```

```
('1016277', 6, 3, 'b')
('1017023', 9, 0, 'b')
('1017122', 1, 8, 'm')
In  [8]: report_results.report_results(results_list)
Out [8]: Of  6  patients, there were  0 inaccuracies
```

10.5 RUNNING THE CLASSIFIER ON FULL DATA

Now comes the real test. We have assembled all the functions and tested them in parts. Now, we need to put the full code together and test it on the entire breast cancer data set.

10.5.1 Training versus Testing

We need to take the full 699 patients and divide them into two files: one file to train the classifier and one file for testing. There are many strategies for testing the accuracy of a classifier. The goal is to train the classifier on as many examples as possible while still testing many patient values. We will take a simple approach and just divide the original file in half: 349 for training, and 350 for testing. We put all our code together and run it as indicated in this example getting the following result.

```
In  [1]: import bcancer_classifier
In  [2]: bcancer_classifier.main()
Out [2]: Reading in training data...

Traceback (most recent call last):
  File "<stdin>", line 1, in <module>
  File "bcancerClassifier.py", line 74, in main
    training_set_list = make_data_set(training_file)
  File "bcancerClassifier.py", line 14, in make_data_set
    int(a5),int(a6),int(a7),int(a8),int(a9)
ValueError: invalid literal for int() with base 10: '?'
```

What happened? The error message says that we have the error in the fourteenth line of the `make_data_set` function. Apparently, Python tried to convert a `'?'` into an integer. Why?

A look at the data files shows the problem. There are a number of patients out of the 699 that have an unknown value as part of their data, indicated by a `'?'` instead of an integer. That is the source of our problem. We missed that in testing because we looked at only a small portion of the data.

We have a few choices. We can throw out the "bad" data (there are 16 patients that have a `'?'` instead of an integer), or we can fix the problem in the `make_data_set` function. It may be a bad idea to throw away the 16 patients with a `'?'` for an attribute. However, it may also be a bad idea to "make up" a substitute value for the missing data.

We chose to modify `make_data_set` to ignore any patient with a `'?'`. We do that at Line 16–17, providing a test to see whether there is a `'?'` in the line. If so, we ***continue***, meaning that we skip the rest of the loop and go on to the next patient. That probably deserves a comment, so we place one in.

The final code and session output are shown in Code Listing 10.15.

Code Listing 10.15

```
1  # naming protocol:
2  #     1. names are strings
3  #     2. counts and indexes are ints
4
5  def make_data_set(file_name):  # file_name is a string
6      '''Read file file_name (str); return list of tuples in format:
7         id, diagnosis, 9 attributes.'''
8      input_set_list = []
9
10 # open file. Fix the error checking
11     input_file = open(file_name)
12
13     for line_str in input_file:
14         line_str = line_str.strip()  # strip off end-of-line character "\n"
15         # if a '?' in the patient data, skip that patient
16         if '?' in line_str:
17             continue
18         id_str,a1,a2,a3,a4,a5,a6,a7,a8,a9,diagnosis_str = line_str.split(',')
19         if diagnosis_str == '4': # diagnosis is "malignant"
20             diagnosis_str = 'm'
21         else:
22             diagnosis_str = 'b'  # diagnosis is "benign"
23         patient_tuple=id_str,diagnosis_str,int(a1),int(a2),int(a3),int(a4),\
24             int(a5),int(a6),int(a7),int(a8),int(a9)
25         input_set_list.append(patient_tuple)
26     return input_set_list
27
28
29 def sum_lists(list1,list2):
30     """Element-by-element sums of two lists of 9 items."""
31     sums_list = []
32     for index in range(9):
33         sums_list.append(list1[index]+list2[index])
34     return sums_list
35
36 def make_averages(sums_list,total_int):
37     """Convert each list element into an average by dividing by the total."""
38     averages_list = []
```

```
    for value_int in sums_list:
        averages_list.append(value_int/total_int)
    return averages_list

def train_classifier(training_set_list):
    """Build a classifier using the training set."""
    benign_sums_list=[0]*9    # list of sums of benign attributes
    benign_count=0            # count of benign patients
    malignant_sums_list=[0]*9 # list of sums of malignant attributes
    malignant_count=0         # count of malignant patients

    for patient_tuple in training_set_list:
        if patient_tuple[1]=='b':  # if benign diagnosis
            # add benign attributes to benign total
            benign_sums_list=sum_lists(benign_sums_list,patient_tuple[2:])
            benign_count += 1
        else:                      # else malignant diagnosis
            # add malignant attributes to malignant total
            malignant_sums_list=sum_lists(malignant_sums_list,patient_tuple[2:])
            malignant_count += 1

    # find averages of each set of benign or malignant attributes
    benign_averages_list=make_averages(benign_sums_list,benign_count)
    malignant_averages_list=make_averages(malignant_sums_list,malignant_count)

    # separator values for each attribute averages benign and malignant
    classifier_list=make_averages(sum_lists(benign_averages_list,
malignant_averages_list),2)

    return classifier_list

def classify_test_set(test_set_list, classifier_list):
   '''Given test set and classifier, classisfy each patient in test set;
      return list of result tuples:(id,benign_count,malignant_count,diagnosis)'''
    result_list = []
    # for each patient
    for patient_tuple in test_set_list:
        benign_count = 0
        malignant_count = 0
        id_str, diagnosis_str = patient_tuple[:2]
        # for each attribute of the patient,
        for index in range(9):
            # if actual patient attribute is greater than separator value
            #      "+2" skips id and diagnosis in list
            if patient_tuple[index+2] > classifier_list[index]:
                malignant_count += 1
```

```
        else:
            benign_count += 1
    result_tuple = (id_str,benign_count,malignant_count,diagnosis_str)
    result_list.append(result_tuple)
return result_list

def report_results(result_list):
    '''Check results and report count of inaccurate classifications.'''
    total_count=0
    inaccurate_count = 0
    for result_tuple in result_list:
        benign_count, malignant_count, diagnosis_str = result_tuple[1:4]
        total_count += 1
        if (benign_count > malignant_count) and (diagnosis_str == 'm'):
            # oops! wrong classification
            inaccurate_count += 1
        elif diagnosis_str == 'b':  # and (benign_count < malignant_count)
            # oops! wrong classification
            inaccurate_count += 1
    print("Of ",total_count," patients, there were ",\
          inaccurate_count," inaccuracies")

def main():

    print("Reading in training data...")
    training_file = "training_data.txt"
    training_set_list = make_data_set(training_file)
    print("Done reading training data.\n")

    print("Training classifier...")
    classifier_list = train_classifier(training_set_list)
    print("Done training classifier.\n")

    print("Reading in test data...")
    test_file = "test_data.txt"
    test_set_list = make_data_set(test_file)
    print("Done reading test data.\n")

    print("Classifying records...")
    result_list = classify_test_set(test_set_list, classifier_list)
    print("Done classifying.\n")

    report_results(result_list)

    print("Program finished.")
```

```
In  [1]: import bcancer_classifier
In  [2]: bcancer_classifier.main()
Out [2]: Reading in training data...

Done reading training data.

Training classifier...
Done training classifier.

Reading in test data...
Done reading test data.

Classifying records...
Done classifying.
Of  348  patients, there were  7 inaccuracies
Program finished.
```

10.6 OTHER INTERESTING PROBLEMS

Here are some other, interesting problems. We don't solve them fully, but we provide you the background information for you to solve them yourself.

10.6.1 Tag Clouds

VideoNote 10.1
Program Development: Tag Cloud

Tag clouds are a useful way to provide a visual description of the word content of a document. In a tag cloud, words that are used more frequently have a larger font—less frequently used words have a smaller font. For example, Figure 10.3 shows a tag cloud for the Declaration of Independence. Common words, called *stop words*, such as "a," "and," "the," and so on, are usually removed before the analysis because their frequency isn't usually

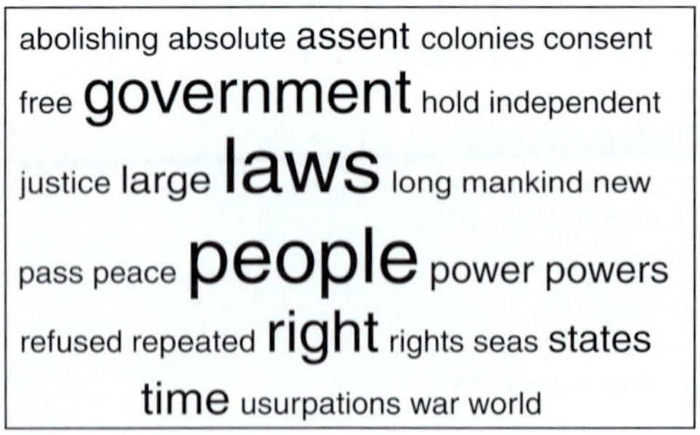

FIGURE 10.3 Tag cloud for the U.S. Declaration of Independence.

of interest. As this tag cloud illustrates, one can quickly see the words emphasized in the declaration.

Most of the work with a tag cloud is similar to what we did for the Gettysburg Address earlier in Section 7.5.2: get a count of each word in the document. As with every problem, there are many details to be handled: "stop words" need to be removed from consideration, punctuation needs to be eliminated, non-ASCII characters need to be removed, and so on. Also, it isn't interesting to display all words, so, as we did with the Declaration of Independence we display only words that occur three or more times are shown. Finally, one must come up with a way to translate word counts into font sizes for display.

A common way to display tag clouds is on the Web. The language of the Web is HTML. You create a document with HTML tags and then point your web browser to it. Two tasks are needed to create the HTML document: first, you need to create words with different font sizes in HTML, and second, you need to pack those words into a box. Code Listing 10.16 shows two functions which accomplish those two tasks.

Code Listing 10.16

```
# Functions adapted from ProgrammingHistorian (updated to Python3)
# http://niche.uwo.ca/programming-historian/index.php/Tag_clouds

# Take one long string of words and put them in an HA BTA BMA BL box.
# If desired, width, background color & border can be changed in the function
# This AB function AB stuffs AB the AB "body" AB string AB into AB the AB
  the ABHA BTA BMA BLAB formatting AB string AB.
def make_HTML_box(body):
    box_str = """<div style=\"
    width: 560px;
    background-color: rgb(250,250,250);
    border: 1px grey solid;
    text-align: center\" >{:s}</div>
    """
    return box_str.format(body)

# Take AB word(str) AB and AB fontsize(int), AB and AB create AB an
  ABHA BTA BMA BLAB word AB in AB that AB fontsize AB.
# These AB words AB can AB be AB strung AB together AB and AB sent AB
  to AB the AB make ABHA BTA BMA BLbox() AB function AB.
# This AB function AB stuffs AB the AB body AB and AB fontsize AB into AB
  an ABHA BTA BMA BLAB word AB format AB string AB.
def make_HTML_word(body, fontsize):
    word_str = '<span style=\"font-size:{:s}px;\">{:s}</span>'
    return word_str.format(str(fontsize), body)
```

10.6.2 S&P 500 Predictions

The S&P 500 is a stock market index containing the stocks of 500 large corporations. It is one of a number of important bellwethers of the stock market—showing trends in overall market performance. A number of sites on the Web collect stock market data and make it available. One such site is Yahoo! Finance.[1] The site provides a download in CSV format—the first few lines are shown in Figure 10.4. We selected to download weekly values.

```
Date,Open,High,Low,Close,Volume,Adj Close
8/17/15,2089.699951,2102.870117,2079.300049,2102.439941,2867690000,2102.439941
8/10/15,2080.97998,2105.350098,2052.090088,2091.540039,3501872000,2091.540039
8/3/15,2104.48999,2112.659912,2067.909912,2077.570068,3768210000,2077.570068
7/27/15,2078.189941,2114.23999,2063.52002,2103.840088,3850828000,2103.840088
```

FIGURE 10.4 CSV file downloaded from Yahoo!® Finance.

The first line of the file is a header line that labels each of the comma-separated fields in each line. Let's consider the "Date" and "Adj Close" values—the latter is the final, adjusted value for the index at the end of the week. To smooth out the data, let's consider 13 weeks at a time—13 weeks is one-quarter of a year. Finally, let's consider data over the last 20 years—roughly the lifetime so far of a college student. Here are some questions we might ask:

- What is the greatest difference between the max and min values in any 13-week interval?
- What is the smallest difference between the max and min values in any 13-week interval?
- What is the greatest change between the first and last values in any 13-week interval?
- What is the smallest change between the first and last values in any 13-week interval?
- If we fit a line to 20 years of data, what is the slope of the line?
- What does the 20 years of data look like with a line fit to it?

Note that as we phrased the questions, the first two values will always be positive, and the next three could be negative. That is, the last value may be less than the first value. Also, a line fit to the data may be sloping downward (negative slope).

How might we approach this problem? We can go through the data line by line and split on commas yielding date as the first value and close as the last value in the resulting list (or use the `csv` module; see Section 14.2). We can gather 13 values together into a list and find the differences and changes over that 13-week interval. Using the `max` and `min` functions we can find the difference as `max - min` on each 13-week list. We can find the change by subtracting the first week from the last week: `thirteen_week_list[-1]-thirteen_week_list[0]`. We can then put the differences into one list and changes into another list. The `max` and `min` of those latter lists provide the answers to the first four questions.

[1] S&P 500 data: http://finance.yahoo.com, ©YAHOO! and the YAHOO! logo are registered trademarks of Yahoo! Inc.

The slope of a line made from the data is a bit trickier. Fitting a line to data is called a linear least squares fit; a search on the Web provides the following formula, which can be put in a function. The x values will be 0 to the number of data values (length of the list), and the `range()` iterator will be useful for generating those values. The y values will be the closing values. The formulas for p, q, r, and s look intimidating, but the Python `sum` function does that summation calculation for us. For example, to calculate q you simply sum over the list: `q = sum(thirteen_week_list)`.

$$slope = \frac{ns - pq}{nr - p^2}$$

where

$$p = \sum_{k=1}^{n} x_k$$

$$q = \sum_{k=1}^{n} y_k$$

$$r = \sum_{k=1}^{n} x_k^2$$

$$s = \sum_{k=1}^{n} x_k y_k$$

We formatted our output as follows:

```
Twenty years of S&P 500 in 13-week intervals.

max and min difference between highest and lowest values in 13 weeks: 482.80, 25.58
max and min change from first week to 13th week: 482.80, -244.84
The slope over 20 years is 0.76
```

From that output we can observe that over 20 years:

- The biggest difference between the `max` and `min` in any 13-week interval was 482.
- The smallest difference between the `max` and `min` in any 13-week interval was 26.
- The biggest increase from the first to last week in any 13-week interval was 482.
- The biggest decrease from the first to last week in any 13-week interval was −245.
- The slope over 20 years is 0.76.

FIGURE 10.5 20 years of S&P 500 data with a line fit to the data.

Finally, we can see that the index has been volatile and that overall the trend (slope) is positive.

Let's plot the close data along with a line fit to the data as shown in Figure 10.5. If every close data point is put in a list named "data," and we can plot it with simply: `pylab.plot(data)`. Similarly if "m" is the slope of the fit line that we calculated, and "b" is the *y*-intercept (first data value in 1995), we can plot the fit line using slope-intercept form from Algebra II as `pylab.plot(m*x_values+b)` where `x_values` is simply a list of *x* values `pylab.arange(len(data))`. The main part of the program doing the plotting is shown in Code Listing 10.17. See Appendix D for an explanation of how to label the *x*-axis.

Code Listing 10.17

```
# data is a list of weekly close data
# years is a list of year string, e.g. '1995', for each data item

# fit a line to the data: get slope and y-intercept
m = slope(data)   # linear least squares fit formula
b = data[0]

# generate an x-value for each data item and set x-ticks
x_values = pylab.linspace(0,len(data),len(data),dtype=int)
step = len(data)//10  # to get 10 ticks on x axis
pylab.xticks(x_values[::step],years[::step]) # set 10 ticks to years

pylab.plot(x_values,m*x_values + b)  # line to fit data
pylab.plot(x_values,data)            # plot close data
pylab.title("20 years of S&P 500 close")
pylab.show()  # display
```

FIGURE 10.6 Flag of Andorra.

With some real data and a little Python programming, we were able to do some real analysis of stock market data. One could easily substitute another index or individual stock performance to do the same or similar analysis.

10.6.3 Predicting Religion with Flags

The design of a flag is influenced by the political and cultural roots of a country. Is it possible to determine the predominate religion of a country simply by looking at its flag?

Characteristics of flags were collected from a book of flags and are available online.[2] Twenty-eight different characteristics of flags were collected, such as number of vertical bars, horizontal stripes, colors, circles, crosses, or stars. Some characteristics were Boolean—that is, they exist or do not—such as crescent, triangle, some icon, some animate object, or some text. Finally, some non-numeric data was collected: dominate color, color in upper-left corner, and color in the bottom-right corner. The data set was augmented with the predominate religion of the country. Roughly half the 194 countries in the data set were Christian, so using the techniques we used for the breast cancer study, we created a flag classifier to predict whether the predominate religion of a country is Christian or not.

The simple classifier correctly predicted the predominate religion from flag characteristics 70% of the time. It was better at predicting that a country was *not* Christian (88% correct) than it was a predicting that a country was Christian (52% correct).

Here is a sample of the data set:

```
Andorra,3,1,0,0,6,0,3,0,3,1,0,1,1,0,0,0,gold,0,0,0,0,0,0,0,1,1,1,blue,red
Angola,4,2,1247,7,10,5,0,2,3,1,0,0,1,0,1,0,red,0,0,0,0,1,0,0,1,0,0,red,black
Anguilla,1,4,0,0,1,1,0,1,3,0,0,1,0,1,0,1,white,0,0,0,0,0,0,0,0,1,0,white,blue
```

Fields 1–6 are country characteristics such as location, size, population, and language, so they are ignored for this exercise. Consider the flag of Andorra in Figure 10.6. Using brackets to note indices in the data line above: it has 3 vertical bars[7], 0 stripes[8], 3 colors[9], red[10],

[2] Richard Forsyth (1990). UCI Machine Learning Repository. http://archive.ics.uci.edu/ml/machine-learning-databases/flags/flag.names. Irvine, CA: University of California, School of Information and Computer Science.

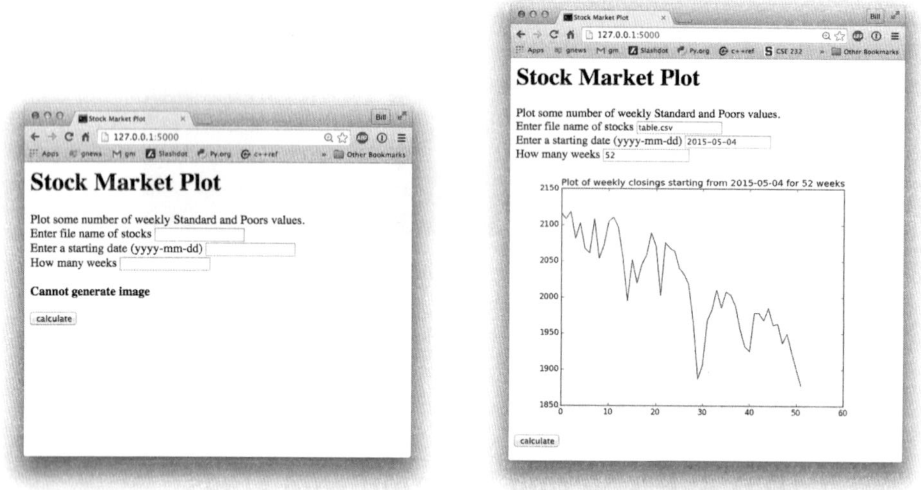

FIGURE 10.7 S&P Plot. [William F. Punch, Richard J. Enbody.]

blue[12], gold[13], gold dominates[17], an icon[25], an animate object[26], text[27], blue in the top left[28], and red in the bottom right[29].

As with the breast cancer data, averages were calculated for each field and then a midpoint was found. If a country's data fell on the correct side of the midpoint for a field, the score was increased by 1. A high score was considered to be a match, that is, a predominately Christian country. The non-numeric color fields were handled by determining the dominant color for Christian flags—listing, counting, sorting, and selecting the dominant color. If a field matched the Christian-dominate color, the score was increased. As the dominant color for the bottom right was red for both Christian and non-Christian, it was not used as a discriminator.

Because the overall accuracy is barely 70%, it is easy to find countries that are identified incorrectly by our simple predictor. In the following output, we illustrate with two correct and two incorrect input:

```
Flags

Enter a country: UK
UK is Christian
Enter a country: China
China is not Christian
Enter a country: Spain
Spain is not Christian
Enter a country: Qatar
Qatar is Christian
Enter a country: done
```

10.7 GUI TO PLOT THE STOCK MARKET

We are going to use the data discussed in Section 10.6.2, the weekly stock endings for the S&P, and do a plot of the final, adjusted value for the index at the end of the each week.

Let's take a look at what we want and then talk about the various parts. The GUI is shown in Figure 10.7.

We covered a lot of what has to be done to plot an image in our GUI approach in Section E.5, but let's look again at the new parts.

10.7.1 Function Model

As we noted in Section E.5, we have to do a lot of work here to get the plotting right, as well as gather the data from the CSV file. Thus a lot of the work is here. The function Model program is shown in Code Listing 10.18.

Code Listing 10.18

```
import matplotlib.pyplot as plt
import string
import random
import os
import glob

def make_plot(lst, date, week):
    # empty list means something went wrong
    if not lst:
        return None
    else:
        # new random file name
        fname = "static/" + ''.join(random.choice(string.ascii_letters +
                                     string.digits) for _ in range(8)) + ".png"

        #### your plotting stuff here
        plt.figure()
        plt.plot(lst)
        plt.title("Plot of weekly closings starting from {:s} for {:d} weeks".
                  format(date, week))
        ####

        if not os.path.isdir('static'):
            os.mkdir('static')
        else:
            # Remove old plot files
```

```
27            for filename in glob.glob(os.path.join('static', '*.png')):
28                os.remove(filename)
29        plt.savefig(fname)
30        return fname
31
32 # our model
33 def compute(file_str, date_str, week_int):
34     file_obj = open(file_str)
35     # get rid of header line
36     file_obj.readline()
37     result_lst = []
38     for line in file_obj:
39         line = line.strip()
40         fields = line.split(',')
41         # if we found our date
42         if date_str == fields[0]:
43             # get the next week_int lines and store the last of each line in a
                 list as a floating point value
44             for _ in range(week_int):
45                 result_lst.append(float(fields[-1]))
46                 fields = file_obj.readline().split(',')
47             # we did our week list
48             break
49     # return the filename or None
50     return make_plot(result_lst, date_str, week_int)
```

For the `compute` function (our Model essentially), our goal is to find a particular date (the first string element of each line) and, having found that date, get the next `week_int` number of lines and store up the last field in each line, the adjusted value, and store them as a float in a list. We ***break*** on **Line 46** to exit the line loop once we have gathered the required adjusted values. The function returns the result of running `make_plot` on the gathered list.

As for the `make_plot` function, we do a lot of what we covered in Section E.5.

- We are going to generate a `.png` file and place it in a special directory called `static` in the directory where our code runs. If the directory does not exist, we will create it.
- If there are any `.png` files in `static`, we are going to delete them so as to not fill up our disk with variations on the same image.
- We will generate a file name that is some sequence of random characters and save the new image under that name. We do this because many browsers **cache** (save) an image locally once loaded. By changing the name, we force the browser to reload the image.
- We return either the newly created file name or `None` if the list was empty.

In fact, the provided `make_plot` function is going to be pretty much the same for any plot, where you need only change the elements bracketed by the #### elements. A plot with fancier labels is in Section 10.6.2 and a description of how the x-axis labels were made can be found in Appendix D.

10.7.2 Controller and View

For the controller (Code Listing 10.19), we need two `TextFields` (one for the file name and one for the date) and an `IntegerField` for the number of weeks. These are passed to the view as we have done in the past. We also have separated the model as a separate file and import the `compute` function as we have done previously on **Line 3**.

Code Listing 10.19

```
1 from flask import Flask, render_template_string, request
2 from wtforms import Form,  IntegerField, TextField, validators
3 from program10_compute import compute
4
5 app = Flask(__name__)
6
7 # html page is the view.
8 page = '''
9 <html>
10    <head>
11       <title> Stock Market Plot</title>
12    </head>
13
14    <body>
15       <h1>Stock Market Plot</h1>
16
17       <form method=post action="">
18          Plot some number of weekly Standard and Poors values.
19       <br>
20       Enter file name of stocks
21          {{ template_form.stock_field }}
22       <br>
23       Enter a starting date (yyyy-mm-dd)
24          {{ template_form.date_field }}
25       <br>
26       How many weeks
27          {{ template_form.weeks_field }}
28       <br>
29         {% if result != None %}
30            <img src="{{ result }}" width=500>
31         {% else %}
32            <br>
```

```
33                 <b> Cannot generate image </b>
34                 <br>
35             {% endif %}
36         <br>
37             <input type=submit value=calculate>
38         </form>
39     </body>
40 </html>
41 '''
42
43 # InputForm and below is our controller
44 class InputForm(Form):
45     stock_field = TextField(validators=[validators.InputRequired()])
46     date_field = TextField(validators=[validators.InputRequired()])
47     weeks_field = IntegerField(validators=[validators.InputRequired()])
48
49 @app.route('/', methods=['GET', 'POST'])
50 def index():
51     result_str = None
52     form = InputForm(request.form)
53     if request.method == 'POST' and form.validate():
54         stock_val = form.stock_field.data
55         date_val = form.date_field.data
56         weeks_val = form.weeks_field.data
57         result_str = compute(stock_val, date_val, weeks_val)
58     return render_template_string(page, template_form=form, result=result_str)
59
60 if __name__ == '__main__':
61     app.run(debug=True)
```

In the view, we need to display the file we just created. To display an image in HTML, we use the tag `<img our_file_name.png width=500>` on **Line 30**. You can change the width of the image to suit your needs.

Finally, if something goes wrong, we have set `result` to `None` and display the message `Cannot generate image`.

Summary

In this chapter, we showed how Python could be applied in a variety of domains. We walked through one problem in detail and outlined approaches to a few very different problems. One interesting observation about this chapter is the complexity of problems that you now have the tools to solve.

Rules

- **RULE 1:** Think before you program!
- **RULE 2:** A program is a human-readable essay on problem solving that also happens to execute on a computer.
- **RULE 3:** The best way to improve your programming and problem skills is to practice!
- **RULE 4:** A foolish consistency is the hobgoblin of little minds.
- **RULE 5:** Test your code, often and thoroughly!
- **RULE 6:** If it was hard to write, it is probably hard to read. Add a comment.
- **RULE 7:** All input is evil, until proven otherwise.
- **RULE 8:** A function should do one thing.

Exercises

1. The function `sum_lists` works only with two lists of exactly nine elements.
   (a) Fix the function to work with lists of any size.
   (b) Fix the function to work even if the lists are of different sizes.
   (c) Rewrite the function using list comprehension. Can you reduce the function to one line, yet have it still be readable?

2. The function `make_averages` works only with lists of exactly nine elements.
   (a) Fix the function to work with lists of any size.
   (b) Rewrite the function using list comprehension. Can you reduce the function to one line, yet have it still be readable?

3. Write a program that will design a new set using the cross product of two sets `set_1` and `set_2`.

4. Refactor the breast cancer code to collect data in to 18 lists and then create the averages using `sum` and `len`. Compare the refactored code to the original code: is it more readable?

5. Find an online transcription of a political debate online, and download the file.
   (a) Generate separate tag clouds for each participant.
   (b) Analyze the tag clouds and write a one-page essay on what the tag clouds tell about the debate.

6. Find online voter polls, and download the data. Pick an interesting election cycle.

(a) Choose a feature of the polls that you find interesting and write a program that analyzes the data.

(b) Write a one-page analysis of your output.

7. Complete the program to plot the S&P 500 weekly close as described in Section 10.6.2. You will need to read in the data and write the slope function for fitting a curve.

8. Choice of appropriate data structure is an important step in designing algorithms. Suppose a text file contains student records on each line and each record is of the format: Name of Student, Student ID, GPA. Now consider reading that file to create a list of lists, a list of tuples, or a tuple of tuples.

(a) If you just want to create a report using the data, would you choose a list or a tuple as the underlying data structure for the record?

(b) If you want to modify the name or student ID or GPA, would you choose a list or a tuple as the underlying data structure for the record?

9. A major holiday is coming, and you need to keep track of all the things to do to prepare for the relatives coming to your place to celebrate. What data structure do you use to keep track?

Programming Projects

1. Classifier: Income predictor

An alternative classifier assignment can be constructed from another data set out of the UCI Machine-Learning Repository. The "Adult Data Set" can be used to predict whether someone's income will be greater than $50,000 or not. The process is the same as for classifying cancer as benign or malignant.

In this case, there are three information fields that can be ignored. They are labeled "Fnlwgt" (field 3), "Native-country" (field 14), and "Education" (field 4). The last one is ignored because that value is captured in the adjacent field "Education-num."

The other difference in this data set is that some fields have discrete attributes. Calculating averages for attributes such as "Hours per week" is simple: just add up all the values and divide by the count of values. The discrete attributes are a little more interesting. Imagine that we have 10 records, all of which are examples of the >50K examples. If the "Relationship" attribute for 2 of these 10 records is "Wife," 3 is "Own-child," 2 is "Husband," 1 is "Not-in-family," 1 is "Other-relative," and 1 is "Unmarried," then the "Relationship" attribute in the >50K model would be as follows:

Relationship	Wife:	0.2
	Own-child:	0.3
	Husband:	0.2
	Not-in-family:	0.1
	Other-relative:	0.1
	Unmarried:	0.1

Follow the six steps outlined for the cancer classifier.

2. **Tag Cloud**
Choose a document to analyze and use the tag cloud function of Section 10.6 to create a tag cloud web page. An interesting alternative is to use a transcript of a political debate for analysis.

3. **Stock Analysis**
Using the formulas of Section 10.6 gather and analyze stock trends. An interesting alternative is to analyze a particular stock.

4. **Flag Analysis**
Using the outline of Section 10.6 and the URL provided, recreate the flag analysis.

PART 4

Classes, Making Your Own Data Structures and Algorithms

CHAPTER 11

Introduction to Classes

> Controlling complexity is the essence of computer programming.
>
> B. Kernighan, co-author of the first book on the C programming language

WE HAVE DISCUSSED AT LENGTH THE USE OF BUILT-IN DATA STRUCTURES AND METHODS for problem solving. What we have not addressed is how to build our *own* data structures. What if our problem requires a data structure and methods of our own design? In this chapter, we will introduce *classes* and how they can help us do exactly that.

11.1 QUICKSTART: SIMPLE STUDENT CLASS

To get a flavor of classes let's define a simple `Student` class. The class definition and a session using it are shown in Code Listing 11.1. Our class has a few attributes such as a first name, last name, and ID. Once the class is defined, we can create an instance object named `stu1` and then print its attributes in the accompanying session. You will notice a number of unusual features such as names beginning and ending with underscores, and the name *`self`* appearing in many places. We will explain these and many other interesting aspects of classes in this chapter.

Code Listing 11.1

```
class Student(object):
    """Simple Student class."""
    def __init__(self,first='', last='', id=0): # initializer
        self.first_name_str = first
        self.last_name_str = last
        self.id_int = id
```

```
def __str__(self): # string representation , e.g. for printing
    return "{} {}, ID:{}".format\
        (self.first_name_str, self.last_name_str, self.id_int)
```

```
In [1]: stu1 = Student('Terry', 'Jones', 12345)
In [2]: print(stu1)
Terry Jones, ID:12345
```

11.2 OBJECT-ORIENTED PROGRAMMING

A common concept in modern programming languages design is the *object-oriented* programming paradigm. Object-oriented programming (OOP) is a general approach to programming that grew out of a need to handle the increasing complexity of programming. It is not the only approach—and hopefully you will be exposed to others—but it is common and has a number of advantages.

OOP is really a point of view. That point of view is that a program is a set of *objects*, where each object can interact with other program objects to accomplish the programmer's goal.

- Each object has some number of *attributes* (e.g., color, make) that are stored within the object.
- The object responds to some *methods*, which are also attributes, that are particular for that kind of object (e.g., move_forward, print).

11.2.1 Python Is Object-Oriented!

The good news is that we have been working with the OOP paradigm all along because Python is fundamentally an OOP language. We have spoken often of Python objects and their associated methods. When we call a constructor such as `list` or `str` (or their shortcuts `[ ]` and `' '`), we are making a new object. Those objects have attributes. Both a list and string object are collections with multiple parts. Those objects respond to methods. We can sort a list by calling the method `my_list.sort()`, change a string to lower case with the method `my_str.lower()`. We know how to work with objects; now we are moving on to making our own.

In Python, there is a strong similarity between a type and a class. We have seen many examples of the difference among objects that are of type `str`, `list`, `int`, and many others. They store different things (strings only strings, lists any object, integers just non-floating point numbers) and respond to different methods, even the same methods in different ways (the binary operator minus (−) is set difference for a set, subtraction for an integer).

OOP compels the programmer to think of the items in a program as objects. We have a lot of experience with this point of view in the programs we have written to date!

11.2.2 Characteristics of OOP

There are three characteristics typically associated with the OOP paradigm. They are:

- Encapsulation
- Polymorphism
- Inheritance

It is difficult to define these characteristics exactly at this point, so we will return to them after we get a better understanding of OOP. Keep them in mind as we lead you through the concepts of OOP.

We will begin with a discussion of OOP in general and then examine the implementation of those concepts in Python.

11.3 WORKING WITH OOP

There are some terms commonly associated with OOP that we introduce here. We acknowledge that OOP terminology is not universally accepted, but there are some general things we can discuss that will span most OOP approaches. We will begin with a generic view of OOP and then consider Python's view.

11.3.1 Class and Instance

The terms *class* and *instance* are important for understanding OOP. They can be surprisingly tricky to understand at first, so we will approach the concepts slowly.

The viewpoint we take in this book is that a *class* is a *template* for making a new object, and that an object made by a class template is called an *instance* of that class. Using a simple analogy, class and instance have a relationship similar to that between a cookie cutter and a cookie. A cookie cutter is a template for stamping out cookies. Once the template is made, we can stamp out any number (an infinite number, in fact) of cookies, each one formed in the likeness defined by the cutter (template). See Figure 11.1.

OOP works similarly. A class is a template for making an instance, and the instance reflects the structure provided by the template, the class. The class can "stamp out" any number (in fact, an infinite number) of instances, each in the likeness of the class.

As we said earlier, a class operates in much the same way as a type. The type `int` is in fact a template; a general model of the attributes of an integer and the operations that can be performed on an integer. In contrast, the specific integers 1, 2, 3, 145, 8857485, and so on, are each instances of the `int` type. Because they are of the same type, each integer instance shares the operations that can be performed on *all* integers, but each integer instance has local, individual characteristics, that is, their individual value.

The class template defines the two major aspects of an instance: the attributes that might be contained in each instance and the operations that can be performed on each instance. It is important to remember that the class defines the structure and operations of an instance,

FIGURE 11.1 Analogy: cookie cutter is to cookie as class template is to instance. [Image courtesy of Jupiterimages/Getty Images.]

but that those operations are operations for class instances, not the class itself.[1] If we stay with the cookie analogy, the operations to be performed on the instance (cookie), such as eat a cookie, or dunk it in milk, are not operations that can be performed on the cookie cutter (at least, we hope not!). We can again look to the integers. We can add two integers, 1 + 2, but what does it mean to perform the same operation on the type `int` itself, `int + int`?

The traditional view is that class defines the instance, the potential attributes (though not the values) of the instance, and the operations that can be performed on that instance. In this first take, the most important operation that a class can do is the "instance-making" operation. All other operations are associated with the instance.

11.4 WORKING WITH CLASSES AND INSTANCES

Let's take a look at some real classes and instances in Python and see what we can do with them.

11.4.1 Built-In Class and Instance

We can apply our new terminology, class and instance, to the programming we have been doing. Any of the built-in data structures are defined as a class: a list is a class, as is a string, set, tuple, or dictionary. These classes can be used to make individual instances using

[1] Note that it is possible to make new classes as instances of other classes with associated methods, the so-called *metaprogrammng*. We leave this for more involved discussions of OOP, but Python does support metaprogramming; see http://www.onlamp.com/pub/a/python/2003/04/17/metaclasses.html

either the constructor (respectively, *list*, *str*, *set*, *tuple*, *dict*) or their short cuts where available. The constructor creates a new object, which is an instance of the class. These instances have internal attributes and associated methods that may be applied to those instances.

The type function helps us understand this detail. Look at the following session:

```
In  [1]: my_list = [1,2,3]
In  [2]: type(my_list)
Out [2]: list

In  [3]: my_str = 'abc'
In  [4]: type(my_str)
Out [4]: str

In  [5]: my_dict = {1:'a',2:'b',3:'c'}
In  [6]: type(my_dict)
Out [6]: dict

In  [7]: my_list
Out [7]: [1, 2, 3]

In  [8]: my_list.sort(reverse=True)
In  [9]: my_list
Out [9]: [3, 2, 1]

In  [10]: my_str.upper()
Out [10]: 'ABC'

In  [11]: my_dict.values()
Out [11]: ['a', 'b', 'c']

In  [12]: my_str.sort()
Traceback (most recent call last):
  File "<stdin>", line 1, in <module>
AttributeError: 'str' object has no attribute 'sort'

In  [13]: my_list.values()
Traceback (most recent call last):
  File "<stdin>", line 1, in <module>
AttributeError: 'list' object has no attribute 'values'
```

When an instance is made of any of the built-in data structures, the new instance has a type: the type of the class it was created from. As a result, certain methods defined by the class are available to those instances. However, when an instance attempts to use a method *not* defined as part of the class, an error results. The error message is also very telling—for example: `AttributeError: 'str' object has no attribute 'sort'`. It clearly states that the attribute being sought is not part of an element of this type (of this class).

11.4.2 Our First Class

Take a look at the following Python session. In the session, we create a class named `MyClass` and create an instance of that class that we name `my_instance`.

```
In  [1]: class MyClass (object):
...:     pass

In  [2]: dir(MyClass)
Out [2]: '__class__', '__delattr__', '__dict__', '__doc__', '__eq__',

'__format__', '__ge__', '__getattribute__', '__gt__', '__hash__',
'__init__', '__le__', '__lt__', '__module__', '__ne__', '__new__',
'__reduce__', '__reduce_ex__', '__repr__', '__setattr__',
'__sizeof__', '__str__', '__subclasshook__', '__weakref__']

In  [3]: my_instance = MyClass()
In  [4]: dir(my_instance)
Out [4]: ['__class__', '__delattr__', '__dict__', '__doc__', '__eq__',

'__format__', '__ge__', '__getattribute__', '__gt__', '__hash__',
'__init__', '__le__', '__lt__', '__module__', '__ne__', '__new__',
'__reduce__', '__reduce_ex__', '__repr__', '__setattr__',
'__sizeof__', '__str__', '__subclasshook__', '__weakref__']

In  [5]: type(my_instance)
Out [5]: __main__.MyClass
```

Figure 11.2 shows the basic components of a class definition.

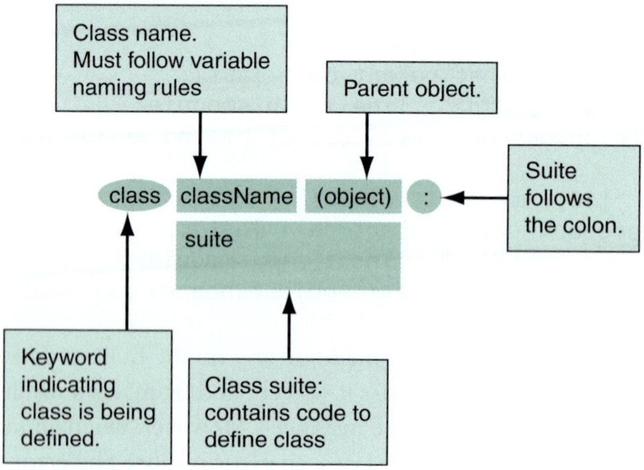

FIGURE 11.2 The basic format of a class definition.

A class definition starts with the **`class`** keyword, followed by the class name. As with all names, the class name must adhere to normal Python naming rules (see Section 1.4.6). Class names use what is called the *CapWords* approach. Each word is capitalized, joined together *without* underscores. After assignment and **`def`**, the keyword **`class`** is our third example of making a new association in a namespace. The name that follows the keyword is the name of the class and that name becomes associated with a class object. After the class name we include, in parentheses, the name of the parent class of our class. In Section 12.6, we will cover more on parent and base classes, but for now we always include the class `object` in parentheses followed by a colon.

What follows the colon, as in previous Python compound statements, is a suite that defines the class. The suite can contain any relevant Python code, typically methods or variable assignments. This particular class has what is essentially an empty suite, except, Python will not syntactically allow a truly empty suite. We use the Python keyword ***pass***, as we have before, to indicate that the suite is indeed empty. In this context, the keyword ***pass*** is an indication of intent. We, the class designers, did not forget to add content; we intended to have no content.

Once the class is defined, we can inspect what we have made with the Python function `dir`. The function `dir` lists all of the *attributes* of the class. Python uses the word "attribute" to indicate both the methods of an object and the names of any values stored in an object. An attribute is a name associated with another object.

You may have noticed something strange about the previous paragraph. We said that `dir` lists all the attributes of an object and used it on our class `MyClass`. Yes, a class is also an object. We will talk more about a class as an object later, but every class, every instance—in fact, nearly everything *in* Python is an object!

The function `dir` with the argument `MyClass` produced a long list attributes. Most of these were provided, by default, by Python through the special object named `object`. Even though we provided no attributes to `MyClass`, that class does indeed have a set of attributes, most of which begin and end with double underscore characters (__). Python reserves a number of special methods and variables that begin with with a pair of underscore characters. These have predefined meaning to Python in its OOP class system. We will be seeing more of these special names shortly.

A Simple Instance

Even though we have included nothing in our class definition, `MyClass` comes with one very important, built-in ability. It has the ability to *make* an instance. We, as class designers, are given the opportunity to affect the instance-creation process, but even if we choose not to avail ourselves of it, our class can make an instance.

We invoke any class's instance-making function by using the *name of the class as a function*. In our case, the name of our class is `MyClass`, so the name of the instance creation function is `MyClass()` and is termed a *constructor*. This is the normal approach in Python. Every constructor we have seen is named the same as the class name it is associated with.

We can see this action in the previous session. Because our class is empty, we use the default instance-making ability of Python.

What is created is an instance of the class. We can use the `dir` function to see what attributes the instance contains. Not surprisingly, the instance attributes look like the class attributes because the instance was made from the class as a template. More importantly, what type is the instance? It is an instance of the class `MyClass` as indicated by the result from the `type` function. An instance is made from a class and carries that class as its type. We have created a new type by creating a class and can make instances of that type!

11.4.3 Changing Attributes

Now we have a class and an instance. How can we change them?

In general, you can reference any object using the standard dot notation we have been using. Also, as in any other assignment, we need only assign a value to a variable for a variable to be created. However, in this case, we assign the variable *internally* to the object when we use the dot notation. That is, as with other objects, a class and instance have a namespace, and when we make a new assignment we add the name to the namespace. Look at the following session.

```
In  [1]: class MyClass (object):
...:     pass

In  [2]: my_instance = MyClass()
In  [3]: dir(MyClass)
Out [3]: ['__class__', '__delattr__', '__dict__', '__doc__', '__eq__',

'__format__', '__ge__', '__getattribute__', '__gt__', '__hash__',
'__init__', '__le__', '__lt__', '__module__', '__ne__', '__new__',
'__reduce__', '__reduce_ex__', '__repr__', '__setattr__',
'__sizeof__', '__str__', '__subclasshook__', '__weakref__']

In  [4]: dir(my_instance)
Out [4]: ['__class__', '__delattr__', '__dict__', '__doc__', '__eq__',

'__format__', '__ge__', '__getattribute__', '__gt__', '__hash__',
'__init__', '__le__', '__lt__', '__module__', '__ne__', '__new__',
'__reduce__', '__reduce_ex__', '__repr__', '__setattr__',
'__sizeof__', '__str__', '__subclasshook__', '__weakref__']

In  [5]: MyClass.class_attribute = 'hello'
In  [6]: print(MyClass.class_attribute)
hello
In  [7]: dir(MyClass)
Out [7]: ['__class__', ..., 'class_attribute']
```

```
In  [8]: my_instance.instance_attribute = 'world'
In  [9]: print(my_instance.instance_attribute)
world
In  [10]: dir(my_instance)
Out [10]: ['__class__', ,..., 'class_attribute', 'instance_attribute']

In  [11]: print(my_instance.class_attribute)
hello
```

To create a variable in Python, you assign it a value. You do much the same for an object attribute. To create a new attribute in an object, the programmer assigns a value to an object attribute, that is, to `object_name.attribute_name` using the dot notation. In the previous session, we made the assignment `MyClass.class_attribute = 'hello'`, resulting in the attribute `class_attribute` being added to `MyClass` with the value `'hello'`. We can print that value back using a normal ***print*** statement and the full name, that is, ***print*** (`MyClass.class_attribute`). Furthermore, we can see that using the `dir` function on `MyClass` clearly shows that `class_attribute` is now part of `MyClass`.[2]

As we have mentioned, a namespace is actually a dictionary that establishes a relationship between names and objects. The namespace for a class is named `__dict__` and that name can be seen in the previous session.

We can also add an attribute to the instance, `my_instance`, again using dot notation and assignment. As before, we can view the attribute's value by printing it. However, look closely at the result of the `dir` function on `my_instance`. See anything odd?

11.4.4 The Special Relationship Between an Instance and Class: instance-of

The oddity is the fact that the attribute `class_attribute`, set to be part of `MyClass`, shows up as an attribute of `my_instance` even though we never assigned `class_attribute` to the instance. How can that be?

Look at the following session.

```
In  [1]: class MyClass (object):
...:    pass

In  [2]: my_instance = MyClass()
In  [3]: MyClass.class_attribute = 'hello'
In  [4]: my_instance.instance_attribute = 'world'
In  [5]: dir(my_instance)
Out [5]: ['__class__', ... , 'class_attribute', 'instance_attribute']
```

[2] For the sake of brevity, we indicate with . . . the repetition of most of the default attributes in the remaining sessions.

```
In  [6]: print(my_instance.__class__)
<class '__main__.MyClass'>
In  [7]: type(my_instance)
Out [7]: __main__.MyClass

In  [8]: print(my_instance.instance_attribute)
world
In  [9]: print(my_instance.class_attribute)
hello
In  [10]: print(MyClass.instance_attribute)

Traceback (most recent call last):
  File "<pyshell#11>", line 1, in <module>
    print MyClass.instance_attribute
AttributeError: type object 'MyClass' has no attribute 'instance_attribute'
```

A special relationship holds between a class and its instance. This relationship is often called an *instance-of* relationship. That is, every instance is related to its respective class by the instance-of relationship: the instance is an instance-of its template class. In fact, we can even see how that relationship is established. In the previous session we printed the value of `my_instance.__class__`, an attribute of `my_instance`. When an instance is created, the class from which it was created is recorded in the special attribute name `__class__` in the instance. In this way, an instance always "remembers" its class, the template from which it was created. When we `print(my_instance.__class__)`, we see that it is an instance of the class `MyClass`. This is shown in Figure 11.3.

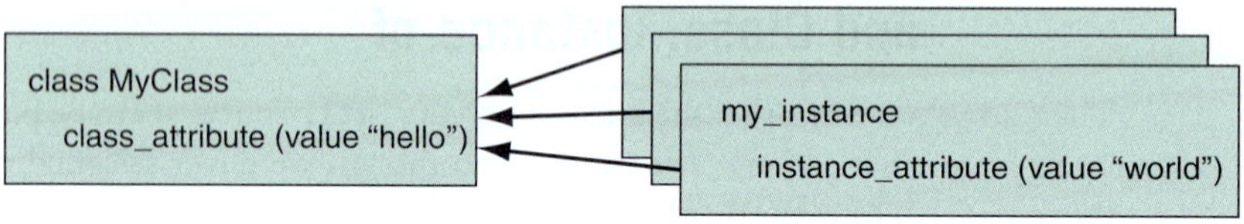

FIGURE 11.3 The instance-of relationship.

Again, if we ask Python to indicate the type of `my_instance` using the `type` function, it reports that `my_instance` is of type `MyClass`, the value stored in the `__class__` attribute.

Part of the Python Scope Rules for Objects: Instance, then Class

You saw in Section 8.1 that the scope of a variable is related to the namespace that defines where a variable is referenced. The previous rule was called the LEGB rule; that is, we look for a variable: first in the local namespace (L), second in the enclosing (function) namespace (E), third in the global namespace (G), and then finally in the built-in namespace (B). If it cannot be found in that search process, then the variable is undefined.

A similar rule applies to objects. We can search through different namespaces to find the value associated with a name. The instance-of relationship provides half of the object rule (Section 12.6 reveals the full rule). If the name cannot be found in the *instance* itself, Python will look up the instance-of relation to see whether the name can be found in the associated *class* namespace. In this way, OOP provides an economy of definition. A name defined in the class namespace is available to *all* instances of that class. The class acts as a kind of global repository for attributes to be used and shared by all its instances. This is how `class_attribute` becomes available to `my_instance`; it is not found in the instance itself, but is found in the class, `MyClass`, that formed `my_instance`. Note that the relationship does not hold both ways. Python throws an error if we ask to print `MyClass.instance_attribute`. The direction of the arrows in Figure 11.3 illustrates that one-way relation.

Interestingly, a programmer is free to override the class-global definition. Because the rule is to first look in the instance, *then* the class, defining any attribute in the instance overrides the definition in the class.

What happens if the class resets the attribute `class_attribute`, as in `MyClass.class_attribute='goodbye'`? That invocation is perfectly legal Python, but now *every instance* of `MyClass` will be affected by the change *unless* they have changed the attribute locally. Look at the following session.

```
In  [1]: class MyClass (object):
...:     pass

In  [2]: inst1 = MyClass()
In  [3]: inst2 = MyClass()
In  [4]: inst3 = MyClass()
In  [5]: MyClass.class_attribute = 27
In  [6]: inst1.class_attribute = 72
In  [7]: print(inst1.class_attribute)
72
In  [8]: print(inst2.class_attribute)
27
In  [9]: print(inst3.class_attribute)
27
In  [10]: MyClass.class_attribute = 999
In  [11]: print(inst1.class_attribute)
72
In  [12]: print(inst2.class_attribute)
999
In  [13]: print(inst3.class_attribute)
999
```

The instance `inst1` set the attribute locally. It is not affected by the class attribute change, and it does not affect the value of the attribute as seen by `inst2` and `inst3`. However, when the class changes the attribute value, both `inst2` and `inst3` reflect the

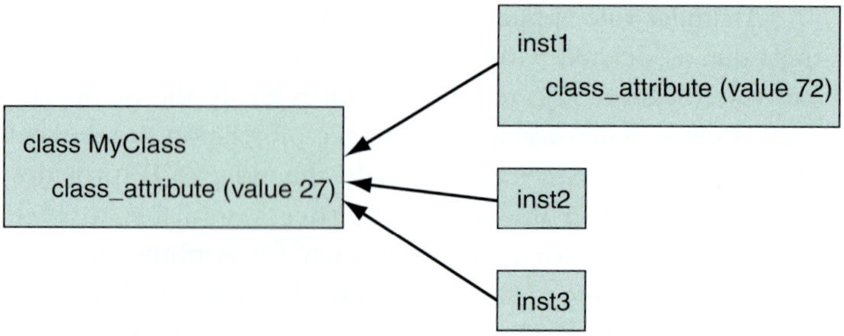

FIGURE 11.4 A mixture of local and instance-of attribute relationships.

change, as they are using the instance-of link to find the value. This situation is shown in Figure 11.4.

11.5 OBJECT METHODS

We added attributes to objects, but not methods. How do we add methods to an object? In fact, exactly what is a method? How do we use methods?

11.5.1 Using Object Methods

We alluded earlier to the fact that a method and a function are different. In Chapter 8, we discussed functions and what they can do. A function is a small program—an encapsulation of an operation. It takes in parameters and returns a value. By providing encapsulation of a task, we can write more readable code.

Functions that define the operations that can be done on an object are called *methods*.

We know a lot about calling methods. We first discussed how a method is called in Chapter 4, but here's a refresher. Consider a string and the string's `count` method. The `count` method takes a single argument, a string, and counts the number of occurrences of the argument string in the calling string. For example, to count the number of times the "m" character occurs in the `a_str` string:

```
In  [1]: a_str = "hi mom"
In  [2]: print(a_str.count("m"))
2
In  [3]: print(a_str.count)
<built-in method count of str object at 0xcb0f20>
```

The variable `a_str` is associated with an instance of the string class, the string "hi mom". If we want to call a method on `a_str`, we use the the same dot notation that we used for attributes. The notation works because a method *is* just another attribute of an object. It just so happens that a method is a callable, or invokable, attribute. Just to make that clear, when we ***print***(a_str.count), we get a value back indicating that this particular attribute is a method of the ***str*** object. To invoke it, we use parentheses after the method name.

To invoke the method, we must do so in the context of a string object, in this case the object associated with a_str. We can call count in the context of a string instance because count works only with string instances. There might be other count methods (there is one for list instances, for example), but this particular method works only for strings while the other count works only for lists. The names may be the same, but their operation depends on the type of object being used.

The invocation is:

```
a_str.count('m')
```

which can be read as "Call the string method count using the string a_str along with the argument '*m*'." The result is how many times '*m*' shows up in the calling string, a_str.

The important thing to note is that a_str is the object that is used in the calling of count. This observation points out two important issues:

- We know which method to call. Both the type of the object (type *str* for a_str, in this case) and the method name (count in this case) are used to find the correct method. Using both names directs Python to the correct method even if it is overloaded (Section 1.7).
- The calling object (a_str, in this case) is *part* of the invocation. In a very real sense, it is another argument to the method.

The method, written specifically for a particular type of object, is specialized for working with just that type.

11.5.2 Writing Methods

Now we need to define our own methods. When defining a method there are really only a few differences between it and a function:

- Where a method is defined.
- An extra argument that is added to every method.

Methods are added to a class by defining functions in the suite of a class. By providing these specialized functions in the class, those functions become available to every instance made from the class using the class-instance scope rules we discussed previously.

The code in Code Listing 11.2 adds a method to our simple class.

Code Listing 11.2

```
class MyClass (object):
    class_attribute = 'world'

    def my_method (self, param1):
        print('\nhello {}'.format(param1))
        print('The object that called this method is: {}'.\
              format(str(self)))
        self.instance_attribute = param1

my_instance = MyClass()
print("output of dir(my_instance):")
print(dir(my_instance))
my_instance.my_method('world')                    # adds the instance_attribute
print("Instance has new attribute with value: {}".\
      format(my_instance.instance_attribute))
print("output of dir(my_instance):")
print(dir(my_instance))
```

```
output of dir(my_instance):
['__class__', ..., 'class_attribute', 'my_method']

hello world
The object that called this method is: <__main__.MyClass object at 0x1020c7610>
Instance has new attribute with value: world
output of dir(my_instance):
['__class__', ..., 'class_attribute', 'instance_attribute', 'my_method']
```

The method is called `my_method` and takes a single argument, as evidenced by the invocation—one can also see the parameter `param1` in the method definition. We invoke it as we described, calling the method in the context of an instance of the class. The scope search process looks first in the instance and, not finding the method there, looks next in the class and, finding the method in the class, runs that method.

The `dir` command shows that the method `my_method` and the attribute `class_attribute`, both defined in the class, are available to the instance `my_instance`.

11.5.3 The Special Argument `self`

There is an oddity about the definition of our method that you may have noticed. We noted in the invocation that only one argument was passed, but in fact two parameters show up

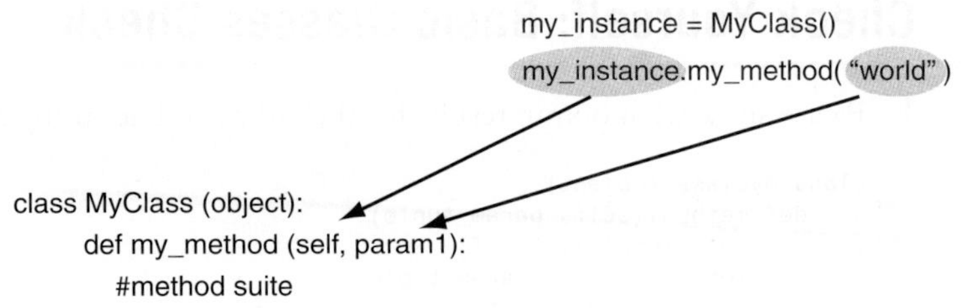

FIGURE 11.5 How the calling object maps to `self`.

in the definition of the method: `self` and `param1`. Our argument mapped to `param1`, but what is `self`?

Python automatically maps the first parameter in a method definition *to the object that called the method*. This mapping is shown in Figure 11.5.

Traditionally, this first parameter is called `self`, indicating that the object we are calling this method on is the object *itself*. The variable can be called anything, but `self` is the expected name. Any other name would be confusing to other programmers who have to read the code.

The name `self` allows us to always have a way to reference the object that called the method. Anywhere in the method where the code references `self`, we are referencing the object that called the method. In this way, we can perform the method's operation on the object that called it.

Look again at the previous code example. In the class definition, `my_method` prints the value of `self` and also performs the following operation `self.instance_attribute = param1`. This means that the object that called the method (in this case `my_instance`) is associated with `self`, and `self` has a new attribute added to it called `instance_attribute`. In the code following the class definition of Code Listing 11.2, we see that we can `print (my_instance.instance_attribute)` to see that `my_method` really assigns `param1` to the `instance_attribute`.

PROGRAMMING TIP

The method parameter `self` must *always* be placed as the first parameter in any method definition. Further, any reference to the calling object must be made *through* `self`. That is, when we refer to a part of the calling object, we use dot referencing as in `self.instance_attribute`. This is a reference to the attribute `instance_attribute` in `self`, where `self` is associated with the calling object.

Check Yourself: Basic Classes Check

1. Please show what output results for the indicated lines using the following program.

```
class MyClass (object):
    def method1(self, param_tuple):
        self.local_list = []
        for element in param_tuple:
            if element > 10:
                self.local_list.append(element)

    def method2(self):
        self.sum_int = 0
        for element in self.local_list:
            self.sum_int += element
        return self.sum_int

inst1 = MyClass()
inst2 = MyClass()
inst1.method1([1,2,3])
print(inst1.local_list)       # Line 1
inst1.method1([10,11,12])
print(inst1.local_list)       # Line 2
print(inst1.method2())        # Line 3
# inst2.method2()             # Line 4
```

(a) What output is produced by Line 1 of the above program?
(b) What output is produced by Line 2 of the above program?
(c) What output is produced by Line 3 of the above program?
(d) Line 4 is commented out. What result would occur if Line 4 were executed by the program. Why?

11.5.4 Methods Are the Interface to a Class Instance

The methods of a class object define what the object can do and, at the same time, define the interface to the object. That is, a user's interaction with an instance of a class is defined by the methods the class has to offer.

Consider the interface to an MP3 player such as an iPod. The only interaction you can have with the iPod is through the functions (for us, methods) available in the interface. Those functions define what you can do with the iPod. You could perform other actions: open up the case and modify the electronics, but that is outside the design of the object itself. If the interface provided is sufficient, then the object is, in a very real sense, defined by that interface for the normal user.

The class designer, in designing the class, provides an interface by defining a set of methods. The expectation is that a well-designed class definition need not be modified, only accessed through the provided methods. If the class is well written, then all the user of the class should ever need to use are those methods. How those methods accomplish their job should not be that user's concern. Should we be required to understand the underlying electronics of our iPod? No, the interface provided should be sufficient.

Whatever the underlying structure of an instance, its methods (which come from the class it was created from) define everything the user needs to know about that instance. In particular, manipulation of the internal structure of an instance should be defined by and limited to the available methods.

11.6 FITTING INTO THE PYTHON CLASS MODEL

Every OOP approach provides an underlying class model that the class designer uses. Python does as well, and if we are to effectively use classes, we must understand a little more about Python's class model. We have seen an introduction in the previous pages; now we will delve a little more deeply into the model. To do so, we must first build a class.

11.6.1 Making Programmer-Defined Classes

How do we decide what should or should not be a class in our program? What counts as an object depends on the context of the program. It should be something recognizable to someone familiar with the problem, regardless of their ability to write a program. For example, if the program is a racing game, an object might be a car. A car's actions might include move-forward, turn-right, and report-position. The car object might have attributes such as color, make, or top-speed. By making objects that *make sense* in the context of the program, it is easier to design the program.

The other components of the car game should also be recognizable objects. You will have other cars as well as a racetrack—all objects. Obstacles that appear in the track will also be objects. People will be objects. By designing the objects and how they interact, an overall design unfolds.

11.6.2 A Student Class

VideoNote 11.1
Designing a Class

Let's got back to our very first class, the `Student` class. The `Student` class had three attributes: `id_int`, `last_name_str`, and `first_name_str`. It will also have three methods described in detail next. One method initializes the class, the second allows updates, and the third defines how information about the class is organized for printing. We will explain this class over the next few sections. See Code Listing 11.3.

Code Listing 11.3

```
class Student(object):
    def __init__(self, first='', last='', id=0):
        # print 'In the __init__ method'
        self.first_name_str = first
        self.last_name_str = last
        self.id_int = id

    def update(self, first='', last='', id=0):
        if first:
            self.first_name_str = first
        if last:
            self.last_name_str = last
        if id:
            self.id_int = id

    def __str__(self):
        # print "In __str__ method"
        return "{} {}, ID:{}".\
            format(self.first_name_str, self.last_name_str, self.id_int)
```

11.6.3 Python Standard Methods

We mentioned earlier in Section 11.4.2 that Python reserves some special methods that begin and end with two underscore characters (`__`). The first method in our `Student` class is one of those special Python methods, the constructor `__init__`. We call the `__init__` method a *constructor* because it is part of the sequence of constructing a new instance of a class.[3] When an instance is made of the class by using the name of the class as a function, the user can affect the creation of that instance through `__init__`. How that happens is shown in Figure 11.6.

Beginning at the bottom of Figure 11.6, Python creates a default instance when a constructor is called (that is, when the name of a class is used as a function, for example, `MyClass ('world')`. After the default instance is made, Python searches for an `__init__` method in the class. If it is found, then the newly created default instance is passed to the parameter `self` of `__init__`, the remaining arguments are passed to the method's parameters (e.g., `'world'` passed to `param1`). The instance is modified according to the `__init__` method suite. The updated instance is then returned from `__init__`. If no such `__init__` method

[3] Strictly speaking, `__init__` is not a constructor in the strictest sense of OOP terminology; rather, it is an *initializer*.

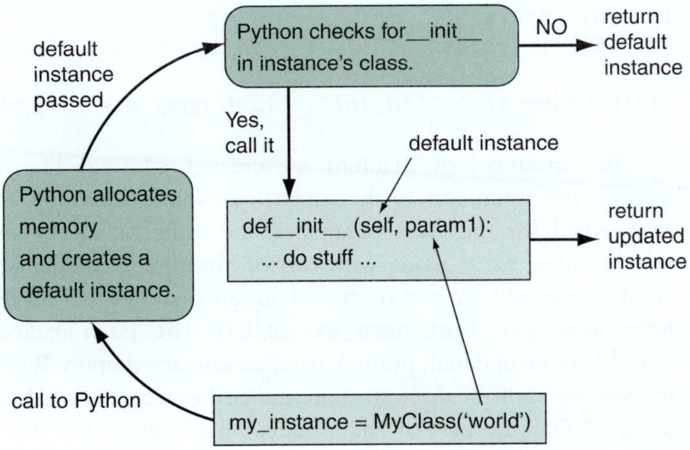

FIGURE 11.6 How an instance is made in Python.

exists, then the default instance is returned. In this example, the instance returned is assigned to `my_instance`.

It is very important to note that `__init__` does not have an explicit ***return*** statement. In fact, a return statement is forbidden for this method. This is because `__init__` is part of the instance creation cycle, so Python handles the return automatically.

Initializing the Instance

By providing an `__init__` method, the class designer can add attributes to any instance made of that class. Because the dot-notation assignment creates attributes, the designer must make an assignment to `self.new_attribute`, creating the attribute as part of the instance (remember, `self` is associated with the instance being made). It is also important to assign some value to each attribute, as assignment is how a value attribute is created. For example, in the `Student` class `__init__`, we have `self.first_name_str = first`.

Following is a session using our `Student` class of Code Listing 11.3.

```
In  [1]: s1 = Student()
In  [2]: print(s1.last_name_str)

In  [3]: dir(s1)
Out [3]: ['__class__', ...,'__init__', ..., '__str__', ...,

'first_name_str', 'id_int', 'last_name_str', 'update']
In  [4]: s2 = Student(last='Python', first='Monty')
In  [5]: print(s2.last_name_str)
Python
```

```
In  [6]: dir(s2)
Out [6]: ['__class__', ...,'__init__', ..., '__str__', ...,

'first_name_str', 'id_int', 'last_name_str', 'update']
```

Two instances of `Student` are created: `s1, s2`. The first instance, `s1`, is created without any arguments to the constructor call: `Student()`. Since a default value (empty) is specified for the `last` parameter, the value of `last_name_str` is empty. The second instance, `s2`, is made with two of the three arguments `Student(last='Python', first='Monty')`. A `dir` of the `s1` instance shows that all three attributes were created: `first_name_str`, `last_name_str`, and `id_int`. Each instance and its attributes are now available to be updated, printed, or otherwise acted upon. Remember, each instance carries its own copies of the three attributes, since they were created by assignment in the `__init__` method. They are part of the instance's namespace. The `dir` also shows the three methods we defined in the class: `__init__, update, __str__` which are also available to the instance.

Printing the Instance

The next special Python method in Code Listing 11.3 is the `__str__` method. As you might guess from the name, it is a method to provide a string that represents the instance. This method is most useful in calls to the ***print*** statement, as the ***print*** statement attempts to convert any object it is provided into a string. By providing a `__str__` method, we can print a representation of our object.

For the `Student` class, the `__str__` method creates a single string that brings together the three attributes and returns that string. When a ***print*** function is called, the object is "converted" to a string and printed. Converted may not necessarily be the best word—clearly there is more to our object than the string we produce, but that is essentially what Python tries to do.

Following is a session that utilizes the `__str__` method.

```
In  [1]: s1 = Student()
In  [2]: s2 = Student(first='Monty', last='Python')
In  [3]: print(s1)
 , ID:0
In  [4]: print(s2)
Monty Python, ID:0
```

You may notice some commented print statements in the definition of our methods. Sometimes it is useful to print out *when* a method is invoked so that you can track more clearly when Python calls your methods. Here is the same session with the comments removed:

```
In  [1]: s1 = Student()
In __init__ method
```

```
In  [2]: s2 = Student(last='Punch', first='Bill')
In __init__ method
In  [3]: print(s1)
In __str__ method
 , ID:0
In  [4]: print(s2)
In __str__ method
Bill Punch, ID:0
```

By turning these print statements on and off, you can better trace the interplay between Python's class model and your methods.

PROGRAMMING TIP

Make *sure* that the `__str__` returns a value and that the value is a *string*. Odd things can happen otherwise.

Changing an Instance

In Python, the initialization of each instance by `__init__` ensures that every instance of the class is created in the same way. Each instance will contain the same number of attributes (though the values of the attributes may be different) and has access to the the same number of methods from the class. However, Python does not restrict the programmer from changing an instance once it is made. This is in keeping with our cookie and cookie cutter example. When the cookie is first stamped out, all of the cookies are the same. However, once made the cook is free to decorate or change each cookie individually.

Similarly, one may add a new attribute to an instance and even add a method directly to the instance's namespace (not easy to do, but it can be done). This ability differs from some other OOP languages such as Java and C++ in that those languages can prevent a user from changing an instance once it is created.

However, no matter the language, most OOP models agree that the *interface* to the object should be through its methods. In this way, the class designer can ensure that the instance is only modified in class designer-approved ways. The user may be free to "mess with" an instance, but they do so at his or her own risk. If the class designer provides an interface to the instance, then that is what the user should use.

In that spirit, we provide the `update` method to our `Student` class of Code Listing 11.3. This method is the class designer's interface for modifying the three attributes of a `Student` instance. Very similar to the `__init__` method, it provides the user with access to the instance's internal attributes.

Check Yourself: Defining Special Methods

1. Show the output that results for the indicated lines using the following program.

```
class NewClass(object):
    def __init__(self,param_int=1):
        self.the_int = param_int
        if param_int%2==0:
            self.parity='even'
        else:
            self.parity='odd'
    def process(self,instance):
        sum_int = self.the_int + instance.the_int
        if sum_int < 0:
            return 'negative'
        elif sum_int % 2==0:
            return 'even'
        else:
            return 'odd'
    def __str__(self):
        return 'Value {} is {}'.format(self.the_int,self.parity)

inst1=NewClass(4)
inst2=NewClass(-5)
inst3=NewClass()
print(inst1)                        # Line 1
print(inst1.parity)                 # Line 2
print(inst1.process(inst2))         # Line 3
print(inst3.process(inst1))         # Line 4
```

(a) What output is produced by Line 1 of the example program?
(b) What output is produced by Line 2 of the example program?
(c) What output is produced by Line 3 of the example program?
(d) What output is produced by Line 4 of the example program?

11.6.4 Now There Are Three: Class Designer, Programmer, and User

So far, we have discussed two kinds of players in our programming world: the programmers that make the programs and the users who use those programs. With the introduction of classes, we introduce a third player, the *class designer.*

The class designer is *also* a programmer, but this programmer's goal is to write code to be used by *other programmers* to use. In designing a class, the class designer provides a tool that, ideally, is intended to only be used and not modified by other programmers. Therefore, the class designer creates the class with other programmers in mind, and the programmer creates the program with the user in mind.

The programmer has a different view of the class than the class designer. The programmer sees the class only through the interface that the class designer provides. The programmer is shielded from the details of how the class does its job and is only aware of the interface—in particular, the operations, that the class designer provides. This structure is the promise of encapsulation. By designing the class well, the class stands as a library to be used by other programmers, providing those programmers with a more abstract, functional unit to solve their problems.

The class designer provides the class; the programmer uses it. When we design a class, we are designing it to be used by other programmers. Our job is to provide a reasonable interface to the class so that it:

- Does its job.
- Can be updated or modified with minimal impact on the users.

11.7 EXAMPLE: POINT CLASS

Let's tackle an example using Cartesian coordinates: dealing with points in a graph—something you should be familiar with from middle-school mathematics. We want to represent the two-dimensional points on the Cartesian coordinate plane. Each point is completely described by its coordinate pair: (x, y). We will choose two instance attributes, x and y, to represent the pair of values.

Once we have the instance attributes in place, we can consider what operations we wish to perform on these objects and write methods to take those actions. For illustration, we will choose finding the distance between two points and the sum of two points (also known as a vector sum).

More specifically we will implement these methods:

- `distance`: returns a distance (a floating-point number) between two points using the standard distance formula: The distance between (x_1, y_1) and (x_2, y_2) is:

$$distance = \sqrt{(x_1 - x_2)^2 + (y_1 - y_2)^2}$$

- `sum`: returns a *new point* that is the vector sum of two points. First, the new point must be created. Then for points (x_1, y_1) and (x_2, y_2), the new point's coordinates are updated to be:

$$(x_1 + x_2, y_1 + y_2)$$

We'll show the code and output, and then describe it. To run this class code you simply run the program as normal (e.g., F5 from SPYDER), which loads the class into the Python shell so that it can then be used as shown in the following Python shell session. At this moment, the output isn't very interesting because the points we create are all (0, 0). See Code Listing 11.4.

Code Listing 11.4

```
import math  # need sqrt (square root)

# a Point is a Cartesion point (x,y)
# all values are float unless otherwise stated
class Point(object):
  def __init__(self): # create and initialize
    self.x = 0.0
    self.y = 0.0

  def distance (self,param_pt): # standard distance formula
    """Distance between self and a Point"""
    x_diff = self.x - param_pt.x  # (x1 – x2)
    y_diff = self.y - param_pt.y  # (y1 – y2)
    # square differences, sum, and take sqrt
    return math.sqrt(x_diff**2 + y_diff**2)

  def sum (self,param_pt): # new point from vector sum
    """Vector Sum of self and a Point"""
    new_pt = Point()        # create a new point
    new_pt.x = self.x + param_pt.x  # calculate x value sum from self and pt
    new_pt.y = self.y + param_pt.y
    return new_pt
```

```
In  [1]: p1 = Point() # create a Point named "p1"
In  [2]: p2 = Point()
In  [3]: print(p1.x, p1.y) # print the Point's x and y values
0.0 0.0
In  [4]: print(p2.x, p2.y)
0.0 0.0
In  [5]: print(p1.distance(p2)) # find distance from p1 to p2
0.0
In  [6]: p3 = p1.sum(p2) # find sum of p1 and p2
In  [7]: print(p3.x, p3.y)
0.0 0.0
```

11.7.1 Construction

The `__init__` method creates two attributes: the coordinates `x` and `y` in each instance. We can show this by printing the two attributes of each of the `Point` instances: `p1` and `p2`. Note that the coordinates are each set to 0 in all instances.

11.7.2 Distance

To find the distance from `p1` to `p2`, we can call the `distance` method using the normal dot-notation: `p1.distance(p2)`. When the method is invoked, `self` is set to the calling object, the one associated with `p1`, and the second parameter `param_pt` is set to the object associated with `p2`.

Within the method, we apply our distance formula. We must first find the difference as indicated in the formula $(x_1 - x_2)$. We have two parameter points: `self` and `param_pt`. The difference in x for those two points is expressed as `x_diff = self.x - pt.x`. Be careful that you understand that particular statement! The expression `self.x` is the x attribute of the calling object, and `param_pt.x` is the x attribute of the second object, the parameter object. We must also calculate `y_diff` using a similar expression. We can then determine the distance using the formula $distance = \sqrt{(x_1 - x_2)^2 + (y_1 - y_2)^2}$. We implement this as `math.sqrt(x_diff**2 + y_diff**2)`. The resulting distance floating-point value is then returned.

Because distance is commutative, reversing the invocation—that is `p2.distance(p1)` —would yield the same result. Which object gets associated with `self` and which with the paramater `param_pt` for this invocation[4]?

11.7.3 Summing Two Points

First it is interesting to note that we named the operation `sum`. Isn't there a `sum` operation in Python already, and wouldn't that affect the default function? That answer is no, and the reason is interesting. The default `sum` is a function in the Python global namespace. The method `sum` we are defining is part of the `Point` class. We can call the default function just by invoking it, but to call the method, we must invoke it in conjunction (using dot notation) with a `Point` object. Python can keep these two separate because of how they are invoked.

On to the method. To sum two points `p1` and `p2` the invocation would again be done in dot notation: `p3 = p1.sum(p2)`. We are calling the `sum` using `p1` as the invoking object and `p2` as an argument. Therefore, when the method is invoked, `self` is associated with the `p1` object and the second parameter `param_pt` is associated with the `p2` object.

What is the right type to return from the summation of two points? With a little thought, it should be clear that a `Point` object is what should be returned. It would be unusual to

[4] p2 is associated with `self`, p1 with `param_pt`.

return any other type as we would expect to apply Point methods to the result. The same would be true of other objects we already know. What should be returned from the sum of two floats, of two strings, of two lists?

Since we need to return a Point instance, we must first create a new Point instance in the method and store the sum in that instance: new_pt = Point(). Once set with the proper attribute values, new_pt will be the return object. For the *x* attribute, we add the *x* values of the two parameter points and assign the result to the *x* attribute of the return object: new_pt.x = *self*.x + param_pt.x. We do the same for the y values: new_pt.y = *self*.y + param_pt.y. Finally, we return new_pt. In the original invocation, the returned point associated with new_pt is assigned to p3.

As with the distance method, the sum method is commutative so a reverse invocation would return the same Point object result.

The output isn't interesting because the points we are creating are all initialized to (0, 0) so both the distance and sum are zero. We start the session by running the program which loads the class into the Python shell so we can use it.

11.7.4 Improving the Point Class

Default Initialization

VideoNote 11.2
Improving a Class

The __init__ method is like any other method, in that it too can take parameters. These parameters are typically used to set the attribute values of each new instance.

A useful feature for the __init__ method is the default parameter value (see Section 8.2). By using defaults, the user is not required to specify all the instance attributes, but every attribute is still created in the instance with some value. Remember that an attribute must be assigned a value to be created in an instance. The following example has parameters x and y each with default value of 0.0. If the user, in invoking the method, provides arguments, then those argument values will be used. If not, the default values of 0.0 will be used.

Code Listing 11.5 is the improved __init__ method—the rest of the class is unchanged.

Code Listing 11.5

```
import math # need sqrt (square root)

# a Point is a Cartesion point (x,y)
# all values are float unless otherwise stated
class Point(object):
    def __init__(self, x_param = 0.0, y_param = 0.0):
        ''' Create x and y attributes. Defaults are 0.0'''
        self.x = x_param
        self.y = y_param
```

```
    def distance (self,param_pt):
        """Distance between self and a Point"""
        x_diff = self.x - param_pt.x  # (x1 - x2)
        y_diff = self.y - param_pt.y  # (y1 - y2)
        # square differences, sum, and take sqrt
        return math.sqrt(x_diff**2 + y_diff**2)

    def sum (self,param_pt):
        """Vector Sum of self and a Point
           return a Point instance"""
        new_pt = Point()
        new_pt.x = self.x + param_pt.x
        new_pt.y = self.y + param_pt.y
        return new_pt
```

Let's use the improved version in a session. This time the point p1 will have some non-zero values for *x* and *y*.

```
In [1]: p1 = Point(2.0,4.0) # create a point with x and y values specified
In [2]: p2 = Point() # create a point with default values
In [3]: print(p1.distance(p2)) # find and print the distance
4.47213595499958
In [4]: p3 = p1.sum(p2) # calculate the sum and then print it
In [5]: print(p3.x, p3.y)
2.0 4.0
```

When the instance is made, you can now pass arguments to initialize the attributes of an instance. We see that in the creation of `p1 = Point(2.0,4.0)`, which initializes p1's *x* attribute to 2.0 and similarly its *y* attribute to 4.0.

You do not have to explicitly set the values for an instance's *x* and y attributes: you can use default arguments. We see that with the creation of `p2 = Point()`, no arguments are passed to `__init__` so the specified default values of 0.0 are used for p2's *x* and *y* attributes.

As with earlier constructor invocations, `p1 = Point(2.0,4.0)` calls the `__init__` method with `self` associated with the new instance being created. In the method, `self.x = param_x` initializes that new object's *x* attribute and similarly for the *y* attribute. Python automatically returns that object (a specific **return** statement is forbidden in `__init__`) and that object is assigned to p1.

"Do the Right Thing": Printing the Values

It is painful to have to print each value of a class instance, especially if it is a complex object with many instance variables. Moreover, we have come to expect Python to "do the right thing" when it comes to operations like printing. As much as possible, when we create a new class it should "do the right thing" with respect to standard Python operations. This is so important that we make it a new rule:

Rule 9: Make sure your new class does the right thing.

Again, by "right thing" we mean it should operate in a way that is familiar to a Python user of your class. The sum of two `Point` instances should return a new `Point` instance. When using a ***print*** function, an instance should respond to that function and *print itself*.

For printing, it means that we need to provide a `__str__` method in `Point`, which gets called when we ***print*** an instance. Code Listing 11.6 adds that method to the `Point` class.

Code Listing 11.6

```
import math  # need sqrt (square root)

# a Point is a Cartesion point (x,y)
# all values are float unless otherwise stated
class Point(object):
    def __init__(self, x_param = 0.0, y_param = 0.0):
        ''' Create x and y attributes. Defaults are 0.0'''
        self.x = x_param
        self.y = y_param

    def distance (self,param_pt):
        """Distance between self and a Point"""
        x_diff = self.x - param_pt.x  # (x1 - x2)
        y_diff = self.y - param_pt.y  # (y1 - y2)
        # square differences, sum, and take sqrt
        return math.sqrt(x_diff**2 + y_diff**2)

    def sum (self,param_pt):
        """Vector Sum of self and a Point
           return a Point instance"""
        new_pt = Point()
        new_pt.x = self.x + param_pt.x
        new_pt.y = self.y + param_pt.y
        return new_pt

    def __str__(self):
        """Print as a coordinate pair."""
        print("called the __str__ method")
        return "({:.2f}, {:.2f})".format(self.x,self.y)
```

Let's look at a session using our improved `Point` class with the ability to print:

```
In [1]: p1 = Point(2.0, 4.0)
In [2]: print(p1)
called the __str__ method
(2.00, 4.00)
```

In this example, we create a `p1` instance as before with initial values for *x* and *y*, 2.0 and 4.0 respectively. With the new `__str__` method, when can now call the ***print*** function, as in ***print***`(p1)` and print a reasonable representation of a point. As we will do occasionally to make flow of control more obvious, we have placed a ***print*** in the `__str__` method to indicate when it gets called. These statements should be removed (or at least commented out) when the class is finished but it helps us, the class designer, understand the flow of control when we are creating our class. Note that when we call the ***print*** function the `__str__` method is implicitly called (as demonstrated by our printing the "called" string) with *`self`* being set to the argument `p1` object. This syntax gives us access to the instance's attributes and allows us to create a string, which *must* be returned by this method. We are free to format this string in any way we feel is suitable for the object we are creating. This returned string is then printed.

Updated Point Class

Now let's take a final look at the whole class in Code Listing 11.7. This review provides us an opportunity to refactor the code to make it better. For example, we could refactor the `sum` method. With initialization of values in the `__init__` method, we can simplify the `sum` method by creating the new point using initialization. Having done that, we can just ***return*** this new point, combining all the previous statements into one. The previous statements are commented so that you might compare the two approaches. Which is more readable? What do you think, and why?

Code Listing 11.7

```python
import math # need sqrt (square root)

# a Point is a Cartesion point (x,y)
# all values are float unless otherwise stated
class Point(object):
    def __init__(self, x_param = 0.0, y_param = 0.0):
        '''Create x and y attributes. Defaults are 0.0'''
        self.x = x_param
        self.y = y_param
```

```
    def distance (self,param_pt):
        """Distance between self and a Point"""
        x_diff = self.x - param_pt.x  # (x1 - x2)
        y_diff = self.y - param_pt.y  # (y1 - y2)
        # square differences, sum, and take sqrt
        return math.sqrt(x_diff**2 + y_diff**2)

    def sum (self,param_pt):
        """Vector Sum of self and a Point
           return a Point instance"""
        # new_pt = Point()
        # new_pt.x = self.x + param_pt.x
        # new_pt.y = self.x + param_pt.x
        return Point(self.x + param_pt.x, self.x + param_pt.x)

    def __str__(self):
        """Print as a coordinate pair."""
        # print("called the __str__ method")
        return "({:.2f}, {:.2f})".format(self.x,self.y)
```

11.8 PYTHON AND OOP

In the introduction, we noted that OOP had three concepts:

- Encapsulation
- Inheritance
- Polymorphism

Python addresses all these issues, though we may not fully explore all of those issues in this introductory book. It is worth noting that different languages might address the issues in ways that differ from Python.

11.8.1 Encapsulation

Python, and really all languages with OOP support, addresses the issue of *encapsulation*. That is, understanding the details of underlying class structure should not be necessary to utilize an instance of a class. Python gives the class designer the ability to create methods as the interface a class's instances. If the class is well designed, then a user of the class need only use the provided methods to use the class instance. The class designer is free to place information in the class that is important to the design, but not the use, of the class. That is, the class designer can hide implementation details of the class, providing the methods as the public face of the class.

11.8.2 Inheritance

Inheritance allows the class designer to utilize the design of an existing class to create a new class. That is, we can create a new class the *specializes* an existing class by utilizing the existing class's attributes, specializing only those attributes that distinguish the new class. In this way, classes can *share* common elements and change only those attributes that distinguish the new class.

How do we do this? Essentially, there are two important elements. First, we impose a relationship on our *classes*, much like the relationship found between instance and class, of parent and child class. Second, we create an approach that allows us to search for an attribute, not only in an instance or its parent class, but utilizing the relationship between classes as well. This relationship allows us to *inherit* attributes found in a class that is *above* it in the relationship scheme. By inheriting those attributes, we can share common code. Consider the car analogy we discussed earlier. Imagine there exits a `Vehicle` class with attributes such as `number_of_wheels`, `engine_size`, `fuel_source`, and so on. A specialization of `Vehicle` could be a more specialized kind of vehicle, for example, a `Truck` class. If the `Truck` class has as its parent the `Vehicle` class, then `Truck` can inherit attributes common to both. That is, we do not need to add attributes to the `Truck` class that already exist in the `Vehicle` class. However, we are free to add more particular attributes to `Truck` such as `carrying_capacity` and `trailer_size`. A different specialization might be a `Sedan` class that also inherits the same common attributes of `Vehicle` but adds a different set of special attributes (i.e., `trunk_size`). The next chapter, Chapter 12 will cover inheritance in more detail.

11.8.3 Polymorphism

Polymorphism is the process of using an operator (such as plus +) or method (such as `count`) to perform different operations depending on the types that invoke them. We have shown that Python has this ability. For example, plus is the addition operation with integers or floats but concatenation with strings or lists. In the next chapter, you will see how to write class methods with polymorphism.

11.9 PYTHON AND OTHER OOP LANGUAGES

Although Python does provide class and OOP support, it differs from some other OOP languages in some of the details. We review those here.

11.9.1 Public versus Private

Given the nature of the two groups using a class (class designer and programmer), one can differentiate the access that a member of each group can have. That is, the class designer may want to control and protect internal class structure from access other than that provided by methods. In so doing, the designer guarantees (or attempts to guarantee) that the provided interface remains constant, but the designer can still modify the internal structure otherwise to meet changing demand. This demarcation of roles, designer and programmer, makes changes to code more manageable.

In OOP terminology, this protection is often discussed in terms of *public* versus *private* attributes:

- Public attributes (variables, methods) are available to everyone (designer and programmer).
- Private attributes (variables, methods) are available only to the designer.

The impetus for separation is to help with large software development. Guarantees of public access to an object, while providing flexibility on private aspects of the object, allows code to be written that can be more easily adapted to changing demands and requirements. Note that large can be quite large indeed. For example, an operating system such as Microsoft Windows will have tens of *millions* of lines of code. Partitioning responsibility is critical for containing potential chaos.

11.9.2 Indicating Privacy Using Double Underscores (__)

Python does not enforce this separation between the designer and programmer. All methods and instance variables are public, so both designers and programmers have access. Python *does* provide support for the designer to indicate attributes that the programmer *should not* modify directly.

Whenever a class designer names an attribute with two leading underscores, this is a message to anyone using the class that the designer *considers this a private variable.* No one should change or modify its value. To prevent this change from accidentally happening, Python *mangles* the name of the attribute for outside use (outside of the class). The verb "mangle" here means that the attribute name is actually changed. The transformation is as follows: an attribute named `__attribute` is changed to be `_ClassName__attribute` for outside use. Look at the code and session in Code Listing 11.8.

Code Listing 11.8

```
class NewClass (object):
    def __init__(self, attribute='default', name='Instance'):
        self.name = name                      # public attribute
        self.__attribute = attribute          # a "private" attribute
    def __str__(self):
        return '{} has attribute {}'.format(self.name, self.__attribute)
```

```
In  [1]: inst1 = NewClass(name='Monty', attribute='Python')
In  [2]: print(inst1)
Monty has attribute Python
In  [3]: print(inst1.name)
Monty
In  [4]: print(inst1.__attribute)

Traceback (most recent call last):
  File "<pyshell#3>", line 1, in <module>
    print(inst1.__attribute)
AttributeError: 'newClass' object has no attribute '__attribute'

In  [5]: dir(inst1)
Out [5]: '_NewClass__attribute', '__class__', ... , 'name']

In  [6]: print(inst1._NewClass__attribute)
Python
```

In the `__init__` method, we assign two attributes: `name` and `__attribute`. By preceding the second with two underscores, we are indicating that `__attribute` is private and should not be accessed. Python changes that attribute name so that, if the provided attribute name (`__attribute`) is referenced outside of the class, an error is thrown. However, using the original attribute name *within* the class, such as in a method of the class (e.g., `__str__`), is allowed.

Look at the `__str__` method. It makes reference to the name directly as `self.__attribute`. The `__str__` method is permitted this access, as it is within the class. However, in the session, we see that if we try to print `inst1.__attribute`, we get an error. Printing in the interpreter is a use of the attribute outside the class and the name is no longer correct. Interestingly, if we do `dir(inst1)` we see that, indeed, the name has been changed (mangled) to `_NewClass__attribute`.

This change of name *does not* prevent the programmer from accessing the attribute value. It only provides a layer of obfuscation. The programmer can get around the class designer if they choose, but they do so in violation of the designer's intent. Perhaps in the future, the class will change and the programmer's code will no longer work because of their disregard for the rules. When an attribute is marked with the double-underscore prefix, it means leave it alone!

11.9.3 Python's Philosophy

The philosophy that Python promotes is best summarized by the phrase "We are all adults here." If the designer indicates something should be private, then a programmer violates privacy at their own peril. By reducing the overhead of indicating what is and what is not private, the code is simpler and, using some simple rules, what *should* be private can be easily indicated.

11.9.4 Modifying an Instance

Many OOP languages use the class to define the state of the instance: what methods are defined that the instance can use and what attributes are parts of the instance. Their class model supports this view. Once the instance is made, it cannot be modified. Attributes cannot be added or removed.

Python, on the other hand, takes a less restrictive stance. A Python class, like the other OOP languages, provides the template for the initial state (variables and methods). However, after the instance is created, that instance can be modified as the programmer sees fit. Again, the phrase "We are all adults here" applies. Why restrict what the programmer might do? As class designers, we indicated what we think a programmer *should* do, but trying to *prevent* a programmer from doing something clutters the language. Besides, if a programmer really does want to do something, even if the designer does not, there is always a way.

11.10 WHAT'S WRONG WITH MY CODE?

Here are suggestions for finding problems with classes. Refer to Appendix C for details.

- **Forgot self:** If you forget `self` as the first parameter in a method you will get a mismatch in the number of parameters. Remember, **every** class method has `self` as its first parameter, even if the method takes no arguments when it is called. Python **automatically** associates the calling object and passes it as the first method parameter. The error message looks like this (for a method named `my_method`): **TypeError: my_method() takes 0 positional arguments but 1 was given**
- **Method __str__ must return a string:** If you forget to return a string from the `__str__` method, you will get this message: `TypeError: __str__ returned non-string (type int)`
- **AttributeError** often happens because you have mistyped the name of a method or an attribute is private.
  - If you mistyped the method, you can use your IPython history to bring it back and retype it.
  - If you can't remember the proper spelling, you can make an instance of the class, put a dot behind it and type the tab key. IPython will list all the potential methods.
  - If that doesn't work, remember the privacy rule covered in Section 11.9.1. If you prepend double underscores to an attribute name, special naming rules apply. For example, if the attribute is named `__my_attribute` in the class `MyClass`, the following are the rules:
    * **Inside MyClass**: The name remains `__my_attribute`, including in the context of any other `MyClass` methods.
    * **Outside MyClass**: The name outside of the `MyClass` namespace, you refer to the attribute as `_MyClass__my_attribute`.
- **NameError** often happens when you do not specify a class attribute correctly. This often occurs when you forget to prepend `self` to the name of a method in the class.

- **Forgot __init__:** If you forget to define an `__init__` method, you may get either unexpected results or an error such as an **AttributeError**. A class definition is not required to have an `__init__` method defined (a default one exists), in which case class instances are created with no attributes. However, by having `__init__` in your class, you can define, by assignment, attributes that you want to exist in every instance. Set a breakpoint after an instance is created to make sure it contains the attributes you expect. If not, check your `__init__`, or create one if you don't have one.

Summary

The concept of OOP is a powerful development tool. It is particularly supportive of the divide-and-conquer style of problem solving. If you can organize your design thoughts around OOP, you can design large programs around basic objects.

The concept of `self` is important in understanding how class objects work, especially in the creation and use of instances. Reread this chapter, if you feel that you have not yet grasped the concept of `self` in Python classes.

Classes

- Classes are objects.
- Object-Oriented Programming (OOP) has three concepts: Encapsulation, Inheritance, Polymorphism.
- Creating a new class creates a new type.
- A class is to its instance as a cookie cutter is to a cookie.
- Classes have attributes and methods that act on those attributes.
- Attributes are usually created within the `__init__` method.
- The identifier `self` refers to the current instance.
- The first parameter of methods is `self`.
- Class structure

```
class ClassName(object):
    def __init__(self,param1=4):
        self.att = param1 # create attribute.
    def __str__(self):
        return "some string" # return a string for printing
    def some_method(self,param):
        # do something
```

Rules

- **RULE 1:** Think before you program!
- **RULE 2:** A program is a human-readable essay on problem solving that also happens to execute on a computer.
- **RULE 3:** The best way to improve your programming and problem skills is to practice!
- **RULE 4:** A foolish consistency is the hobgoblin of little minds.
- **RULE 5:** Test your code, often and thoroughly!
- **RULE 6:** If it was hard to write, it is probably hard to read. Add a comment.
- **RULE 7:** All input is evil, until proven otherwise.
- **RULE 8:** A function should do one thing.
- **RULE 9:** Make sure your new class does the right thing.

Exercises

1. In your own words, describe the purpose of the `__init__` method.

2. Write a Shopping Cart class to implement a shopping cart that you often find on websites where you could purchase some goods. Think about what things you could store in a cart and also what operations you could perform on the cart.

   To simplify matters, you could consider the website to be an electronics e-store that has goods like flat-panel TVs, boomboxes, iPods, camcorders, and so on.

3. Consider a table fan. Write a Table Fan class. What would be the attributes of this class? Examples of attributes could be speed levels of fan, side-to-side movement (on/off, and degrees of movement), manufacturer name, cost, used/new, and so on. Think about it this way. You want to be able to *get* information about the fan; for example, if you want to buy or sell a fan from some website such as Craigslist, what features would you be interested in? Also, consider control (operations) you might want to have over the fan such as setting the fan speed or having it pan from side to side.

4. There are many websites where you could listen to music, for example, rhapsody.com. A music album contains many soundtracks and each soundtrack has a name, time duration, name of artist, year, and other data.

   Design classes for the album and soundtrack. Think about the methods appropriate for the classes. For soundtrack, some methods could be play, pause, stop, and so on.

5. Write a class to hold the measurements for a rectangle. Some of the parameters of a square are length, breadth, area, perimeter, internal angles, and length of diagonals. Think about the methods appropriate for the class.

6. Write a class an investor might use to track their investments. Fields might include: type of investment, amount invested, investment period, expected returns, taxes owed and taxes paid. Think about the methods appropriate for the class than an investor might use.

7. Consider a hospital scenario. Design classes for:
   - Patients. The class might have fields like unique ID for the patient, name, male or female, age, address, phone number, date of birth, height, and weight.
   - Doctor. Fields might include the doctor's name, unique registration number, qualification (DO or MD), specialization (surgeon, pediatrician, etc.), phone number, office hours, and office location.
   - Patients' records in a hospital. The record might have fields like last date of check-up, doctor's unique ID, patient's unique ID, list of health problems in the patient, list of medicines prescribed, cost of the checkup, final report, and so on.

   Methods of these classes would be mostly `get` and *`set`* methods for the corresponding fields.

8. Consider the design of a class for managing the Olympics—to simplify things, consider management of Olympic medal awards. Design a medal class.
   - Fields: Name of the athlete, country, event, medal type (gold, silver, bronze)
   - Methods: `get`, *`set`*, and so on.

9. Design a schedule class for classes that a student (you!) take during a semester.

10. In a supermarket, all vegetables have a product code, name, some description, and price per unit. Design a class called "Vegetable" to represent the vegetables. Provide get and set methods for the class.

11. Design a class called Sentence that has a constructor that takes a string representing the sentence as input. The class should have the following methods:
    - `get_first_word`
    - `get_all_words`
    - `replace(index, new_word)`—Change a word at a particular index to "new_word". For example, if sentence is "I'm going back." and `set_word_at_index(2, "home")`, then sentence becomes "I'm going home."

12. Create a class named `Robot` with internal attributes that can't be accessed from outside the class. It should have private attributes to hold its physical and psychological state. A robot's `condition` is the sum of the values of its physical and psychological state. The `condition` property should return the robot instance's condition.

13. Create a class named `Attendee` which will keep track of the number of people joining and leaving a meeting. It should have methods to increase the number of people in the meeting if a new attendee joins, and to decrease the number of people in the meeting if someone leaves. Write a program that will display a welcome message and the number of people currently in the meeting every time a new Attendee object is created.

Programming Projects

1. Solitaire: Using Classes

Writing a program to play the popular card game of solitaire offers an opportunity to work with classes while developing problem solving skills. A large number of variations of solitaire exist—the website `http://worldofsolitaire.com` alone has over 50 variations. In this exercise, your program will enforce the rules of the game—the user will be playing the game.

We provide a module `cards.py` that contains two classes: `Card` and `Deck`. A `Deck` is a collection of `Cards`. We also provide a sample piece of code that demonstrates how to use the cards module. The Card and Deck classes are general-purpose for developing card games, so they contain many methods that may not be used in any particular implementation.

Each `Card` has two primary attributes: `rank` and `suit`. In an English deck, there are four suits—spades, diamonds, hearts, and clubs—that we represent by their first letters: `'S'`, `'D'`, `'H'`, `'C'`. Each suit has thirteen cards—Ace, 2–10, Jack, Queen, and King—with ranks 1–13 in that order. Each card has a **value** that for most cards is the same as its rank, but for face cards (Jack, Queen, King), the value is 10.

Some card games such as poker have an Ace with a rank greater than a King; other games such as Blackjack allow the Ace to have a value of 1 or 11. The Card class does not incorporate those alternative ranks and values, so those differences need to be added to the class for those games or incorporated into the game program itself.

The primary methods for the Card class are:

- `get_rank` returns the rank of a Card (*int*).
- `get_suit` returns the suit of a Card (`string`).
- `get_value` returns the value of a Card (*int*).

There are other methods that are explained in the module, but two are worth mentioning because they are useful when debugging: `set_rank` and `set_suit`. They allow you as the programmer to set up particular scenarios when testing your code.

A `Deck` is a collection of cards; in fact it is a sequence because we expect a deck to be ordered.

Although there are many methods in the class, the primary methods for the `Deck` class are:

- `shuffle` randomly rearranges the cards in the deck (returns nothing).
- `deal` returns one card and removes the card from the deck (`Card`).
- `empty` returns *True* if there are no cards in the deck (`bool`).

Both classes have `__str__` and `__repr__` defined to make printing easy.

Here is a sample session illustrating a few `Card` and `Deck` methods:

```
In  [1]: import cards
In  [2]: a_deck = cards.Deck()
In  [3]: a_deck.shuffle()
In  [3]: a_card = a_deck.deal()
In  [3]: print a_card
Out [3]:  8D

In  [4]: a_card.get_suit()
Out [4]: 'D'

In  [5]: a_card.get_rank()
Out [5]: 8

In  [6]: jack_of_clubs = cards.Card('J','C')
In  [7]: print jack_of_clubs
  JC
In  [8]: print a_deck

  5C  QS  6S  2D  4D 10C  8H  6D  4C  AH  9S  AD  8C
  9H  4H  7S  3H 10H  QD  7C  6C  2H  5S  3S  AS  QC
  KC  3C  8S  7H  JH  KD  KH  JD  7D  AC  9C  2C  JS
  2S  KS 10S  5H  9D  3D  5D 10D  QH  6H  JC  4S
```

Every solitaire game has three main components: the stock, the tableau, and the foundation. The *stock* is the source of new cards, that is, the deck of cards. The *foundation* is where the cards get stacked in four stacks (one for each suit) in order from Ace to King—four complete stacks in the foundation indicate winning the game. The `tableau` is where the main part of solitaire is played and varies significantly from game to game. A losing game is when no more moves can be made in the tableau and the stock is empty.

Write a program to play the *Easthaven* version of solitaire—complete rules and versions to play with to learn the game can be found online (e.g., `http://worldofsolitaire.com`).

Easthaven solitaire (tableau rules):

- The tableau begins with seven columns with three cards in each column. In each column, initially, only the top card is visible.
- Build down by rank and by alternating color. For example, you can play a two of Hearts on a three of Spades (the column goes down by rank, and alternates colors).
- Either the top card may be moved or complete or partial correctly ranked piles may be moved as a pile. If a pile is moved, the top card of the pile must follow the rules (down rank and alternating color) and all the rest of cards in the pile must also follow the rules.
- An exposed face-down card may be turned face up.

- An empty spot may be filled with any card or correctly ranked pile.
- If you cannot make any moves on the tableau, or any moves from the tableau to the foundation, you can take cards from the stock.
- **Different!** When the stock is used, a card is added to the end of *each* tableau column.
- Any fully exposed card can be moved to the foundation as long as the foundation rules are adhered to: placement in the foundation must follow both suit and rank (Ace up to King).

Create a main program that is a loop that drives the game. Repeatedly prompt for commands such as move_within_tableau, move_to_foundation, and deal_from_stock. Each command suggests its own method, but you are likely to want many more helping methods.

Note: This set-up can be used for any of the solitaire games so this exercise provides a framework for many, many exercises: simply adjust the tableau rules appropriately. The `cards.py` module can be also used for any card game, but the single-player solitaire is an excellent exercise.

2. GPS Unit for Hikers

GPS has been built into a wide variety of consumer devices. They share many features, but differ in details. Here we consider the GPS unit used by hikers and back-country explorers. An important feature of such units is the ability to mark *waypoints*, including the ability to collect them into a path that can be retrieved later. Another important feature is distance and bearing to a waypoint: you have a target waypoint, and you want to know what direction it is in and the distance to that target. This last feature is particularly useful in geocaching or locating your starting point, if you are lost.

When queried the GPS hardware generates the current longitude and latitude: a pair of floating-point values. The range of longitude is −180 degrees to +180 degrees (the reference point (0) is the meridian through Greenwich, England). The range of latitude is −90 degrees to +90 degrees (the reference point (0) is the equator with positive values in the northern hemisphere). For example, according to the "Farmer's Almanac" the "middle" of the United States is at latitude 39.83333 degrees, longitude −98.5833 degrees. That is near the town of Lebanon, in Smith County, Kansas. We need to simulate that capability in this exercise. Write a method named `gps_get_long_lat` that returns a longitude and latitude pair. The method uses the Python `random` module to generate the pair.

A waypoint will be a position, a longitude—latitude pair, with a name.

Implement the following capabilities:

- Your GPS unit should be able to save the current waypoint, that is, save the current position as a waypoint, and associate a name with the position.
- Your GPS unit should be able to save and retrieve named paths consisting of a sequence of waypoints.

- It should also be able to find the length of a given path—assuming a straight line between each waypoint.
- Your GPS unit should be able to calculate the distance to a waypoint (from the current location).

Write a main program that loops and prompts the user for functionality provided by the GPS unit. Create a session that tests all methods.

Optional: add a method to calculate a bearing between the current position and a waypoint. Hint use the math inverse tangent (`atan`) function, but the `atan2` function may be slightly easier to work with.

CHAPTER 12

More on Classes

> It is only in the world of objects that we have time and space and selves.
>
> T. S. Eliot, poet

OBJECT-ORIENTED PROGRAMMING NOT ONLY HELPS YOU CREATE AND ORGANIZE NEW data structures, but also affects how you think about problem solving. In this chapter, we take a look at more capabilities provided by object-oriented thinking.

12.1 MORE ABOUT CLASS PROPERTIES

As mentioned in Chapter 11, there are three major object-oriented programming (OOP) characteristics: encapsulation, inheritance, and polymorphism.

We have focused so far on encapsulation, which:

- *Hides details* of implementation to aid reading and understanding.
- Provides *modularity* that makes it easier to use a class in other contexts.
- Provides an *interface* in the form of methods to access and manipulate a class instance.

We add a new concept to encapsulation: *consistency*. There are two characteristics to consider with respect to consistency:

- A new class should be consistent with the rules and syntax of the language.
- A new class should respond to "standard methods" (such as construction, printing, and iteration) that are appropriate for the object.

This is really just an expansion on **RULE 9**. New classes should "do the right thing." A class you create should behave like any other object so that it can be used in a natural way—just like they have used other objects. In a similar vein, one would expect familiar methods to work in familiar ways. For example, the "+" operator sums integers and concatenates strings. The operations are quite different, but each operation is appropriate for its specific type.

In this section, you will see how to make the classes we create behave in a way that is consistent with built-in objects.

12.1.1 Rational Number (Fraction) Class Example

Python, like most computer languages, has built-in objects for integers and "decimals" (floating points). However, only with the release of Python 2.6 did Python provide support for rational numbers with the `fractions` module and the `Fraction` class. We implement here a rational numbers class of our own design which, when it is completed, you can compare to Python's built-in class.

Rational numbers have two parts, a numerator and a denominator, that our class implementation must represent. Furthermore, the class should behave in a way that is consistent with other number objects we have become familiar with such as *int* and *float*. In particular, the following kinds of operations should be applicable to a rational number:

- Construction
- Printing
- Arithmetic operators (+, −, *, /)
- Comparison operators (<, >, ==, etc.)

Assuming that we have written the class (or are using the built-in `Fraction` class), a rational number should have the kinds of behavior shown in the following session. Later in this chapter we will see how you can build the class to achieve this consistency. This session establishes, before we even design the class, what "do the right thing" means for a rational number class.

```
# get our rational number class named frac_class
In [1]: from frac_class import *
In [2]: r1 = Rational(1,2) # create the fraction 1/2
In [3]: r2 = Rational(3,2) # create the fraction 3/2
In [4]: r3 = Rational(3) # default denominator is 1, so really creating 3/1
In [5]: r_sum = r1 + r2 # use "+" in a familiar way
In [6]: print(r_sum) # use "print" in a familiar way
4/2
In [7]: r_sum # display value in session in a familiar way
Out [7]: 4/2

In [8]: if r1 == r1: # use equality check "==" in a familiar way
...     print('equal')
... else:
...     print('not equal')
...
equal
In [9]: print(r3 - r2) # combine arithmetic and printing in a familiar way
3/2
```

In this session, a Rational instance looks like any other number. It responds syntactically to methods as we expect and uses operators as we expect. It is consistent and does the right thing. One thing to note about the right thing to do. We get to make choices as to what we, the class designers, thing is right. For example, when a rational number is printed, it has not been reduced, for example, 4/2 is printed instead of the reduced value 2. Not reducing the value is a design decision made by the designer of the class (the text authors, in this case). It would be equally reasonable to have decided that all values should be reduced before printing.

Variation on Import, from

In the previous session, the import line is somewhat different. That first line uses the general form ***from*** module ***import*** *. This is a variation on the syntax we have been using up to this point. A normal ***import*** frac_class would require us to precede every member of that module with the module name, for example frac_class.Rational() to call a constructor. While this is a very clear statement, we want the Rational() constructor in the frac_class method, it is also tedious to repeatedly type. This alternate syntax imports contents of the module directly into the top level of Python. That is, every element of the module becomes part of the global scope of the Python interpreter. The following session shows a more concrete example using the math module.

```
In  [1]: globals(>>>)
Out [1]: {'__builtins__': <module 'builtins' (built-in)>, '__name__': '__main__',
  '__doc__': None, '__package__': None}

In  [2]: import math
In  [3]: globals(>>>)
Out [3]: {'__builtins__': <module 'builtins' (built-in)>, '__name__': '__main__',
  '__doc__': None, 'math': <module 'math' from '/Library/Frameworks/Python.
framework/Versions/3.2/lib/python3.2/lib-dynload/math.so'>, '__package__': None}

In  [4]: math.sqrt(4)
Out [4]: 2.0

In  [5]: from math import *
In  [6]: globals(>>>)
Out [6]: {'__builtins__': <module 'builtins' (built-in)>, '__name__': '__main__',
  '__doc__': None, 'math': <module 'math' from '/Library/Frameworks/Python.
framework/Versions/3.2/lib/python3.2/lib-dynload/math.so'>, '__package__': None
  'sqrt': <built-in function sqrt>, 'pow': <built-in function pow>, 'fsum':
  <built-in function fsum>, 'cosh': <built-in function cosh>,  'pi': 3.
141592653589793, 'e': 2.718281828459045, 'tanh': <built-in function tanh>, ...}

In  [7]: sqrt(4)
Out [7]: 2.0
```

This session shows how the global value dictionary (returned by the function `globals`) changes using the two types of import. After the first import, the only change to the global dictionary is the inclusion of the math package name (with a value pointing to the math package library). Having done so, we can invoke the `sqrt` function in the module using `math.sqrt(4)`. However, if we use the new import syntax, look at change to the global dictionary. *All* of the elements of math are now directly available without the package prefix (not all are shown, it's a long list). They are all now part of the global namespace of Python. We can now type `sqrt(4)` and the appropriate operation will occur.

As with all things, there are good and bad points to this new syntax. Clearly the good is the shortened name for everything. Instead of typing `frac_class.Rational()`, we can type `Rational()` to run the constructor. The bad is the pollution of the global namespace. What if the module you import has a function with the same name as one in the global namespace? Imagine if the `math` module had a `sum` method.[1] When we did the second kind of import, the `math` version would over-ride the default version. We would change how `sum` works. This could be very bad indeed.

The syntax is such that you can be more specific. You are allowed to say *what* you want to import from a module. For example, we could have said `from math import sqrt`. In that case only the `sqrt` function would have been imported into the global namespace. This is a good compromise if you know what you need from a module.

The bottom line is: be careful when you do a `from module import *`. It is preferable to `import module` or to specifically import names with `from module import name1, name2`.

12.2 HOW DOES PYTHON KNOW?

How can Python "know" what operators and methods can apply to a new class we create?

- Python can distinguish operators and methods to apply based on the *type* of the objects being used.
- Python provides some special method names that represent typical operators (binary operators, standard functions, etc.) in the language.

12.2.1 Classes, Types, and Introspection

When we first introduced classes we stated that *a class is just a type*. When we create a new class, we are effectively creating a new type. With numbers we had *`int`* as a type, and now we have created our own class, `Rational`, that can be used as a type. Remember that

[1] It doesn't, but we're pretending here.

type does not go with a variable name, but instead with the object with which the name is associated.

Because the type associated with any variable name can change, it is useful to be able to inquire about the type of the object presently associated with a variable. This process is called *introspection*. That is, while the program is running, we can ask an object (or a variable associated with an object) what type the object is.

Python provides two different introspection functions, one of which we have seen before:

- We have discussed the `type` function a number of times (see Section 1.6). Again, `type (some_variable)` returns the type of the object associated with `some_variable`. Though we have seen this in sessions, we have not used it in programs. We will here!
- A slightly different version of introspection is the `isinstance` function. `isinstance (some_variable,some_type)` returns a Boolean indicating whether `some_variable` is of type `some_type`.

Here is a session showing these functions in action:

```
In  [1]: import math # get some objects to play with
In  [2]: float # what is the "value" of "float"?
Out [2]: float

In  [3]: list # list?
Out [3]: list

In  [4]: type(math.pi) # try the introspection functions
Out [4]: float

In  [5]: isinstance(math.pi,float)
Out [5]: True

In  [6]: isinstance(math.pi,list)
Out [6]: False

In  [7]: type(float) # ask what the type of float is? it is a "type"!
Out [7]: type

In  [8]: type(list)
Out [8]: type

In  [9]: class MyClass(object): # create a new class with nothing in it
...     pass                  #      ("pass" does that)
...:
In  [10]: my_instance = MyClass() # create an instance of our new class
In  [11]: type(my_instance) # check the type of our new instance
Out [11]: __main__.MyClass
```

```
In  [12]: type(MyClass) # a class is a type!
Out [12]: type

In  [13]: isinstance(my_instance,MyClass)
Out [13]: True
```

Things to note from the session:

- Every type has a name, and that name is associated with a Python object. For example, *float* and *list* are names associated with types *float* and *list* respectively. These are the names you may use when doing a comparison such as `isinstance()`.
- The `type` of a type such as *float* or *list* is type (specifically `type`). How about that, the type of Python types is `type`.
- The type of `math.pi` is *float* because the object associated with that variable is the value of π—a floating-point number.
- We make an empty class called `MyClass`. It is empty because it has no structure or any associated methods—only the filler statement ***pass***. It is still a class.
- Even though we don't define a constructor for `MyClass`, one is provided by default and we can make an instance, called `my_instance` using the class name as a constructor.
- *Very Important:* what is the type of `my_instance`? It is of type `MyClass`.
- Finally, `MyClass` is of type `type`, just like *float* and *list*.

We can write code that takes advantage of the types of variables to produce different results. Code Listing 12.1 is a function that does addition for both integers and strings of integers. It returns a 0 for any other type.

Code Listing 12.1

```
1  def special_sum(a,b):
2      ''' sum two ints or convert params to ints
3      and add. return 0 if conversion fails '''
4      if type(a)==int and type(b)==int:
5          result = a + b
6      else:
7          try:
8              result = int(a) + int(b)
9          except ValueError:
10             result = 0
11     return result
```

Notes on the `special_sum` function:

- **Lines 4–5**: The function checks the types of the two parameters. If they are both integer, the function adds the two integers and assigns it to the `result` variable.

- **Line 7–8**: Otherwise, it tries to convert both parameters to integers and add them after conversion. This will work for a *float* (with truncation) or with a string of digits.
- **Line 9–10**: Otherwise, the *int()* conversion will throw a `ValueError` and set the `result` variable to zero.
- **Line 11**: The result is returned.

The choice of returning a zero value upon error is a programmer's choice. Depending on the circumstances, that may not be the correct decision (maybe `None` would be appropriate). In any event, it needs to be documented in the doc string (**Lines 2–3**).

12.2.2 Remember Operator Overloading

We first mentioned the topic of overloading in Section 1.7 and further showed its effects on strings in Section 4.2.2. Remember the concept:

- `4 + 3` is integer addition, producing an integer result.
- `'four' + 'three'` is string concatenation, producing a string result.
- `'four'+ 3` is undefined—no "+" operation is defined for those mixed types.

How can Python tell which operation to use when presented with the "+" operator? Python does so in a way similar to our `special_sum` function: it examines the types of the arguments using introspection. By examining the types, it can look up the appropriate operation. If no such operation is found (no operation exists for that particular combination of values), an error is raised.

12.3 CREATING YOUR OWN OPERATOR OVERLOADING

You can create your own operator overloads for the new class (type) you have created. In the previous section (Section 12.2), we said there were two requirements for such overloading: a way to do introspection and a way to relate operators and methods. We have already discussed introspection, now we need to understand how Python relates operators and methods.

Python establishes a relationship between operators and methods as part of its standard class mechanism. The relationship is fixed by Python: which operators can use and the method name that Python associates with each operator. If you provide one of these special method names in your class, then instances of that class can respond to the associated operator through this method name.

Consider the example of `var1 + var2`. Python associates the `+` operator with the special method name `__add__`. As mentioned, performing this operation has two steps. First, Python determines the type of `var1`. Once determined, Python looks for the special method `__add__` in the class of `var1`. The details of how the Python does the invocation are discussed below in Section 12.3.1.

Overall, Python associates special method names with operators of the following three general classes:

- math-like operators, such as +, −, *, /
- collection operators, such as [ ], `len`
- general class operators, such as methods for printing, construction, etc.

Table 12.1 lists some of the more commonly overloaded operators.[2]

Expression	Method name	Description
Math-like Operators		
x + y	`__add__()`	Addition
x − y	`__sub__()`	Subtraction
x * y	`__mul__()`	Multiplication
x / y	`__div__()`	Division
x == y	`__eq__()`	Equality
x > y	`__gt__()`	Greater Than
x >= y	`__ge__()`	Greater Than or Equal
x < y	`__lt__()`	Less Than
x <= y	`__le__()`	Less Than or Equal
x != y	`__ne__()`	Not Equal
Sequence Operators		
len(x)	`__len__()`	length of the sequence
x in y	`__contains__()`	does the sequence y contain x
x[key]	`__getitem__()`	access element *key* of sequence x
x[key]=y	`__setitem__()`	set element *key* of sequence x to value y
General Class Operations		
x=myClass()	`__init__()`	constructor
print (x), str(x)	`__str__()`	convert to a readable string
	`__repr__()`	print a representation of x
	`__del__()`	finalizer, called when x is garbage collected

TABLE 12.1 Python special method names.

12.3.1 Mapping Operators to Special Methods

The details of how + get mapped to `__add__` are particular to Python's standard class structure. We, as class designers, have to fit into the Python mold for this mapping by providing the appropriate methods. An example mapping:

`var1 + var2` ⇒ `var1.__add__(var2)`

[2] For a full list see `http://docs.python.org/py3k/reference/datamodel.html#special-method-names1`

These are equivalent expressions. Either one does exactly the same thing, but the first is more familiar.

The first variable in a binary operation (in this case, `var1`) becomes the variable that calls the associated method (in this case, `__add__`) and the second variable becomes the argument (in parentheses). For example, if we reverse the operands:

`var2 + var1` ⇒ `var2.__add__(var1)`

Order matters, so we will have to pay attention to it! We will have more to say about order in Section 12.5.2.

Let's examine a simple example that illustrates how these special methods can be defined. In Code Listing 12.2, there is one "math-like" method that performs addition (`__add__`), and one general method that performs conversion to a string (`__str__`). A few extra **`print`** statements have been added to the methods to illustrate *when* these functions are called. As we have shown before, such print statements can help when developing and debugging functions and should be removed once the code is working correctly.

Code Listing 12.2

```
1  class MyClass(object):
2      def __init__(self, param1=0):
3          ''' constructor, sets attribute value to
4          param1, default is 0'''
5          print('in constructor')
6          self.value = param1
7
8      def __str__(self):
9          ''' Convert val attribute to string.'''
10         print('in str')
11         return 'Val is: {}'.format(str(self.value))
12
13     def __add__(self,param2):
14         ''' Perform addition with param2, a MyClass instance.
15         Return a new MyClass instance with sum as value attribute'''
16         print('in add')
17         result = self.value + param2.value
18         return MyClass(result)
```

Let's examine a few lines in the example:

- **Line 6**: The constructor sets a local instance variable named `value` to the value of `param1`. `param1` has a default value of zero. We will assume it is a number (not safe, but this is a simple example).

- **Line 11**: The string conversion method must return a string! We use *str*.
- **Line 13**: The add method. The name *self* is bound to the variable that calls the method (the first operand in the binary expression), and param2 is bound to the second operand in the binary expression. That is, $x + y$ associates x with *self* and associates y with param2.
- **Line 18**: After calculating the sum, we create a new MyClass instance and return it after setting that instance's value attribute to the sum. Again, it makes sense to return an instance of MyClass from addition.

Here is a session that exercises the little class:

```
In  [1]: from program12_2 import * # shortcut to reference contents directly
In  [2]: inst1 = MyClass(27)
in constructor
In  [3]: type(inst1)
Out [3]: program12_2.MyClass

In  [4]: type(MyClass)
Out [4]: type

In  [5]: print(inst1) # calls __str__
in str
Val is: 27
In  [6]: a_sum = inst1 + inst1 # calls __add__
in add
in constructor
In  [7]: print(a_sum)
in str
Val is: 54
In  [8]: type(a_sum)
Out [8]: program12_2.MyClass
```

Here are a few observations about the session:

- When we created inst1, the constructor (via the __init__ method) was called and we see the associated print statement "in constructor" printed in the session.
- The name inst1 is of type MyClass, and MyClass is of type type. We have made a new type!
- The statement ***print***(inst1) calls __str__ to convert the instance to a string. We see the "in str" line in the session as a result.
- When we invoke the line a_sum = inst1 + inst1, we see that we get a call to the add method (Python translates "+" to __add__ as described above) as well as a call to the constructor when we make a new instance of MyClass in __add__ (in line 18 of the code).
- The variable a_sum is assigned to an object of type MyClass since __add__ returned a new MyClass instance.

Again, the ***print*** statements showing "in constructor," "in add," and "in str" help show where these functions are called.

12.4 BUILDING THE RATIONAL NUMBER CLASS

At the beginning of this chapter, we showed a session in which rational numbers were used in a standard way, responding to standard operations. In that session, we explicitly used the "+", "−", and "==" operators. Therefore, to implement the `Rational` class used in that session, we need to have the following methods:

- `__init__()` which we always need
- `__str__()` which we also always need
- `__add__()` for the "+" operator
- `__sub__()` for the "−" operator
- `__eq__()` for the "==" operator
- and, any other supporting functions

12.4.1 Making the Class

The first step in designing a class is to define the structure of the class; in particular, define the `__init__` method that establishes the attributes included in each instance. For the rational number class, each instance will have numerator and a denominator, both integers. We also need to print a rational number instance in a nice way. We must implement `__init__` and `__str__` to accomplish both of those tasks. Let's take a first cut at our rational number class implementing those methods. As before, we include some ***print*** statements to help us recognize when these methods are called.

Within the interpreter, we also expect to be able to type the name of a variable and have its associated object displayed. The method that Python calls to accomplish this is named `__repr__` (short for representation). If we do not have the `__repr__` method, then Python types a default value. For clarity, it is good to include it in our basic class. Our `__repr__` implementation simply calls the `__str__` method, which is sufficient for most cases when you are first learning to construct classes. Note the dot notation and the use of *self* in the call to the `__str__` method in Code Listing 12.3.

Code Listing 12.3

```
class Rational(object):
    """ Rational with numerator and denominator. Denominator
    parameter defaults to 1"""
    def __init__(self,numer,denom=1):
        print('in constructor')
        self.numer = numer
        self.denom = denom
```

```
8
9      def __str__(self):
10         """ String representation for printing"""
11         print('in str')
12         return str(self.numer)+'/'+str(self.denom)
13
14     def __repr__(self):
15         """ Used in interpreter. Call __str__ for now """
16         print('in repr')
17         return self.__str__()
```

Things to note in our first pass at a rational number class:

- `__init__` assigns the two attributes to each instance: `numer` and `denom`.
- `__init__` also takes a default argument on parameter two, `denom`. If only the numerator is provided, the denominator will be 1, meaning that the fractional value will be the value of the numerator (this default will be very useful later on).
- `__str__` creates a new string by concatenation. It converts the numerator and denominator to strings and places a slash (/) between them. It then returns that combined string.
- The `__repr__` method, called when an instance value is required by the interpreter, simply calls the `__str__` method. Note how it is called. The variable `self` is the instance being printed. We get the string by invoking `self.__str__()`, an explicit call (not implicit through `print`) to `__str__`.
- We add debugging print calls at lines 5, 11, and 16, so we may see when the methods are called.

Let's exercise these methods in a session. As before, the embedded print statements help illustrate when each method is called.

```
In  [1]: from program12_3 import * # shortcut, call Rational directly
In  [2]: inst1_Rational = Rational(1,2)
in constructor
In  [3]: print(inst1_Rational)
in str
1/2
In  [4]: inst1_Rational # interpreter calls __repr__ to print
Out [4]: in repr

in str
1/2
In  [5]: inst2_Rational = Rational(2)
in constructor
In  [6]: inst2_Rational
```

```
Out [6]: in repr

in str
2/1
In  [7]: type(inst2_Rational)
Out [7]: program12_3.Rational
```

This session reinforces what we have seen before, namely:

- When a new `Rational` instance is created, the constructor (`__init__`) is called, indicated by the ***print*** statement "in constructor."
- When a `Rational` instance is printed, the `__str__` is called.
- When we type a variable name in the shell containing a `Rational` instance, Python calls `__repr__` (which we have programmed to call `__str__`).
- If only one value is provided to the `Rational` constructor, it is assumed to be the numerator, so the denominator is set to 1 by default.
- The type of a `Rational` instance is the `Rational` class.

Now that we have the basics of a class, let's include addition.

12.4.2 Review Fraction Addition

Do you remember how to add fractions? An important component was the common denominator. We'll review the elementary arithmetic and then use what we remember to create an algorithm for adding fractions.

How do you add $\frac{1}{5} + \frac{2}{5}$? How about $\frac{1}{5} + \frac{1}{3}$?

- The first case is easy because both fractions have a common denominator. If the denominators are the same, we simply add the numerators and keep the common denominator in the answer: $\frac{1}{5} + \frac{2}{5} = \frac{3}{5}$.
- The second case does not have a common denominator, so we have to manipulate the fractions so that they have a common denominator. Once accomplished, addition is simple like the first case. One method to determine the common denominator is the *least common multiple* (also known as LCM) of the two denominators. The LCM is the smallest number that each of the denominators divides into evenly, that is, *without* a remainder. By inspection, we know that in this case that number is 15, but what algorithm can we use to find it in general?

The LCM is most easily computed in terms of another value, the *greatest common divisor* (also known as GCD). The GCD is the largest value that divides two values without a remainder. The relation between LCM and GCD is shown in Equation 12.1.

$$\text{LCM}(a, b) = \frac{a * b}{\text{GCD}(a, b)} \tag{12.1}$$

Just to be clear, here are some examples:

- By inspection, LCM of 6 and 15 is 30 and is expressed as $LCM(6, 15) = 30$. Let's see if the LCM using Equation 12.1 is also 30. To begin with, the GCD of 6 and 15 is 3; represented as $GCD(6, 15) = 3$. Plugging $a = 6$ and $b = 15$ into the LCM Equation 12.1, we get $LCM(6, 15) = (6 * 15)/GCD(6, 15) = (90)/3 = 30$, the expected value.
- Similarly, by inspection, the LCM of 8 and 20 is 40 and is expressed as $LCM(8, 20) = 40$. Let's check those values in the LCM Equation 12.1. Beginning again with the GCD, the GCD of 8 and 20 is 4 and is expressed as $GCD(8, 20) = 4$. Again, using the LCM Equation 12.1, we plug in $a = 8$ and $b = 20$ to get $LCM(8, 20) = (8 * 20)/GCD(8, 20) = (160)/4 = 40$, the expected value.

Our task has been reduced to finding an algorithm for the GCD. Once we have that algorithm, we can use Equation 12.1 to find the LCM, which we can use as a common denominator.

Euclid and the GCD

It turns out that one of the oldest known algorithms is a method to calculate the GCD of two numbers. It was first recorded by Euclid in his book titled *Elements*, written approximately 300 B.C.E., but it was likely known earlier than that.

Euclid happened to have used geometry to derive it, but the algorithm is the same. Euclid's algorithm uses two positive integers, where both are not 0.

Euclid's GCD algorithm (on two positive integers):

1. If one of the numbers is 0, return the other number and halt.
2. Otherwise, find the integer remainder of the larger number divided by the smaller number.
3. Reapply the algorithm to the smaller number from the previous iteration and the just calculated remainder.

Using the values from the previous example, let's apply Euclid's algorithm to find GCD(8,20).

Step 1 Neither number is 0; proceed.
Step 2 The integer remainder of 20/8 is 4 (i.e., 20%8 = 4).
Step 3 Reapply the algorithm using the previous smaller number (8) and the remainder (4) to find the GCD(8,4).
Step 4 Neither number is 0; proceed.
Step 5 Remainder of 8/4 is 0 (i.e., 8%4 = 0).
Step 6 Reapply the algorithm to find the GCD(4,0).
Step 7 One number is 0; return the other (4) and halt.

The final result is that GCD(8,20) is 4 as expected.

This algorithm can easily be implemented in a *recursive* function, but we aren't quite there yet (see Chapter 15).

Let's rewrite our GCD algorithm so that it is easier to implement in Python. We'll begin by naming the two positive integers `bigger` and `smaller` to help keep them straight. Also because the algorithm refers to one number as the smaller number, let's arbitrarily assume that `bigger > smaller` (if `bigger < smaller`, we can swap their values). Here is an updated version of the algorithm:

Euclid's GCD algorithm (on two positive integers, `bigger` and `smaller`, such that `bigger > smaller`):

1. If `smaller == 0`, return `bigger` and halt.
2. Find the remainder of `bigger` divided by `smaller`: `bigger% smaller`.
3. Reapply the algorithm using `smaller` and the remainder.

Notice that the algorithm continues until `smaller == 0`, which is equivalent to continuing while `smaller != 0`.

After we find a remainder in step 2, we reapply the algorithm using `smaller` and the remainder. That is, we must set `bigger` and `smaller` to be respectively `smaller` and `remainder` from the previous iteration. To accomplish this, we use multiple assignment (Section 2.2.7). We include a ***`print`*** statement in line 7, so we can observe how the function is working—it can be removed later. The code is shown in Code Listing 12.4.

Code Listing 12.4

```
1  def gcd(bigger, smaller):
2      """Calculate the greatest common divisor of two positive integers."""
3      if not bigger > smaller:          # swap if necessary so bigger > smaller
4          bigger, smaller = smaller, bigger
5      while smaller != 0:                          # 1. if smaller == 0, halt
6          remainder = bigger % smaller             # 2. find remainder
7          print('calculation, big:{}, small:{}, rem:{}'.\
8                 format(bigger, smaller, remainder)) # debugging
9          bigger, smaller = smaller, remainder  # 3. reapply
10     return bigger
```

Let's observe our `gcd` function in operation:

```
In  [1]: from program12_4 import gcd
In  [2]: gcd(8,20)
Out [2]: calculation, big:20, small:8, rem:4

calculation, big:8, small:4, rem:0
4
In  [3]: gcd(22,8)
Out [3]: calculation, big:22, small:8, rem:6
```

```
calculation, big:8, small:6, rem:2
calculation, big:6, small:2, rem:0
2
```

Once we have a `gcd` function, we can use our LCM relation from Equation 12.1 to write an `lcm` function. Note the integer division (`//`) so an integer quotient is returned. Remember that we need to have the `gcd` function loaded before we can call the `lcm` function because `gcd` is used in `lcm`. Note that in Code Listing 12.5 we commented out the print in `gcd` because we have completed development of the `gcd` function and no longer need to debug it—at least not now!

PROGRAMMING TIP

If you write ***print*** statements in your code for debugging purposes, you can comment or uncomment them as needed. Commenting them reduces the "print load" you get when your algorithm runs, but they are always good to have around, if you want to uncomment them and test something out again.

Code Listing 12.5

```python

def lcm (a,b):
    """Calculate the lowest common multiple of two positive integers."""
    return (a*b)//gcd(a,b)  # Equation 12.1, // ensures an int is returned
```

Here is a session using the same values from the previous exercise:

```
In  [1]: from lcm import lcm
In  [2]: lcm(8,20)
Out [2]: 40

In  [3]: lcm(22,8)
Out [3]: 88
```

12.4.3 Back to Adding Fractions

Armed with some basic arithmetic, we can return to the original problem of adding two fractions. In the `__add__` method, we need to do the following:

1. Find the LCM of the two `Rational` instance denominators.
2. Modify the two `Rational` instances
   - to have the LCM as the denominator.
   - the new numerator is the LCM times the rational number.

3. Now we can find the sum of the modified numerators. Note the `int` conversion so the number will correctly be an `int`. Effectively, we are truncating away any floating-point rounding errors.
4. Create a new `Rational`, with the sum as the numerator and the LCM as the denominator, and return it.

Subtraction is basically the same. We show the next version of the class in Code Listing 12.6.

Code Listing 12.6

```python
def gcd(bigger, smaller):
    """Calculate the greatest common divisor of two positive integers."""
    print('in gcd')
    if not bigger > smaller:          # swap if necessary so bigger > smaller
        bigger, smaller = smaller, bigger
    while smaller != 0:               # 1. if smaller == 0, halt
        remainder = bigger % smaller  # 2. find remainder
        # print('calculation , big:{}, small:{}, rem:{}'.\
        #       format(bigger, smaller, remainder)) # debugging
        bigger, smaller = smaller, remainder  # 3. reapply
    return bigger

def lcm (a,b):
    """Calculate the lowest common multiple of two positive integers."""
    print('in lcm')
    return (a*b)//gcd(a,b)   # Equation 12.1, // ensures an int is returned


class Rational(object):
    """ Rational with numerator and denominator. Denominator
    parameter defaults to 1"""
    def __init__(self,numer,denom=1):
        print('in constructor')
        self.numer = numer
        self.denom = denom

    def __str__(self):
        """ String representation for printing"""
        print('in str')
        return str(self.numer)+'/'+str(self.denom)

    def __repr__(self):
        """ Used in interpreter. Call __str__ for now """
        print('in repr')
        return self.__str__()
```

```
36
37
38      def __add__(self, param_Rational):
39          """ Add two Rationals"""
40          print('in add')
41          # find a common denominator (lcm)
42          the_lcm = lcm(self.denom, param_Rational.denom)
43          # multiply each by the lcm, then add
44          numerator_sum = (the_lcm * self.numer/self.denom) + \
45                          (the_lcm * param_Rational.numer/param_Rational.denom)
46          return Rational(int(numerator_sum), the_lcm)
47
48      def __sub__(self, param_Rational):
49          """ Subtract two Rationals"""
50          print('in sub')
51          # subtraction is the same but with '-' instead of '+'
52          the_lcm = lcm(self.denom, param_Rational.denom)
53          numerator_diff = (the_lcm * self.numer/self.denom) - \
54                           (the_lcm * param_Rational.numer/param_Rational.denom)
55          return Rational(int(numerator_diff), the_lcm)
```

Comments on the `Rational` class so far:

- **Line 42** calculates the `lcm`.
- **Line 44** both modifies each numerator and then sums them as the new numerator.
- **Line 46** returns a new instance of a `Rational` because the sum of two rational numbers is a rational number. The new instance is created by calling the `Rational` constructor with the two new values for numerator and denominator.
- In our example code, every method and function prints out a line when it is called. Tracking code is easier, but it must be commented out when done debugging.

Let's look at an output session to see how this expanded example works:

```
In  [1]: from program12_6 import *
In  [2]: one_half = Rational(1,2)
in constructor
In  [3]: type(one_half)
Out [3]: program12_6.Rational

In  [4]: two_fifths = Rational(2,5)
in constructor
In  [5]: sum_Rational = one_half + two_fifths
in add
in lcm
```

```
in gcd
in constructor
In  [6]: print(sum_Rational)
in str
9/10
In  [7]: sum_Rational
Out [7]: in repr

in str
9/10
In  [8]: type(sum_Rational)
Out [8]: program12_6.Rational

In  [9]: two = Rational(2)
in constructor
In  [10]: print(two - one_half)
in sub
in lcm
in gcd
in constructor
in str
3/2
```

Here are some observations on that session:

- We begin by creating two Rationals: `one_half = Rational(1,2)` and `two_fifths = Rational(2,5)`
- When we add `one_half` and `two_fifths`, note how many functions and methods get called. First, the system converts the binary operation into a method call by calling `__add__` with `one_half` bound to *self* and `two_fifths` as `param_Rational`. The `__add__` method calls `lcm`, which in turn calls `gcd`. The `lcm` value is then returned to the `__add__` method. Because we need to return a `Rational`, a call is made to the `Rational` constructor to construct the result. Note that we convert the numerator to an *int* before calling the constructor; `lcm` returned an *int* so it didn't need conversion.
- We test the default denominator in the constructor by creating a `Rational` number object $\frac{2}{1}$ using the constructor call `Rational(2)`.
- Finally, we test that subtraction of $2 - \frac{1}{2}$ correctly produces the result $\frac{3}{2}$.

The overall process is a bit complicated, but each step is fairly simple and the organization is accomplished by us, the class designers.

Assignment

You likely noticed that we used assignment (=) with rational numbers in the sessions without defining an assignment operator within the `Rational` class. Assignment is different from the other operators because it is simply a manipulation of the namespace. Assignment only associates an object with a name, so, no matter the object, assignment establishes that association. No special operator is needed for assignment based on an object type. Assignment works, as is, with all objects.

Check Yourself: Check Defining Your Own Operators

1. Provide the indicated output for the following code:

```
class TestClass(object):
    def __init__(self,param_str=''):
        self.the_str=''
        for c in param_str:
            if c.isalpha():
                self.the_str += c
    def __add__(self,param):
        if type(param)==TestClass:
            the_str = self.the_str + param.the_str
            return TestClass(the_str)
        else:
            return self

    def __str__(self):
        return 'Value: {}'.format(self.the_str)

inst1 = TestClass('abc')
inst2 = TestClass('123ijk')
sumInst1 = inst1 + inst2
sumInst2 = inst1 + 'xyz'
print(inst1)                           # Line 1
print(sumInst1)                        # Line 2
print(sumInst2)                        # Line 3
print(isinstance(sumInst2,TestClass))  # Line 4
```

(a) What output is produced by Line 1 when executing the indicated code?
(b) What output is produced by Line 2 when executing the indicated code?
(c) What output is produced by Line 3 when executing the indicated code?
(d) What output is produced by Line 4 when executing the indicated code?

12.4.4 Equality and Reducing Rationals

In this section, we consider the task of comparing two rational numbers to see whether they are equal.

The simple case is to compare the two numerators and two denominators. If both are the same, then the fractions are the same. So is $\frac{1}{2} == \frac{1}{2}$? Sure.

However, checking equality is complicated by the fact that two different rational numbers can be equal because their reduced values are equal, for example, $\frac{12}{16} == \frac{6}{8}$ because they both reduce to $\frac{3}{4}$.

Therefore, to check for equality, we need to reduce the fractions. That begs for a reduction function. To check for equality, we will reduce both fractions and then compare.

Fortunately, we already have the tools (functions) to accomplish this task. The first step in reducing a fraction is to find the greatest number that will divide into both the numerator and denominator. That is, the GCD, and we already have that function. Having found that divisor, we divide both the numerator and denominator by that value, creating a new `Rational` instance that has been reduced.

Once we can reduce a fraction, we can then compare the numerators and denominators. The methods in question are shown in Code Listing 12.7.

Code Listing 12.7

```
1  def reduce_rational(self):
2      """ Return the reduced fractional value as a Rational"""
3      print('in reduce')
4      # find the gcd and then divide numerator and denominator by gcd
5      the_gcd = gcd(self.numer,self.denom)
6      return Rational(self.numer//the_gcd, self.denom//the_gcd)
7
8  def __eq__(self,param_Rational):
9      """ Compare two Rationals for equality, return Boolean"""
10     print('in eq')
11     # reduce both; then check that numerators and denominators are equal
12     reduced_self = self.reduce_rational()
13     reduced_param = param_Rational.reduce_rational()
14     return reduced_self.numer == reduced_param.numer and\
15         reduced_self.denom == reduced_param.denom
```

Comments on our `Rational` class:

Line 5: `reduce_rational` finds the GCD of the provided `Rational` object now associated with *`self`*.

Line 6: A new `Rational` object is created and returned in reduced form. The numerator and denominator of this new object are made by dividing *`self`*`.numer` and *`self`*`.denom` by the GCD.

Lines 12–13: The method `reduce_rational` is called on both *`self`* and `param_Rational`. Both return new `Rational` objects, which are assigned to `reduced_self` and `reduced_param`, respectively. Neither `param_Rational` nor *`self`* are modified! The result of testing two rational numbers should not modify those numbers.

Lines 14–15. Finally, we return the result of the ***and*** of two comparisons: the equality of both the reduced numerators and the reduced denominators. This is a Boolean, as should be returned by a comparison.

For the reduce_rational method, if the fraction is already in its reduced form, then the GCD is 1. We still divide, even if it is 1, as that is simpler to do than to check for that special case.

An alternate way to design a rational number class would be to *always* keep fractions in reduced form. That is, if you create a fraction $\frac{12}{16}$, it will be reduced to $\frac{3}{4}$ when the fraction is created. Arithmetic operations would operate similarly. It is not obvious that one design is better than the other: both have merits. If you work with the Fraction class in Python 2.6 fractions module, you will see that they always reduce their fractions.

The session that exercises Code Listing 12.7 is interesting:

```
In  [1]: from program12_7 import *
In  [2]: one_half = Rational(1,2)
in constructor
In  [3]: five_tenths = Rational(5,10)
in constructor
In  [4]: five_tenths.reduce_rational()
Out [4]: in reduce

in gcd
in constructor
in repr
in str
1/2
In  [5]: one_half == five_tenths
Out [5]: in eq

in reduce
in gcd
in constructor
in reduce
in gcd
in constructor
True
```

- The method five_tenths.reduce_rational() returns the appropriate result, $\frac{1}{2}$. The value in five_tenths is not modified.
- Can you follow the sequence of invocations of functions and methods for five_tenths.reduce_rational()?
  - reduce_rational method is called.
  - gcd is called from reduce_rational.
  - Once reduced, a new Rational is created by calling the constructor. This Rational instance is returned.
  - The returned Rational is to be displayed by the shell, which calls __repr__ to do that.
  - __repr__ calls __str__.

- one_half == five_tenths converts to one_half.__eq__(five_tenths), which produces *True*. Neither value is modified. Note that reduce_rational is called twice, once for *self* and once for param_Rational.

12.4.5 Divide and Conquer at Work

VideoNote 12.1
Augmenting a Class

Notice again how we applied a divide-and-conquer approach to solving this problem. We broke the problem of performing operations on rational numbers into smaller pieces, each of which was easily testable, for example, lcm, gcd, and reduce_rational. We then combined the parts to solve the problem at hand. Reemphasizing this approach is important, especially when building your own classes. Many small functions are easier to develop and debug than a few large ones. The interactive nature of Python makes testing of small functions and methods easy. It is a hallmark of object-oriented code to build in this way.

12.5 WHAT DOESN'T WORK (YET)

Our testing sessions seem to indicate that our class is sufficient, but look at the following session. Why don't these expressions work?

```
In  [1]: from rationalNumber3 import *
In  [2]: one_half = Rational(1,2)
in constructor
In  [3]: one_half + 1
Out [3]: in add

Traceback (most recent call last):
  File "<stdin>", line 1, in <module>
  File "rationalNumber3.py", line 35, in __add__
    the_lcm = lcm(self.denom,f.denom)
AttributeError: 'int' object has no attribute 'denom'

In  [4]: 1 + one_half
Traceback (most recent call last):
  File "<stdin>", line 1, in <module>
TypeError: unsupported operand type(s) for +: 'int' and 'Rational'
```

First, it is reasonable to expect that we should be able to mix other numeric types with our new Rational class, but at this point it seems we cannot. Second, we get two different error messages for the two expressions:

- one_half + 1: error is trying to find denom in 1.
- 1 + one_half: error is unsupported types for +.

It is useful to try to interpret what these error messages are telling us. Let's begin by reviewing how these expressions get translated. The first expression translates as

one_half + 1 ⇒ one_half.__add__(1).

However, in our __add__ method, we assume that the argument being passed is of type Rational. In this case, it isn't: 1 is of type *int* so it doesn't have a denom attribute.

In the second example, 1 + one_half doesn't even make it to our __add__ method. This second expression translates as

1 + one_half ⇒ 1.__add__(one_half).

In this case the first argument is an *int*, so the system looks in the *int* type for operations defined on *int*'s and Rational's. This is none so this is an error, different from the previous error.

We need to fix both errors, but they will each require their own solution.

12.5.1 Introspection

To fix the first problem, namely one_half + 1, we need to fix our assumptions about the __add__ method. Take a look at that code. When we designed the method, we assumed that the type of the passed parameter is Rational. We try to access the numer and denom attributes of the parameter. What if the parameter is not a Rational? We, the class designers, need to check the type first and then take appropriate action. We need to utilize introspection. Remember, we discussed introspection in Section 12.2.1. Introspection allows us to query the type of a variable while the program is running, and take appropriate action.

Our __add__ method presently works correctly with two Rational parameters. What other types might it work with? Clearly it should work with integers. We might do other types as well, but let's work with *int* for now.

We need to check the type of the parameter as it comes in. If the parameter is an *int*, then we need to convert the *int* to a Rational. Once converted, we can continue as before. Conveniently, if we call the Rational constructor with a single integer argument, it does create a Rational (with a default denominator of 1)—good design!

To save space, we show only relevant parts of the class in Code Listing 12.8.

Code Listing 12.8

```
    def __add__(self, param):
        """ Add two Rationals. Allows int as a parameter"""
        print('in add')
        if type(param) == int:  # convert ints to Rationals
            param = Rational(param)
        if type(param) == Rational:
```

```
7              # find a common denominator (lcm)
8              the_lcm = lcm(self.denom, param.denom)
9              # multiply each by the lcm, then add
10             numerator_sum = (the_lcm * self.numer/self.denom) + \
11                 (the_lcm * param.numer/param.denom)
12             return Rational(int(numerator_sum),the_lcm)
13         else:
14             print('wrong type')  # problem: some type we cannot handle
15             raise(TypeError)
```

Line 4: We check the parameter's type with the `type` function. If it is of type *`int`*, then the parameter is converted to a `Rational` by calling the `Rational` constructor, passing the `param` as the single argument. It re-assigns `param` to the returned `Rational`

Line 6: We have either converted an *`int`* to a `Rational` or had received a `Rational` initially to get past this ***`if`*** statement. If so, we then do what we did previously to add the two fractions.

Line 13: If we get to this line, then we did not end up with a `Rational` type for the passed parameter. We print an error message then *raise* an error. The command *raise* is a way to signal to Python that an error has occurred that will be dealt with if possible. We have dealt with handling exceptions, but this is the first time that we raised one on our own. More detail about raising exceptions will be explained in Chapter 14.

Let's test it!

```
In  [1]: from program12_8 import *
In  [2]: one_half = Rational(1,2)
in constructor
In  [3]: one_half + one_half
Out [3]: in add

in lcm
in gcd
in constructor
in repr
in str
2/2
In  [4]: one_half + 1
Out [4]: in add

in constructor
in lcm
in gcd
in constructor
in repr
```

```
in str
3/2
In  [5]: one_half + 3.14159
Out [5]: in add

wrong type
Traceback (most recent call last):
  File "<stdin>", line 1, in <module>
  File "program12_6.py", line 52, in __add__
    raise(TypeError)
TypeError
In  [6]: 1 + one_half
Traceback (most recent call last):
  File "<stdin>", line 1, in <module>
TypeError: unsupported operand type(s) for +: 'int' and 'Rational'
```

In our session, testing indicates that regular `Rational` addition still works (we didn't break it!), as does `Rational` + *`int`*. `Rational` + `anything_else` raises the TypeError exception—correctly, as that's how we designed it. However, *`int`* + `Rational` still does not work, so we have more to do.

12.5.2 Repairing `int + Rational` Errors

VideoNote 12.2
Create a Class

Introspection allows us to examine the type of the parameter(s) passed into a method, but we still cannot address the problem of an expression such as `1 + one_half`. The problem is that because the first element of the binary operation is an *`int`*, there is no way for us to automatically route the addition (+) operation to the `__add__` method of `Rational`. This is because our translation of binary operator to method depends on the type of the *first* operand. The first operand is an *`int`*, and we cannot (and likely wouldn't want to) change the underlying functionality of *`int`*'s for every new type (class) we define.

Python provides a way around this problem. For each math-like method predefined by the system, a reversed method exists: `__radd__`, `__rsub__`,`__rmul__`,`__rdiv__`, `__rand__`, `__ror__`.[3] The Python process here is a little complicated, so follow carefully for the expression `1 + Rational(1,2)`.

1. Python tries to find an appropriate `__add__` method for *`int`*s. However, no such method exists with a parameter of type `Rational`.
2. Given that error, Python looks for the existence of an `__radd__` method in the *second* operand (`Rational` in this case). If it exists, then Python *automatically* reverses the expression and calls `__radd__`. In this case, that expression will be `Rational(1,2).radd__(1)`.
3. If neither of these work, Python raises an error.

[3] Others exist for mod, shift, and so on, but *not* for comparison operations.

In our case of *int* + `Rational`, the `__radd__` maps the `Rational` to *self* and the *int* to the parameter. For addition because addition is commutative (order doesn't matter), we just call the existing non-reversed `__add__` with the now properly ordered expression. Because introspection allows us to have *int*'s as a parameter, all should be well. Let's take a look at just that method in Code Listing 12.9.

Code Listing 12.9

```
def __radd__(self,param):
    """ Add two Rationals (reversed)"""
    # mapping is reversed: if "1 + x", x maps to self, and 1 maps to f
    print("in radd")
    # mapping is already reversed so self will be Rational; call __add__
    return self.__add__(param)
```

Take a look at a session to see that it works:

```
In  [1]: from program12_9 import *
In  [2]: one_half = Rational(1,2)
in constructor
In  [3]: one_half + one_half
Out [3]: in add

in lcm
in gcd
in constructor
in repr
in str
2/2
In  [4]: one_half + 1
Out [4]: in add

in constructor
in lcm
in gcd
in constructor
in repr
in str
3/2
In  [5]: 1 + one_half
Out [5]: in radd

in add
in constructor
```

```
in lcm
in gcd
in constructor
in repr
in str
3/2
```

Make sure you can follow along. The `1 + one_half` begins with a call to `__radd__` because an `int + Rational` method doesn't exist. If a `__radd__` method exists in `one_half`, Python invokes that method and reverses the order of the original binary operation, mapping `one_half` to `self` and 1 to the parameter. *Read the previous sentence again carefully*! Python reverses the order of the operands when it calls a reverse method.

Because addition is commutative, we can simply call the non-reversed method using the now properly ordered arguments: `self.__add__(param)`. That is, `1 + one_half` through `__radd__` will map `one_half` to `self` and 1 to `param`, which our `__add__` can handle. We see "in add" printed followed by the first "in constructor," where the `int` 1 is converted to a `Rational`. The final "in constructor" is when we construct a `Rational` to return. Phew!

Mixed-Type Comparisons

What about handling mixed-type comparisons? Unfortunately, comparisons do not have "reversed" versions of methods, so something that does a comparison between an `int` and a `Rational` cannot be solved so easily. That is, `1 == oneHalf`, which compares an `int` with a `Rational` will fail, and a reversed equality operator does not exist to help us out. A solution exists, but it is messy and beyond the scope of this introductory text. The complexity comes from the fact that comparisons behave quite differently from simple arithmetic, and the concept of "equality" or "greater-than" can get messy at the language implementation level. Therefore, at this stage, mixed-type comparisons such as "equal," "greater-than," "less-than," "not-equal," and so on are left for a more-advanced text.

Collection Operators and Iteration

If the class we are constructing is a collection, we can also define operators such as indexing (`[ ]`) and iteration. Please see the Python manual for details.

12.6 INHERITANCE

As we have mentioned, one of the hallmarks of a OOP system is inheritance. Let us finally get down to details and examine what inheritance means. We'll first see *what* it is and then get into *why* it is a good idea.

12.6.1 The "Find the Attribute" Game

In Section 11.4.3 we discussed how information is shared between instances and classes. Remember:

- A single class can have many instances, where each instance is initialized by the class's constructor method, `__init__`.
- When constructed, one of the instance's attributes is the `__class__` attribute, indicating the class the instance was created from. This establishes the *instance-of* relationship. Every instance remembers what class it is an instance of.
- When referencing a value in an attribute (e.g., `my_instance.attribute_name`), Python first looks in the instance for the attribute and, if not found there, it then looks in the class the instance was derived from. In this way, attributes stored in the class are available to every instance derived from that class.

We want to extend the "find the attribute" search algorithm from Section 11.4.4 to include other classes besides the one the instance is derived from. But how? As it turns out, classes can also have a relationship with other classes, a relationship independent of the class-instance relationship. Let's explore that a bit.

Class "is-a" Relationship and the Class Hierarchy

Remember when we wrote our first class, shown in Section 11.4.2? In every definition of a Python class, the final element is a parenthetical list of classes that we called the "parent object." We noted at that time that, until we got to inheritance, this list was always to contain the special class `object`. Now that we are at inheritance, we can explain this argument in more detail.

Every class maintains at least one *parent* class. The two classes are said to have a "parent-child," "superclass-subclass," or "base-derived class" relationship depending on who is doing the describing. However you describe the two classes, the relationship is meant to represent the specialization of an object. It is often called an *is-a* relationship. For example, if you create a `Car` class, then a `Ford` class "is-a" `Car`, but a more particular kind of `Car`. Subsequently, a `Mustang` class "is-a" `Ford` class, but a more particular kind of `Ford`. Remember, these are still classes, not instances! A `Mustang` is a general class of `Car`, not a single, particular car, such as "Bill's 1967 Green Shelby Cobra Mustang" (don't I wish!), which is an individual car, an instance. `Car`, `Ford` and `Mustang` are still classes of vehicles—templates from which individual instances are derived.

The "is-a" relationship is "one-way," much as the "instance-of" relationship is "one way." The instance remembers who its class is, but the class does not track its instances. A class remembers who its parent class is, but the parent class does not track its child classes.

Each Python class indicates specifically in its class definition who its parent class is. This relationship gets recorded in the `__bases__` attribute of each class.

Taken together, all the classes and their parent relationships form a *hierarchy* of classes. The *Oxford English Dictionary* includes the following as one of the definitions of hierarchy:

> **hierarchy**: A body of persons or things ranked in grades, orders, or classes, one above another.

A hierarchy of Python classes is an organization, through the parent class of each class, indicating how classes are related to one another via an "is-a" relation. Figure 12.1 shows the situation.

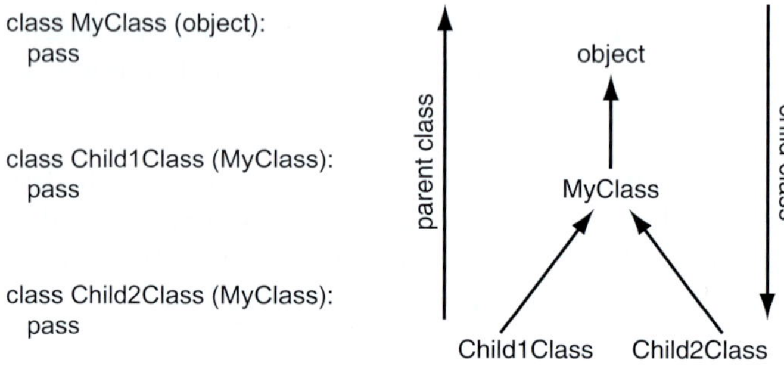

FIGURE 12.1 A simple class hierarchy

The figure shows three, rather empty, classes. The important point is that this figure shows that the parent class value in each class establishes an "is-a" relationship, and how, taken together, the "is-a" relationships establish a hierarchy. One class that is shown in the hierarchy but never defined is `object` (note the lowercase!). Python provides the object named `object` as the "top object" in the Python class hierarchy. *Every* class defined in Python ultimately ends up at `object` by following the parent class links. All of the built-in objects (list, set, tuple, dictionary, etc.) are objects whose parent is `object`. Code Listing 12.10 shows this. Note who the parent class of `object` is.

Code Listing 12.10

```
class MyClass (object):
    ''' parent is object'''
    pass

class MyChildClass (MyClass):
    ''' parent is MyClass '''
    pass
```

```
my_child_instance = MyChildClass()
my_class_instance = MyClass()

print(MyChildClass.__bases__)          # the parent class
print(MyClass.__bases__)               # ditto
print(object.__bases__)                # ditto

print(my_child_instance.__class__)   # class from which the instance came
print(type(my_child_instance))       # same question, asked via function
```

```
(<class '__main__.MyClass'>,)        # print(MyChildClass.__bases__)
(<class 'object'>,)                  # print(MyClass.__bases__)
()                                   # print(object.__bases__)
<class '__main__.MyChildClass'>      # print(my_child_instance.__class__)
<class '__main__.MyChildClass'>      # print(type(my_child_instance))
```

Back to the Game

Now we know of two relationships: "is-a" between classes and "instance-of" between an instance and the class it was created from. We can now update the "instance-of" relationship of Figure 11.3 by including the "is-a" relationship as shown in Figure 12.2. We call the illustrated process of determining relationships, the "find the attribute" game.

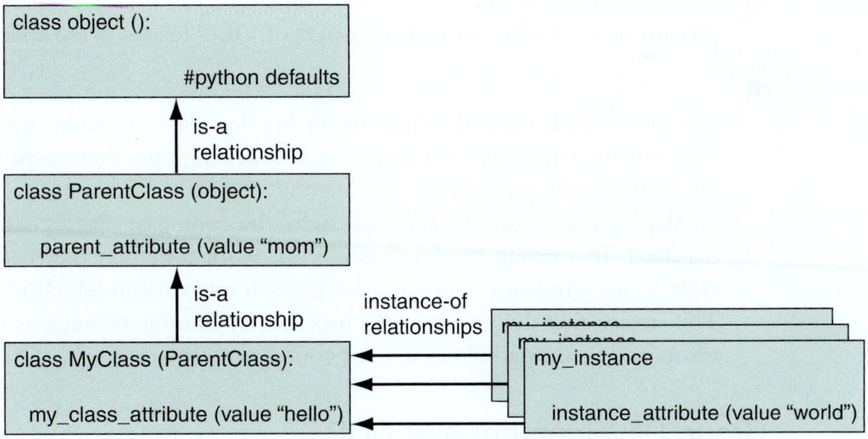

FIGURE 12.2 The players in the "Find the Attribute" game.

The order of search is now:

1. Look in the instance; if not found there, go on.
2. Look in the class of the instance (up the "instance-of" relation); if not there, go on.

3. Look up the class parent link, the "is-a" relation, and look in the parent class. Continue looking up the "is-a" links until the attribute is found or there are no more "is-a" links to follow (meaning that ultimately you arrived at `object` and the attribute was not found).

Using Figure 12.2, how does Python find `my_instance.parent_attribute`? Following the rules:

- Python first looks in the instance itself. The attribute is not in the instance, so on to step 2.
- Python then looks in the class from which it was instantiated, via the "instance-of" link, `MyClass`. The attribute is not in the class, so on to step 3.
- Python moves up the class hierarchy via the "is-a" link to `ParentClass`. It finds the attribute there and returns it.

If the process gets to the class `object` and it doesn't find the attribute, the search fails and Python generates an error.

12.6.2 Using Inheritance

Let's review. We can now impose a structure on a set of classes using the "is-a" ("parent-of") relationship. This organization fits into the already existing "instance-of" relationship and extends the search process for finding attributes of an instance (and remember, attributes include methods). So what?

The promise of inheritance as an aspect of OOP relates to the ability to share common code:

- If a new class is created as part of an existing class hierarchy, then the new class can *reuse* existing code from the hierarchy, specializing only those aspects or attributes that are unique to the new class.
- By sharing code from the class hierarchy, the coding of classes can be somewhat standardized. If a group of developers must work together, they can establish standard code to accomplish common tasks and a framework in which to develop new tasks. This means that the group works together by sharing as much as possible, preventing errors and incompatibilities in their code.

Group Development and OOP

The last of the previous points is important because it emphasizes a need that OOP often fills: group development. One of the main reasons that OOP has been successful is that it helps in coordinating group development of software. It is a drawback of an introductory course that group development is often not emphasized (students can only do so much in a single course!), but OOP works best in a group environment.

More importantly, a group environment is how modern software is developed. It is rare that a single programmer (or even a small group of programmers) does an entire development cycle. It requires too much work and takes too much time. Developers need to work together to create software, and OOP is a tool to help in that regard. That is why the term *software engineering* is so often used in regards to development. Software engineering is concerned with developing tools to make development, especially group development, easier to accomplish. OOP is one of those tools.

How does OOP help in a group setting? Let's look at the various aspects we have used. Encapsulation means that a class designer can write code for another programmer to solve a problem. The details of the class are hidden from the programmer; only the interface is made available. If the class must be modified in some way (to be faster, to use less memory, to interact with a new device, etc.), then the class designer can modify the class as long as he can maintain the interface, the methods made available to the programmer. This division of duty—class design and class use—makes it easier to share code.

Inheritance does much the same thing. By providing standard methods via a class hierarchy, the group can make decisions as to how their code should be developed and shared.

12.6.3 Example: The Standard Model

Physicists who investigate the nature of the atom have worked for many years to develop a model of matter and the forces that act on that matter. The results of this research are currently termed the *Standard Model*. The Standard Model is a description of all the fundamental pieces from which matter is constructed and three of the fundamental forces of nature (gravity not yet being incorporated). It is a crowning achievement of an enormous amount of work, but its description is relatively easy to provide. Figure 12.3 shows a summary of the model.[4]

Each of the 12 particles shown in the model have a number of attributes including: mass, spin, charge, and name. They also have intrinsic attributes, such as location (in three-dimensional space) and velocity (direction of movement in three-dimensional space). This classification of particles is perfect for a class hierarchy. Let's try and develop at least part of it.

Every particle has both a *name* and the quantity called *spin* as well as a position in 3D space and a velocity. Our base class then will be called `Particle` and the `__init__` and `__str__` methods will manipulate those values. A second class called `MassParticle` will be a child class of `Particle`. It will add the quantity `mass` to any instance. The final class will be called `ChargedParticle`. It will add the quantity `charge` to any instance. An example of this hierarchy is shown in Figure 12.4. An implementation is shown in Code Listing 12.11.

[4] It should be noted that the Standard Model is a working hypothesis, well-established, but not fully proven. This version of the model ignores some particles, such as anti-particles.

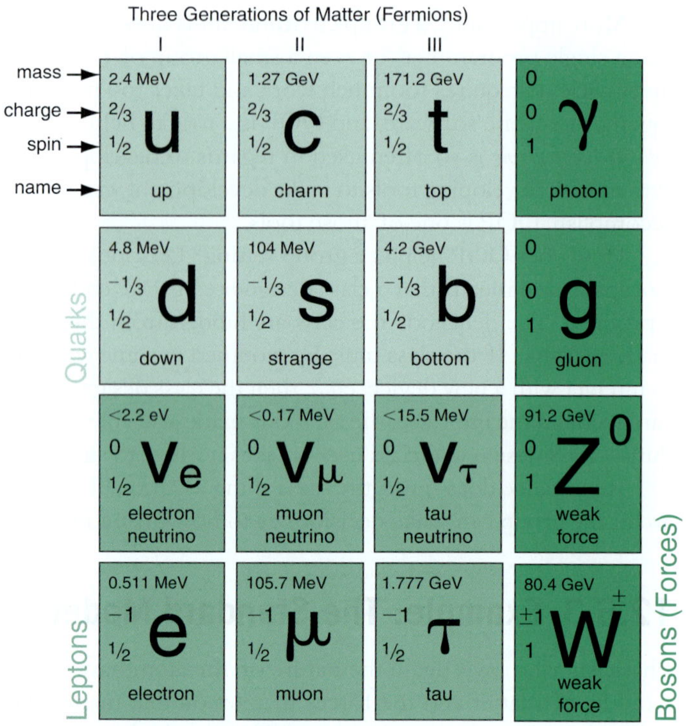

FIGURE 12.3 The Standard Model of physics.

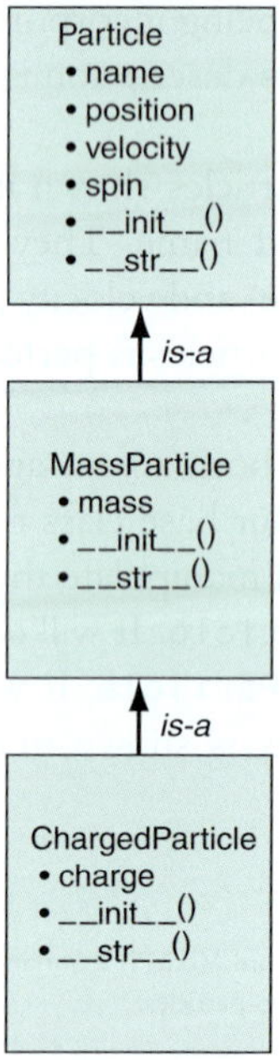

FIGURE 12.4 The particle class hierarchy.

Code Listing 12.11

```
class Particle (object):
    def __init__ (self, name='', position=(0.0,0.0,0.0), \
                  velocity=(0.0,0.0,0.0), spin=0.0):
        self.position = position
        self.velocity = velocity
        self.name = name
        self.spin = spin

    def __str__ (self):
        print('in particle str')
        pos_str = '({}:{}:{})'.\
            format(self.position[0],self.position[1],self.position[2])
        vel_str = '({}:{}:{})'.\
            format(self.velocity[0],self.velocity[1],self.velocity[2])
        result_str = "{} at {} with velocity {} and spin {}".\
              format(self.name, pos_str, vel_str, self.spin)
        return result_str

class MassParticle (Particle):
    def __init__ (self, name='',position=(0.0,0.0,0.0), \
                  velocity=(0.0,0.0,0.0), spin=0.0, mass=0.0):
        Particle.__init__(self, name, position, velocity, spin)
        self.mass = mass

    def __str__(self):
        print('in mass str')
        result_str = Particle.__str__(self)
        result_str = result_str + ' and mass {}'.format(self.mass)
        return result_str

class ChargedParticle(MassParticle):
    def __init__(self, name='', position=(0.0,0.0,0.0), \
                 velocity=(0.0,0.0,0.0), spin=0.0,mass=0.0, charge=0.0):
        MassParticle.__init__(self,name,position,velocity,spin,mass)
        self.charge = charge

    def __str__(self):
        print('in charged str')
        result_str = MassParticle.__str__(self)
        result_str = result_str + ' and charge {}'.format(self.charge)
        return result_str
```

Using Parent Class Methods

```
In  [1]: from program12_11 import *
In  [2]: photon = Particle(name='photon', spin=1.0)
In  [3]: print(photon)
in particle str
photon at (0.0:0.0:0.0) with velocity (0.0:0.0:0.0) and spin 1.0
In  [4]: tau = ChargedParticle(name='tau', spin=0.5, charge=-1.0, mass=1.777)
In  [5]: print(tau)
in charged str
in mass str
in particle str
tau at (0.0:0.0:0.0) with velocity (0.0:0.0:0.0) and spin 0.5 and mass 1.777 and
charge -1.0
```

As you have seen, Code Listing 12.11 implements our class hierarchy. For simplicity, we implement only the `__init__` and `__str__` methods.

If you look carefully at the `__init__` and `__str__` methods of the two child classes, you will see something odd. An example would be the `__init__` of `MassParticle`. It contains the line: `Particle.__init__(self,name,position,velocity,spin)`. What is that? All of our previous work used instances to call methods. Here, we are calling the method with a *class* and passing `self` in the argument list.

The problem is this. When we make a child class, we want it to have an `__init__` method just like every other class. However, if it is a child class, we *also* want to make sure we call its parent class's `__init__` as well. In this way, we do locally to any instance what needs to be done for our class, but we also must do what the *parent* class requires.

We cannot do this initialization with something like `self.__init__` in the local class's `__init__`. That just calls the same method again! We need a way to call the parent class `__init__` (and any other inherited method).

Python provides a way to do this. We are used to doing method calls in the context of a calling object. For example, in `inst1.update` the object `inst1` is calling the method `update`. This is called a "bound method." This usage means that the first parameter of `update`, the parameter `self`, is *automatically* bound by Python to the object `inst1`. On the other hand, the method can be called without automatically assigning the calling object to `self`, but the *user* must then provide the calling instance explicitly. This latter case is called an "unbound method." With an unbound method, we specifically indicate the method (what class, what method) using dot notation and then explicitly pass the argument that will bind to the `self` parameter of the method.

In Code Listing 12.11, there are some print statements in each of the `__str__` methods to indicate which method is being called to show which methods are in fact being used.

Changing Code Using Class Inheritance

The print output of the `__str__` method is not very well formatted. The good news is that we can fix most of the problems by changing the `__str__` in `Particle`. Fixing the code in `Particle` updates the formatted output that occurs for *all* particles (remember the "find the attribute" rules). An updated version and session output are shown in Code Listing 12.12.

Code Listing 12.12

```
# multi-class model for the standard model, showing
# inheritance along __str__ use.

class Particle (object):
    def __init__ (self, name='', position=(0.0,0.0,0.0),\
                  velocity=(0.0,0.0,0.0), spin=0.0):
        self.position = position
        self.velocity = velocity
        self.name = name
        self.spin = spin

    def __str__ (self):
        # print 'in Particle str'
        pos_str = '({:.2}:{:.2}:{:.2})'.\
              format(self.position[0],self.position[1],self.position[2])
        vel_str = '({:.2}:{:.2}:{:.2})'.\
              format(self.velocity[0],self.velocity[1],self.velocity[2])
        result_str = "{}\n at {}\n with velocity {}\n and spin {}\n".\
                format(self.name, pos_str, vel_str, self.spin)
        return result_str

class MassParticle (Particle):
    def __init__ (self, name='',position=(0.0,0.0,0.0),\
                  velocity=(0.0,0.0,0.0), spin=0.0, mass=0.0):
        Particle.__init__(self, name, position, velocity, spin)
        self.mass = mass

    def __str__(self):
        # print 'in mass str'
        result_str = Particle.__str__(self)
        result_str = result_str + ' and mass {}\n'.format(self.mass)
        return result_str

class ChargedParticle(MassParticle):
    def __init__(self, name='', position=(0.0,0.0,0.0),\
                 velocity=(0.0,0.0,0.0), spin=0.0,mass=0.0, charge=0.0):
        MassParticle.__init__(self,name,position,velocity,spin,mass)
        self.charge = charge
```

```
    def __str__(self):
        # print 'in charged str'
        result_str = MassParticle.__str__(self)
        result_str = result_str + ' and charge {}'.format(self.charge)
        return result_str
```

```
In  [1]: from program12_12 import *
In  [2]: photon = Particle(name='photon', spin=1.0)
In  [3]: tau = ChargedParticle(name='tau', spin=0.5, charge=-1.0, mass=1.777)
In  [4]: print(photon)
photon
 at (0.0:0.0:0.0)
 with velocity (0.0:0.0:0.0)
 and spin 1.0

In  [5]: print(tau)
tau
 at (0.0:0.0:0.0)
 with velocity (0.0:0.0:0.0)
 and spin 0.5
 and mass 1.78
 and charge -1.0
```

This is the beauty of inheritance. If the parent class is doing work, we just call the parent class method and then, in our local method, add on whatever we need. If we need to modify any common functionality, we do it in the class where it resides and all inheriting classes "see" the effect.

In this session, we can see that even though we did not change the `__str__` method of the `chargedParticle` we inherited the changes made in `Particle` so the print of the `chargedParticle` is also nicely formatted.

12.7 WHAT'S WRONG WITH MY CODE?

Here are suggestions for finding problems with classes. Refer to Appendix C for details.

- **Return class type with arithmetic methods:** The most common mistake with arithmetic methods such as `__add__` is to forget to return objects of the class type. For example, if you add two Rational numbers, you expect the result to be a Rational number. The solution is `return Rational(num,denom)` where you create a Rational object before you return it.

Summary

In this chapter, you learned how to increase the capabilities of classes that we design. You learned the value of consistency, the use of introspection, and how to overload some operators.

Classes

- Overloading operators:
  `A + B` maps to `A.__add__(B)`
  which maps to `__add__(self,param)`
  by mapping `A` to `self` and mapping `B` to `param`.
- Inheritance: inherit properties of the superclass.
- Expanded class organization:

```
class ClassName(object):
    def __init__(self,param):
        self.value == param
    def __add__(self,param):
        the_sum = self.value + param.value
        return ClassName(the_sum)
    def __radd__(self,param):
        return self.__add__(param)
    def __eq__(self,param):
        return self.value == param.value

class ChildClass(ClassName):
    def __init__(self,param):
        ClassName.__init__(self,param)
```

Rules

- **Rule 1:** Think before you program!
- **Rule 2:** A program is a human-readable essay on problem solving that also happens to execute on a computer.
- **Rule 3:** The best way to improve your programming and problem skills is to practice!
- **Rule 4:** A foolish consistency is the hobgoblin of little minds.
- **Rule 5:** Test your code, often and thoroughly!
- **Rule 6:** If it was hard to write, it is probably hard to read. Add a comment.

- **RULE 7:** All input is evil, until proven otherwise.
- **RULE 8:** A function should do one thing.
- **RULE 9:** Make sure your new class does the right thing.

Exercises

1. Describe what the `isinstance` function does, and give an example of its use.
2. Augment the Rational number class to include multiplication and division. Include the ability to accommodate operands of type *`int`*.
3. The human body has many organs (heart, lungs, brain, and kidneys, to name a few). We could think of the human body as a complex object made up of simpler objects (organs).
   (a) Create classes for heart and brain. Think about what the functions of the heart and brain are in our body and map these functions into methods.
   (b) Create an `Organ` class as the base class for the organs and derive the classes created earlier from the base class.
4. There are websites such as `http://www.kbb.com` that provide information about second-hand vehicles. Design a base class for vehicle with fields such as model year, total mileage, Vehicle Identification Number (VIN), EPA class, EPA mileage, engine, transmission, and options.

   Design subclasses for car, truck, SUV, and minivan. Think about the specific fields and methods required for the subclasses.
5. Write a class called `Movie` that has fields to store the name of the director, the lead actors, the supporting cast, production house, the total production budget, and the revenue it earned. Create an overloaded compare operator so that when you compare two movies, you get to know whether they made the same amount of profit or not.

   You could also have other overloaded Boolean operators.
6. In Newtonian physics, we know that two velocities in the same direction add to each other; in the opposite direction, they subtract from each other to give a net result in the direction of the bigger velocity.

   Design a simple class called `Velocity` that has a field for the speed in meters per second. (Forget about the direction for now).

   The default constructor would work with meters/sec metric.

   Write a constructor that takes three parameters: (a) distance, (b) time, and (c) whether the velocity is in meters/sec or feet/sec.

   This constructor should accordingly convert the feet/sec into meters/sec. Create overloaded unary, addition, and subtraction operators for velocity.

A more advanced version of this class would consider the directions other than same or opposite directions.

7. Every semester, students take a number of courses, and at the end of the semester, they get their final grades. Design a SemTranscript class that stores the name of the student, list of courses taken by the student and the corresponding grades, and the average grade for that semester. Also, create a overloaded addition operator so that you can add two semester grades to get courses taken in two semesters and calculate the final grade for a year.

   Note: In the overloaded operator, you cannot just directly take an average of the grades of the two SemTranscript objects to get the average final grade of the year.

8. File Concatenation: Many operating systems allow one to concatenate files. Design a class called `TextDocument` that reads the contents of a text file only. Create a constructor that takes the path of a text file. Create an overloaded addition operator for this class that adds (concatenates) two `TextDocument` objects (appends the second one at the end of the first one) and creates a new text file. Handle all possible error cases, such as for file existence.

9. Consider a specific type of chemical reaction that takes in two compounds and returns a new compound. Design a class called `Compound` with fields for the name of the compound (such as hydrochloric acid), chemical formula of the compound (HCl). Create an addition operator for the compound class so that when you add two compounds, you get a new one. In the operator function, just print a string indicating the two compounds being added.

10. Design a class called `Color`. The fields of the class are three decimals for Red, Green, and Blue components in the range 0 to 1, inclusive (0 indicates Black and 1 indicates White). Add checks to ensure that the values are always in the given range. Provide addition and subtraction operators for the color class. Include saturation in the addition and subtraction: if any component goes less than 0 or greater than 1, assign them 0 or 1, respectively.

11. Write a program to extend the *`list`* class by adding a `push` method.

12. Vectors, in Physics, are objects that have both magnitude and direction. Design a class to represent vectors. Provide addition and subtraction operators - remember to adjust directions appropriately.

---

13. Write a `wholeNumber` class. The whole numbers are the nonnegative integers: 0,1,2, . . . Your class must handle addition, subtraction, and multiplication of whole numbers—no division or mixed-type (whole number and integer) operations need be handled. Your class must also handle printing, for example, if x is an instance of the `wholeNumber` class, you must be able to write: `print(x)`.

Two cases must not be allowed: (1) you must not be able to create a `wholeNumber` that has a negative value; (2) an arithmetic operation cannot be allowed to have a negative result. In both cases, an error message must be printed.

Remember that arithmetic must return a whole number. That is, if x and y are whole numbers, the result of $x + y$ must be a whole number.

Include sample code that uses your class and demonstrates the use of all methods as well as error handling.

14. Write a class for linear equations. A generic linear equation is of the form $y = mx + b$ where m and b are constants. Include the following methods:

(a) `__init__`, `__str__`, `__repr__`.
(b) `value(x)`, which returns the value of the equation given x.
(c) `compose(linearEquation)` that composes two linear equations. That is, if $y = x + 1$ and $z = 2a + 5$, then $y(z) = 2x + 6$ and will be called as `y.compose(z)`. Note that the `compose` operation is not commutative.
(d) `__add__` returns the sum of two linear equations. That is, if $y = ax + b$ and $z = cx + d$, then $y + z = (a + c)x + (b + d)$.

Include sample code that uses your class and demonstrates the use of all methods as well as error handling.

15. Write an `Odometer` class. An odometer is the gauge on your car that measures distance traveled. In the United States, an odometer measures miles; elsewhere, it measures kilometers. Many vehicles with electronic odometer interfaces have the ability to switch between miles and kilometers. The accuracy is 1/10 of a mile (kilometer).

Something to consider: if an odometer gets replaced, a new one must be able to be set to some specified mileage.

Include the following methods:

(a) `__init__`, `__str__`, `__repr__`.
(b) The constructor must take two arguments that both have default values: one is mileage, and the other specifies units.
(c) Addition and subtraction both have one odometer operand and one numeric operand, where the numeric operand represents the miles being added/subtracted (not two odometer operands).
(d) Addition should be commutative (but not subtraction).
(e) Output should always be rounded to a 1/10 of a mile (kilometer), but the odometer itself should maintain full floating-point accuracy.

Include sample code that uses your class and demonstrates the use of all methods as well as demonstrating error handling.

16. Write a `Clock` class that measures hours, minutes, and seconds.

Include the following methods:

(a) `__init__`, `__str__`, `__repr__`.

(b) Addition allows for both clock-to-clock operations and clock-to-integer operations. If one argument is an integer, the integer is assumed to represent hours. Addition should be commutative!
(c) Output should always be rounded to the second.
(d) If inappropriate values are passed to the constructor, the created clock instance should get a value of 0 hours, 0 minutes, and 0 seconds.

Include sample code that uses your class and demonstrates the use of all methods as well as error handling.

17. Write a `Compass` class. A compass provides bearings. A bearing is a measure of direction as indicated by clockwise rotation around a circle. There are 360 degrees in a bearing and within each degree are 60 minutes. Thus a legal bearing would be 270 degrees, 36 minutes (approximately due west). There are never more than 359 degrees in a bearing, or more than 59 minutes in a bearing. Both degrees and minutes are integer values.

Include the following methods:

(a) `__init__`, `__str__`, `__repr__`.
(b) Addition allows for both bearing-to-bearing operations and bearing-to-integer operations. If one argument is an integer, the integer is assumed to represent degrees. Addition should be commutative!
(c) Output should always be rounded to the minute.
(d) If inappropriate values are passed to the constructor, the created bearing instance should get a value of 0 degrees, 0 minutes.

Include sample code that uses your class and demonstrates the use of all methods as well as error handling.

18. Write a class `RedirectOutput` which redirects all output to a text file and displays a message before and after writing to the file.

CHAPTER 13

Program Development with Classes

> I paint objects as I think them, not as I see them.
>
> Pablo Picasso, artist

IN THIS CHAPTER, WE WILL DEVELOP A MORE IN-DEPTH EXAMPLE USING CLASSES SO you can see how problem-solving design can be accomplished using classes (objects).

13.1 PREDATOR–PREY PROBLEM

For this problem, we will consider a simulation of a natural habitat: a predator–prey problem. Predator–prey problems are a study of the varying sizes of populations as two groups of animals interact. One group constitutes the prey, a population of animals that are the food source for the other population of animals, the predators. The simulation shows the dynamic interaction of these two populations. It represents a kind of habitat war as the two populations struggle to survive or thrive.

Typically, both groups have a fixed birthrate. The prey usually procreate faster than the predators, allowing for a growing prey population. However, as the population of prey increases, the habitat can support a higher number of predators. This in turn leads to an increasing predator population and, after some time, a decreasing prey population. Around that time the population of predator grows so large as to reach a critical point, the point where the number of prey can no longer support the present predator population and the predator population begins to wane. As the predator population declines, the prey population recovers and the two populations continue this interesting interaction of growth and decay. Though predator–prey relationships have been modeled with equations[1] it is interesting to simulate the relationship on a computer and observe how they interact. The classic simulation may be the WAT-OR game, based on a "Scientific American" article by A. K. Dewdney.[2] We choose a slightly different model here.

As with any simulation, the programmer gets to choose what is represented, as no reasonably sized computer program could encompass the complexity of a full habitat. Within such a simulation, the user can adjust the identified parameters, such as birth and death rates of each population, and observe the impact on each cycle, and each population.

An actual example of studying predator–prey relationships in their habitat is the one between wolves and moose on Isle Royale in Lake Superior, as shown at the website `http://www.isleroyalewolf.org`. Isle Royale is located in the northwest of Lake Superior and its population of wolves and moose are isolated to the island (occasionally, Lake Superior does freeze enough for walking to land). Its isolation is a perfect laboratory for studying the effects of predator–prey interaction. A graph of the varying population sizes as actually has occurred since 1959 can be found at: `http://www.isleroyalewolf.org/data/data/home.html`.

13.1.1 The Rules

These are the rules we will use for our simulation:

- The habitat updates itself in units of time called clock *ticks*. During one tick of our habitat clock, every animal in the island gets an opportunity to do something.
- All animals are given an opportunity to move into an adjacent space, if an empty adjacent space can be found. One move per clock tick is allowed.
- Both the predators and prey can reproduce. Each animal is assigned a fixed *breed time*. If the animal is still alive after breed-time ticks of the clock, it will reproduce. The animal does so by finding an unoccupied, adjacent space and fills that space with the new animal—its offspring. The animal's breed time is then reset to zero. An animal can breed at most once in a clock tick.
- The predators must eat. They have a fixed *starve time*. If they cannot find a prey to eat before starve-time ticks of the clock, they die.
- When a predator eats, it moves into an adjacent space that is occupied by prey (its meal). The prey is removed and the predator's starve time is reset to zero. Eating counts as the predator's move during that clock tick.
- At the end of every clock tick, each animal's local event clocks is updated. All animals' breed times are decremented and all predators' starve times are decremented.

This is the model we will need to support. It doesn't perfectly model the actual environment, but it does sufficiently well to provide insight into predator–prey interactions.

[1] Lotka–Volterra equations.

[2] *Scientific American*, December Issue, 1984.

13.1.2 Simulation Using Object-Oriented Programming

Simulation is perfectly suited for object-oriented programming (OOP). In OOP, we need to identify objects and define their interactions to create a program. Simulations naturally require these kind of identifications. It is for this reason that OOP evolved out of the programming language Simula, a programming language for writing simulations.

What objects do we need for our simulation? We need an island, some moose (the prey), and a few wolves (the predators). We also need all the methods that govern how they interact with each other, as well as a main program. Let's focus on the classes we need for the moment. We need:

- `Island` Class
- `Prey` Class
- `Predator` Class

Having a single `Prey` class and a single `Predator` class, we can create many instances of these classes and have the instances interact. Very efficient!

We now need to identify for each class:

- *What* we need to have represented in each class instance.
- *How* these instances can be manipulated, that is, what methods are needed.

Next, look at each class and try to sketch out what is required.

13.2 CLASSES

13.2.1 *Island* Class

Isle Royale is shaped like an elongated rectangle, but to keep our example simple, we choose to model an `Island` instance as a square, an $n \times n$ grid. Every element in the grid could potentially have *one* of three values. Either it contains nothing, a predator or a prey.

To begin with, the grid is initialized to be empty at every grid position. The value 0 will be used to represent an empty grid position. Every class needs a constructor (`__init__`) and it is generally useful to have a `__str__` method so that we can easily display an `Island` instance. When we create an instance, we need to specify only its size—in our case, we'll specify the length of a side since the island is square. This will be an argument to our constructor. See Code Listing 13.1.

Code Listing 13.1

```
class Island():
    """Island
       n X n grid where zero value indicates an unoccupied cell."""
```

```
    def __init__(self, n):
        '''Initialize cell to all 0's, then fill with animals
        '''
        self.grid_size = n
        self.grid = []
        for i in range(n):
            row = [0]*n     # row is a list of n zeros
            self.grid.append(row)

    def __str__(self):
        '''String representation for printing.
           (0,0) will be in the lower-left corner.
        '''
        s = ""
        for j in range(self.grid_size-1,-1,-1):   # print row size-1 first
            for i in range(self.grid_size):       # each row starts at 0
                if not self.grid[i][j]:
                    # print a '.' for an empty space
                    s+= "{:<2s}".format('.' + "  ")
                else:
                    s+= "{:<2s}".format((str(self.grid[i][j])) + "  ")
            s+="\n"
        return s
```

```
In  [1]: from island1 import *
In  [2]: royale = Island(10)
In  [3]: print(royale)
.  .  .  .  .  .  .  .  .  .
.  .  .  .  .  .  .  .  .  .
.  .  .  .  .  .  .  .  .  .
.  .  .  .  .  .  .  .  .  .
.  .  .  .  .  .  .  .  .  .
.  .  .  .  .  .  .  .  .  .
.  .  .  .  .  .  .  .  .  .
.  .  .  .  .  .  .  .  .  .
.  .  .  .  .  .  .  .  .  .
.  .  .  .  .  .  .  .  .  .
```

In the `__init__` constructor, we save the size of the instance and the grid that represents the instance. Those two items are sufficient to represent the present state of the `Island` instance—essentially, the location in the grid of all the predators and prey.

A grid of n rows and n columns can be thought of as a list of n rows—each of length n. We create a row that is a list of n items of value 0 using the repeat (*) operator. We then add n rows to our instance grid, making the $n \times n$ grid.

The `__str__` method prints the contents of each grid element. To keep with standard Cartesian coordinates, we have the method print in such a way that (0,0) is in the lower-left corner. This means we have x increasing to the right and y increasing to the top. However, because printing occurs from the top down, we must print the highest-numbered row first.

The output in the previous session shows the creation of a 10×10 `Island` instance named "royale" followed by printing of the current state of the instance: empty.

13.2.2 Predator and Prey, Kinds of Animals

At this point, it is worth our time to think a little about the rest of our simulation design. If we look at the requirements for the two kinds of animals in our simulation, predator and prey, we can see that they share some important characteristics. They occupy locations on the `Island` instance, and they must be able to move and breed. Because they share these characteristics, it makes sense that they *inherit* those characteristics from a common parent, the `Animal` object.

`Animal` Object

What state does each animal instance need? Each instance needs to know where it is on the `Island` instance. The question is: where do we keep that location information—with the `Animal` instance, with the `Island` instance, or with both? Each `Animal` instance needs to know where it is, its local information, but it also needs to be aware of what else is in its surroundings, the global information. In addition, we will probably want to control how many animals can be at the same place at the same time. For those reasons, an `Animal` instance will have as *local* state its location on the island grid, its x and y coordinates. We let the `Island` instance keep *global* state information on all the inhabitants by marking in each grid location what is presently there, including nothing.

Therefore, our `Animal` object will need the following:

- Its name (string, e.g., 'moose' or 'wolf').
- Its location: (x, y) coordinates on the island.
- The `Island` instance, that is, the island the animal is on.

The `__init__` constructor will need to take in each of these values as parameters. The x and y values indicate where on the island the animal will be placed. The `Animal` instance will also need to know the island it is located on. Finally, the instance will need its name: moose and wolf.

We need to inform the `Island` instance when a new `Animal` instance is added to the island. For that purpose we create the `register` method in the `Island` class. This method will "place" (register) the `Animal` instance in the `Island` grid at the x and y coordinates stored in the instance. In this way, we coordinate the local information (x and y coordinates stored in the `Animal` instance) with the global information (location of each instance in the `Island` instance grid) for the simulation.

Also, each `Animal` instance will need to know how big the `Island` instance is so that it can move around without falling into the surrounding water. For that purpose, we will also create a `size` method in the `Island` class.

Our communication between the animal and the island will be:

- `n = island.size()   # get the size from the island instance`
- `island.register(self)   # register an animal (self) location with the island instance`

Let's add those two methods to the `Island` class. Also, let's create the bare bones of the `Animal` class so that we can begin to work with the interaction between animals and the island. This is shown in Code Listing 13.2.

Code Listing 13.2

```
class Island (object):
    """Island
       n X n grid where zero value indicates not occupied."""
    def __init__(self, n, prey_count=0, predator_count=0):
        '''Initialize grid to all 0's, then fill with animals
        '''
        print n,prey_count,predator_count
        self.grid_size = n
        self.grid = []
        for i in range(n):
            row = [0]*n    # row is a list of n zeros
            self.grid.append(row)
        self.init_animals(prey_count,predator_count)

    def size(self):
        '''Return size of the island: one dimension.
        '''
        return self.grid_size

    def register(self,animal):
        '''Register animal with island, i.e. put it at the
        animal's coordinates
        '''
        x = animal.x
        y = animal.y
        self.grid[x][y] = animal

    def __str__(self):
        '''String representation for printing.
           (0,0) will be in the lower left corner.
        '''
```

```
        s = ""
        for j in range(self.grid_size-1,-1,-1):  # print row size-1 first
            for i in range(self.grid_size):       # each row starts at 0
                if not self.grid[i][j]:
                    # print a '.' for an empty space
                    s+= "{:<2s}".format('.' + "  ")
                else:
                    s+= "{:<2s}".format((str(self.grid[i][j])) + "  ")
            s+="\n"
        return s

class Animal(object):
    def __init__(self, island, x=0, y=0, s="A"):
        '''Initialize the animal's and their positions
        '''
        self.island = island
        self.name = s
        self.x = x
        self.y = y

    def __str__(self):
        return self.name
```

```
In  [1]: royale = Island(10)
In  [2]: animal1 = Animal(island=royale,x=4,y=8,s='a1')
In  [3]: animal2 = Animal(island=royale,x=6,y=4,s='a2')
In  [4]: royale.register(animal1)
In  [4]: royale.register(animal2)
In  [4]: print(royale)
.   .   .   .   .   .   .   .   .   .
.   .   .   .   a1  .   .   .   .   .
.   .   .   .   .   .   .   .   .   .
.   .   .   .   .   .   .   .   .   .
.   .   .   .   .   .   .   .   .   .
.   .   .   .   .   .   a2  .   .   .
.   .   .   .   .   .   .   .   .   .
.   .   .   .   .   .   .   .   .   .
.   .   .   .   .   .   .   .   .   .
.   .   .   .   .   .   .   .   .   .
In  [5]: print(animal1)
a1
```

Notice how the printing of an `Island` is accomplished in its `__str__` method. We access the grid with `self.island[i][j]`, but what is located there? Examine the `Island` `register` method. It is passed an `Animal` instance as a parameter. It is this instance value that is stored in the grid. Thus `self.island[i][j]` is a reference to that `Animal` instance, and because that call is within `__str__`, it is asking for the string representation of that particular animal. That is found in the Animal's `__str__` method. At the end of the session, we show an explicit call to the Animal's `__str__` method by way of a **`print`** statement.

For debugging purposes, it would be nice to confirm that the `Animal` instance grid coordinates agree with the island grid location. Printing the `Island` instance indicates the location that instance is maintaining for each `Animal` instance. The opposite, accessing position information for an `Animal` instance, requires a new `Animal` method. Let's call it `position`, and we will have it simply return the `Animal` instance's (x, y) coordinate pair. Code Listing 13.3 shows the method (without the rest of the Animal class). We can see in the accompanying session that both the `Island` instance and the `Animal` instance have the same location coordinates for that `Animal` instance.

Code Listing 13.3

```
def position(self):
    """Return coordinates of current position."""
    return self.x, self.y
```

```
In  [1]: royale = Island(10)
In  [2]: animal1 = Animal(island=royale,x=0,y=8,s='a1')
In  [3]: animal1.position()
Out [3]: (0, 8)

In  [4]: print(royale)
.   .   .   .   .   .   .   .   .   .
a1  .   .   .   .   .   .   .   .   .
.   .   .   .   .   .   .   .   .   .
.   .   .   .   .   .   .   .   .   .
.   .   .   .   .   .   .   .   .   .
.   .   .   .   .   .   .   .   .   .
.   .   .   .   .   .   .   .   .   .
.   .   .   .   .   .   .   .   .   .
.   .   .   .   .   .   .   .   .   .
.   .   .   .   .   .   .   .   .   .
```

13.2.3 Predator and Prey Classes

The `Predator` and `Prey` classes share many characteristics, which are collected in the `Animal` class. We can take advantage of this sharing by having each be a subclass of

Animal. Each Predator and Prey class will require particular methods, but they can also share many methods and variables by being subclasses of the Animal class.

In particular, remember that the __init__ method of the subclass must call the __init__ of the parent class to fully initialize the instance. Code Listing 13.4 shows the two new classes with just their respective __init__ methods. Note that we do not need to define a __str__ method for either subclass, as this method already exists in the Animal class.

Code Listing 13.4

```
class Animal(object):
    def __init__(self, island, x=0, y=0, s="A"):
        '''Initialize the animals and their positions
        '''
        self.island = island
        self.name = s
        self.x = x
        self.y = y

    def __str__(self):
        return self.name

class Prey(Animal):
    def __init__(self, island, x=0,y=0,s="O"):
        Animal.__init__(self,island,x,y,s)

class Predator(Animal):
    def __init__(self, island, x=0,y=0,s="X"):
        Animal.__init__(self,island,x,y,s)
```

13.2.4 Object Diagram

It is useful to create a diagram of the objects we have created to help understand the relationships among them. See Figure 13.1.

13.2.5 Filling the Island

VideoNote 13.1
Improve Simulation

Now that we have the Prey, Predator, and Island classes, we need a way to fill an Island instance with instances of both Predator and Prey. We could leave this as a separate function to be written as part of the main program, but it makes sense that the Island instance should be able to fill itself given some counts for each class.

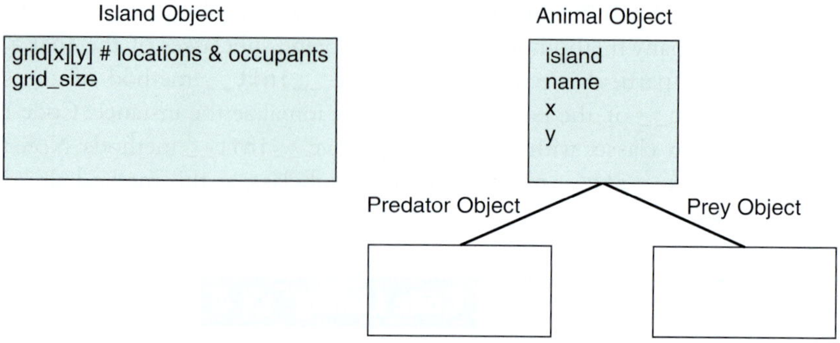

FIGURE 13.1 Objects: island, animals, predators, and prey.

To accomplish this we add the `init_animals` method of `Island`. It takes two parameters, the predator and prey counts, and fills the island with the correct number of instances of these two classes.

We would like to place the animal instances at random spots on the `Island` instance. That means that we will need to import the `random` module and use the `randint` method to get the x and y coordinates to place an animal. The value generated will be between 0 and the island's size. See Section 16.1.5 for more information on the `random` module.

The generated values must place the new instance at an unoccupied grid location. If the present (x, y) is occupied, another pair must be generated.

Querying a Grid Location

We need some way to query an `Island` instance to see if an `Animal` instance is at a location. To do that, the island needs a method to respond to that query. Let's call that method `animal()`. It will take the x and y coordinates as arguments:

```
def  animal(self,x,y):
    if 0 <= x < self.size   and   0 <= y < self.size:
        return   self.island[x][y]
    else:
        return   -1 # outside island boundary
```

The method returns an instance (if one occupies the position), a 0 (if the position is empty), or a −1 to indicate that the coordinates are off the island (explained later).

Repeat Until Full

With these pieces in hand, we can do the following to fill the island:

- Generate an (x, y) pair using `random.randint(0,grid_size)`
- Check to see whether that position is empty or has an animal instance using the `animal` method

- If the position is empty:
  - Create the new instance, record the *x* and *y* values in the instance, then register the instance.
  - Increment the count of created instances. Initialization of that animal (predator or prey) ends when the count reaches the goal count for the animal (passed as an argument to the constructor).
- If the position is occupied:
  - The ***while*** loop continues, but the count of created instances is not incremented.

If the `Island` instance is very full, this process could be rather inefficient. Perhaps you could improve it? (See the Exercises.)

The remaining detail of this section is to make two small changes to the `Island` `__init__` method. First, two more parameters are passed to `Island`: the counts for the `Predator` and `Prey` instances. They default to 0, if not specified. Second, a line is added to the end of the constructor to call the `init_animals` method. The `Island` class with these additions is shown in Code Listing 13.5, but to avoid clutter we have omitted the unmodified methods: `size`, `register`, and `__str__`.

Code Listing 13.5

```
class Island (object):
    def __init__(self, n, prey_count=0, predator_count=0):
        '''Initialize grid to all 0s, then fill with animals
        '''
        # print n,prey_count,predator_count
        self.grid_size = n
        self.grid = []
        for i in range(n):
            row = [0]*n    # row is a list of n zeros
            self.grid.append(row)
        self.init_animals(prey_count,predator_count)

    def animal(self,x,y):
        '''Return animal at location (x,y)'''
        if 0 <= x < self.grid_size and 0 <= y < self.grid_size:
            return self.grid[x][y]
        else:
            return -1  # outside island boundary

    def init_animals(self,prey_count, predator_count):
        ''' Put some initial animals on the island
        '''
        count = 0
```

```
        # while loop continues until prey_count unoccupied positions are found
        while count < prey_count:
            x = random.randint(0,self.grid_size-1)
            y = random.randint(0,self.grid_size-1)
            if not self.animal(x,y):
                new_prey=Prey(island=self,x=x,y=y)
                count += 1
                self.register(new_prey)
        count = 0
        # same while loop but for predator_count
        while count < predator_count:
            x = random.randint(0,self.grid_size-1)
            y = random.randint(0,self.grid_size-1)
            if not self.animal(x,y):
                new_predator=Predator(island=self,x=x,y=y)
                count += 1
                self.register(new_predator)

    ## Unmodified methods not shown: size, register, __str__
```

13.3 ADDING BEHAVIOR

We have a start with our simulation. We have an `Island` instance on which we can place `Predator` and `Prey` instances. Now we need to have these animals do something—let's begin with movement.

13.3.1 Refinement: Add Movement

Neither the `Predators` nor `Prey` instances should stay still, so let's add movement. Immense complexity of movement can be modeled, but we will begin with simple "random" movement (truly random movement will added later). Because both kinds of instance needs to move, we will add a new method to `Animal`.

The movement we allow is to move to a neighboring region, if it is empty. If no neighboring locations are empty, the animal instance cannot move and remains at its present location.

Our algorithm to find a location to move to is as follows:

1. for each neighboring location:
   (a) if neighboring location is empty:
      i. move to neighboring location
      ii. break (stop looking for a place to move to)

What is a "neighboring region"? Any square not only shares edges with four neighbors, but also shares a corner with another four neighbors. See Figure 13.2. A reasonable argument can be made for moving only to the four neighboring regions sharing edges. However, let's allow these animals more freedom of movement and let them jump to any of the eight neighboring regions.

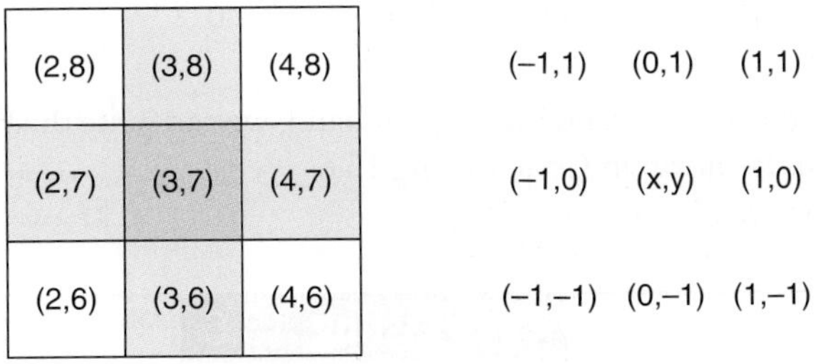

(a) Example centered on (3,7) (b) Offset values from location x,y

FIGURE 13.2 Eight neighbors.

If an animal is at a particular location (particular coordinates), what are the coordinates of the eight neighboring locations that it might move to? Figure 13.2(b) shows the offsets of the eight neighbors. We can add the offset to an animal's current coordinates to find the coordinates of a neighbor. For example, if an animal is at (3,7), the location immediately below it has offset (0,–1) so the neighboring coordinates are (3+0,7–1) = (3,6). See Figure 13.2(a).

To implement movement, we can loop through the neighbors, but what is the best way to represent neighbors for looping? The offsets provide regularity that can be worked into a loop. Let's make a list of offsets and then refer to the offset list each time we want to determine coordinates for a neighbor. Examining each neighbor becomes a walk through the offset list, applying each offset to an animal's current location. A refinement of our algorithm now looks like this:

1. for each offset:
   (a) neighbor_x = current_x + offset_x
   (b) neighbor_y = current_y + offset_y
   (c) if neighboring location is empty:
      i. move to neighboring location
      ii. break (stop looking for a place to move to)

We now have two new actions to consider. First, how do we know if a neighbor is empty? We can use the `animal` method previously defined for the `Island` class. That method returns an `Predator` or `Prey` instance, if it exists at the specified location.

Second, how do we move to a neighboring location? We can update the local location, the *x* and *y* coordinates in the animal instance, but we also need to update the island to keep the global information in synch. We also need to remove the animal from its current location and then register it in its new location. Therefore, the `Island` class needs a method to remove an animal from a given location. Removal simply sets the grid location to 0.

```
def  remove(self,x,y):
    self.grid[x][y]  =  0
```

With those two island methods in hand, we can write the `Prey's move` method and test it. This is shown in Code Listing 13.6.

Code Listing 13.6

```
def move(self):
    """Move to an open, neighboring position."""
    # neighbor offsets
    offset = [(-1,1),(0,1),(1,1),(-1,0),(1,0),(-1,-1),(0,-1),(1,-1)]
    for i in range(len(offset)):
        x = self.x + offset[i][0]  # neighboring coordinates
        y = self.y + offset[i][1]
        if self.island.animal(x,y) == 0: # neighboring spot is open
            self.island.remove(self)  # remove from current spot
            self.x = x  # new coordinates
            self.y = y
            self.island.register(self) # register new coordinates
            break  # finished with move
```

```
In  [1]: royale = Island(5) # create island
In  [2]: moose1 = Prey(royale,"m1") # create two moose
In  [3]: moose2 = Prey(royale,"m2")
In  [4]: print(royale) # print initial state of island
.    .    .    .    .
.    .    .    .    .
.    .   m1    .    .
.   m2    .    .    .
.    .    .    .    .

In  [5]: moose1.move() # move each moose
In  [5]: moose2.move()
```

```
In  [5]: print(royale) # observe island after moves
.   .   .   .   .
.   m1  .   .   .
m2  .   .   .   .
.   .   .   .   .
.   .   .   .   .
```

Note how each neighboring coordinate is calculated using `offset`. Each item in the `offset` list is a tuple: `(x,y)`. To get the x value of offset "i" we use `offset[i][0]`, that is, the first item of the pair. The y value is similar. Also, note how the first offset is up-and-left so each animal in the test moves up one and left one position.

Falling off the Island?

Some of you may be asking, "How do we keep from falling off the island?" It is a good question. Some models of a "world" allow the world to "wrap" at the edges. That is, if you walk off the island going left (an x value less that 0), you reset yourself to the right (to an x value of 9, or whatever the size of the island is). Other approaches simply prevent you from making a "bad" move.

Our particular approach is the latter: we prevent a bad move. This prevention is done in the `animal` method of `Island`. If the passed arguments are out of range, the method returns a -1 indicating the problem.

Is this a good approach? See the exercises for other options.

13.3.2 Refinement: Time Simulation Loop

Let's add a `main` function to initialize our world and a loop to drive our simulation. We add a number of each of the `Predator` and `Prey` instances to an `Island` instance. Then, in the main loop, each trip through the loop constitutes one unit of time. In that unit of time, we give each instance the opportunity to move. We do this by moving through each grid element in the `Island` instance and, if the element holds an animal, allow it to move.

Here is an outline of our driving loop:

1. Create `Island` instance with a set number of `Predator` and `Prey` instances.
2. Loop for a specified number of time ticks:
   (a) Move each instance.

Let's take a look in Code Listing 13.7 at how that driving loop might be implemented in Python. We included a ***`print`*** statement so we can observe the movement in each time step. However, we only print the first two time steps here.

Code Listing 13.7

```
def main ():
    # initialization of the simulation
    royale = Island(5,1,1) # 5x5 island, 1 predator, 1 prey
    time_steps = 20

    # run the event loop
    island_size = royale.size()
    count = 0
    while count < time_steps:
        print(royale) # print the island
        for x in range(island_size):
            for y in range(island_size):
                animal = royale.animal(x,y)
                if animal:
                    animal.move()
        count += 1
```

```
.   m   .   .   .
.   .   .   w   .
.   .   .   .   .
.   .   .   .   .
.   .   .   .   .

m   .   .   w   .
.   .   .   .   .
.   .   .   .   .
.   .   .   .   .
.   .   .   .   .
< rest of simulation not shown >
```

Notice again how animals tend to move up and to the left. That is because our `move` method always works through the offsets in the same order. Improving on that movement is left as an exercise.

13.4 REFINEMENT: EATING, BREEDING, AND KEEPING TIME

The next refinements introduce a number of complications that require close attention. First, we need to add breeding to the `Animal` class, allowing both `Predator` and `Prey` instances to breed. Second, we differentiate `Prey` and `Predator` classes by introducing the eating behavior to the `Predator` class. In our simple model only predators eat and, if they cannot eat, they starve. Third, the time span in which prey and predators breed must be different. For the simulation to work, prey must breed at a faster rate than predators—otherwise, predators quickly starve. Finally, yet another time span must be introduced in which predators must eat or, if they cannot, starve.

The ability to set these time spans is important as their values are critical for the simulation. If `Prey` instances cannot breed quickly enough, then they will *all* be consumed, ending the simulation. If not enough `Prey` instances are provided, the `Predator` instances will *all* starve and the simulation will end. Part of the interest in the simulation is examining what values will work and how they affect the simulation. We must therefore find a way for the user to easily changes these values.

13.4.1 Improved Time Loop

We can start by improving the main function, both for initialization of values and for introducing the new (yet unwritten) behaviors into the main loop. The new main function will now take seven parameters to establish the various aspects of the simulation. Those parameters are:

`predator_breed_time`: the time span that must pass before a `Predator` instance can breed.
`predator_starve_time`: the time span that a `Predator` instance must eat within, otherwise it will starve.
`initial_predators`: the number of `Predator` instances that will initially be placed on the Island.
`prey_breed_time`: the time span that must pass before a `Prey` instance can breed.
`initial_prey`: the number of `Prey` instances that will initially be placed on the island.
`size`: the size of a single side of the `Island` instance (which, you remember, is a square).
`ticks`: the number of time "ticks" that will pass before the simulation ends.

We can also provide default values for these parameters that constitute a runnable version of the simulation. However, the user is now free to change them by simply indicating which ones to override when calling the new main function.

Remembering the Breed and Starve Time Spans

Where can we place the breeding and starving time spans (`predator_breed_time`, `prey_breed_time`, `predator_starve_time`)? They are set as variables in the main function (as parameters), but this does not make them available to each individual prey and predator instance. One option would be to set the values outside of the main function as global variables, but global variables are undesirable, for a number of reasons. Another option would be to pass them as arguments when we create `Predator` and `Prey` instances—adding another parameter to the classes. That is a good option, but let's choose yet another option that shows off some of Python's object-oriented capabilities.

Remember how a variable is searched for in a class hierarchy (see Section 12.6). First Python looks in the instance, then in the class, then up the class hierarchy through the class's parent class. If we place a variable in both the predator and prey *classes* (not the instance, the class), that value will be globally available to all instances of the two classes. A potential issue is that if we later change the value of that variable, it is changed for all instances, so we must be careful! That issue may be desirable or undesirable, depending on our needs. In our case, we will use these values only in the constructor (`__init__`) so any changes to the values will impact instances as they are created. We create three variables in the `main` function with the initial parameter values: `Predator.breed_time`, `Predator.starve_time`, and `Prey.breed_time`. Because each specifies a class name (`Predator` or `Prey`), these assignments augment the respective class definitions; that is, these names are added to the class namespace. These values will now be available for all the instances of those classes when we create them.

We then extend the event loop to include eating and breeding (for `Predator` instances only in the listing). We also include at the end of the event loop a new method, `clock_tick`. This method will "change" each instance based on its type. Anything that must happen every time tick for an instance is handled here. The updated driver is shown in Code Listing 13.8.

Code Listing 13.8

```
def main(predator_breed_time=6, predator_starve_time=3, initial_predators=10,\
        prey_breed_time=3, initial_prey=50, size=10, ticks=300):
    ''' main simulation; sets defaults, runs event loop, plots at the end
    '''
    # initialization values
    Predator.breed_time = predator_breed_time
    Predator.starve_time = predator_starve_time
    Prey.breed_time = prey_breed_time

    # make an island
    isle = Island(size,initial_prey, initial_predators)
    print(isle)

    # event loop.
    # For all the ticks, for every x,y location.
    # If there is an animal there, try eat, move, breed and clock_tick
    for i in range(ticks):
        for x in range(size):
            for y in range(size):
                animal = isle.animal(x,y)
                if animal:
                    if isinstance(animal,Predator):
```

```
                animal.eat()
            animal.move()
            animal.breed()
            animal.clock_tick()
```

Updating the `__init__` Methods

We need to include these new time spans in the instance. Each instance will have its own clock to keep track of its breeding time. The `Predator` instance will have a second clock to keep track of its starvation time. That is, when an instance is created its internal clocks need to be initialized. Both `Predator` and `Prey` instances should be initialized with a `breed_clock` whose value is set to the respective class `breed_time` value. Each instance will then update its clock during every clock tick via that `clock_tick` method. When their individual breeding clocks hit 0, they may breed. Similarly, `Predator` instances should be initialized with a `starve_clock`, initialized to the value in `Predator.starve_time`.

The updated methods are shown in Code Listing 13.9.

Code Listing 13.9

```
class Prey(Animal):
    def __init__(self, island, x=0,y=0,s="O"):
        Animal.__init__(self,island,x,y,s)
        self.breed_clock = self.breed_time

class Predator(Animal):
    def __init__(self, island, x=0,y=0,s="X"):
        Animal.__init__(self,island,x,y,s)
        self.starve_clock = self.starve_time
        self.breed_clock = self.breed_time
```

Where did `self.breed_time` and `self.starve_time` get set? They are not assigned in the `Predator` or `Prey` class definitions. As mentioned earlier, they were added to the class namespace in the `main` function where we assigned `Predator.breed_time`, `Predator.starve_time`, and `Prey.breed_time`. When we assigned those values, they were added to the respective classes' namespace, so they were available when the constructors were called. Notice how in the `Predator` and `Prey` classes the `self` in `self.breed_time` was resolved to the respective class name (`Predator` or `Prey`) when in the `main` function we assigned values to `Predator.breed_time` and `Prey.breed_time`. The starve time worked similarly.

Taking this approach with the `breed_time` and `starve_time` shows how class definitions can be dynamically augmented in Python—a powerful capability, but one that must be used carefully to ensure that readability is maintained.

13.4.2 Breeding

The breeding method is common to both subclasses (except for their time spans, as described in the previous section) so we place the `breed` method in `Animal`.

The rules described for the simulation said that when an animal breeds, the local neighborhood is examined for the first unoccupied location. If such a location is found, the new instance (the offspring) is placed at that location. It is unspecified what to do if an unoccupied location cannot be found—something we will have to resolve.

The "Neighbor" Method and Updating Move

Again, a little introspection is useful here. The process of looking for an unoccupied space used for breeding looks quite like the `move` method already described, which also requires an unoccupied neighbor. In fact, when we get to the `eat` method we will need to do something similar again, though in the eating case it will be to look for a neighbor that is `Prey`, not an unoccupied neighbor. It seems that we might be able to abstract out the "check neighbors" function and use it in many places.

We separate the "check neighbors" method from the existing `move` method so we can abstract the neighbor-checking aspect. That is, we *refactor* the move code! We call the new method `check_grid`, also part of the `Animal` class. It checks the eight neighbors for a location and returns either the location or 0.

One change is that we add a new parameter to `check_grid`, the `type_looking_for` parameter. Instead of looking only for empty grid locations, we look for a location that contains the `type_looking_for` type. If we want an unoccupied location, we are looking for a grid location with type `int` since an unoccupied location has a 0 value. However, we could also look for a location that has a `Prey` instance (for eating).

The updated move code and added `check_grid` are shown in Code Listing 13.10.

Code Listing 13.10

```
def check_grid(self,type_looking_for=int):
    ''' Look in the 8 directions from the animal's location
    and return the first location that presently has an object
    of the specified type. Return 0 if no such location exists
    '''
    # neighbor offsets
```

```
        offset = [(-1,1),(0,1),(1,1),(-1,0),(1,0),(-1,-1),(0,-1),(1,-1)]
        result = 0
        for i in range(len(offset)):
            x = self.x + offset[i][0]  # neighboring coordinates
            y = self.y + offset[i][1]
            if not 0 <= x < self.island.size() or \
               not 0 <= y < self.island.size():
                continue
            if type(self.island.animal(x,y))==type_looking_for:
                result=(x,y)
                break
        return result

    def move(self):
        '''Move to an open, neighboring position '''
        location = self.check_grid(int)
        if location:
                # print('Move, {}, from {},{} to {},{}'.format( \
                #          type(self), self.x, self.y, location[0], location[1]))
            self.island.remove(self)     # remove from current spot
            self.x = location[0]         # new coordinates
            self.y = location[1]
            self.island.register(self) # register new coordinates
```

Back to Breeding

Now we have a method that can check the eight neighbors for a location of a particular type. If our instance's local `breed_clock` hits 0, we will look for an open neighbor. Using the `check_grid` method, we will look for a location that contains an *`int`*. If one is found, we can initialize the breed process. That requires the following steps:

- We must reset the instance's `breed_clock` to the standard `breed_time` contained in the class so it may breed again.
- We must create a new instance (for the offspring) with the proper *x* and *y* values—from the open neighboring location.
- We must register the new offspring instances with the `Island` instance.

Interestingly, if this is an `Animal` method, how do we know which kind of instance to make, a `Predator` or a `Prey`? We want the method to be flexible so it will make either under the correct circumstances. Usefully, every instance knows the class to which it belongs, stored in the special variable `__class__`. We capture that class in the

the_class variable, then call the constructor on that class. The breed method is shown in Code Listing 13.11.

Code Listing 13.11

```
def breed(self):
    ''' Breed a new Animal.  If there is room in one of the 8 locations,
    place the new Prey there. Otherwise, you have to wait.
    '''
    if self.breed_clock <= 0:
        location = self.check_grid(int)
        if location:
            self.breed_clock = self.breed_time
            the_class = self.__class__
            new_animal = the_class(self.island,x=location[0],y=location[1])
            self.island.register(new_animal)
```

13.4.3 Eating

Interestingly, the eat method has much in common with both the move and breed methods given the existence of the check_grid method. There are some differences, though. This eating method *must* be in the Predator class, as Prey instances are not allowed to eat. Further, there is a little more manipulation that must be done to deal with eating.

Remember the rules. A Predator instance can look in the local neighborhood for a Prey instance. If one is found, the Predator instance moves to that location and removes the Prey instance from the Island instance. In particular, the eating method must do the following:

- Call the check_grid method passing the Prey class as the type_looking_for argument.
- If a location is found with a Prey instance:
  - Remove the Prey instance from the island.
  - Remove the Predator instance—the instance indicated by the *self* variable, from the Island instance.
  - Update the Predator instance to the new *x* and *y* coordinates, the coordinates of the Prey that was just removed.
  - Re-register the Predator instance, now at the new location.
  - Set the starve_clock of the Predator instance to the original Predator.starve_time value (so it will not starve and will continue to operate).
- If no Prey instance is found, the method does nothing.

The code for eating is shown in Code Listing 13.12.

Code Listing 13.12

```
def eat(self):
    ''' Predator looks for one of the eight locations with Prey. If found,
    moves to that location, updates the starve clock, removes the Prey.
    '''
    location = self.check_grid(Prey)
    if location:
        self.island.remove(self.island.animal(location[0],location[1]))
        self.island.remove(self)
        self.x=location[0]
        self.y=location[1]
        self.island.register(self)
        self.starve_clock=self.starve_time
```

13.4.4 The Tick of the Clock

Every pass through the event loop should update each instance's present status. In particular, the individual clocks that were initialized to their class values (breed and starve times) must be decremented. Therefore, we need a method for each class that updates the internal instance clocks on each tick of the clock. We create two methods in each subclass, called `clock_tick`.

The `Prey` `clock_tick` decrements the instance's `breed_clock`. The `Predator` `clock_tick` method decrements its `breed_clock`, but it also checks to see whether the `starve_clock` has hit 0. If so, then the instance has starved and must be removed.

The two methods are shown in Code Listing 13.13:

Code Listing 13.13

```
class Prey(Animal):
    # ...
    def clock_tick(self):
        '''Prey updates only its local breed clock
        '''
        self.breed_clock -= 1

class Predator(Animal):
    # ...
    def clock_tick(self):
```

```
''' Predator updates both breeding and starving
'''
self.breed_clock -= 1
self.starve_clock -= 1
if self.starve_clock <= 0:
    self.island.remove(self)
```

13.5 REFINEMENT: HOW MANY TIMES TO MOVE?

Remember our picture of the eight neighbors available for a local move? (Figure 13.2)

Our present event loop does the following:

- It moves through the `Island` instance a row a time, through each y value.
- If there is an animal instance in that row (the x value) and y value, it gives that animal an opportunity to:
  – Potentially eat, if it is a `Predator` instance.
  – Move if it can
  – Breed if it can
  – Do whatever must be done to the instance every clock tick

If our animal moves up or to the left, things seem to work fine. But what happens if our animal moves down or to the right? In those cases, either x is incremented (moving down) or y is incremented (moving right). Lets look at the "moving down" case. From wherever the instance starts, it moves to a new location with an x value one greater. The event loop processes x and y values by incrementing first all the y values in a row, then incrementing the x value to begin a new row. This ordering means that the instance we just moved will be given the opportunity to move again because it moved into the next row. If it moves down again, it will get yet another chance to move. Thus, a single instance may move multiple times during the same clock tick. A `Predator` instance could similarly eat multiple times, if—every time it eats—it eats going down or to the right.

The result may or may not be the behavior we wanted, but in truth it makes sense to have one move (eat) per clock tick per instance. Each instance should move (eat) at most one time-event clock tick. The problem is really one of isolating the global state, the grid of `Predator` and `Prey` instances, in time. Each clock tick should have its own global state, but in the implementation we present, we have a common global state across all ticks of the clock.

How can we repair this? There are a number of approaches we might take. We could:

- Have *two* grids, one for the present clock tick and one for the next. Moves would be from the location in the present grid to the future grid of the next clock tick, as would

eating. When the present clock tick ends the new grid becomes the present grid and a fresh empty grid, created for the next clock tick.
- Create a list of instances from the global state and move only instances from the list. Once moved, they are removed from the list and not moved again during this clock tick.
- Mark each instance with a flag, indicating movement. During the present clock tick, if an instance is moved, its flag is changed. All of the movement methods pay attention to the flag and will not move it again if the flag is set. All the movement flags must be cleared on every instance after the present clock tick.

Each approach has its advantages and disadvantages. The multiple-grid approach is more realistic, and more in tune with having multiple global states for different time periods. However, the changes to the present code to include multiple grids would be extensive. Moreover, instances that cannot move must still be copied into the new grid. The list approach is easy for movement, but complicated for eating. If a `Predator` instance eats a `Prey` instance, we have to search through the list to make sure it is also removed. Marking is conceptually simple and requires minimal code updates, but it is time consuming. We have to manipulate all the instances on every cycle to clear their move flags.

Ultimately, we chose the marking approach because it fit best with our existing design. To implement it, we need to make changes in the following locations:

- The `Animal __init__` method must add a new variable `moved` to every instance and initialize it to *`False`* (the instance has not been moved).
- The `move` and `eat` methods must be modified to check whether the instance has its moved flag set to *`True`*. If so, it should not be moved again. If the flag is not set, the instance can be moved and its `moved` flag should be set to *`True`* (so it cannot move again during this clock tick).
- The `Island` class gains a new method, `clear_all_moved_flags`. This method clears the `moved` flag of every instance on the island to *`False`*.
- The main loop must call the `clear_all_moved_flags` at the beginning of every clock tick.

VISUAL VIGNETTE

13.6 GRAPHING POPULATION SIZE

One of the original ideas of predator–prey simulations is to follow the change in population size during the course of the simulation. Watching the print outs of the `Island` instance does not convey that well. It would be useful to add graphing to observe the changes. Pylab to the rescue!

In this situation, it would be useful to plot both the `Predator` and `Prey` population counts during the course of the run. Pylab works best by collecting the y values of each clock tick. We do so for both `Predator` and `Prey` by creating two lists: `predator_list` and `prey_list`. These lists will contain the counts of each population at a particular clock tick: index 0 will have the value for clock tick 0, and so on.

We need methods to actually find the counts for both predator and prey on the Island. We add two methods: `count_predators` and `count_prey`. Each will count the number of each type of instance and return the value. At the end of every clock tick we query the island for the counts and append them to the appropriate list.

Once the counts are collected and the simulation ends, we plot each list individually and then display the results.

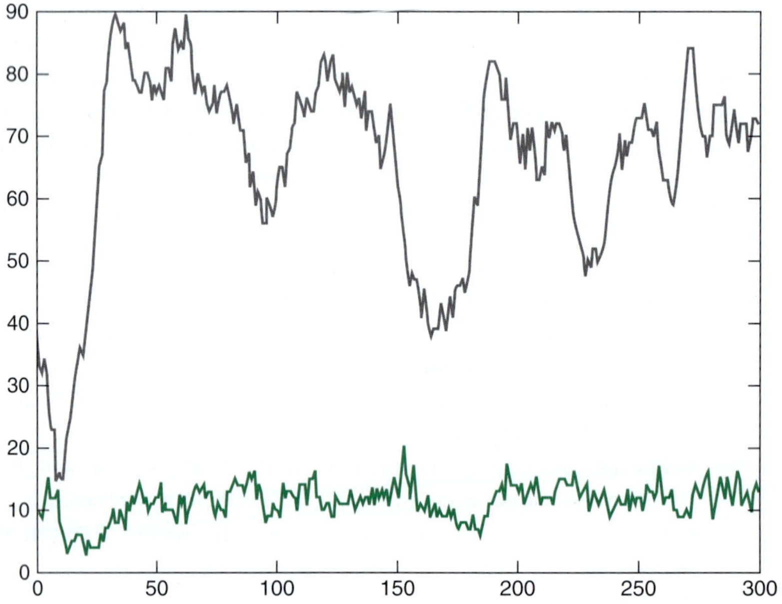

FIGURE 13.3 Graph of population sizes using our simulation

A typical graph is shown in Figure 13.3 for the following parameter settings (the defaults for the main function): `predator_breed_time=6`, `predator_starve_time=3`, `initial_predators=10`, `prey_breed_time=3`, `initial_prey=50`, `size=10`, `ticks=300`. The population swings are more pronounced for the `Prey` instances than the `Predator` instances, which is typical of the real situation. Note that when the `Predator` population rises (around tick 160), the `Prey` population falls dramatically. This results in `Predator` loss and `Prey` recovery, just as predicted!

The final code is available online.

Summary

In this chapter, we developed a predator–prey simulation simulator to illustrate the use of classes in problem solving.

Exercises

1. Add randomness to the direction chosen in `move`.
2. Have `Prey` move away from neighboring `Predators`.
3. Add the ability to look two "hops" away to see `Predators` or `Prey`, and move toward or away from them as appropriate.
4. Adjust survival rules so `Predators` starve quickly.
5. Adjust survival rules so `Prey` reproduce quickly.
6. `init_animals` can be inefficient, especially if the island is quite full. Improve it.
7. Test the code to determine situations in which multiple moves can occur.
8. Implement one of the `move` improvements:
   - Multiple grids
   - List
   - Marking

PART 5

Being a Better Programmer

CHAPTER 14

Files and Exceptions II

> The young man knows the rules, but the old man knows the exceptions.
>
> Oliver Wendell Holmes Jr., Supreme Court jurist

WE HAVE WORKED A NUMBER OF TIMES WITH BOTH FILES AND EXCEPTIONS IN THE course of our programming travels. However, there are many interesting details on both topics that we have not yet had time to explore. We will do so in this chapter.

14.1 MORE DETAILS ON FILES

Let's review what we know about files so far and then move on with new details.

- A file is a collection of bytes of information that usually resides permanently on a disk. Files fall into two broad categories: text files and binary files. For this text, we are working with text files.
- To access a file from Python you must open a connection between the Python shell and the file residing on a disk. The ***open*** command sets up that connection and returns the file object that represents the connection. All subsequent actions we perform on a file are done through this object.
- We can open a file to read or write content to a file. The second argument to ***open***, a string consisting of `'r'`, `'w'`, or `'a'` indicates the type of access. See Table 6.1.
- We also learned in Section 9.3.1 that files can have different Unicode encodings, translation of the bytes of the file into readable characters. We can alter the decoding of a file by providing a third named argument to the ***open*** function, the `encoding` argument. The default is `utf_8`.
- All access text files is via *strings*. We read and write strings to a file.
- To read a line from a file, we have been using iteration via a ***for*** loop over a file object as the collection. Each iteration through the loop yields one line of text.

- To write a string to a file, we have used the ***print*** function with the name argument `file`. The argument is an opened file object (with write access) that will be the target of printing. All output from the ***print*** is then written to the file object provided.

Code Listing 14.1 reviews what we know so far.

Code Listing 14.1

```
# Prompt for three values: input file, output file, search string.
# Search for the string in the input file, write results to the
# output file

import sys
def process_file(i_file, o_file, a_str):
    '''if the a_str is in a line of i_file, add stars
       to the a_str in line, write it out with the
       line number to o_file'''
    line_count_int = 1
    for line_str in i_file:
        if a_str in line_str:
            new_line_str = line_str.replace(a_str, '***'+a_str)
            print('Line {}: {}'.format(line_count_int, new_line_str),\
                  file=o_file)
        line_count_int += 1

try:
    in_file_str = input("File to search:")
    in_file = open(in_file_str, 'r', encoding='utf_8')
except IOError:
    print('{} is a bad file name'.format(in_file_str))
    sys.exit()

out_file_str = input("File to write results to:")
out_file = open(out_file_str, 'w')
search_str = input("Search for what string:")
process_file(in_file, out_file, search_str)
in_file.close()
out_file.close()
```

```
File to search:inFile.txt
File to write results to:outFile.txt
Search for what string:This
```

```
In  [1]: runfile('/Users/user/python/file.py', wdir='/Users/user/python')

File to search:fred.txt
fred.txt is a bad file name
Traceback (most recent call last):
  File "/Users/bill/tpocup/ch14/programs/program14-1.py", line 23, in <module>
    sys.exit()
SystemExit
```

For the first, successful run, here are the contents of inFile.txt and outFile.txt

inFile.txt	outFile.txt
This is a test	Line 1: ***This is a test
This is only a test	
Do not pass go	Line 2: ***This is only a test
Do not collect $200	

The following are some of the important features of the program.

Lines 6–16: Define a function `process_file`. It takes an input file, an output file, and a string. The function looks for the string in a line of the input file and, if found, writes a modified version of the line to an output file.

Line 13: Use the `replace` method to change each occurrence of `a_str` to have stars appended to the front.

Lines 14–15: Print the modified line, with the line number, to the file. Note the use of the `file` = parameter in ***`print`***.

Lines 18–20: Prompt for a file to open. Open in a ***`try`*** block to catch a bad file name. Note the use of `encoding=utf_8`.

Lines 21–23: The ***`except`*** clause catches a bad file name. Prints a message and calls `sys.exit()` (note ***`import`*** `sys` on **Line 5**). This function exits the program by raising the `SystemExit` exception. Compare with `os._exit()`, which stops the program *and* stops the iPython kernel that was running. You will get a message that you can restart the kernel, just select the console menu in the top right of the console (not of Spyder, the console) and select "Restart Kernel".

14.1.1 Other File Access Methods, Reading

So far, we have only used iteration to read a file. However, Python provides a number of methods to read the contents of a file:

- `readline`: read a single line.
- `readlines` (note the plural): read *all* the file lines, and store as a list of lines.

- read(size_in_bytes): read as many bytes as indicated in the argument into a single string. The default is *the entire* file.

Let's take a look at these methods using the file ''temp.txt'' with the following contents:

```
First Line
Second Line
Third Line
Fourth Line
```

The method readline reads a single line and returns that line as a string. It does essentially what one file iteration does, reads a single line. You can observe this functionality in the following session that has both a readline and a **for**. If you precede the loop with some number of readline calls, the **for** picks up where the readline left off in the file. Notice how the line stored in first_line_str contains a "carriage return" at the end of the string represented by the backslash-n character sequence (\n) which, of course, could be removed by the string strip method. It is because we did not strip the lines in the loop that the output looks double spaced (the carriage return from the read line, and the carriage return added by the **print** statement). Finally, what happens when you try to read a line when the file contents have been completely read? All the file methods will simply return an empty string (''). No error is reported, just an empty string returned. We will see more about how to manipulate a "read" file in Section 14.1.4.

```
In  [1]: temp_file = open("temp.txt","r") # open file for reading
In  [2]: first_line_str = temp_file.readline() # read exactly one line
In  [3]: first_line_str
Out [3]: 'First line\n'

In  [4]: for line_str in temp_file: # read remaining lines
...:     print(line_str)

Second line

Third line

Fourth line

In  [5]: temp_file.readline() # file read, return empty str
Out [5]: ''

In  [6]: temp_file.close()
```

The readlines method (again, note the plural) reads the *entire contents* of the file and stores each line as an element in a list. The list is what the method returns. The following session demonstrates readlines on the same input file previously noted.

```
In  [1]: temp_file = open("temp.txt","r") # open file for reading
In  [2]: file_contents_list = temp_file.readlines() # read all file lines into a list
In  [3]: file_contents_list
Out [3]: ['First line\n', 'Second line\n', 'Third line\n', 'Fourth line\n']
```

As simple as this looks, there is some danger in using `readlines`. If the file is very large, then the entire contents are read and placed in a list of lines, which will also be very large. Reading in gigabytes of file and storing the contents in this way can be very slow and inefficient.

Finally, there is the `read` method. This method takes a single integer argument which is the number of bytes to be read from the file (where 1 byte is typically 1 character, at least given the use of a utf_8 file encoding). However, if no such size argument is provided, the default is to read the *entire contents* of the file. However much of the file is read, the return value is a single string. Again, once the contents have been read, any more use of the method results in an empty string. The following session demonstrates this method.

```
In  [1]: temp_file = open("temp.txt","r") # open file for reading
In  [2]: temp_file.read(1) # read 1 char
Out [2]: 'F'

In  [3]: temp_file.read(2) # read the next 2 chars
Out [3]: 'ir'

In  [4]: temp_file.read() # read remaining file
Out [4]: 'st line\nSecond line\nThird line\nFourth line\n'

In  [5]: temp_file.read(1) # file read, return empty string
Out [5]: ''

In  [6]: temp_file.close()
```

14.1.2 Other File Access Methods, Writing

So far, we have seen how to write to a file using the ***print*** function with a `file=` parameter. However, like reading, there are a number of methods available for writing to files:

- `write`, write a string to a file. It returns the number of bytes (characters) written to the file.
- `writelines`, write a sequence (e.g. a list of lines) to a file

The simplest method to write a string to the file is the `write` method. This method writes *only* strings to the file (so conversion from other types is necessary). If you want multiple lines output to the file, you must insert the carriage-return character sequence (`\n`) between the lines yourself. A common approach in Python is to assemble a string from various pieces and then write the final string to a file. Not surprisingly, it can be difficult to keep track of very long strings, so there is good reason to have multiple writes, often writing a single line on each iteration of the algorithm. Every `write` appends to the end of the file's present contents, making the file longer with each `write`. Let's look at a sample.

```
In  [1]: word_list = ['First', 'Second', 'Third', 'Fourth']
In  [2]: out_file = open('outFile.txt', 'w')
In  [3]: for word in word_list:
...        out_file.write(word + ' line\n')
...
In  [4]: out_file.close()
```

This session recreates the original input file `''temp.txt''` we used in the file reading section previously. Note that we must append the (`\n`) at the end of each line before we write it, to get multiple lines in the output file.

The `writelines` method is the counterpart of the `readlines` method. Remember that `readlines` read the contents of the file, returning a list of lines. The `writelines` takes a list of lines as an argument and writes that list to the file. Again, if you want multiple lines output to the file, you must insert the carriage-return character sequence (`\n`) between the lines yourself. See the following session.

```
In  [1]: out_file = open('out.txt', 'w')
In  [2]: line_list = ['First\n', 'Second\n', 'Third\n', 'Fourth\n']
In  [3]: out_file.writelines(line_list)
In  [4]: out_file.close()
```

Note that each of the lines in the list ends with a (`\n`), which creates a new line in the written file.

PROGRAMMING TIP

It is common to write other types than strings to files (or to expect values from a file other than strings). All interaction with text files is done only with strings. Any other type must be converted to a string before it can be written to a text file. If not, you will get a `TypeError`, indicating that the value you are trying to write needs to be converted to a string.

14.1.3 Universal New Line Format

It is an interesting fact that different operating systems (OS X, Windows, Linux) have different characteristics with regard to files. In particular, depending on the operating system, there is a particular character, or set of characters, that represent the newline character: the character placed at the end of a string to indicate that the next character goes on the following line of text. There have been a number of ways to indicate a new line through the history of computer operating systems, but two characters are used most commonly: `'\n'` and `'\r'`. Though not strictly true, they are usually referred to as the "newline" character and the carriage-return character, respectively. Commonly used combinations are shown in Table 14.1.

Operating System	Character Combination
Unix & Mac OS X	`'\n'`
MS Windows	`'\r\n'`
Mac (pre-OS X)	`'\r'`

TABLE 14.1 End-of-line characters.

What an inconvenience! To avoid having to worry about this issue, Python provides what is called the Universal New Line format. This process translates the operating specific values to "\n" on read and from "\n" to the operating specific values on write. By default, this translation is turned on. However, the *open* function provides a named argument `newline=` which specifies what get's translated.

The main point is that Python is smart about doing the translation. *By default*, if you do not provide a `newline=` in the open statement, Python will do the right thing. Very nice!

For completeness, here is what you *could* do. This is reprinted (mostly) from the Python documentation.

- On input, if `newline=None` or is not provided, universal newlines mode is enabled. Lines in the input can end in `'\n'`, `'\r'`, or `'\r\n'`, and these are translated into `'\n'` before being returned. If `newline=''`, universal newline mode is enabled, but line endings are returned to the caller untranslated. If `newline` is set to any of the other legal values, input lines are only terminated by the given string, and the line ending is returned untranslated.
- On output, if `newline=None` or is not provided, any `'\n'` characters are translated to the system default line separator. This is indicated in the special value of the `os` module, `os.linesep`. If `newline=''`, no translation takes place. If `newline` is any of the other legal values, any `'\n'` characters are translated to the given string.

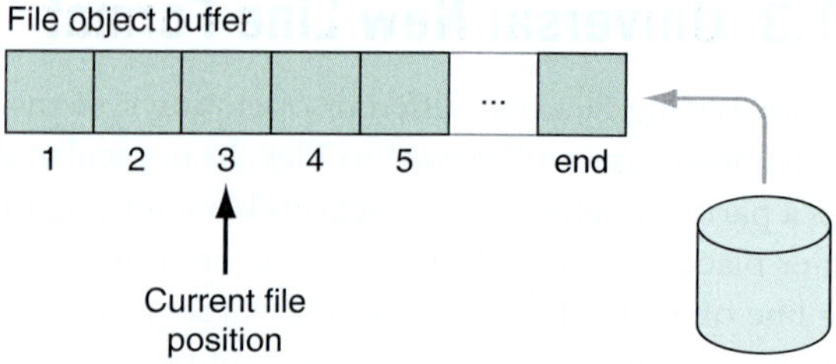

FIGURE 14.1 Current file position.

14.1.4 Moving Around in a File

Table 6.1 indicates where reads and writes will begin in a file by default. However, Python provides a way to control *where* we are in a file when we read or write, and to change the position of where a read or write occurs.

Remember how the file object gains access to the contents of a disk file: the *open* function creates a buffer—a location in memory—where the disk contents are copied. Once the contents are read into the file object buffer, the file object treats the buffer as a very large list in which each element of the list has an index. A file object counts each byte (roughly each character) as an index into the file object buffer. Furthermore, the file object maintains a *current file position*, which is the present index where reads or writes are to occur. See Figure 14.1.

Many of the file methods implicitly use the current file position. For example, after a `readline` occurs, the current file position moves to the position after the next carriage return. The `write` method writes at the current file position.

Python provides methods to work with the current file position. The first is the `tell` method. The `tell` method reports the position of the current file position relative to the beginning of the file in bytes. The second is the `seek(n)` method. This methods shifts the current file position to a new position `n` bytes into the file object buffer.

A common usage is `seek(0)` to go to the beginning of the file. An idiomatic expression `seek(0,2)` will take you to the end of the file. Other seek options are available for binary files.

To illustrate these concepts let's experiment with the same `''temp.txt''` file used earlier.

```
In  [1]: test_file = open('temp.txt','r')
In  [2]: test_file.tell() # where is the current file position?
Out [2]: 0

In  [3]: test_file.readline() # read first line
Out [3]: 'First Line\n'
```

```
In  [4]: test_file.tell() # where are we now?
Out [4]: 11

In  [5]: test_file.seek(0) # got to beginning
Out [5]: 0

In  [6]: test_file.readline() # read first line again
Out [6]: 'First Line\n'

In  [7]: test_file.readline() # read second line
Out [7]: 'Second Line\n'

In  [8]: test_file.tell() # where are we now?
Out [8]: 23

In  [9]: test_file.seek(0,2) # go to end
Out [9]: 46

In  [10]: test_file.tell() # where are we now?
Out [10]: 46

In  [11]: test_file.readline() # try readline at end of file: nothing there
Out [11]: ''

In  [12]: test_file.seek(11) # go to the end of the first line (see tell above)
Out [12]: 11

In  [13]: test_file.readline() # when we read now we get the second line
Out [13]: 'Second Line\n'

In  [14]: test_file.close()
In  [14]: test_file.readline() # Error: reading after file is closed
Traceback (most recent call last):
  File "<pyshell#65>", line 1, in <module>
    test_file.readline()
ValueError: I/O operation on closed file.
```

There are a few things to note about this session:

- `arthur_file.tell()` reports the position in bytes.
- When you try to read information from a file and the current file position is at the end of the file, the read returns an empty string.
- Trying to read a file after closing it generates an error.

The most common operation is probably to seek to the beginning of the file. Remember `a_file.seek(0)`!

14.1.5 Closing a File

Closing a file is the process of tearing down the connection between the program and a file, separating the stream from the file. In particular, everything in the buffer that is in memory is written back to the disk so that the contents of the buffer and the contents of the file are in sync. Closing a file ensures that the synchronization between the file and the buffer is done properly and no information is lost.

PROGRAMMING TIP

Not closing a file, especially a file that is being written, risks losing the contents of the file. Because the program writes data to the file object in memory (not directly to the file on disk), the operating system will occasionally *synchronize* the contents of the file object and disk file contents, to make sure that everything that was written to the file object gets written to the disk file. Closing the file ensures this synchronization. Although Python is very good about closing files if you forget, it is always best to close your files when you are done with it.

14.1.6 The *with* Statement

The process of opening and closing a file is a common enough event that Python provides a shortcut, the `with` statement. This statement makes it a little easier to open and file and ensures that a file, once opened, gets closed automatically without requiring the programmer to provide the actual `close` statement.

The general form of a `with` statement is:

```
with expression as variable:
    # with suite
```

and a typical example of its usage is shown in the following session, using the same file `temp.txt` as previously.

```
In  [1]: with open('temp.txt') as temp_file:
Out [1]: ...      temp_file.readlines()

...
['First line\n', 'Second line\n', 'Third line\n', 'Fourth line\n']
```

The `with` expression performs its action and the returned value is associated with the variable of the statement. That variable can then be used in the following suite. The advantage of the `with` statement is that, if an error occurs in the suite, Python will automatically close the opened file before the suite is exited.

We will examine more of how this might work in Section 14.5.1 on exceptions.

14.1.7 Text File Encodings; Unicode

We saw a discussion concerning the encoding of files in different Unicode encodings, which Python references as a **codec**. A codec, as it applies to text files, is the Unicode code point used to encode the characters in the file. As we saw in Section 9.3.1, how a file gets generated might affect the encoding of the Unicode characters used in the file. If we do not specify the file's encoding, then by default some of the characters cannot be interpreted and you get an error, something like "UnicodeDecodeError: `'utf8'` codec can't decode byte 0xb1."

The solution is to open the file using the associated text encoding, indicating the proper interpretation of the bytes of the file as we saw in Section 9.3.1:

```
periodic_file = open("Periodic-Table.csv", "r",encoding="windows-1252")
```

These encodings, in this case `windows-1252` can be thought of as a dictionary (sometimes called a map or mapping), indicating how the bytes "map" to the particular character they represent.

There are a lot of these text encodings available for Python, representing the many languages and characters available in the myriad languages of the world. The Python documentation lists them at `https://docs.python.org/3.4/library/codecs.html#standard-encodings`, but we mention some of the more common ones here:

ascii: The classic ASCII character set

utf-8: The ASCII set in Unicode

utf-16: A two byte encoding that covers a large set of characters from the Latin and Greek character set. A good listing of the characters can be found at `http://www.fileformat.info/info/charset/UTF-16/list.htm`

latin_1: Also known as iso-8859-1. This is identical for ASCII from 0 to 128, with different characters from 129 to 255. Used by MSDOS.

windows-1252: Also known as cp1252, used by Microsoft Windows. See `https://msdn.microsoft.com/en-us/goglobal/cc305145.aspx`

Check Yourself: Basic File Operations

1. Given the file "input.txt" whose contents are:

```
First Line
Second Line
Third Line
```

Answer the questions regarding the following program:

```
with open('input.txt') as my_file:
    print(my_file.readline(),end='')
    print('--something--')
    for r in my_file:
        print(r,end='')
```

What is the output?

(a)
```
First Line
--something--
First Line
Second Line
Third Line
```
(b)
```
--something--
First Line
Second Line
Third Line
```
(c)
```
First Line
--something--
Second Line
Third Line
```
(d) None of the above.

14.2 CSV FILES

We have shown the use of CSV (comma-separated value) files in a couple of examples. Here we will discuss those files in a little more detail.

A CSV is not a different kind of file, but rather a different kind of file *format*. A CSV is actually a text file and can be used in conjunction with the functions and methods we have discussed. However, the arrangement of data in the file is special, and we can take advantage of that.

Name	Exam1	Exam2	Final Exam	Overall Grade
Bill	75.00	100.00	50.00	**75.00**
Fred	50.00	50.00	50.00	**50.00**
Irving	0.00	0.00	0.00	**0.00**
Monty	100.00	100.00	100.00	**100.00**
Average				**56.25**

FIGURE 14.2 A simple spreadsheet from Microsoft Excel 2016. [Excel 2016, Windows 10, Microsoft Corporation.]

The problem with this file format, as we have mentioned previously, is that the standards for reading and writing do not really exist, especially given the age of the format. Nonetheless, it is a very useful way to exchange data between applications and therefore an important format for us to understand.

14.2.1 CSV Module

As we have mentioned many times, one of the great advantages of Python is the community that supports its use. When common problems arise, the Python community provides powerful, free solutions. Such is the case with CSV files. In the case of CSV files, different venders have annoying variations in how they generate the CSV format. To help alleviate the difficulties of dealing with multiple variations in CSV files, Python provides the `csv` module. The `csv` module provides an easy way to read and write CSV files.

To work with CSV-formatted files, we need some new objects: a `csv.reader` object to read the file and a `csv.writer` object to write a CSV file. We will use the following example to show reading and writing to such a file. We created a simple spreadsheet using Microsoft Excel 2016, shown in Figure 14.2. The values in bold are calculated values using simple Excel formulas to average the four rows for a grade, then average grades for an overall grade average. The corresponding CSV file is also shown here:

```
Name,Exam1,Exam2,Final Exam,Overall Grade
Bill,75.00,100.00,50.00,75.00
Fred,50.00,50.00,50.00,50.00
Irving,0.00,0.00,0.00,0.00
Monty,100.00,100.00,100.00,100.00

Average,,,,56.25
```

First, it is important to note that some information from the original Excel file is lost. The CSV format preserves only values. For example, the four grades and the grade average are no longer formulas. Changes to one of the row values will *not* update the corresponding averages. Second, series of commas in the last line of the CSV file indicate empty values for that field.

14.2.2 CSV Reader

To create a `csv.reader` object, we use the constructor method `reader`. Interestingly, the `reader` method takes as an argument a file object, meaning that you must have already opened a file for reading and created a file object. The `reader` constructor returns a reader object that can be used to iterate through a CSV file, much like a file object can be used to iterate through the contents of a text file.

The difference, however, is that the `csv.reader` returns a single *row* of the file for each iteration (not necessarily a line). Further, the returned value from the iteration is not a string but a *list of strings*, where each element of the list represents one of the fields of the row. The code and its results are shown here in Code Listing 14.2.

Code Listing 14.2

```
import csv
workbook_file = open('Workbook1.csv','r')
workbook_reader = csv.reader(workbook_file)

for row in workbook_reader:
    print(row)

workbook_file.close()
```

```
['Name', 'Exam1', 'Exam2', 'Final Exam', 'Overall Grade']
['Bill', '75.00', '100.00', '50.00', '75.00']
['Fred', '50.00', '50.00', '50.00', '50.00']
['Irving', '0.00', '0.00', '0.00', '0.00']
['Monty', '100.00', '100.00', '100.00', '100.00']
[]
['Average', '', '', '', '56.25']
```

A few things to note:

- By default, files open in Universal New Line mode. That is good. It is important here: for this particular Excel spreadsheet, it was required—otherwise, an error is generated. The error is even very helpful, suggesting you use that mode.[1] Isn't Python nice?

[1] _csv.Error: new-line character seen in unquoted field–do you need to open the file in universal-newline mode?

- The blank line of the CSV file between the "Monty" row and the "Average" row does appear in the output as an empty list. Every row, even blank rows, are returned by the `reader` object.
- If a field in a row is not filled in, the row is still marked with an empty string, as shown in the last row.

14.2.3 CSV Writer

Like the `reader`, we create a `csv.writer` object using the `writer` constructor. As with the reader, the required argument is a file object, but in this case that file must have been opened for writing.

The `csv.writer` object has a method `writerow` that will write a row of data to the file.

14.2.4 Example: Update Some Grades

As an example, let us update Irving's final grade to 100.00. In so doing, we have a lot of work that must be done, as all the formulas for updating the spreadsheet are missing. We must update Irving's average as well as the grade average. Code Listing 14.3 follows.

Code Listing 14.3

```
import csv
workbook_file = open('Workbook1.csv','r')
workbook_reader = csv.reader(workbook_file)

sheet_list = []
for row in workbook_reader:
    sheet_list.append(row)
workbook_file.close()

sheet_list[3][3] = '100.00'   # give Irving a break, 100 on the final

# update Irving's average
sum_float = 0.0
for field_str in sheet_list[3][1:-1]:   # fields 1, 2 and 3: the grades
    sum_float += float(field_str)
avg_float = sum_float/3
# we have to write a string, convert to two decimal places using str formatting
```

```
18 sheet_list[3][4] = '{:.2f}'.format(avg_float)
19
20 # list comp shortcut for update Irving's average
21 # sheet_list[3][4]='{:.2f}'.format(sum([float(field_str)\
22 #                              for field_str in sheet_list[3][1:-1]])/3)
23
24 # update the overall grade average
25 sum_float = 0.0
26 for row in sheet_list[1:-2]:          # rows 1,2,3,4: the student rows
27     sum_float += float(row[-1])       # the average of that row
28 grade_average_float = sum_float/4
29 # we have to write a string, convert to two decimal places using str
   formatting
30 sheet_list[-1][-1] = '{:.2f}'.format(grade_average_float)
31
32 # list comp shortcut for update overall average
33 # sheet_list[-1][-1] = '{:.2f}'.format(sum([float(row[-1])\
34 #                                   for row in sheet_list[1:-2]])/4)
35
36 newbook_file = open('NewWorkbook1.csv','w')
37 newbook_writer = csv.writer(newbook_file)
38 for row in sheet_list:
39     newbook_writer.writerow(row)
40 newbook_file.close()
```

There is a lot of slicing going on here, which is a good exercise for us. Let's take a look.

Lines 2–5: We do the normal opening and reading of the CSV file. However, we create a variable `sheet_list` as an empty list to collect all the rows.

Lines 6–8: Iterate through the rows and append them to the `sheet_list`. At the end, `sheet_list` contains a list of lists (the inner lists are the rows).

Line 10: Give Irving a break; update his final exam grade to 100.00 as a string. Remember, CSV files are text files!

Lines 12–18: This code updates Irving's average based on the new grade. Check to make sure you understand the slicing there! Look at the CSV file contents in the example. The comments give some hints (as they should). Line 18 is interesting. We need to write a string for the final average (a floating-point number). We want to write it with only two decimal places, so we use string formatting to do the work.

Lines 20–22: These lines are a list comprehension that do all the work of Lines 12–18. Is it readable? Readability depends on the reader, but this code is more dense and therefore more likely to have a mistake.

Name	Exam1	Exam2	Final Exam	Overall Grade
Bill	75	100	50	**75**
Fred	50	50	50	**50**
Irving	0	0	100	**33.33**
Monty	100	100	100	**100**
Average				**64.58**

FIGURE 14.3 The updated Excel spreadsheet created from the new CSV file. [Excel 2016, Windows 10, Microsoft Corporation.]

Lines 25–30: Now we must update the overall average based on the new averages. Again, lots of slicing going on—make sure you can follow it.

Lines 32–34: As we did earlier, these lines are a list comprehension that does all the work of Lines 25–30.

Lines 36–40: Having updated `sheet_list`, we now write it out to a new file using the `writerow` method, one row a a time.

The updated CSV file is shown here. The Excel spreadsheet created from reading in that file is shown in Figure 14.3.

```
Name,Exam1,Exam2,Final Exam,Overall Grade
Bill,75.00,100.00,50.00,75.00
Fred,50.00,50.00,50.00,50.00
Irving,0.00,0.00,100.00,33.33
Monty,100.00,100.00,100.00,100.00

Average,,,,64.58
```

Some of the formatting is lost in the spreadsheet, but the values are correct. Again, no formulas are preserved.

14.3 MODULE: *OS*

Let's take a look at the `os` module ("os" is an abbreviation for "operating system"). It is a module included with the Python distribution—like the `math` module. The `os` module has many capabilities, but we will look at the file-related ones here. You can find the full list of functions in the documentation that comes with Python, or you can simply search online for "Python os module." To appreciate some of the capabilities we have at hand, let's begin with a look at how files are organized on your disk.

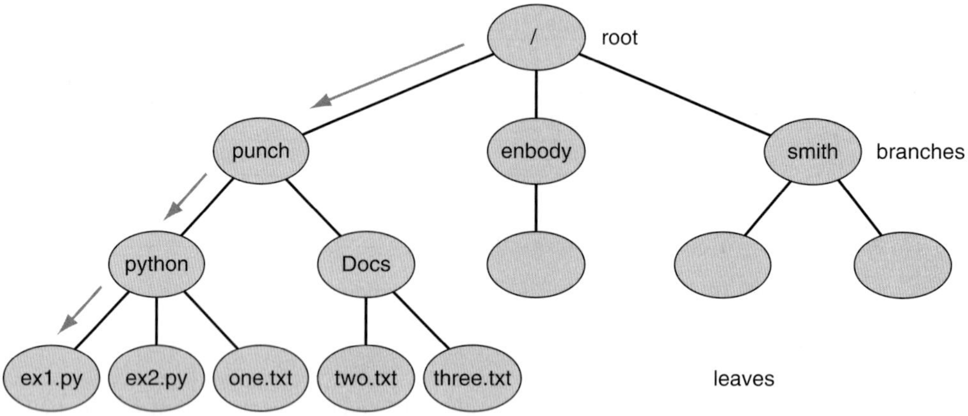

FIGURE 14.4 Directory tree with path /punch/python/ex1.py highlighted.

14.3.1 Directory (Folder) Structure

Part of the role of an operating system is to keep files organized. The currently popular operating systems such as Microsoft Windows, Linux, and Apple's OS X maintain files in a *directory structure*. This assumes the existence of a special container called a *directory* in Linux and OS-X, or a *folder* in Windows.[2] Each directory can hold three things:

- A list of files that are in the directory.
- A list of other directories, also contained in the directory.
- A link to the directory's parent in the directory structure.

Directories are organized by the last two items: directories they contain and the parent directory they are connected to. The organization is typically referred to as a *hierarchy*, or often by computer scientists as a *tree*. The tree contains the relationship of each directory to its "parent" and "children." The "children" of a directory are those directories that it contains. The parent of a directory is the directory that contains it. We can draw the *tree structure* of the directories as shown in Figure 14.4. However, it is an odd tree. It has a root, branches, and leaves, but it is upside down: the root is at the top and the leaves are at the bottom. Each inner circle in the tree is a directory (more generally a *node*) and each line connecting nodes is the relationship between directories (more generally called an *edge*). The root is a special directory, alone at the top, whereas leaves are special nodes at the bottom: nodes with no children (files).

The operating system finds files by beginning at the root, represented by "/" (spoken as "slash"). The operating system moves down the tree structure by following edges and directories until it finds the desired file (contained in a directory) or a directory itself. The

[2] We'll continue to just use the word "directory" from now on, but be aware that in Windows it would be called a "folder."

path taken through the tree structure is called just that: a *path*. The path represents an ordered list of directories traversed to get to the desired directory. For example, in Figure 14.4 the file "ex1.py" is found in the directory "python", which is a child of the directory "punch", which is a child of the directory "/". The full path is indicated by separating each directory with a "/", thus "/punch/python/ex1.py" is the *fully qualified name* of the file. That path is highlighted with arrows in Figure 14.4. Every leaf node (usually a file) can be represented by a fully qualified name, indicating a path from the root. Of importance to us is that a path can be represented as a string in Python: `"/punch/python/ex1.py"`.

Paths are represented slightly differently by different operating systems. The path shown in the example is the Unix style used in Linux and OS X (underneath OS X is a flavor of Unix). Microsoft Windows uses backslashes (\) instead of forward slashes and starts its paths with the device name, for example, C:\punch\python\ex1.py. Fortunately, Python understands which operating system it is working on, so it automatically converts whichever style you use to the appropriate one.

There are two special directory (folder) names: "." (spoken as "dot") and ".." (spoken as "dot-dot"). The single dot represents the directory you are currently working in. For example, if you are working in punch's python directory, the "." is synonymous with the path "/punch/python/" so whenever you use ".", the operating system will fill in the current path "/punch/python". The double-dot is synonymous with the parent directory (folder), that is, the node "above" where you are currently working. For example, if your current directory (folder) is "/punch/python" then ".." is "/punch/".

PROGRAMMING TIP

In Python, if you type a file name without a full path, the assumption is that the file is in the directory where the program currently running resides. Thus, if you run your program from a directory, you can open any file in that directory without fully qualifying the path. Otherwise, Python requires that the full path be provided.

14.3.2 *os* Module Functions

Let's look at a few sessions illustrating a small subset of the many functions available in the `os` module. The directory tree we use in this example is shown in Figure 14.4.

The first session illustrates functions that allows one to move about the directory tree and list the contents of any directory:

- `os.getcwd`: Here *getcwd* stands for "get cwd" and "cwd" stands for "current working directory"—the directory or folder that you are currently working in. The cwd is returned as a string. By default, the current working directory is set to the directory from where the program started (see the previous programming tip).

- `os.chdir`: Here the *chdir* stands for "change directory," so it changes the current working directory to the path that was used as an argument (side effect). All paths are strings in Python, where the directories are separated by "/" as mentioned earlier.
- `os.listdir`: Here *listdir* stands for "list directory" that lists the files and directories in the node specified by the path argument. A list of strings is returned.

```
In  [1]: import os # load the os package
In  [2]: os.chdir("/punch/python") # change to the example starting point
In  [2]: os.getcwd() # check that we are there
Out [2]: '/punch/python'

In  [3]: os.listdir(".") # list contents of current directory , indicated by "."
Out [3]: ['ex1.py', 'ex2.py', 'one.txt']

In  [4]: dir_list = os.listdir(".") # we can give that list a name
In  [5]: dir_list
Out [5]: ['ex1.py', 'ex2.py', 'one.txt']

In  [6]: os.listdir("/punch") # list the contents at some path
Out [6]: ['Docs', 'python']
```

The second session illustrates functions that manipulate path and file names. Notice how this group begins with `os.path`, indicating the "path" subset of the `os` module. The first return Booleans (`True` or `False`) to indicate whether the path "is a file" (`isfile`), "is a directory" (`isdir`), or generically if such an item exists (`exists`). The final functions manipulate path names (strings). They can extract a file name from a path (`basename`) or extract the directory part of the path from the whole path (`dirname`). Some can create a list by splitting off the file name from a path (`split`) or splitting off only the file extension from a path (`splitext`). Finally, there is a `join` function to combine partial paths into a complete path—note how it inserts a slash (`/`) character as needed.

```
In  [1]: import os # load the os package
In  [2]: os.path.isfile("/punch/python/ex1.py") # check if a file exists
Out [2]: True

In  [3]: os.path.isfile("/punch/python/ex3.py")
Out [3]: False

In  [4]: os.path.isdir("/punch/python") # check if a directory exists
Out [4]: True

In  [5]: os.path.exists("/punch/python") # check if file or directory exists
Out [5]: True

In  [6]: os.path.basename("/punch/python/ex1.py")# split a file name off a path
Out [6]: 'ex1.py'
```

```
In  [7]: os.path.dirname("/punch/python/ex1.py") # split the directory from a path
Out [7]: '/punch/python'

In  [8]: os.path.split("/punch/python/ex1.py") # split path to [directory, file]
Out [8]: ('/punch/python', 'ex1.py')

In  [9]: os.path.splitext("/punch/python/ex1.py")# split off extension (after ".")
Out [9]: ('/punch/python/ex1', '.py')

In  [10]: os.path.join("/punch/python", "ex1.py") # join a path to a file name
Out [10]: '/punch/python/ex1.py'

In  [11]: path_str = os.getcwd() # name a path
In  [12]: path_str
Out [12]: '/punch/python'

# join directory in path_str to new filename
In  [13]: os.path.join(os.path.split(path_str)[0], "dummy.py")
Out [13]: '/punch/dummy.py'

In  [14]: os.path.join("/punch/python/", "ex1.py")
Out [14]: '/punch/python/ex1.py'
```

The final session illustrates the `os.walk(path_str)` function. This is a particularly useful function for moving through the contents of a directory tree. It takes a `path_str` argument (a valid path string) and yields three values: the name of the current directory, a list of subdirectories in the directory, and a list of files in the directory, for *every directory* on the tree under the directory argument provided. If you put `os.walk` in a ***for*** loop, it will visit every node in the directory tree under the `path_str` directory. In the following session, we walk through the directory tree of Figure 14.4, starting in `/punch`.

```
In  [1]: os.getcwd() # check our starting point
Out [1]: '/punch'

In  [2]: for dir_name, dirs, files in os.walk("."): # "walk" in the current
                                                        directory
...:      print(dir_name, dirs, files)

. ['Docs', 'python'] [] # current directory, list of 2 subdirectories, no files
./Docs [] ['three.txt', 'two.txt']    # Does directory, no subdirectories, 3 files
./python [] ['ex1.py', 'ex2.py', 'one.txt'] # directory, no subdirectories, 3 files
```

14.3.3 *os* Module Example

Here is an example that shows something you can do with the `os` module functions. The task is to write a Python program that searches a directory tree for any text file that contains a particular string. We'll walk down the directory tree, starting in the current working directory.

In addition, we will make a list of text files that contain the string and a list of directories those files are in.

The basic idea is this. In each directory, we look at each file in the directory to see if it is a text file (extension ".txt"). If it is a text file, we open it, read it in, and then check to see if our search string is in the file. If so, we add the file to our list of files and add the directory to the list of directories. Once we finish with the files in the directory, we output what we found.

We begin with a function that does most of the work:

I. Walk the directory tree, starting at the current directory.
  1. For each `file` in the directory:
     (a) If `file` is a text file:
        i. Add to the count of text files examined.
        ii. Open the file and read its contents into a string.
        iii. If `search_str` is in the `file` string:
           A. Create path for file.
           B. Add file to list of files containing `search_str`.
           C. Add directory to list of directories.

The program prompts for a search string, initializes the count and lists, and then calls the function. After the function call, the information is output.

When looking at Figure 14.4, assume that files "one.text" and "two.txt" contain the string "red." Code Listing 14.4 is the program and the output.

Code Listing 14.4

```
#  search for a string:
#  starting from the current directory, walk a directory tree
#  look in all text files (extension ".txt") for the string

import os

# walk the directory subtree starting at the current directory
# search for search_str, count files examined,
# keep lists of files found and directories
def check(search_str,count,files_found_list,dirs_found_list):
    for dirname,dir_list,file_list in os.walk("."):   # walk the subtree
        for f in file_list:
            if os.path.splitext(f)[1] == ".txt":  # if it is a text file
                count = count + 1               # add to count of files examined
                a_file = open(os.path.join(dirname,f),'r')  # open text file
                file_str = a_file.read()        # read whole file into string
                if search_str in file_str:      # is search_str in file?
                    filename = os.path.join(dirname,f) # if so, create path
                                                          for file
```

```
                files_found_list.append(filename)  # and add to file list
                if dirname not in dirs_found_list:  # if directory is not
                    dirs_found_list.append(dirname) # and directory list
            a_file.close()
    return count

search_str = input('What string to look for: ')
file_list = []     # list of files containing string
dir_list = []      # list of directories of files containing string
count = 0          # count of text files examined

# call our function that examines directory tree for string
count = check(search_str,count,file_list,dir_list)

print('Looked at {} text files'.format(count))
print('Found {} directories containing ".txt" files and target string:{}'.\
    format(len(dir_list),search_str))
print('Found {} files ".txt" files containing the target string: {}'.\
    format(len(file_list),search_str))
print('\n*****Directory List*****')
for a_dir in dir_list:
    print(a_dir)

print('\n-----File List-----')
for a_file in file_list:
    print(a_file)
```

```
What string to look for: red
Looked at 3 text files
Found 2 directories containing files with ".txt" suffix and target string:red
Found 2 files with ".txt" suffix containing the target string: red
*****Directory List*****
./Docs
./python

-----File List-----
./Docs/two.txt
./python/one.txt
```

14.4 MORE ON EXCEPTIONS

In Chapter 6 we first touched on the basic use of Python exceptions. In particular, we introduced the idea of an exception in the context of **RULE 7**, all input is evil until proven otherwise. We need to write our code to deal with issues that might arise that are unforeseen, especially when dealing with user input. Let's review what we have already seen.

14.4.1 Basic Exception Handling

The basic syntax of Python exception handling is called a ***try-except*** suite:

```
try:
    # code to watch here
except ParticularErrorName:
    # some code to handle the named error, if it occurs
```

There are two parts to the handling of exceptions:

try suite: the suite of code after ***try***. It contains the code we want to "watch" to see whether any exception occurs. If an exception occurs anywhere in the ***try*** suite, Python will halt execution of the suite at the error line and look for some exception code to handle the particular error that occurred. If no handler is found, Python will halt the entire program and print the exception.

exception suite: the suite of code associated with an exception—almost always a particular exception as indicated by Python's standard error names, for example, `ValueError` and `KeyError`. There may be multiple exception suites, with each one written to handle a particular kind of error that might have happened in the ***try*** suite.

If no error occurs, the ***try*** suite finishes normally; all exception suites are ignored (not executed) and control passes to whatever code follows the ***try-except*** group. The flow is illustrated in Figure 14.5.

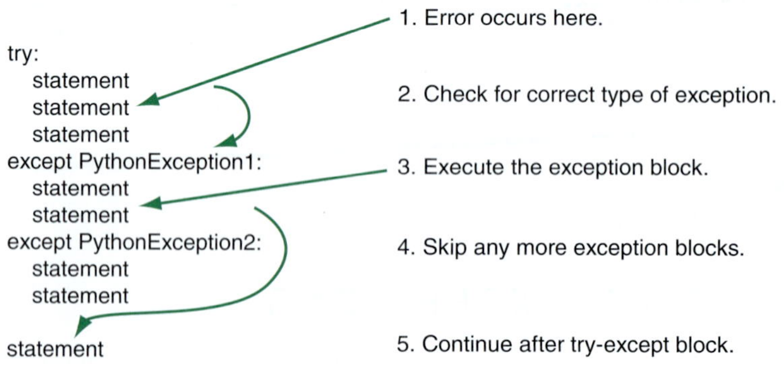

FIGURE 14.5 Exception flow.

14.4.2 A Simple Example

VideoNote 14.1
Dictionary Exceptions

Let's take a look at an example that shows the flow of control. Code Listing 14.5 prompts for two-floating point numbers where the first (the dividend) is to be divided by the second (the divisor). Two errors are possible here. The first occurs if the provided input cannot be converted to a floating-point number: a `ValueError`. The second occurs if the divisor value is a 0, Python raises a `ZeroDivisionError` exception. The ***print*** statements at the beginning and the end of the ***try*** suite help indicate what parts of the ***try*** suite are executed. The code also provides two `except` suites—one for each of those specific errors. In this simple example, the handling code simply prints that the error occurs. The code ends with a ***print*** statement, something to illustrate what gets executed **after** the ***try-except*** group is finished.

Code Listing 14.5

```
try:
    print("Entering the try suite")
    dividend = float(input("Provide a dividend to divide:"))
    divisor = float(input("Provide a divisor to divide by:"))
    result = dividend/divisor
    print("{:2.2f} divided by {:2.2f} yields {:2.2f}".\
        format(dividend,divisor,result))
except ZeroDivisionError:
    print("Divide by 0 error")
except ValueError:
    print("Value error, could not convert to a float")

print("Continuing on with the rest of the program")
```

```
Entering the try suite
Provide a dividend to divide:10
Provide a divisor to divide by:2
10.00 divided by 2.00 yields 5.00
Continuing on with the rest of the program


In  [1]: runfile('/Users/user/python/file.py', wdir='/Users/user/python')

Entering the try suite
Provide a dividend to divide:10
Provide a divisor to divide by:a
Value error, could not convert to a float
Continuing on with the rest of the program
```

```
In [2]: runfile('/Users/user/python/file.py', wdir='/Users/user/python')

Entering the try suite
Provide a dividend to divide:10
Provide a divisor to divide by:0
Divide by 0 error
Continuing on with the rest of the program

In [3]: runfile('/Users/user/python/file.py', wdir='/Users/user/python')

Entering the try suite
Provide a dividend to divide:

Traceback (most recent call last):
  File "/Users/bill/book/v3.5/chapterExceptions/divide.py", line 3, in <module>
    dividend = float(input("Provide a dividend to divide:"))
KeyboardInterrupt
```

Four examples of input are provided for Code Listing 14.5, shown in the previous session. It is useful to go through the four examples and follow the control of the program:

No Error: The input values are 10 and 2. This session has no errors. The entire ***try*** suite is executed (Lines 2–6), the two exception suites are skipped, and the code finishes by executing Line 13.

Value Error: The input values are 10 and `'a'`. In this case the conversion of the second value to a float will generate an exception. The flow of control gets through lines 1–4. Line 4 ends in an exception, meaning that lines 5–6 of the ***try*** suite are skipped. Control then skips to Line 10, the `ValueError` handler, and executes Line 11, the `exception` suite. The ***try-except*** group ends and the program finishes by executing Line 13.

Zero Division Error: The input values are 10 and 0. The ***try*** suite executes lines 2–5. Line 5 results in an exception, meaning that line 6 of the ***try*** suite is skipped. Control skips to Line 8, the `ZeroDivisionError` handler, which then executes Line 9, the `exception` suite. The ***try-except*** group ends and the program finishes by executing line 13.

Keyboard Interrupt: Lines 1–3 are executed. At the first prompt for input, the user enters a Control-C (holding down the Ctrl key and then typing C). This is an event sent to the program to indicate "stop processing," resulting in an exception, the `KeyInterrupt` exception. The lines 3–6 of the ***try*** suite are skipped. Python finds no handler for this exception, so Python halts the program with an error and prints the error message shown.

As we mentioned previously, it can be difficult to remember the specific names for exceptions. One can always take a look at the documentation `https://docs.python.org/3/library/exceptions.html`, but the easiest way to find the correct error name is to simply cause the error and see what Python prints. For example, here is a Python shell generating a couple of errors:

```
In  [1]: 1/0
Out [1]:

Traceback (most recent call last):
  File "<pyshell#9>", line 1, in <module>
    1/0
ZeroDivisionError: integer division or modulo by zero
In  [2]: open("junk")
Out [2]:

Traceback (most recent call last):
  File "<stdin>", line 1, in <module>
FileNotFoundError: [Errno 2] No such file or directory: 'junk'
```

Multiple Exceptions in One *except*

An ***except*** statement can take a parenthetical list of comma separated exceptions that it can handle. If *any* of the listed exceptions occur, then that statement is activated.

No Exception *except*

It is legal to have an exception handler with no particular exception name specified. Such a handler will catch *all* exceptions, but that is generally not a good idea. Consider what that handler must do. Any error that occurs it must handle. That is as general a problem as just passing control to Python and the shell. Specific exception handlers can be created with strategies to handle specific exceptions. A general exception handler can do very little, as it does not have enough specific information about the error.

14.4.3 Events

Besides input and related errors, another major type of exception that occurs in programs comes from *events* that need to be handled. These are not errors, but "things that happened" and that need to be addressed. Handling events as they occur is an important task. For example, in an operating system an event occurs every time someone clicks a mouse button. The operating system, also a program (and typically a very large one), may be working on something else such as processing information coming from a network when the mouse-click event happens. However, the mouse-click event needs attention right now! The operating system needs to divert its "attention" to that mouse-click event now (waiting a long time to deal with a mouse click would not be good for the user). Once it's finished handling that mouse click, it can go back to deal with other events (keyboard clicks, network information arrival, video updates, etc.). Exception handling is a way for the developer to handle such an event. In this chapter, we will focus on exceptions with respect to errors. However, the topic of *event-driven* programming is very important in computer science.

14.4.4 A Philosophy Concerning Exceptions

There are really two ways to look at dealing with errors, both of which can be summarized with pithy expressions: "Easier to Ask Forgiveness than Permission," EAFP, or "Look Before You Leap," LBYL. First-time programmers, when they think of dealing with errors at all, tend to take the LBYL approach. In this approach, the programmer will provide conditional expressions that test for all the possible error conditions that might occur and, if none are found, then the associated code is run. However, as you gain more experience with programming, you might find EAFP to be easier to work with and, subsequently, to read: try to do something, whatever it is, but catch any potential errors that occur and handle them. It is a kind of "clean up any messes" approach. It focuses on creating good code to solve the problem and then, in a separate construct, deal with any errors. This means that EAFP better separates the main intent of the code from the error conditions that might arise.

Take a look at two examples in Code Listing 14.6 that convert a string value to an int using the two different philosophies.[3]

Code Listing 14.6

```
# check whether int conversion will raise an error, two examples.
# Python Idioms, http://jaynes.colorado.edu/PythonIdioms.html

# LBYL, test for the problematic conditions
def test_lbyl (a_str):
    if not isinstance(a_str, str) or not a_str.isdigit:
        return None
    elif len(a_str) > 10:     # too many digits for int conversion
        return None
    else:
        return int(a_str)

# EAFP, just try it, clean up any mess with handlers
def test_eafp(a_str):
    try:
        return int(a_str)
    except (TypeError, ValueError, OverflowError): # int conversion failed
        return None
```

Which approach seems more readable? The EAFP is more succinct and the list of errors being caught is clearly labeled. We can certainly understand the other, LBYL, approach, but EAFP seems clearer.

[3] Taken from the *Python idioms page*. Copyright © 2010 by Rob Knight. Used by permission of Rob Knight.

In general, if you are adding code to test for possible error conditions, it makes sense to just *try* what you intend and then *handle* the errors you are concerned about. That is what **`try-except`** groups are for.

14.5 EXCEPTION: *ELSE* AND *FINALLY*

Another clause that can be added to a **`try-except`** group is the **`finally`** clause. The finally suite is run as you exit the **`try-except`** group *no matter whether an error occurred or not*. If something absolutely, positively has to be done, whether an error occurs not, this is the place for that code. For example, if you are working with files, the file should be closed at the end of processing, regardless of whether an error occurred. The **`finally`** clause gives you an opportunity to clean up as the **`try-except`** group ends.

The **`try-except`** group also can have an **`else`** clause. The else suite is executed only if the **`try`** suite does *not* encounter an error. One can think of the **`try`** as a kind of conditional execution: if an exception occurs, you jump to the exception handler, otherwise (else) you jump to the **`else`** suite and perform a "normal" exit from the group.

14.5.1 *finally* and *with*

Understanding the **`finally`** statement brings us back to the `with` statement and understanding how it works. Python provides a special concept called a *context*, typically viewed as a resource that persists for some period of time and must be managed. Some objects in Python provide context management which can be manipulated by the `with` statement. Objects which provide these contexts could be web transactions, database access, a user login or any object that needs to manipulate some available resource. The most obvious such object is a file, which needs to be opened and closed.

What the `with` statement guarantees is that when its associated suite is exited, then access to the resource is closed no matter whether the exit is planned or by error. In this way, a `with` statement can be viewed as working with objects that have an associated **`finally`** clause that closes the resource. No matter what, when the suite ends, however it ends, the closing of a resource utilized by a `with` statement, is executed.

14.5.2 Example: Refactoring the Reprompting of a File Name

We saw an example in Section 6.6.3 how you might use exceptions to reprompt for a file name when the user-provided name does not exist. Here we refactor that code to be more complete and show how the **`else`** and **`finally`** clauses can be used. Assume that a file named "test.txt" exists with the following content:

This is a test.
It is only a test.

Code Listing 14.7

```
# all aspects of exceptions

def process_file(data_file):
    """Print each line of a file with its line number."""
    count = 1
    for line in data_file:
        print('Line ' + str(count) + ': ' + line.strip())
        count = count + 1

while True:     # loop forever: until "break" is encountered
    filename = input('Input a file to open: ')
    try:
        data_file = open(filename)
    except FileNotFoundError:    # we get here if file open failed
        print('Bad file name; try again')
    else:
        # no exception so let's process the file
        print('Processing file',filename)
        process_file(data_file)
        break           # exit "while" loop (but do "finally" block first)
    finally:            # we get here whether there was an exception or not
        try:
            data_file.close()
        except NameError:
            print('Going around again')

print('Line after the try-except group')
```

```
Input a file to open: aaaa          # bad input raises exception
Bad file name, try again            # line from except block
Going around again...               # line from finally block
Input a file to open: test.txt      # good file name this time
Processing the file test.txt        # in else block we call function to process file
Line 1: This is a test.
Line 2: It is only a test.
Line after the try/except block.    # line after try/except block
```

As before, the goal of this code is to repeatedly ask the user for a file name until the name provided can be opened. Once opened, the file is processed and subsequently the file is closed.

We create a `while` loop that loops forever, `while True:`, requiring that a `break` statement occur somewhere in the subsequent code so that the loop can end. In the loop, we prompt for a file name to open.

The `try` suite monitors the `open` function. Either the file opening succeeds or it does not. That is, there are two possible cases: the error case or the success case.

ERROR CASE: If the `open` fails, it raises an `FileNotFoundError`. Control jumps to the `except` suite, which prints an error message, finishes, and control moves to the `finally` clause (finally is *always* executed) where the `finally` suite is executed. What we would like to do here is close the file that was opened, but in this case (the error case), no file was opened and the variable `dataFile` has not been assigned a value. Nonetheless, in EAFP tradition, we close it anyway, but monitor *that* closure in a `try` suite. If the closure fails, as it does here, we catch the error, in this case a `NameError` because the variable `data_file` has not yet been assigned a value (because of the opening error). The `except` suite prints a message and the loop continues, reprompting for a file to open.

SUCCESS CASE: If the `open` succeeds, `data_file` is assigned the file descriptor and no exception is raised. Therefore, control moves to the `else` clause and executes the `else` suite. The `else` suite executes the `process_file` function, which prepends the line number to each line of the file and prints the new line. When `process_file` ends, control flows back to the `else` clause of the `try-except` group, which executes a `break`. The `break` will end the loop, but as always, the `finally` suite must be executed before the `try-except` group can end. The `finally` suite executes `data_file.close()`, which now succeeds because `data_file` was defined by the assignment in the open process earlier. The `finally` suite finishes, the `break` leaves the loop, and the last `print` line of the code is executed.

14.6 MORE ON EXCEPTIONS

14.6.1 *Raise*

It is possible for you to *raise* an exception anytime you wish, instead of having Python raise it for you. Simply use the keyword `raise` followed by the exception name:

```
raise ExceptionName
```

Raising an exception allows you to also pass a particular value to the exception handler. You pass the argument by calling the Exception with the argument following in parentheses. In Code Listing 14.8, we use an `if` statement to identify the problem and then use the `raise` command to pass the offending value. This example is not compelling because in this case a simple `if-else` would suffice. However, in a very large program, the `except` block may be in a distant calling function.

Code Listing 14.8

```
dig_str = input("Input an integer: ")
try:
    if dig_str.isdigit():
        dig_int = int(dig_str)
    else:
        raise ValueError(dig_str)  # raise an exception here!
except ValueError:
    print("Conversion to int Error: ", dig_str)
```

Check Yourself: Basic Exception Control

1. Answer the questions regarding the following program:

```
my_dict = {'bill':100, 'zach':'hi mom', 'laurie':'bye mom'}

try:
    result = ''
    key_str = input("Enter a key:")
    val = my_dict[key_str]
    result = result + val
except KeyError:
    result = 'hi mom'
except TypeError:
    result = '100'
else:
    result = result+" "+'all done'
finally:
    if result.isdigit():
        result = int(result) + 10

print(result)          # Line 1
```

(a) What output does Line 1 produce with the input '*bill*'?
(b) What output does Line 1 produce with the input '*zach*'?
(c) What output does Line 1 produce with the input '*fred*'?
(d) What output does Line 1 produce with the input 0?

14.6.2 Create Your Own

It is also possible to create your own exceptions. In Python, exceptions are classes. To make your own exception, you must create a subclass of one of the existing exception classes. By using inheritance, all the essential features of exceptions are preserved. However, the new exception provides a way for you to communicate unique errors for user-built classes. Though this can be done in more detail, all that is really required is to make a subclass of an existing exception class. No body is required of this new class. Thus the expression ***class*** `NewException (Exception):` ***pass*** is sufficient to make a new exception. The class definition is empty (hence the keyword ***pass***), but the characteristics of base `Exception` class are inherited by `NewException`.

14.7 EXAMPLE: PASSWORD MANAGER

The following example creates a new class that is a password manager. It can be used to validate a user's name and password or to add a new user to the password database. For simplicity's sake, in this example we do not securely manage our password database. It is just a dictionary. However, it would not be too much work to import an encryption module and securely manage the dictionary data. We leave that as an exercise for those interested.

The code for the `passManager` class is shown in Code Listing 14.9.

Code Listing 14.9

```
import string

# define our own exceptions
class NameException (Exception):
    ''' For malformed names'''
    pass
class PasswordException (Exception):
    ''' For bad password '''
    pass
class UserException (Exception):
    ''' Raised for existing or missing user '''
    pass

def check_pass(pass_str, target_str):
    """ Return True, if password contains characters from target."""
    for char in pass_str:
        if char in target_str:
            return True
    return False

class PassManager(object):
    """A class to manage a dictionary of passwords with error checking."""
    def __init__(self, init_dict=None):
        if init_dict==None:
            self.pass_dict={}
```

```
26         else:
27             self.pass_dict = init_dict.copy()
28
29     def dump_passwords(self):
30         return self.pass_dict.copy()
31
32     def add_user(self,user):
33         """ Add good user name and strong password to password dictionary."""
34         if not isinstance(user,str) or not user.isalnum():
35             raise NameException
36         if user in self.pass_dict:
37             raise UserException
38         pass_str = input('New password:')
39         # strong password must have digits, uppercase and punctuation
40         if not (check_pass(pass_str, string.digits) and\
41                       check_pass(pass_str, string.ascii_uppercase) and\
42                       check_pass(pass_str, string.punctuation)):
43             raise PasswordException
44
45     def validate(self,user):
46         """ Return True, if valid user and password."""
47         if not isinstance(user,str) or not user.isalnum():
48             raise NameException
49         if user not in self.pass_dict:
50             raise UserException
51         password = input('Passwd:')
52         return self.pass_dict[user]==password
```

Here are some notes about this class:

Lines 4–12: Define three new exceptions. The doc strings indicate their purpose.

Lines 14–19: The function `check_pass` looks to see whether parameter `pass_str` contains any character of the parameter `target_str`.

Lines 23–27: The `__init__` method takes a default argument for the password dictionary, `None`, which can then be checked for in the code (see the programming tip in Section 8.2.1) Using `None` and then checking for its use avoids the issues of modifying a mutable default value. If a parameter value is provided, it should be a dictionary and we make a shallow copy of it. Given that all the values should be strings, this approach should be sufficient.

Lines 32–43: The `add_user` method ensures three conditions. First, the `user` parameter should be a string and consist only of letters or digits. Second, the user being added should not already be in the dictionary. Third, the password provided should have at least one uppercase letter, at least one punctuation mark and at least one digit. The second and third conditions are checked using `check_pass` and the appropriate string from the `string` module. Any violation of these conditions raises one of our user-defined errors.

Lines 45–52: The `validate` method does most of the checks done in `add_user`. It makes sure that the name is a valid name (only letters and digits), and it makes sure the user *is* in the dictionary. Finally, it returns a Boolean indicating whether the dictionary password matches the provided password.

Code Listing 14.10 utilizes `PassManager` for validating a user. Notice that, except for the return value from `validate`, most of the interaction between the main program and the module is via monitoring of exceptions. The comments should be fairly helpful, so we point out only the most interesting points.

Code Listing 14.10

```
from program14_9 import *

def main ():
    pm = PassManager({'bill':'$4Donuts', 'rich':'123ABC!'})

    max_tries = 3  # three tries allowed
    cnt = max_tries
    valid_bool = False
    while cnt > 0 and not valid_bool:
        user_str = input('User name:')
        try:
            valid_bool = pm.validate(user_str) # validate prompts for password
        except NameException:
            print('Bad name!')
        except UserException:
            if input('No such name, add as new user (Y or y)? ') in 'Yy':
                try:
                    pm.add_user(user_str)
                    # only get here if no exceptions raised in add_user
                    valid_bool = True
                except NameException:
                    print('Bad name!')
                except UserException:
                    print('User already exists!')
                except PasswordException:
```

```
26                print('Bad password!')
27        finally:
28            cnt -=1
29    if not valid_bool:
30        print('Session timed out.')
31    else:
32        print('Welcome user',user_str)
```

Line 1: We import, using the ***from*** statement, the new exception classes, and the `PassManager` class.

Lines 4–8: We establish some variables. We instantiate a `PassManager` and pass a dictionary as a initial value. Again, this is not a secure password approach, but it is simple and useful for this example. The maximum times a password can be guessed is three times (stored in `cnt`). The Boolean `valid_bool` is what is returned from `validate`.

Lines 9–12: As long as the number of tries is greater than 0 and `valid_bool` is *`False`* (validation has not yet succeeded), we will try to validate the user. Note that if `validate` raises an exception, `valid_bool` will not be set to *`True`*.

Lines 15–26: This `UserException` occurs if no such user exists in the `PassManager` as determined by the validate call of Line 12. In this case, we provide the option to add a new user. We add a new ***try-except*** block to add the new user. If `add_user` does not raise an exception, then `valid_bool` will be set to *`True`*.

Line 27: The ***finally*** statement goes with the outer ***try-except*** block. No matter what finally ensues, every time through the loop `cnt` is decremented, so that only three tries are allowed.

The following session shows a basic interaction of the two modules:

```
In  [1]: program14_10.main()
User name:bill
Passwd:$4Donuts
Welcome user bill

In  [2]: program14_10.main()
User name:fred
No such name, add as new user (Y or y)? y
New password:abc123
Bad password!
User name:fred
No such name, add as new user (Y or y)? y
New password:Good4You!
Welcome user fred
```

Summary

In this chapter, we explained file input and output in greater detail. We also looked at handling CSV-formatted files in more detail. Finally, we showed more complex file handling using the `os` module. We also included exceptions in more detail. It is particularly useful for ensuring that input is valid. We provided a couple of code snippets for checking input and checking file openings.

Files

- `readline()`: read one line; return a string.
- `readlines()`: read all lines; return a list of strings.
- `read(n)`: read n bytes; return a string.
- `write(s)`: write string s.
- `writelines(l)`: write list of strings.
- `tell()`: return position in file as bytes from beginning.
- `seek(n)`: go to n bytes from beginning of file.
- `seek(0,2)`: go to end of file.
- `with open(s) as f`: open, do something to f, close.
- **CSV**

```
import csv
f = open(s)
r = csv.reader(f)
for row in r:
    # do something to each row
```

- `import os`
  - `os.getcwd()`: get curent working directory (cwd); return path string.
  - `os.chdir(p_str)`: change cwd to path string p_str.
  - `os.listdir()`: return a list of files and directories is cwd.
  - `for dir_name, dirs, files in os.walk(p_str)`: walk the directory.
- `import os.path`
  - `os.path.isfile(p_str)`: is p_str a file? Returns Boolean.
  - `os.path.isdir(p_str)`: is p_str a directory? Returns Boolean.
  - `os.path.exists(p_str)`: does p_str exist? Returns Boolean.
  - `os.path.basename(p_str)`: return file name from p_str.

– `os.path.dirname(p_str)`: return directory prefix from p_str.
– `os.path.split(p_str)`: split p_str as (directory, file_name).
– `os.path.join(path,file_name)`: inverse of split–builds p_str.
– `os.path.splitext(p_str)`: split p_str as (path, file_extension).

Exceptions

- ***else***: suite executed if no errors occur in ***try*** suite.
- ***finally***: suite always executed.
- ***raise*** `ErrorName`: raise an error.
- Create your own exception:

```
class SomeException(Exception):
    pass
```

Exercises

1. A `KeyError` exception exists if you attempt to access a dictionary with an invalid key. Write a small program that illustrates using a ***try-except*** block to handle a `KeyError` exception. Create a small dictionary and write a special error message if an attempt is made to access the dictionary with an invalid key.

2. Given dictionary D, rewrite this code using exceptions:

```
if x in D:
    D[x] += 1
else:
    D[x] = 1
```

3. Write a function that takes a string of words and integers as an argument and returns two lists: one a list of the words, the other a list of the integers. Use exceptions to distribute words and integers to their respective lists.

4. Phone Records.
Telecom operators such as AT&T or Verizon maintain records of all the calls made using their network (named "call detail records" or CDRs). Usually, the CDRs are collected at the routers within the telecom networks, and millions of CDRs are stored in a single file. Although most of the records are in correct format, some records (a handful) either do not contain all the requisite fields or contain garbled data; these records cause problems during any data processing.

Consider a simplified version of a CDR that has only four fields: date and time of the call, source number, destination number, and duration of the call. Create a comma-separated file containing multiple CDRs. In that file include some erroneous or incomplete records that:

- Do not have duration of the call (no duration, no billing!).
- Have garbled phone numbers like 12-345-6789 or 123-45?-6789.

Also, create some records in which the source or destination number is recorded as null (this happens sometimes if it was an international call). It's a valid record. Create some records in which the comma is missing between the source and destination numbers, for example, 123-456-7890 987-654-3210.

Note: If a comma is missing between the source and destination or they have null values, you can still get the required information and it should not be counted as an erroneous record.

Also, create another file containing all the North American area codes (see `http://www.bennetyee.org/ucsd-pages/area.html`).

(a) Find the call that had the longest duration and find its source and destination regions.
(b) Find the number of garbled or incomplete CDRs.
(c) How many international calls were made?
(d) List of all calls made on a particular date.
(e) List of all calls made during a particular hour.
(f) Optional: Plot a distribution of the arrival times of the calls. This plot could help in identifying busy and idle periods of the network.

Use exceptions (`IndexError`, `ValueError`, `TypeError`) to handle erroneous CDRs rather than checking individual cases using if-else constructs.

5. Assume that a file has opened as "somefile," such as `somefile = open('test.txt', 'r')`. Try the following (note the "s" in the second method name).

(a) What will `somefile.readline()` return?
(b) What will `somefile.readlines()` return?

6. Given a test file named "test.txt" containing the following three lines:

Line One
Line Two
Line Three

Consider the following code:

```
someFile = open('test.txt','r')
for line in someFile: # Loop 1
        print line
for line in someFile: # Loop 2
        print line
```

(a) What will be printed by Loop 1?
(b) What will be printed by Loop 2?
(c) How can you modify the code so that both Loop 1 and Loop 2 print the same thing (other than having them both print nothing)?

7. Suppose that a text file contains student records on each line and each record is of the format:

```
Name of Student, Student Id, GPA.
```

Write code to read the file line by line and store all the records in lists or tuples. Hint: you need to create a list of lists or list of tuples.

8. Write a function that takes one argument: a string file name. The function should return a list of lists such that each list is a list of the words in each line. In addition

(a) Remove all whitespace from each word and remove all punctuation. The string module constants will be useful for the last task.
(b) Clean the words before placing them in the list. Specifically, convert all words to lower case and throw out any "words" that contain anything other than letters.

9. Write a function that takes one argument: a string file name. The function reads lines from the file and performs the following operations on them.

(a) Remove all special characters and write all text to a new file.
(b) Search for email addresses in the text file and write them to a new file.

Programming Projects

1. Spreadsheets.

Spreadsheet programs such as Microsoft Excel or OpenOffice Calc have an option to export data into CSV files). In this exercise, you will create a program that will read in a spreadsheet (in CSV format), and manipulate it. Provide the following capabilities:

- Print the data
- Delete a row or column
- Insert a row or column
- Change a value in a cell
- Output the data in csv format

Issues to consider:

- Use Python's `csv` module to read in a spreadsheet. Choose an appropriate data structure to store the data. Should you use lists, tuples, or dictionaries?
- Construct a driving loop in your program that will prompt for the operations specified previously. A useful interface is to allow choices to be specified with a single letter related to the operation, for example, "d" for delete.

2. File copy.

All operating systems have commands that will create a copy of a file. In this exercise, you are to create a program that will make an *exact* copy of a file. Provide the following capabilities:

- Copy only files that end with a ".txt" extension. Generate an appropriate error if something else is specified.
- Using the `os` module, check whether the source file exists.
- Using the `os` module, check whether the destination file exists. If so, ask the user if he or she wants to overwrite it.
- If no paths are specified, assume that the file is in the current folder (directory). Otherwise, use the `os` module to separate the path from the file name. If a path is specified for the destination file, check whether the path exists—otherwise, generate an error.

CHAPTER 15

Recursion: Another Control Mechanism

> A journey of a thousand miles begins with a single step.
>
> Lao-Tzu (老子), *The Way of Lao-Tzu*

Earlier you learned about looping and selection as control techniques. In this chapter, you learn about another control mechanism: recursion. Recursion does not add any power to our programming, as looping and selection are sufficient for all programs, but there are some solutions that are easier to both understand and implement with recursion. In fact, there is a class of languages called *functional programming languages*, such as Haskell, Scheme, and Lisp, that feature recursion as their primary control mechanism. Once understood, recursion can be a natural way to express a solution to a problem, so we need it in our problem-solving tool box.

15.1 WHAT IS RECURSION?

Syntactically, recursion is simple: it is a function that calls itself. For example:

```
def f(n):
    ...
    f(n-1)
```

At first blush, however, it looks rather odd. Take a look ahead at the recursive function `factorial` in Section 15.2. It seems that there is nothing there. It looks quite "circular," defining something in terms of itself. How could that work?

The key is to understand that recursion is not circular, if there is a condition under which the circularity ends: it "bottoms out" at some point. That is the key. Understanding recursion implies understanding two parts of your problem:

- How to break your problem into smaller pieces, each of which can be addressed by your function and then "put back together."
- Determining when the recursive invocation of a function ends, when the recursion "bottoms out."

Recursion ends up being an algorithm that, in itself, uses a form of divide and conquer, our frequently applied approach for designing algorithms. Recursion breaks a problem down into pieces, down to the "smallest" piece, solves that smallest piece, and then reassembles the smaller solutions into an overall answer.

Correctly controlling recursion requires dealing with two different cases. The first case terminates a recursive sequence and is known as the *base case*. If the base case is missing, the recursive function calls go on forever. Such a program never halts with an answer—known as *infinite recursion*. The second case is the *recursive step*. It both breaks the problem down and reassembles the partial solutions.

Recursion can occur in many situations. The English language allows for recursion and a classic (and humorous) case of infinite recursion is a recursive definition that simply refers to itself. Here is an actual, and useless, definition of a "recursive definition" from the Jargon File:[1]

> **Recursion:**
> *see Recursion*

Another example of a recursive definition of an English word is a definition of one's *ancestors*:

> **def** ancestors:
> One's parents are one's ancestors (base case).
> The parents of one's ancestors are also one's ancestors (recursive step).

We can think of Lao-Tzu's quote at the beginning of this chapter as a recursive description of how to make a long journey. For the purpose of illustrating recursion, let's rewrite the quote as: "a journey of a thousand *steps* begins with single step." If you have taken 999 steps, you can easily take that 1000th step. If you have taken 998 steps, you can easily take the 999th step. The process continues recursively until you get to that first step (the base case), and you know how to take that first step.

Written recursively, our modified version of Lao-Tzu's quote becomes:

> **def** journey:
> The first step is easy (base case).
> The nth step is easy after already completing the previous $n - 1$ steps (recursive step).

[1] A glossary of the so-called "computer hacker" slang, see: http://www.catb.org/jargon/html/R/recursion.html

We can express this journey of a thousand steps as a Python function that expresses each step as a string—the first step is the string "Easy." All other steps are strings in the form of step (n). A call to `takeStep(4)` results in the string `'step(4) + step(3) + step(2) + Easy'`. Recursively, the `takeStep` function begins with `n = 4`, then calls itself with `n = 3`, and so on until it is called with `n = 1`. At that point, the calling sequence reaches its end, and we return from the calls backwards from `n = 1` with string "Easy". See Code Listing 15.1.

Code Listing 15.1

```
def take_step(n):
    if n == 1:  # base case
        return "Easy"
    else:
        this_step = "step(" + str(n) + ")"
        previous_steps = take_step(n-1)       # recursive call
        return this_step + " + " + previous_steps
```

```
In  [1]: takeStep(4)
Out [1]: 'step(4) + step(3) + step(2) + Easy'
```

We'll look at how the control is managed a little later. An astute reader will notice that the ***else*** is not necessary, because if `n != 1`, the first ***return*** will not happen, and the program will proceed to the ***else*** clause anyway.

15.2 MATHEMATICS AND RABBITS

Let's consider a recursive definition from mathematics. The factorial function may be familiar to you. The factorial function is so frequently used in mathematics and statistics that the shorthand expression uses an exclamation point. That is, `factorial(4)` is written as 4! and its value is $4! = 4 \times 3 \times 2 \times 1$. Because 1! is defined to have a value of 1, we can define the factorial function recursively as follows:

```
factorial(n):
    factorial(1) = 1                          # base case
    factorial(n) = n * factorial(n-1)         # recursive step
```

Our base case, where we "bottom out," is when the factorial function gets an argument of 1. At that point, we know the answer (no calculation is required), and we return the value 1.

The recursive step both breaks the problem down and reassembles the partial answer. At every step, we divide the problem into two parts:

- The value n
- The value of factorial(n − 1)

Once those two parts are calculated, we combine them (the conquer step) by multiplying the two values and returning that product.

Code Listing 15.2

```
def factorial(n):
    """Recursive factorial."""
    if n == 1:
        return 1                        # base case
    else:
        return n * factorial(n-1)    # recursive case
```

That is, to find factorial(4) recursively (see Code Listing 15.2):

4! = 4 * 3!		
but we know	3! = 3 * 2!	
but we know	2! = 2 * 1!	
but we know	1! = 1	*base case*
so	2! = 2 * 1 = 2	
so	3! = 3 * 2 = 6	
so	4! = 4 * 6 = 24	

Written to look more like Python, we can write the function as:

```
factorial(n):
    if n == 1, return 1                              # base case
    if n > 1, return n * factorial(n-1)              # recursive case
```

```
In  [1]: factorial(4)
Out [1]: 24
```

Another classic example of recursion is the Fibonacci sequence, which first appeared in print almost a thousand years ago. The author, Fibonacci, presented the sequence as an artificial example of how rabbits might breed. If you start with two rabbits, they will breed, to created a third rabbit. The three rabbits will produce two more offspring, to yield a total of five. Fibonacci's pattern to find the number of rabbits in the next generation was to add the totals from the two previous generations:

```
1           # first rabbit
1           # second rabbit
2 = 1 + 1   # two rabbits (summing the first and second rabbits)
3 = 1 + 2   # three rabbits (summing the previous two generations)
5 = 2 + 3   # five rabbits (summing the previous two generations)
8 = 3 + 5   # eight rabbits (summing the previous two generations)
...
```

What is our base case? In the case of the Fibonacci sequence, there are two base cases because we are summing the previous *two* generations in our recursive step. That is, our first base case is the "first rabbit" and the second base case is the "second rabbit."

For the recursive step, we divide the data into two parts:

- The value for `fibonacci (n — 1)`
- The value for `fibonacci (n — 2)`

The conquer stage is to sum those two values together, once calculated, and return that sum as the function value.

The resulting recursive definition is (in English first):

```
fibonacci (n):
    For the first two cases (n=0 or n=1): there is 1 rabbit    # base case
    if n > 1: sum the previous two generations                 # recursive case
```

The definition translated into Python is shown in Code Listing 15.3.

Code Listing 15.3

```
def fibonacci(n):
    """Recursive Fibonacci sequence."""
    if n == 0 or n == 1:     # base cases
        return 1
    else:
        return fibonacci(n-1) + fibonacci(n-2)  # recursive case
```

```
In  [1]: fibonacci(4)
Out [1]: 5

In  [2]: fibonacci(6)
Out [2]: 13
```

fibonacci(4) = fibonacci(3) + fibonacci(2)	
so we next determine	fibonacci(3) = fibonacci(2) + fibonacci(1)
and	fibonacci(2) = fibonacci(1) + fibonacci(0) *base case*
the base case yields	fibonacci(2) = 1 + 1 = 2
so	fibonacci(3) = 2 + fibonacci(1) = 2 + 1 = 3
and	fibonacci(4) = fibonacci(3) + fibonacci(2) = 3 + 2 = 5

PROGRAMMING TIP

Recursion must have a base case, and it must appear *first* in the function.

15.3 LET'S WRITE OUR OWN: REVERSING A STRING

VideoNote 15.1
Recursion

You've seen some examples—now let's write our own recursive function. Let's reverse a string. You already know an easy way to reverse a string (what is it? remember the slicing with a negative step in Section 4.1.5), but let's write a recursive function that does the same job.

As always, we need to define the base case and the recursive step. In the recursive step, we need to define the divide process and the conquer process. A skeleton function would then look like Code Listing 15.4.

Code Listing 15.4

```
# recursive function to reverse a string

def reverser (a_str):
    # base case
    # recursive step
        # divide into parts
        # conquer/reassemble

the_str = input("Reverse what string:")
result = reverser(the_str)
print("The reverse of {} is {}".format(the_str,result))
```

What is the base case for a string reversal? Well, what string is easy to reverse? Certainly a string with a length of 1 is trivial to reverse—it is just the string itself! We put that in as the base case as shown in Code Listing 15.5.

Code Listing 15.5

```
# recursive function to reverse a string

def reverser (a_str):
    # base case
    if len(a_str) == 1:
        return a_str
    # recursive step
      # divide into parts
      # conquer/reassemble

the_str = input("Reverse what string: ")
result = reverser(the_str)
print("The reverse of {} is {}".format(the_str,result))
```

Now let's consider the divide-and-conquer step. We need to answer the two questions: how to divide the data up and how to reassemble (conquer) that data once the parts are calculated. As you have seen previously, these two steps are often done together.

What to do? Let's assume that `reverser` does what it is supposed to do: reverse a string. If that is true, how can we take advantage of that? If we were to break a string into two pieces: one sent to the reverser function recursively and one not, what data should we send?

Consider the string `'abcde'`. If the reverser function works as advertised, we could just take the first letter, in this case, `'a'`, and append that to the *end* of the rest of the string if that string was reversed. That is,

beginning with:	first-character + rest-of-string
the reverse is:	reverse of rest-of-string + first-character

or, in Python,

```
reverser(a_str[1:]) + a_str[0].
```

This approach reverses the position of the first letter and leaves the work of reversing the rest of the string to a recursive call. In typical recursive fashion, we continue with the process until we hit a string of length 1, and then we can begin reassembly.

Code Listing 15.6 shows the final product. We add some ***`print`*** statements just to show the "divide" steps as they happen, the "bottoming out" of the base case, and then finally the reassembly.

Code Listing 15.6

```
# Reverse a string using a recursive function.

def reverse (a_str):
    """Recursive function to reverse a string."""
    print("Got as an argument:",a_str)
    # base case
    if len(a_str) == 1:
        print("Base Case!")
        return a_str
    # recursive step
    else:
        new_str =reverse(a_str[1:]) + a_str[0]
        print("Reassembling {} and {} into {}".format(a_str[1:],a_str[0],
new_str))
        return new_str

the_str = input("What string: ")
print()
result_str = reverse(the_str)
print("The reverse of {} is {}".format(the_str,result_str))
```

```
>python reverser.py
What string:abcde

Got as an argument: abcde
Got as an argument: bcde
Got as an argument: cde
Got as an argument: de
Got as an argument: e
Base Case!
Reassembling e and d into ed
Reassembling de and c into edc
Reassembling cde and b into edcb
Reassembling bcde and a into edcba
```

15.4 HOW DOES RECURSION ACTUALLY WORK?

How is it possible for a function to call itself, and how does the computer keep track of all the function calls that result?

15.4.1 Stack Data Structure

The computer keeps track of function calls on a data structure known as a *stack*. A stack is a data structure that grows and shrinks only at one end. Imagine a stack of plates, as you might find in a cafeteria (see Figure 15.1).

FIGURE 15.1 A stack of plates, cafeteria-style. [Image courtesy of Jupiterimages/Getty Images.]

The stack of plates is spring-loaded. You may add more plates to the stack, but only the top plate is available. If you remove a plate from the top, the stack of plates lifts up, presenting the next user with a new "top" plate. The process can continue until the stack fills up or the stack empties out. One can imagine a data structure with much the same behavior. You can add and remove new data to and from the stack. The order of availability is often called *LIFO*, meaning **L**ast **I**n, **F**irst **O**ut. The last data item you add to the stack is the first item you can retrieve. Such a stack might fill to capacity or run out of data items to provide. A data structure stack is shown in Figure 15.2. A stack has three standard operations: pop, push, and top. The names are really quite descriptive of our "stack of plates":

pop: Pop removes the item at the top of the stack and returns it. The stack is one element smaller as a result. In our plate analogy, this action removes the top plate from the stack of plates.

push: Push takes a parameter and adds that parameter as an element to the top of the stack. The stack is one element larger as a result. The item just pushed becomes the top

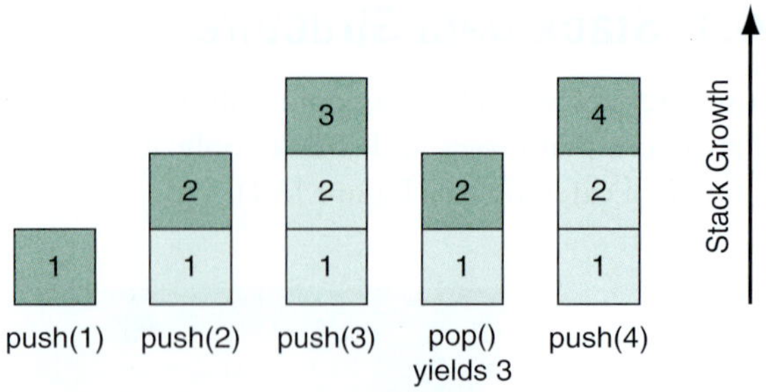

FIGURE 15.2 The operation of a stack data structure.

element of the stack. In our plate analogy, this action puts a plate on top of the stack of plates.

top: Top returns, but does not remove, the top element of the stack. The stack is not modified. In our plate analogy, in this action we simply look at the top plate.

We can implement a stack data structure using a Python list. Remember, `append` adds an element to the end of the list (the *top*), and `pop` removes an element from the end of a list (the *top*). The `top` method corresponds the last element of the list. The correspondence is shown in Table 15.1.

Stack Terminology	Python Terminology	Action
top()	`List[-1]`	Return the value of top of stack
push(x)	`List.append(x)`	Push x onto top of stack
y = pop()	`y = List.pop()`	Pop top off of stack and assign to y

TABLE 15.1 Stack terminology translated to Python.

Here is a Python session illustrating stack behavior using Python list methods. We name the stack "stack_list" and illustrate pop, push (Python append), and top:

```
In  [1]: stack_list = [1,2,3] # create a stack
In  [2]: x = stack_list.pop() # pop an item off the stack
In  [3]: x # the poped item was assigned to x
Out [3]: 3

In  [4]: stack_list # pop removed the item
Out [4]: [1, 2]

In  [5]: stack_list.append(7) # push 7 onto the stack (using append)
In  [6]: stack_list
Out [6]: [1, 2, 7]
```

```
In  [7]: stack_list[-1] # top()
Out [7]: 7

In  [8]: stack_list # top() doesn't change the stack
Out [8]: [1, 2, 7]
```

15.4.2 Stacks and Function Calls

Python keeps track of function calls by pushing the namespace for each function call onto a stack. Examining the stack during recursive calls illustrates how Python keeps track of the many calls to the same function.

Remember the recursive factorial function of the previous section:

```
factorial(n):
    if n == 1, return 1                          # base case
    if n > 1, return n * factorial(n-1)          # recursive case
```

Let's examine the stack when we execute `factorial(4)`. First, let's adjust our factorial function to print information about the state of each recursive function call. An `indent` variable was added so that deeper recursion gets more indentation so that it is easier to visualize the recursion. Printed statements with the same indentation are made within the same function instance. Also, the recursive function call is moved to a separate line to allow us to print a line right after the recursive call returns. Included in that line is the value returned by the recursive call. See Code Listing 15.7.

Code Listing 15.7

```
def factorial(n):
    """Recursive Factorial with print to show operation."""
    indent = 4*(6-n)*" "  # more indent on deeper recursion
    print(indent + "Enter factorial n = ", n)
    if n == 1:             # base case
        print(indent + "Base case.")
        return 1
    else:                  # recursive case
        print(indent + "Before recursive call f(" + str(n-1) + ")")
        # separate recursive call allows print after call
        rest = factorial(n-1)
        print(indent + "After recursive call f(" + str(n-1) + ") = ", rest)
        return n * rest
```

```
In  [1]: factorial(4)
Out [1]:         Enter factorial n =  4
```

```
            Before recursive call f(3)
                Enter factorial n =  3
                Before recursive call f(2)
                    Enter factorial n =  2
                    Before recursive call f(1)
                        Enter factorial n =  1
                        Base case.
                    After recursive call f(1) =  1
                After recursive call f(2) =  2
            After recursive call f(3) =  6
24
```

Notice the the pattern of calls. First, is a series of "Enter-Before" pairs that reflect entering each function call ("Enter ...") followed by a recursive call ("Before ..."). This series of "Enter-Before" pairs reflects the ever deeper recursive calls until we finally reach the base case. Each is indented as we go deeper. The base case is followed by a series of "After ..." lines, one after each return from a recursive call. Notice how each "After ..." line matches up with a corresponding "Before ..." line—identical indentation indicates that the lines are being printed in the same function instance.

The overall pattern is a series of recursive calls that go deeper and deeper until the base case is reached. This is followed by an unwinding of the sequence of calls, each completing and returning a value until the original factorial value is computed.

To see how Python actually keeps track of the values and recursive function calls, see Figure 15.3. The figure shows the call stack for `factorial(4)`. As time moves from left to right we see the stack grow until the base case is reached and then shrink until we get back to the original call. To fit the notation into the figure, we abbreviated "factorial(n)" to "f(n)". Values that are yet to be determined are labeled with a question mark (?). For example, in

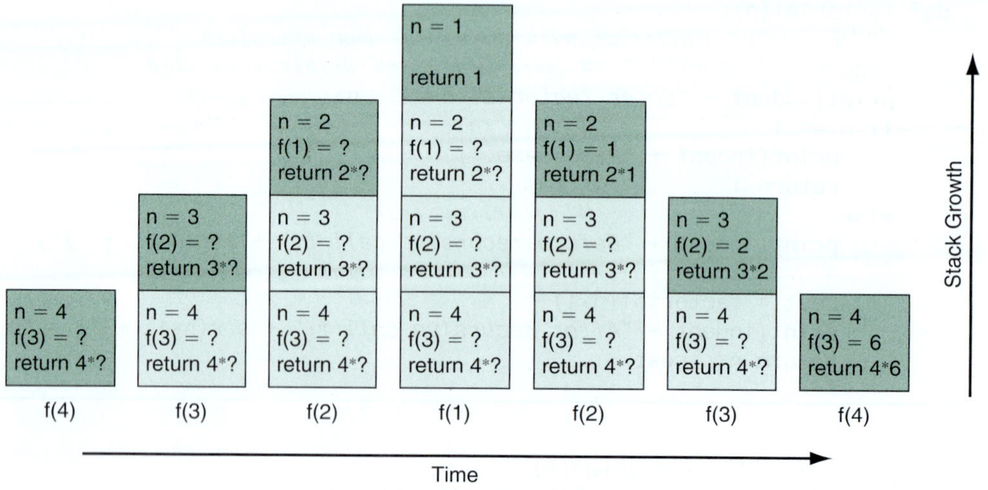

FIGURE 15.3 Call stack for `factorial(4)`. Note the question marks.

the first call to `factorial(4)`, we see that $n = 4$, $f(3) = ?$ (the recursive call hasn't been completed), and we will eventually execute ***return*** `4 * ?` once "?" is resolved by the recursive call. The second stack shows a frame added for the recursive `factorial(3)` call. Note the question marks that remain in the bottom frame as well as in this new frame because we have not yet determined what those values are. In fact, no question marks are resolved until we reach the base case at `factorial(1)`. At that point, we finally have a value (1) to return. After that point, the rightmost stacks successively shrink as the recursive function calls return and the question mark values are resolved. Eventually, we see a final ***return*** `6*4` that yields our final value of 24.

Compare Figure 15.3 to the output we printed earlier for the same `factorial(4)`call earlier. There is a direct correspondence between the height of the stack in the figure and the amount of indentation in the output. Also, observe the values of n and the recursive calls $f(n - 1)$ in both the output and in the figure. It is important to be able to see the correspondence between the stack and the values output by the program.

15.4.3 A Better Fibonacci

Now that we know a little about how recursion works, let's revisit our Fibonacci solution. While the recursion in Code Listing 15.3 does work, it turns out to be a pretty expensive calculation. Figure 15.4 shows why.

This tree of recursive calculations in Figure 15.4 shows that the Fibonacci value of 3 is calculated 8 times when calculating the Fibonacci value of 8. As you try larger and larger numbers, this recalculation penalty becomes prohibitive. If you have nothing else to do, try calculating the Fibonacci of 50 using Code Listing 15.3. You might have to wait awhile, and remember that Control-C will exit the calculation when you get bored.

This can be fixed fairly simply by using a dictionary. If we remember every Fibonacci calculation we make in a dictionary and check the dictionary before we make the calculation,

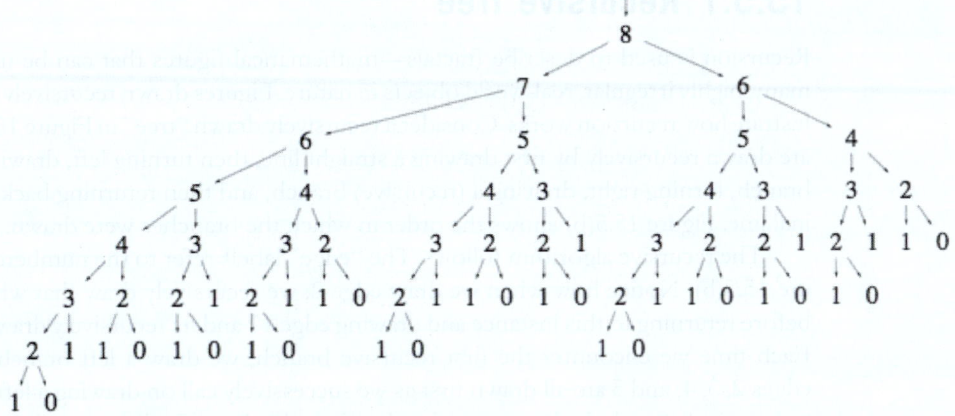

FIGURE 15.4 The simple Fibonacci code recalculates the same value.

we ensure that every number has its Fibonacci value calculated exactly once. See the Code Listing 15.8.

Code Listing 15.8

```
def fibonacci(n):
    """Recursive fibonacci that remembers previous values"""
    if n not in fibo_dict:
        # recursive case, store in the dict
        fibo_dict[n] = fibonacci(n-1) + fibonacci(n-2)
    return fibo_dict[n]

# global fibonacci dictionary.
fibo_dict = {}

# enter the base cases
fibo_dict[0] = 1
fibo_dict[1] = 1

fibo_val = input("Calculate what Fibonacci value:")
print("Fibonnaci value of",fibo_val,"is",
      fibonacci(int(fibo_val)))
```

The change in the computational complexity is pretty dramatic. Try the Fibonacci of 50 with this code.

15.5 RECURSION IN FIGURES

15.5.1 Recursive Tree

Recursion is used to describe fractals—mathematical figures that can be used to describe many, highly irregular, real-world objects in nature. Figures drawn recursively can also help illustrate how recursion works. Consider a recursively drawn "tree" in Figure 15.5(a). Branches are drawn recursively by first drawing a straight line, then turning left, drawing a (recursive) branch, turning right, drawing a (recursive) branch, and then returning back along the original line. Figure 15.5(b) shows the order in which the branches were drawn.

The recursive algorithm follows. The "edge" labels refer to the numbered edges in Figure 15.5(b). Notice how when we draw edge 2, we recursively draw that whole left branch before returning to this instance and drawing edge 17 and its recursively drawn right branch. Each time we encounter the first recursive branch, we draw a left branch. For example, edges 2, 3, 4, and 5 are all drawn first as we successively call on drawing a left branch. When we eventually reach the base case after drawing edge 5, we finally return from a (left) branch

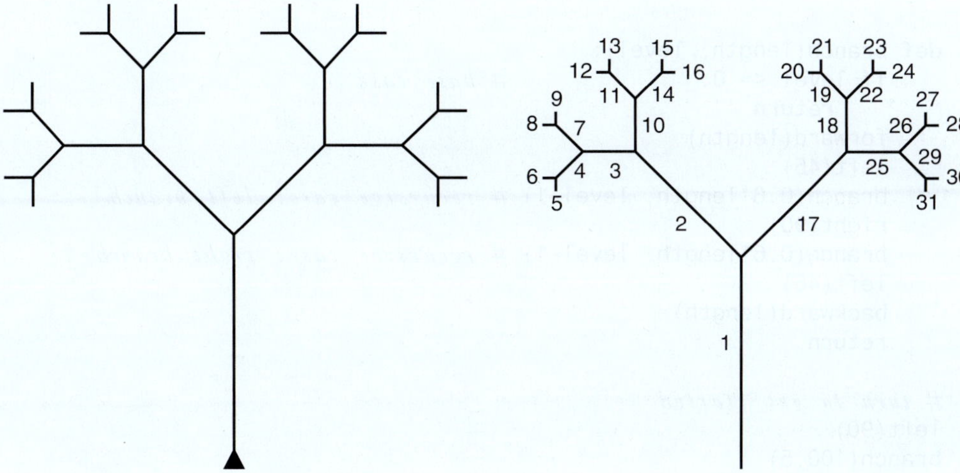

FIGURE 15.5 Recursive tree: (a) Python-drawn on left; (b) order-of-drawing on right.

call, turn right 90°, and draw a right branch (edge 6). We then move backward along edge 4, which completes that recursive branch instance, so we can turn right and recursively execute a right branch starting with edge 7. And so on.

At the highest level, our drawing looks like this:

```
draw edge 1
turn left
draw edge 2 and left branch          # recursive case
turn right
draw edge 17 and right branch        # recursive case
turn left
move back
```

Figure 15.5(a) was drawn using the following Python program with Turtle Graphics. Notice how the `level` parameter is reduced on each call, so it provides a way to work down to the base case. We added a length parameter to our program so that branches become shorter as we progress to lower levels. Since Turtle Graphics draws relatively slowly, it is instructive to watch as the branches are drawn. Notice the pattern: forward, turn left, recursive call, turn right, recursive call, move back. See Code Listing 15.9.

Code Listing 15.9

```
# Breadth−first tree

from turtle import *
```

```
def branch(length, level):
    if level <= 0:                # base case
        return
    forward(length)
    left(45)
    branch(0.6*length, level-1) # recursive case: left branch
    right(90)
    branch(0.6*length, level-1) # recursive case: right branch
    left(45)
    backward(length)
    return

# turn to get started
left(90)
branch(100,5)
```

15.5.2 Sierpinski Triangles

Drawing fractal patterns is a fun way to experiment with recursion. Here is another fractal figure, the Sierpinski triangle (Figure 15.6). Like the tree we drew previously, it has a simple pattern: forward, recursive call, backward, turn left 120°. It must also keep track of levels,

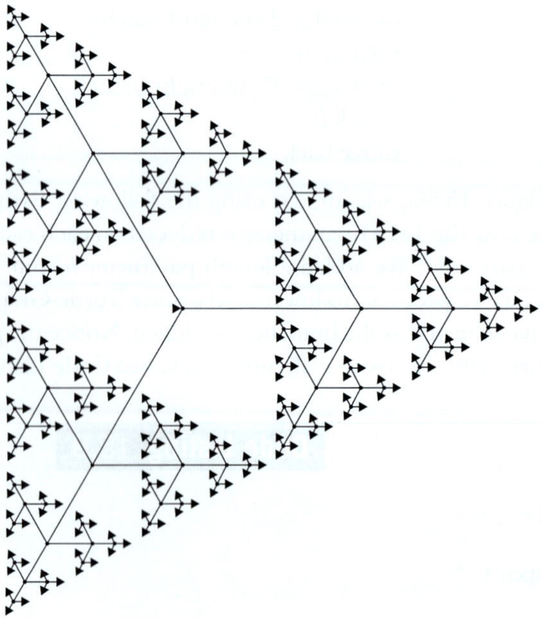

FIGURE 15.6 Sierpinski triangle.

so we can define a base case to stop, and there is a length parameter, so the edges get smaller with each recursive call. When it reaches the base case, it stamps a triangle shape at that spot. Finally, a dot marks the start of each recursive call to help us observe the calls. As with the tree example, it is instructive to watch the Turtle Graphics slowly draw the triangle so that you can observe the recursive calls in action. See Code Listing 15.10.

Code Listing 15.10

```
# Draw Sierpinski figure

from turtle import *

def sierpinski(length, depth):
    if depth > 1: dot()  # mark position to better see recursion
    if depth == 0:       # base case
        stamp() # stamp a triangular shape
    else:
        forward(length)
        sierpinski(length/2, depth-1)  # recursive call
        backward(length)
        left(120)
        forward(length)
        sierpinski(length/2, depth-1)  # recursive call
        backward(length)
        left(120)
        forward(length)
        sierpinski(length/2, depth-1)  # recursive call
        backward(length)
        left(120)

sierpinski(200,6)
```

15.6 RECURSION TO NON-RECURSION

We mentioned earlier that recursion provides a different way to view a problem, but it does not add any computing power to our tool kit. In fact, there exists an algorithm that can convert a recursive algorithm to a non-recursive algorithm. Such an algorithm can be found in an algorithms textbook.[2] Because there is overhead in calling functions, the many function calls in a recursive algorithm can be slower than the non-recursive version. When that is the case, one can think of a solution recursively, write and test a recursive solution, and then convert the solution into a more efficient non-recursive one.

[2] For example, Sedgewick, R., *Algorithms*, Addison-Wesley, 1988.

15.7 GUI FOR TURTLE DRAWING

15.7.1 Using Turtle Graphics to Draw

Just a bit of a warning here. What we are going to do here is a bit complicated as we are using Turtle Graphics in a way that it wasn't really designed for. Turtle Graphics was all about being able to watch the turtle move around the screen and draw. It was therefore intended as a kind of interactive media experience.

However, if we want to do our typical GUI drawing as we have done in Section 10.7, what we want is not interactive drawing but a drawing as an image that we can pull up in a web page. What to do?

There are packages out there that support 2D, even 3D drawing, but they are not part of the Anaconda package that we are supporting, and they are rather more complicated than we want. Besides, we have **learned** how to draw using Turtle Graphics! Why can't we just generate an image of the drawing and skip all the interactive stuff!

The answer is that we can bend Turtle Graphics to do what we want, but it is a bit ugly. We are going to have to take over from what Turtle Graphics does for us, making our life easier by creating a screen and so on, and do it ourselves so that we have some control over the process.

Thus, you might choose to ignore some of the details, and rightly so. However, as we have done with a lot of the GUI work, a good example can act as a template that will allow you to insert your own Turtle Graphics function to do the drawing you want and give you functionality needed to draw a Turtle image for your web GUI.

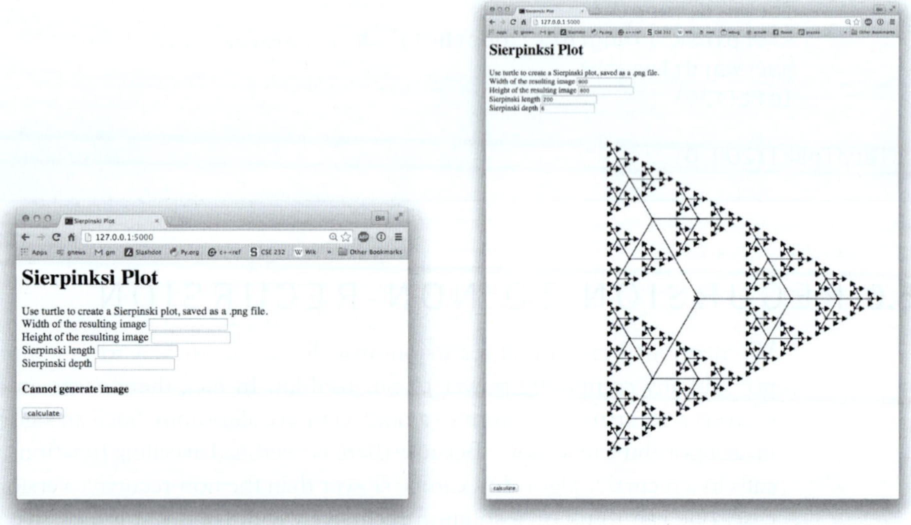

a) Startup b) Sierpinski drawing

FIGURE 15.7 Sierpinski GUI. [William F. Punch, Richard J. Enbody.]

15.7.2 Function Model

We are going to reuse the Sierpinski code from Section 15.5.2 to do some Turtle drawing as shown in Figure 15.7. We are going to incorporate that function into our `compute` function where all the dirty work occurs to get an image quickly from a Turtle drawing. Code Listing 15.11 has comments to indicate how it is done, but here are highlights.

Code Listing 15.11

```
def compute(width_int, height_int, length_int, depth_int):
    ''' Complicated, but here is the deal:
    1) create a window, root, with nothing in it. We have control of the
       window this way
    2) grab the canvas (drawing surface) from root
    3) use that canvas for our Turtle screen
    4) make a raw turtle on the screen we just made from the root canvas
    5) withdraw (hide) the window. You might still get a flash of the window.
       Must be after the turtle creation as no object stuff can occur after
       a withdraw. Drawing window now hidden
    6) go fast: no delay, no tracing at all, only draw once, full dump, at the
       end with update
    7) do the random file thing, clean out the old files in static (make
       static dir if necessary)
    8) dump the canvas as a postscript file, our only option
    9) convert eps file to png using PIL
    '''
    root = tkinter.Tk()
    canv = tkinter.Canvas(root, width=width_int, height=height_int)
    scr = turtle.TurtleScreen(canv)
    canv.pack()
    t = turtle.RawTurtle(scr)
    root.withdraw()

    # draw as fast as possible
    scr.delay(0)
    scr.tracer(0,0)

    ###### actually do some turtle drawing with a function ######
    sierpinski(t, length_int, depth_int)

    # one update of the screen/canvas, all drawing done here and all at once
    scr.update()

    if not os.path.isdir('static'):
```

```
35          os.mkdir('static')
36      else:
37          f_eps = "static/sier.eps"
38          f_png = "static/" + ''.join(random.choice(string.ascii_letters +
string.digits) for _ in range(8)) + ".png"
39          for filename in glob.glob(os.path.join('static', '*')):
40              os.remove(filename)
41          # dump the screen as postscript, our only option from a canvas
unfortunately
42          canv.postscript(file=f_eps)
43          # remove the window, we're done
44          root.destroy()
45          # use PIL to convert eps to png
46          im = Image.open(f_eps)
47          im.save(f_png)
48          return f_png
49
50  if __name__ == "__main__":
51      compute(900, 800, 200, 6)
```

On **Line 29** is a call to our Turtle Graphics program. The rest of the code, explained in the comments, is to make Turtle behave the way we want quickly and to draw an image we can display.

The code for drawing (not shown) is exactly the code in Section 15.5.2 with one change: the turtle is passed in as an argument and prefixes every turtle command. For example, `forward(length)` becomes `t.forward(length)`.

15.7.3 Controller and View

The Controller and View is similar to what we saw in Section 10.7 in that we are going to prompt for some information using fields, then generate a file name from a call to `compute` to load in the web page. We gather the width and height of the canvas and the length and depth of the drawing and pass those to `compute`.

Summary

In this chapter, we introduced the concept of recursion. Some problems are naturally recursive, and this technique can be particularly effective for crafting a solution to such problems. For example, we show that fractals can be very complex, but many can be expressed with relatively simply recursive algorithms.

The recursive function syntax is simple: a function simply calls itself. However, a base case is needed at the beginning of the function so that the series of recursive calls will eventually terminate.

Exercises

1. A common task in an editor application, such as WordPad or TextEdit, is parentheses matching. For example, "(()())" is a valid string of parentheses because each opening bracket has a corresponding closing bracket. On the other hand, "(()" is not a valid string. Another invalid example would be ")(", as the opening bracket should precede the closing bracket.

Write a recursive function that takes a string as input and returns True if the string is valid with respect to matched parentheses. To simplify matters, begin by considering that the input string has only "(" or ")" and no other characters.

2. Pascal's triangle is a triangular array of the binomial coefficients. To create the triangle, you start with 1 at the top, and add numbers such that each number is the sum of the two numbers above it. The first four rows would be

```
      1
     1 1
    1 2 1
   1 3 3 1
```

Write a recursive function that takes a value *n* from the user and generates the first *n* rows of Pascal's triangle.

3. When developing the Rational class, we created a function to calculate the greatest common denominator: `gcd`. Refactor the function to be recursive.

4. A recursive function to calculate the Fibonacci numbers was presented in this chapter. However, each time a number was calculated, it recalculated previous Fibonacci numbers. Refactor your recursive function to retain previous, already calculated Fibonacci numbers and reference them instead of recalculating them. A list could be used, but a dictionary works better. The name for this technique is "memoization."

5. A formula exists for calculating the amount of money in a savings account that begins with an initial value (the initial principal, P) and earns interest with an annual interest rate i, for n years: $P(1 + i)^n$.

Write a recursive function that calculates that same value, and check your result against the formula.

6. Converting decimal numbers to binary numbers can be done recursively. Write a function that takes a positive int argument and returns the corresponding binary number as an int composed of only ones and zeros. For example, `convert(5)` returns the int: 101.

The insight for this problem comes from the fact that the rightmost digit of a decimal n is easy to calculate. It is the remainder when dividing by the base 2: $n\%2$. To get the next rightmost digit, you take the resulting quotient, that is, $n_2 = n/2$, and find its remainder, $n_2\%2$, which is the next digit. Unfortunately, that generates the digits from right to left and we want them from left to right. We could easily do that non-recursively using string concatenation or string reversal, but in this exercise you are to use recursion to recursively calculate the digits. Effectively, you are letting recursion reverse the ordering: think in terms of calculating the rightmost digit as described previously, but then let recursion reverse the digits.

7. The United States still uses the traditional English system of measurement. Each inch on a ruler is marked off as fractions, using tick marks that look like this:

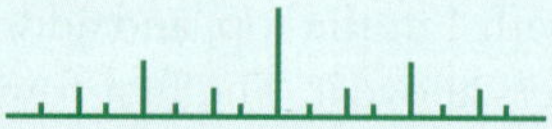

The tallest tick mark falls at the center dividing into halves, two shorter tick marks indicate the quarter divisions, and even shorter ones are used to mark the eighths and sixteenths, and so on. Write the following recursive function:

```
drawRuler(x, y, width, height)
```

where `(x,y)` represents the lower-left corner of a rectangle that has dimensions `width` × `height`. The ruler will be drawn within that rectangle. The function draws a line along the rectangle's bottom edge and then recursively draws vertical tick marks. The rectangle itself is not drawn. The middle-most tick mark is centered in the rectangle and is as tall as the rectangle height. Each smaller tick mark is half the height of the next larger one. Once the tick marks become sufficiently small, the recursion terminates. The recursive insight to this problem is to recognize that the middle-most tick mark subdivides the rectangle into two smaller rectangles, each of which is a smaller ruler of its own. Use Turtle Graphics to draw the figure.

CHAPTER 16

Other Fun Stuff with Python

> People rarely succeed unless they have fun in what they are doing.
>
> Dale Carnegie, author/lecturer

WE HAVE COME A LONG WAY IN OUR PROGRAMMING JOURNEY, AND WE HAVE LEARNED to do many interesting and useful things using Python. The experience you have gained will serve you well in your nascent Python career.

However, we would be remiss in leaving you with the impression that we have covered all of Python. We most definitely have not! Python has many features that we have overlooked for the sake of teaching you the fundamentals of programming. That is, when we had to make a choice, we chose to *not* introduce a new Python feature when the programming concept we were introducing could be done using our existing Python skills. We hoped to focus on programming and less on Python when such a choice was presented.

However, we *really* do want to talk about some of the cool things you can do in Python, so we have added those topics here at the end of the book. These things may not be essential to understanding programming or even Python, but they are useful tools that allow you to solve problems in interesting ways.

So, enjoy these interesting aspects of Python.

16.1 NUMBERS

Python provides support for various number representations that you might find useful, and here are a few of them.

16.1.1 Fractions

We did a lot of development on our own `Rational` number class in Chapter 12 but, as we mentioned there, Python does provide its own version of a Rational number in the `fractions` module (note the plural!).

Remember, a rational number is a number that can be expressed as the ratio of two integers, for example, a fraction p/q where p and q are integers and $q! = 0$. Real numbers that are not rational are called irrational numbers such as π or $\sqrt{2}$.

Much like we did in our own work, the `fractions` module provides a `Fraction` class for our use. Typically one does the following: `from fractions import Fraction`.

An instance of `Fraction` can be treated very much like any other number:

- You can construct them, using a variety of constructor methods.
- You can add, subtract, multiply, and divide `Fraction` instances.
- You can mix types and get a result.
- You can print them.
- You can control how a float is converted to `Fraction`.

We'll take a look at these following properties.

Fraction Construction

The `Fraction` has a particularly rich set of constructors. Look at the examples in the session and the discussion that follows.

```
In  [1]: from fractions import Fraction
In  [2]: half = Fraction(1,2)
In  [3]: half
Out [3]: Fraction(1, 2)

In  [4]: also_half = Fraction(8,16)
In  [5]: also_half
In  [5]: bad = Fraction(5,0)
Traceback (most recent call last):
  File "<stdin>", line 1, in <module>
  File "/opt/local/Library/Frameworks/Python.framework/Versions/3.4/lib/python3.4/
        fractions.py", line 167, in __new__
    raise ZeroDivisionError('Fraction(%s, 0)' % numerator)
ZeroDivisionError: Fraction(5, 0)
Fraction(1, 2)
In  [6]: two = Fraction(2)
In  [7]: two
Out [7]: Fraction(2, 1)
```

```
In  [8]: fourth = Fraction(0.25)
In  [9]: fourth
Out [9]: Fraction(1, 4)

In  [10]: import math
In  [11]: pi_fraction = Fraction(math.pi)
In  [12]: pi_fraction
Out [12]: Fraction(884279719003555, 281474976710656)

In  [13]: 884279719003555/281474976710656
Out [13]: 3.141592653589793

In  [14]: math.pi
Out [14]: 3.141592653589793

In  [15]: third = Fraction("1/3")
In  [16]: third
Out [16]: Fraction(1, 3)

In  [17]: tenth = Fraction("0.10")
In  [18]: tenth
Out [18]: Fraction(1, 10)

In  [19]: three = Fraction("3")
In  [20]: three
Out [20]: Fraction(3, 1)
```

numerator, denominator: You can provide two integers: a numerator and a denominator. Note that the denominator cannot be zero or it will throw a `ZeroDivisionError`.

If the instance is not in reduced form, then Python will reduce it as it did with the variable `also_half`.

numerator: You can provide a single integer, a numerator, and the denominator is assumed to be 1.

float: If you provide a floating-point number, Python will create an exact fraction if it can or the best approximation if it cannot. Here **cannot** means that either the number cannot be represented exactly as a Rational number, such as (math.pi), or that the floating-point accuracy being used can only represent an approximation.

Python could accurately represent the float 0.10 but could only approximate `math.pi`, though the approximation is good to 15 decimal places!

string: If a string is provided, Python will do a conversion based on a couple of factors:

- If the string has a "/" in it, it is assumed to represent two separate integers (a numerator and a denominator) and the instance is created based on those numbers.
- If the string represents a float or an integer, then the rules listed previously will be used to do the conversion.

Fraction Operations

Please look at the session below.

```
In  [1]: from fractions import Fraction
In  [2]: fourth = Fraction(1,4)
In  [3]: eighth = Fraction(1,8)
In  [4]: fourth + eighth + eighth
Out [4]: Fraction(1, 2)

In  [5]: fourth - eighth
Out [5]: Fraction(1, 8)

In  [6]: fourth * eighth
Out [6]: Fraction(1, 32)

In  [7]: fourth / eighth
Out [7]: Fraction(2, 1)

In  [8]: fourth + 0.5
Out [8]: 0.75

In  [9]: fourth + 0.1
Out [9]: 0.35

In  [10]: fourth + 2
Out [10]: Fraction(9, 4)

In  [11]: fourth + 22
Out [11]: Fraction(89, 4)

In  [12]: float(fourth)
Out [12]: 0.25

In  [13]: data_lst = [fourth, eighth]
In  [14]: max(data_lst)
Out [14]: Fraction(1, 4)

In  [15]: sum(data_lst)
Out [15]: Fraction(3, 8)

In  [16]: fourth.numerator
Out [16]: 1

In  [17]: fourth.denominator
Out [17]: 4
```

```
In  [18]: half.numerator = 3
Traceback (most recent call last):
  File "<stdin>", line 1, in <module>
AttributeError: can't set attribute
In  [19]: import math
In  [20]: math.pi
Out [20]: 3.141592653589793

In  [21]: pi_frac = Fraction(math.pi)
In  [22]: pi_frac
Out [22]: Fraction(884279719003555, 281474976710656)

In  [23]: 884279719003555/281474976710656
Out [23]: 3.141592653589793

In  [24]: pi_frac.limit_denominator(100)
Out [24]: Fraction(311, 99)

In  [25]: 311/99
Out [25]: 3.1414141414141414

In  [26]: pi_frac.limit_denominator(10000)
Out [26]: Fraction(355, 113)

In  [27]: 355/113
Out [27]: 3.1415929203539825

In  [28]: pi_frac.limit_denominator(100000)
Out [28]: Fraction(312689, 99532)

In  [29]: 312689/99532
Out [29]: 3.1415926536189365
```

Binary operations: As mentioned, the standard binary operations (+, −, *, /) work with a `Faction` instance, yielding a new `Fraction` instance. If the operation results in an instance that can be reduced, Python will reduce the `Fraction` instance.

You can also do comparisons (<, >, <=, ==, etc.), membership operations (in) and most any other numeric operation.

Mixed types: You can mix a `Fraction` instance with a float or an integer. If the mixed type is an integer, a new `Fraction` is produced. If it is a float, a float is produced. Note that the conversion of the float to a `Fraction` instance might be an approximation.

Other Operators: You can do basic conversions, using functions such as *`float`* and `str`. You can also use built in functions such as `max`, `sum`.

Accessors: You can access the instance elements with the `.numerator` or `.denominator` methods.

It is important to note that, once an instance is made, it is **immutable**. You cannot change either the numerator or denominator of an instance once it is constructed.

Float conversion: When converting a float to a `Fraction`, you can limit the size (the limit of the value) of the denominator to a particular value. In so doing you can control how accurate the approximation is. The method is `.limit_denominator`. The single argument indicates the largest denominator size that is allowed. Python looks for the best approximation within that size.

16.1.2 Decimal

We have talked previously about the approximate nature of floating-point values (see Section 1.6.1). Remember this example:

```
In  [1]: 2.0 / 3.0
Out [1]: 0.6666666666666666

In  [2]: 1.1 + 2.2
Out [2]: 3.3000000000000003

In  [3]: 0.1 + 0.1 + 0.1 - 0.3
Out [3]: 5.551115123125783e-17
```

This represents two problems with floating-point numbers. The first is that some numbers, say the fraction 1/3 are an infinite repeating sequence and therefore cannot be exactly represented. This is handled by the `fractions` module in Section 16.1.1.

The second is the approximate nature of some floating-point operations. For example, $5.551115123125783e - 17$ is a really small number, but it is not the result we expected from $0.1 + 0.1 + 0.1 - 0.3$, which should be 0.

The `decimal` module and its associated class `Decimal` allow us to work with floating-point values that:

- Can do exact floating-point calculations for decimal numbers, even if those numbers cannot be exactly represented in binary floating-point format.
- Allows you to keep a floating-point result using **significant places**.
- Allows you to control the **precision** of decimal operations

We will discuss each of those in more detail later. The bottom line of why the `decimal` module exists is this: a `Decimal` instance can represent any decimal number exactly, round up or down, and apply a limit to the number of significant digits and the level of precision.

Decimal Construction

If we include `from decimal import Decimal` we get access to the `Decimal` class. There are three ways to construct a `Decimal` instance:

```
In  [1]: from decimal import Decimal
In  [2]: one = Decimal(1)
In  [3]: one
Out [3]: Decimal('1')

In  [4]: one_one = Decimal('1.1')
In  [5]: one_one
Out [5]: Decimal('1.1')

In  [6]: one_one_float = Decimal(1.1)
In  [7]: one_one_float
Out [7]: Decimal('1.100000000000000088817841970012523233890533447265625')

In  [8]: two_two = Decimal('2.2')
In  [9]: one_one + two_two
Out [9]: Decimal('3.3')

In  [10]: one_one_float + two_two
Out [10]: Decimal('3.300000000000000088817841970')
```

integer: If you provide a single integer, you construct a `Decimal` instance of that value.

string: If you provide a string representation of a decimal number, that value will be stored **exactly** in the instance. All operations using that instance will reflect the use of that exact value, without any floating-point inaccuracy.

float: If you provide a floating-point number, then the underlying floating-point representation will be used in constructing the instance. Thus, any floating-point inaccuracies will exist in the resulting instance. This is enough of an annoyance (and against the whole idea of the module) that one can set an option to trigger an exception if a float is used in the constructor.

Decimal Operations

As with the `Fraction` class, instances of `Decimal` can be used with most operations.

```
In  [1]: from decimal import Decimal
In  [2]: one_one = Decimal('1.1')
In  [3]: six_six = Decimal('6.6')
In  [4]: one_one + six_six
Out [4]: Decimal('7.7')

In  [5]: one_one - six_six
Out [5]: Decimal('-5.5')
```

```
In  [6]: one_one * six_six
Out [6]: Decimal('7.26')

In  [7]: one_one / six_six
Out [7]: Decimal('0.1666666666666666666666666667')

In  [8]: one_one_with_zeros = Decimal('1.1000')
In  [9]: one_one_with_zeros + six_six
Out [9]: Decimal('7.7000')

In  [10]: one_one > six_six
Out [10]: False

In  [11]: six_six > one_one
Out [11]: True

In  [12]: one_one_with_zeros == one_one
Out [12]: True

In  [13]: one_one + 1
Out [13]: Decimal('2.1')

In  [14]: one_one + 1.1
Traceback (most recent call last):
  File "<stdin>", line 1, in <module>
TypeError: unsupported operand type(s) for +: 'decimal.Decimal' and 'float'
In  [15]: data_lst = [one_one, six_six]
In  [16]: sum(data_lst)
Out [16]: Decimal('7.7')

In  [17]: max(data_lst)
Out [17]: Decimal('6.6')

In  [18]: one_one in data_lst
Out [18]: True

In  [19]: float(one_one)
Out [19]: 1.1
```

Binary operations: As mentioned, the standard binary operations (+, −, *, /) work with a `Decimal` instance, yielding a new instance. In division, the result is a full floating-point representation.

Note that the example using `one_one_with_zeros` preserves **significant digits**. That is, the result will contain accuracy that matches the rules for significant digits, in this case maintaining the number of trailing zeros required. Look up the topic of significant digits for more details.

You can also do comparisons (<, >, <=, ==, etc.), membership operations (in) and most any other numeric operation.

Mixed types: You can mix a `Decimal` instance with an integer **but not a float**. If the mixed type is an integer, a new `Decimal` is produced. If it is a float, then an exception is thrown.

Other Operators: You can do basic conversions, using functions such as *`float`* and *`str`*. You can also use built-in functions such as `max` and `sum`.

Finally, note that a `Decimal` instance is **immutable**, as was the case for a `Fraction` instance. However, note there are no accessors for a `Decimal` instance.

Other Decimal Properties

The specification for Decimal follows some very complicated rules for the datatype as specified by the Institute of Electrical and Electronics Engineers (IEEE).[1] It is a bit beyond this text to examine this complicated topic, but there are a few things we can note.

You can access some of the general properties used by the `decimal` package by examining a special variable called the **context**. You can access the context by using the function `getcontext()`, which returns a context variable with a number of fields that can be set by the user which controls the behavior of the `decimal` package. Here are some of the highlight elements.

```
In  [1]: import decimal
In  [2]: from decimal import Decimal
In  [3]: one_one = Decimal('1.1')
In  [4]: six_six = Decimal('6.6')
In  [5]: context = decimal.getcontext()
In  [6]: one_one / six_six
Out [6]: Decimal('0.1666666666666666666666666667')

In  [7]: context.prec = 4
In  [8]: one_one / six_six
Out [8]: Decimal('0.1667')

In  [9]: context.prec = 10
In  [10]: one_one / six_six
Out [10]: Decimal('0.1666666667')

In  [11]: context.rounding()
Traceback (most recent call last):
  File "<stdin>", line 1, in <module>
TypeError: 'str' object is not callable
In  [12]: context.rounding
Out [12]: 'ROUND_HALF_EVEN'
```

[1] http://grouper.ieee.org/groups/754/

```
In  [13]: context.capitals
Out [13]: 1

In  [14]: big = Decimal('6.022e23')
In  [15]: big
Out [15]: Decimal('6.022E+23')

In  [16]: context.capitals=0
In  [16]: big
Out [16]: Decimal('6.022e+23')
```

precision:. You can control the level of precision by setting the `.prec` field of the context. The value to be stored is the number of floating-point elements to be maintained for any operation. The default is 28. Whatever the precision is set to, the result will be rounded to that many elements.

rounding: You can set the method of rounding used using the `.rounding`. Python provides eight, predefined methods of rounding, the default being ROUND_HALF_EVEN, meaning round to nearest with ties going to nearest even integer. You can look at the other 7 in the documentation.

Exponent: You can control whether exponent numbers display with a lowercase or uppercase "e" by the `.capitals` field, which can take either a 1, representing a capital "E" or 0, representing a lowercase "e".

There is much more to the `decimal` package, including dealing with **Infinity**, dealing with an undefined/unrepresentable numbers called "Not A Number" (**NaN**s), various exceptions of **signals** that can be caught, and so on.

16.1.3 Complex Numbers

Complex numbers are important numbers with applications in fields such as electromagnetics, chemistry, and economics. They are a topic that requires some background but the basics are:

- Each complex number consists of two parts: a **real** part and an **imaginary** part, typically written as $a + bj$ where a is the real part, b is the imaginary part, and j is $\sqrt{-1}$.[2]
- A complex number is not a point on the Real number line, but a coordinate in a plane with the x-axis representing the real number and the y-axis representing the imaginary number.
- A real number then is properly represented by $a + 0j$; that is, its imaginary part is 0. A **pure imaginary** number would be $0 + bj$; that is, the real part is 0. Thus, the complex numbers are a superset of the real numbers.

[2] Sometimes mathematicians use i in place of j.

Python Complex Numbers

No special module need be imported for construction and basic operations using complex numbers.

```
In  [1]: c1 = 1 + 2j
In  [2]: c2 = complex(2,1)
In  [3]: c2
Out [3]: (2+1j)

In  [4]: c1.real
Out [4]: 1.0

In  [5]: c2.imag
Out [5]: 1.0

In  [6]: c1 + c2
Out [6]: (3+3j)

In  [7]: c1 - c2
Out [7]: (-1+1j)

In  [8]: c1 * c2
Out [8]: 5j

In  [9]: c1 / c2
Out [9]: (0.8+0.6j)

In  [10]: c1 == c2
Out [10]: False

In  [11]: c1 < c2
Traceback (most recent call last):
  File "<stdin>", line 1, in <module>
TypeError: unorderable types: complex() < complex()
In  [12]: data_lst = [c1, c2]
In  [13]: c1 in data_lst
Out [13]: True

In  [14]: sum(data_lst)
Out [14]: (3+3j)

In  [15]: import cmath
In  [16]: cmath.sqrt(c1)
Out [16]: (1.272019649514069+0.7861513777574233j)

In  [17]: cmath.sin(c1)
Out [17]: (3.165778513216168+1.959601041421606j)
```

To construct a complex number, you can use one of two notations:

a + bj: Just typing in the number in the proper format is a valid way to construct a complex number. Thus 1 + 2j creates the complex number $1 + 2j$.

complex(): The `complex` function can also be used to construct a complex number. Thus `complex(2,1)` creates the complex number $2 + 1j$.

accessors: You can access the real or imaginary part of a complex number using the `.real` of the `.imag` accessors. As with `Fraction` and `Decimal` numbers, the complex numbers are **immutable** and you cannot change a complex number's value using its accessors.

Basic operations are also defined, though you need to be careful about multiplication and division.

arithmetic: The operations +, −, *, and / are different for complex numbers and Python implements them correctly.

Comparison Operations:. Except for direct equality, none of the comparison operators work as there is no ordering of the complex numbers. Since there is no ordering, operations such as `max`, `min`, and `sort`, which depend on an ordering, also do not work. You **can** do a `sum` of a list of complex numbers or test for membership with ***`in`***. Other math operators are specialized for complex numbers, see the next section.

Complex Numbers and cmath

Most other math operations on complex numbers are special. Python provides a `cmath` module for complex number operations. We leave it to you to take a look at the documentation for more details[3] but the general classes of `cmath` operations include power and log functions such as `cmath.sqrt` and trigonometry functions such as `cmath.sin` and a number of other categories. Be aware that, for most calculations beyond simple math, you need special modules to work with complex numbers.

16.1.4 Statistics Module

Of all the elements in Section 16.1, the `statistics` module is probably the most useful since `statistics` has a place in every branch of science.[4] There is probably the most useful, as statistics has a place in every branch of science. This module does not provide a new number representation, but a set of functions that can be used to do statistical calculations on all the numbers, except complex, which we have just seen.

- All of these functions require a sequential data structure (a list, a tuple, a set) to process. That is, every function returns a value based on a data set from "list-like" data structures.

[3] `https://docs.python.org/3.4/library/cmath.html`

[4] `https://docs.python.org/3.4/library/statistics.html`

- All of the functions can take a "list" of int, *float*, `Decimal`, or `Fraction` and perform their operations. Again note that complex numbers **cannot** be used.
- It is recommended to **not mix** types. That is, the list contents should be of uniform type. Python does not guarantee results on mixed types, which could be implementation dependent.
- The `statistics` module has its own exception, `StatisticsError`, which is thrown if an assumption about the function is not met. For example, passing an empty list to any statistics function throws this error.

Following is a session that covers some of the functions and a description.

```
In  [1]: from decimal import Decimal
In  [2]: from fractions import Fraction
In  [3]: import statistics
In  [4]: fraction_list = [Fraction(1,2), Fraction(3,4), Fraction(1,8)]
In  [5]: decimal_list = [Decimal('1.1'), Decimal('5.6'), Decimal('3.14159')]
In  [6]: float_list = [123.45, 678.90, 1126.574]
In  [7]: statistics.mean(fraction_list)
Out [7]: Fraction(11, 24)

In  [8]: statistics.mean(decimal_list)
Out [8]: Decimal('3.28053')

In  [9]: statistics.mean(float_list)
Out [9]: 642.9746666666666

In  [10]: statistics.median(float_list)
Out [10]: 678.9

In  [11]: statistics.median([1,2,3,4])
Out [11]: 2.5

In  [12]: statistics.mode([1,1,2,3,4])
Out [12]: 1

In  [13]: statistics.mode([1,2,3,4])
Traceback (most recent call last):
  File "<stdin>", line 1, in <module>
  File "/opt/local/Library/Frameworks/Python.framework/Versions/3.4/lib/python3.4/
statistics.py", line 434, in mode
    'no unique mode; found %d equally common values' % len(table)
statistics.StatisticsError: no unique mode; found 4 equally common values
In  [14]: statistics.variance(float_list)
Out [14]: 252532.41202533332

In  [15]: statistics.stdev(float_list)
Out [15]: 502.5260311917516
```

Averages and Central Location

This set of functions provide information about the "centrality," the "middleness" if you will, of the list of data. There are a number of such functions but let's look at three in particular:

mean: Another word for mean is "average," the sum of all the data divided by the number of data. It is the average of the values found in the list.

median: The median returns one of two values. If the number of values in the list is odd, then the middle element in the sorted list will be returned (the list need not be sorted to begin with). If the numbers of values in the list is even, then the average of the two middle elements is returned.

mode: The mode returns the most common element in the list. Note that if there is not a "most common" element, that is there is more than one element with the same, largest occurrence count, an error is thrown.

Measures of Spread

This set of functions provides information on how spread the values are from the mean of the data.

variance: The variance is an indication of spread, how dispersed, the data is from the mean. Its units are the square of the list's units. A high value indicates more dispersion, a low value less dispersion. Note that the function requires a list of at least two values to operate, otherwise the `StatisticsError` is thrown.

stdev: The function measures the standard deviation, the square root of the variance. As it is a square root, its unit value is the same type as the list elements units. It is commonly used in measures for normal distributions.

If more sophisticated data analysis is needed, Python has a `pandas` module (included with the Anaconda distribution). It has many similarities to R so someone familiar with R[5] and Python will feel comfortable using `pandas`.

16.1.5 Random Numbers

We have mentioned random numbers and a few methods from the `random` module. However, just what does it mean to have a "random number" module and what does it do? Take a look at the following session:

```
In  [1]: random.seed(1)
In  [1]: for r in range(4):
Out [1]:         print(random.random())
```

[5] https://www.r-project.org/about.html

```
0.13436424411240122
0.8474337369372327
0.763774618976614
0.2550690257394217
In  [2]: random.seed(1)
In  [2]: for r in range(4):
Out [2]:         print(random.random())

0.13436424411240122
0.8474337369372327
0.763774618976614
0.2550690257394217
```

The session uses two of the module's functions:

seed(obj): Initializes the random number generator.
random(): Generates a random number in the range from 0.0 to 1.0.

Look what happened. We set the seed and then generated four random numbers. We set the seed again, to the same value, and generated four more random numbers. However, those four numbers were the same as the previous four! How is that random?

What the `random` package has are functions to generate what are called *pseudo-random* numbers. They are random numbers in the following sense: when looking at a sequence of generated "random" numbers, it is hard to predict what the next generated random number will be. The *sequence* looks random. However, the algorithm that generates the numbers *is* an algorithm. If you initialize it with the same seed, it will generate the same sequence. The sequence generated isn't random, but the elements within the sequence appear random relative to each other, even to sophisticated statistical tests.

To simulate what most people would consider random numbers, a random sequence, the `seed` function with no arguments will generate a seed value based on the present clock value on the local computer. As that value changes from microsecond to microsecond, it generates a sufficiently random sequence for most purposes.

Here is a list of functions that you might find useful in the module `random`.

randint(a,b): Generate a random integer N in the range $a \leq N \leq b$.
choice(sequence): Select a random element from the sequence and return it.
shuffle(sequence): Shuffle the order of the sequence in place.
sample(sequence, num): Generate a new sequence by sampling k elements from the original sequence.

The following session shows the use of some of these functions.

```
In  [1]: random.seed() # seed it to the clock
In  [1]: random.random()
Out [1]: 0.8906539974571333
```

```
In  [2]: random.randint(1,100)
Out [2]: 1

In  [3]: random.randint(1,100)
Out [3]: 31

In  [4]: random.randint(1,100)
Out [4]: 13

In  [5]: random.choice('abcdefgh')
Out [5]: 'f'

In  [6]: random.choice('abcdefgh')
Out [6]: 'h'

In  [7]: random.choice('abcdefgh')
Out [7]: 'f'

In  [8]: random.shuffle([1,2,3,4,5]) # shuffle is in place
In  [8]: a_list = [1,2,3,4,5]
In  [8]: random.shuffle(a_list)
In  [8]: a_list
Out [8]: [1, 3, 4, 5, 2]

In  [9]: random.shuffle(a_list)
In  [9]: a_list
Out [9]: [4, 1, 3, 5, 2]

In  [10]: random.shuffle(a_list)
In  [10]: a_list
Out [10]: [1, 3, 2, 4, 5]

In  [11]: random.sample(a_list,2)
Out [11]: [3, 4]

In  [12]: random.sample(a_list,2)
Out [12]: [4, 2]

In  [13]: random.sample(a_list,2)
Out [13]: [3, 2]
```

16.2 EVEN MORE ON FUNCTIONS

Because functions are such an important aspect of programming, Python has added quite a few features that make the programming and use of functions easier. They may not be essential to writing functions, but they can definitely be very useful! Let's take a look.

16.2.1 Having a Varying Number of Parameters

Imagine that you are faced with the task of reimplementing the standard Python **`print`** function with the same basic operation. You might start by writing a skeleton definition as we have frequently done, providing the name of the function and the list of parameters it needs.

However, at that point you already have a problem. How many parameters should a reimplementation of **`print`** have? That turns out to be a hard question to answer. Think about it, how many arguments might be provided in a **`print`** function call: 0, 2, 10, 100? The answer is that it varies, and having a varying number of arguments (and hence parameters) is a bit of a problem. What should we do? We could write the function with some large number of parameters, most with defaults, but that seems unwieldy.

What Python does (and other programming languages do as well) is to provide a way to pass a varying number of arguments to a function. In fact, Python provides *two* ways to deal with this problem.

Let's review two concepts: the difference between positional arguments and keyword arguments. Positional arguments are arguments that are provided in the function call at some position in the argument list. The argument is passed to the parameter based on their positions: the first argument to the first parameter and so on. Keyword arguments are designated in the call with an equal (=) sign. Keyword arguments are passed to parameters based on the name of the parameter.

It can be messy to mix keyword arguments and positional arguments in one function call. There is a detailed algorithm for how such a mix can occur, but here are two pieces of advice:

- Don't mix positional and keyword arguments because it can be tangled. If you don't do it right, you can get syntax errors.
- If you mix the two anyway, provide all the positional arguments first followed by keyword arguments, making sure you are not trying to "double assign" a parameter with both a positional and keyword argument.

With that in mind, let's look at the two approaches.

Multiple Positional Arguments

Python allows you to define a special parameter in the parameter list of a function definition that will gather all the extra positional arguments provided by a function call. What makes this parameter special is that it is preceded by an asterisk (*), sometimes called a star. Take a look at the following session.

```
In  [1]: def my_function (param1, param2, *param_rest):
...:     print('p1={}, p2={}, p3={}'.format(param1, param2, param_rest))

In  [2]: my_function(1,2)
Out [2]: p1=1, p2=2, p3=()
```

```
In  [3]: my_function(1,2,3,4,5)
Out [3]: p1=1, p2=2, p3=(3, 4, 5)

In  [4]: my_function('hi','mom','how','are','you')
Out [4]: p1=hi, p2=mom, p3=('how', 'are', 'you')

In  [5]: my_function(1) # need to provide at least 2 args
Traceback (most recent call last):
  File "<pyshell#7>", line 1, in <module>
    my_function(1)
TypeError: my_function() takes at least 2 arguments (1 given)
In  [6]: my_function(param1=1, param2=2, 3,4,5,6)
Out [6]: SyntaxError: non-keyword arg after keyword arg   # keyword args after
                                                           positional
```

Placing a single star in front of a parameter name means that any extra position arguments are gathered as a tuple and associated with that parameter. If no extra arguments are passed, then the starred parameter (such as `*param_rest`) has the value of an empty tuple. This means that, no matter how many arguments you pass, the starred parameter will store them. Note that in the session, the two arguments are required (two positional arguments before `*param_rest`) for the function call to proceed. The session demonstrates the "positional arguments first" error mentioned earlier.

Note you *cannot* use a starred parameter as a keyword argument. It is forbidden by Python syntax rules.

Multiple Keyword Arguments

Having provided a way to pass multiple positional arguments, Python also provides a way to pass an unknown number of keyword arguments where keyword parameters have not all been provided. That is, you can write an argument of the form `my_key=value` where `my_key` has not been defined as a parameter of the function. The following session demonstrates this process.

```
In  [1]: def a_function(param1, param2, **param_dict):
...:     print(param1, param2, param_dict)


In  [2]: a_function(1,2)
Out [2]: 1 2 {}

In  [3]: a_function(param2=1, param1=2)
Out [3]: 2 1 {}

In  [4]: a_function(param2=1, param1=2, new_key=10, another_key=20)
Out [4]: 2 1 {'new_key': 10, 'another_key': 20}
```

```
In  [5]: a_function(1,2, new_key=10, another_key=20)
Out [5]: 1 2 {'new_key': 10, 'another_key': 20}

In  [6]: a_function(1,2,3) # too many positional args
Traceback (most recent call last):
  File "<pyshell#28>", line 1, in <module>
    a_function(1,2,3)
TypeError: a_function() takes exactly 2 positional arguments (3 given)
```

In this case, the special parameter requires two stars (**). The two stars indicate that any extra keyword arguments are assigned to a dictionary stored in the two-starred parameter (such as `**param_dict`). The keywords are assigned as string keys in the dictionary. Thus, the call `bill=100` would create an entry `'bill':100` in the dictionary.

Using a two-starred parameter allows more freedom in mixing positional and keyword arguments. Positional arguments can be provided first in the argument list, followed by keyword arguments. However, only the number of positional arguments in the function definition can be used positionally. That is, a two-starred parameter will not pick up extra positional arguments.

As with a starred parameters, two-starred parameter names *cannot* be used as a keyword argument.

Both starred and two-starred parameters can be used in the same function as long as positional (starred) parameters preceded named (two-starred). Code Listing 16.1 illustrates such parameters in a program that creates a grade dictionary. It accepts the dictionary and a default grade as two positional arguments, then a variable number of students (who will be assigned the default grade), then a variable number of keyword arguments (student=grade) that will also be entered in the dictionary. The associated session is also shown.

Code Listing 16.1

```

def setup_grades (grade_dict, default_grade, *student_tuple, **special_dict):
    ''' Setup a grade dictionary. All students (variable number) get
        the default grade except for any keyword pairs provided
    '''
    for student in student_tuple:
        grade_dict[student] = default_grade

    for student,grade in special_dict.items():
        grade_dict[student] = grade


grade_dict = {}

```

```
setup_grades(grade_dict, 0, 'wanda', 'fred', 'irving', bill=100, rich=100)

for key,val in grade_dict.items():
    print('{:10} | {:5}'.format(key,val))
```

```
wanda      |     0
bill       |   100
irving     |     0
rich       |   100
fred       |     0
```

16.2.2 Iterators and Generators

Iterators have been discussed multiple times, especially iteration over a collection of elements. We know that all collections can be placed in a ***for*** loop and that, subsequently, the loop will move through every element of the collection.

We have not talked much about *how* iteration is done. In so doing, we can gain some insight into the underlying structure of Python, and even get an idea of how we might write our own classes so that they to could do iteration.

Iterator Objects

Like nearly everything else in Python, iterators are objects. As an object iterators support two attributes, a `__next__()` method and an `__iter__()` method. Both of these methods are more easily accessed using their respective Python built-in functions: `next` and `iter`. These two functions are relatively easy to understand:

next(an_iterator): The `next` function takes a single argument, an iterator, and returns the next element of the iteration. It raises a `StopError` exception when it reaches the end of the elements it can provide.

iter(an_iterator): The `iter` function takes as an argument an iterator and returns that iterator.

It is the `next` function that is at the heart of iteration. Consider the following session, which iterates through a file named "test.txt" with contents we have seen previously, namely:

```
First Line
Second Line
Third Line
Fourth Line
```

```
In  [1]: test_file = open('test.txt', 'r')
In  [2]: test_file
Out [2]: <_io.TextIOWrapper name='test.txt' mode='r' encoding='UTF-8'>
```

```
In  [3]: iter(test_file)
Out [3]: <_io.TextIOWrapper name='test.txt' mode='r' encoding='UTF-8'>

In  [4]: next(test_file)
Out [4]: 'First line\n'

In  [5]: next(test_file)
Out [5]: 'Second line\n'

In  [6]: next(test_file)
Out [6]: 'Third line\n'

In  [7]: next(test_file)
Out [7]: 'Fourth line\n'

In  [8]: next(test_file)
Traceback (most recent call last):
  File "<pyshell#7>", line 1, in <module>
    next(test_file)
StopIteration
In  [9]: next(test_file)
Traceback (most recent call last):
  File "<pyshell#8>", line 1, in <module>
    next(test_file)
StopIteration
```

A file object is, in fact, an iterator object. It can be used as an argument in both the `iter` and `next` function calls. When used in a `next` call, it yields the next item in iteration, a line of the file. Every subsequent call yields the next item (next line in this case) until no more items are available, at which point the `next` call yields a `StopIteration` exception, and will continue to do so for subsequent calls.

Iterator objects are interesting because they store some state information about the elements they are iterating over. That is, they "remember" what the last call of `next` provided and provide the following element (whatever the order may be for the elements of that type) for subsequent calls.

Collections and Iterator Objects

Collections themselves are not iterators. They cannot be used as an argument to the `next` method. However, all collections are iterable objects. By that we mean, we can create an iterator from any collection. We do this by use of the `iter` function.

iter(a_collection): Creates an iteration object for the particular collection.

When called with a collection as an argument, `iter` yields an iterator object specific for the type of collection (a *str* yields a `str_iterator`, a *list* a `list_iterator`, etc.). It is specific for the type as it matters what elements are provided and their order, depending on the type (a `str` the next character in the sequence, a `dict` one of the keys but without any implicit order, etc.). Each call of `next` on the iterator yields the next value. Note that if we use the `list` function with the iterator object as an argument, all the elements are provided and a list of the elements created. The session below shows working with iterators from collections.

```
In  [1]: range_object = range(10)
In  [2]: type(range_object)
Out [2]: range

In  [3]: next(range_object)
Traceback (most recent call last):
  File "<pyshell#32>", line 1, in <module>
    next(range_object)
TypeError: range object is not an iterator
In  [4]: range_iter = iter(range(10))
In  [5]: type(range_iter)
Out [5]: range_iterator

In  [6]: next(range_iter)
Out [6]: 0

In  [7]: next(range_iter)
Out [7]: 1

In  [8]: dict_iter = iter({'a':1, 'b':2, 'c':3})
In  [9]: type(dict_iter)
Out [9]: dict_keyiterator

In  [10]: next(dict_iter)
Out [10]: 'a'

In  [11]: next(dict_iter)
Out [11]: 'c'

In  [12]: next(dict_iter)
Out [12]: 'b'

In  [13]: next(dict_iter)
Traceback (most recent call last):
  File "<pyshell#41>", line 1, in <module>
    next(dict_iter)
StopIteration
In  [14]: = iter({'a':1, 'b':2, 'c':3})

['a', 'c', 'b']
```

*How **for** Works*

Given what we know now, it should be clear how a ***for*** loop works. When started, a ***for*** loop uses the `iter` function to create an iterator object from its target. If the target is already an iterator object, then `iter` returns that object. If the target is a collection, `iter` returns a new iterator object specific for that collection. The loop then calls the `next` function on the iterator object during each iteration of the loop. It continues to do so until the `next` function call results in a `StopIteraton` exception, which the ***for*** loop captures and uses to end the loop.

Generators

We can write our own functions that act like iterator objects. These are functions that yield a sequence of elements as a result of their operation, but yield them one at a time in response to a `next` call. As a result, these functions "remember" what element they yielded last and know what element to yield next.

We used the word "yield" in the previous paragraph, and there is a good reason for that. The only thing that differentiates a regular, every day function and a generator is a single Python keyword, `yield`. Instead of a ***return*** statement, generators use the `yield` statement to return values. In so doing, the function changes significantly. When a `yield` expression is evaluated, the associated function generates its next value, only its next value, returns it, and then *waits* for its next function call at the `yield`. When the function ends (cannot yield more data), the next call raises a `StopIteration` error. If you take a look back at the paragraph above, this generator looks a lot like an iterator. It is, in fact, a way to write your own iterator. Let's look at a session.

```
In  [1]: def regular_function(int_list, an_int):
        result_list=[]
        for num in int_list:
                result_list.append(num * an_int)
        return result_list

In  [2]: def generator_function(int_list, an_int):
        for num in int_list:
                yield num * an_int


In  [3]: regular_function([1,2,3], 5)
Out [3]: [5, 10, 15]

In  [4]: generator_function([1,2,3],5)
Out [4]: <generator object generator_function at 0x1018c1e10>

In  [5]: gen_object = generator_function([1,2,3],5)
In  [6]: next(gen_object)
Out [6]: 5
```

```
In  [7]: next(gen_object)
Out [7]: 10

In  [8]: next(gen_object)
Out [8]: 15

In  [9]: next(gen_object)
Traceback (most recent call last):
  File "<pyshell#62>", line 1, in <module>
    next(gen_object)
StopIteration
In  [10]: gen_object = generator_function([1,2,3],5)
In  [11]: list(gen_object)
Out [11]: [5, 10, 15]
```

We wrote two versions of a function that multiplies each element of a list of integers by an integer argument. The first, `regular_function`, iterates through the list, multiplies each element by the integer parameter, and collects up the results in a list `result_list`. This list is returned. The second version, `generator_function`, performs the same operation but with two differences:

- This function uses the `yield` statement instead of the ***`return`*** statement.
- As a result, no intermediate `result_list` is created and returned. Each result is yielded individually.

It is also interesting to note the result of the invocations of the two functions. The first yields a list result as expected. The second simply returns a *generator object*. That generator object can then be used as an argument to the `next` function to yield the next result in the sequence. When all the results have been provided, subsequent calls to `next` raise a `StopIteration` error. If we use a generator object as the argument to the *`list`* function, it captures all the elements of the generator in a list. See, a generator looks very much like an iterator!

Why Generators?

Why would having such a thing as a generator be useful? You can write a generator to *represent* a sequence of elements without actually having to generate all the elements in that sequence. Like the *range* function, a generator is a representation of a sequence that could be very long, but only a representation, not the sequence. In fact, you can write a generator to represent a sequence that is *infinitely* long. Remember the Fibonacci sequence from Section 15.2? We wrote the solution to that sequence recursively, but here is a generator version of the Fibonacci sequence (Code Listing 16.2).

Code Listing 16.2

```
def fibo_generator():
    first, second = 0,1
    while True:
        yield first
        first,second = second, first + second

fibo_generator_object = fibo_generator()

print(next(fibo_generator_object))
print(next(fibo_generator_object))

for count in range(100):
    print(next(fibo_generator_object), end=', ')
```

How many elements of the series will this program generate. As many as you like. Every call to `next` will yield the next value. This generator really does represent the series, and *all* the elements of the series can be generated by this function. Yet, we only get as many as we wish. Generators can be very useful in this way.

16.2.3 Other Functional Programming Ideas

Though we have not talked explicitly about it, we have really worked with two different programming paradigms in Python:

Procedural: Procedural programming is the use of instructions, followed line by line, that changes the values of variables and other elements using built-in or user-defined functions.

Object Oriented: Object-oriented programming uses classes and instances as a way to encapsulate programming elements and provide interfaces to those elements via methods

There is another (there are in fact many other) programming paradigm that Python also provides access to, called **Functional** programming. Functional programming is focused on the use of functions, but functions that do not have "side effects" as we have often seen. A function in this paradigm focuses on taking inputs, doing a computation, and providing outputs without side-effects.

The use of generators, iterators, and comprehensions are a kind of functional programming. These are functions that take inputs, provide outputs but without side effects. You can chain the output of one as the input of another and create complicated programs that rarely set values, only pass data elements through functions. There are a few other functional elements you can find in Python. Let's look at a few.

Anonymous Functions, Lambda

There is a special way to define a function called a *lambda expression*. The word *lambda* is a kind of homage to the original method used to define functional programming, the lambda calculus.[6] However, for our purposes it is a regular function definition with three restrictions:

- The body of a lambda expression can contain only a single line.
- The body can only contain an expression (something which returns a value), no statements or other elements.
- The result of the expression is automatically returned, no **return** statement is required (or allowed).

The form of a lambda is:

```
lambda arg_list: expression
```

The following session shows some examples.

```
In  [1]: def add_func (int1, int2):
...:     return int1 + int2

In  [2]: add_lambda = lambda int1,int2: int1 + int2
In  [3]: add_func(2,3)
Out [3]: 5

In  [4]: add_lambda(2,3)
Out [4]: 5
```

You might ask as why this style is useful? It has two uses. One, anywhere an expression can be used, you can use a lambda as it is, in effect, an expression (it always returns something, it has to). Second, if you need a function for something but only for some small task, you can use a lambda. A lambda is essentially an "anonymous function," a function without a name. Some applications that follow will show how you might use a lambda.

16.2.4 Some Functional Programming Tools

The three functions `map`, `filter`, and `reduce` (reduce is in in the module `functools`) are good examples of functional programming tools.

map: This function takes as arguments a function and one or more iterables. For one iterable, the function should take one argument: two iterables, two arguments. It applies the provided function to each element of the iterable(s). It returns an interable, a map object.

[6] http://palmstroem.blogspot.com/2012/05/lambda-calculus-for-absolute-dummies.html

filter: This function takes as arguments a Boolean function and an iterable. It applies the function to each element of the iterable and collects those elements for which the function returns True. It returns an iterable, a filter object.

reduce: This function is part of the `functools` module. It takes as arguments a function of two arguments and an iterable. The function is applied first to the first two elements of the iterable, then reapplied to the previous result and the third element of the iterable, then reapplied to the previous result and the fourth element, and so on. It returns the value that results from the application.

An example of their use is shown in the following session.

```
In  [1]: map_result1 = map(lambda x: x + 1, [1,2,3,4,5])
In  [2]: map_result1
Out [2]: <map object at 0x1018c7290>

In  [3]: list(map_result1)
Out [3]: [2, 3, 4, 5, 6]

In  [4]: list(map_result1)
Out [4]: []

In  [5]: map_result2 = map(lambda x,y: x + y, [1,2,3,4,5], [10,20,30,40,50])
In  [6]: list(map_result2)
Out [6]: [11, 22, 33, 44, 55]

In  [7]: filter_result1 = filter(lambda x : x.isdigit(), 'abc123')
In  [8]: filter_result1
Out [8]: <filter object at 0x1018c75d0>

In  [9]: list(filter_result1)
Out [9]: ['1', '2', '3']

In  [10]: from functools import reduce
In  [11]: reduce_result = reduce(lambda x,y: x + y, [1,2,3,4,5])
In  [12]: reduce_result
Out [12]: 15
```

A couple of things to note:

- With both `map` and `filter`, the return result is an iterable. If you use the result as an argument to *`list`*, the contents of the iterable are shown.
- Again, with both `map` and `filter`, the result, once iterated over, is exhausted. Further iteration yields no value.
- We used only lambda expressions in the examples (since we just talked about them), but any function with the correct number of arguments would work.

16.2.5 Decorators: Functions Calling Functions

Of all the interesting things you can do with functions, the Python *decorator* is not only one of the most interesting, but also one of the hardest to understand, at least the first time through. Once you understand it, we think you will find them very useful, but it takes a little work. Here we go.

Imagine you have written a set of functions that each perform the same task, say add up all the integers in a list of integers, but you'd like to know which one is faster. How can you do this without changing the functions?

One way is shown in Code Listing 16.3.

Code Listing 16.3

```python
import time

def add_list1 (int_list):
    ''' add a list of ints, iteration '''
    result_sum=0
    for num in int_list:
        result_sum = result_sum + num
    return result_sum

def add_list2(int_list):
    ''' add a list of ints, use builtin sum'''
    return sum(int_list)

def timer_func(int_list):
    t1 = time.time()
    add_list1(int_list)
    t2 = time.time()
    print("First function took {:7f} seconds".format(t2 - t1))

    t1 = time.time()
    add_list2(int_list)
    t2 = time.time()
    print("First function took {:7f} seconds".format(t2 - t1))


# big list
int_list = list(range(100000))

# run timer
timer_func(int_list)
```

We define the two functions, `add_list1` and `add_list2` which are the functions we want to test. The first iterates through the list, adding up the values. The second uses the built-in `sum` function.

We then define a third function, `timer_func`. The `timer_func` uses the `time` module, in particular the `time.time` function (the function time in the module time). The `time.time` function returns the present time to some number of fractions of a second depending on the operating system you are using.

To time a particular invocation of one of our two functions, we then *wrap* around the function call two invocations of `time.time`. The difference between the two times should be the difference it took to run the function. We do this for both functions.

The following session shows the result of running our code. Note that the time varies depending on how much other stuff is going on in your computer, but the general difference is shown: the built-in approach is definitely faster.

```
In  [1]: runfile('/Users/user/python/file.py', wdir='/Users/user/python')

First took 0.0063229 seconds
Second took 0.0014639 seconds


In  [2]: runfile('/Users/user/python/file.py', wdir='/Users/user/python')

First took 0.0077262 seconds
Second took 0.0019238 seconds


In  [3]: runfile('/Users/user/python/file.py', wdir='/Users/user/python')

First took 0.0072241 seconds
Second took 0.0014629 seconds


In  [4]: runfile('/Users/user/python/file.py', wdir='/Users/user/python')

First took 0.0072711 seconds
Second took 0.0018129 seconds
```

What we showed was that we can write an extra timer function, and every time we need to time a function we can modify the timer function to include the new function to time. That works, but it is inconvenient. We don't have to rewrite the function we want to time but we do have to rewrite the timer function. That seems kind of silly in a way, because what we do, the wrapping part, is *exactly* the same except for the particular function we are timing. Can we get around that?

Well, the answer is yes, but let us do it in two parts.

Passing a Function Object as a Parameter

We have said this before, but let us say it again. Everything in Python is an object, and a function is no different. As such, we can pass a function as a parameter to *another* function (in this case, our `timer_func`) and have the parameter-function invoked inside `timer_func`. That's worth saying again. We can pass a function as a parameter and invoke the passed function wherever we pass it to. How to do that? Execution of a function is indicated by adding an argument list to the end of the function name. If it is a function, it is invoked. If not, you get an `TypeError`, indicating it is not a callable item. Take a look at Code Listing 16.4 and session.

Code Listing 16.4

```python
import time
import functools

def add_list1 (int_list):
    ''' add a list of ints, iteration'''
    result_sum=0
    for num in int_list:
        result_sum = result_sum + num
    return result_sum

def add_list2(int_list):
    ''' add a list of ints, use builtin sum'''
    return sum(int_list)

def add_list3(int_list):
    ''' use a map to do the addition '''
    return functools.reduce(lambda x,y: x + y, int_list)

def timer_func(int_list, *func_tuple):
    ''' time a tuple of functions and report '''
    func_counter = 1

    for func in func_tuple:
        t1 = time.time()
        func(int_list)
        t2 = time.time()
        print("Function {} took {:7f} seconds".format(func_counter, t2 - t1))
        func_counter += 1

# big list
int_list = list(range(100000))

# run timer
timer_func(int_list, add_list1, add_list2, add_list3)
```

```
Function 1 took 0.006709 seconds
Function 2 took 0.001549 seconds
Function 3 took 0.015519 seconds
In  [1]: add_list1
Out [1]: <function add_list1 at 0x1020cee20>

In  [2]: add_list1(int_list)
Out [2]: 4999950000

In  [3]: renamed_func = add_list1
In  [4]: renamed_func
Out [4]: <function add_list1 at 0x1020cee20>

In  [5]: renamed_func(int_list)
Out [5]: 4999950000

In  [6]: my_int = 10
In  [7]: my_int(int_list)
Traceback (most recent call last):
  File "<pyshell#10>", line 1, in <module>
    my_int(int_list)
TypeError: 'int' object is not callable
```

We did a few things here. First, we added yet another test function, `add_list3` that used `reduce` and a lambda function.

Second, the session shows that a function is just like any other object. We can assign the function object to another name, here `renamed_func` and still invoke it under the new name. Only a function is callable, and Python reports an error if you try to call a non-function.

Third, and more importantly, we really changed `timer_func`. Instead of taking a single parameter, a list of integers to add, we also provided a varying length, positional argument of *functions*. We pass in the functions we want to run, and run them. For each function we run, we wrap the function with time checks and invoke the function with the list of integers. We can pass as many functions to test as we like to `timer_func` and it will time all of them! Note how `timer_func` is invoked. It now passes all the functions we want to test as parameters. Note that the `reduce` lambda combination is the slowest.

Decorators

The previous example was an improvement because we wrote a function that accepts other functions as parameters. We can then invoke the passed function and wrap whatever we need around the invocation, such as timing information. Can we do better than that?

Yes, a little better. It would be even better if we could find a way to automatically do the wrapping *on the function* itself instead of calling a separate wrapper function. That is, could we easily turn on or turn off the kind of wrapping we are doing by somehow augmenting the function itself? That, in essence, is what a decorator does. Let's look at it first in Code Listing 16.5 then explain it.

Code Listing 16.5

```
import time
import functools

def timer_decorator(func):
    ''' time a tuple of functions and report '''
    def wrapper(int_list):
        t1 = time.time()
        result = func(int_list)
        t2 = time.time()
        print("Function took {:7f} seconds".format(t2 - t1))
        return result
    return wrapper

# decorate add_list1
@timer_decorator
def add_list1 (int_list):
    ''' add a list of ints, iteration '''
    result_sum=0
    for num in int_list:
        result_sum = result_sum + num
    return result_sum

# @timer_decorator comment out decoration
def add_list2(int_list):
    ''' add a list of ints, use builtin sum'''
    return sum(int_list)
# and do it by hand
add_list2 = timer_decorator(add_list2)

@timer_decorator
def add_list3(int_list):
    ''' use a map to do the addition '''
    return functools.reduce(lambda x,y: x + y, int_list)

int_list = list(range(100000))

print(add_list1(int_list))
print(add_list2(int_list))
print(add_list3(int_list))
```

```
Function took 0.007209 seconds
4999950000
Function took 0.001441 seconds
4999950000
Function took 0.013848 seconds
4999950000
```

The big idea here is found in the `timer_decorator` function. Note that it takes a function parameter as we have seen before. The `timer_decorator` function also wraps the function parameter with timing calls as before. However, the big differences are:

Line 6: Inside `timer_decorator` we defined another function, here called `wrapper`, that does the wrapping.

Line 12: What `timer_decorator` returns is the internally define function `wrapper`.

What does all that mean, wrapping the provided parameter function inside another function and returning that function? Take a look at **Line 15** and **Line 29**. **Line 29** decorates the function `add_list1`, and **Line 29** does the decoration by hand. Look at that **Line 29**. What we have done is pass, as an argument, the original function (`add_list2`) to the decorator. The decorator creates a new function, which wraps the original function, then *reassigns* the new wrapper function to the same name as the parameter function. Having run that code, the parameter to `time_decorator`, used in `wrapper`, points to the original function we are trying to wrap, and the original name of that function we are trying to wrap is associated with the returned function `wrapper`. Since the `wrapper` function (which is now also the `add2_list` function) takes a single argument, we call the new function with that single argument. That's all a decorator does: change the original function to be associated with the new wrapped function.

Note a couple of things:

- Running a decorator *changes* the function that is decorated to be the wrapped function in the decorator.
- It is easy to turn decoration on and off. Just comment/uncomment the decorator and reload the code.

Why Is This a "Good Thing"

With decorators, we now have the ability to modify the operation of a function without ever changing the definition of the function. We just "wrap" whatever changes we want around the function to change its behavior. We can even wrap built-in functions, functions to which we do not have the definition, and change their behavior *and* we can turn it on and off at will. Very handy indeed!

16.3 CLASSES

Writing your own classes is an important part of Python programming. Python provides some advanced tools to aid in the writing of classes. We will look at a few of them here.

16.3.1 Properties

VideoNote 16.1
Properties

You are probably familiar with writing spreadsheets using applications such as Excel. When writing a spreadsheet, there are two kinds of elements (more really, but we care about two here) that you can put in the spreadsheet: actual values or a calculation that depends on actual values. Figure 16.1 shows a very simple spreadsheet.

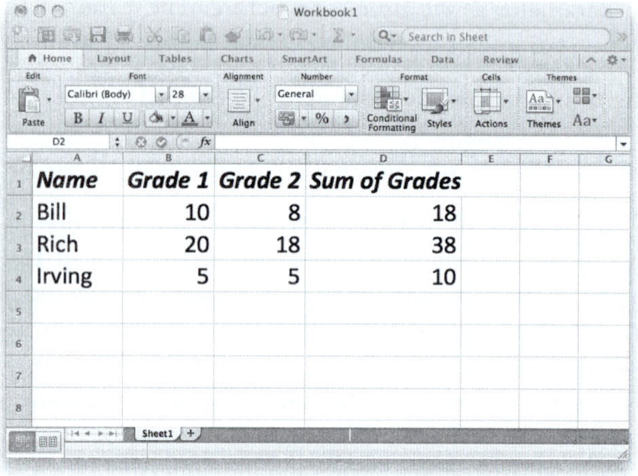

FIGURE 16.1 A simple spreadsheet with a formula. [Excel 2016, Windows 10, Microsoft Corporation.]

The fourth column, labeled "Sum of Grades" is not a value, it is a formula. It adds the previous two values in the row, creating the sum value. If either of those two values are ever modified, the formula will upgrade the sum to reflect that change. One way to phrase this is to say that any change to one of the grade values will *trigger* a change to the formula result. It triggers this update automatically, which is why spreadsheets are so useful.

It would be nice to have the same kind of "trigger" mechanism in our instances. If we need a particular attribute of an instance to depend on other attributes, then whenever the other attributes are changed, the trigger attribute will update itself based on these changes, just like a spreadsheet. How can we do this?

Python provides *properties* as a way to write trigger functions for an attribute. It does this in a very nice way. The normal way to fetch or set a value from the point of view of the person using the attribute does not change. They can `print(my_instance.attribute)` or `my_instance.attribute = 10` just like they normally would. However, we the class designers can change these attributes to be functions (triggers), not just values.

Python provides three activities that can be "triggered": the setting of an attribute, the fetching of an attribute, and the deletion of an attribute (though this is less commonly used). The first two are often called "setters" and "getters": functions used to set and get an attribute values.

Let's take a look at a simple example. We will create a `Circle` class that has attributes `radius`, `area`, and `circumference`. The behavior we want is that, whenever `radius` is set then the other two values are properly updated. Furthermore, neither `area` nor `circumference` should be settable: only `radius`. Lets take a look at Code Listing 16.6.

Code Listing 16.6

```python
from math import pi

class Circle (object):
    ''' only allows setting radius. When radius is set, area and circumference
        are updated. Neither area nor circumference can be set
    '''
    def __init__(self, rad=1):
        self.__radius = rad
        self.__circumference = 2*pi*rad
        self.__area = rad*rad*pi
    def __str__(self):
      return 'Radius={:.2f}, Circumference={:.2f}, Area={:.2f}'.\
            format(self.__radius, self.__circumference, self.__area)

    # propety functions
    def get_radius(self):
        print('in get_radius')
        return self.__radius
    def set_radius(self,rad):
        print('in set_radius')
        self.__radius = rad
        self.__circumference = 2*pi*rad
        self.__area = rad*rad*pi
    def get_area(self):
        print('in get_area')
        return self.__area
    def get_circumference(self):
        print('in get_circumference')
        return self.__circumference

    #property attributes
    radius = property(fget=get_radius,fset=set_radius)
    circumference = property(fget=get_circumference)
    area = property(fget=get_area)
```

```
In [1]: default_circle = Circle()
In [2]: new_circle = Circle(2)
In [3]: print(default_circle)
```

```
Radius=1.00, Circumference=6.28, Area=3.14
In  [4]: print(new_circle)
Radius=2.00, Circumference=12.57, Area=12.57
In  [5]: new_circle.radius
Out [5]: in get_radius

2
In  [6]: new_circle.radius = 4
in set_radius
In  [7]: print(new_circle)
Radius=4.00, Circumference=25.13, Area=50.27
In  [8]: new_circle.area = 4
Traceback (most recent call last):
  File "<pyshell#19>", line 1, in <module>
    new_circle.area = 4
AttributeError: can't set attribute
In  [9]: dir(new_circle)
Out [9]: ['_Circle__area', '_Circle__circumference', '_Circle__radius',
          '__class__', '__delattr__', '__dict__', '__doc__', '...

 '__sizeof__', '__str__', 'area', 'circumference', 'get_area', 'get_circumference',
          'get_radius', 'radius', 'set_radius']
```

Some important ideas to pay attention to:

- The `__init__` function defines three attributes with double underlines (__) (**Lines 8–10**). These indicate privacy. However, remember how to access them. Inside the class methods they are accessed normally. Outside the class methods, they get "mangled" with the class name: so `__area` gets mangled to `_Circle__area`. The `dir` function shows this for the class instance `new_circle`.
- We define four methods as our trigger functions: three getters (`get_radius`, `get_area`, and `get_circumference`) and one setter (`set_radius`).
- All four of the trigger methods work with the *private* variables defined in `__init__`. We'll see why in a minute.
- Finally, the interesting part. At the very end (**Lines 32–34**) we define three new attributes and set them as properties using the `property` function. The `property` function takes three keyword arguments: `fget`, `fset`, and `fdel`. Each is a function that gets triggered under the appropriate access:
  - `fget` is the function triggered on a get (a fetch of the property value).
  - `fset` is the function triggered on a set (a setting of the property value).
  - `fdel` is the function triggered on the deletion of a property value

We defined three properties in our class. We can access those properties as if they were normal attributes. To make that obvious we have placed ***`print`*** statements in the getters and setters (**Lines 17, 20, 25, 28**). We don't need these prints for the class, but they let us know what functions are being run (we can comment them out later).

In the session, when we write `new_circle.radius`, it triggers the `get_radius` method as that is the function we associated with the `fget` property of `radius` (**Line 32**). Note what happens when we try to do `new_circle.area=4`. Since we did not provide an `fget` for the `area` property (**Line 34**), there is no way to set that attribute. We have made it a read only attribute!

Effectively, we have made two sets of attributes in our class: the private attributes and the public property attributes. If the class user only uses the property attributes, then by setting the `radius`, all other values are updated automatically. If the user tries to update the other attributes, they get an error. The associated methods manipulate the private variables, which store the actual values. Thus, the properties are the public face of the class, and the private attributes are "hidden."

Properties give us a more powerful way to control how a class user accesses our class. Properties are an *active* control on how the class gets used.

16.3.2 Serializing an Instance: `pickle`

Imagine you have developed a GradeClass for recording grades. Inside this class is a dictionary, where the dictionary keys are the names of the students and the values are a tuple of the recorded grades. You want to create an instance of this GradeClass for each class, develop a nice interface to initialize, modify the contents of the instance. All very nice!

However, let's imagine that you want to work with this class instance over the course of the semester (grades come in over time, remember?). Therefore, you want to be able to store and reload the instance and its contents so you can save the *state* of the instance. You don't want to forget any grades, and you want to update them over time. How are you going to do this? You could develop your own way to record the contents of an instance and reestablish it, but that is likely a lot of work. Again, Python to the rescue.

Python implements what is called a *serialization* protocol. It is a big word, but serialization means that we take a set of elements (objects, variables, etc.) and turn them into a sequence that we can save, hence the serializing of the objects. The sequence that serialization creates is a series of instructions which, when executed, recreate the original object and its contents. This means you can save your data structures and their contents, and later reload them and pick up where you left off. Very nice.

Python provides a couple of ways to serialize objects, but the best is the `pickle` module (and its close cousin, the `cPickle`, which is much faster). The main methods are:

dumps(obj): This method creates the serialization string that can recreate the provided object.

dump(obj, file) This method stores the serialization string of the object to a file object. The file must have been opened for writing as a binary file.

load(file): This method loads from a file object whose file contains pickle strings and recreates the object. The file associated must be opened for reading as a binary file.

Code Listing 16.7 creates a *very* simple implementation of a `Grades` class. The session creates a `Grades` instance, fills it with grades, dumps the contents of the `Grades` instance to a file and then reloads it.

Code Listing 16.7

```python
import pickle

class Grades(object):
    ''' grades are a list of tuples: test,grade'''
    def __init__(self, name='', semester='FS12'):
        self.grades_dict = {}
        self.class_name = name
        self.semester = semester

    def add_name(self, name):
        self.grades_dict[name] = []

    def add_grade(self, name, grade):
        try:
            self.grades_dict[name].append(grade)
        except KeyError:
            print("Bad name, can't add grade")

    def __str__(self):
        ''' print in alphabetical order'''
        grade_list = list(self.grades_dict.items())
        grade_list.sort()
        result_str = ''
        result_str += 'Class:'+self.class_name+', Semester:'+self.semester+'\n'
        for student in grade_list:
            result_str += 'Student:{:10}, Grades:{}\n'.format(student[0],
                         student[1])
        return result_str
```

```
In  [1]: grades = Grades("cse231", "FS11")
In  [2]: for name in ['bill', 'rich', 'irving']:
...:     grades.add_name(name)

In  [3]: print(grades)
Class:cse231, Semester:FS11
Student:bill      , Grades:[]
Student:irving    , Grades:[]
Student:rich      , Grades:[]
```

```
In  [4]: grades.add_grade('rich', ('mid1', 100))
In  [4]: grades.add_grade('rich', ('mid2', 50))
In  [4]: grades.add_grade('rich', ('final', 75))
In  [4]: grades.add_grade('bill', ('mid1', 50))
In  [4]: grades.add_grade('bill', ('mid2', 50))
In  [4]: grades.add_grade('bill', ('final', 50))
In  [4]: print(grades)
Out [4]: Class:cse231, Semester:FS11

Student:bill      , Grades:[('mid1', 50), ('mid2', 50), ('final', 50)]
Student:irving    , Grades:[]
Student:rich      , Grades:[('mid1', 100), ('mid2', 50), ('final', 75)]

In  [5]: pickle.dumps(grades)
Out [5]: b'\x80\x03c__main__\nGrades\nq\x00)\x81q\x01}q\x02(X\n\x00\x00\
x00class_nameq\x03X\x06\x00\x00\x00cse231q\x04X\x08\x00\x00\x00semesterq\x05X\x04\
x00\x00\x00FS11q\x06X\x0b\x00\x00\x00grades_dictq\x07}q\x08(X\x04\x00\x00\x00billq\
t]q\n(X\x04\x00\x00\x00mid1q\x0bK2\x86q\x0cX\x04\x00\x00\x00mid2q\rK2\x86q\x0eX\x05
\x00\x00\x00finalq\x0fK2\x86q\x10eX\x06\x00\x00\x00irvingq\x11]q\x12X\x04\x00\x00\
x00richq\x13]q\x14(X\x04\x00\x00\x00mid1q\x15Kd\x86q\x16X\x04\x00\x00\x00mid2q\
x17K2\x86q\x18X\x05\x00\x00\x00finalq\x19KK\x86q\x1aeuub.'

In  [6]: grade_file = open('cse231.grades', 'wb')
In  [7]: pickle.dump(grades, grade_file)
In  [7]: grade_file.close()

In  [7]: runfile('/Users/user/python/file.py', wdir='/Users/user/python')

Traceback (most recent call last):
  File "<pyshell#16>", line 1, in <module>
    grades
NameError: name 'grades' is not defined
In  [9]: grade_file = open('cse231.grades', 'rb')
In  [10]: reloaded_grades = pickle.load(grade_file)
In  [11]: print(reloaded_grades)
Class:cse231, Semester:FS11
Student:bill      , Grades:[('mid1', 50), ('mid2', 50), ('final', 50)]
Student:irving    , Grades:[]
Student:rich      , Grades:[('mid1', 100), ('mid2', 50), ('final', 75)]
```

We load the program, which restarts Python, and proceed to create some grades which we store in the class instance associated with `grades`. We `dumps` the object associated with `grades` to see the (mostly unreadable) serialization of the object. We then open a *binary* file for writing. It must be binary because the serialization object is a series of `bytes` (bytes is a Python type, see the next section), not a string or other "readable" type. We `dump` the object to the file and close the file.

We can then restart Python and load the `Grades` class file. We need the definition of the `Grades` class to be loaded into the shell so that the saved instructions will operate properly, recreating the saved instance. We then open the same file for reading as a binary file and call the `load` function. The new object is associated with a new variable name, which when we ***print***, showing we reobtained the same values.

Restrictions

There are some restrictions on serialization that we have to pay attention to:

- By default, we cannot serialize a file object's connection to a file. In general, we cannot serialize any resource connected to the operating system of the machine we are running on.
- Serializing instances (as we did) requires that the class definition be loaded and not nested inside another class or other scope. It must be available at the top-level of the shell or module.
- Pickle is not considered secure. The file that is created can be modified and the resulting loaded object changed.

16.4 OTHER THINGS IN PYTHON

The list of things we have not covered is quite long, but here are a couple of other things in Python you might want to take a look at:

16.4.1 Data Types

Python has the following built-in data types that we have not covered:

bytes, bytearray The `bytes` type is an immutable array of 8-bit bytes ($0 \leq byte \leq 255$). The `bytearray` is a mutable array of the same type.

frozenset An immutable set.

collections There are a number of other datatypes in the `collections` module.

namedtupel: A way to create a new subclass of *`tuple`* that has all the properties of a *`tuple`* but also named attributes.

OrderedDict: A dictionary that "remembers" the order in which elements were added. It can be used to create a sorted dictionary.

deque: Pronounced "deck," this is a listlike data structure with fast access (`append` or `pop`) to either end.

16.4.2 Built-in Modules

Python has a large number of built-in modules. Here are a few interesting ones:

calendar: Module to support making calendars.

functools: More tools to support functional programming.

array: Sequence of same-type numeric values, more efficient.
shelve: A "permanent" dictionary, whose keys and values are stored in a file via `pickle`.
e-mail: A module to manipulate MIME types and e-mail contents.
urllib.request: A way to request web content over the Internet via Python calls.
http.server: A way to establish a web server in Python.
tkinter: Python's default 2D graphics library and GUI development system.
pdb: The Python debugger, for understanding the cause of errors and fixing them.
timeit, trace: Profiling tools to figure out where your Python programming is spending all of its computational resources.

16.4.3 Modules on the Internet

Of course, one of the best things about Python are the large numbers of modules that other developers make available to share with Python users. The best way to look at such modules is through the Python Package Index (pypi) at `http://pypi.python.org`. Here are some great modules that you might want to take a look at.

pygame: Module for developing graphics and audio to support gaming in Python.
Vpython: Visual Python is a stunning package that makes it very easy to create 3D graphics with animation.
nltk: The Natural Language Toolkit, a Python implementation of many tools to work with natural language.
django: A framework for the development of websites using Python.
pyWemSMS: pyWebSMS is a program, which let you send sms through Internet without opening any browser.
python-itunes: A simple python wrapper to access the iTunes Store API.
biopython: Tools for computational molecular biology.
ephem: A toolkit for high precision astronomical calculations.
ChemKit: Artificial Chemistry Kit, a spin-off topic of Artificial Life. AChem is aimed at emergence of life from nonliving environment—primordial soup.
music21: A Toolkit for Computer-Aided Musical Analysis and Manipulation.

There are so many more than that are available. Take a look and see if you can find the Python module that fits your needs, or write your own and publish it in pypi.

CHAPTER 17

The End, or Perhaps the Beginning

> Every new beginning comes from some other beginning's end.
>
> Lucius Annaeus Seneca, Roman philosopher

We have reached the end of our programming journey. However, it is really not the end. You will surely continue on, learning more about programming, expanding your problem-solving abilities, and hopefully doing wonderful things with Python.

We feel the same way. Programming is a dynamic process, with new topics popping up all the time. Please check the Pearson website for the book at `http://www.pearsonhighered.com/educator/product/Practice-of-Computing-Using-Python-plus-MyProgrammingLab-with-Pearson-eText-Access-Card-Package-The/9780132992831.page`

At this site, we plan on posting new material that we think you, as Python programmers, might find interesting. They might be proto-chapters that we are working on, new exercises, other web connections, anything of interest to us and, hopefully, to you as well.

So please stop by and see what is new and exciting. We wish you a happy programming journey.

APPENDIX A

Getting and Using Python

A.1 ABOUT PYTHON

A.1.1 History

PYTHON WAS CONCEIVED IN THE 1980'S BY GUIDO VAN ROSSUM, AND THE FIRST version was published in 1991. It was designed around a philosophy that emphasized the importance of programmer effort over computer effort, so it prioritized readability. Python is often characterized as minimalist, but only with respect to the core language's syntax and semantics. Both of these characteristics make it appropriate for a first language. The large number of modules developed to support Python allows it to be used in a wide variety of environments, which greatly enhances its utility beyond a first language. That is, it offers the best of both worlds: it's readable and powerful to use.

An important goal of the Python developers was to make it fun to use. This goal is reflected in the origin of the name (after the television series *Monty Python's Flying Circus*), in the common practice of using Monty Python references in example code, and in an occasionally playful approach to tutorials and reference materials. For example, although many programming languages choose the nonsense words *foo* or *bar* for arbitrary variable names in examples, one is more likely to find *nit* and *spam* in Python literature. We will hold to that Python tradition.

A.1.2 Python 3

In December of 2008 Python 3.0 was released, which is a new version of the language that is both more stable and more consistent. The change was significant in that the new Python was designed such that older (e.g., Python 2) programs would not run under it.

Python 3 is not a wholesale re-writing of the Python language, but it does fix many fundamental issues. One of the downsides of such a big change is that existing packages have to be rewritten. Changes are proceeding, and Python 3 is fast becoming the new standard for Python programming.

In this book, we focus strictly on Python 3 programs. We do not even discuss conversion from Python 2 to Python 3. If you are starting to program today (and that is the intended audience of this book), you should start with Python 3.

A.1.3 Python Is Free and Portable

An important characteristic of Python is that the language and many of its components are *free*. It is also important to note that Python is *mostly* agnostic when it comes to operating systems. You can run Python on a Windows machine, a Macintosh machine, or under any of the Unix variants out there, especially Linux. Even more useful is that a Python program written on one kind of machine should run exactly the same on another (except when you use operating-system-specific code). This portability means that you can work in *your* favorite environment. You can also move to a new environment, and your Python program should run there as well. Very convenient!

There are many ways to obtain a Python distribution and its associated modules. Many operating systems, such as OS X (apple) and Linux, typically come with a Python pre-installed. However, it can be difficult to assure that the Python version is consistent (is your preinstalled Python a 3.x version or the older 2.x version, for example) and that packages are pre-installed for your convenience.

As a result, we are recommending using the Anaconda distribution of Python available at `https://continuum.io/downloads`. This distribution has many advantages over using a pre-installed version or even doing it yourself including:

- Despite the fact that this is a distribution from a company, it is still free!
- You can select which version to install. We are using the Python 3.5 version.
- It comes with a large number of packages pre-installed, saving you a lot of work. If you want to experiment with new packages, they are likely already there. Take a look at `http://docs.continuum.io/anaconda/pkg-docs` under the Python 3.x tab.
- It installs Python and all the packages to a separate directory. If you need another version (say the pre-installed version) you can use that separately from the Anaconda distribution. If you decide you don't like Anaconda, deleting the directory will remove it from your system completely.

A word about downloading. Anaconda provides a number of versions that you can download. It is important for *this* book that you get the Python 3.x version as we assume that version for the work we do. If you go to the download page, `https://continuum.io/downloads` make sure you notice the "Python 3.5" link so you can get the correct version as shown in Figure A.1.

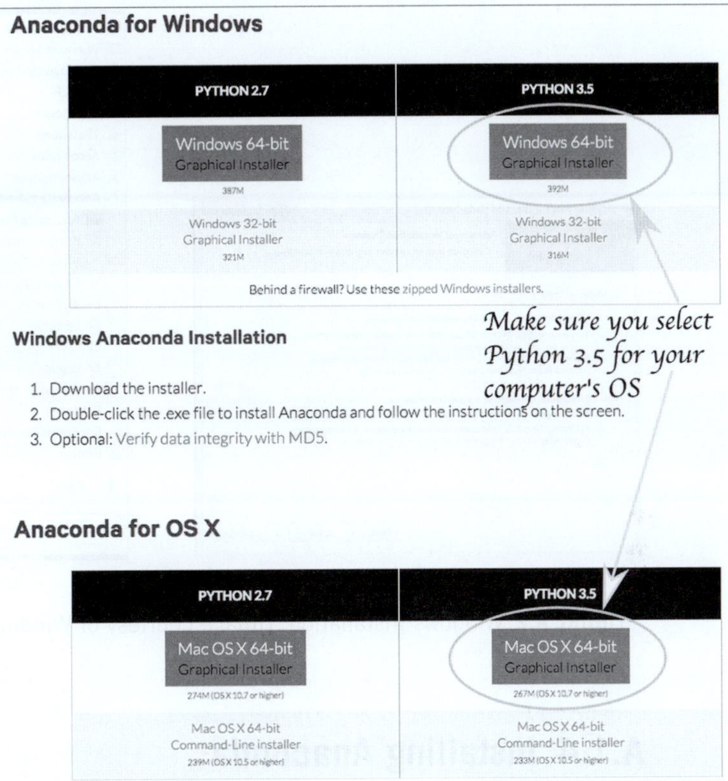

FIGURE A.1 Get Python 3.x! [Image courtesy of Continuum Analytics.]

Some of the packages that are pre-installed include the SPYDER Integrated Development Environment (IDE) as well as Pylab, the numerical and plotting packages. If you prefer the basic distribution, get it from `http://www.python.org`. Go to the download section and download the Python 3 version for your operating system. Once installed you are now all set to begin experimenting!

As we mentioned, included in the Anaconda distribution are hundreds of packages. However, there are many more than that! You can also browse the list of more packages (at the time of this writing, over 60,000) at `http://pypi.python.org/pypi`, and many of them are Python 3 compatible. However, remember to check! Python 2 programs will not run under Python 3.

What You Get

When you install Python on your computer, you typically get the following tools:

- A Python *shell*, a window into which you can directly type Python commands, and where interaction between you and programs you write typically occurs.
- An editor in which you can type programs, update them, save them to disk, and run them.

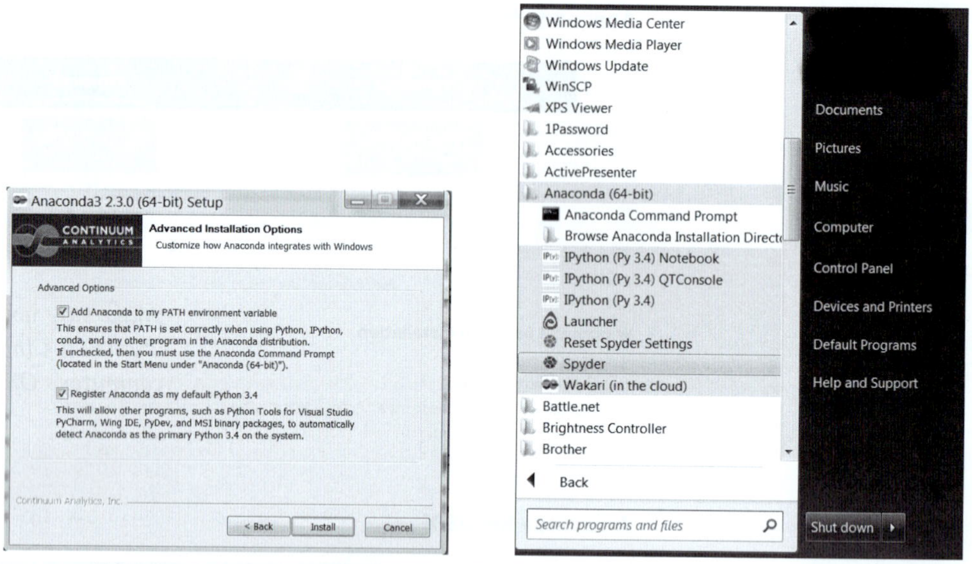

a) Windows installation options b) Start

FIGURE A.2 Windows Installation. [Image courtesy of Windows 10, Microsoft Corporation.]

A.1.4 Installing Anaconda

The Anaconda folks provide some great directions on how to do an install for the various operating systems. Take a look at their install directions at: `http://docs.continuum.io/anaconda/install`

When installing with Windows you will get Advanced Installation Options that you might want checked (see Figure A.2). With Windows 7 SPYDER defaults to the Anaconda3 directory; Windows 8 and 10 is an app.

A.1.5 Starting Our Python IDE: SPYDER

As we mentioned, we will be working with a Python IDE called SPYDER. Let's start SPYDER! On both Windows and Mac, after the install an application called **Launcher** is available to launch various Python applications.

- On Windows, you would go to the *Start Menu*, select *All Programs* and then find the entry for *Anaconda*. Within the *Anaconda* label is *Launcher*. Running *Launcher* brings up the window shown in Figure A.3. Select *spyder-app*.

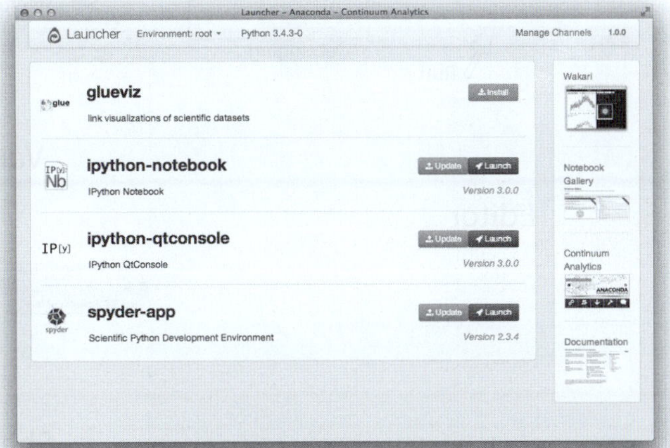

FIGURE A.3 Anaconda Launcher. [Screenshot from Python. Copyright © by Python. Used by permission of Python.]

- On the Mac, the *Launcher* application should be available under the standard *Applications* menu. Running *Launcher* brings up the same window shown in Figure A.3. Select *spyder-app*.
- On Linux you would enter *spyder* in a terminal. You will see the SPYDER start-up icon (Figure A.4) in your list of applications.

FIGURE A.4 Spyder startup icon. [Image courtesy of Continuum Analytics.]

A.1.6 Working with Python

The Anaconda distribution of Python, the shell, and editor are combined into one tool, the SPYDER IDE is shown in Figure A.5. The editor is in the left window; the shell is in the lower-right window. The upper-right window is very useful, but we'll discuss that later.

The shell is the lower-right window in SPYDER and is labeled *iPython console*.

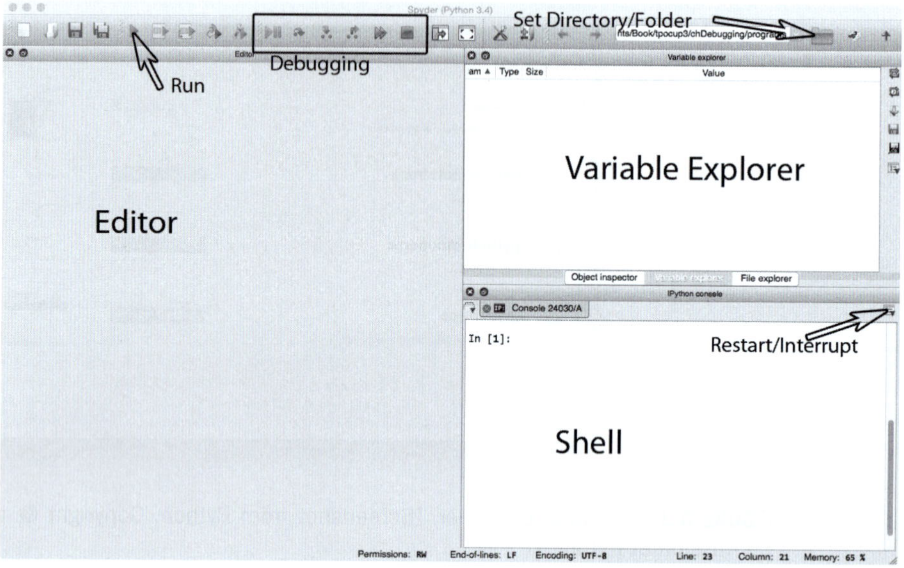

FIGURE A.5 Anaconda's Spyder IDE. [Screenshot from Python. Copyright © by Python. Used by permission of Python.]

In the iPython shell, each prompt is numbered within square brackets so you can refer back to them. What you type shows up after the *In [1]:* prompt. When you type something and hit the Enter key, the result shows up on the next line(s). For example, go to the Python shell and type in the following:

```
1 + 1 <Enter Key>
print( "Hi Mom") <Enter Key>
```

If you begin to type a command, such as the `len` command (which gives the length of the element in parentheses) but don't complete it, Python will prompt you with some information on the command and what it expects. Figure A.6 shows an example of interactive input.

Sometimes you can get results you expect; sometimes an error. For example, try entering:

```
1 + 1.2 <Enter Key>
print(hello) <Enter Key>
```

The results would look like Figure A.7: The last output shows that an error occurred. Because `hello` was not a variable and did not have quotes around it, ***`print`*** failed to perform.

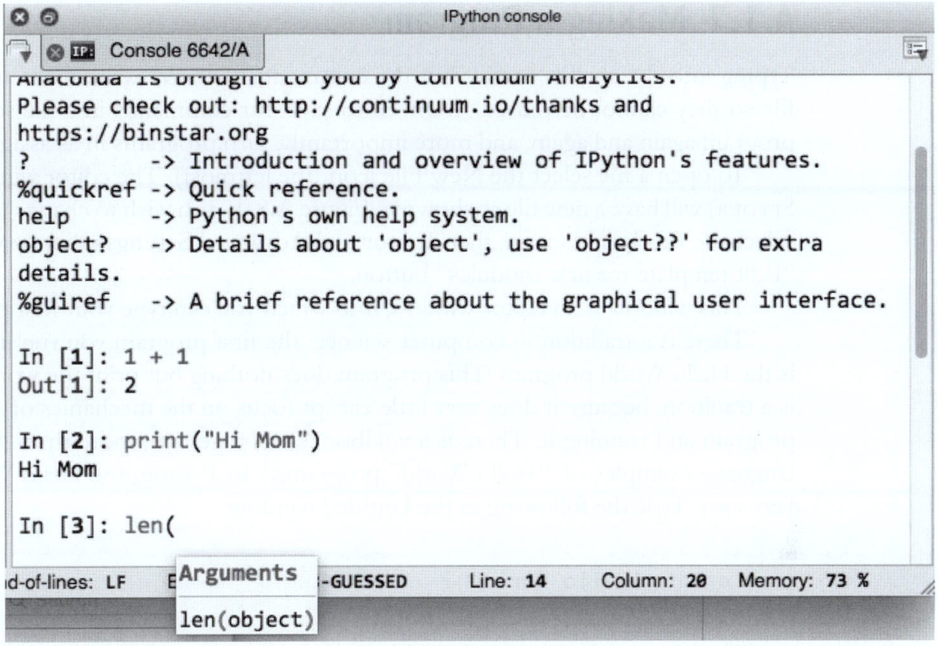

FIGURE A.6 Typing your first Python commands. [Screenshot from Python. Copyright © by Python. Used by permission of Python.]

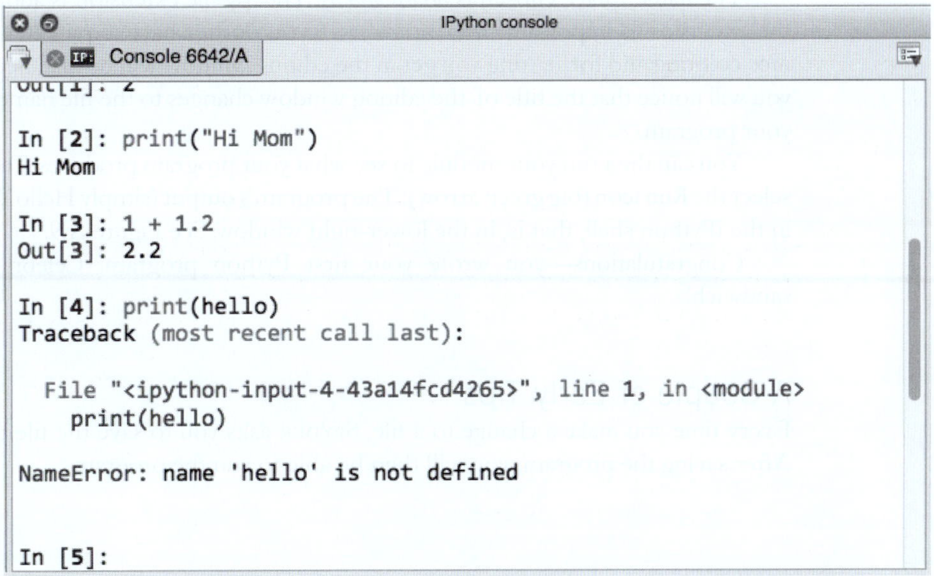

FIGURE A.7 How Python shows errors. [Screenshot from Python. Copyright © by Python. Used by permission of Python.]

A.1.7 Making a Program

Typing into the shell is useful, but the commands that you write there are not saved as a file so they cannot be reused. We need to save our commands in a file so we can run the program again and again, and more importantly, turn programs in as assignments!

To open a file select the New File icon (the leftmost). The editor window (left side of SPYDER) will have a new file as shown in Figure A.8. If you wish to change the *@author* label, select the Preferences icon, then Editor and Advanced Settings where you will see a large "Edit template for new modules" button.

This window is an editor window, into which you can type your first program.

There is a tradition in computer science: the first program you run in a new language is the Hello World program. This program does nothing but print the words *Hello World.* It is a tradition, because it does very little except focus on the mechanics of writing your first program and running it. There is a wikibooks.org page with more than 200 programming language examples of "Hello World" programs.[1] In Python, the Hello World program is very easy. Type the following in the Untitled window:

```
print( 'Hello World')
```

The phrase after ***print*** should be in quotes (either single or double quotes is fine). Having done that, save your first program so you can use it again. Select the Save File icon (third from left).

The name I have chosen is *helloWorld.py*. The .py file extension is added by default, but the extension is important–*very important.* If you do not have a .py extension, then all the nice coloring and formatting you get in the editing window will be lost. Second, once saved, you will notice that the title of the editing window changes to the file name you used to save your program.

You can then run your module to see what your program produces. To run the program select the Run icon (big green arrow). The program's output (simply Hello World) will appear in the iPython shell, that is, in the lower-right window. See Figure A.9.

Congratulations—you wrote your first Python program. Celebrate with a Spam sandwich!

A Couple of Early Tips

Every time you make a change to a file, SPYDER asks you to save the file before you run it. After saving the program, you will then be able to run the program.

[1] https://en.wikibooks.org/wiki/Computer_Programming/Hello_world

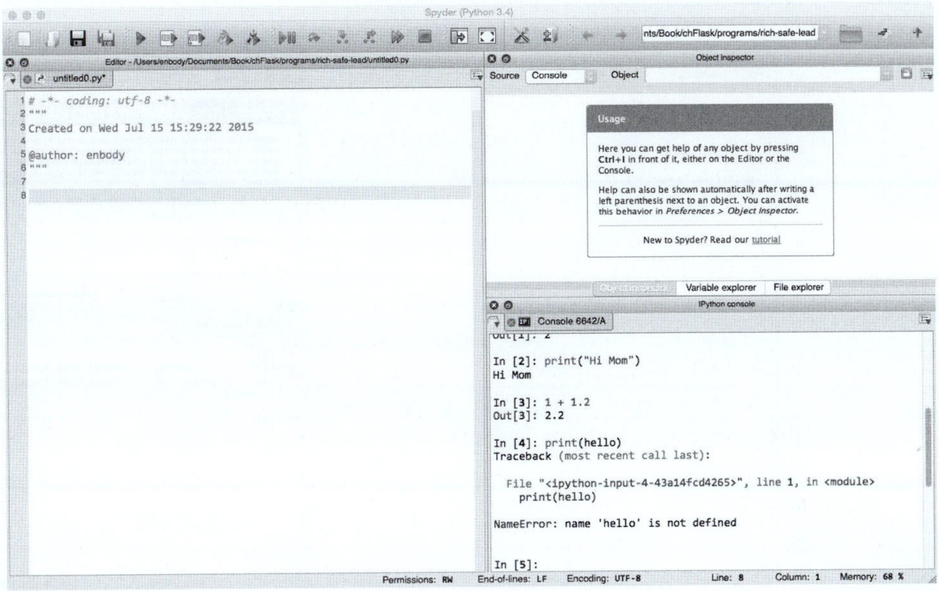

FIGURE A.8 Opening an editing session in Spyder to make a Python program. [Screenshot from Python. Copyright © by Python. Used by permission of Python.]

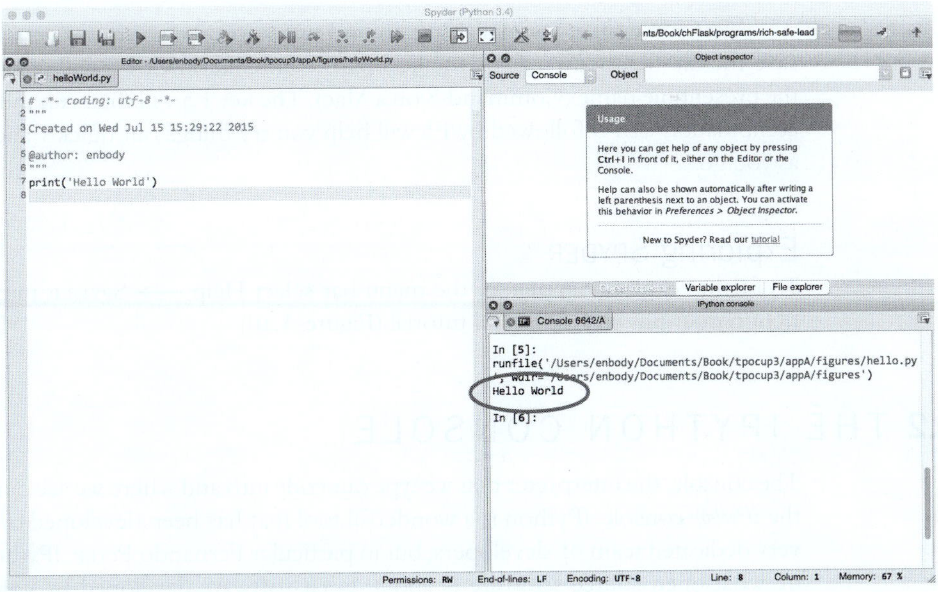

FIGURE A.9 Running your Python program. [Screenshot from Python. Copyright © by Python. Used by permission of Python.]

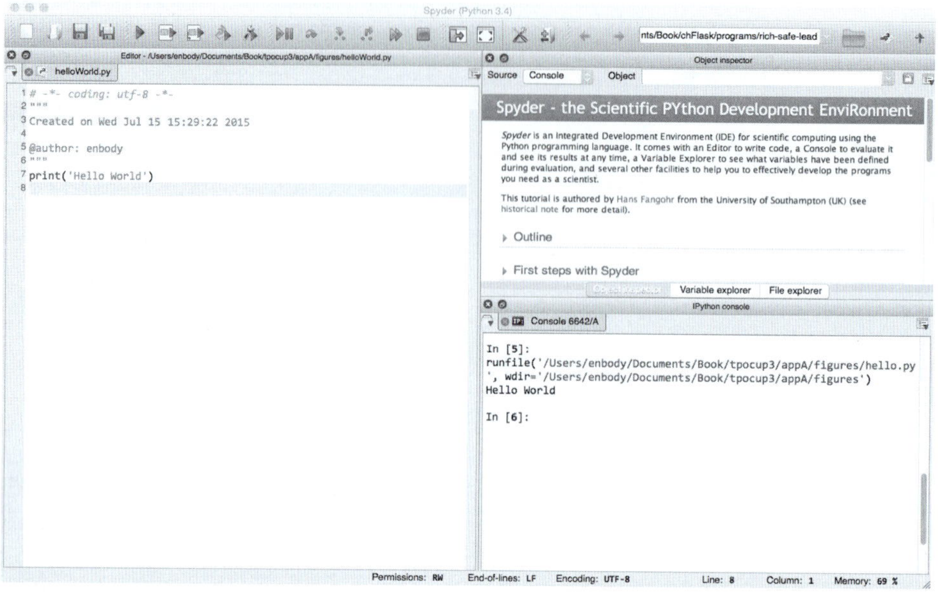

FIGURE A.10 Helpful Spyder tutorial. [Screenshot from Python. Copyright © by Python. Used by permission of Python.]

After some time, you will come to find two keyboard shortcuts very useful. After you save the file for the first time, the keyboard combination Ctrl-S will re-save the file under the present file name (Command-S on a Mac). The key F5 will then run the program. So the combination Ctrl-S followed by F5 will help you try things out quickly and clean up errors as you go.

Exploring SPYDER

To further explore SPYDER, in the menu bar select Help ⟶ SPYDER tutorial. The upper-right corner fills with a helpful tutorial (Figure A.10).

A.2 THE IPYTHON CONSOLE

The console, the interpreter that we type our code into and where we see our results, is called the *iPython* console. iPython is a wonderful tool that has been developed over the years by a very dedicated team of developers, but in particular Fernando Perez. iPython is an example of what open source software is about; great software developed by volunteers working together.

iPython is designed to *make your coding life easier.* As such it is something that is worth becoming more familiar with. There is a lot to iPython, but we would like to cover some of the basics here.

A.2.1 Anatomy of an iPython Session

The following is a small iPython session. Let's note a couple of things:

- Some lines start with `In`, short for input. These are lines where you typed in some information for iPython to interpret.
- Some line start with `Out`, short for output. These are return values that were produced when the associated input line was run.
- Both the `In` and the `Out` have a number in square brackets. This is the *history* number. iPython keeps a history of what you typed in and what was returned. The history numbers of `In` and the `Out` match up. Thus when `my_int + 27` was entered, `In[2]`, the resulting output `31` was returned as `Out[2]`. The history numbers are the same.
- Some lines start with neither `In` nor `Out`. These are *side-effect* lines, usually the result of printing something. They are **not** returned values from executing Python code, but they are output that was produced. Take a look at Section 1.4.2 for more on side-effect versus return. For example, `In [5]: print(my_int)` did print 4, but no associated `Out` was produced. A `print` statement has no return value, thus no `Out`.

```
In [1]: my_int = 4

In [2]: my_int + 27
Out[2]: 31

In [3]: import math

In [4]: math.sqrt(my_int)
Out[4]: 2.0

In [5]: print(my_int)
4

In [6]: new_int = input("Give me an int:")
Give me an int:123

In [7]: new_int
Out[7]: '123'

In [8]:
```

A.2.2 Your Top Three iPython Tips

iPython can do a lot of things, but there are a couple that are hard to live without. We list those here in a separate section since, if you learn nothing else about iPython, you should learn these!

The Arrow Keys and Your History

The ↑ (up arrow) and ↓ (down arrow) of your keyboard allow you to scroll back and forth through the history of what you typed into iPython. This may sound trivial, but it is a real time saver. Every time you hit the ↑, iPython reprints the previous entry. Every time you hit ↓, iPython reprints the following entry. Continuing with the preceding session, the console is sitting at `In [8]` waiting for input. The following shows what happens when you press:

↑ first time: `In [8]: new_int`
↑ second time: `In [8]: new_int = input("Give me an int:")`
↑ third time: `In [8]: print(my_int)`
↓ first time: `In [8]: new_int = input("Give me an int:")`
↓ second time: `In [8]: new_int`

Once you have searched for the line you want, you can do one of two things:

- If you press the Enter key, that line will be resubmitted.
- You can also use the ← or → to move through the line so that you can edit it. You can remove characters, add characters as you please. When you hit enter, the newly edited line is then submitted. In Spyder, you can use the mouse as well to edit the line.[2]

Now if you type something and misspell it, or you want to redo something you did earlier, you can use the arrow keys to enter your code!

A.2.3 Completion and the Tab Key

It can be frustrating when you cannot remember the exact name of a method (of string, of dictionaries, etc.) you know you learned. How was that spelled? What was it exactly? The same is true of a module. What are the functions in the module? What are the arguments to that function?

iPython provides a straightforward way to answer those kinds of questions. It's the **tab key**. The tab key is kind of magical in iPython. It tells you all the information you need to know about functions, methods, arguments in Python.

Let's look at a session. Note that the "..." indicate more information was presented than is shown here. Try it and see!!!

[2] On a command line interface, the mouse will likely not be available for editing.

```
In [1]: import math

In [2]: math.        # hit the TAB key
math.acos       math.degrees    math.fsum       math.log2
math.acosh      math.e          math.gamma      math.modf
math.asin       math.erf        math.hypot      math.pi
math.asinh      math.erfc       math.isfinite   math.pow
math.atan       math.exp        math.isinf      math.radians
math.atan2      math.expm1      math.isnan      math.sin
math.atanh      math.fabs       math.ldexp      math.sinh
math.ceil       math.factorial  math.lgamma     math.sqrt
math.copysign   math.floor      math.log        math.tan
math.cos        math.fmod       math.log10      math.tanh
math.cosh       math.frexp      math.log1p      math.trunc

In [2]: math.s       # hit the TAB key
math.sin   math.sinh  math.sqrt

In [2]: math.sqrt(4)
Out[2]: 2.0

In [3]: my_str = "abc"

In [4]: my_str.    # hit the TAB key
my_str.capitalize    my_str.isidentifier  my_str.rindex
my_str.casefold      my_str.islower       my_str.rjust
my_str.center        my_str.isnumeric     my_str.rpartition
my_str.count         my_str.isprintable   my_str.rsplit
my_str.encode        my_str.isspace       my_str.rstrip
my_str.endswith      my_str.istitle       my_str.split
my_str.expandtabs    my_str.isupper       my_str.splitlines
my_str.find          my_str.join          my_str.startswith
...

my_str.isdigit       my_str.rfind

In [4]: my_str.find?       # question mark is documentation
Docstring:
S.find(sub[, start[, end]]) -> int

Return the lowest index in S where substring sub is found,
such that sub is contained within S[start:end].  Optional
arguments start and end are interpreted as in slice notation.

Return -1 on failure.
Type:      builtin_function_or_method
```

```
In [5]: my_str?
Type:        str
String form: abc
Length:      3
Docstring:
str(object='') -> str
str(bytes_or_buffer[, encoding[, errors]]) -> str
...

encoding defaults to sys.getdefaultencoding().
errors defaults to 'strict'.

In [6]:
```

When I imported math, I couldn't remember what the square root function is in Python (OK, I remembered but let's pretend shall we). So for `In [2]` I typed `math.` followed by the tab key. iPython lists all the members of the module. On `In [3]` I typed `math.s` followed by the tab key. All the members that start with "s" are listed. Ah, its "sqrt", and off we go.

On `In [3]` I made a string `my_str`. What can I do to my string? On `In [4]` I typed `my_str.` followed by the tab key, and all the methods of string were listed.

As best it can, iPython will try to complete your command when you hit a tab key. If there are options on how to complete the command, iPython will list all the options so that you may choose among them.

Get used to using the tab key, it is truly a life saver!

A.2.4 The ? Character

The "?" character also plays a special role. In the previous session, I looked through all the string methods and noticed one called `find`. What does that function do? What are its arguments? What does it return? On `In [4]` I typed `my_str.find?` and hit return. At that point iPython prints out its documentation on the string `find` function. Now I know what `find` does!

If you are bad about naming your variables and you cannot figure out what a variable contains, you can use the ?. On `In [5]` I typed `my_str?` and hit return. Python tells me: what type it is, what its present value is, its length and all kinds of other good information.

Use the ? whenever you have a question. That's what it is for!

A.2.5 More iPython Tips

If you want to learn more about how to use iPython, there are plenty of websites with tutorials. Try `http://ipython.org/ipython-doc/stable/interactive/`

tutorial.html to get more information. However, here are a couple more useful tidbits.

```
In [1]: my_int = 4

In [2]: my_int + 123
Out[2]: 127

In [3]: my_str = "abc123"

In [4]: loc = my_str.find("a")

In [5]: loc
Out[5]: 0

In [6]: hist -no
   1: my_int = 4
   2: my_int + 123
127
   3: my_str = "abc123"
   4: loc = my_str.find("a")
   5: loc
0
   6: hist -no

In [7]: recall 2

In [8]: my_int + 456
Out[8]: 460

In [9]: _oh[2]
Out[9]: 127

In [10]: result = _oh[2]

In [11]: _oh
Out[11]: {2: 127, 5: 0, 8: 460, 9: 127}

In [12]: _ih
Out[12]:
['',
 'my_int = 4',
 'my_int + 123',
 'my_str = "abc123"',
 'loc = my_str.find("a")',
 'loc',
 "get_ipython().magic('hist -no')",
```

```
 "get_ipython().magic('recall 2')",
 'my_int + 456',
 '_oh[2]',
 'result = _oh[2]',
 '_oh',
 '_ih']

In [13]:
```

history: As we have said, iPython keeps a history of what you have typed and entered to be evaluated. The ↑ and ↓ allows you to move through the history one at a time, but what if you have stuff far back in your history?

Take a look at the session above. The `hist` command shows you what you typed previously; that is, everything that showed up as an `In [ ]` in your session. If you type `hist -n` iPython will show your history with their history numbers. If you type `hist -no`, iPython will show: the line number, what you typed and, if there was any output, what that output was. Knowing a history number will come in handy in the upcoming tips.

Working with History: There are a couple of ways you may get around using ↑ and ↓ for things far back in your history **if you know the history number**!

- **recall**: The `recall` command brings back the input line associated with a particular history number. For example, on `In [7]`, I typed `recall 2` and subsequently got `In [8]: my_int + 123`. I edited that line and resubmitted it with the new results.

  As a shortcut for recall, you can type `_num`. Thus I could have typed `In [7]: _2` and gotten the same result.
- **_ih** and **_oh**. The variable `_ih` is a *list* of all the inputs that you have typed. You can type it and see its contents.

  Similarly, `_oh` is a `dictionary` of all the outputs. The key for the dictionary is the history number, and the value is the output. Thus for `In [9]` I typed `_oh[2]` and directly received **without rerunning the code** the result obtained in history element 2.

```
In [1]: pwd
Out[1]: '/Users/bill/python'

In [2]: ls
NumPy Cookbook/     copyFile.py~        pyside/            teaching/
NumPy Cookbook.zip  copymp3.py          search.py
PADS/               ipython/            searchTitle.py
copyFile.py         nbconvert/          stuff/

In [3]: cd ipython
/Users/bill/python/ipython
```

```
In [4]: ls
PyCon2012-IPythonTutorial-Intro.pdf       notebooks.tar
PyCon2012-IPythonTutorial-Notebook.pdf    parallel/
ipython.pdf                               parallel.tar
notebooks/

In [5]: cd ..
/Users/bill/python

In [6]:
```

Operating System Commands: From iPython you can run many of the operating system commands that you could use from a Unix Command Line Interface (CLI). If you already know these commands, you can try them out in iPython, even from a Windows machine!

If you don't know many Unix CLI commands, there are a couple that can be really useful. They are a little odd in that they are very terse (remember, computer scientists are really lazy typists) but a few that are worth memorizing:

- **pwd**: That's short for "print working directory." This is helpful for the so-called "file directory problem." As described in Section 14.3.1, any file you open without a fully qualified path needs to be in the directory that the Python file started from. Where is that exactly? If you type `pwd`, iPython will tell you where you are in your directory structure. This is called the **current working directory** or **wdir**. Where the wdir is when iPython starts depends on a number of things, but wherever it is you can tell now where your wdir is.
- **ls**: That short for "list files." If you type `ls` in iPython, it will provide a list of the files in your wdir. Convenient if you are looking for a file you are trying to open and cannot remember how to spell it, or if it is even in the wdir.
- **cd**: That's short for "change directory." The `cd` command allows you to move up and down your directory/folder structure to set the wdir to be where you need it to be.

  If there is a directory you wish to move "down" to, then you can `cd directory`. If you want to move "up" from a directory you are in to its parent, you can `cd..` (two dots).

A.3 SOME CONVENTIONS FOR THIS BOOK

Looking at screen shots can be a bit tedious as the fonts can be small and hard to read. We have adopted the following conventions for both interactive and edited code in this book.

A.3.1 Interactive Code

When we type code that is interactive—that is, typing directly into the Python shell—we will frame the interaction as follows:

```
In  [1]: print("Something")
Something
In  [2]: len("Something")
Out [2]: 9

In  [3]: 3 + 4 * 7
Out [3]: 31

In  [4]: 3.14159/2
Out [4]: 1.570795
```

A.3.2 Program: Written Code

When we display a program, we will use code listings, as shown in Code Listing A.1:

Code Listing A.1

```
# calculate area of a triangle

base = 4
height = 3

area = 1.0/2.0 * base * height

print("Area is: ", area)
```

A.3.3 Combined Program and Output

Sometimes we will display both a program and its output (after it was "run"), so we use a code listing as shown in Code Listing A.2:

Code Listing A.2

```
# calculate area of a triangle

base = 4
height = 3

area = 1.0/2.0 * base * height

print("Area is: ", area)
```

```
Area is:  6.0
```

A.4 SUMMARY

Now you have Python. You can begin to learn to program!

APPENDIX B

Simple Drawing with Turtle Graphics

TURTLE GRAPHICS IS A SIMPLE WAY TO DO GRAPHICS THAT DATES BACK TO THE 1960S. A `turtle` module has been included with standard distributions of Python, starting with Python 2. The "turtle" is a cursor that you can control to draw on a two-dimensional palette. The last half-century of experience indicates that it is relatively easy for novice programmers to control a turtle by imagining that they are the turtle as it moves around. The turtle graphics module provides an easy way to do two-dimensional drawing in Python.

B.0.1 What Is a Turtle?

The programming language LOGO was created in the 1960s as a teaching tool for children to experiment with math and programming. One of its main features was a "turtle robot." Literally, they imagined that a tethered robot could be controlled from a workstation, with a pen attached to the robot, so that children could draw. Typically, they used an artificial turtle (a cursor on the screen) as a way to learn to control the robot.

This approach to drawing was a very important concept. All the drawing was done *relative to the present position* of the turtle. It could turn, move forward, and position the pen to create drawings. This approach has proven to be simpler than trying to teach the concepts of Cartesian absolute coordinates. Children could literally "be the turtle" and imagine what would be drawn.

Thus was born turtle graphics. As such, our artificial turtle graphics system has a number of characteristics:

- A two-dimensional drawing screen
- One (or more) turtles. Each turtle has:
  - A position

FIGURE B.1 The initial turtle screen. [Screenshot from Python Turtle Graphics. Copyright © by Python. Used by permission of Python.]

– An orientation or direction
– A pen, with attributes such as color, width, up/down, and so on.

When turtle graphics are started, with the ***import*** `turtle` line, a window is created with a small "turtle" cursor in the center. The default screen is 400 × 300, though it can be modified. The default turtle is actually an arrow that points in the direction of its current orientation. The turtle starts in the middle of the screen facing east (right), with increasing angles going counter clockwise (turtle facing 0 degrees, standard Cartesian angle settings). See Figure B.1.[1]

[1] All figures in this chapter were done on Mac OS X.

We create drawings on the screen by giving the turtle(s) a series of commands. Let's look at some of those commands.

B.0.2 Motion

As mentioned, commands move a turtle relative to its current position, for example, "move forward 10 pixels" or "turn right 45 degrees." The distance moved (pixels) or degrees turned can be integer or floating-point numbers. These values can be positive or negative as well. Many of the commands have shortcuts, but these tend to be a bit cryptic (fd for forward, bk for backward) so we only show the full command names. See the official Python documentation (`http://docs.python.org/py3k/library/turtle.html#module-turtle`). Table B.1 shows some of these commands.

forward(*distance*)	Move forward *distance* in current direction.
backward(*distance*)	Move backward *distance* in the opposite direction.
right(*angle*)	Turn right by *angle* units.
left(*angle*)	Turn left by *angle* units.
goto(*x,y*)	Move turtle to absolute screen position (*x,y*).
home()	Move turtle to origin (0,0) facing the default direction (typically east)
speed(*speed*)	Set turtle drawing *speed* as int in range 0–10

TABLE B.1 Turtle movement commands.

Speed can be a particularly useful attribute. First, calling `speed()` with no arguments will yield the present setting. This is true for most of the attribute settings of the turtle graphics module: calling them without arguments yields the present setting.

Second, the turtle is purposefully set to be animated so you can see the process of drawing. However, with longer, more complicated drawings, the animation can be tedious. The default setting is 3, with the range of 1–10 indicating slower to faster. However, a setting of 0 (zero) should mean *no* animation, making 10 the fastest setting. However, if the driving program itself is slow, the turtle can still look slow, but this is not because of the speed setting.

B.0.3 Drawing

Drawing is what turtle graphics is all about, and the `turtle` module provides many command for just that purpose. We list the important ones in Table B.2.

The `circle` command is a little tricky. Here are some details that are good to know when using it:

- Draws a circle of size `radius`. Turtle position is unchanged, and the circle center is `radius` distance *left* of the turtle. Thus just changing the orientation, not the position, of the turtle draws a different circle.

pendown()	Put the pen down—drawing when moving.
penup()	Pull the pen up—no drawing when moving.
pensize(*width*)	Set the line thickness to *width*, a positive int.
circle(*radius*, *extent=None*, *steps=None*)	Draw a circle (see below)
dot(*size=None*, color)	Draw a filled dot.
stamp()	Stamp a copy of the turtle at the present position. Returns a `stamp_id`
clearstamp(*stamp_id*)	Remove stamp with `stamp_id`
clear()	Clear the screen. Leave the turtle position and orientation unchanged
reset()	Clear screen Reset turtle to initial configuration (at (0,0) facing east)

TABLE B.2 Turtle drawing commands.

- The argument `extent` is an angle. By setting this value, you can draw semicircles, where `extent` is the number of degrees completed. Both the turtle position and orientation are changed when `extent` is provided.
- The argument `steps` is the number of straight line segments used to draw the circle. By default, the circle is drawn smoothly (many steps) but by setting the value to a particular number, you can create polygons. For example, `steps=6` will draw a hexagon.

Code Listing B.1 exercises some of these commands. Figure B.2 is the result of the process.

Code Listing B.1

```
# draw a smiley face

from turtle import *
import time

speed(10)     # draw fast!

penup()       # right side of face
forward(75)
```

```
pendown()       # draw an eye
right(90)
circle(25)
circle(10)

penup()         # left side of face
right(90)
forward(150)

pendown()       # draw an eye
right(90)
circle(25)
circle(10)

penup()         # center and down
right(90)
forward(75)
right(90)
forward(50)

pendown()        # draw a nose
left(45)
forward(40)
right(135)
forward(56.56)
right(135)
forward(40)

penup()          # center, down, then 100 left
right(135)
forward(50)
right(90)
forward(100)
left(90)         # need to face east

pendown()
circle(100, 180)  # smile

time.sleep(3)   # hold for 3 seconds so we can see
```

B.0.4 Color

What would good drawing be without color! The `turtle` module provides ways to specify color and to apply color to your drawing.

FIGURE B.2 Our first turtle figures. [Screenshot from Python Turtle Graphics. Copyright © by Python. Used by permission of Python.]

Specifying Color

There are three ways to specify color in Python turtle graphics, two of which are very common:

- A colorstring.
- A tuple of three values, each value in the range of 0–255 (usually as `int`, but `float` is accepted).
- A tuple of three values, each value in the range of 0.0–1.0 (less common, so not discussed).

For colorstrings, Python accepts any of the standard color strings provided by Python's built in drawing module, **Tk**. Tk provides a long list of predefined color strings, whereas in all things Python the case of the string matters. Common strings such as "green", "blue", "red", and "yellow" are obvious but others such as "BlanchedAlmond" or "CornflowerBlue" are less so. The full list can be found at `http://www.tcl.tk/man/tcl8.5/TkCmd/colors.htm`.

In general, color can be complicated to specify, and there are various ways to do it. One way is *additive color* where a mixture of red, green, and blue is sufficient to reproduce any color. Therefore, a common way to specify a color is to provide the mixture of the color's red, green, and blue content, often referred to as the *rgb* color. The use of rgb specifications of color is common as most television and monitors used three pixel colors (red, green, and blue) to create color. Specifying color as three integer values between 0 and 255 is a common way to represent color in computer applications. Thus, specifying a tuple of (0,0,0) (zero red, zero green, and zero blue) is another way to specify black. Blue would be (0,0,255), red (255,0,0), yellow (255,255,0), and CornflowerBlue (100, 149, 237).

B.0.5 Drawing with Color

You can specify two different drawing colors: the color of the pen and the color used to fill a region drawn on the screen. Not surprisingly, the first is set by the `pencolor` command and the second by the `fillcolor` command. Table B.3 lists the commands.

pencolor(*a_color*)	a_color is either a colorstring or an rgb tuple
fillcolor(*a_color*)	a_color is either a colorstring or an rgb tuple
colormode(255)	Sets rgb values to be 0–255 (defaults to 0.0–1.0, better to set to 255)
color(*pen_color*, *fill_color*)	Set both with one function
begin_fill()	Mark where region to color in begins
end_fill()	Mark where region to color in ends

TABLE B.3 Turtle pen commands.

Some things to note.

- The `color` command will set*both* colors in one call. If you provide one argument, both the pen and fill colors are set to the argument color. If you provide two arguments, the first is the pen color and the second is the fill color.
- Filling an area is done by bracketing drawing with the two commands `begin_fill()` and `end_fill()`. The area filled is whatever occurs between the two calls. When `end_fill()` is executed, the area is filled using the line between end and begin as the final part of the filled area.
- As with most of the commands we have seen, calling any of these commands without arguments will yield the present values.

Code Listing B.2 exercises some of these calls. Figure B.3 shows the result of using this code.

Code Listing B.2

```
# draw squares, change the pen size and color
# just to show off

from turtle import *
import time

colormode(255)  # colors in range 0–255

def square(length, fill_tuple):
    ''' Draw a square, side length, color fill_tuple'''
    fillcolor(fill_tuple)
    begin_fill()
    for i in range(4):
        forward(length)
        right(90)
    end_fill()

# init values, fun to change
red = 100
green = 0
blue = 50
color_inc = 10
side_length = 50
pen_width = 1
pen_inc = 1
pen_limit = 5

speed(0)
for i in range(36):
    square(side_length, (red,green,blue))
    right(10)
    red = (red + color_inc) % 255          # range 0–254
    blue = (blue + color_inc) % 255
    green = (green + color_inc) % 255
    side_length += 3
    # range 1–pen_limit
    pen_width = ((pen_width + pen_inc) % pen_limit) + 1
    pensize(pen_width)

time.sleep(5)
```

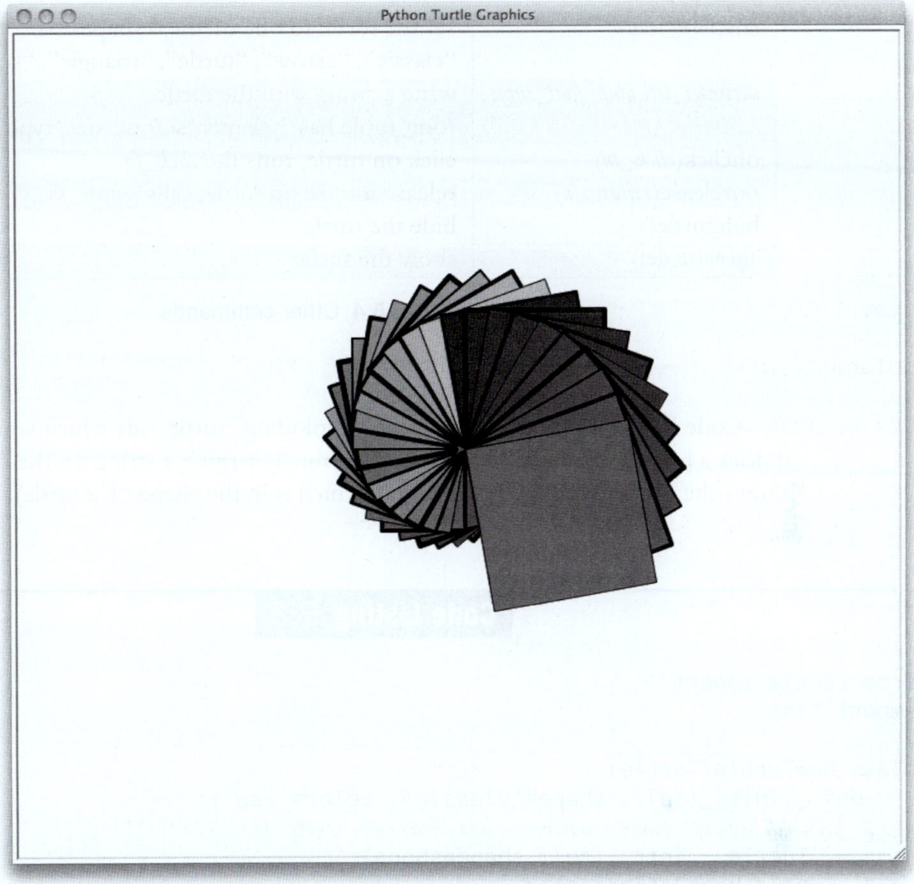

FIGURE B.3 Turtle squares. [Screenshot from Python Turtle Graphics. Copyright © by Python. Used by permission of Python.]

B.0.6 Other Commands

There are over 90 turtle commands, so there are many things you can do with turtle graphics. Here are some commands we have not yet mentioned.

The `write` command is a bit tricky in that you have to know something about fonts to use it. A typical font tuple would be something like `('Arial','14','normal')`, but you need to know what fonts you have on your system. The hide and show turtle functions are useful. When you hide the turtle drawing goes much faster. Also, you can hide the turtle and move the pen somewhere to write a string, then move it back and show the turtle again.

Finally, you can subclass that `Turtle` class and create new kinds of turtles. You can also create multiple turtles on the screen and move them around in parallel.

shape(*a_shape*)	set the turtle to one of the 6 shapes: "classic", "arrow", "turtle", "triangle", "square", "circle"
write(*a_str, font=font_tuple*	write a string with the turtle font_tuple has 3 elements: font, size, type
onclick(*click_fn*)	click on turtle, runs the *click_fn*
onrelease(*release_fn*)	release mouse on turtle, calls *release_fn*
hideturtle()	hide the turtle
showturtle()	show the turtle

TABLE B.4 Other commands.

Code Listing B.3 shows making an "exploding" turtle, one which you can click on and it does a brief animation of an explosion, finally writing a string on the screen. Figure B.4 shows the result of clicking on a turtle (which is in the shape of a turtle).

Code Listing B.3

```
from turtle import *
import time

class NewTurtle(Turtle):
    def __init__(self, shape='classic', color='red'):
        ''' store boom color, call parent with the rest '''
        Turtle.__init__(self,shape=shape)
        self.boom_color=color

    def explode(self,x,y):
        ''' quick animation, draw expanding dots, then clear'''
        self.dot(5, self.boom_color)
        self.dot(20, self.boom_color)
        self.dot(50, self.boom_color)
        self.dot(50,'white')        # clear the color
        self.write('      boOOOM!', font=("Arial", "14", "normal"))

t1 = NewTurtle(shape='turtle')
t1.onclick(t1.explode)
t1.forward(100)
```

FIGURE B.4 Turtle Explosion! [Screenshot from Python Turtle Graphics. Copyright © by Python. Used by permission of Python.]

B.1 TIDBITS

B.1.1 Reset/Close the Turtle Window

The drawing window will stay open with your present drawing. If you want to clear the window and start again do:

```
turtle.reset()
```

This will clear the window and reset the turtle to the start position.

If you want to close the window, do:

```
turtle.bye()
```

APPENDIX C

What's Wrong with My Code?

> "We have met the enemy and he is us."
>
> Pogo by Walt Kelly

C.1 IT'S YOUR FAULT!

A computer does what you tell it to do, not necessarily what you intended it to do. If the program *you wrote* is not working as you intended, it's your fault. Who else could be at fault after all! The real question though is, how do I find the problem and fix it? That is the goal of this chapter.

Programmers make mistakes when writing programs. These mistakes come in many different forms: assumptions about the data, misunderstanding of the algorithm, incorrect calculations, poorly designed data structures, and—best of all—just plain blunders. Testing is a way to protect us from ourselves. If we make a mistake, it would be most useful to be informed *before* we release code for use. Without some form of testing, how will we ever really know how well our program works? In addition, testing done well indicates where the error which is the first step to fixing it.

C.1.1 Kinds of Errors

There are at least three classes of errors:

- Syntactic errors
- Runtime errors
- Design errors

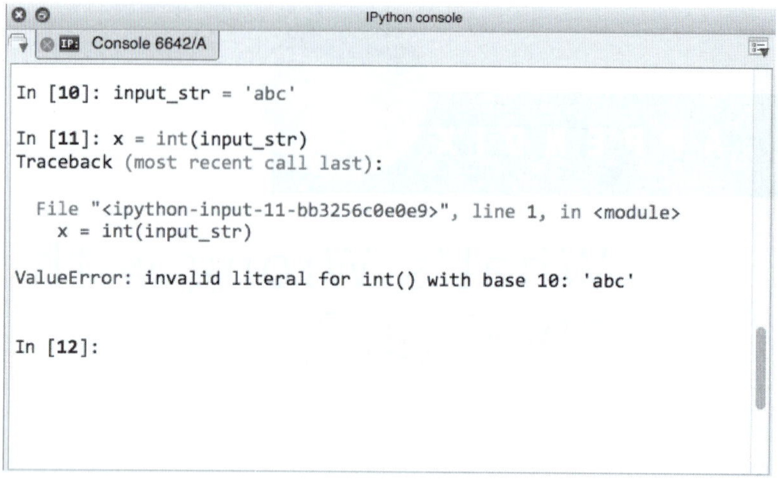

FIGURE C.1 Syntax error. [Screenshot from Python. Copyright © by Python. Used by permission of Python.]

Syntactic errors are the easiest to detect and are detected for us by the interpreter. They are errors in the use of the programming language. Examples of syntactic errors include forgetting a colon (:) at the end of a header, a misplaced parenthesis, and a misspelling of a Python command—the list is long. When a program is run that contains a syntax error, Python reports the error and (as best it can) identifies where the error occurred. Figure C.1 illustrates a ValueError generated by trying to convert a string of characters to an integer.

Runtime errors are errors of intent. They are legal language statements; they are syntactically correct, but they ask Python to do something that cannot be done. Their incorrectness cannot be detected by the Python interpreter syntactically, but occur when Python attempts to run code that cannot be completed. The classic example is to make a list of length 10 (indices 0–9) and then at some point during processing ask for the list element at index 10. There is no syntactic error; requesting a value at some index is a reasonable request. Furthermore, requests of values at index 0–9 provide results. Only when the tenth index value is requested does Python encounter the problem. Python cannot provide that value at index 10 because it doesn't exist, hence the runtime error shown in Figure C.2. Runtime errors can be hard to find, even with testing. They may occur intermittently: we may only occasionally ask for the index 10 element, depending on our calculations. Runtime errors may occur only under special circumstances. For example, if the name of the file we open has a suffix ".txt" and an error is triggered, any other suffix might be fine. Whatever the cause, just because you haven't seen the error doesn't mean it isn't there!

Design errors are a broad class of errors that basically cover everything else that is neither a syntactic nor a runtime error. The program is syntactically correct and we do not ask Python to do something that it inherently cannot do. However, the results we get are simply wrong. Design errors are just that: errors. We didn't write our averaging equation

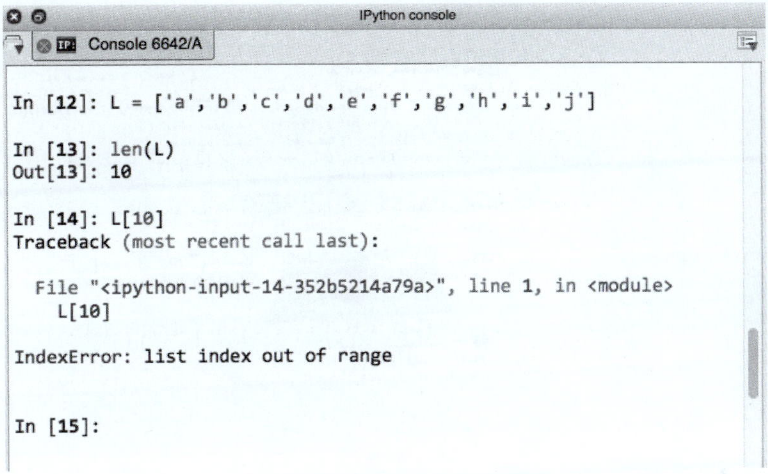

FIGURE C.2 Run-time error. [Screenshot from Python. Copyright © by Python. Used by permission of Python.]

correctly, we skipped a value in the list, we multiplied instead of dividing, we didn't reset a default value in our function call, and so on. We made a mistake and, through no fault of the language, we got the wrong answer.

Testing for Runtime and Semantic Errors

Testing is about minimizing our errors as we program. We will make errors—that's a given. Can we recover from them, find them early, and minimize their effect? These are important questions.

C.1.2 "Bugs" and Debugging

Programmers often talk about bugs in their programs. The source of the term "bug" is something much discussed in computer science. The source of the term is not clear, but it is clear that it pre-dates computers. There are a number of documented letters of Thomas Edison using the term "bug" to indicate defects in his inventions.[1] There is some evidence that the term dates back to telegraphy equipment and the use of semi-automatic telegraph keys that were called "bugs" and, though efficient, were difficult to work with.[2] One of the most famous computer examples is traced to Admiral Grace Hopper. See Figure C.3.

[1] http://theinstitute.ieee.org/technology-focus/technology-history/did-you-know-edison-coined-the-term-bug

[2] http://id.answers.yahoo.com/question/index?qid=1006052411732

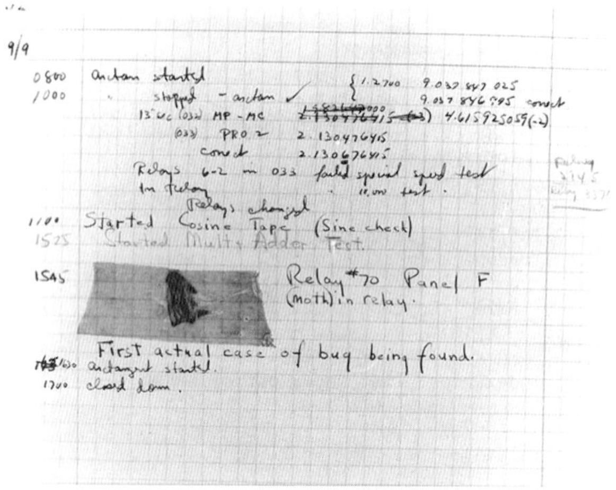

FIGURE C.3 A real hardware bug! [Courtesy of the Naval Surface Warfare Center, Dahlgren, VA., 1988. – U.S. Naval Historical Center Online Library Photograph.]

> In 1946, when Hopper was released from active duty, she joined the Harvard Faculty at the Computation Laboratory where she continued her work on the Mark II and Mark III. Operators traced an error in the Mark II to a moth trapped in a relay, coining the term *bug*. This bug was carefully removed and taped to the log book. Stemming from the first bug, today we call errors or glitch's [sic] in a program a *bug*.[2]

Removing bugs from a program has been called "debugging," likely from this incident.

To call these errors "bugs" is a bit self-forgiving of us. It implies that these errors were not our fault. Rather, they slipped into our program without our knowing. We may not have known it at the time, but they are our errors. Edsger Dijkstra, who was a famous professor of computer science, said the following about the word "bug":

> We could, for instance, begin with cleaning up our language by no longer calling a bug "a bug" but by calling it an error. It is much more honest because it squarely puts the blame where it belongs, viz., with the programmer who made the error. The animistic metaphor of the bug that maliciously sneaked in while the programmer was not looking is intellectually dishonest as it is a disguise that the error is the programmer's own creation. The nice thing of this simple change of vocabulary is that it has such a profound effect. While, before, a program with only one bug used to be "almost correct," afterwards a program with an error is just "wrong."[3]

[2] http://ei.cs.vt.edu/~history/Hopper.Danis.html

[3] From "EWD 1036 – On the cruelty of really teaching computing science." Copyright by Rutger M Dijkstra. Used by permission of Rutger M Dijkstra.

C.2 DEBUGGING

There are three steps to finding errors in your code:

1. Test: run tests to determine if the program works correctly.
2. Probe: insert probes to determine where the error occurs.
3. Fix: fix the error.

C.2.1 Testing for Correctness

Part of the specification of most problems in an introductory course often includes input with corresponding expected output. However, such specifications are usually incomplete so you need to develop your own tests.

When developing your code it is often useful to begin with small test cases that are easy to verify. If the sample file has 1000 lines, create a test file with the first 5 lines from the sample file.

Once you think your code is working take an adversarial approach: try to break your code. What input might cause a problem? The specifications included a few sample inputs so consider variations on that input. If integer input is expected, test what happens when non-integers are input.

We will return later to testing.

C.2.2 Probes

Once you know that an error exists the next step is to figure out where in the code the error occurs. Simply reading your code is a good place to start, and explaining your code to someone else is surprisingly effective (this is known as *code review*). Sometimes what made sense late last night seems quite stupid today when you are trying to explain it to someone else. They ask: why did you do that? You reply: I have no idea!

If simply reading (inspecting) the code doesn't reveal the error, insert *probes*. Probes allow you to view the values that variable actually have as opposed to what you think they have. There are two ways to probe your code:

- Insert *print()* probes into the code.
- Use a debugger (such as is available in SPYDER).

Let's take a look at two programs with errors and see how to use the debugger to help find and fix them. The first program uses topics only from Chapters 1 and 2. The second program uses later topics so it can be used to illustrate more debugging features.

C.2.3 Debugging with SPYDER Example 1

This first example will sum the numbers from 1 to 100 inclusive. We have already seen this example, but will revisit it to learn about debugging.

Code Listing C.1 shows our first version of the code—with errors (can you find them?).

Code Listing C.1

```
# sum the numbers from 1 to 100
while number = 100:
    the_sum = the_sum + number
print("Sum:", the_sum)
```

If you copy the code into SPYDER, the first thing you will notice is the tiny warning flag with an embedded exclamation point with the line numbers. If you hover your mouse over it, you will see the message: invalid syntax (Figure C.4). Often the syntax error is on the flagged line, but frequently the error is on the previous line—the interpreter got confused

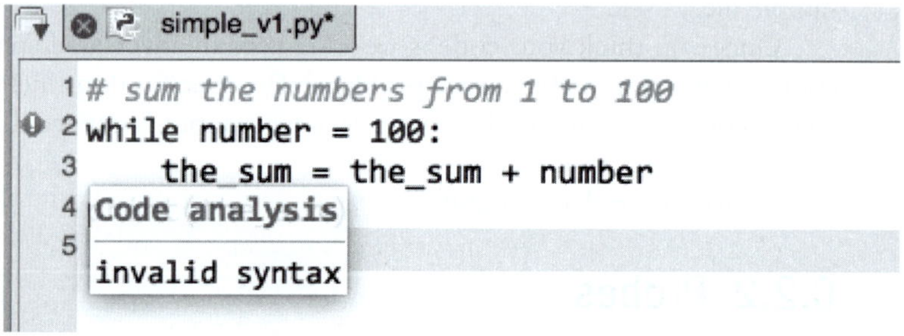

FIGURE C.4 Flagged syntax error. [Screenshot from Python. Copyright © by Python. Used by permission of Python.]

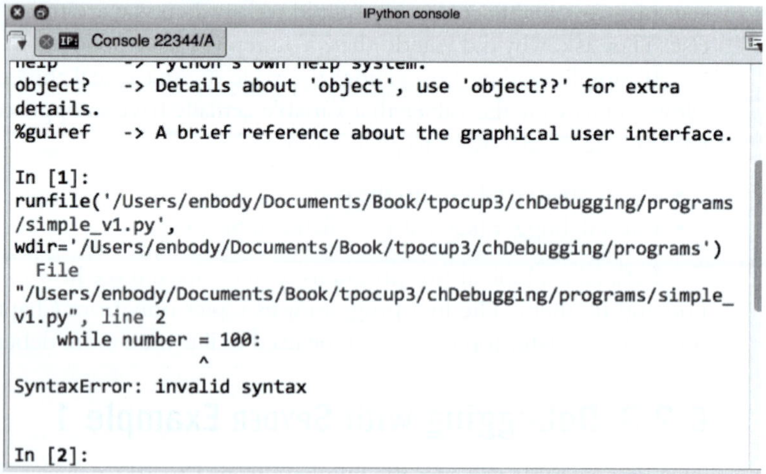

FIGURE C.5 Syntax error flagged in the shell. [Screenshot from Python. Copyright © by Python. Used by permission of Python.]

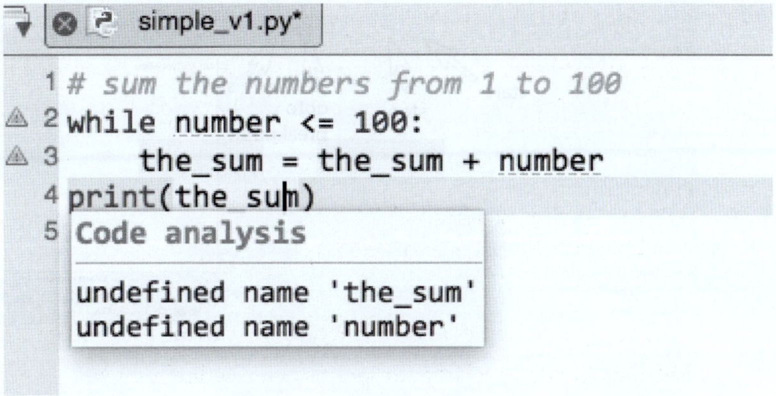

FIGURE C.6 Undefined name error. [Screenshot from Python. Copyright © by Python. Used by permission of Python.]

when it got to this line. Unfortunately, the error message is not very helpful. If you run the program, you will see the same error message in the shell, but the interpreter will also try to point to where in the line it thinks the error is. In Figure C.5 you can see that the "=" sign is indicated. Oops, we have an assignment rather than the "less than or equal" test we wanted: change "=" to "<=".

When we make that fix, the error flag disappears but a new one appears as shown in Figure C.6. In fact two new error flags appear indicating two "undefined name" errors. Neither `number` nor `the_sum` has been given an initial value. That is, neither has appeared on the left side of an assignment statement. Since we are collecting values into a sum, the additive identity zero is the appropriate initial value. Since we are adding numbers starting at 1, that is an appropriate initial value for `number`.

Code Listing C.2 shows our second version of the code–still with errors (can you find them?).

Code Listing C.2

```
# sum the numbers from 1 to 100
the_sum = 0
number = 1
while number <= 100:
    the_sum = the_sum + number
print("Sum:", the_sum)
```

We have now removed syntax errors that the interpreter could find. Let's move on to other errors that occur when the program runs. When we execute this code nothing happens—usually that means that there is an infinite loop. We could find it by inspection (can you see it?), but how can I use the debugger to help? First, let's set a breakpoint—a spot where we will stop the program so we can examine the namespace for the values of

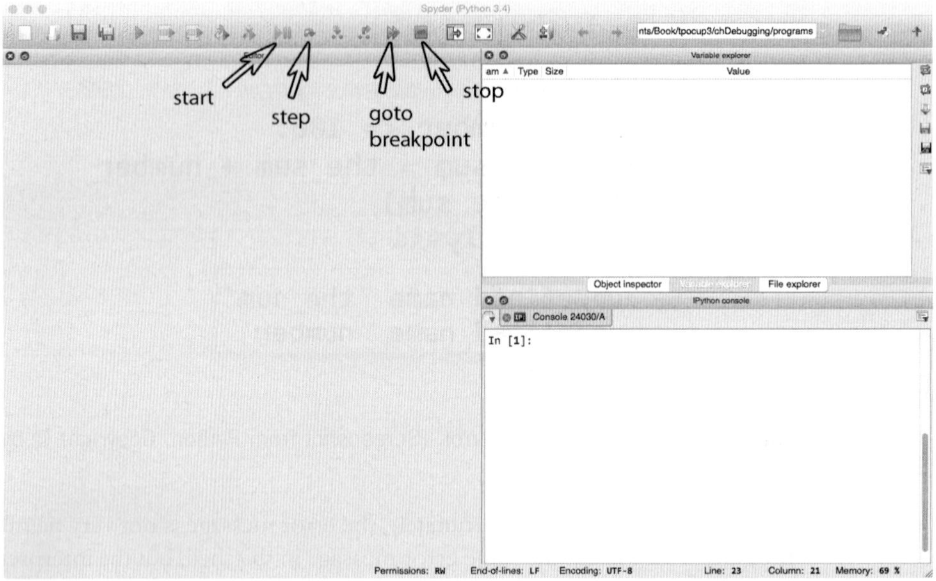

FIGURE C.7 Debugging command icons. [Screenshot from Python. Copyright © by Python. Used by permission of Python.]

variables. We can have an unlimited number of breakpoints, but fewer is easier to manage. There is only one loop so let's put a breakpoint there. The best place is the first line of the loop, line 5 (in this case there is only one line). We can set a breakpoint there by double-clicking on the number 5. A small red circle marks a set breakpoint. The mark can be seen along the left side in Figure C.13.

With a breakpoint set we need to fire up the debugger and run the program to the breakpoint. The debugger symbols are in blue at the top of SPYDER (Figure C.7). You can start the debugger from the drop down under "Debug" or select the start debugging symbol, a right-facing blue arrow with two vertical bars. This sets up the debugger. To run the debugger to the breakpoint, execute to the next breakpoint by selecting the double, blue, right-facing arrow symbol. (To stop debugging select the blue square.) With the Variable Explorer selected in the upper right of SPYDER, you can see the active variables in the program's namespace.

Here are the steps:

1. Set the breakpoint (double-click the line number for line 5)
2. Check that the Variable Explorer is selected in the upper-right window
3. Start the debugger (the blue right-arrow and two bars symbol) 
4. Execute to the breakpoint (the blue, double right-arrow symbol) 
5. Step one line at a time (blue curved arrow with one dot) 
6. When you are done hit the "stop debugging" button 

Figure C.7 indicates the stepping symbol. The Variable Explorer window shows the variables in the program's namespace. Every time you click the step symbol one line of code is executed. That line is highlighted in the editor window and is indicated in the shell. As you step through the code observe variable changes in the Variable Explorer window in the upper right. What you notice as you step through this code is that the variable `number`, the loop control variable, never changes so that is the reason for the infinite loop. It needs to be incremented within the loop suite at the end.

With that error fixed we have the Code Listing C.3.

Code Listing C.3

```
# sum the numbers from 1 to 100
the_sum = 0
number = 1
while number <= 100:
    the_sum = the_sum + number
    number+= 1
print("Sum:", the_sum)
```

Running that code produces the sum 5050. Is that correct? The formula for the sum of a sequence of n integers starting at 1 is $n(n-1)/2$, which for $n = 100$ also produces the sum 5050 so the code is correct.

C.2.4 Debugging Example 1 Using *print()*

How might I find the error of Example 1 without using the debugger? You might not have access to a debugger or might find it inconvenient for the information you need to gather. The idea here is to get to information about the state of the program while it is running. The technique is to carefully place `print()` statements to display the values of variables—much like we examined values in the Variable Explorer. The rule is to place `print()` statements where we set breakpoints. For example, place a `print()` statement at the beginning of a loop to discover the state in each iteration. A useful protocol is to label your output. Code Listing C.4 shows Example 1 with a labeled print statement at the beginning of the loop.

Code Listing C.4

```
# sum the numbers from 1 to 100
the_sum = 0
number = 1
while number <= 100:
```

```
    print("number:",number,"; the_sum:",the_sum)
    the_sum = the_sum + number
print("Sum:", the_sum)
```

When we run this version of the code the infinite loop is apparent. Figure C.8 shows the output displayed in the shell. In the time it took to take a snapshot of the screen the program had generated over half-a-million print statements. The only way to halt SPYDER is to Restart the kernel by selecting the icon shown in Figure C.8. Restarting loses the printed information, but it is easy to observe that `number` never changes, as we noted earlier. We need to increment `number` at the bottom of the loop suite as shown earlier.

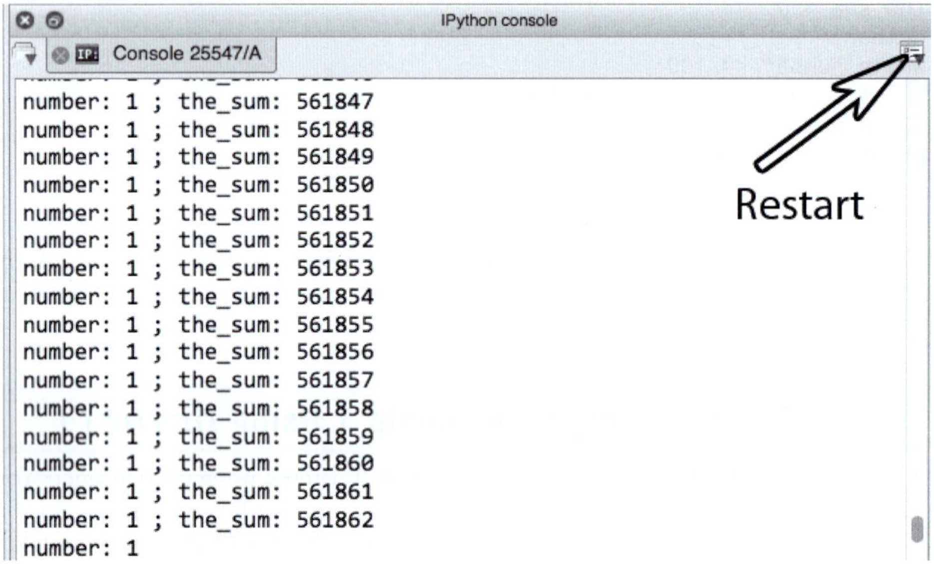

FIGURE C.8 Infinite loop printing. [Screenshot from Python. Copyright © by Python. Used by permission of Python.]

One nice feature of using print statements is that you watch the values change in "real" time. For example, when this program is corrected you can see the sum accumulate as shown in Figure C.9.

C.2.5 Debugging with SPYDER Example 2

To explore the debugger further let's find the median of a list of values. For example, given the sorted list [1, 3, 5] the median is 3, the middle value. That list had an odd number of values. If there are an even number of values, take the average of the two middle values.

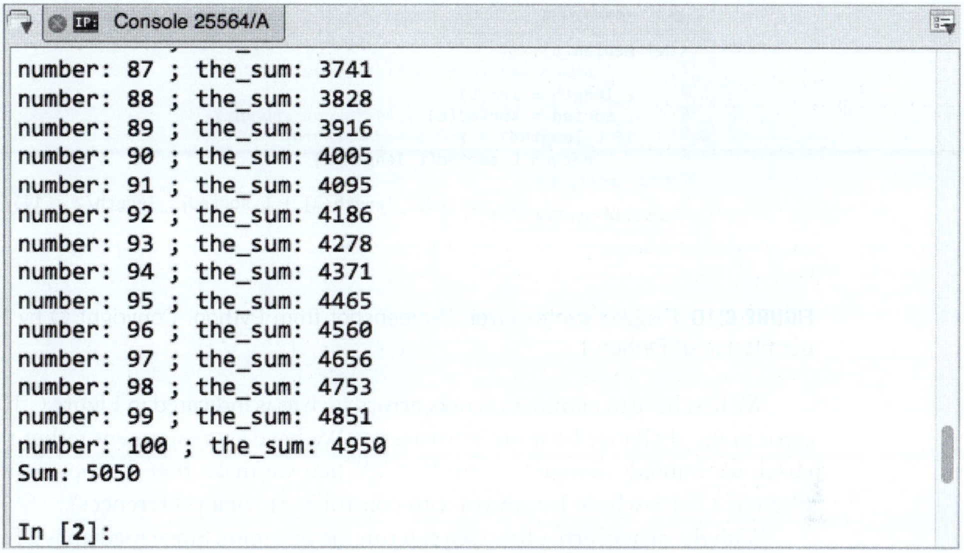

FIGURE C.9 Loop printing. [Screenshot from Python. Copyright © by Python. Used by permission of Python.]

That is, the even-length sorted list [1, 3, 5, 7] has median 4.0, which was calculated using $(3 + 5)/2$.

Our algorithm is:

- Find the length of the list.
- if the length is odd, divide the length by two to get the index of the middle
- else find the indices of the two middle values and find their average

Code Listing C.5 shows our first version of the code—with errors (can you find them?).

Code Listing C.5

```
def median(L):
    '''return median of a list of values'''
    L_length = len(L)
    L_sorted = sorted(L) # Let's not change L
    if L_length%2 = 1:  # even length
        return L_sorted[L_length/2]
    else:               # odd length
        return (L_sorted[L_length/2] + L_sorted[L_length/2 + 1])/2
```

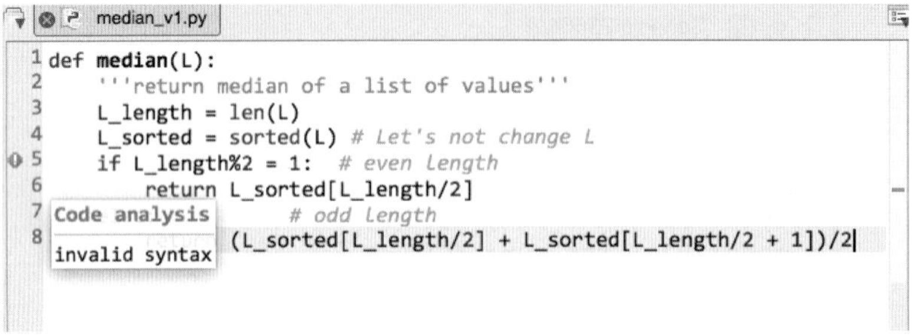

FIGURE C.10 Flagged syntax error. [Screenshot from Python. Copyright © by Python. Used by permission of Python.]

We first have to eliminate syntax errors such as is indicated in Figure C.10. As before, the error in the shell may be more informative. We have an assignment rather than the equality check we wanted: change "=" to "==". When we make that fix the error flag disappears (there is a delay whose length you can control in SPYDER preferences).

With the syntax error fixed we can run the program. Since median is a function we must call it in the shell with some list, for example, `median([1,5,3])` as shown in Figure C.11. We now see a new error: *TypeError: list indices must be integers, not float.* The error message indicates that we have an error in the index to a list. The indicated line indexes the `L_sorted` list as `L_sorted[L_length/2]`. Since the division "/" in our index `L_length/2` returns a float that is the source of the error. We can fix that with integer division("//"), but we made the same mistake in line 8 so let's fix those, too.

With those errors fixed we can test that `median([1,5,3])` returns a result, but is it correct? What is the right answer? In this case, we can call on a statistics module so let's ***import*** `statistics` and find out what the correct answer is. See Figure C.12. Calling

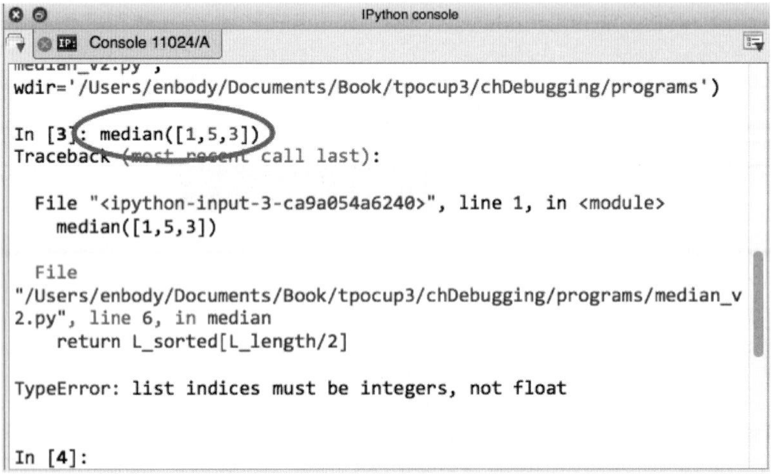

FIGURE C.11 Syntax error in shell. [Screenshot from Python. Copyright © by Python. Used by permission of Python.]

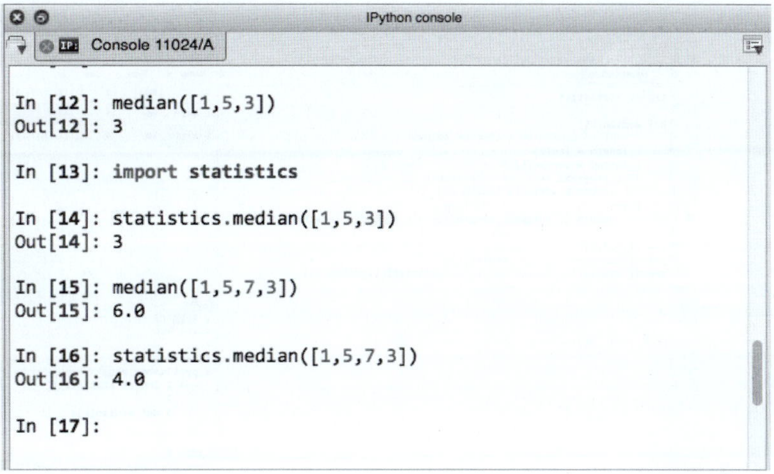

FIGURE C.12 No error, but still not correct. [Screenshot from Python. Copyright © by Python. Used by permission of Python.]

median in the statistics module yields the same result. Note that we have only tested an odd-length list so let's test an even-length list, `median([1,5,7,3])`, and compare it to the result from the statistics module. Again, we find a problem as shown in Figure C.12.

By this time you may be tiring of typing and retyping the testing code so let's build it into our program as shown in Code Listing C.6.

Code Listing C.6

```
import statistics

def median(L):
    '''return median of a list of values'''
    L_length = len(L)
    L_sorted = sorted(L) # Let's not change L
    if L_length%2 == 1:  # even length
        return L_sorted[L_length//2]
    else:                # odd length
        return (L_sorted[L_length//2] + L_sorted[L_length//2 + 1])/2

L = [1,5,7,3]
print("Median of",L,"is",median(L))
print("Statistics median of",L,"is",statistics.median(L))
```

With the call to median embedded in the program, we can now call up the debugger and set a breakpoint. Upon inspecting our code we have only one line related to odd length

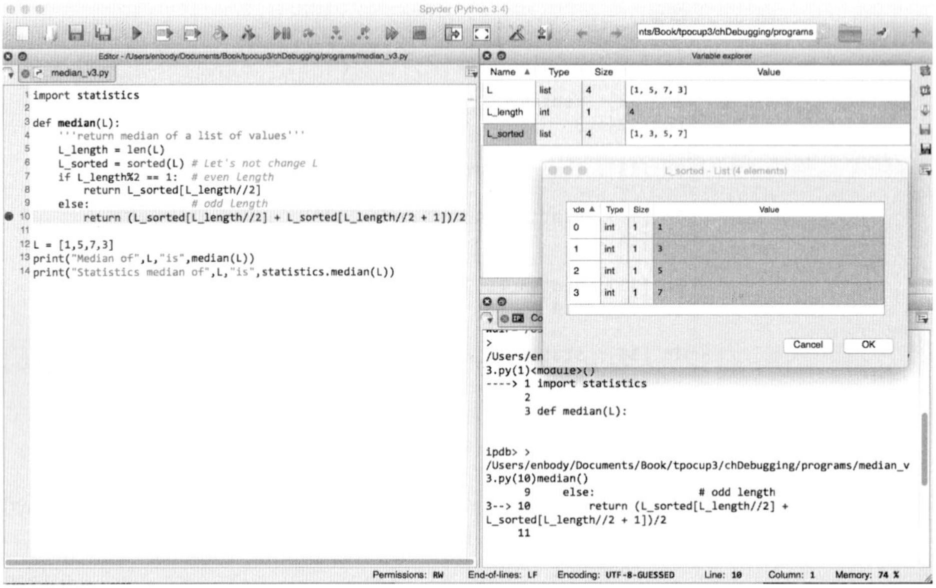

FIGURE C.13 Collection pop-up in Variable Explorer. [Screenshot from Python. Copyright © by Python. Used by permission of Python.]

lists, and it is likely that our problem is again with the indices. That is line 10, so we can set a breakpoint there by double-clicking on the number 10. A small red circle marks a set breakpoint. The mark can be seen along the left side in Figure C.13.

With a breakpoint set we need to fire up the debugger and run the program to the breakpoint. As shown earlier in Figure C.7,

1. Set the breakpoint (double-click the line number for line 10).
2. Check that the Variable Explorer is selected in the upper-right window.
3. Start the debugger (the blue right-arrow and two bars symbol).
4. Execute to the breakpoint (the blue, double right-arrow symbol).
5. When you are done hit the "stop debugging" button.

In the Variable Explorer, you can see the active variables in the function's namespace. What is new in the example is that we can double-click on the name of a collection, such as a list, Variable Explorer. The Variable Explorer then pops up a window with information about the collection.

In our example, you can see `L_sorted` as [1,3,5,7] as well as `L_length` whose value is 4. Our index calculations are `L_length//2` and `L_length//2 + 1` yielding indices of 2 and 3 respectively. Those indices select values 5 and 7 in `L_sorted` rather than the 3 and 5 values we want (indices 1 and 2). Therefore, we are "off by one," a common problem. We can fix it by subtracting 1 from each index as shown in Code Listing C.7. Since the second index had a "+1" now subtracting 1 cancels that increment.

Code Listing C.7

```python
import statistics

def median(L):
    '''return median of a list of values'''
    L_length = len(L)
    L_sorted = sorted(L) # Let's not change L
    if L_length%2 == 1:  # even length
        return L_sorted[L_length//2]
    else:                 # odd length
        return (L_sorted[L_length//2-1] + L_sorted[L_length//2])/2

L = [1,5,7,3]
print("Median of",L,"is",median(L))
print("Statistics median of",L,"is",statistics.median(L))
```

We now get the correct answer for this list, but we should not stop testing. Next test is the edge cases—in this case what happens if we pass an empty list to the median function? It generates an *IndexError: list index out of range* because any index we generate will be out of range. One fix would be to return `None`, if the length of the list is zero. An alternative would be ***if not*** `L`.

We are still not done. We need to test more. Let's generate random lists and use that to explore the debugger further. We'll begin with lists of length 10 containing 10 random integers, but we can randomize the length, too. Code Listing C.8 adds a `gen_list` function, but with errors so we can explore the debugger.

Code Listing C.8

```python
import statistics, random

def gen_list(count,max):
    '''return a list of length count of random integers from 0 to max '''
    L = []
    i = 1
    while i < count:
        L.append(random.randint(0,max))
    return L

def median(L):
    '''return median of a list of values'''
    if len(L) == 0:
        return None
```

```
15      L_length = len(L)
16      L_sorted = sorted(L) # Let's not change L
17      if L_length%2 == 1:  # even length
18          return L_sorted[L_length//2]
19      else:                # odd length
20          return (L_sorted[L_length//2-1] + L_sorted[L_length//2])/2
21
22  L = gen_list(10, random.randint(0,100))
23  print("L=",L)
24  print("My median of L is",median(L))
25  print("Statistics median of L is",statistics.median(L))
```

When we run the code in Code Listing C.8 nothing happens—there must be an infinite loop. We could find it by inspection (can you see it?). As before we can set a breakpoint and step through the function one line at a time. There is only one loop and that is in the `gen_list` function so let's put a breakpoint there. The best place is the first line of the loop, line 8 (in this case there is only one line).

Let's review our steps (Refer to Figure C.7):

1. Set the breakpoint (double-click the line number for line 8).
2. Check that the Variable Explorer is selected in the upper-right window.
3. Start the debugger (the blue right-arrow and two bars symbol).
4. Execute to the breakpoint (the blue, double right-arrow symbol).
5. Step one line at a time (blue curved arrow with one dot).
6. When you are done hit the "stop debugging" button.

Figure C.14 was grabbed after four items were added to the list. Every time you click the step symbol, one line of code is executed. That line is highlighted in the editor window and is indicated in the shell. As you step through the code, observe variable changes in the Variable Explorer window in the upper right. What you notice as you step through this code is that the variable `i`, the loop control variable, never changes so that is the reason for the infinite loop. It needs to be incremented within the loop suite at the end.

Now we generate correct medians, but there is still a problem. We specified lists of length 10, but end up with lists of length 9. Why? (Can you spot it?) The `count` variable is suspect since it controls the loop that builds the lists so let's use the debugger to find this error. This time set *two* breakpoints: one at the top of the loop suite and the other right after the loop as shown in Figure C.15. Everything looked fine when stepping through the loop until it exited too early. Figure C.15 shows what the Variable Explorer looks like after the loop. We see that the value of `i` is 10 so what happened? Our loop-control Boolean is wrong. If with start with `i=1`, the Boolean should be `i <= count`. Alternatively, we could start with `i=0` and use `i < count` as the Boolean.

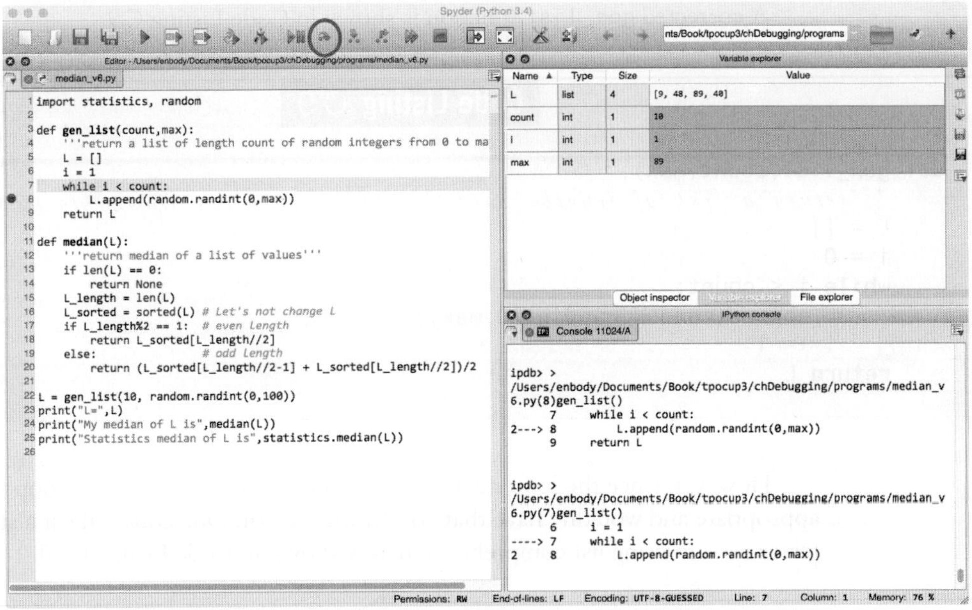

FIGURE C.14 Stepping one line at a time in the debugger. [Screenshot from Python. Copyright © by Python. Used by permission of Python.]

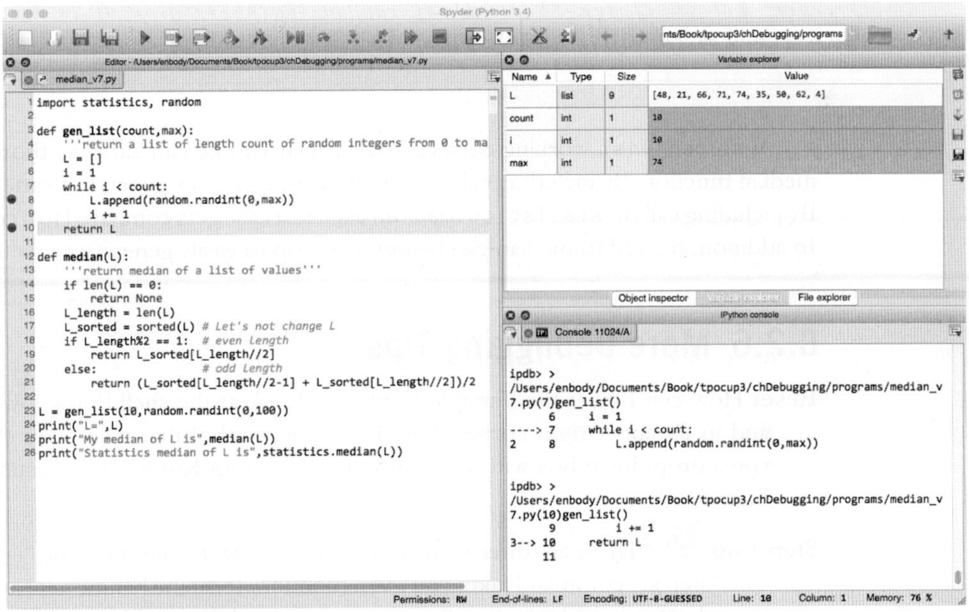

FIGURE C.15 Two breakpoints. [Screenshot from Python. Copyright © by Python. Used by permission of Python.]

A corrected `gen_list` function is shown in Code Listing C.9.

Code Listing C.9

```
def gen_list(count,max):
    '''return a list of length count of random integers from 0 to max '''
    L = []
    i = 0
    while i < count:
        L.append(random.randint(0,max))
        i += 1
    return L
```

However, since the loop iterates a fixed number of times a "for" loop would be more appropriate and wouldn't have that "off by one" error. One could take it a step further to a terser version using list comprehension as is shown in Code Listing C.10.

Code Listing C.10

```
def gen_list(count,max):
    '''return a list of length count of random integers from 0 to max '''
    return [random.randint(0,max) for i in range(count)]
```

With `gen_list` working correctly many tests can be run easily to thoroughly test the median function. By including calls to `randint` we can easily generate a variety of test cases. By including calls to `statistics.median` each test case gets compared to a correct solution. In addition, the call to median can be put in a loop to easily generate many test cases.

C.2.6 More Debugging Tips

Reset How can I reset the Variable Explorer? Look at the shell in the lower right corner and in its upper right corner there is a small symbol that when you click on it gives you a drop-down box with the option to "Interrupt Kernel" or "Restart Kernel". See Figure C.7.

Step Into  There are three step commands. We have seen the basic "step" command. The "step in" command takes you *into* a function. It can be handy, but can have difficult-to-understand results because sometimes you end up stepping into system or module functions. For example, if there is a simple print statement you will be taken into the messy details of the print operation. If you end up there, stop debugging and restart. It is usually easiest to set a breakpoint where you want to go.

Step Over  The third step command is the "step over" command that takes you past a function. It's stated operation is "Run until the current function or method returns." However, like the "step in" command it can take you into the messy details of functions or methods.

C.3 MORE ABOUT TESTING

Testing is a very broad category; it would be difficult to cover it in sufficient depth in an introductory programming book. However, it is an interesting topic and one often ignored in introductory books. We think it is important enough to take a quick look. Let's get started.

There are various philosophies on how, when, and why testing should be done. Some of these include:

- Planning versus code testing. This might be better phrased as *static* versus *dynamic* testing. Static testing is work done without running the code. You might think of it as the various stages of understanding the requirements of the code and then planning to achieve those goals. Dynamic testing is the kind of testing done with the code, during execution of the code. It should be noted that in good software development, developing static tests is an important part of the overall software development process. However, this chapter will focus on dynamic testing, that is, testing with code.
- When to test: *post-coding* versus *pre-coding* testing. Traditionally, code is developed and then handed off to an independent testing group. The testing group develops the tests and, when errors are found, passes that information back to the developers, all in a cycle. However, more modern testing approaches, including *agile* and *extreme* programming, focus on developing the tests to be applied to code *before* the code is written. As the code is written and updated, these tests are used as the standard for gauging progress and success.
- Levels of testing. *Unit* testing is focused on the individual pieces (modules, functions, classes) of code as they are developed. *Integration* testing focuses on bringing tested modules together to see whether they work as intended. *System* testing focuses on the entire system to see whether it meets the goals of the project.
- What to test? This is probably a category all unto itself, as there are many goals one might focus on for testing. They would include:
  - **Correctness**. Are the results produced correct? What counts as correct? Do we know all the cases?
  - **Completeness**. Are all the potential cases covered: all user entries, all file formats, all data types, and so on?
  - **Security**. Is the program safe from being broken into by another user, through the Internet, or otherwise?

- **Interface**. Is the interface usable? Are its features complete? Does the user get what he or she expects when using the program?
- **Load**. Does the program respond well if it is presented with a heavy load: many users, large data sets, heavy Internet traffic, and so on?
- **Resources**. Does the program use appropriate amounts of memory, CPU, and network?
- **Responsiveness**. Does the program respond in a reasonable amount of time? If there are time limits, does it meet those limits?

And on and on. Testing is a complicated business!

C.3.1 Testing Is Hard!

One of things we want to convey is that testing is hard—at least as hard as writing the program in the first place. That is one of the reasons we have left testing to the end. You have had enough on your hands, learning to design programs, implement them in code, and then fix them.

Correctness

How hard is testing? Let's just pick one of the examples mentioned earlier: correctness. How does one determine whether a program is correct? One type of correctness would be a *proof*. There is a branch of software engineering that focuses on that very topic: taking a program, turning it into a mathematical expression, and proving its correctness. However, that is a very difficult task. In fact, at this time it is not possible to take an arbitrary program and prove it correct. So correctness is often practically measured against a specification of behavior provided by the user. However, even that measurement can be difficult.

In 1993, Intel released its first Pentium™ desktop CPU. It was a new architecture and required many years of development, including new software to make the chip run. In 1994, it was discovered that the floating-point division instruction had a small flaw, due to an error in tables that the algorithm used for its calculations (these tables were stored on the chip). It resulted in a rare error in some divisions. *Byte* magazine in 1994 estimated that about 1 in 9×10^9 divisions of random numbers would show the defect. How many cases should Intel have tested to see whether it was correct? Yet a professor at Lynchburg college performing some mathematical calculations *did* hit the error in his work, rare or not.[4] To further illustrate the insidiousness of this example, Intel *had* developed both the correct algorithm and table, but when the table was loaded into the chip, a portion was inadvertently set to zeros!

[4] See more information at the wikipedia page on the FDIV error, http://www.trnicely.net/pentbug/pentbug.html.

C.3.2 Importance of Testing

Testing is important. In fact, many modern software developers put testing as the first problem to be solved! As we mentioned earlier, *agile* software development focuses on writing the tests before the code is written. In so doing, a developer accomplishes two very important tasks:

- Focus on what the code *should* do before actually coding the implementation. It relates to our old maxim: think before you program. By writing the tests first, you focus on what the code should do.
- Once tests have been set up, every new piece of code or change to existing code has a test-base in place to assure the developer that their code is correct, at least as far as the measures provided.

Even beginning programmers should try to integrate testing into their development process. Python embeds tools to make this process easier. We will introduce some examples here and hope that you will be exposed to more in your programming career.

C.3.3 Other Kinds of Testing

Python provides a number of support modules for testing. The `unittest` module provides a much greater level of control to run testing. The module `nose`[5] also provides a greater level of control, and both can do some system testing. In-depth coverage of that module is beyond the scope of an introductory book and is left to the reader.

C.4 WHAT'S WRONG WITH MY CODE?

Here we have collected in one place all the suggestions that were at the end of each chapter.

C.4.1 Chapter 1: Beginnings

Here are suggestions for finding problems with Python beginnings.

The most important thing to do is: "Read the Error message!." Learning to read error message helps tremendously when deciphering errors.

Error messages can appear in two places:

- **In the SPYDER editor:** an error flag appears to the left of line numbers. You can mouse over error marker to see the error. If not a syntax error, the error is likely a kind of `NameError` (see later).
- **In the shell:** Two types of errors

[5] http://code.google.com/p/python-nose

Static Errors that SPYDER can also point out in the editor. These include syntax errors, missing modules and misnamed variables.

Run-time Errors that can only be found when running the program.

Types of Error messages that are likely to occur from topics in this chapter.

- **ValueError** These are often a conversion error, for example, `float('abc')`.
  `ValueError: could not convert string to float: 'abc'`
- **TypeError** These often result from trying to do an operation on two different types that are not permitted in Python. For example, mismatched types, for example, `'abc' - 2` `TypeError: unsupported operand type(s) for -: 'str' and 'int'` The Variable Explorer shows type so it is a good place to check for helpful information.

  Also remember our naming conventions in Section 1.4.6. If you append type information to your variables it is easier to track down this kind of error.
- **NameError** This error usually means that the name is not in the namespace. This often means that you never gave the identifier (name) an initial value. Since Variable Explorer shows your namespace you will see that the name isn't there. There are generally two reasons:
  - *Identifier not initialized*, for example, `x = y` # but y never initialized
    `NameError: name 'y' is not defined`
  - *Forgot import*, for example, you forgot to import math or forgot to prepend math
    `x = sqrt(y)`
    `NameError: name 'sqrt' is not defined`
- **Syntax Error** For example,
  `x === 3`
  `SyntaxError: invalid syntax`
  In the shell, the message will point to the error.
- **ZeroDivisionError:** Self-explanatory

There are other errors that either do not generate an error or the error generated is not helpful. Watch for these!

- **Mismatched Parentheses** can occur for many reasons and can be hard to find. If you have many parentheses or wonder if you have them correct, the IDE such as Spyder can help by matching corresponding pairs. One trick is to delete parenthesis at the end of a line or expression and watch the IDE highlight the corresponding one as you add parentheses back in one at a time. Also, Spyder automatically fills in all matching parenthesis as you type. An important thing to keep in mind is that errors with parenthesis can be generated by Python a few lines *after* where the error actually occurred—Python got confused and finally gave up and generated an unhelpful error message.

Note, error messages indicate a line number for the error, but sometimes, especially with a `SyntaxError`, the error actually happens on an earlier line. This is because the interpreter tries hard to understand what was given to it, but gives up at some point, usually down the program from where the error initially occurred.

Finally, be careful that you do not select a variable name that is already in use by Python as a built-in or module name. For example, you might run the following code `str = "abc"`, assigning a value to the variable `str`. The only problem is the Python is using `str` as the name of the string type. However, Python is happy to oblige. During the remainder of your program, `str` is a variable and not a type. Pay attention to **colors** when creating variable names. SPYDER colors Python keywords. If a color pops up on your variable, perhaps you should look and see if it is a Python keyword. Finally, if you fix the problem (change the variable name) then, when you start Python up again, the problem will go away.

C.4.2 Chapter 2: Control

Here are suggestions for finding problems with control.

- **Conditional**:
  - *Boolean expression error*: Test your Boolean expression in the shell.
  - *Value errors*: Insert a breakpoint on the header line to examine the values in the Boolean expression.
  - *Incorrect indentation* Is rare: inspection is the only solution.
- **Repetition**:
  - ***Started wrong***: The initialization expression is wrong: insert a breakpoint (or print the value) right before your Boolean expression first checks it.
  - ***Stopped wrong***: The Boolean expression is wrong: insert a breakpoint on the loop's header line and examine the loop-control variable (or print the loop-control variable as the first instruction in the suite). It may be useful to put a breakpoint immediately **after** the loop to examine the final value of the loop-control variable (or print it).
  - ***Incremented wrong***: The change expression is wrong or in the wrong place. A breakpoint (or print) at the first instruction in the suite is helpful.
  - **Problem with the loop variable:** Generally the way to isolate these problems is to observe the loop variable. When you see the values changing that is often a valuable clue to the problem. There are three things you can try:
    - *Print* the loop variable and watch it change.
    - *Set a Breakpoint:* An alternative to printing is to break at the beginning of the loop and examine the loop value in the Variable Explorer.
    - *Print range:* Printing the range values with your expression can help understand what your code is actually iterating over. However, you need to wrap `list(...)` around range to see the values, for example, `print(list(range(5)))`.

    Here are some common causes:

    * *Modified loop variable in for*: modifying the loop variable in a *for* loop can cause unexpected problems. That is, if you have `for i in range(5):` do not modify `i` within the loop suite.

  * *Range value is wrong*: a common problem is to forget that `range` generates a half-open interval in that it doesn't include the final value. That is, `range(5)` generates 0, 1, 2, 3, and 4, but **not** 5.
  * *Range value is zero*: sometimes `range(x)` will be a problem because `x` is either zero or `None`.

C.4.3 Chapter 4: Strings

With strings the error message itself is more useful than the type of error message generated. Two types of error messages dominate string errors: `IndexError` and `TypeError`. Many string errors manifest themselves as `TypeError` so it is the error message itself that is most useful.

The two most common error messages are:

- **IndexError: string index out of range** clearly describes the problem, for example, `s='hello'` and you try `s[15]` whose index is beyond the end of the string `s` (indices 0:4).
- **TypeError: 'str' object does not support item assignment** occurs when indexing appears on the LHS of an assignment statement, for example, `s[0]='x'`. Since a string is immutable, individual characters cannot be modified and this is the resulting error message.

Less common errors are these; both are `TypeErrors`.

- **TypeError: replace() takes at least 2 arguments (1 given)** or something similar occurs when the wrong number of arguments are used for the method. In this case, `replace` expects at least two arguments, but only one was provided: `s.replace('e')`. A similar error can occur for other string methods, or for a function with the wrong number of arguments such as `len()`; that is, providing no arguments when one is expected.
- **TypeError: unorderable types: str() < int()** occurs when two different types are compared, but such a comparison is not permitted in Python, for example, `'x'<5`. The problem is obvious in that example, but less obvious when comparing two identifiers, for example, `x<y` unless you know the types. Observing the types in SPYDER's variable explorer can help, as can the naming practices we have described (appending type info to the variable name, see Section 1.4.6).

Other errors which are less likely.

- **String arithmetic errors:** string arithmetic allows some operations, but not others. For example, `'hello'*2` is fine; it results in `'hellohello'`. However, the following cause problems:
  - `'hello'*'a'` generates the error: `TypeError: can't multiply sequence by non-int of type 'str'`. While multiplication by an integer is allowed, multiplying a string by another string is not permitted by Python.

– `'hello'+2` generates the error: `TypeError: Can't convert 'int' object to str implicitly`. While multiplication is allowed, there is no corresponding operation for adding a string and a number. In this case, the interpreter thinks you might be trying to add two strings together (something it understands) and that the second argument, a number, should be converted to a string. However, as the error message indicates, there isn't a rule for automatically converting a number to a string. If your intent is to convert the number to a string, then you must do so explicitly: `'hello'+ str(2)`.

- **String formatting errors** come from a missmatch of either types or number of items to be formatted.
  – **Type missmatch** occurs when the format specifier type doesn't match the provided item, for example, specifying an integer format (`"{:d}"`) while providing a string argument; that is, `"{:d}".format("abc")`. The resulting error message is: `ValueError: Unknown format code 'd' for object of type 'str'` which effectively says that the 'd' format isn't defined for use with a string (it is for use with an integer).
  – **Wrong number of arguments** occurs when you specify say two items to format, but there is a mismatch in the number of format elements and arguments for example, `"{}{}".format("a")`. The resulting error message seems unrelated: `IndexError: tuple index out of range`. We don't describe 'tuples' until a later chapter, but the argument to the format method is implicitly a tuple and this message is saying that two items were expected, but only one was found, hence "out of range."
- **Missing Parenthesis in Method:** Some string methods such as `lower()` and `upper()` take no arguments so it is easy to forget the parenthesis. If you type such an expression into the interpreter you don't get an error message. Instead you get unexpected output such as `<function str.upper>` or `<built-in method upper of str object at 0x106e85998>`. Effectively you not asking Python to **run** the method, which would require the parentheses, but are instead asking Python to **report** what "lower" **is**, which Python dutifully reports.

  Even worse would be the following code: `f = "abc".lower`. Again, no error occurs but what is assigned to the variable `f` is the **function** "lower," not the result of **running** `lower`. Probably not what you wanted

C.4.4 Chapter 5: Functions

Here are suggestions for finding problems with functions.

- **Test Functions Independently:** A particularly useful trick is the ability to run individual functions within Spyder. That allows us to test functions independently. Within the Spyder IDE highlight the function and under the "Run" drop-down select "Run Selection or current line" to run the highlighted function. After it has been "run" you can now call the function from within the shell. Run the function with sample arguments and see if it produces the results you expect. *Testing functions independently is one of the most important approaches to programming you can learn!*

- **Examine the Function's Namespace:** Setting a breakpoint within a function allows you to examine the function's namespace within the Variable Explorer window of Spyder (upper right of IDE). Knowing the value of variables, particularly the provided arguments, is useful for finding problems.
- **Stepping through a Function:** Set a breakpoint at the beginning of the function and then step through the function, one instruction at a time. This is useful for observing what is the function is actually doing. Pay particular attention to which parts of control (loops or selection) that you step through. Often there is a problem with a Boolean expression or the values of variables within the expression.
- **Mismatched arguments and parameters:** This kind of error message is self explanatory and helpful with its information. Here is an example.
  `TypeError: square() missing 1 required positional argument: 'x'`
- **None:** When a variable has an unexpected value such as `None` of a function definition such as `<function str.lower>` it is often due to that variable being incorrectly assigned a value from a function call in one of two ways: First, mistakenly assigning the result of a function call that **has no return**, that is, `result = [1,3,2].sort()`. Such non-return functions are usually associated with mutable data structures such as lists. The other is forgetting the parenthesis in the function call, that is, `f = "ABC.lower"`. The function was never **run**, and you don't get the result you expected.
  When you see such an error, walk the code back to find the function that provided a value to that variable. It likely is missing a return statement.
- **TypeError:** Sometimes you get a `TypeError` when there is mismatch of types between the provided argument and how that argument is used in the function. For example, maybe you passed a string to a function that is performing integer arithmetic that is not defined for strings. Again, either the Variable Explorer or proper naming can help sort out this problem.

C.4.5 Chapter 6: Files and Exceptions

Here are suggestions for finding problems with files.

Here are three common errors or problems you will find when opening and writing to files:

- **FileNotFoundError:** The error message describes the problem, but not what caused it. Here are the two most common causes:
  - **Misspelled file name:** If you misspelled the file name, Python cannot find it.
  - **File not in the same folder as the program:** By default a program looks for a file in the same directory as the program. If it isn't there, Python cannot find it. If the file

is in another directory by choice, you must give a fully qualified path to that file; that is, "/Users/bill/Documents/file.txt".

- Remember that the IPython console can help with the previous two errors in two ways:
  - In the console itself, when you **Run** your edited file a line shows up in the console of the form: `runfile('/Users/user/python/file.py', wdir='/Users/user/python')` where the `wdir` is the working directory, the assumed location of any files you are trying to open. Is that the correction working directory?
  - You can use the IPython history commands (the up and down arrow on your keyboard) to get the previous command back and fix any misspellings of the filename.
- **Empty or partially written file:** If you forget to *close* a file, some of what you wrote to the file might be missing. Python tries to deal with this, but it is not always successful. *Always remember to close files!*
- **Accidentally overwriting a file:** Python does not warn you if you are about to overwrite a file. For example, if you open a file with "w" as the modifier, the contents of the file, if it already exists, will be lost.

Here are some errors you might run into when reading the contents of a file, especially when iterating through the file's contents line by line.

- **TypeError**: Remember that what is returned by iterating through a file is a string. Even if that file's contents contain a number on that particular line, that number is returned as a **string**, not an integer (or a float, or anything else). You must explicitly convert the numeric-string to its appropriate arithmetic value before you can use it in an arithmetic calculation.
- **Extra Line**: Not a Python error per se, but if you print out your lines of input and get an extra line (like double spacing), what happened? Did you remember to `strip` your line when you got it? Otherwise it is carrying a extra "*n*".
- **IndexError**: Remember that some of the file lines may only have a "*n*", basically a blank line in the file. When you `strip` such a line you are left with an empty string. You cannot index any character in an empty string as it has none, thus leading to the `IndexError`.

C.4.6 Chapter 7: Lists and Tuples

Here are suggestions for finding problems with lists.

As a sequence, lists have similar issues with ranges as we saw in strings. Tuples, being immutable, cannot have their elements changed, as we also saw in strings. Lists do not have as many methods (11) as strings (44) so there are fewer errors associated with method use. However, there are some errors that tend to happen with lists that are really control problems.

- **None:** a common way to end up with `None` with lists is to combine assignment with append, for example, `x=my_list.append(y)`. Since append has a side effect of updating the end of the string and **no return**, the value of *x* will be `None`. A similar thing happens by mixing up the `sorted` function (which returns a sorted list) versus the `sort` method (with has a side effect of sorting the list and no return). The problem manifests itself with `x=my_list.sort(y)`, which results in *x* having a value of `None`.
- **[ ]:** an unexpected empty list is usually a control error—your `append` statement was never executed. Usually that is a problem with the Boolean expression or its values. Set a breakpoint and check Variable Explorer for errant values.
- **IndexError:** as with other collections such as strings an `IndexError` comes from two sources:
  - The list has a different length than expected. Often the list is empty, but another common problem is "off by one"; that is, the list is one element smaller or larger than expected. Remember, indices in lists begin with 0 and the last index is at length −1. This is often a control problem so set a breakpoint and examine your Boolean expression.
  - The index variable is wrong—again, "off by one" is common.
- **Tuples are immutable** so item assignment is not allowed. This problem is similar to what happens with strings, the other immutable collection. For example, `my_tuple[2]=5` will generate this error: `TypeError:'tuple'object does not support item assignment.`
- **IndexError**: Finally, there is a way to generate an `IndexError` other than "off by one" error or the like. Unlike other sequences, lists are mutable. Thus, as you iterate through a list it is possible to modify the list as you iterate. However, **never modify a mutable during iteration**. We mentioned this as a programming tip in Section 7.2.4 but `IndexError` is one way this manifests itself.

C.4.7 Chapter 8: More Functions

The problems we encounter here all center on the use of mutable parameter objects such as lists.

- If you pass a mutable, such as a list, to a function, then a change in that mutable is preserved across the call. That is, the mutable **argument** in the calling program will be changed by any change to that mutable **parameter** in the function. You can check for this by setting a breakpoint before and after the function call in SPYDER and watching how the mutable value is updated.
- Another problem discussed in some detail in Section 8.2.1 is using a mutable, such as a list, as a default parameter value. The short answer is **don't**. A default value is created once, and only once, when the function is defined. If the default is modified in the function, then as a mutable that change persists and you get changing default values. As

mentioned, if you need a mutable default value, assign a value of `None` as the default and check for it in the function code.

C.4.8 Chapter 9: Dictionaries

Here are suggestions for finding problems with dictionaries, sets, and scope.

- **Dictionaries**
  - **TypeError: 'builtin_function_or_method' object is not iterable:** happens when you forget the parenthesis in `for k,v in D.items():`. Similarly for the `keys()` or `values()` methods. You must invoke the method (use parentheses) to generate the results you require.
  - **KeyError** occurs when the key doesn't exist in the dictionary, similar to "out of range" for lists and strings. The error message prints the errant key.
  - **Empty dictionary:** When you unexpectedly find that your dictionary has no values, that is a *control* error. Suggestions include setting a breakpoint and examining your control Boolean expression and values.
  - **Unexpected value:** If you find unexpected values in a dictionary, you may have overwritten an existing key-value pair by reusing a key with a new value. Remember, dictionaries are mutable and the key can be updated with a new value.
  - **TypeError: unhashable type: 'list':** happens when you use a mutable for a key. Remember, you cannot use mutable items as a key in a dictionary. As in this example error, you cannot use a List as a key.
- **Sets**
  - **AttributeError: 'dict' object has no attribute 'add':** happens when you initialized a set with `s={}` instead of `s=set()`; that is, you created a dictionary when you wanted a set. You can observe the type in the Variable Explorer.
- **Scope**
  - **Global:** The most common "error" with respect to scope is using global variable references. A global variable is set in the outermost scope of the program and available to all other program elements. While not specifically an error, resolving why a global variable is being properly set can be difficult to debug. It is better to pass arguments to functions specifically to indicate the values being operated on by the function, making debugging easer. Setting a breakpoint at the end of a function lets you observe a function's namespace in Variable Explorer.

    More difficult is the **shadowing problem** discussed in Section 9.6. You can have the same name in different namespaces, and the **LEGB** rule is used to resolve the value. Thus you may try to refer to a variable's value and not get the expected result because **LEGB** resolved the value in an unexpected way. In particular, if you assign a variable inside of a function, that variable is now **local to the function namespace**. Again, passing arguments explicitly to functions can help make debugging the problem easier.

  - **NameError** for a name you know exists usually occurs because the name is in a different namespace. Variable Explorer is helpful for seeing what names are in the current namespace.
  - **UnboundLocalError** can occur when you unintentionally reference a global variable within a function. In this case you get a helpful error message: *UnboundLocalError: local variable 'i' referenced before assignment.* How did this happen? Consider the following code. In the `test()` function the `i + 1` on the RHS refers to `i`, which is local to the function because `i` first occurs on the LHS, but the local name has not been initialized.

```
def test():
    i = i + 1

i = 0
test()
```

C.4.9 Chapter 11: Classes I

Here are suggestions for finding problems with classes.

- **Forgot self:** If you forget `self` as the first parameter in a method you will get a mismatch in the number of parameters. Remember, **every** class method has `self` as its first parameter, even if the method takes no arguments when it is called. Python **automatically** associates the calling object and passes it as the first method parameter. The error message looks like this (for a method named `my_method`): **TypeError: my_method() takes 0 positional arguments but 1 was given**
- **Method __str__ must return a string:** If you forget to return a string from the `__str__` method, you will get this message: `TypeError: __str__ returned non-string (type int)`
- **AttributeError** often happens because you have mistyped the name of a method or an attribute is private.
  - If you mistyped the method, you can use your iPython history to bring it back and retype it.
  - If you can't remember the proper spelling, you can make an instance of the class, put a dot behind it and type the tab key. iPython will list all the potential methods.
  - If that doesn't work, remember the privacy rule covered in Section 11.9.1. If you prepend double underscores to an attribute name, special naming rules apply. For example, if the attribute is named `__my_attribute` in the class `MyClass`, the following are the rules:
    * **Inside MyClass**: The name remains `__my_attribute`, including in the context of any other `MyClass` methods.
    * **Outside MyClass**: The name outside of the `MyClass` namespace, you refer to the attribute as `_MyClass__my_attribute`.

- **NameError** often happens with you do not specify a class attribute correctly. This often occurs when you forget to prepend `self` to the name of a method in the class.
- **Forgot __init__:** If you forget to define an `__init__` method, you may get either unexpected results or an error such as an **AttributeError**. A class definition is not required to have an `__init__` method defined (a default one exists), in which case class instances are created with no attributes. However, by having `__init__` in your class, you can define, by assignment, attributes that you want to exist in every instance. Set a breakpoint after an instance is created to make sure it contains the attributes you expect. If not, check your `__init__` or create one if you don't have one.

C.4.10 Chapter 12: Classes II

Here are suggestions for finding problems with classes.

- **Return class type with arithmetic methods:** The most common mistake with arithmetic methods such as `__add__` is to forget to return objects of the class type. For example, if you add two Rational numbers, you expect the result to be a Rational number. The solution is `return Rational(num,denom)` where you create a Rational object before you return it.

Summary

In this chapter, we introduced the built-in debugging and testing capabilities of Python. These techniques assist in developing better code.

APPENDIX D

Pylab: A Plotting and Numeric Tool

> None of us is as smart as all of us.
>
> Ken Blanchard

As we have said previously, one of the strengths of Python is its fantastic user base—in particular, the many useful modules that those users provide. In fact, this is exactly what open source software is about—the sharing of effort for the good of all users.

In this chapter we take a brief look at the `pylab` module (which combines the `matplotlib` plotting and `numpy` numeric modules). Examples of its use are sprinkled throughout the book, so this appendix provides details.

D.1 PLOTTING

We will use pylab to create graphs. As its documentation says,

> pylab tries to make easy things easy and hard things possible.

As you have seen in some of the examples (see Figure 2.10 or Figure 2.11 and their associated code), it is relatively easy to do simple 2D plotting. However, pylab is *not* part of the standard Python distribution, but it is built into Anaconda's distribution which is one of the reasons we like it. An alternative packaged distribution is Enthought Canopy (`http://www.enthought.com/products/epd`). If you are not using a distribution that packages many of the common modules such as Anaconda or Canopy, you will need to download extra packages into your existing Python environment. *Matplotlib.org* is a good place to start, but note that you must install numpy from *numpy.org* first.

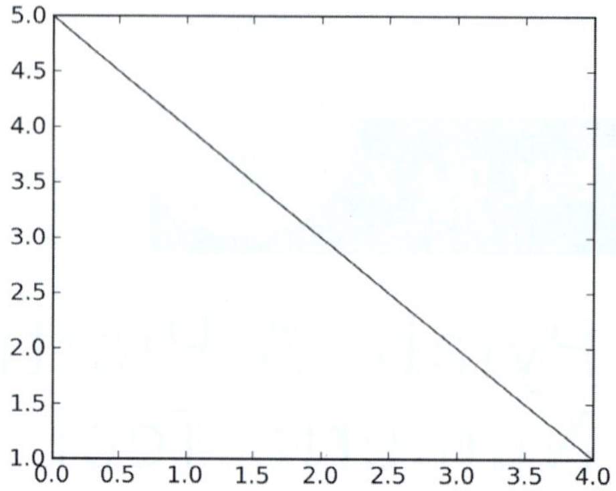

FIGURE D.1 First plot

Try the following in the shell to see if your plotting package is installed properly:

```
In  [1]: import pylab
In  [2]: pylab.plot([5,4,3,2,1])
```

You should get a plot such as Figure D.1. Note that if you want to draw the same plot in a program (instead of the shell), you need to add a final line, `pylab.show()`, to display the plot.

If you are not using Anaconda, but are using the standard IDLE with pylab, they do not always "play well" with each other. They are essentially sharing the graphics routines that draw to your screen and they sometimes get confused. You may be required to stop Python and restart. If this is a problem, you can always run your programs from a command line.

D.2 WORKING WITH PYLAB

Examples of working pylab code will be sprinkled throughout the book, but there are some wonderful repositories of more complicated examples. In particular, the gallery (`http://matplotlib.org/gallery.html`) provides a number of beautiful examples of what you can do with Python's plotting!

Let's quickly review some of the basic plotting commands. Remember, the online documentation is very good and provides a great deal of detail as well as examples.

D.2.1 Plot Command

The `plot` command allows you to make two-dimensional line drawings. We first ***import*** `pylab`, then we can do plots of the following kinds:

`pylab.plot(x-values,y-values)`

x-values *optional* list of x-values (default is 0 to `len(y-values)-1`)
y-values list of y-values

Examples:

- `pylab.plot(x_vals,y_vals)`: Assumes two lists of numeric values of equal length. Plot with default properties.
- `pylab.plot(y_vals)`: Creates x values in range of 0 to `len(y_vals)-1`. Plot with default properties.
- `pylab.plot(x_vals, y_vals, 'bo')`: Plot the x and y values, modify the line type to blue circles.
- `pylab.plot(x_vals,y_vals, 'gx', x_vals2, y_vals2, 'y+')`: Plot with two graphs in the same window. First plot is x_vals versus y_vals with green x's, second plot is x_vals2 vs. y_vals2 with yellow +'s. An equivalent double graph can be achieved with a separate `plot` command for each graph.

Try the following in the shell to place two plots in one figure:

```
pylab.plot([1,2,3,4,5,6,7,8,9,10],'ro',[5,5,5,5,5,5,5,5,5,5],
'gx')
```

D.2.2 Colors, Marks, and Lines

The pylab `plot` command allows one to plot with different colors, different marks, and different line characteristics such as line width or dashed.

color The standard colors are: 'blue', 'green', 'red', 'cyan', 'magenta', 'yellow', 'black', 'white'. Each can be specified by their first character, for example, 'r' for 'red', except 'black' which is 'k' because 'b' is for 'blue'.

marker There are 19 markers. Here are some common ones: 'o' for circle, '+' for plus, '*' for star, 'x' for x.

style There are seven line styles. Here are a few: '-' for line (default) , '–' for dashed , '-.' for dashes and dots.

linewidth A linewidth can be specified in pixels.

For example, here is a dashed red line with x-marks at data points with a line thickness of 3:

```
pylab.plot([1,2,3,4,5,6,7,8,9,10],'rx--',linewidth=3)
```

D.2.3 Generating X-Values

Often when you generate a plot you want to start with a list of x-values that act as input to some function, where the function's results are plotted as the y-values. For example, plotting graph where the y-values are the sin(x) for x-values from 0 to 4*pi. Pylab provides `linspace` for this purpose. `linspace` generates a specified number of elements between a provided range. The increment between elements is determined by the range and the number of elements:

```
pylab.linspace(start,stop,num)
```

start starting value of the sequence (included)
stop final value of the sequence (included)
num *optional* number of values (default is 50)
dtype *optional* type of values (default is float)

To create 100 *x*-values from 0 to 4*pi: `pylab.linspace(0, 4*math.pi, 100)`.

An alternative to `linspace` is `arange`. It takes four arguments as well but differs in the meaning of the third. The third argument for `arange` provides the increment between each element, which determines the number of elements that are generated. In general, `linspace` is preferred as it works more reliably.

D.2.4 Plot Properties

There are a number of properties you can attach to a plot. Here are some common properties:

pylab.xlabel('a_str') Labels the x-axis with 'a_str'
pylab.ylabel('a_str') Labels the y-axis with 'a_str'
pylab.title('a_str') Titles the plot at the top with 'a_str'
pylab.grid(True) Superimposes a grid on the plot area.

The program in Code Listing D.1 shows a sine plot with labels, as shown in Figure D.2.

Code Listing D.1

```
# Plot sine with labels
import math, pylab

x_values = pylab.linspace(0, math.pi*4, 50)
y_values = [math.sin(x) for x in x_values]
pylab.plot(x_values,y_values)
pylab.xlabel('x values')
pylab.ylabel('sine of x')
pylab.title('Plot of sine from 0 to 4pi')
pylab.show()
```

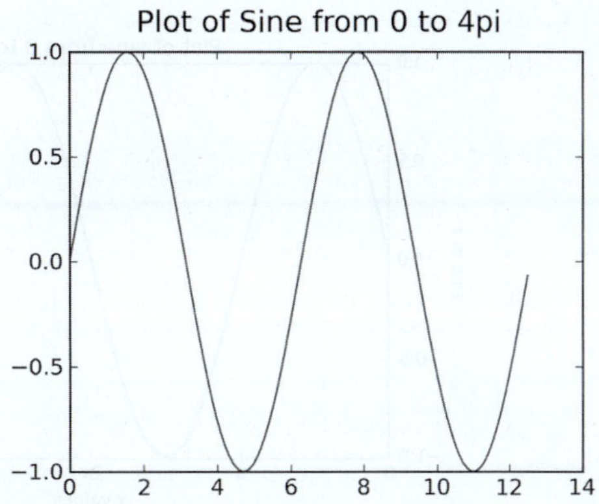

FIGURE D.2 Labeled sine wave code and resulting plot.

D.2.5 Tick Labels

Pylab provides a command to orient and label each axis entry. These entries are often called "ticks," so the commands to label them are called `xticks` and `yticks`. If you do not provide such a command, matplotlib will label the ticks with the x-values it uses. However, you have the option to say what each tick label should be and where it should be located. We show `xticks` below, the same approach can be used for `yticks`.

```
pylab.xticks(locations,labels,rotation=degrees)
```

locations list of location values
labels list of labels for location values
rotation *optional* rotation in degrees (default is 0)

Examples:

- `pylab.xticks([0,1,2,3],['Graham','Eric','Terry','John'])`
- `pylab.xticks([0,math.pi/2,math.pi],['0',u'\u03C0'+'/2',u'\u03C0'])`

The second example uses the Unicode character for π in the labels. Such labels would improve Figure D.2. For example, adding this line:

```
pylab.xticks([0, math.pi, 2*math.pi, 3*math.pi, 4*math.pi],
['0', u'\u03C0', '2'+u'\u03C0', '3'+u'\u03C0','4'+u'\u03C0'])
```

results in Figure D.3.

Arithmetic can be used on *locations* to center labels such as centering labels on a bar chart. A `linspace` can be used to center the label in the middle of the tick by adding a

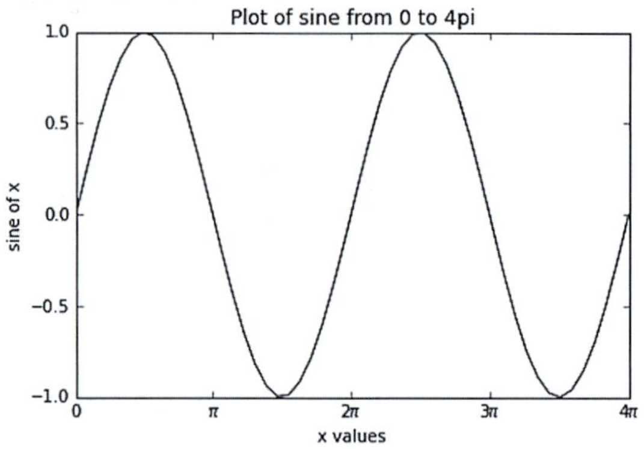

FIGURE D.3 Sine with improved labels.

bar width to each element and divide by 2 to center, such as `pylab.linspace(0,4,5)+bar_width/2`. See Section 9.8 for an example.

Figure 10.5 is an interesting example of labeling an axis. There were over 1000 data points over 20 years, but the most sensible labeling was a small set of years, for example, '1995', '1997', . . . , '2013', '2015'. That is, we wanted 10 labels out of 1044 (the length of the data list), which is $1044//10 = 104$ calculated as $step = len(data)//10$. Therefore, we wanted labels spaced out at intervals of 104. Slicing is the answer: `pylab.xticks(x_values[::step],years[::step])` where x_values is a list of 1044 ints and years is a list of year strings of the same length as x_values.

D.2.6 Legend

It can be useful to place a legend on a graph. There are two parts to creating a legend:

1. *associate a name with a plot:* Add a `label = 'a_str'` to the `plot` call to associate the string 'a_str' with that plot.
2. *create and place the legend:* Call `pylab.legend(location,title)`

location a string specifying legend placement, e.g. 'upper left'
title a string legend title

Code Listing D.2 and the associated Figure D.4 illustrate three plots with a legend: $y = x$, $y = x^2$, and $y = x^3$. Each is drawn with a different color and line width (the line width helps distinguish each plot in the monochrome of the text). Each has a `label` specified that shows up in the legend. Exponents in the label are achieved using the appropriate Unicode character. The `pylab.legend` command specifies 'upper right' and the simple title string

'Legend.' The *y*-values in the plots take advantage of the fact that arithmetic operations can be specified across pylab lists (which are really numpy arrays) so X**2 squares every item in the list.

Code Listing D.2

```
import pylab

# generate x values
X = pylab.linspace(0, 20, 100)

# Plot line with a blue continuous line of width 1 (pixels)
pylab.plot(X, X, color="blue", label="y=x")

# Plot squared with a green continuous line of width 2 (pixels)
pylab.plot(X, X**2, color="green", linewidth = 2, label="y=x"+u'\u00B2')

# Plot cube with a green continuous line of width 3 (pixels)
pylab.plot(X, X**3, color="red", linewidth = 3, label="y=x"+u'\u00B3')

pylab.legend(loc='upper right', title='Legend')

# Set y limits to make the graph look nicer
pylab.ylim(0.0, 100.0)

# Show result on screen
pylab.show()
```

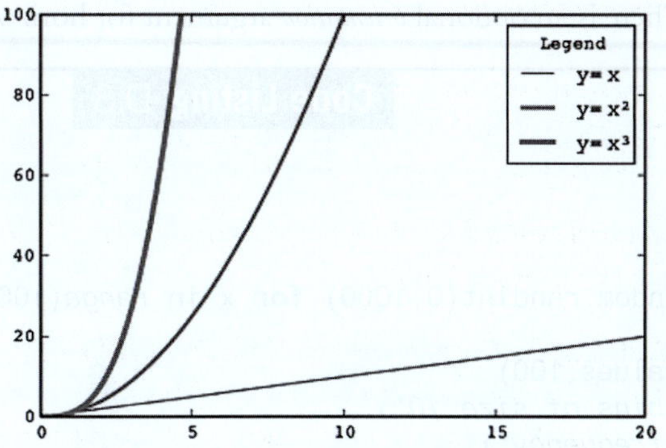

FIGURE D.4 Three plots with legend.

D.2.7 Bar Graphs

Bar graphs can have either vertical (`bar`) or horizontal (`barh`) bars. There are two required arguments and ten optional ones–we illustrate two of the most common. See Section 9.9 for an example.

```
pylab.bar(x-values,y-values,width=w,color=c)
```

x-values list of x-values (bar locations)
y-values list of y-values (the bar height)
width] *optional* width of each bar (default is 0.8)
color *optional* color of each bar (default is 'blue')

There is a similar `barh` that creates horizontal bars.

D.2.8 Histograms

A histogram is a graph that shows the number of elements within a range of values. The range, called a *bin*, is used uniformly for all the data in the histogram. Thus, the *x*-axis indicates the various bins and the *y*-axis the number of elements in each bin.

The command for a histogram is `pylab.hist`. There are 15 arguments that can be provided, but the two most important are the list of values and the number of bins. For example, the program in Code Listing D.3 generates 10,000 values, randomly distributed between 0 and 1000. We allow for 100 bins (thus each bin is of size 10, 100 bins for a range from 0 to 1000). Note that the distribution is fairly, but not exactly, equal in all bins. See Code Listing D.3 with the associated Figure D.5.

```
pylab.hist(values,bins)
```

values list of values to be binned
bins *optional* number of bins (default is 10)

There is an optional *orientation* argument for horizontal or vertical bars.

Code Listing D.3

```
import pylab
import random

x_values = [random.randint(0,1000) for x in range(10000)]

pylab.hist(x_values,100)
pylab.xlabel('bins of size 10')
pylab.ylabel('frequency')
pylab.title('plot of 10,000 random ints 0-1000, bins of size 10')
pylab.show()
```

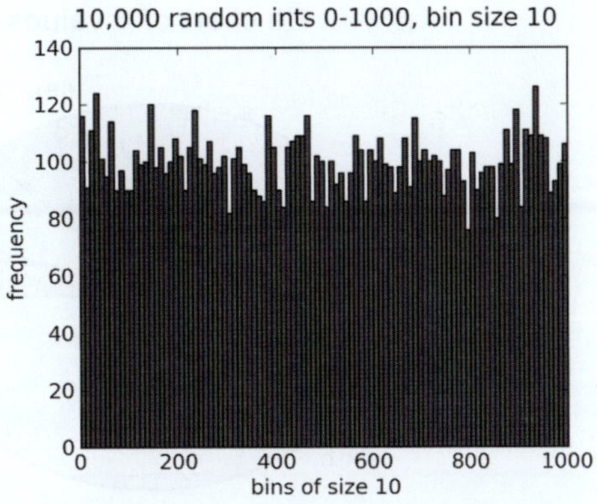

FIGURE D.5 Histogram code and its associated plot.

D.2.9 Pie Charts

Pie charts show the percentage of the whole that each value in the list occupies. That is, for each element in the given value list the percentage (one_value/sum(values)) that each value occupies in a list. It takes a dozen optional arguments; we show two very useful ones are.

```
pylab.pie(values,labels=label_list,colors=color_list)
```

values list of values
labels *optional* list of labels for pie slices
colors *optional* list of colors for pie slices

An example pie chart is provided in Figure D.6 for Code Listing D.4.

Code Listing D.4

```
import pylab
pylab.axes(aspect=1)  # pie chart looks best when aspect ratio of figure is 1

values = [10,20, 50,100,200,1000]
pie_labels = ['first','second','third','fourth','fifth','sixth']

# these are the default colors. You get these if you do not provide any
color_list = ['b', 'g', 'r', 'c', 'm', 'y', 'k', 'w']

pylab.pie(values,labels=pie_labels,colors=color_list)
pylab.title('Pie chart of 6 values')
pylab.show()
```

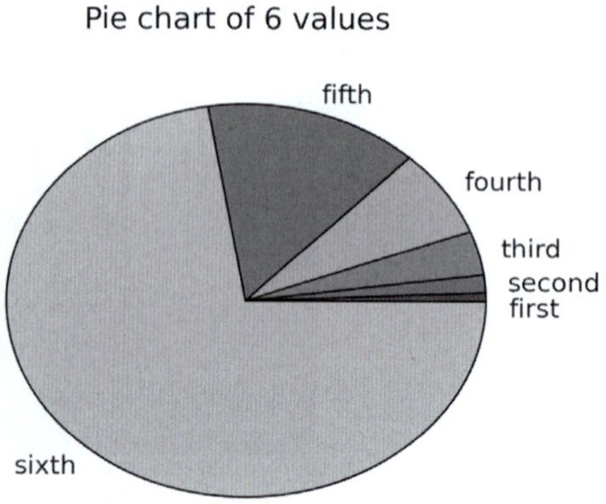

FIGURE D.6 Pie chart code and its associated plot.

D.2.10 How Powerful Is pylab?

In this appendix we have barely scratched the surface of what is possible in pylab. To illustrate what can be done under the heading of "make hard things possible" consider this 3D plot from the matplotlib gallery. We list the code as Code Listing D.5 and its Figure D.7 without explanation.

Code Listing D.5

```
from mpl_toolkits.mplot3d import axes3d
import matplotlib.pyplot as plt
from matplotlib import cm

fig = plt.figure()
ax = fig.gca(projection='3d')
X, Y, Z = axes3d.get_test_data(0.05)
ax.plot_surface(X, Y, Z, rstride=8, cstride=8, alpha=0.3)
cset = ax.contourf(X, Y, Z, zdir='z', offset=-100, cmap=cm.coolwarm)
cset = ax.contourf(X, Y, Z, zdir='x', offset=-40, cmap=cm.coolwarm)
cset = ax.contourf(X, Y, Z, zdir='y', offset=40, cmap=cm.coolwarm)

ax.set_xlabel('X')
ax.set_xlim(-40, 40)
ax.set_ylabel('Y')
ax.set_ylim(-40, 40)
ax.set_zlabel('Z')
ax.set_zlim(-100, 100)

plt.show()
```

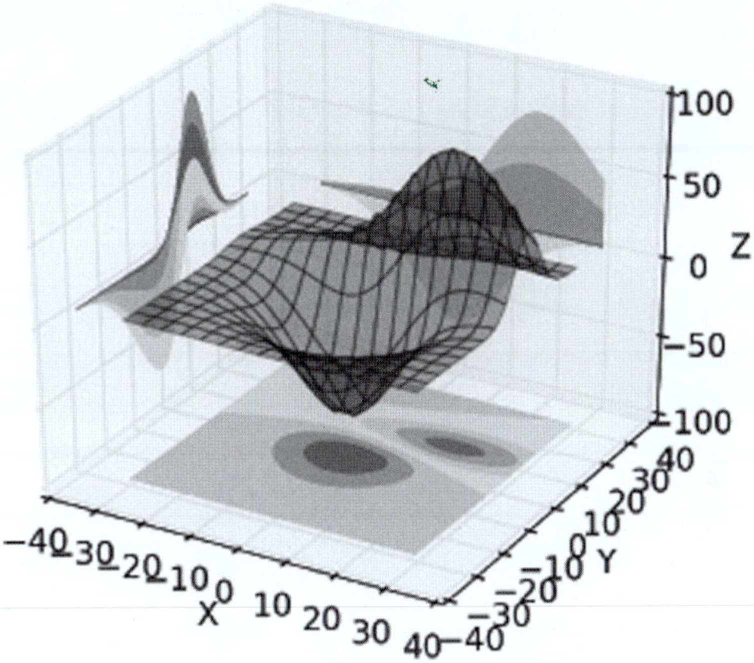

FIGURE D.7 Impressive demonstration of Python plotting.

APPENDIX E

Quick Introduction to Web-based User Interfaces

> As far as the customer is concerned, the interface is the product.
>
> Jef Raskin

We have worked hard on understanding the Python language and finding ways to apply our new-found knowledge to the development of programs to solve problems, usually problems concerned with analyzing data.

However, as the quote above shows, from the point of view of the user the *interface* to that underlying program is the only real window that the user has to the program. Programs are often judged, not on the underlying code, but on the interface provided to that code and how well it serves the user's needs. Thus, a good programmer must not only do a good job of solving a problem using code, but also do a good job designing the interface to that code.

The design of a computer interface can be a complex. In fact, it is an entire area of study termed **H**uman **C**omputer **I**nteraction or **HCI**. HCI practitioner's interests cover a broad range, from hardware to psychology, from software libraries to cognitive science. It is a big area, but it is important to provide some access to an interface, especially a **G**raphical **U**ser **I**nterface or **GUI** (often pronounced "gooey") as modern users have come to expect graphically oriented interfaces.

Since we cannot possibly cover all HCI topics, we will focus on software libraries that support the development of interfaces that are more intuitive than the **C**ommand **L**ine **I**nterfaces (CLI), we have been using. Not surprisingly, there are many (many, many) software libraries to support the development of GUIs. Unfortunately, many require users to install extra components, which can be a problem.

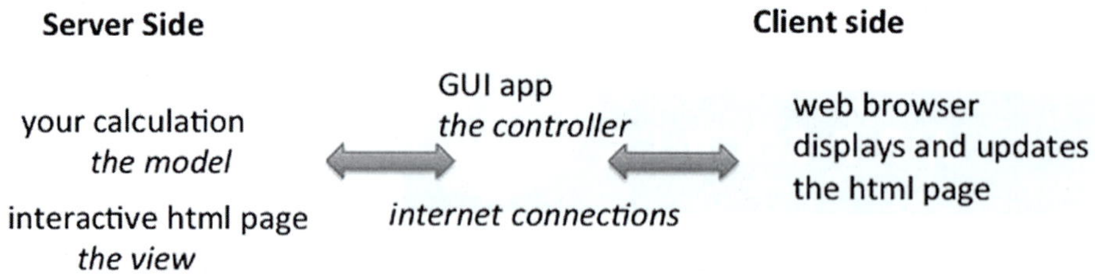

FIGURE E.1 MVC: Model-View-Controller.

Fortunately, an interface is available: the web browser. Advances in web browser technology and standardization combine to make web elements for interface design accessible to Python programmers. It is somewhat messy, but it is possible to structure a Python program to essentially be a template that allows a novice programmer to build a web-based GUI interface to most of their programs. Not surprisingly, components will have to be imported, but they come with the Anaconda distribution. An interesting advantage of this approach is that a programmer can have their program running on their own computer while making it available to a user working through a browser on the user's computer.

E.0.1 MVC Architecture

There is another advantage to a web-based interface. It can act as a **M**odel-**V**iew-**C**ontroller (**MVC**) architecture, an organization that allows us to more easily create a template-like program structure for a novice. Figure E.1 shows the MVC architecture.

In this organization, our application Python code is called the *Model* and provides the data that we want to provide to others on the Internet via web pages. Our code may reside on our computer or on a server machine somewhere else on the Internet. The user, possibly somewhere else on the Internet, through their browser connects to an Internet server (our computer), which serves up a web page, termed the *View*. The View provides a way to "see" the data from the Model, determined by the creator of the View. Potentially the user interacts with the web page in their browser by filling out elements of that interface (a "form") and then submitting that information back to the server for the calculation by the Model (e.g., by pushing a "submit" button). The web page is subsequently updated with new Model results and displayed in the browser. A component called the *Controller* controls the flow of information back and forth between the user's browser and our program on the server. We will show you how to create a small program that contains those three pieces: the Model, the View, and the Controller.

E.1 FLASK

Wow, that is pretty complicated and intimidating! A web server serves up web pages as a View or interface, we connect information through the web page to our calculation or Model on the server and then somehow update the information, the View or web page, on the user's browser. How do we go about all that? This *Controller* application seems pretty complicated!

Fortunately there are some Python libraries that aid in developing just exactly this kind of software. The one we will focus on, mostly for its simplicity, is called Flask. Flask does everything we need:

- Provides a ubiquitous interface for users through a web interface.
- Does not require *any* special software for **the user** to bring up the interface except a browser.
- Allows us to develop an MVC architecture, meaning that our Python code can sit on a server and be accessed over the Internet.
- Allows both input from the View to be passed to the Model and the View updated with new results all through a web browser.

E.2 QUICKSTART FLASK, HELLO WORLD

Remember our first program (in Section A.1.7) from when we started with Python? Let's do the same thing with a Flask program that serves up "Hello World". Consider Code Listing E.1. We'll show how to run it, examine its output, and then go back and look at the details.

Code Listing E.1

```python
from flask import Flask
app = Flask(__name__)

@app.route('/')
def hello_world():
    return 'Hello World!'

if __name__ == '__main__':
    app.run(debug=True)
```

To run this code, execute in a terminal window as shown in this session:

```
>python 1-hw.py
 * Running on http://127.0.0.1:5000/ (Press CTRL+C to quit)
127.0.0.1 - - [21/Jul/2015 12:59:47] "GET / HTTP/1.1" 200 -
^C
```

The session indicates that Flask is now serving web pages, which by default can only be visited by someone on your local computer (in a moment we will fix it so anyone on the web can visit the web page being served). The session lists the web address, which for local-only

FIGURE E.2 Hello World Web page. [William F. Punch, Richard J. Enbody.]

browsers is `http://127.0.0.1:5000`. If you paste that address into the address bar of a web browser on your computer, you will see the web page shown in Figure E.2. Note that the web server continues running until you end the program: from the command line one typically types Control-C, that is hold down the Control/Ctrl key and then press the C key.

E.2.1 What Just Happened?

Quite a lot actually, and it is worth taking a look at in detail using the line numbers from Program E.1. However, you can simply copy and run the code without fully understanding it. It is the first step toward building a program to act as a template.

Lines 1–2: We import from the `flask` module the `Flask` class (notice the capitalization). Readers who have not read Chapter 11 can simply accept these two lines and move on. For those who have done classes, we create a variable `app`, an *instance* of `Flask`. The `__name__` parameter to the `Flask` class constructor is needed, but difficult to explain so we'll skip that.

Line 4: We use a decorator (see Section 16.2.5 for more details) to accomplish two tasks:

- What page on the web server to server up.
- What function should be run when that web page is accessed.

In this case the `@app.route('/')` means that we are defining the behavior for accessing the default web page. The `route` function is a method from the `Flask` class.

Line 5: We define a function under the decorator indicating what will be called when the route (from **Line 4**) is accessed. The function is called `hello_world`; it takes no arguments and returns a single string, "Hello World".

Lines 8–9: This code is a Python short-cut to invoke `app.run` if the Python file is started from the command line. The special variable `__name__` is the name of the current module. If that module is named `__main__`, then this means that the code was invoked from the command line, that is,

```
python 1-hw.py
```

In this case, the `app.run` is invoked and the entire flask process started.

So what is the flask process? After `app.run` is started, flask creates a local web server that "listens" for incoming connections to the address it provides (for the local process `http://127.0.0.1:5000`). If a web browser accesses that address, it looks to see which page is accessed. The `'/'` page is the root (default) page and when that page is accessed, the function in the next line, `hello_world` in this case, is invoked, and the returned string is displayed to the requesting browser.

Very cool indeed! For a very small amount of code we set up our own web server, served up pages for incoming connections, and displayed the specified content.

E.2.2 Multiple Routes

We can have our web server serve up multiple pages, one server serving multiple pages, where we define the content for each page. See Code Listing E.2.

Code Listing E.2

```
from flask import Flask
app = Flask(__name__)

@app.route('/')
def hello_world():
    return 'Hello World!'

@app.route('/login')
def login_page():
    return 'Welcome to the login page'

@app.route('/login/message')
def message_page():
    return 'The message is: xyzzy'

if __name__ == '__main__':
    app.run(debug=True)
```

a) / page

b) /login page

c) /login/message page

FIGURE E.3 Three pages, one web server. [William F. Punch, Richard J. Enbody.]

The only differences between this program and our first program is that we have now have three routes:

Line 4: Route is `app.route('/')` with the associated function `hello_world`.
Line 8: Route is `app.route('/login')` with the associated function `login_page`.
Line 12: Route is `app.route('/login/message')` with the associated function `message_page`.

Thus, we can visit three different pages depending on which page of our web server we visit. See Figure E.3 for the three pages.

E.2.3 Stacked Routes, Passing Address Arguments

Continuing with our simple example, we can be both more efficient about routes, having multiple routes use the same function, and use information from the web address as information for that function.

Code Listing E.3

```
1  from flask import Flask
2  app = Flask(__name__)
3
4  @app.route('/')
5  @app.route('/<name>')
6  def hello_name(name="Stranger"):
7      return "Hello {}!".format(name)
8
9  if __name__ == '__main__':
10     app.run(debug=True)
```

What's new in Code Listing E.3?

Lines 4–5: There are two decorators now sitting atop the function `hello_name`, and we can interpret this to mean that if either web page is visited, this function will be invoked. Two routes, one function.

Line 5: What's interesting about the second route is the fact that the route itself has a variable name enclosed in angle brackets, `'/<name>'`. What this means is that `name` is indeed a variable and takes on the value of the web page visited. For example, if the web page was `'/fred'`, then `name` would be assigned the string value `'fred'`. If the page visited was instead `/bill`, then `name` would be assigned the string value `'bill'`.

Line 6: The variable `name` is passed to the function. If `name` has not been assigned a value (if the route used was `'/'`), then `name` is assigned the value `'Stranger'` (see parameter defaults in Chapter 8). Otherwise, it is assigned the value of the web page visited.

In this way the web address can be used to pass information to your program for processing. Frequently on the web, information you provide is passed as part of the web address.

One thing that will not work is to pass a longer web address to our server, for example, `/bill/login`. That will generate a 404 error, a "missing web page" error. You can also see this in the session. In the session, message 200 indicates success in serving the page, and again 404 indicates the "page not found" error. For more info on http error codes see `http://www.w3.org/Protocols/rfc2616/rfc2616-sec10.html`

```
>python 3-helloName.py
 * Running on http://127.0.0.1:5000/ (Press CTRL+C to quit)
```

```
 * Restarting with stat
127.0.0.1 - - [22/Jul/2015 11:11:42] "GET / HTTP/1.1" 200 -
127.0.0.1 - - [22/Jul/2015 11:11:42] "GET /favicon.ico HTTP/1.1" 200 -
127.0.0.1 - - [22/Jul/2015 11:12:33] "GET /bill HTTP/1.1" 200 -
127.0.0.1 - - [22/Jul/2015 11:12:33] "GET /favicon.ico HTTP/1.1" 200 -
127.0.0.1 - - [22/Jul/2015 11:12:49] "GET /bill/login HTTP/1.1" 404 -
127.0.0.1 - - [22/Jul/2015 11:12:49] "GET /favicon.ico HTTP/1.1" 200 -
```

E.3 SERVING UP REAL HTML PAGES

Up to this point all our server has served up are single strings. That's not an interesting web page.

Typically a web page uses a special language called **H**yper **T**ext **M**arkup **L**anguage or **HTML** to format and structure a web page. A markup language[1] is a way to augment text with **tags** that describe extra information that can be used to augment the text, often to organize it in some fashion. In particular, HTML[2] has information that not only organizes the text, but also indicates how the page should be displayed when interpreted by a web browser.

So how can we serve up a real web page? We must have the function we decorate with a route return an HTML-encoded web page. To do that we must know at least a little HTML.

E.3.1 A Little Bit of HTML

HTML is not a topic that can be covered in a couple of paragraphs. Rather it is more like a book topic, potentially multiple books depending on the details. Nonetheless, we can cover enough here for the bare essentials. You can visit a "cheat sheet" to see a quick list of the tags (e.g., `http://www.simplehtmlguide.com/cheatsheet.php`) but it can take some time to get a sufficient understanding to build a complex HTML page.

E.3.2 HTML Tags

HTML tags always come in pairs (well, almost always, see `<br>`). The pair of tags denote a section of text (the text between the tags) that is to be organized according to the command of that tag. The beginning of a tagged area begins with `<some_command>` and the area ends with a tag with the same command but prefixed with a \, so `<\some_command>`. Anything, text or HTML, is affected within a tagged area, with the effect determined by the tag command.

[1] https://en.wikipedia.org/wiki/Markup_language
[2] https://en.wikipedia.org/wiki/HTML

Tag	**Meaning**
Structure Tags	
<html>…<\html>	Defines an area as an HTML web page
<head>…<\head>	Introductory Elements (logo, title, etc.)
<title>…<\title>	Title, only in header, shows up in browser tab
<body>…<\body>	The body contents of the web page
<h1>…<\h1>	A header, larger text for a section start. Tags include <h1> to <h6>
<p>…<\p>	A paragraph starting with line break. New lines in text are ignored.
 	Insert line break. No matching end tag
Text Formatting	
<i>…<\i>	tag area is in italics font
<b>…<\b>	tag area is in boldface font

TABLE E.1 Some HTML tags.

While browsers are pretty good at rendering even badly formatted HTML, it is a good practice to try and write your HTML code as properly formatted pairs.

List of HTML Tags

Table E.1 has a very abbreviated list of HTML tags and their meanings. We can combine tags to make an HTML web page. The page and how it is rendered is shown in Figure E.4b.

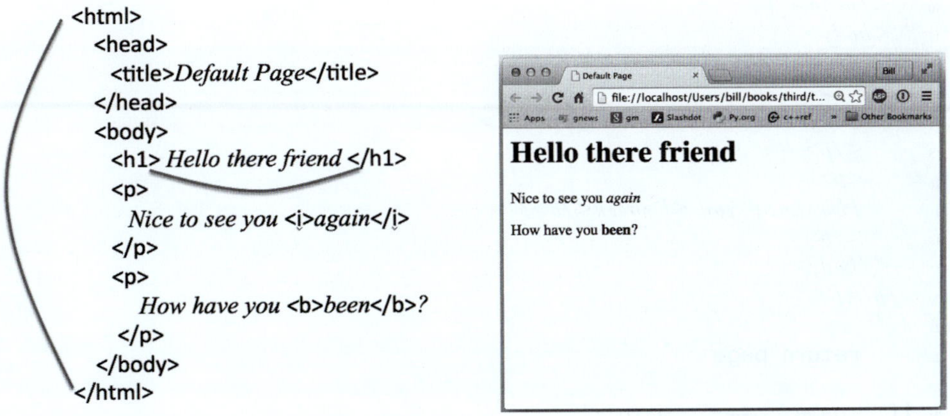

FIGURE E.4 (a) It shows HTML, with italics as plain text and dark lines as tag pairs. (b) It shows the rendering of that text in a browser. [William F. Punch, Richard J. Enbody.]

To render the page we saved it as a file with an .html extension and then double clicked the file, by default the .html extension caused it to be opened in the browser. Notice that the address is a `file://` address, meaning the browser is rendering a local file, not something on the Internet. Also, notice how the title text, `Default Page`, shows up as the title of the tab in the browser.

E.3.3 Flask Returning Web Pages

It is a small change to fix our program to return fully specified HTML web pages instead of just a single string. We simply return a triply quoted string that is the HTML specified page instead of just a single string.

We use a triply quoted string because such a string preserves the vertical spacing of the page. While space preservation is not required (a browser can render a single string as a web page) the spacing makes it much easier to read. Consider Code Listing E.4 and the page it served, as shown in Figure E.5.

Code Listing E.4

```
from flask import Flask
app = Flask(__name__)

@app.route('/')
def index():
    page = '''
<html>
  <head>
    <title>Default Page</title>
  </head>
  <body>
    <h1>Hello there friend </h1>
    <p>
    Nice to see you <i>again</i>
    </p>
    <p>
    How have you <b>been</b>?
    </p>
  </body>
</html>
 '''
    return page

if __name__ == '__main__':
    app.run(debug=True)
```

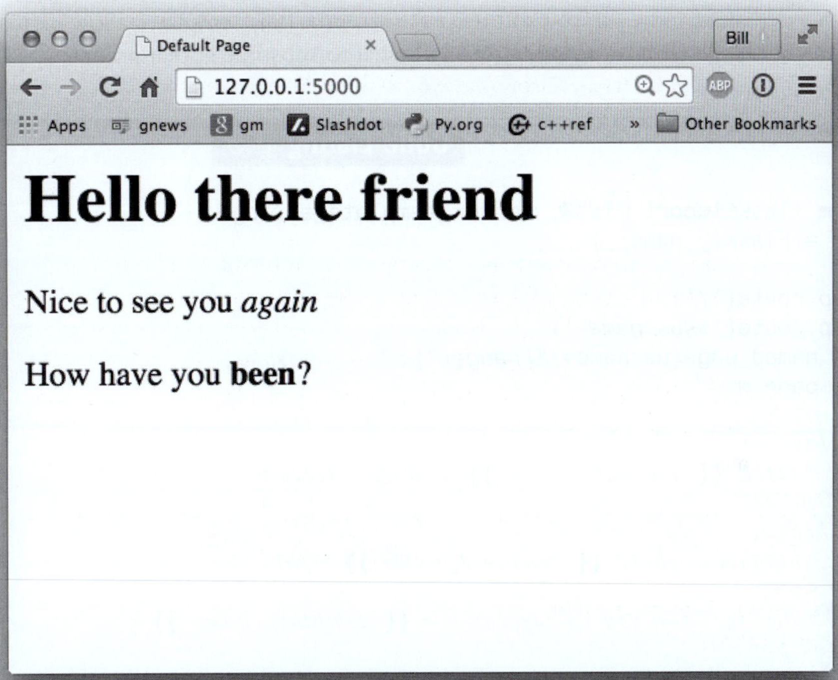

FIGURE E.5 Flask serves up our web page. [William F. Punch, Richard J. Enbody.]

The only real difference from the previous program is the address. Our new web page is at `http://127.0.0.1:5000/`, a web page not a file. If we open up our flask app to serve web pages outside of our own machine (and we can), then anyone else on the Internet can see the page! Pretty neat.

E.3.4 Getting Arguments into Our Web Pages

Next we'd like to do what we did before: retrieve information from the web address and display it in our web page. However, this time we will display a real HTML page, not simply a string.

That poses a bit of a problem. We have to find a way to mark **where** we want to substitute our address argument into the web page, and then we have to decide **what** to substitute.

Part of the flask application is a templating language called **Jinja** (pronounced like the spice ginger if you roll the r at the end). Jinja templates allow us to mark where in a web page we want to substitute and what to substitue at that point.

Code Listing E.5

```
1  from flask import Flask, render_template_string
2  app = Flask(__name__)
3
4  @app.route('/')
5  @app.route('/<usrname>')
6  def named_page(usrname="Stranger"):
7      page = '''
8  <html>
9    <head>
10     <title>{{ template_name }}'s Page</title>
11   </head>
12   <body>
13     <h1>Hello there {{ template_name }} </h1>
14     <p>
15     Nice to  see you <i>again</i> {{ template_name }}
16     </p>
17     <p>
18     How have you <b> been </b> {{ template_name}}
19     </p>
20   </body>
21 </html>
22     '''
23     return render_template_string(page, template_name=usrname)
24
25 if __name__ == '__main__':
26     app.run(debug=True)
```

Consider Code Listing E.5. It is similar to the previous program, and the web page it displays is nearly the same. Let's look at the differences.

Line 1: We have included a new element from flask called `render_template_string`. Ultimately that function is going to do the work of creating our web page with some substitutions.

Lines 4–5: We have two routes as we did in Code Listing E.3. We allow for a default page and an address of a single string. The variable `usrname` is assigned the address string.

Lines 7–22: This is our triply quoted string HTML page just like before with the exception of the use of `{{template_name}}`.

The elements between {{...}} mark a **template**, a place where a substitution of text can occur. The element within the {{...}} is the name of the element we can substitute. Thus, {{template_name}} means that at some point we want to substitute template_name with some other text at this location.

Note that Lines 10, 13, 15, and 18 all have this template element.

Line 23: This is where the substitution occurs. Function render_template_string takes two arguments. The first is the variable that is assigned a template string, in this case page, our HTML triply quoted page description. The second (and potentially others if multiple substitutions occur) indicate what is assigned. The expression template_name = usrname indicates that wherever {{template_name}} occurs, the function will replace it with the value contained in usrname.

What is returned is the string, in this case an HTML page, where all the templates have been replaced with the value of usrname.

We run the code as before in the command line and paste the url into our browser. What is different this time is that whatever we append to the url becomes username when the page is redrawn. For example, if our original url is http://127.0.0.1:5000/, we get the default "Stranger" version displayed. However, if we append "bill" to the url as http://127.0.0.1:5000/bill we get the "bill" version displayed. Multiple versions are shown in Figure E.6. Note the differences in the urls displayed. Also, note the tab on each browser. It reflects the setting of the title tag of the page.

E.4 ACTIVE WEB PAGES

We can create a web server that serves up static pages, but we have not yet discussed how we can have our web page setup up so that we can enter data and then subsequently update the web page with results. That is our overall goal so we make that addition next.

E.4.1 Forms in wtforms

Since the HTML 2.0 specification, HTML has included a tag <form>...<\form> to denote a region that contains input elements such as text boxes, pull down menus, radio buttons, and so on. These elements can then be connected to scripts that perform some action when input is provided. Thus, these forms provide an "active" part of the web page, which is a kind of GUI.

We will do much the same thing using **wtforms** in flask. Using these forms provide a number of benefits:

- We can use Python to do something with the input.
- We are provided a class Form with the functionality of a web form.
- The Form class provides various functionality, including validation of input.

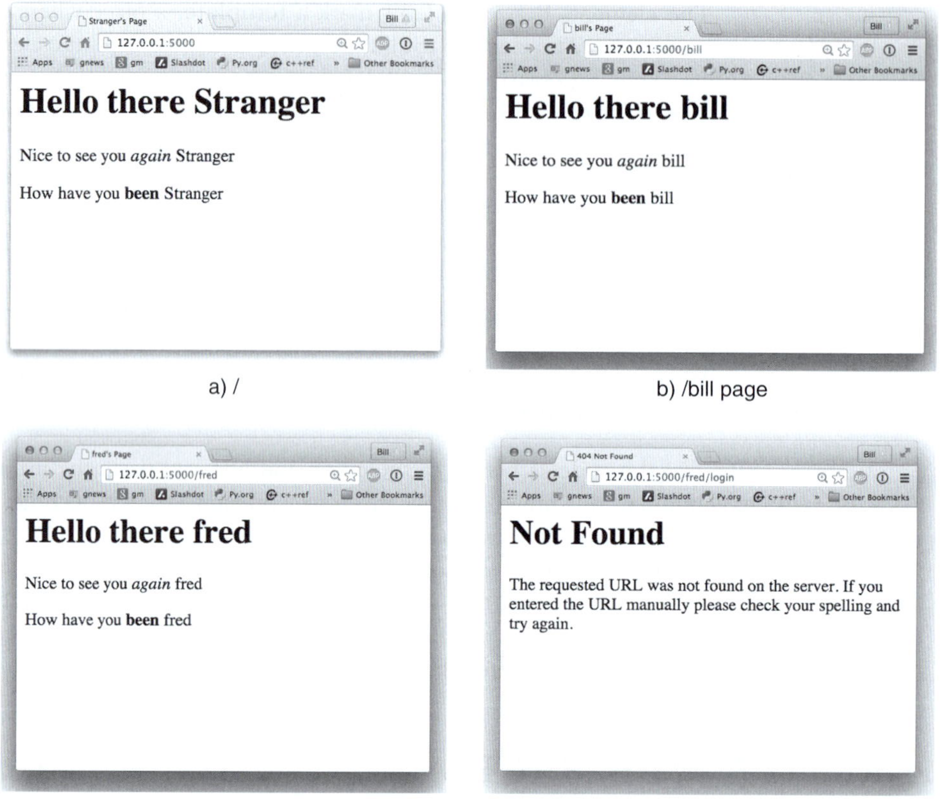

a) /

b) /bill page

c) /fred page

d) /fred/login page

FIGURE E.6 Passing web address to our display function. [William F. Punch, Richard J. Enbody.]

Like HTML `form` elements, `wtforms` provides **fields** which represent input types such as floats, integers, buttons, pulldowns, and so on. Once data is provided through these elements, the data can be gathered (by our Controller), made available to us for update (by our Model) and regenerated as a new version of the web page (our View) to reflect updates.

The `wtforms` do not come included by default in the the Anaconda distribution, but can easily be included. If you are working with Anaconda, then the Anaconda package manager is called `conda`. You request a new package by typing `conda install flask-wtf` into a Terminal window. If you are using a standard Python distribution, you by entering the following command into a Terminal window: `pip install flask-wtf`.

E.4.2 A Good Example Goes a Long Way

There is a lot going on here and you may not understand all of it, but one good thing is the following: if we have an example that is close to what we want to do, we can learn enough

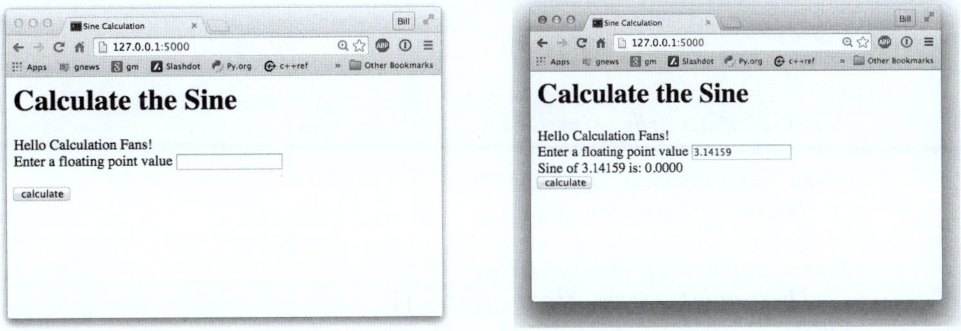

FIGURE E.7 (a) It shows the web page before the calculation occurs, (b) It shows the same web page after the calculation.

to modify the example to fit our needs. That is the goal of the rest of this appendix. We will show you generic examples and show where to change the examples to fit your needs. You can grow into your understanding as you use the examples. You don't have to fully understand it to start with, which is great for our needs.

Here is our first example. It prompts the user to enter a value and then updates the page with the sine of that entered value. We'll show the code (Code Listing E.6) and what the web page it generates looks like (Figure E.7), then describe how it works and what to modify to meet your needs.

Code Listing E.6

```
from flask import Flask, render_template_string, request
from wtforms import Form, validators, FloatField
import math

app = Flask(__name__)

# function is the model. Calculate sine and return a formatted string
def compute(val):
    result = math.sin(val)
    result_str = "Sine of {} is: {:.4f}".format(val,result)
    return result_str

# html page is the view.
page = '''
<html>
    <head>
        <title> Sine Calculation</title >
```

```
    </head>

    <body>
        <h1>Calculate the Sine</h1>

        <form method=post action="">
            Hello Calculation Fans!
        <br>
        Enter a floating-point value
            {{ template_form.float_field }}
        <br>
            {% if result != None %}
                {{ result }}
            {% endif %}
        <br>
            <input type=submit value=calculate>
        </form>

    </body>
</html>
'''

# InputForm and below is our controller

# form with a single FloatField
class InputForm(Form):
    float_field = FloatField(validators=[validators.InputRequired()])

@app.route('/', methods=['GET', 'POST'])
def index():
    sine_val = None
    form = InputForm(request.form)
    if request.method == 'POST' and form.validate():
        input_val = form.float_field.data
        sine_val = compute(input_val)
    return render_template_string(page, template_form=form, result=sine_val)

if __name__ == '__main__':
    app.run(debug=True)
```

Let's start our analysis by pointing out a couple of areas of the code. Remember, we don't necessarily have to fully understand how all this works (though it certainly helps). We need to see how to modify the code to meet our needs. As before, pay attention to the three major parts: the Model, the View, and the Controller.

Line 2: We added more imports, in particular the `Form` class, which we will subclass for our own purposes, and `FloatField`, which is an input element we will be using. We'll discuss `validators` later.

Lines 8–11: This is our **Model**, a Python function that will take in input from our web page `Form` elements, and return a value which can be used to update the web page with results, dynamically updating the page when input is provided.

Lines 16–38: This is our **View**, the web page (defined as a triply quoted string) that will contain our input elements using Jinja templates and will update the page with results generated by our **Model**.

Lines 43–57: This is the our **Controller**.

More About the Controller

Lines 43–44

Here we create our first form—a web page with places to enter values. This will make more sense if you have learned classes from Chapter 11, but you really only need to understand how to mimic the structure. We are making a new class, here called `InputForm` as a subclass of the provided `Form` class. You might remember subclassing and inheritance from Section 12.6. Briefly, when we create a subclass of an existing class, we can first **inherit** the methods and variables of the class and second add our own specializations to the new subclass. Thus, `InputForm` has all the capabilities and methods of the provided class `Form`.

For this program, we want a text box in our form so we can enter a floating-point value. To do that we create an attribute, `FloatField`, which is a class. `FloatField`, when invoked in a web page, provides a text box specialized to collect floating-point values from that web page. We instantiate `FloatField` as the variable `float_field`, a ***`class attribute`*** of our `InputForm`. As a class attribute, every instance of `InputForm` will share that class variable. When we construct `float_field`, we add some parameters to the constructor. In this particular case, we add a **validator**, a way to check that what we got from the field was what we wanted and expected. Here we require that input be provided before we can pull the data.

Lines 49–53

On **Line 49** we instantiate our new class and assign it to the variable `form`. As it is created inside of a route function, the function is only called when the web page represented by the route has been accessed by a user. We use the class `request` as a constructor argument. The `request` contains information about the web page request that we can use later.

On **Line 50** we want to know if the request we received was a "POST" (data is being passed to the web server) and if the form is valid, that is, it passed the validation test associated with the field, in this case that input is required. If those two conditions are true, we can gather the data from the form.

On **Line 51**, we get the data entered into the form by accessing `form.float_field.data`. That is, from our form, from the class attribute `float_field` in that form, we get the data. It should be there because we have already passed the validate test, which indicated that data had been entered.

On **Line 52** we pass the gathered data to our Model and receive a result.

On **Line 53** we update our HTML template page with the information.

More About the View

The View is the HTML that describes how the web page will be laid out. In particular, where to place things such as the input text box for floats that was described in the controller.

On **Lines 23–35** we define an input form, and it is within the `form` region that we can define our input elements.

On **Line 23** we initiate the form to capture `post` requests with no associated actions (we'll take care of that below).

On **Line 27** we have included a template for `template_form.float_field`. In the `render_template_string` on **Line 54** we assigned the `form` variable, an instance our our `InputForm`, and pass it to the Jinja template engine as `template_form`. The statement `template_form.float_field` invokes the field and has it display itself (as a text box) in the web page. Whatever kind of form we pass, this is how we call it so that it renders itself.

Lines 29–31

Jinja also allows one to define some simple control within the page to dynamically display information. These commands are bracketed with `{%...%}`. Common commands are `{%if condition%}` or `{%for var in collection%}` or the like. They always end with a tag ending (just like other HTML tags) such as `{%endif%}` or `{%endfor%}`. Note the similarity to Python control statements.

Line 30 is querying whether a result ≠ `None` had been received. If so, then the template `{{result}}` passed from `render_template_string` is displayed in the web page. If it was not received, the area is left blank.

Line 33 creates a button that can be pressed on the web page. The second argument ("calculate") is the label of the button. When it is pressed the form is activated.

More About the Model

The Model is your Python code to solve the particular problem in hand. Therefore, it is hard to provide too much advice about the Model, as this is the crux of the particular problem you are trying to solve. Here are some suggestions:

- You might consider putting the Model code in another file to keep things tidy and more readable. Large amounts of code that support some Model can clutter the file when included with the View and Controller.
- You might consider returning formatted strings for text or an image element (such as a png). In this way you have better control over what will show up on your web page.

You can use Code Listing E.6 as a template for creating a GUI that takes in a value as input and displays a result as output.

- Modify the Model to be your Python code that solves your problem.
- Modify the View by changing strings or adding more input forms to collect input and display output.
- Modify the Controller to collect the needed input, for example, instead of a float maybe you need an int or a string.

With that basic template in hand we can next take a look at a few of the input types that are available.

E.4.3 Many Fields Example

This example is not all that different from the sine calculation we just did. In fact, it is simpler as there is really no Model. The Model here simply returns the values passed in by the Controller so you can see how it works.

The goal here is to show off the different kinds of fields (and there are more than indicated here) that you might want to use in your GUI.

The first thing we are going to do is clean up a bit. As we mentioned, it can get messy with everything in one file. We are going to break the files up into their three component parts: the Model, the View, and the Controller. This is what we do:

- Move the Model `compute` function to a different file, which we name "compute.py". We can import the compute function from compute.py in our Controller.
- Move the View to a file called "view.html." The standard in flask is to put View in a subdirectory to the Controller called "templates." Thus our View is "templates/view.html".
- Move everything else into the Controller part, which we conveniently call "controller.py". This is the element we can call Python on.

OK, let's take a look at the code and the page it displays (shown in Figure E.8).

The Model

Code Listing E.7 shows the "compute.py" file. There isn't much to the Model. It takes in the various inputs we provide from the Controller and prints them. Note it still provides a formatted string for output. You can imagine taking in all kinds of data and doing complicated calculations before you do the return, but this simple code provides a basic template.

Code Listing E.7

```python
# function is the model
def compute(f,r,s,b,t):
    view_str = "Text:{}, Float:{:.4f}, Radio:{}, Select:{}, Boolean:{},".
                format(t,f,r,s,b)
    return view_str
```

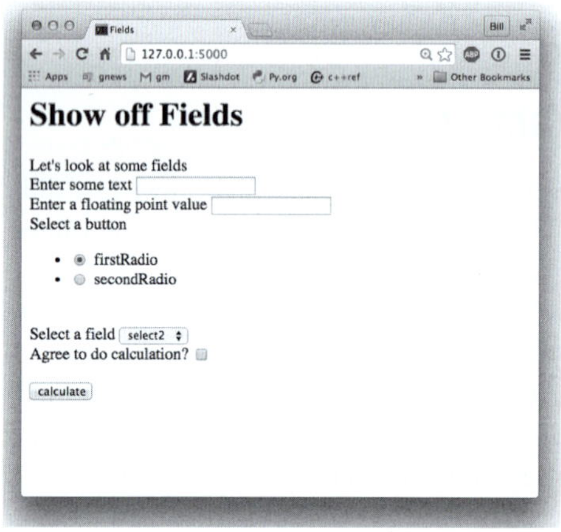

a) Startup

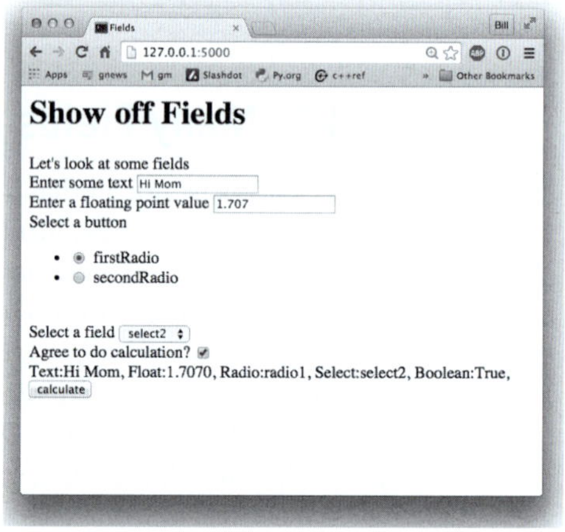

b) Data submitted, results displayed

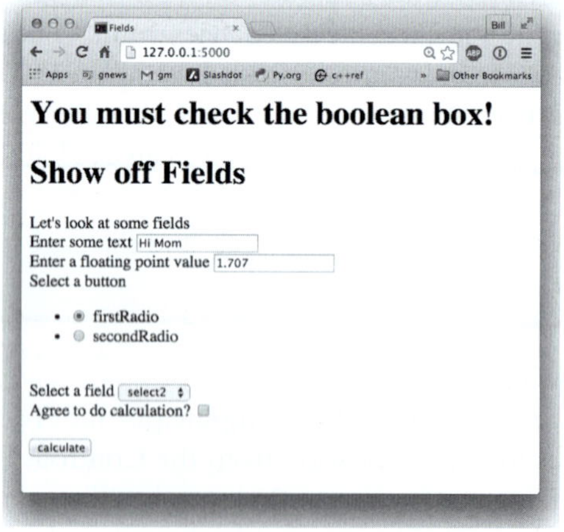

c) Error, didn't check the box

FIGURE E.8 The Many Forms example. [William F. Punch, Richard J. Enbody.]

The View

Code Listing E.8 shows the "templates/view.html" file that contains the View. It is basically our standard HTML web page with a few changes. Note that it is a file, not a triply quoted string, but that is a small change that requires a small change in the controller.

Code Listing E.8

```
<html>
   <head>
      <title> Fields</title>
   </head>

   <!-- get flashed messages -->
   {% with messages = get_flashed_messages() %}
      {% if messages %}
         {% for message in messages %}
            <h1> {{ message }} </h1>
         {% endfor %}
     {% endif %}
   {% endwith %}

   <body>
      <h1>Show off Fields</h1>

      <form method=post action="">
      Let's look at some fields
      <br>
      Enter some text
         {{ template_form.text_field }}
      <br>
      Enter a floating point value
         {{ template_form.float_field }}
      <br>
      Select a button
         {{ template_form.radio_field }}
      <br>
      Select a field
         {{ template_form.select_field }}
      <br>
      Agree to do calculation?
         {{ template_form.boolean_field }}
      <br>
         {% if result != None %}
            {{ result }}
         {% endif %}
      <br>
```

```
40         <input type=submit value=calculate>
41       </form>
42
43    </body>
44 </html>
```

The form is on **Lines 18–41** and looks much like we had before except a number of new field elements have been introduced. We display all of them and collect all the data to pass into our Model.

In **Lines 6–13** we do something a little fancy (which you can ignore if you like). We are requiring that you check the check box in order to proceed. Error messages can be passed through the system using the `flash` facility. If a `flash` has occurred, then we display that message as an error.

The Controller

Code Listing E.9 is the "controller.py" file containing the Controller. There are a number of differences here from our previous example.

Code Listing E.9

```
from flask import Flask, render_template, request, flash
from wtforms import Form, FloatField, BooleanField, SelectField, TextField,
RadioField, validators
from compute import compute

app = Flask(__name__)
app.secret_key = 'some_secret'

# InputForm and below is our controller
class InputForm(Form):
    float_field = FloatField(validators=[validators.InputRequired()])
    radio_field = RadioField(choices=[('radio1','firstRadio'),('radio2','
secondRadio')], validators=[validators.InputRequired()])
    select_field = SelectField(choices=[('select1','select1'),('select2','
select2')], validators=[validators.InputRequired()])
#    boolean_field = BooleanField( [validators.Required()])
    boolean_field = BooleanField()
    text_field = TextField([validators.InputRequired()])

@app.route('/', methods=['GET', 'POST'])
def index():
    result_str = None
```

```
20      form = InputForm(request.form)
21      if request.method == 'POST' and form.validate():
22          float_val = form.float_field.data
23          radio_val = form.radio_field.data
24          select_val = form.select_field.data
25          text_val = form.text_field.data
26          boolean_val = form.boolean_field.data
27          if boolean_val != True:
28              print("Got to Flash")
29              flash ("You must check the boolean box!")
30          else:
31              result_str = compute(float_val, radio_val, select_val, boolean_val
    , text_val)
32
33      return render_template("view.html", template_form=form, result=result_str)
34
35  if __name__ == '__main__':
36      app.run(debug=True)
```

Imports

Line 1: We import `render_template` now, **not** `render_template_string`. The `render_template` allows us to have a file as a View, not a string.

Line 2: We pull in a number of new field types just to illustrate how we set them up and how they work:

- `FloatField`, for floating-point numbers
- `BooleanField`, a check box returning True or False
- `SelectField`, a pull down menu
- `TextField`, returns regular text
- `RadioField`, radio buttons

We'll use all of them in an example.

Line 3: We import the compute function, our Model, from the compute module (really just "compute.py").

InputForm

We augment our subclassed `InputForm` with many more Fields, mostly just showing off. Some things to note:

For both the `RadioField` and the `SelectField` we initialize them with a list of pairs, here called `choices`. The pairs are such that the first element of every pair is displayed (as a button, and a menu element), and the second element is the value returned if that subelement is selected.

Route Function

There isn't much new here. We gather the data from all the fields so we can submit them to the Model. We do make one check.

On **Lines 27–29** we check to see if the value returned from the `BooleanField` instance `boolean_val` has been assigned the value True. If not, we `flash` a message that can be caught by the View and dealt with accordingly.

Line 33 is only different in that we use `render_template` where the first argument is the View element, in this case "view.html", which is assumed to be stored in the "templates" subdirectory.

We now have a more elaborate template with a greater variety of input types so a more complex GUI can be constructed. That template will take care of most GUIs you will want to build. One missing capability is the ability to display images. That is the topic of the next section.

E.5 DISPLAYING AND UPDATING IMAGES

Let's add an image to our GUI. It would be great if, as a result of entering some information through our GUI, we could then output, or update, an image on the web page. Adding an image requires little work on the web page (`flask`) side of things. Most new work will be in our Model to output a webpage with an **embedded** image, something we can easily do. The example we examine displays a sine wave plot based on parameters that the user enters into form fields. The web page is shown in Figure E.9.

Code Listing E.10 shows the "controller.py" file with the Controller code. This Controller is similar to previous ones. The only difference is the number of forms and their location in the web page.

Code Listing E.10

```
from flask import Flask, render_template, request
from wtforms import Form, FloatField, validators
from compute import sine_plot

app = Flask(__name__)


class InputForm(Form):
    A = FloatField(
        label='x^2 +',
        validators=[validators.InputRequired()])
    B = FloatField(
        label='x +',
        validators=[validators.InputRequired()])
```

```
    C = FloatField(
        label='x +',
        validators=[validators.InputRequired()])


@app.route('/', methods=['GET', 'POST'])
def index():
    form = InputForm(request.form)
    result = None
    if request.method == 'POST' and form.validate():
        A = form.A.data
        B = form.B.data
        C = form.C.data
        result = sine_plot(A,B,C)

    return render_template("view.html", form=form, result=result)

if __name__ == '__main__':
    app.run(debug=True)
```

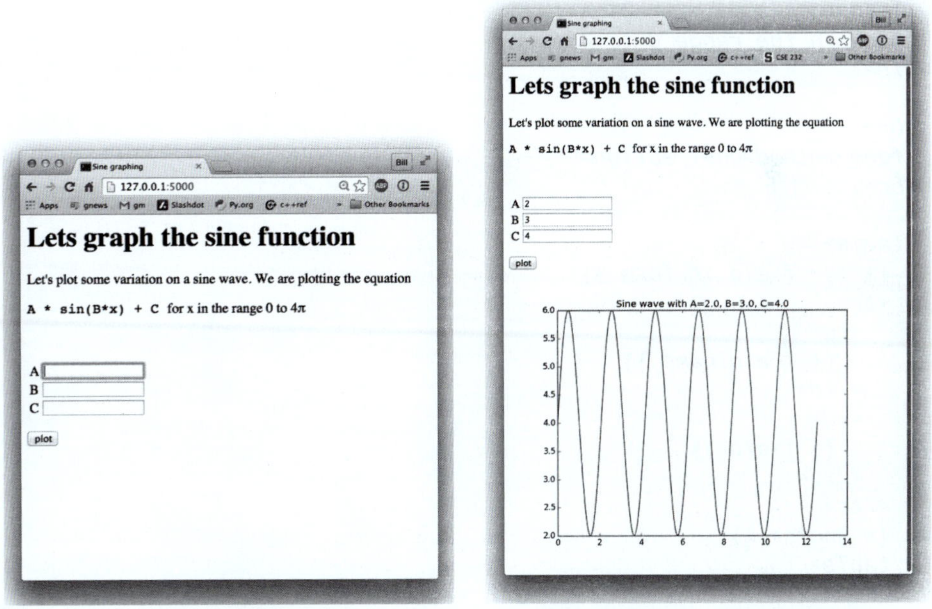

a) Startup b) Data submitted, results displayed

FIGURE E.9 Sine wave plot. [William F. Punch, Richard J. Enbody.]

Code Listing E.11 is the "templates/view.html" file containing the View. The View is a little different in how we lay out the fields. In **Lines 22–33** we use a ***for*** iterator to iterate through all the fields in the class and lay out each field on a separate line of a table. This is a pretty handy approach to having all the fields (no matter how many fields there are) show up as a line in the HTML. It lays them out in a table so that each field shows up in a new table line.

Code Listing E.11

```
1 <html>
2 <head>
3 <title> Sine graphing</title>
4 </head>
5
6 <body>
7 <h1>Lets graph the sine function</h1>
8
9 Let's plot some variation on a sine wave. We are plotting the equation
10 <p>
11 <font face="Courier">
12 A * sin(B*x) + C
13 </font>
14
15 for x in the range 0 to 4&pi;
16 </p>
17
18 <br>
19 <form method=post action="">
20 <br>
21
22 <table>
23   {% for field in form %}
24   <tr>
25     <td>
26       {{ field.name }}
27     </td>
28     <td>
29       {{ field }}
30     </td>
31   </tr>
32   {% endfor %}
33 </table>
34
```

```
35 <p>
36 <input type=submit value=plot>
37 </form>
38 </p>
39
40 <p>
41 {% if result != None %}
42 <img src="{{ result }}" width=500>
43 {% endif %}
44 </p>
45
46 </body>
47 </html>
```

To display our image in **Line 42** we introduce a new HTML tag, the `img` tag. Our new Model returns a file name of an image and we embed that image in the web page using the tag.

The Model ("compute.py" in Code Listing E.12) relies on our understanding of **pylab** plotting that we cover in some detail in Appendix D. Nonetheless, there are a few details worth noting.

Code Listing E.12

```
from numpy import sin, linspace, pi
import matplotlib.pyplot as plt
import string
import random
import os
import glob

# our model
def sine_plot(A,B,C):
    fname = "static/" + ''.join(random.choice(string.ascii_letters + string.
                                                digits) for _ in range(8)) + ".png"
    x = linspace(0,4*pi,500)
    y = (A * sin(B * x)) + C
    plt.figure()
    plt.plot(x,y)
    plt.title("Sine wave with A=%s, B=%s, C=%s" % (A,B,C))
    if not os.path.isdir('static'):
```

```
18          os.mkdir('static')
19      else:
20          # Remove old plot files
21          for filename in glob.glob(os.path.join('static', '*.png')):
22              os.remove(filename)
23      plt.savefig(fname)
24      return fname
```

Ultimately our Model is going to generate a `.png` file that contains the result of our plot. The Model will return the name of that file, which will then be displayed by the `img` tag in the HTML View. However, this is a problem. If we reuse the same file name every time, we might have a problem with the browser. You see, for efficiencies sake most browsers perform **image caching**. By **caching** (pronounced like "cashing") we mean that once an image is downloaded, the browser stores it locally and, if the image is required to be displayed again, it simply uses its local copy. That's great as long as the image has not changed, and bad if it has. Typically to get the image updated we have to reload the image. That's a problem as our user may not understand that.

One way to get around that is to generate every image file with a **random file name**. By random, I mean some random combination of letters and digits. If we randomize, then every time the Model is updated, and subsequently a new image generated, a new file is generated. That can still be a bit of a problem in that we can accumulate a lot of files if we are not careful.

Given all that, here is what we will do:

Line 10: First, the "standard" flask place to store such images is in a directory called "static". Just like "templates" is where Views go, "static" is where images go.
So we generate a file name that has "static/" as the first part of its name, and then generate 8 characters randomly from the combination of the `string.ascii_letters` and `string.digits` all ending with the suffix `.png`. For example, a generated file name might be `static/IuoBjJab.png`, which it was at one time on my laptop!

Lines 11–15: These lines generate the plot, add a title, and anything else to make our plot look nice.

Lines 16–17: Make sure that a static directory exists in the current directory. We cannot store a file to the static directory if it does not exist. If not, we create it.

Lines 19–21: This is our clean up routine. If the static directory does exist, then we must have used it to store a file in the past. **Lines 20–21** look through the directory for any files ending in `.png` and delete them.

Lines 22–23: Finally, we use the `.savefig` method to save our file to the file name we generated above. We then return that file name to the Controller for use in the View.

You now have a template for a GUI that takes in input and displays a plot.

E.6 ODDS AND ENDS

Clearly we cannot cover the entirety of flask, HTML and web forms in such a short appendix. We have only hit the high points. To end this appendix, we cover some odds and ends that might be useful if you dive deeper into the topic.

Remember, the idea is to use the existing examples as prototypes to build your own applications. Just make a copy and modify them to suit your needs.

Flask class

The line `app = Flask(__name__)` seems a little strange. What is that `__name__` variable and what is it doing there? It also shows up at the end of our controller.py scripts when we invoke `if __name__ == "__main__"`. It is this latter expression that is a common expression in Python code. When a Python file is run from the command line, that `__name__` variable gets set to `"__main__"`.

On the `Flask` class, here is what the documentation says:

> The idea of the first parameter is to give Flask an idea what belongs to your application. This name is used to find resources on the file system and can be used by extensions to improve debugging information and a lot more.
> So it's important what you provide there. If you are using a single module, `__name__` is always the correct value. If you however are using a package, it is usually recommended to hardcode the name of your package there.

Here's the important, take-away idea: For any module you write, `app = Flask( __name__)` is the correct way.

Flask instance.**run** parameters

Without really explaining it, we have been running our Controller application with a parameter, namely `app.run(debug=True)`. The `run` method can take a number of parameters, and here are some of the useful ones:

- **debug=True**: This means just what it says—turn on the debugger. If not provided, then debugging is turned off. If you write some code that is incorrect, the resulting web page will show a list of errors. The bad news is that the error list is pretty long and has little to do with your code. Take a look at Figure E.10.

  The useful elements are the first text line, "AttributeError: 'FloatField' object has no attribute 'data'" and the last couple of lines of the stack, in particular "File "/Users/bill/books/third/tpocup3/chFlask/programs/8-sinePlot/controller.py", line 25. These tell you what and where to look for the problem.

  Without this parameter being set, errors go undetected.
- **host = '0.0.0.0'**: By default the web page is only available on your local machine (no one from the outside world can see it). However, if you have debugging turned off (set to False or just don't provide it) and use the parameter above, then if your machine can be seen from the Internet, then the webpage can be seen by the outside world.

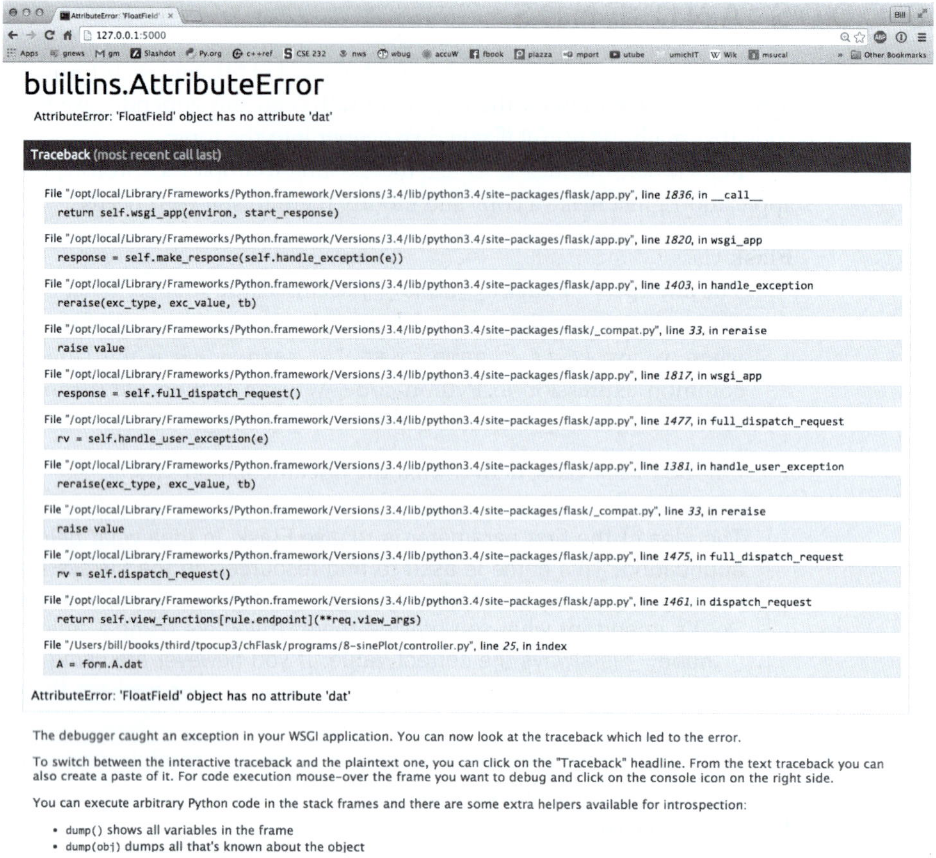

FIGURE E.10 Error. [William F. Punch, Richard J. Enbody.]

- **port=1234**: To provide a little further protection you can also change the port on your web page. The default is 5000, but you can change it to any other number you want, though it is preferable to be above 1024 to avoid conflict with other software.

APPENDIX F

Table of UTF-8 One Byte Encodings

UTF-8 IS A MULTI-BYTE ENCODING OF THE UNICODE CHARACTER SET. AS IT IMPLEMENTS the original ASCII character set unchanged, it is the most popular Unicode encoding in use on the web. Below is shown the single byte encodings of UTF-8, which are in fact the same at the original ASCII encoding. See Table F.1.

Char	Dec	Char	Dec	Char	Dec	Char	Dec
NUL	0	SP	32	@	64	`	96
SOH	1	!	33	A	65	a	97
STX	2	"	34	B	66	b	98
ETX	3	#	35	C	67	c	99
EOT	4	$	36	D	68	d	100
ENQ	5	%	37	E	69	e	101
ACK	6	&	38	F	70	f	102
BEL	7	'	39	G	71	g	103
BS	8	(	40	H	72	h	104
HT	9	)	41	I	73	i	105
LF	10	*	42	J	74	j	106
VT	11	+	43	K	75	k	107
FF	12	,	44	L	76	l	108
CR	13	-	45	M	77	m	109
SO	14	.	46	N	78	n	110
SI	15	/	47	O	79	o	111
DLE	16	0	48	P	80	p	112
DC1	17	1	49	Q	81	q	113
DC2	18	2	50	R	82	r	114
DC3	19	3	51	S	83	s	115
DC4	20	4	52	T	84	t	116
NAK	21	5	53	U	85	u	117
SYN	22	6	54	V	86	v	118
ETB	23	7	55	W	87	w	119
CAN	24	8	56	X	88	x	120
EM	25	9	57	Y	89	y	121
SUB	26	:	58	Z	90	z	122
ESC	27	;	59	[	91	{	123
FS	28	<	60	\	92	|	124
GS	29	=	61	]	93	}	125
RS	30	>	62	^	94	~	126
US	31	?	63	_	95	DEL	127

TABLE F.1 Table of single byte UTF-8 (ASCII) characters.

APPENDIX G

Precedence

Operator	Description
()	Parentheses (grouping)
f(args…), x[i:i], x[i], x.attr	Fuction call, slicing, subscript, dot
**	Exponentiation
+x, -x, ˜x	Positive, negative, bitwise NOT
*, /, %,//,@	Multiplication, division, remainder
+, -	Addition, subtraction
<<, >>	Shifts
&	Bitwise AND
^	Bitwise XOR
|	Bitwise OR
<, <=, >, >=, !=, ==, is, is not, in, not in	Comparisons, identity, membership
not x	Boolean NOT
and	Boolean AND
or	Boolean OR
lambda	Lambda expression

TABLE G.1 Precedence of Python operators: highest to lowest.

APPENDIX H

Naming Conventions

You have heard it many times before and we summarized in **RULE 2**: programs should be readable. Part of that readability is good naming. We have focused in the book on naming variables and functions based on what they are used for. However, there are also conventions on *how* elements should be named and the format of that naming.

Whatever the style you prefer, one consideration in choosing a programming style is fitting in with the programming style of the group you are working with. Groups establish naming conventions so that reading a program is even easier. Conventions make it easier to recognize different programming elements just by how they are formatted.

Python has established such a naming convention. Python provides a special process called the *PEP* process, short for Python Enhancement Process for changes proposed to Python. A PEP is described as follows `http://www.python.org/dev/peps/pep-0001/`

> We intend PEPs to be the primary mechanisms for proposing new features, for collecting community input on an issue, and for documenting the design decisions that have gone into Python. The PEP author is responsible for building consensus within the community and documenting dissenting opinions.[1]

You can see that Python is very open to the community at large when it comes to improving the language. One of the early PEPs, PEP-8, was focused on a Style Guide for writing Python programs (see `http://www.python.org/dev/peps/pep-0008/`).

For the most part, we have followed the style guidelines provided in PEP-8. Not all of those guidelines apply to what we have done in this book (there is a *lot* in Python you have yet to see), but we did stick with those parts that applied to our book. Some prove difficult to use in a book (where space is at a premium) but we did as much as we felt we could. Also, remember **RULE 4** (which, by the way, shows up prominently in PEP-8). We followed the rules as long as they helped in readability, but we diverged when we thought there was a better way!

[1] Excerpt from "PEP 0001-PEP Purpose and Guidelines" by Barry Warsaw, Jeremy Hylton, David Goodger and Nick Coghlan. Published by Python Software Foundation, © 2000.

H.1 PYTHON STYLE ELEMENTS

If you read all of PEP-8, you can see that it is quite detailed! In fact, there are enough details that Python has a package you may download called *pep8* (`http://pypi.python.org/pypi/pep8`) that will check for you how well you adhere to the style standards. How you write Python code is prescribed to a level that might surprise many people. Remember, if we as Python programmers follow these conventions, then our code is likely to be more readable.

These are some of the highlights that we adhered to in the book:

H.2 NAMING CONVENTIONS

There are a couple of naming conventions in use in Python:

- *lower_with_underscores*: Uses only lower case letters and connects multiple words with underscores.
- *UPPER_WITH_UNDERSCORES*: Uses only upper case letters and connects multiple words with underscores.
- *CapitalWords*: Capitalize the beginning of each letter in a word; no underscores.

With these conventions in mind, here are the naming conventions in use in the book.

Variable Names: lower_with_underscores
Constants: UPPER_WITH_UNDERSCORES
Function Names: lower_with_underscores
Function Parameters: lower_with_underscores
Class Names: CapitalWords
Method Names: lower_with_underscores
Method Parameters and Variables: lower_with_underscores

- Always use *self* as the first parameter to a method
- To indicate privacy, precede name with a double underscore. This invokes the name mangling rules (see Section 11.9.2)

H.2.1 Our Added Naming Conventions

We adopted two other naming conventions that we use throughout the book.

First, we often (though not always) append a type name to the end of a variable, preceded with an underscore. As we know, this does not affect our ability to associate whatever type we wish with a variable, but it helps us as programmers remember the types we intended to store with this variable. We violate this rule when the type is clear (making the naming tedious) and usually add a comment in the code to indicate what a name without type is assumed to be.

Second, when we create variable names that are used to demonstrate some attribute of programming, as opposed to performing some operation in a program, we name variables as `my_str` or `my_list`. That is, we precede the name with *my* just to indicate we need a "throw away" variable for some demonstration.

H.3 OTHER PYTHON CONVENTIONS

- Indentation should be done using four spaces per indentation level. If you use Spyder, you get this kind of indentation "for free," that is Spyder does it for you. However, remember that you are using spaces, not tabs, when you do indentation. This difference might matter, if you use an editor that does not understand Python.
- Lines that get too long should be aligned in a "reasonable" fashion, for example aligned with an open delimiter and at a different indentation level than any following indented suites.
- Lines should be less than 80 characters. This rule ensures compatibility with many display formats.
- Blank lines are recommended in many circumstances, which we list below. However, writing a book and trying to minimize spacing requires that we violated these rules occasionally.
  - Separate functions and class definitions with two lines.
  - Separate method definitions with one line.
  - Use blank lines to group related elements.
- Do individual imports on a separate line at the top of the file.
- Use of whitespace:
  - White space should be used to separate binary operators and assignment statements from other elements (just one space is sufficient).
  - No white space around default parameter assignments in function definitions.
  - No space between a function call and its argument list's first parenthesis.

APPENDIX I

Check Yourself Solutions

I.1 CHAPTER 1

Variables and Assignment

1. (a), (d), (e)
   (b) is invalid because it begins with a number.
   (c) is invalid because it has a character that is not a number, letter or underscore.
2. (b), (c)
3. (a) 6
   (b) 10
   (c) 5

Types and Operators

1. (a) 1.1666666666666667
   float
   (b) 1
   int
   (c) 1
   int
   (d) 2
   int
   (e) 7.0
   float
2. (a) 16
   (b) 26
   (c) 9
   (d) 10

I.2 CHAPTER 2

Basic Control Check

(a) 4
(b) 0
(c) string
(d) assignment (to update count)
(e) separate the loop header from the suite

Loop Control Check

1. (a) 1
   2
   10
   20

   (b) 0
   0
   20
   20

   (c) 10, 10
   15, 5
   20, 0
   25, -5
   30, -10
   . . .

More Control Check

1. (a) 3
   (b) 0
   (c) 4
   (d) 1
   (e) iv

for and *range* Check

1. (a) 12
   (b) 8
   (c) iv
   (d) v (Line 3 will always print 0)

I.3 CHAPTER 4

Slicing Check

1. (a) bbcc
   (b) abb
   (c) abc
   (d) aabb
   (e) a b

String Comparison Check

1. (a) the empty string is printed
   (b) cb
   (c) cc
   (d) infinite loop (loop control variable never changes)
   (e) IndexError: string index out of range

I.4 CHAPTER 5

Simple Functions Check

1. 5
   TypeError: Can't convert 'int' object to str implicitly
   7
   8

2.
```
def make_even(n):
    return 2*n
```

   The expression 2*n works fine with a string: it concatenates two copies. The reason is that the '*' operator is defined for strings and 'n' is a string. However, in make_odd the expression 2*n+1 mixes strings and ints.

I.5 CHAPTER 6

1. (b) and (c) are both correct

Exception Check

1. (c)

Function Practice with Strings

1. (a) bcd45
   cd456
   (b) aaabbc
   aabbcd

I.6 CHAPTER 7

Basic Lists Check

1. (a) ['hi', 'mom', 'dad', 1, 57, 25]
   (b) ['hi', 25]
   (c) None
   (d) ['hi', 'mom', 'dad', [1, 57, 25]]
   (e) TypeError: unorderable types: list() < str()
   (f) ['hi', 'mom', 'dad', [1, 57, 25]]
   (g) None
   (h) ['hi', 'mom', 'dad', [1, 57, 25], 127, 256]
   (i) 256
   (j) ['hi', 'mom', 'dad', [1, 57, 25], 127]

Lists and Strings Check

1. (a) [1.6, 2.7, 3.8, 4.9]
   (b) [['1', '6'], ['2', '7'], ['3', '8'], ['4', '9']]
   (c) [1, 2, 3, 4]
   (d) ['4', '9']
   (e) 4:9

Mutable List Check

(a) ['bye', 'mother', 'dad', ['nanna', 'grandpa']]
(b) ['bye', 'mother', 'dad', ['nanna', 'grandpa']]
(c) ['hi', 'mom', 'father', ['nanna', 'grandpa']

I.7 CHAPTER 8

Passing Mutables Check

1. (a) ['a', 'b', 'c', 'd']
   (b) ['goodbye', 'mother', 'and', 'father']
   (c) sister

More on Functions Check

1. (a) (10, [10, 20, 30])
   (b) (5, [5, 10, 15, 20])
   (c) (3, [3, 6, 9])
   (d) (7, [7, 14, 21, 28, 35])
   (e) 2

I.8 CHAPTER 9

Dictionary Check

1. (a) 33
   (b) walter
   (c) True
   (d) 'walter': 20, 'bill': -1, 'rich': 2, 'fred': 10

Set Check

1. (a) {'ab', 'cd'}
   (b) set()
   (c) {'ab'}

I.9 CHAPTER 11

Basic Classes Check

1. (a) []
   (b) [11, 12]
   (c) 23
   (d) AttributeError: 'MyClass' object has no attribute 'local_list'
   Since method1 was never called, local_list was not created.

Defining Special Methods

1. (a) Value 4 is even
   (b) even
   (c) negative
   (d) odd

I.10 CHAPTER 12

Check Defining Your Own Operators

1. (a) Value: abc
   (b) Value: abcijk
   (c) Value: abc
   (d) True

I.11 CHAPTER 14

Basic File Operations

1. (a) c

Basic Exception Control

1. (a) Enter a key: bill
   110
   (b) Enter a key: zach
   hi mom all done
   (c) Enter a key: fred
   hi mom
   (d) Enter a key: 0
   hi mom

INDEX

D

E

Q

R